AMNESTY INTERNATIONAL REPORT

1991

This report
covers the period
January to December
1990

Amnesty International U.S.A.
322 Eighth Avenue
New York, NY 10001

First published 1991
by Amnesty International Publications
1 Easton Street, London WC1X 8DJ, United Kingdom

© Copyright Amnesty International Publications 1991

ISBN: 0-939994-61-5
AI Index: POL 10/01/91
Original Language: English

Typesetting and page makeup by:
Accent on type, 2-4 Tyson Street, London EC1R 4QR

Printed by: The John D. Lucas Printing Company, Baltimore, Maryland, USA

Cover design: Tessa Pellow
(The languages shown are the official languages of the United Nations. *Amnistie Internationale* is the term used by the francophone branch of Amnesty International in Canada.)

All rights reserved
No part of this publication may be reproduced,
stored in a retrieval system, or transmitted,
in any form or by any means,
electronic, mechanical, photocopying, recording and/or otherwise
without the permission of the publishers.

This report documents Amnesty International's work and its concerns throughout the world during 1990. The absence of an entry in this report on a particular country does not imply that no human rights violations of concern to Amnesty International have taken place there during the year. Nor is the length of a country entry any basis for a comparison of the extent and depth of Amnesty International's concerns in a country. Regional maps have been included in this report to indicate the location of countries and territories cited in the text and for that purpose only. It is not possible on the small scale used to show precise political boundaries, nor should the maps be taken as indicating any view on the status of disputed territory. Amnesty International takes no position on territorial questions. Disputed boundaries and cease-fire lines are shown, where possible, by broken lines. Areas whose disputed status is a matter of unresolved concern before the relevant bodies of the United Nations have been indicated by striping only on the maps of the country which has *de facto* control of the area.

CONTENTS

Introduction / **1**
Amnesty International: A Worldwide Campaign / **3**
Work with International Organizations / **10**
Amnesty International photograph exhibition: 1991 campaign / **21**

Afghanistan (The Republic of) / **27**
Albania (The People's Socialist Republic of) / **28**
Algeria (The People's Democratic Republic of) / **31**
Angola (The People's Republic of) / **32**
Antigua and Barbuda / **34**
Argentina (The Argentine Republic) / **34**
Australia / **36**
Austria (The Republic of) / **36**

Bahamas (The Commonwealth of the) / **38**
Bahrain (The State of) / **38**
Bangladesh (The People's Republic of) / **40**
Benin (The People's Republic of) / **42**
Bermuda / **43**
Bhutan (The Kingdom of) / **44**
Bolivia (The Republic of) / **44**
Brazil (The Federative Republic of) / **46**
Brunei Darussalam / **49**
Bulgaria (The Republic of) / **50**
Burkina Faso / **51**
Burma (see **Myanmar**)
Burundi (The Republic of) / **52**

Cambodia (The State of)/Democratic Kampuchea / **54**
Cameroon (The Republic of) / **55**
Canada / **57**
Central African Republic (The) / **58**
Chad (The Republic of) / **59**
Chile (The Republic of) / **61**
China (The People's Republic of) / **64**
Colombia (The Republic of) / **67**
Comoros (The Islamic Federal Republic of the) / **70**
Congo (The People's Republic of the) / **71**
Côte d'Ivoire / **72**
Cuba (The Republic of) / **73**
Cyprus (The Republic of) / **76**
Czechoslovakia (The Czech and Slovak Federal Republic) / **76**

Denmark / **77**
Djibouti (The Republic of) / **78**

CONTENTS

Dominica (The Commonwealth of) / **78**
Dominican Republic (The) / **79**

Ecuador (The Republic of) / **80**
Egypt (The Arab Republic of) / **81**
El Salvador (The Republic of) / **84**
Equatorial Guinea (The Republic of) / **87**
Ethiopia (The People's Democratic Republic of) / **88**

Fiji / **91**
Finland (The Republic of) / **92**
France (The French Republic) / **92**

Gabon (The Gabonese Republic) / **93**
Gambia (The Republic of the) / **95**
Germany (The Federal Republic of) / **95**
Ghana (The Republic of) / **97**
Greece (The Hellenic Republic) / **99**
Grenada / **100**
Guatemala (The Republic of) / **101**
Guinea (The Republic of) / **104**
Guinea-Bissau (The Republic of) / **106**
Guyana (The Cooperative Republic of) / **107**

Haiti (The Republic of) / **108**
Honduras (The Republic of) / **110**
Hong Kong / **112**

India (The Republic of) / **113**
Indonesia (The Republic of) **and East Timor** / **117**
Iran (The Islamic Republic of) / **119**
Iraq (The Republic of) **and Occupied Kuwait** / **122**
Ireland (The Republic of) / **125**
Israel (The State of) **and the Occupied Territories** / **126**
Italy (The Italian Republic) / **129**

Jamaica/ **130**
Japan / **132**
Jordan (The Hashemite Kingdom of) / **133**

Kampuchea (see **Cambodia**)
Kenya (The Republic of) / **135**
Korea (The Democratic People's Republic of) / **137**
Korea (The Republic of) / **137**
Kuwait (The State of) / **140**

Laos (The Lao People's Democratic Republic) / **141**
Lebanon (The Lebanese Republic) / **142**

CONTENTS

Lesotho (The Kingdom of) / **144**
Liberia (The Republic of) / **145**
Libya (The Great Socialist People's Libyan Arab Jamahiriya) / **147**

Madagascar (The Democratic Republic of) / **148**
Malawi (The Republic of) / **149**
Malaysia / **150**
Maldives (The Republic of) / **151**
Mali (The Republic of) / **151**
Mauritania (The Islamic Republic of) / **153**
Mauritius / **155**
Mexico (The United Mexican States) / **156**
Morocco (The Kingdom of) **and Western Sahara** / **159**
Mozambique (The People's Republic of) / **162**
Myanmar (The Union of) / **163**

Namibia / **166**
Nepal (The Kingdom of) / **167**
Nicaragua (The Republic of) / **169**
Niger (The Republic of the) / **171**
Nigeria (The Federal Republic of) / **172**
Norway / **174**

Pakistan (The Islamic Republic of) / **175**
Panama (The Republic of) / **178**
Papua New Guinea (The Independent State of) / **179**
Paraguay (The Republic of) / **181**
Peru (The Republic of) / **182**
Philippines (The Republic of the) / **185**
Poland (The Polish Republic) / **189**
Portugal (The Portuguese Republic) / **189**
Puerto Rico (see **United States of America**)

Romania / **191**
Rwanda (The Rwandese Republic) / **193**

Saint Vincent and the Grenadines / **194**
São Tomé and Príncipe (The Democratic Republic of) / **195**
Saudi Arabia (The Kingdom of) / **195**
Senegal (The Republic of) / **198**
Sierra Leone (The Republic of) / **199**
Singapore (The Republic of) / **200**
Somalia (The Somali Democratic Republic) / **201**
South Africa (The Republic of) / **204**
Spain (The Kingdom of) / **207**
Sri Lanka (The Democratic Socialist Republic of) / **209**
Sudan (The Republic of the) / **212**
Suriname / **215**

CONTENTS

Swaziland (The Kingdom of) / **216**
Sweden (The Kingdom of) / **217**
Switzerland (The Swiss Confederation) / **218**
Syria (The Syrian Arab Republic) / **219**

Taiwan (The Republic of China) / **221**
Tanzania (The United Republic of) / **222**
Thailand (The Kingdom of) / **223**
Togo (The Togolese Republic) / **225**
Trinidad and Tobago (The Republic of) / **226**
Tunisia (The Republic of) / **227**
Turkey (The Republic of) / **228**

Uganda (The Republic of) / **231**
Union of Soviet Socialist Republics (The) / **233**
United Arab Emirates (The) / **236**
United Kingdom (of Great Britain and Northern Ireland, The) / **237**
United States of America (The) (inc. Puerto Rico) / **240**
Uruguay (The Eastern Republic of) / **243**

Venezuela (The Republic of) / **245**
Viet Nam (The Socialist Republic of) / **247**

Yemen (The Republic of) / **249**
Yugoslavia (The Socialist Federal Republic of) / **251**

Zaire (The Republic of) / **254**
Zambia (The Republic of) / **256**
Zimbabwe (The Republic of) / **257**

APPENDICES

I: Amnesty International Visits, 1 January to 31 December 1990 / **262**
II: Statute of Amnesty International: Articles 1 and 2 / **265**
III: Amnesty International News Releases 1990 / **267**
IV: Amnesty International Around the World / **270**
V: International Executive Committee / **272**
VI: Selected International Human Rights Treaties / **273**
VII: Selected Regional Human Rights Treaties / **278**
VIII: Overdue Reports / **280**
IX: United Nations Basic Principles on the Use of Force and Firearms by Law Enforcement Officials / **283**
X: United Nations Basic Principles on the Role of Lawyers / **286**
XI: Protocol to the American Convention on Human Rights to Abolish the Death Penalty / **289**
XII: Selected Statistics / **290**

INTRODUCTION

The new decade opened against a background of dramatic political changes. Respect for fundamental human rights was at the heart of events. Across Eastern and Central Europe, prisoners of conscience were being freed – one, Vaclav Havel, became President of his country, and many others were assuming important roles in the new order. As the first year of the decade ended, Albania became the last country in Europe to legalize peaceful political dissent.

In Africa, Namibia voted strong human rights provisions into its new constitution, and the release of Nelson Mandela and other political prisoners signalled the start of negotiations for change in South Africa. Released prisoners of conscience re-entered political life in Benin and Zaire, but only a minority of prisoners of conscience had survived to do so when the Chadian Government was overthrown.

Protection of human rights was a central issue in efforts to resolve long-standing conflicts in El Salvador and Cambodia. In Chile, once synonymous with gross human rights violations such as "disappearances", extrajudicial executions and torture – abuses which still afflict several countries in the Americas – a new elected government was facing the complex task of establishing the truth about past violations.

An immediate or eventual end to executions was increasingly recognized as an essential aspect of respect for human rights. The death penalty was abolished in the Czech and Slovak Federal Republic, Hungary, Mozambique and Namibia, as well as in Andorra, Ireland, and São Tomé and Príncipe. It was also abolished for ordinary offences in Nepal, while moratoriums on executions began in Bulgaria and South Africa.

But as the world struggled to keep up with one set of events, it was overtaken by another. The Iraqi invasion of Kuwait in August was accompanied by mass extrajudicial killings, summary executions, torture and arrests of prisoners of conscience. Elsewhere in the Middle East, Syrian military action in Lebanon also saw summary executions; the Israeli response to Palestinian demonstrations or riots resulted in dozens of deaths; and Yemeni migrant workers were tortured before their expulsion from Saudi Arabia.

One lesson emerged clearly from both sets of events. There were many people in and out of government at the end of 1990 who had reason for deep shame – and sometimes self-interested regret – at their failure to stand up against human rights violations in the past. It was only those brave individuals who had not bowed down to the repression of freedom of expression who commanded full respect when it was restored in countries of Eastern and Central Europe.

The Iraqi Government headed by President Saddam Hussein had been committing gross and widespread human rights abuses for many years before the 1990 crisis. These included repeated massacres of Kurdish civilians by the Iraqi armed forces, sometimes using chemical weapons. In the face of such gross abuse, Amnesty International had appealed directly to the United Nations (UN)

INTRODUCTION

Security Council in September 1988 for urgent action and publicized gruesome evidence of the atrocities. However, the world's governments and media took only token interest, and none of the UN bodies took action.

In early 1989 Amnesty International published harrowing accounts of the torture and killing of children in Iraq. In early 1990 the organization again pressed the UN Commission on Human Rights to take action on the grave human rights situation in the country. The Commission voted not to act on a draft resolution on Iraq. It took the same decision concerning a resolution on China, thus avoiding action on the two countries which particularly cried out for international concern.

The response to Amnesty International's information on Iraq changed dramatically on 2 August 1990, the day Iraq invaded Kuwait. Suddenly, the telephones at the organization's International Secretariat in London were busy with inquiries about Iraq's human rights record. Pictures of the victims of chemical weapons appeared widely on television. Exiled Kurds, who had battled for so long to have their stories heard, were invited to speak to the media. Amnesty International's own reporting of the abuses perpetrated in Kuwait following the Iraqi invasion made front pages across the world and was cited by heads of government. The UN Sub-Commission on Prevention of Discrimination and Protection of Minorities finally adopted a resolution on Iraq when it met in August, and in December the General Assembly expressed grave concern about Iraqi abuses in occupied Kuwait.

Yet at the same time, lengthy Amnesty International reports on grave human rights violations in countries such as Chad, Egypt, El Salvador, Iran, India, Mauritania, Myanmar, Sri Lanka, Sudan and Turkey were fortunate to be given reasonable space in the media, let alone to be taken up at a high level by governments.

The governments of the world stand in danger of sabotaging the hope of a new era for human rights – a hope for which millions of ordinary people are struggling, often risking their lives or freedom. Some governments are sabotaging it by the violations they commit directly; others by the selectivity with which they exert their influence. Even those governments which are committed to protecting the rights of their own citizens have other interests to pursue in their foreign relations, and these frequently conflict with their obligation to defend human rights worldwide. Sometimes, human rights concerns become the short-term beneficiary of this self-interest; more often they become the casualty of political expediency.

It is for this reason that the existence of a worldwide human rights movement, independent of the political and economic interests of nation states, remains so necessary. The foremost contribution to this movement is made by those men and women who struggle to defend human rights at the local and national level in countries where they are violated daily. Without their courage, persistence and resilience, Amnesty International and other international organizations would often know little about the abuses: their struggle requires the strongest possible support across national frontiers. Where no open stand for human rights is feasible, the international human rights movement must proclaim the rights of those who are not permitted to proclaim their own.

Amnesty International has been a part of this movement since its foundation in 1961. The organization was born out of a sense of outrage at violations of human rights perpetrated despite the assent of governments to the Universal Declaration of Human Rights. Thirty years on, its members remain outraged. This report, covering 141 countries, shows why. Accounts of prisoners of conscience, unfair trials of political prisoners, torture, "disappearances" after arrest and judicial and extrajudicial executions still arrive at Amnesty International's offices every day from different corners of the earth.

There have never been valid excuses for the commission of these gross violations of human rights. The first excuse for the sin of omission – of failure to act – is ignorance. The human rights movement acting at local, national, regional and international levels has today deprived governments and most peoples of that excuse. The world has also too often heard governments' excuses that political and economic interests override human rights issues – the events of 1990 should have put an end to these excuses once and for all.

In the last decade of the 20th century it is not enough for some people to feel vindicated and others ashamed because of the changes which have improved respect for human rights in some countries. It is a time to act to secure those improvements, especially as many are already threatened by new conflicts or the resurgence of old ones. It is a time to remain outraged by the continuation of gross violations of human rights – and to identify the situations which individuals, governments and the international community will be ashamed of tomorrow if we do not act today. This report contains not only descriptions of these situations, but also an account of what Amnesty International, acting alongside other human rights activists worldwide, has done to prevent them. After 1990, there can be no more excuses.

AMNESTY INTERNATIONAL – A WORLDWIDE CAMPAIGN

"We cannot and will not again be a country cited as violent in reports by Amnesty International.... We will not allow the 'new Brazil' to accept any form of disrespect for human rights." This pledge was given by President Collor of Brazil in a nationally televised speech on 22 June 1990, just three days after Amnesty International had launched an action on torture and extrajudicial executions in Brazil. Three months later the President called for a full investigation into all cases of torture and extrajudicial execution of children highlighted in an *Amnesty International Newsletter* article. In November a leading Brazilian human rights activist received death threats after denouncing the death squad murders of children in Rio de Janeiro. Amnesty International members sent thousands of urgent appeals to the Brazilian government. Within the month he had received federal police protection.

The men and women who helped persuade the Brazilian Government to

INTRODUCTION / AMNESTY INTERNATIONAL – A WORLDWIDE CAMPAIGN

recognize and investigate human rights violations were drawn together by the common belief that ordinary people can take effective action to protect the human rights of others. They are all inspired by the United Nations Universal Declaration of Human Rights, which forms the basis of Amnesty International's work. The organization's strength lies in its membership and supporters – people from over 150 countries who are prepared to write letters, send telegrams and organize campaigns to stop human rights abuses wherever they occur. In 1990 the number of Amnesty International members and regular donors surpassed 1,000,000 – one reminder to all governments of the depth of feeling that exists around the world about human rights.

Many members work through one of more than 6,000 volunteer groups active in over 70 countries worldwide. To ensure impartiality and independence, no group is asked to work on the case of a prisoner in its own country. In 45 countries Amnesty International sections coordinate the work of the local groups and organize campaigns, publicity and fund-raising. New groups are being formed all the time and the movement has expanded to reach all corners of the world. Eastern Europe achieved rapid membership development in 1990; by the end of the year there were about 700 international members and between 30 and 40 functioning groups in the region. Groups existed or were in formation in every country in Eastern Europe except Albania, and even in Albania developments in late 1990 promised a brighter future for human rights work in the country. In Sub-Saharan Africa groups were formed in Benin and Togo, joining those already active in Zambia and Mauritius, and a fifth African section was established in Sierra Leone. In the Middle East and North Africa members were active in eight countries although members in the Sudan and Kuwait were forced to severely restrict their activities owing to political developments in both countries. In the Asia/Pacific region Amnesty International sections existed in five countries with less formal groupings in a further 11. In the Americas and the Caribbean, sections continued their activites in 11 countries and there were functioning groups in a further eight. It is this surge of interest in Amnesty International in Eastern Europe and the developing world, alongside the organization's still increasing strength in North America and Western Europe, that has pushed membership to record levels. In 1990 Amnesty International groups worldwide were working on behalf of 4,500 prisoners held in 77 countries. At least 1,296 were released during the year.

As has been the case since Amnesty International's foundation in 1961, members campaign for the release of prisoners of conscience – men and women imprisoned solely for their beliefs, ethnic origin, language or religion who have neither used nor advocated violence. Members also work on behalf of victims of torture and unfair trials, those who have "disappeared" or have been extrajudicially executed, and all those who face the death penalty. A variety of methods are used to campaign for these victims. Members write letter after letter to government officials, judges, prison officers – anyone who may be able to help. At the same time, groups seek to publicize the prisoner's plight in their local press, approach embassies, or ask influential people to sign petitions and support protests.

A campaign can take months or years but once the call has been made for the release of a prisoner of conscience, Amnesty International never gives up. The Dunedin group in New Zealand vigorously campaigned for 19 years on behalf of South Korean prisoner of conscience Suh Sung. He was finally released in February 1990, and later said: "It is my hope that those who worked so hard on my behalf will now continue to work to bring about the release of all the other political prisoners in South Korea."

In the course of any campaign, Amnesty International groups must raise money for postage, stationery, leaflets, publications, meeting rooms and the dozens of minor expenses incurred. Members have devised a wide variety of fund-raising events, many of which also provide opportunities to publicize urgent human rights concerns. In 1990 the Hong Kong group participated in sponsored "walkathons". Artists in New Zealand donated their work to a charity auction for Amnesty International. A group in Sierra Leone grew and sold cassavas. Concerts promoting human rights work were organized in the Philippines, New Zealand, India, Chile and Japan. In Kuwait, before the Iraqi invasion, local groups staged a well-publicized art exhibition in Kuwait City.

Large-scale political imprisonment, detention without trial, torture, "disappearances" and extrajudicial executions cannot be confronted solely by highlighting individual prisoner cases. In countries where a pattern of abuse warrants sustained and increased international pressure, Amnesty International organizes country campaigns or actions. In 1990 there were campaigns on countries including Brazil, Chad, China, Myanmar (Burma), Peru, South Korea, Sri Lanka and Sudan.

The campaign on China continued the work begun following the June 1989 massacre in and around Tiananmen Square, Beijing. Then, Amnesty International launched an emergency campaign involving hundreds of thousands of members all over the world. Although the Chinese authorities failed to respond, Amnesty International maintained the pressure throughout 1990. In May the organization published the names of 650 of the thousands of prisoners arrested and held since the June 1989 pro-democracy protests – at that time the longest list of prisoners in China ever compiled by a human rights organization. "One year after the killings in Beijing, the fate of those prisoners is still veiled in official secrecy – but they are not forgotten," Amnesty International said. "We know some of their names and we want to know what has happened to all of them.... Our message to the government is that these human rights violations are an international concern and international pressure will not go away." In September Amnesty International launched a further action on China aimed at maintaining international attention on the continued repression of trade unionists, workers, writers, academics and human rights activists and on the increased use of the death penalty.

Between March and June an action on Chad mobilized groups in Africa, Europe and the Americas to send thousands of letters urging the government to release all prisoners of conscience, stop torture, and account for prisoners whose fate remained unknown. Several actions on Sudan were also launched during the year. Amnesty International members in Egypt were particularly active in collecting signatures for a letter of appeal to President Bashir of Sudan.

Amnesty International frequently asks for support for its campaigns from doctors, lawyers, trade unionists and other groups in the community with special interests, skills or influence. In this "target sector work", members either work through their local sections or join professional groups. There are extensive networks of Amnesty International medical and legal groups, and a growing number of trade unionists, teachers and journalists work on behalf of individual prisoners and in general campaigns.

Between April and September 1990 a target sector action mobilized Amnesty International members and trade unionists from all over the world to appeal on behalf of 12 trade unionists who had been victims of human rights abuses in countries such as El Salvador, Sri Lanka, Syria and Turkey. Several trade unions agreed to bring Amnesty International concerns before the International Labour Conference. Recently formed Amnesty International groups in Algeria, Egypt, Jordan and Kuwait distributed a video and a leaflet in Arabic and collected thousands of signatures for the appeal case petitions.

Amnesty International medical groups in over 30 countries around the world organize actions on behalf of prisoners who are seriously ill, often because of torture or inadequate care. They also campaign for an end to medical participation in human rights violations and raise Amnesty International concerns with medical associations. Medical groups sometimes intervene on behalf of colleagues who are themselves victims of human rights abuses. In 1989 Dr Maamun Mohamed Hussein called a 10-minute meeting to discuss a doctors' strike at a Sudanese hospital. Dr Hussein and his colleague, Dr Sayed Abdallah, were arrested, tried and convicted of "calling and organizing a strike" and "incitement to opposition against the government". In December 1989 Dr Hussein was sentenced to death and Dr Abdallah received a sentence of 15 years' imprisonment. Medical groups began an immediate international campaign to publicize the cases and demand the release of the two men. On the eve of a visit in May by a delegation representing several scientific and medical organizations from the United States of America, both doctors were released. Dr Abdallah was re-arrested in August, and medical groups again organized to put pressure on the Sudanese authorities to release Dr Abdallah and some 20 medical professionals still in detention.

Human rights emergencies are happening all the time all over the world. Amnesty International has to be prepared to act quickly when it learns of a "disappearance", or fears that a prisoner may be facing torture or execution. The Urgent Action network can be mobilized for worldwide action within 48 hours. The network has about 50,000 participants in 60 countries who are prepared to write, fax or telegraph immediate appeals on behalf of victims of human rights violations. One member, a night-watchman in Ireland, writes to every address on every Urgent Action – an average of 2,000 letters a year. In 1990 a total of 823 Urgent Actions were issued, taking up the cases of 3,626 people in 90 countries.

Amnesty International's campaigns are based on the facts gathered, documented and analysed at the International Secretariat in London. The Secretariat's main task is to ensure that Amnesty International members in over 150 countries receive accurate and timely information for effective human rights action. Research teams covering all regions of the world establish networks of contacts, and monitor media reports and government statements. The International Secretariat also communicates with the government authorities in countries where human rights violations have taken place. It submits information to the United Nations and other intergovernmental organizations, and maintains contact with non-governmental organizations such as international trade unions and human rights organizations. Missions are organized to send Amnesty International representatives to various countries to discuss concerns with government officials, collect information about human rights violations or legal procedures, or to observe political trials.

The International Secretariat provides information about cases and campaigns to members, groups, sections and the international news media. It publishes reports on current human rights abuses in individual countries and on pervasive patterns of human rights violations. These reports routinely appear in Arabic, English, French and Spanish, as well as other languages when possible, such as Chinese, Farsi, German, Japanese, Portuguese and Russian. A summary of current human rights news and prisoner of conscience cases for worldwide letter writing appears in the monthly *Amnesty International Newsletter*, which is also produced in Arabic, English, French, Spanish and, from 1991, Russian.

The bulk of Amnesty International's work is carried out by volunteer activists, working on the basis of information provided by the International Secretariat. The membership itself sets the organization's policies through Amnesty International's governing body – the International Council – which is made up of section delegates and meets every two years. The Council elects an International Executive Committee to carry out its decisions and supervise the International Secretariat. All the movement's funds are raised by the members, and impartiality is protected by accepting no contributions from governments and by following strict guidelines on financial donations.

Abolition of the Death Penalty
Amnesty International is unconditionally opposed to the death penalty and works for its worldwide abolition. The organization regularly monitors death sentences and executions around the world and appeals for clemency whenever it learns of an imminent execution.

The trend towards worldwide abolition of the death penalty continued in 1990 with seven countries abolishing the punishment for all crimes and one abolishing it for ordinary offences. By the end of the year nearly half of all countries in the world had abolished the death penalty in law or practice. Forty-four countries had abolished the death penalty for all offences and 17 for all but exceptional offences, such as wartime crimes. A further 25 countries, while retaining the penalty in law, had not carried out any executions for at least 10 years.

A move to reintroduce the death penalty for common crimes was defeated in the House of Commons (lower house of parliament) of the United Kingdom on 17 December by 367 votes to 182 – a margin of 185 votes, larger than in 1988 when a similar motion was rejected. In Argentina a presidential initiative to reintroduce the death penalty for common crimes was withdrawn in the face of opposition from legislators and other sectors of society.

Despite these encouraging trends, the use of the death penalty continued elsewhere. During 1990, 2,029 prisoners are known to have been executed in 26 countries and 2,005 people were sentenced to death in 54 countries. These figures include only cases known to Amnesty International: the true number is certainly higher. As in previous years, a very few countries accounted for the majority of executions recorded.

Refugees
Amnesty International opposes the forcible return of any person to a country where he or she might reasonably be expected to be imprisoned as a prisoner of conscience, to "disappear" or to be tortured or executed. It seeks to ensure that states provide such people with effective and durable protection, which should normally include legal protection, from being sent against their will to a country where they risk any of these human rights violations, or to a third country where they will not be granted such protection. Amnesty International's work for asylum-seekers and refugees is based on international standards, such as the 1951 Convention relating to the Status of Refugees, which it encourages governments to ratify if they have not already done so.

In order that people at risk may be afforded effective protection, Amnesty International seeks to ensure that refugee-determination procedures and the procedures followed at airports and borders are adequate to identify asylum-seekers who would be at risk of human rights violations if sent against their will to the country they have fled or to a third country. It calls on all states to ensure that their procedures include certain minimum safeguards which are essential in helping to identify and ensure the protection of such people.

Amnesty International also works to ensure that no one seeking protection from human rights violations is obstructed from gaining access to a proper refugee-determination procedure. If a government restricts entry to its territory, for example by imposing a visa requirement or some similar restrictive measure, Amnesty International calls on the government to demonstrate that the measure does not obstruct asylum-seekers in need of protection from gaining access to that country's refugee-determination procedure. If the government cannot demonstrate this, Amnesty International opposes the restrictive measure.

Where asylum-seekers or refugees are detained, Amnesty International calls on governments to demonstrate that such detention is lawful according to international standards: the detention must be for legitimate reasons and those detained must be provided with a prompt, fair, individual hearing of the legality of the detention before a judicial or similar authority. The organization opposes any practice of detaining asylum-seekers or refugees which does not fulfil these standards.

A large part of Amnesty International's work on behalf of asylum-seekers and refugees is done by the organization's sections in the countries where people seek protection. For example, during 1990 Amnesty International's Hong Kong and British sections had several meetings with officials in Hong Kong and the United Kingdom (UK), calling on these governments to implement the recommendations set out in the organization's January 1990 Memorandum regarding the protection of Vietnamese asylum-seekers in Hong Kong (see entry on **Hong Kong**).

Amnesty International's Finnish Section raised its concern with the Finnish Government about access to refugee-determination procedures, and in particular reports indicating that visa requirements were being applied in such a way that could obstruct Somali asylum-seekers travelling through the USSR from seeking protection in Finland (see entry on **USSR**).

The British Section submitted to the UK Government over 30 detailed recommendations arising from the organization's concerns about serious deficiencies in policy and practice in the UK which, in Amnesty International's view, put asylum-seekers at risk of being expelled to countries where they faced imprisonment, torture, "disappearance" or execution. For example, the section was concerned about instances in which, on occasion, airport immigration officials had denied asylum-seekers access to the refugee-determination procedure in the UK; the section also expressed concern about the imposition of visa requirements, together with fines imposed on airlines carrying passengers without a valid visa, which had been shown to obstruct asylum-seekers from obtaining access to refugee-determination procedures in the UK.

Members of Amnesty International's United States (US) Section raised with the US Government the organization's concern that for some years the pattern of acceptance and denial of asylum applications in the United States of America (USA) had consistently demonstrated a clear bias against granting asylum to people from certain countries where widespread and serious human rights abuses occurred, in particular asylum-seekers from El Salvador, Guatemala and Haiti. The section also expressed concern about the government's practice of interdiction at sea of Haitians attempting to reach the USA, which could obstruct asylum-seekers at risk of human rights abuses in Haiti from seeking protection in the USA.

Throughout the year Amnesty International sections in member states of the European Community (EC) raised concerns with their governments, and with members of their national parliaments and the European Parliament, about proposals contained in certain draft intergovernmental treaties under discussion among EC member states, and the implications of these proposed measures for the protection of asylum-seekers (see **Introduction/Work with Intergovernmental Organizations**).

These are just a few examples of the substantial work done during 1990 on behalf of asylum-seekers and refugees by Amnesty International's sections; such work is not reflected in the country entries in this report, which cover only the activities of the International Secretariat.

WORK WITH INTERNATIONAL ORGANIZATIONS

The United Nations (UN)
There were some encouraging advances in the development of new international standards for the protection of human rights during the year, in particular the adoption by the Eighth UN Crime Congress of new standards imposing strict limitations on the permissible use of force and firearms by law enforcement officials. However, in some areas the UN did not take adequate measures to ensure full implementation of the existing norms and standards established by its member states. This was particularly evident in the UN's response to serious human rights violations in certain countries, about which some member states continued to be reluctant to take firm action except in the context of other political developments which attract international censure. The most striking example of this during 1990 was the case of Iraq, in respect of which a pattern of grave and widespread human rights violations has been repeatedly drawn to the UN's attention by Amnesty International in recent years.

Once again no action was taken on a draft decision on Iraq at the 46th session of the UN Commission on Human Rights ("the Commission") in February. However, with international attention focused on Iraq following its invasion of Kuwait on 2 August, its human rights record did then come under greater scrutiny. Following this the UN Sub-Commission on Prevention of Discrimination and Protection of Minorities ("the Sub-Commission") adopted a resolution on Iraq at its 42nd session in August calling on the Commission to take stronger action at its 1991 session to investigate the human rights situation there. Later in the year, on 18 December, the UN General Assembly adopted Resolution 45/170 condemning human rights violations by the Iraqi authorities in occupied Kuwait. It called on Iraq to adhere to principles of international law and asked the Commission to consider the human rights situation in occupied Kuwait at its next session. Amnesty International had continued to raise its concerns about human rights violations by the Iraqi Government during all these discussions in different UN bodies. In addition, in December the organization made available its report on human rights violations by Iraqi forces in occupied Kuwait to the UN Security Council which had, in its Resolution 674(1990), invited all states to collate information on such violations and make it available to the Security Council.

The Commission's failure in February to take action on a decision concerning Iraq was all the more disappointing since the text was very moderate; it simply attempted to formalize within the UN framework Iraq's previous invitation to Sub-Commission members to visit the country. The Commission also failed, by two votes, to take action on a draft resolution on another serious human rights situation – that of China – notwithstanding a report of the UN Secretary-General, which included information submitted by Amnesty International, prepared pursuant to a resolution adopted by the Sub-Commission in 1989 (see *Amnesty International Report 1990*, Introduction/Work with International Organizations).

The Commission did, however, take a firmer position in respect of two other countries. It decided to maintain the Special Rapporteur on Romania appointed in 1989, despite the overthrow of the former government. The Romanian Government raised no objections to an extension of the Special Rapporteur's mandate and indicated its willingness to continue to cooperate with him. The Commission also took note of the serious deterioration in the human rights situation in Haiti. It decided to appoint an independent expert to examine the situation in Haiti and to consider his report at its next session under item 12, which deals with violations in particular countries, rather than under the advisory services program.

The Commission also recognized the serious violations occurring in Guatemala, another country being considered under advisory services: it requested the Secretary-General to appoint an independent expert to examine the human rights situation there, although it left open the question of the agenda item under which the report would be considered. Amnesty International, which had been urging the Commission for some time not to allow advisory services to be used as a means of avoiding scrutiny of serious human rights situations, submitted a written statement to the Commission describing the escalation of human rights violations in Guatemala. In respect of Chile, another country which had been on the Commission's agenda for many years, the Commission decided to terminate the mandate of its Special Rapporteur in view of the election of a civilian government due to take office in March 1990. Although this was perhaps a rather premature move at an important time of transition in a new democracy, the Commission did request the Chilean government-elect to report to a special meeting at its 1991 session on the government's follow-up to recommendations adopted by the UN in respect of Chile.

The Commission again adopted resolutions under item 12 on a number of other countries already under consideration – Afghanistan, Albania, Cuba, El Salvador, Iran, the Israeli-Occupied Territories and South Africa. Amnesty International made an oral statement to the Commission drawing attention to the failure of governments to stop the practice of extrajudicial executions and cited examples from Chad, China, Colombia, Iraq, Peru and Sri Lanka. In another oral statement, the organization emphasized the importance of international measures to prevent torture, referring to continuing reports of torture from Brazil, Mauritania, Myanmar (Burma), Papua New Guinea, Syria and Turkey. Amnesty International also submitted written statements on Iran, Israel and the Occupied Territories and Myanmar, as well as on Guatemala.

There was considerable discussion at the Commission about ways to make its work more effective following the General Assembly's Resolution 44/167 in 1989, recommending that the Economic and Social Council (ECOSOC) should take the necessary steps at its 1990 session to expand the membership of the Commission on the basis of equitable geographical distribution. Some of the methods discussed could reduce the Commission's effectiveness in dealing with serious violations of human rights, but no final conclusions on this were adopted. On 25 May ECOSOC adopted a resolution deciding to enlarge the Commission by 10 seats, to be allocated among the regional groups of Africa,

Asia and Latin America and the Caribbean. This will bring its membership to 53, effective from 1992. The resolution also authorized the Commission to meet exceptionally between its regular sessions if a majority of its members agrees, and recommended that the mandates of its "theme mechanisms" – including those on torture, "disappearances" and summary or arbitrary executions – be increased from two to three years.

As noted above, at its 42nd session in August the Sub-Commission took stronger action on Iraq. The resolution adopted expressed concern about the human rights situation there and called on the Commission to consider appointing a Special Rapporteur. In addition, the Sub-Commission again adopted resolutions on East Timor, El Salvador, Guatemala, Iran, Israel and the Occupied Territories and South Africa. With the exception of El Salvador, Guatemala and South Africa, which were adopted by consensus, these country resolutions were adopted by a secret ballot vote. This is an exceptional measure to which the Sub-Commission also resorted in 1989; at the 1990 session it decided to request the Commission to recommend to ECOSOC an amendment to the rules of procedure to allow for secret ballot voting in the Sub-Commission as a matter of course when resolutions concerning violations in individual countries are under consideration.

There was also progress on an important standard-setting exercise in the UN when the Sub-Commission approved at its August session the text of the draft *Declaration on the Protection of All Persons from Enforced or Involuntary Disappearance* (see *Amnesty International Report 1990*, Introduction/Work with International Organizations). The draft Declaration was transmitted to the Commission with the recommendation that it be approved and eventually sent on to the General Assembly for adoption.

In addition, further progress was made at the Sub-Commission on a number of issues of interest to Amnesty International. The Special Rapporteur completed his study of administrative detention; his recommendations were endorsed by the Sub-Commission, which transmitted his various proposals for the establishment of a new "theme mechanism" on detention to the Commission for a decision at its 1991 session. Amnesty International made an oral statement on its concerns regarding the practice of administrative detention, citing examples from Chad, China, Egypt, Ethiopia, Ghana, India, Israel and the Occupied Territories, Mauritania, South Africa and Sri Lanka. A preliminary report was presented by the two Special Rapporteurs of the Sub-Commission studying freedom of opinion and expression. In another of its oral statements Amnesty International had highlighted the plight of prisoners of conscience, giving examples from China, Cuba, Iraq, Malawi, Sudan, Syria, Turkey and Viet Nam. It also named the following 11 countries where such prisoners were being held: Albania, Cameroon, Indonesia, Iran, Israel and the Occupied Territories, Kenya, the Republic of Korea, Morocco, Myanmar, Tunisia and Yugoslavia. The Sub-Commission also requested the Commission (and ECOSOC) to approve its decision to appoint a Special Rapporteur on the independence of the judiciary, who would study measures to strengthen the legal profession and investigate violations in this area. The Sub-Commission's Working Group on Detention decided to continue its discussion of the death penalty, particularly its imposition on juveniles, at its next session. Amnesty International made a statement to the Working Group on the imposition of the death penalty on offenders under the age of 18 years, giving examples from Iran, Nigeria and the USA. It noted the raising of the minimum age for execution in Barbados and the reintroduction of the death penalty for juveniles under 18 and over 16 in St Vincent and the Grenadines. The Working Group also decided to examine the question of the right to *habeas corpus* as a non-derogable right which would complement another on-going Sub-Commission study on fair trial. As at the Commission, there was considerable discussion in the Sub-Commission about methods and organization of work, but no final decisions were taken.

The Eighth UN Congress on the Prevention of Crime and the Treatment of Offenders was held in Havana, Cuba, from 27 August to 7 September. The UN Crime Congresses, which are convened by and report to the General Assembly, are held every five years and are responsible for reviewing and setting the UN's crime prevention and criminal justice program. The Eighth UN Crime Congress, the theme of which was "international cooperation in crime prevention and criminal justice for the twenty-first century", was one of the largest, attended by delegates from 127 countries as well as representatives from intergovernmental and non-governmental organizations (NGOS), and 350 experts. The Congress adopted 46 resolutions, all by consensus, including four new human rights standards described below. These represent an important contribution to the growing body of international instruments for the protection of human rights. The only resolution which was not adopted concerned the death penalty, calling on states which retain this punishment to consider imposing a three-year moratorium on its use in order to permit a study of the effects of abolition. The resolution failed to secure the required two-thirds majority for adoption, although 48 votes were cast in favour of it with 29 against and 16 abstentions.

One of the most important new standards adopted by the Eighth UN Crime Congress in the field of human rights protection was the *Basic Principles on the Use of Force and Firearms by Law Enforcement Officials* (see Appendix IX). This imposes strict restraints on the permissible use of force and firearms and requires governments to introduce regulations governing the use of force and firearms as well as proper reporting procedures and measures to punish arbitrary or abusive use of force or firearms. Another important instrument adopted by the Eighth Congress was the *Basic Principles on the Role of Lawyers* (see Appendix X). This instrument contains measures both to guarantee the basic right of access of individuals to legal assistance and to protect lawyers from interference or intimidation in the carrying out of their professional duties. In addition to these two instruments, the Congress agreed the text of a new set of *UN Rules for the Protection of Juveniles Deprived of Their Liberty*, which was subsequently adopted by the General Assembly in Resolution 45/113 of 14 December 1990. It also adopted *Guidelines for the Role of Prosecutors*, which includes provisions requiring prosecutors to give due attention to the prosecution of grave human rights violations, and requires them to refuse to use evidence which they know or believe to have been obtained by unlawful means, such as torture.

The General Assembly at its 45th session adopted Resolution 45/121 of 14 December welcoming the new instruments and resolutions adopted by the Eighth Congress and inviting governments to be guided by them in the formulation of appropriate legislation and practice and to make efforts to ensure their implementation.

Amnesty International attended the Eighth UN Crime Congress and distributed a paper setting out its recommendations to the participants. During the Congress the organization also held an ancillary meeting on "Worldwide Moves To Abolish the Death Penalty" with the participation of three distinguished guest speakers: Justice P.N. Bhagwati, former Chief Justice of the Supreme Court of India; Professor Sofia Kelina, Deputy Director of the Institute of State and Law, Academy of Sciences of the USSR; and Doctor Carimo Issa, a judge and adviser to the Minister of Justice of Mozambique.

There was some progress during the year in respect of ratifications of international human rights treaties (see Appendix VI). Four countries ratified or acceded to the International Covenant on Civil and Political Rights (ICCPR) and the International Covenant on Economic, Social and Cultural Rights – Burundi, the Republic of Korea, Malta and Somalia – bringing the total number of ratifications of these instruments as of 31 December to 92 and 97 respectively. The Republic of Korea, Malta and Somalia also became Party to the first Optional Protocol to the ICCPR, bringing the total number of ratifications to 51. In addition, Yugoslavia signed the Optional Protocol. The first ratifications of the Second Optional Protocol to the ICCPR Aiming at the Abolition of the Death Penalty took place during the year (see *Amnesty International Report 1990,* Introduction/Work with International Organizations and Appendix IX): Australia, the (former) German Democratic Republic, New Zealand, Portugal and Sweden became Party to it. A further 15 countries signed this Protocol – Belgium, Costa Rica, Denmark, the Federal Republic of Germany, Finland, Honduras, Italy, Luxembourg, Netherlands, Nicaragua, Norway, Romania, Spain, Uruguay and Venezuela. Seven countries ratified or acceded to the Convention against Torture and Other Cruel, Inhuman or Degrading Treatment or Punishment – the Federal Republic of Germany, Guatemala, Liechtenstein, Malta, Paraguay, Romania and Somalia – bringing the total number of States Parties to this treaty to 55.

The Convention on the Rights of the Child, adopted by the UN in 1989, came into force on 2 September 1990 following receipt of the requisite 20 ratifications (see *Amnesty International Report 1990,* Appendix XI). By the end of the year there were 63 States Parties to this Convention and a further 69 states had signed it. A World Summit for Children, convened at UN headquarters in New York on 29 to 30 September, was attended by some 72 heads of state or government. Amnesty International's Secretary General attended and the organization issued a press release and an external document drawing attention to its concerns about the continuing serious abuses to which children are subject in several countries, noting in particular Albania, Argentina, Bolivia, Brazil, Chad, China, El Salvador,

Guatemala, Iraq, Israel and the Occupied Territories, Mauritania, Myanmar, Nigeria, Peru, the Philippines, South Africa, Sri Lanka, Turkey and the USA.

Amnesty International continued throughout the year to submit information about violations of human rights in a wide range of countries to the various mechanisms and procedures established by the UN. The organization submitted to the UN procedure established by ECOSOC Resolutions 728F and 1503 information on six countries: Chad, Colombia, Myanmar, Peru, Somalia and Turkey. Resolution 728F authorizes the UN to receive communications about human rights violations and to bring them to the attention of the government concerned. Under Resolution 1503 the UN examines communications in confidential proceedings to determine whether there is evidence of a "consistent pattern of gross violations of human rights" in a country.

During 1990 Amnesty International brought to the attention of the UN Working Group on Enforced or Involuntary Disappearances information on cases from 19 countries including Colombia, El Salvador, Guatemala, Peru, the Philippines and Sri Lanka. It submitted to the Special Rapporteur on summary or arbitrary executions information on cases of possible or threatened extrajudicial execution from 32 countries including China, Colombia, El Salvador, Guatemala, Iraq, Israel and the Occupied Territories, Peru, Somalia and Sri Lanka. Cases of death sentences imposed in apparent violation of international minimum standards were submitted to this Special Rapporteur from 18 countries including Burkina Faso, India, Iran, Sudan and the USA. Information about cases of torture from 47 countries was submitted to the Special Rapporteur on torture; these included Chad, China, Egypt, Iraq, Kenya, Myanmar, Peru, Sudan and Turkey. The organization also submitted information about Turkey to the Committee against Torture, the monitoring body established under the Convention against Torture, for its consideration under Article 20 of that Convention. Under Article 20 the Committee may initiate an inquiry into the systematic practice of torture in a State Party. Submissions were made to the Special Rapporteur on religious intolerance concerning 14 countries, including China, Egypt and Greece.

Amnesty International continued to submit relevant information to the UN Special Rapporteurs and Representatives on Afghanistan, El Salvador, Iran and Romania and to the Experts on Equatorial Guinea, Guatemala and Haiti. Information was also submitted to the Special Committee to investigate Israeli Practices Affecting the Human Rights of the Palestinian People and Other Arabs of the Occupied Territories and to the *Ad Hoc* Working Group of Experts on southern Africa. Amnesty International made a statement on East Timor to the UN Special Committee on Decolonization in August and submitted a statement to the UN Special Committee against *Apartheid* in October on the occasion of the UN Day of Solidarity with Political Prisoners in Southern Africa.

The United Nations Educational, Scientific and Cultural Organization (UNESCO)
Amnesty International continued to submit information to the Committee on Conventions and Recommendations of UNESCO, which examines human rights violations against writers, teachers and others within UNESCO's mandate.

Amnesty International brought to the Committee's attention new cases from China (Tibet), Egypt, Iran, Myanmar, Peru and Yugoslavia. The organization also attended in June the 22nd Conference of International Non-Governmental Organizations in Consultative Relationship with UNESCO.

The International Labour Organization (ILO)

As in past years, Amnesty International attended the International Labour Conference of the ILO in Geneva in June. It followed the proceedings of the Committee on the Application of Conventions and Recommendations, which forms part of the ILO's supervisory mechanism for the implementation of its conventions. Amnesty International raised its concerns about human rights violations relevant to the Committee's work in Brazil, Colombia and Peru, all of which were taken up by the Committee, and in the Philippines and Sri Lanka. Amnesty International also submitted information to the ILO Commission of Inquiry on Romania.

The Organization of American States (OAS)

Chile ratified the American Convention on Human Rights and Paraguay ratified the Inter-American Convention to Prevent and Punish Torture, bringing the total numbers of ratifications of these instruments to 22 and eight respectively (see Appendix VII). Amnesty International continued its practice of submitting to the Inter-American Commission on Human Rights (IACHR) information relating to its concerns in member states of the OAS, including El Salvador, Guatemala, Peru and Colombia. In June Amnesty International again attended the General Assembly of the OAS as a "special guest". Prior to the session the organization sent a letter to all member states expressing grave concern about the noticeable increase in recent years in attacks suffered by human rights defenders in various countries in the region. Amnesty International referred to the inefficacy or non-existence of investigations into these violations in countries such as Brazil, Colombia, El Salvador, Guatemala, Honduras and Peru, and called on the General Assembly to address these concerns and to promote preventive measures.

An important human rights development in the OAS was the adoption by the General Assembly on 8 June of a Protocol to the American Convention on Human Rights to Abolish the Death Penalty (see Appendix XI). By the end of the year five states had signed the Protocol – Ecuador, Nicaragua, Panama, Uruguay and Venezuela – but none had ratified it. Regrettably the General Assembly did not consider at its 1990 session the draft convention on "disappearances", postponing its consideration until the next session.

The activities of the Inter-American Court of Human Rights substantially increased during the year with the submission to it by the IACHR of a further three "contentious" cases, one against Peru and two against Suriname. So far the Court has only ever ruled on two "contentious" cases, both against Honduras (see *Amnesty International Report 1990*, Introduction/Work with International Organizations). The Court began its consideration of the case against Peru, continued its practice of handing down advisory opinions and adopted an interpretative judgment on one of its previous decisions. In addition, at the request of the IACHR, the Court adopted provisional measures for the protection of witnesses in a case which the IACHR is examining, also concerning Peru.

The Organization of African Unity (OAU)
Forty-one member states of the OAU were parties to the African Charter on Human and Peoples' Rights by the end of 1990 after ratifications by Angola, Malawi and Mozambique became effective during the year (see Appendix VII). The African Commission – a body of 11 experts established under the Charter to monitor its implementation – met in two regular sessions in April and October at its headquarters in Banjul, the Gambia. Amnesty International, which has observer status at the African Commission, attended part of the second session and made a statement. The organization also submitted its first communication under Article 55 of the African Charter concerning human rights violations in Sudan since the 30 June 1989 military coup. In December Amnesty International attended a seminar in Dakar, Senegal, on the future of the Commission and possible amendment of the Charter.

The Council of Europe
On 6 November Hungary became the 24th member state of the Council of Europe, the first Warsaw Pact country to join this organization. On its admission, Hungary signed the European Convention on Human Rights and its Protocol No. 6 concerning abolition of the death penalty. Finland ratified this Convention in May together with its Protocol No. 6 and Liechtenstein also ratified Protocol No. 6 in November, bringing to 16 the number of States Parties to this Protocol (see Appendix VII).

In November the Committee of Ministers adopted the text of the Ninth Protocol to the European Convention. This will permit individuals who have submitted a petition to the European Commission of Human Rights to refer their case to the European Court of Human Rights, following the Commission's determination of the case. At present only the Commission or one of the States Parties involved in the case may do this.

Five countries ratified the European Convention for the Prevention of Torture and Inhuman or Degrading Treatment or Punishment – the Federal Republic of Germany, Finland, Iceland, Portugal and San Marino – bringing the number of ratifications of this treaty to 20 (see Appendix VII). The European Committee for the Prevention of Torture set up under this treaty began its work and Amnesty International began regular submissions to it of relevant information. The Committee carried out its regular periodic visits during the year to Austria, Denmark, Malta and the UK and undertook one *ad hoc* visit to Turkey.

Amnesty International continued to attend as an observer the biannual meetings of the Council of Europe's Steering Committee for Human Rights. In October Amnesty International's Secretary General addressed the Committee as its guest speaker. Amnesty International also attended in January a hearing on Turkey organized by the Parliamentary Assembly's Committee on Legal Affairs and Human Rights, and continued to submit relevant information to it and to the parliamentary Committee on Migration, Refugees and Demography which it attends as an observer.

The European Community (EC)
During 1990 Amnesty International submitted its concerns on a wide range of countries to the governments of the EC acting within the framework of European Political Cooperation (EPC), to members of the European Parliament and to the EC Commission.

EC member states, meeting in the framework of EPC, adopted joint declarations on the human rights situation in several countries, including China, El Salvador, Iraq/Kuwait, Israel and the Occupied Territories, Myanmar, Nigeria, Somalia, South Africa and Sri Lanka. The European Parliament adopted resolutions concerning human rights in various countries, including Brazil, China, Colombia, Cuba, El Salvador, Guatemala, Iran, Iraq/Kuwait, Israel and the Occupied Territories, Morocco, Myanmar, Niger, the Philippines, Somalia, Sri Lanka, Sudan, Syria and Yugoslavia. It also appointed a rapporteur to prepare a report on the use of the death penalty in the world and condemned executions in Indonesia, Iraq and the USA. In April the European Parliament held a public hearing on the human rights situation in Tibet. Amnesty International submitted information about its concerns in Turkey to the EEC-Turkey Joint Parliamentary Committee; these concerns were raised by members of this Committee during its on-going discussions about Turkey's human rights record.

EC governments and the Joint Parliamentary Assembly composed of representatives from the EC countries and 68 African, Caribbean and Pacific (ACP) states began discussions on the implementation of strengthened provisions on the protection of human rights incorporated in the Fourth ACP–EEC Convention on cooperation and aid (Lomé IV). The Convention was signed in December 1989 but was not in force by the end of 1990. In a resolution adopted in September, the ACP–EEC Joint Parliamentary Assembly called for a three-year moratorium on the application of the death penalty in retentionist states.

During discussions on draft intergovernmental treaties related to harmonization of asylum and immigration policies in EC countries, Amnesty International raised its concerns with the EC governments, the EC Commission, members of national parliaments and the European Parliament about the implications of these instruments for the protection of refugees and asylum-seekers at risk of human rights violations. A Convention dealing with the state responsible for examining an asylum request was adopted in June but another draft Convention dealing with border controls remained under discussion at the end of the year. A separate agreement, part of which also dealt with border controls, was adopted and signed by the five members of the "Schengen Group" – Belgium, the Federal Republic of Germany, France, Luxembourg and the Netherlands – in June; Italy also signed this agreement in November. The European Parliament adopted two resolutions in March and June expressing concern at the lack of essential safeguards in these texts to protect the rights of asylum-seekers and refugees and the absence of sufficient public discussion and parliamentary consultation.

The Conference on Security and Cooperation in Europe (CSCE)
The second session of the Conference on the Human Dimension of the CSCE was convened in Copenhagen from 5 to 29 June (see *Amnesty International Report 1990*, Introduction/Work with International Organizations). Albania, the only European country which does not participate in the CSCE, expressed an interest in joining this body and attended the Copenhagen Conference as an observer. Amnesty International attended the Conference, following the liberalization of access for NGOs. Before the Conference the organization circulated its recommendations to all participating states. A detailed concluding document was adopted reaffirming the commitment of participating states to ensure full respect for human rights with particular reference to democracy, the rule of law, minorities, the rights to freedom of conscience, expression, assembly and association and conscientious objection. It was also agreed to keep the death penalty under review and to strengthen the mechanism established in 1989 to monitor compliance with the CSCE human rights agreements.

A summit meeting of CSCE heads of state and government was held in Paris in November, which Amnesty International and other NGOs attended as observers. The Charter of Paris for a New Europe was signed covering the full scope of issues dealt with by the CSCE, including human rights. The Charter also established a more formal structure for the CSCE, with a secretariat based in Prague, biennial Follow-Up Meetings, annual meetings of a Council composed of Foreign Ministers, a parliamentary assembly and provision for *ad hoc* emergency meetings.

Commonwealth
At the last biennial Commonwealth Heads of Government Meeting (CHOGM) in 1989 it was decided to establish two groups to study Commonwealth policy: a governmental Working Group of Experts on Human Rights and a High Level Appraisal Group on the Future of the Commonwealth in the 1990s and Beyond. The High Level Group consists of 10 states: Australia, the Bahamas, Canada, India, Jamaica, Malaysia, Nigeria, Singapore, the United Kingdom and Zambia. The Working Group of Experts presented its report in August, which recommended ways in which the Commonwealth could strengthen its promotion of human rights, particularly in the field of education and in encouraging ratification of human rights treaties. Amnesty International prepared a paper setting out ways in which the Commonwealth could strengthen its protection and promotion of human rights in its member countries, and this was brought to the attention of all member countries and the Commonwealth Parliamentary Association at its meeting in September. Amnesty International also met the new Secretary-General of the Commonwealth, Chief Emeka Anyaoku, in November to discuss its proposals.

Inter-Parliamentary Union (IPU)
The Inter-Parliamentary Union (IPU), a non-governmental organization composed of members of parliament from 111 countries, maintains a special committee to investigate the reported violations of the human rights of members of parliament. During 1990 Amnesty International sent the committee information on the situation of members or former members of parliament in Colombia, Indonesia, Nepal and Sudan. Amnesty International delegations observed the April session of the Inter-Parliamentary Conference in Nicosia, Cyprus, and the October session in Punta del Este, Uruguay.

PHOTO EXHIBITION: 1991 CAMPAIGN
No More Excuses!

Amnesty International was founded in 1961. For 30 years its voice has been raised for victims of human rights violations: for prisoners of conscience; for victims of torture and unfair trials; for those facing execution; for the "disappeared".

These 30 years have seen a growing human rights movement worldwide. But the violations continue.

In 1991 Amnesty International is launching a campaign to highlight the continuing abuses. Its message to all governments is "No More Excuses!"

Thirty posters are to be exhibited around the world. The cases illustrate and symbolize the horrors caused by human rights violations. They stand as examples of the hundreds of thousands of other victims whose tragic stories are never heard.

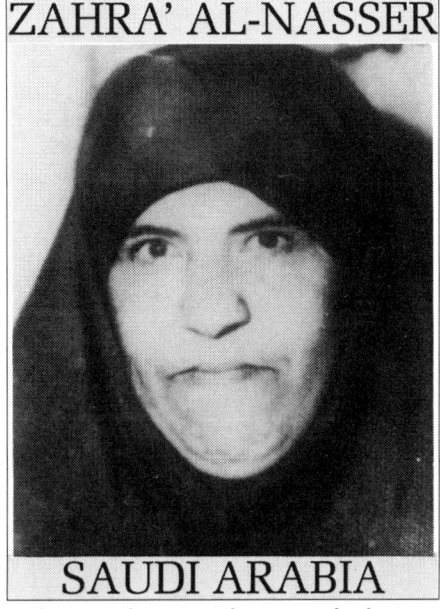

ZAHRA' AL-NASSER
SAUDI ARABIA

Died in custody, apparently as a result of torture, after border police detained her for having a Shi'a prayer book

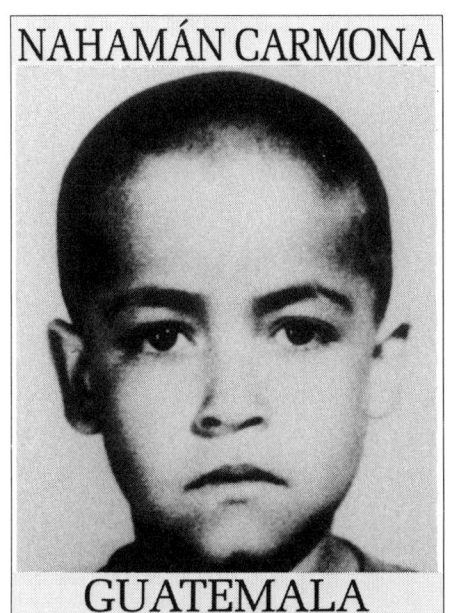

NAHAMÁN CARMONA
GUATEMALA

Kicked to death by police officers

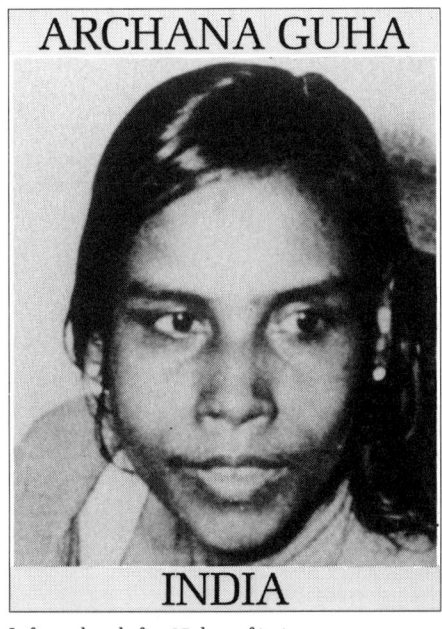

ARCHANA GUHA
INDIA

Left paralysed after 27 days of torture

PHOTO EXHIBITION

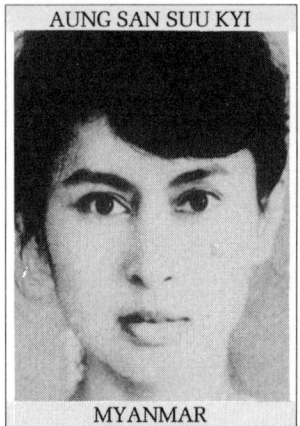

AUNG SAN SUU KYI
MYANMAR
Under house arrest because of her non-violent political beliefs

MULUGETTA MOSISSA
ETHIOPIA
Jailed for over 10 years because of his ethnic origin

REVEREND LAWFORD IMUNDE
KENYA
Six years' imprisonment for writing opinions in his diary

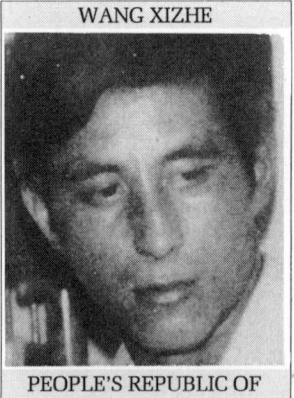

WANG XIZHE
PEOPLE'S REPUBLIC OF CHINA
Jailed since 1981 for advocating democracy

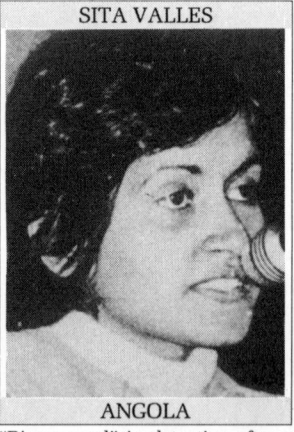

SITA VALLES
ANGOLA
"Disappeared" in detention after a coup attempt in 1977

NASRIN RASOOLI
IRAN
Executed for her non-violent political activities

V. SKANDARAJAH
UNITED KINGDOM
Refused asylum and forcibly returned to Sri Lanka, despite the risk of torture

DR THOMAS WAINGGAI
INDONESIA
Jailed for 20 years for peacefully advocating independence for a province of Indonesia

DR PEDRAZA
COLOMBIA
"Disappeared" in July 1990 while campaigning for the human rights of others

PHOTO EXHIBITION

MOHAMED SRIFI
MOROCCO
Sentenced to 30 years in jail for his peaceful political views

VERA CHIRWA
MALAWI
Jailed for believing that her country should be run differently

ERHAN TUSKAN
TURKEY
Imprisoned for publishing political writings in his magazine

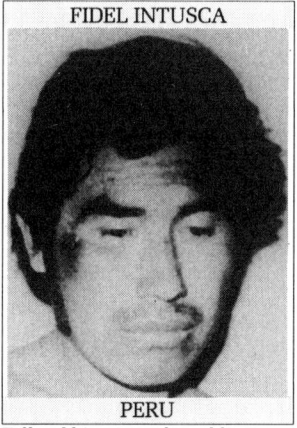

FIDEL INTUSCA
PERU
Tells of his torture by soldiers at a military base

STANZA BOPAPE
SOUTH AFRICA
"Disappeared" in 1988 during his fourth detention in 10 years

ESTEBAN GONZALEZ
CUBA
Jailed for criticizing the political system in his country

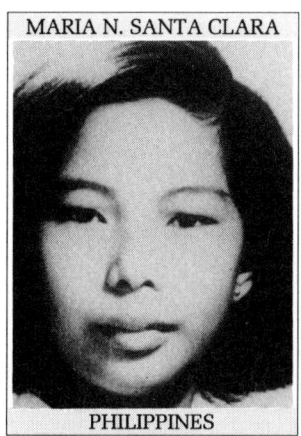

MARIA N. SANTA CLARA
PHILIPPINES
"Disappeared" with a colleague while working for a community organization

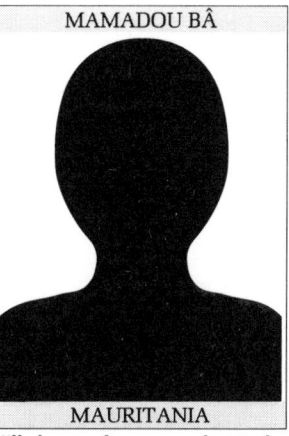

MAMADOU BÂ
MAURITANIA
Killed at the age of 12 by government troops because of the colour of his skin

ANDREAS CHRISTODOULOU
GREECE
Jailed for refusing to perform military service on account of his religious beliefs

PHOTO EXHIBITION

DR USHARI — SUDAN
Jailed for struggling for the human rights of others

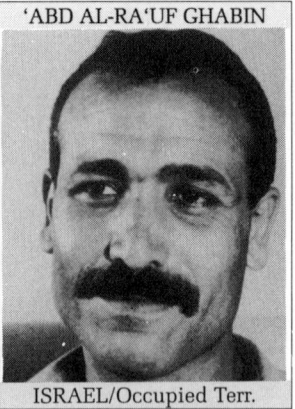

'ABD AL-RA'UF GHABIN — ISRAEL/Occupied Terr.
Tells of being beaten during interrogation and deprived of sleep

NGUYEN CHI THIEN — VIET NAM
A poet who has spent half his life in jail for his political verses

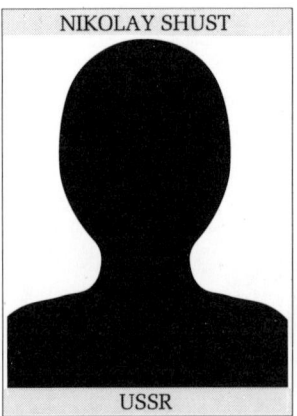

NIKOLAY SHUST — USSR
Jailed for refusing to perform military service on account of his religious beliefs

DALTON PREJEAN — USA
Executed despite a history of mental illness and being a juvenile at the time of his crime

FEBE VELÁSQUEZ — EL SALVADOR
One of 10 trade unionists killed in a bomb attack on their union headquarters

JOSÉ RAMÓN GARCÍA — MEXICO
"Disappeared" after leading a campaign publicizing alleged electoral fraud

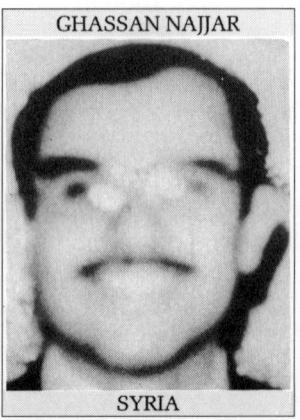

GHASSAN NAJJAR — SYRIA
Serving 11 years in prison for protesting about the abuse of emergency powers

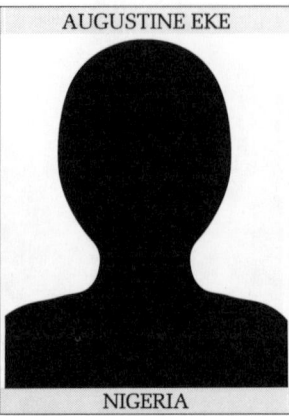

AUGUSTINE EKE — NIGERIA
Facing death by firing-squad though only 14 at the time of the crime

COUNTRY ENTRIES

AFGHANISTAN

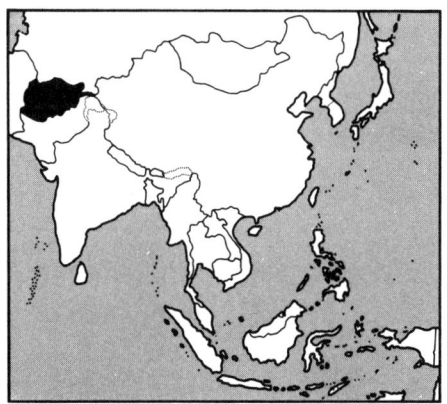

Hundreds of government opponents were believed to be imprisoned, including prisoners of conscience, and dozens of people were said to have been extrajudicially executed following an attempted coup. New information was received about the torture and ill-treatment of prisoners in previous years. At least five people were sentenced to death and six people executed. Armed opposition groups also held many hundreds of prisoners and were responsible for torture and killings.

President Najibullah's government retained control of the capital, Kabul, and other main cities but continued to face armed opposition from a variety of groups – the Mujahideen – which effectively controlled one provincial capital and many rural areas. The continuing conflict made it difficult to obtain accurate and objective information about human rights.

In March the government of President Najibullah survived an attempted coup led by the then Defence Minister, Shahnawaz Tanai, who subsequently fled to Pakistan and formed an alliance with the *Hezb-e Islami* Mujahideen group led by Gulbuddin Hekmatyar. Dozens of people were said to have been extrajudicially executed following the coup attempt, and hundreds arrested. In April Kabul Radio said 623 people had been held, but it was not known how many had been brought to trial by the end of the year. The government, in response to an intervention by Amnesty International, said that their cases would be "examined in strict compliance with both national legislation and international instruments".

At least four but possibly many more alleged members of the National Unity Party (NUP), which had sponsored the establishment of democracy in Afghanistan through peaceful means, were released in the first half of 1990. They had been brought to trial before the Special Court of National Security in 1989. The nature of the charges was not made public, but at least two of those who were released had been convicted: Mohammad Mohsen Formoly, a university professor, received a six-year sentence and Dr Abdul Jalil was sentenced to two years' imprisonment. Those tried had been among dozens of NUP supporters arrested in June 1989, the rest of whom were believed to have been released earlier.

No new information was received about Amin Yusufzai, a possible prisoner of conscience reportedly arrested in 1986 (see *Amnesty International Report 1990*). The government did, however, confirm the continuing imprisonment of two media workers, Seyed Abdul Samad and Mohammad Nazar. It said they had been sentenced for "the crime of participation and cooperation in [the] espionage activities of Alain Guillo", a French journalist (see *Amnesty International Reports 1989* and *1990*) and evasion of military service. Both appeared to be prisoners of conscience.

The government also responded in June to inquiries about Dr Mohammad Younis Akbari, a nuclear physicist sentenced to death in 1984 (see *Amnesty International Report 1985*), stating that he had been executed. The date of execution was not given. No new information was forthcoming about prisoners who reportedly "disappeared" in previous years.

New information about torture was received from former prisoners. One, who was reportedly arrested and tried in 1983, alleged that he had been tortured with electric shocks, beaten and had his teeth broken, and had been forced to sign a statement saying that he had spied for the Mujahideen while visiting Pakistan.

At least five people were sentenced to death in January, including two reportedly aged under 18. In October President Najibullah was reported to have commuted 58 death sentences. However, in the same month Kabul Radio announced that six people had been executed after they had been sentenced to death by a special court of national security on charges of murder, robbery and disruption of public order.

In November the government told Amnesty International that Seyed Hamza, an alleged member of *Jamiat-e-Islami* Mujahideen group, had been sentenced to death in 1988 for violent political offences. It added that the sentence had been referred to President Najibullah for approval but that no decision on the case had yet been announced.

Mujahideen forces reportedly detained, ill-treated and killed people in areas they effectively controlled if they suspected them of links with the government or rival Mujahideen groups. One case reported in 1990 was that of Haji Anaat Khan, a supporter of the former king, Zahir Shah, who was detained together with his assistant in November 1989 while travelling through territory controlled by the *Hezb-e-Islami* (*Hekmatyar*) Mujahideen group. They were forcibly taken over the border to Pakistan and the assistant was reportedly tortured before both were released after eight days. At least 1,500 prisoners were believed to be held by the various Mujahideen groups inside Afghanistan with others said to be held in Pakistan. Several abductions from Pakistan were also attributed by some sources to the Mujahideen. The fate of two people who were abducted in 1989 remained unclear at the end of 1990. Abdul Fatah Wadoud, an Afghan working for the World Food Programme in Peshawar, was reportedly abducted by *Hezb-e-Islami* (*Hekmatyar*); and John Tarzwell, a Canadian relief worker, was abducted by an unidentified Mujahideen group.

The Mujahideen also carried out executions. Four *Hezb-e-Islami* (*Hekmatyar*) supporters were reportedly hanged in public at Taloqan in January by members of the *Jamiat-e-Islami* group under Ahmad Shah Masood's command. They were apparently tried and sentenced under Islamic law in connection with killings in 1989. Two other hangings by Mujahideen forces were reported at Spinboldak in October.

Amnesty International expressed concern to the government about the continued imprisonment of NUP members and, in response, was informed in May that three of those arrested had been released by February under a decree issued by President Najibullah. The authorities did not, however, clarify how many NUP supporters were being held. Amnesty International also inquired about people arrested following the March coup attempt, urging full respect for their human rights, and about prisoners reportedly arrested in previous years. The authorities responded on several cases. Amnesty International also called for the commutation of all death sentences.

ALBANIA

According to official sources nearly 200 political prisoners were pardoned and released between June and December, and several dozen others were released early on parole. At least 600 others remained in detention, including people imprisoned during the year. The majority were prisoners of conscience detained for attempting to exercise their rights to freedom of movement and freedom of expression. In most cases they had been denied legal assistance before and during trial. It was alleged that police and investigators had beaten and otherwise ill-treated suspects following arrest in order to obtain confessions. Prison conditions were harsh. It was alleged that border guards shot without warning scores of people attempting to leave the country. The authorities stated that some three or four death sentences are imposed every year, but owing to official censorship no details of death sentences or executions carried out in 1990 were available.

In January anti-government demonstrations took place in Tirana and Shkodër, followed by reports of unrest in other towns. On 2 July there were further anti-government demonstrations in Tirana, and several groups of people entered foreign embassies. Clashes occurred when security forces tried to prevent others from following them. However, that night and in the next few days almost 5,000 people took refuge in foreign embassies. In mid-July they were allowed to leave the country. In December the authorities decided to legalize opposition parties after mass peaceful demonstrations by students in Tirana, and the first two opposition parties were founded. Anti-government rioting broke out in Shkodër and other towns between 12 and 14 December and some 150 people were arrested.

In May and June the People's Assembly adopted legal reforms which softened some of the harshest restrictions on the rights to freedom of expression, conscience and movement. Other changes restored legal status to lawyers (lost in 1967) and reintroduced provision for early release on parole. In June Albania was granted observer status with the Conference on Security and Cooperation in Europe (CSCE) and in September sought full membership.

Until 1990 the state severely restricted travel abroad and few Albanian citizens, apart from official delegations and a limited number of students, were permitted to leave the country. In June a decree was passed granting citizens the right to a passport, but many people continued to leave the country without official permission.

Among the changes introduced in May was the abolition of a law which had defined attempts to leave the country without official permission as a form of treason punishable by 10 to 25 years' imprisonment or death. Redefined as "illegal border-crossing", this offence became punishable by a maximum of five years' imprisonment. This change was not retroactive for people convicted before May and many prisoners of conscience continued to serve sentences of up to 20 years imposed under the old law.

Among them were Namik Ajazi, who was sentenced to 20 years' imprisonment in May 1988 by the district court of Librazhd, later reduced to 13 years; Aleksander Rexhepi, sentenced to 13 years' imprisonment in April 1988 by the district court of Shkodër, apparently merely for having spoken with friends about his wish to leave the country; and Zeni Jonuzi, sentenced to 13 years' imprisonment in October 1988, also by the district court of Shkodër.

In early July Haxhi Sula, Agim Sula, Petro Mishtari and Ilir Seran were sentenced by the district court of Tirana to between two and three years' imprisonment and up to five years' internal exile for attempted "illegal border-crossing". The four men had been arrested near the town of Librazhd while attempting to cross into Yugoslavia. Another member of the group, Kujtim Xhaja, was shot and killed by border guards. In July Christos Mertyris, a member of Albania's Greek minority, was sentenced to two years' imprisonment for "illegal border-crossing" by the district court of Gjirokastër.

Changes were also made to Article 55 of the criminal code which prohibits "anti-state agitation and propaganda". In May the maximum sentence for this offence was reduced from 25 years' imprisonment or death to 10 years' imprisonment. This change was not retroactive except in the case of people convicted of "religious propaganda", who became eligible for release. Many prisoners of conscience who had non-violently expressed political dissent continued to serve long prison sentences.

Information came to light during the year on the imprisonment of Petrit Ishmi, Alfred Berisha and Xhulieta Cuka, typographers from Tirana, who had been arrested in March 1989 after they produced and distributed a pamphlet calling for demonstrations to protest at restrictions on freedom of speech and the press. In August 1989 a military court in Tirana convicted them under Article 55 and sentenced Petrit Ishmi to 20 years' imprisonment and five years' internal exile and Alfred Berisha to 15 years' imprisonment. Xhulieta Cuka received a 13-year prison sentence but was released in November 1989 under the terms of a general pardon which included almost all women prisoners.

In April 1990 a former political prisoner, Ramiz Kaca, aged 78 and in poor health, was sentenced to five years' imprisonment by Tirana district court for having sent letters to the authorities protesting at violence used by the police against people who had taken part in peaceful demonstrations in Tirana at the end of January. His trial was closed to the public and he was not permitted legal assistance. His sentence was reduced on appeal to three years' imprisonment. In November he was pardoned and unconditionally released.

In June three men, Vasil Dhimitri, Zeqir Gollobani and Faruk Pico, were reportedly tried in Tirana on charges of organizing the 28 January demonstration. According to some accounts they were sentenced to between 14 months and two years' imprisonment, but these sentences could not be confirmed.

The limited information available suggested that most, perhaps all, prisoners of conscience imprisoned for their religious beliefs had been released by the end of the year, including Father Ndoc Luli (see *Amnesty International Report 1985*) who was reportedly released in 1989. Restrictions on religion (which was banned in 1967) were relaxed: in early November President Ramiz Alia indicated that the constitutional ban on religious activities and propaganda would be abolished. On 4 November Roman Catholic worshippers in Shkodër attended a public mass for the first time since 1967 and by the end of the year Greek Orthodox and Muslim services had also been held in a number of places without official interference.

The punishment of "administrative internment" — internal exile imposed by administrative order and without recourse to courts — was abolished. This measure had often been applied to families whose relatives had left the country without official permission, or to political dissenters. However, the available information indicated that people already administratively detained had not, as a result of the change, been automatically allowed to return home. Internal exile continued to exist as a form of supplementary punishment imposed by courts and could still be applied for up to two years as a "preventive measure" against people who had not committed a criminal offence, but whose activities were judged to be "incompatible with good conduct and social morality".

The code of criminal procedure was changed in May to allow defendants the right of access to lawyers throughout criminal proceedings. Lawyers' associations were established in November by the Ministry of Justice (itself re-established in May).

Former political prisoners alleged that following their arrest they had been tortured to force them to confess. They stated that they had been brutally beaten, deprived of sleep and made to wear handcuffs which were deliberately tightened in order to cause intense pain. Several alleged that they had been tortured with electric shocks. People who were arrested during the demonstrations on 2 July in Tirana described how they had been taken to police headquarters and repeatedly interrogated and beaten before being released. There were reports that many of those arrested in connection with the anti-government riots in December had been tortured.

In June Odysseas Prasos (see *Amnesty International Report 1990*), who was reported to have died after being arrested in October 1989 while attempting to leave the country without permission, arrived in Greece after he and two other members of his family had been granted passports. He confirmed, however, that he and his three brothers had been severely beaten following their arrest near the Greek border and afterwards at Sarandë police station, and that they had been dragged through local villages to be denounced and beaten as "traitors". As a result of this ill-treatment Odysseas Prasos was admitted to Tirana prison hospital for treatment. Yorgos Prasos alleged that he had been made to hang by his hands from the ceiling of a cell in Sarandë police station and that on one occasion electric shocks were administered to him. The four brothers were pardoned and released in November 1989.

Former political prisoners reported harsh conditions of imprisonment, including poor food and inadequate medical care. Those who had been held in corrective labour camps in Spaç and Qafë e Barit, where prisoners mine copper and pyrites, complained that prisoners were obliged to achieve high work quotas in dangerous conditions with minimal industrial protection.

Several people were allegedly shot by police while taking part in demonstrations in July in Tirana or while trying to enter embassies; among those said to have been killed were Edmond Hoti and Ramadan Zidri. There were also reports that border guards regularly shot without warning people trying to leave the country. A refugee, Vasilis Mathios, reportedly alleged that his son and three others were killed by border guards with bayonets on 13 December while trying to cross into Greece. However, in the last week of December border guards apparently did not fire on several thousand people, mainly members of the Greek minority, who crossed into Greece.

In May the number of offences punishable by death was reduced from 34 to 11 and women were exempted from the death penalty. Capital offences still included embezzlement or theft of state property, as well as treason, espionage, terrorism and murder. According to official statements, between 1980 and 1990 four death sentences were imposed for political offences and three or four people were sentenced to death every year for ordinary crimes. According to unofficial sources, the bodies of execution victims were sometimes publicly exhibited.

In April Amnesty International wrote to President Alia urging the abolition of the death penalty, and expressing the hope that amendments to the criminal code would ensure that Albanian citizens could enjoy without fear of punishment the non-violent exercise of their human rights. The organization also called on the authorities to ratify the international covenants on human rights. In July Amnesty International asked the government for details of any charges brought against those held in connection with their attempts to leave the country. It called for an investigation into any killings of demonstrators or people seeking refuge in foreign embassies and urged that security forces comply with the UN Code of Conduct for Law Enforcement Officials.

In December the organization called for constitutional changes which would provide effective guarantees for basic human rights. It also expressed concern about the continued detention of prisoners of conscience; allegations of torture and ill-treatment and poor prison conditions; and reports that people trying to leave the country had been killed by border guards. In addition, it urged that those arrested in connection with the riots in December be guaranteed legal safeguards, including adequate time to prepare their defence: 26 of them had been sentenced to up to 20 years' imprisonment within one week of their arrest.

ALGERIA

Fifteen government opponents sentenced after an unfair trial in 1987 were released in July. Some may have been prisoners of conscience. There were renewed allegations of torture and ill-treatment of prisoners. Seven people were sentenced to death *in absentia*.

New legislation was introduced in March under which those convicted of publishing information endangering state security or national unity may be imprisoned for up to 10 years. Penalties of up to three years' imprisonment may be imposed for criticizing Islam or other revealed religions.

By the end of the year over 30 new parties had been registered under legislation introduced in 1989. In June the *Front islamique du salut* (FIS), Islamic Salvation Front, gained the majority of votes cast in the country's first multi-party municipal elections.

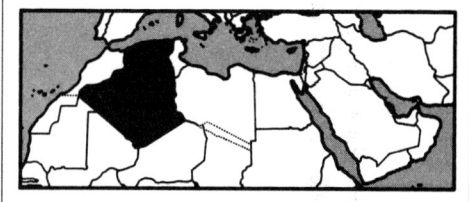

In July the government of President Chadli Benjedid announced an amnesty for those tried and convicted by the former State Security Court (see *Amnesty International Report 1990*) and those found guilty of political offences committed before the new constitution was introduced in February 1989. The amnesty benefited those arrested in connection with the riots of October 1988 (see *Amnesty International Report 1989*) who had been freed on *liberté provisoire*, provisional liberty, as well as members of the security forces accused of torturing detainees during the riots. A further Act established rates of compensation for those who had been tortured during the riots.

The *Direction générale pour la documentation et la securité* (DGDS), General Office for Documentation and Security, a security police force, was dissolved in September. It was widely criticized during the 1988 riots for its involvement in surveillance and repression of government opponents.

Fifteen political prisoners sentenced after an unfair trial in 1987 were released in July. Their sentences had been quashed in 1989 but they had remained in prison pending a retrial. Those freed, some of whom may have been prisoners of conscience, included Mansouri Milyani,

Abdelkader Chbouti and Mohamed A'mamrah, all of whom had originally been sentenced to death. The 15 had been tried before the State Security Court with more than 170 other supporters of radical Islamic groups on charges of plotting to overthrow the government, murder, sabotage, armed robbery and membership of armed gangs (see *Amnesty International Report 1988*). They were the last of those tried to be released.

Torture continued to be reported. About 60 prisoners who escaped from Blida prison in September, including untried members of Islamic groups accused of violent offences and convicted criminal prisoners, alleged that they were tortured after their recapture a few days later. They were said to have been beaten with plastic hoses, electric wires, whips and thongs. They also alleged that they were tortured with a method known as *rabha*, where a stick is tied to a rope binding the victim's feet and tightened so that it cuts into the flesh. They were then reportedly hung upside-down and beaten on the chest, back and head. The government ordered an inquiry, which confirmed the allegations.

Further allegations of ill-treatment were made by more than 20 people arrested in Ténès in October. They were detained following demonstrations and riots in the town and were taken to Ténès police headquarters, where they were allegedly kicked, beaten and urinated on by police officers. Five of the alleged victims, all of whom reportedly faced criminal charges arising from the riots, were aged under 18. The authorities denied that they were ill-treated.

Seven people were sentenced to death *in absentia* after being convicted of carrying out an armed attack in January on a court in Blida. During the attack one gendarme and two of the assailants were killed. The seven were among those who escaped from Blida Prison in September.

Amnesty International welcomed the releases of prisoners. It also expressed concern to the government about continued reports of torture and sought information about the outcome of relevant official inquiries.

ANGOLA

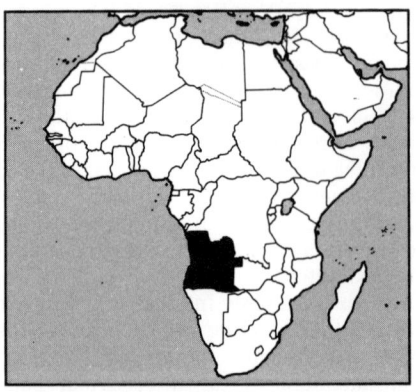

Hundreds of suspected government opponents were arrested. Many political prisoners, possibly thousands, arrested in previous years continued to be held without trial, although the government announced the release of over 3,800. One prisoner was reported to have died as a result of torture, and others were ill-treated. Two people believed to have "disappeared" in 1977 emerged from hiding. At least one death sentence was passed. The armed opposition *União Nacional para a Independência Total de Angola* (UNITA), National Union for the Total Independence of Angola, held thousands of prisoners. Both sides were alleged to have forcibly conscripted civilians into their forces and to have deliberately killed prisoners.

The government and UNITA made some progress in talks to end the war, but did not reach agreement by the end of 1990. The conflict affected all parts of Angola and intensified in the northern provinces. Hundreds of civilians were killed. Cuban troops assisting government forces continued to withdraw in accordance with an international agreement (see *Amnesty International Report 1990*). Hunger caused by war and drought affected several million people and many died as a result.

Legal reforms introduced included the creation in April of a Supreme People's Court, which President José Eduardo dos Santos described as the first practical step towards establishing the independence of the judiciary. In October President dos Santos announced plans to introduce a multi-party political system. A committee began planning constitutional amendments which were to include increased protection of human rights.

Few details about prisoners, both those held from previous years and those arrested in 1990, were released by the government or UNITA. Restrictions on freedom of movement increased the difficulty of obtaining information from areas affected by conflict.

The majority of political prisoners were UNITA combatants or people suspected of assisting UNITA. Others were members or supporters of groups fighting for the independence of Cabinda, an Angolan enclave between Congo and Zaire, and government soldiers suspected of politically motivated offences. Detainees were held without trial in prisons and detention centres in various provinces. They apparently had no opportunity to challenge the legality of their imprisonment: a few, however, reportedly obtained their release through bribery. Some were thought to be imprisoned solely on suspicion of sympathizing with UNITA or opposing government policies, but it was impossible to obtain sufficient information to determine whether they were prisoners of conscience.

Government forces announced the capture of some 200 UNITA combatants during the year. Seven people, including an Evangelical Church pastor, were paraded publicly in May shortly after their arrest: they were accused of planning to plant bombs in Huambo city in central Angola. The pastor was accused of forging identity cards for UNITA members.

There were no trials reported during the year of anyone arrested for political reasons or captured in 1990 or previous years. However, over 3,800 prisoners, mostly former UNITA members, were released, according to official sources.

Among those held without trial were members of Cabinda opposition groups. João Mateus Fuca Baluarte, a member of the *Frente da Libertação do Estado de Cabinda* (FLEC), Cabinda State Liberation Front, who was reportedly arrested in Cabinda in 1987 and tortured by security police, was apparently still held in Bentiaba prison in Namibe province. Andre Gimbi Nzungu, a member of the *União Nacional de Libertação de Cabinda*, National Union for the Liberation of Cabinda, who was arrested in Cabinda in 1989, was also apparently still held.

One prisoner was reported to have died as a result of torture. In February officials reported that Marcolino Nduvale Faustino, a former UNITA officer, had hanged himself in Luanda's high security prison known as Catete Road Prison. Various other sources, however, suggested that he had died as a result of torture. Officials said he had surrendered to the authorities in 1989 and was then allowed to go free until early 1990 when he was arrested as a suspected UNITA spy. According to UNITA sources, however, he was captured in battle in mid-1988 and had been held continuously since then. No inquest into his death was known to have been held by the end of 1990.

Numerous reports were received of prisoners being beaten by soldiers and police in various parts of the country.

In January two people believed to have been arrested after an unsuccessful coup attempt in May 1977 and listed among many hundreds who then "disappeared" returned to Luanda. No action was taken against them by the authorities. They had apparently evaded arrest in 1977 and had been living in hiding elsewhere in Angola. Although about 200 prisoners arrested in connection with the coup attempt were freed in December 1979, the authorities never accounted for hundreds more who "disappeared" in detention and are believed to have been killed.

On several occasions UNITA alleged that government troops had deliberately killed civilians and government army deserters. Government sources alleged that UNITA had deliberately killed civilians. Neither side provided detailed accounts and it was impossible to obtain independent corroboration of the alleged killings.

At least one death sentence was imposed: in January José Pedro da Silva Martins, a former soldier, was convicted by the Luanda Military Court of murdering a Swedish diplomat in September 1989. He appeared to have no right of appeal. At least three people sentenced to death in previous years remained under sentence of death – two pilots convicted in 1989, and Moisés André Lina, an opposition leader convicted in 1987 (see *Amnesty International Reports 1988* and *1990*).

Opposition groups also held prisoners. UNITA reportedly held up to 10,000 prisoners, many of whom were believed to be government soldiers. Tito Chingunji and Wilson dos Santos, former UNITA representatives abroad, reportedly remained restricted in Jamba, UNITA's headquarters in southeast Angola. Former UNITA members compiled a list of about 20 UNITA members who, they alleged, had been deliberately killed by UNITA in previous years (see *Amnesty International Reports 1989* and *1990*).

Both UNITA and FLEC abducted foreign nationals as part of their campaigns for international recognition. A French oil worker captured in northwest Angola in February died from illness or exhaustion in UNITA custody. FLEC abducted over 12 people: all but one were subsequently released.

Amnesty International investigated the cases of possible prisoners of conscience, including the two prisoners from Cabinda. It also sought information from the government about the number and identities of released prisoners, and about the death in custody of Marcolino Nduvale Faustino, but without response. Amnesty International appealed for the commutation of the death sentences.

ANTIGUA AND BARBUDA

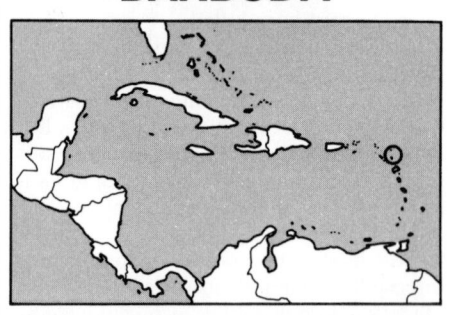

One death sentence was imposed. There were no executions; the last execution was carried out in 1989. Flogging was introduced for rape.

Everette Byers was sentenced to death in April for murder. He was one of two prisoners reportedly under sentence of death at the end of the year.

In June Parliament approved an amendment to the Corporal Punishment Act introducing a sentence of flogging, in addition to a prison sentence, for convicted rapists.

In November Amnesty International wrote to Prime Minister Vere C. Bird Sr, noting that flogging constitutes cruel, inhuman or degrading punishment and as such is prohibited by internationally recognized standards. The organization urged that the punishment of flogging be abolished, and that no flogging sentences be carried out.

ARGENTINA

Allegations of torture and ill-treatment of detainees by the police increased. One person allegedly "disappeared" after being taken into police custody. Investigations were not completed into allegations that in 1989 some members of an opposition group had been extrajudicially executed or had "disappeared", and that others had been tortured or ill-treated. An attempt by the President to reintroduce the death penalty failed. The President pardoned eight former military officers and four others; among them was a former army general who was awaiting trial on 39 murder charges relating to human rights violations.

On 3 December there was a military uprising against the government of President Carlos Menem. The rebellion, involving a few hundred soldiers, was defeated. Thirteen people were killed, including five civilians. The President declared a state of siege on 3 December which was lifted the following day. He said that those involved would be tried by military courts and noted that the penalties provided for rebellion included execution. He subsequently retracted his support for the death penalty.

On 29 December President Menem pardoned and released the leaders of the military government which ruled Argentina between 1976 and 1983, and other high-ranking officers jailed for crimes committed during the "Dirty War". Also included in the presidential pardon and release were the past military government's economy minister, José Alfredo Martínez de Hoz; the former leader of the Montonero guerrilla group, Mario Firmenich; and two former Peronist activists, Duilio Brunello and Norma Kennedy. Among the military officers pardoned by President Menem was former army general Carlos Suárez Mason, extradited from the United States of America in 1988, who had been awaiting trial on 39 murder charges relating to human rights violations.

Reports of torture and ill-treatment of detainees in police custody in Buenos Aires province were more frequent than in previous years. It appeared that the police were reluctant to investigate complaints against members of the police, other security agencies and the armed forces.

In October Luis Patti, the Deputy Police Chief of Pilar, Buenos Aires province, was detained and charged with beating Daniel Bársola and Miguel Angel Guerrero and torturing them by electric shocks. The two men had been detained on 12 September on suspicion of burglary. Following a public outcry against Deputy Police Chief Patti's detention, the judge who had ordered the detention received telephone threats. He was then taken off the case by an appeal court on the grounds that he might not be able to judge the case fairly. Deputy Police Chief Patti was released shortly afterwards, pending the outcome of the judicial investigation.

In September Andrés Alberto Nuñez, from La Plata, Buenos Aires province, reportedly "disappeared" after being taken into custody by the Investigations Force of La Plata. He was reportedly detained at his home on 28 September on suspicion of theft. A witness claimed to have seen Andrés Alberto Nuñez being beaten at the Investigations Force headquarters. The police denied that he had been detained. An investigation into the case was begun by the Criminal Court of La Plata, but Andrés Alberto Nuñez' fate and whereabouts remained unknown at the end of the year.

Argentine human rights organizations alleged that the Human Rights Directorate in the Ministry of the Interior failed to follow up consistently the cases of over 150 children who had "disappeared" with their parents or who had been born to women who were held in secret detention centres during the period of military rule between 1976 and 1983. Many of these children had allegedly been given to police and military families.

Investigations remained open into the treatment in 1989 of members of the *Movimiento Todos por la Patria* (MTP), All for the Fatherland Movement, who had been involved in an armed attack on the Third Infantry Regiment barracks at La Tablada, Buenos Aires province, in January 1989 (see *Amnesty International Report 1990*). Significant evidence had supported allegations that two MTP prisoners were extrajudicially executed after surrender and that three others "disappeared" after giving themselves up to military personnel. There was also evidence that several MTP prisoners were tortured and ill-treated, by beatings and threats among other methods, while in military, police and prison custody.

The investigations into these allegations continued in the Federal Court of the District of Morón, Buenos Aires province, and in other criminal courts. In October 1989 a judge of the 6th Criminal Court of Buenos Aires had ruled that the case against police and prison officers for the alleged assault on five MTP prisoners in the cells of *Tribunales*, the main courthouse in Buenos Aires, should be dismissed. An appeal against this decision was lodged in 1989 by the state prosecutor and by lawyers acting for the complainants. By the end of 1990 the case had not been resolved, nor had other investigations into alleged violations against MTP prisoners resulted in any prosecutions.

In August President Menem sent draft legislation to the Argentine Congress to reintroduce the death penalty for certain crimes, including kidnapping resulting in death, and drug-trafficking. However, the legislation was withdrawn shortly afterwards owing to opposition from most legislators and several influential organizations, including the Roman Catholic Church.

In March Amnesty International published a report, *The Attack on the Third Infantry Regiment Barracks at La Tablada: Investigations into Allegations of Torture, "Disappearances" and Extrajudicial Executions*, which concluded that there was compelling evidence to support allegations that after surrender some MTP prisoners had been extrajudicially executed or had "disappeared", and others had been tortured or ill-treated. The organization urged the government to take swift action to prevent further such abuses and said that delays into the investigations of these allegations amounted to a denial of the right to a prompt, thorough and effective investigation.

In November Amnesty International requested information from the authorities about measures taken in connection with allegations of torture and ill-treatment of detainees in police custody in Buenos Aires province. The organization continued to press the authorities to establish the whereabouts of children who had "disappeared". In August Amnesty International wrote to President Menem urging him not to make further proposals to reintroduce the death penalty. The organization pointed out that the reintroduction of the death penalty would be contrary to both world and regional trends and would contravene the American Convention on Human Rights which provides that the death penalty shall not be re-established in states that have abolished it.

AUSTRALIA

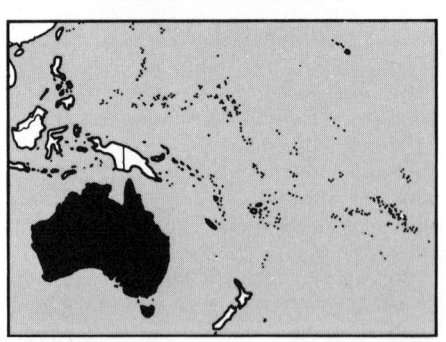

The Royal Commission into Aboriginal Deaths in Custody continued its inquiries into deaths of Aboriginals in previous years. Prisoners in Yatala Labour Prison said that they had been denied food during a protest in January; the authorities denied the allegations.

No deaths said to have been caused by torture or ill-treatment, either in police or prison custody, were brought to the attention of Amnesty International during the year. The Royal Commission into Aboriginal Deaths in Custody (see *Amnesty International Reports 1989* and *1990*) published reports on the deaths of Aboriginals in previous years, but did not find evidence that they resulted from police torture or ill-treatment. The Commission continued its inquiries and held a number of public hearings but had not issued its final report by the end of the year. The Minister for Aboriginal Affairs wrote to Amnesty International in June. He stressed his government's commitment to the prevention of Aboriginal deaths in custody and mentioned several initiatives taken by states and territories to implement the recommendations contained in the Commission's interim report of 1989.

Amnesty International received reports that in January over 120 prisoners in the Yatala Labour Prison in South Australia were denied food for 72 hours as a punishment. In response to Amnesty International's inquiries and expression of concern, the state authorities denied the reports and said that food was available to the prisoners if they returned to their cells.

In October the federal government acceded to the Second Optional Protocol to the International Covenant on Civil and Political Rights Aiming at the Abolition of the Death Penalty.

AUSTRIA

Allegations of torture and ill-treatment in police custody continued. Those who made criminal complaints about ill-treatment risked criminal prosecution or investigation. Two conscientious objectors to military service served prison sentences; both were considered prisoners of conscience.

In June the government announced the implementation of interim measures to combat ill-treatment of detainees held in police custody. It said the measures included improved training of police officers, unannounced visits by police doctors to police stations to make on-the-spot examinations of detainees, the distribution to every detainee of a paper outlining the detainee's rights, and the establishment of an expert panel to examine proposals to prevent ill-treatment.

The Interior Minister stated in January that between 1984 and 1989 he had received 2,622 allegations of ill-treatment by the police, of which 1,142 had resulted in criminal complaints against officers leading to 33 convictions. He said that disciplinary investigations were carried out concerning 120 officers and disciplinary measures were taken against 26 of them.

Allegations of torture and ill-treatment in police custody continued. A number of the alleged victims were reluctant to make complaints, or allow their names to be ublished, for fear of prosecution for defamation.

An 18-year-old Yugoslav was arrested on 16 January on suspicion of attempted theft and taken to Himberg police station for interrogation. He alleged that five or six police officers made him undress, secured his hands behind his back, pushed sharp objects under his fingernails, burned him with a cigarette and beat his genitals with a ruler. He said that this treatment lasted for several hours and that as a result he agreed to sign a confession.

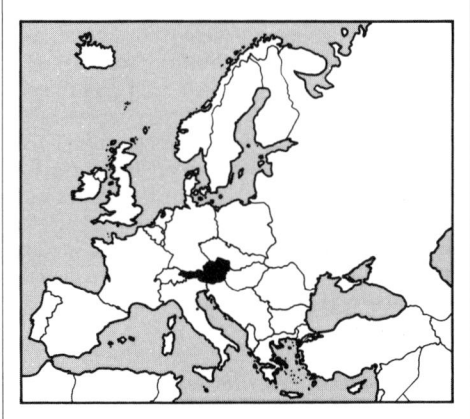

Three days later the investigating judge at the Vienna Juvenile Court ordered a medical examination which was carried out the same day. Doctors noted six second-to-third-degree burns on the man's back and signs of bleeding beneath the nails on two fingers of his left hand. A bruise and swelling were found on his penis, which the doctors said were the effects of being beaten with a blunt instrument. The doctors found that the injuries were at least three days old and could have occurred while he was held in police custody. A police officer testified that the man had not had these injuries when he arrived at the police station.

The Vienna Juvenile Court rejected the man's signed confession because it regarded the allegations of torture as a "possibility [which] could not be excluded". As there was no evidence apart from the confession, the man was convicted only of those offences to which he admitted in open court.

The court also refused to accept the Public Procurator's application to extend the indictment to include the accusation that the man had committed "defamation" by making the allegations of torture. However, the Public Procurator was allowed to pursue this accusation in separate proceedings: the prosecution was later withdrawn owing to lack of evidence. An investigation started by the Public Procurator into the allegations of torture had not been concluded by the end of the year.

In March the Vienna Public Procurator dismissed a criminal complaint lodged by Mustafa Ali against the police about his ill-treatment in police custody in 1989 (see *Amnesty International Report 1990*). His complaint to the Constitutional Court had not been heard by the end of the year.

A 19-year-old woman lodged a formal complaint in June about sexual acts forced upon her at the Karlsplatz police station in Vienna in May. The woman said that she had been detained by two police officers, who forced her to have oral sex with them at the police post and "rewarded" her with drugs in the form of tablets. A third officer was said to have known that the sexual assault was taking place, but failed to intervene. The two police officers were suspended from duty, and the officer who failed to intervene faced disciplinary charges.

Martin Dengscherz and Christian Schwarz served prison sentences for refusing to perform military service on conscientious grounds. The Vienna Higher Alternative Service Commission rejected their applications to be recognized as conscientious objectors, on the grounds that they had not presented their beliefs in a credible manner. Both men were subsequently convicted of refusing to perform military service. Christian Schwarz was released from prison in July after serving a three-month sentence and Martin Dengscherz was released in November after serving a one-month prison sentence.

In January Amnesty International published a report, *Austria: Torture and Ill-treatment*, which focused on allegations of unwarranted and deliberate physical violence, sometimes amounting to torture, in police custody. The organization pressed for additional safeguards during the initial detention period, an effective and impartial complaints mechanism, and full implementation of the United Nations (UN) Convention against Torture. The organization called on the government to ensure that complainants were not discouraged from reporting police abuse through fear of being charged with a criminal offence.

The government responded *inter alia* that a decree of September 1989 required allegations of police ill-treatment to be promptly investigated by a judge unless they were manifestly unfounded. The decree also contained guidelines for public procurators and courts on observing the UN Convention against Torture's prohibition of the use of evidence obtained through torture. The government said that the lodging of counter-complaints, such as defamation, was the exception rather than the rule.

Amnesty International appealed for the release of both prisoners of conscience.

BAHAMAS

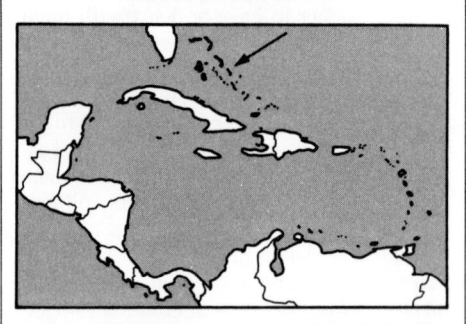

Four prisoners were scheduled for execution but were granted stays. At the end of the year some 21 people were under sentence of death. No executions were carried out in 1990; the last execution took place in 1986.

The executions of four prisoners convicted of murder, set for 21 and 28 August, were stayed. Romain Shephard was granted a stay after he indicated his intention to appeal to the Judicial Committee of the Privy Council in London, which acts as the final court of appeal for the Bahamas. Peter Meadows, Arnold Heastie and Nikita Hamilton were granted stays of execution pending a decision on a constitutional motion in a separate case. The motion argued that it would be unconstitutional to execute anyone in the Bahamas because the method of execution was not specified in the Constitution or any law. The motion was still pending a hearing at the end of the year.

Amnesty International wrote to Prime Minister Lynden Pindling in November expressing concern that death warrants had been issued in August for the execution of the four prisoners and, furthermore, that this action had been taken when a decision was pending on a constitutional challenge to the death penalty. The letter welcomed the stays of execution and urged the government not to issue new death warrants. It also urged the government to commute all death sentences and to take other steps to abolish the death penalty.

BAHRAIN

Dozens of people suspected of opposition to the government, including prisoners of conscience, were arrested and detained without charge or trial. Others were sentenced after unfair trials or continued to serve sentences imposed after unfair trials in previous years. Political detainees alleged that police officers had tortured or ill-treated them in incommunicado detention to make them confess. One death sentence was imposed but there were no executions.

Members of the Shi'a community continued to comprise the majority of those arrested and imprisoned on political grounds. Arrests occurred throughout the year, and dozens of people were detained without charge or trial under the 1974 Decree Law on State Security Measures (see *Amnesty International Report 1990*). Many of those held, among whom were a number of children, were believed to be prisoners of conscience. Some long-term untried detainees were released in August, including al-Sayyed 'Abdullah al-Muharraqi, a Shi'a religious leader.

About 40 people were arrested in June, reportedly for distributing leaflets which expressed solidarity with political prisoners. Most were released within a few weeks. A Sunni religious leader, Nidham Ya'aqoubi, was detained in August, reportedly after criticizing members of the government in his Friday sermons. He was subsequently released uncharged, but forbidden from delivering sermons in the mosque.

Some Bahrainis were arrested on their return from visits or residence abroad and were detained for days or weeks as possible prisoners of conscience. They included six women and their children – families of prisoners sentenced in 1981 for their alleged participation in a coup attempt – who were held for about one week in August and then sent back to Syria.

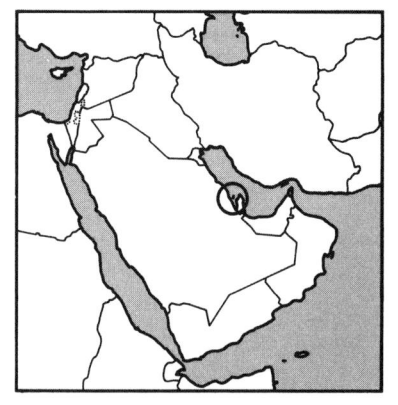

Dozens of political prisoners were sentenced to prison terms after unfair trials. Five were jailed in March at the end of a trial before the Supreme Civil Court of Appeal of nine people arrested in September 1988 (see *Amnesty International Reports 1989* and *1990*). Their arrests had taken place following the brief detention of a prominent religious leader, Sheikh 'Abd al-'Amir al-Jamri, apparently because of his outspoken criticism of government policies.

Muhammad Jamil 'Abd al-'Amir al-Jamri was convicted of membership of an unauthorized organization and other offences and sentenced to 10 years' imprisonment. 'Abd al-Jalil Khalil Ibrahim Hassan received a seven-year term, two others received three-year sentences and the fifth, Hussein Ibrahim al-Qassab, a minor at the time of the offence, was sentenced to six months' imprisonment. Four of the accused were acquitted. All nine defendants alleged that they were tortured by police in pre-trial custody, and prosecution witnesses said they had been threatened by security police to make them give false testimony against the accused. No investigation into these allegations was known to have been carried out.

The trial, like others before the Supreme Civil Court of Appeal, did not satisfy international fair trial standards. The court can convict solely on the basis of uncorroborated confessions obtained by the police in the absence of witnesses, and defendants have no right of appeal against their conviction or sentence. Apart from close relatives of the accused, the public are excluded from the court.

Nineteen other people arrested in 1988 were convicted by the Supreme Civil Court of Appeal in May on charges of forming an unauthorized organization and possession of leaflets. 'Abd al-Ridha Mansour al-Khawaja and 'Abdullah Ibrahim 'Ali al-Sairafi were each sentenced to seven years' imprisonment. Six others received five-year prison sentences. The remaining 11 defendants received one-year prison terms and were released as they had already been in custody for approximately 21 months.

In a separate case, three people charged with membership of an unauthorized organization were acquitted in November, although they were then held for a further week before being released. All three alleged that they had been tortured and beaten in detention. In December nine people from the village of Bani Jamra were sentenced on similar charges. Seven received two-year prison terms, one received a three-year term, and one, Fatima Ibrahim Kadhem, was given a one-year suspended sentence. Two others were acquitted. Most of them had been held since early 1989.

Scores of political prisoners sentenced after unfair trials in previous years remained in prison throughout 1990. They included alleged members of banned organizations such as the Bahrain National Liberation Front (BNLF), the Islamic Liberation Front and the Islamic Enlightenment Society. Other alleged members of these organizations completed their sentences and were released.

Political prisoners, including approximately 70 people sentenced to long prison terms in 1981, complained of harsh prison conditions and mounted a number of hunger-strikes. One took place after Salah al-Khawajah, a political prisoner serving a seven-year term at Jaw Prison, sustained an eye injury, allegedly as a result of torture.

A Pakistani national, convicted of drug-trafficking, was sentenced to death by the

High Criminal Court in July but there were no executions: the last known execution was in 1977.

Amnesty International expressed concern to the government about the imprisonment of possible prisoners of conscience, the use of prolonged incommunicado detention, allegations of torture, unfair trials and the death penalty. It also sought information about a number of specific cases.

Following an inquiry about alleged members of the BNLF imprisoned since 1986, the Minister of the Interior responded in October that one such prisoner was a "trained international terrorist", while other sentenced political prisoners were "criminals...sentenced for using or advocating the use of violence". He denied that the Bahraini authorities were holding prisoners of conscience.

Amnesty International urged the government to ratify the United Nations Convention against Torture and Other Cruel, Inhuman or Degrading Treatment or Punishment, the International Covenant on Civil and Political Rights and other international human rights treaties, and to apply their provisions in order to safeguard human rights.

BANGLADESH

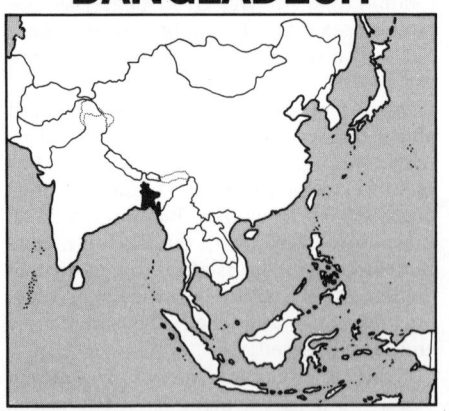

Hundreds of anti-government protesters were arrested, including prisoners of conscience who were detained without charge or trial. Torture of prisoners by police continued, sometimes leading to the death of the suspect. Scores of demonstrators were shot dead by police or paramilitary forces, including some in circumstances suggesting they had been extrajudicially executed. **At least 19 people were sentenced to death. It was not known if there were any executions.**

President Hossain Mohammad Ershad resigned on 6 December following eight weeks of demonstrations and strikes called by opposition parties. He handed over power to a caretaker vice-president nominated by the opposition parties, Chief Justice Shahabuddin Ahmed, who was appointed to head an interim administration lasting up to three months, during which parliamentary elections would be held.

In October, after police shot students dead during a demonstration in Dhaka, the *Sarbodaliya Chhatra Oikya,* All Party Students Unity, was formed to coordinate further protest action. The three main opposition alliances – the eight-party alliance led by the Awami League (AL), the seven-party alliance led by the Bangladesh National Party (BNP) and the leftist five-party alliance – participated jointly in the anti-government protest movement. The *Jamaat-e-Islami*, Party of Islam, and the trade union federation, *Sramik Karmichari Oikya Parishad* (SKOP), also called strikes and demonstrations.

A state of emergency declared on 27 November was lifted on 6 December. Under the state of emergency constitutional guarantees safeguarding human rights were suspended, including the right to challenge arbitrary or illegal detention in court.

In late October communal attacks against the Hindu minority resulted in at least two deaths and numerous rapes. The government imposed a curfew, but there were complaints that the police failed to intervene to protect victims from attacks, which continued in some areas during curfew hours.

Hundreds of opposition party workers, including probable prisoners of conscience, were detained in connection with the anti-government demonstrations. Sheikh Hasina Wajed, the President of the AL, was placed under house arrest from 27 November to 4 December. Several others were also detained in November before the emergency was imposed, including the presidents of the Ramna and Dhaka City branches of the *Jatiya Samajtantrik Dal* (JSD), National Socialist Party; a leader of the BNP youth wing, Mirza Abbas; and a leader of the AL's youth wing,

Mostafa Mohiuddin Monto. Further arrests occurred during the state of emergency. Those detained included Abdul Quyyum Mukul, Secretary of the Dhaka City Committee of the Communist Party of Bangladesh, and Mohammad Rahmatullah of the AL. In Sylhet about 20 people, including five students, were reportedly detained. All these detainees were released after the change of government.

The Special Powers Act (SPA) empowers the government and local authorities to detain without charge or trial anyone alleged to have committed a "prejudicial act" likely or intended "to endanger public safety or the maintenance of public order". Detention orders extending beyond 30 days must be approved by the government and can be renewed indefinitely.

Some government opponents who were detained under the SPA were also charged with criminal offences apparently for political reasons. Pankganj Bhattacharya, General Secretary of the Bangladesh National Awami Party, was detained under the SPA in October and also charged in connection with attacks on private offices in Dhaka during a transport blockade organized by opposition parties. He was released soon afterwards, shortly before a *habeas corpus* action challenging the legality of his detention could be heard in court.

Hundreds of prisoners remained in detention under the SPA, including an unknown number of possible prisoners of conscience and other political prisoners. In December the interim government issued warrants for the arrests under the SPA of former president Hossain Mohammad Ershad and 16 ministers and officials who had served in his government, apparently in connection with investigations into corruption. Hossain Mohammad Ershad was arrested in December, as were former vice-president Moudud Ahmed, former deputy prime minister Shah Moazzem Hossain, former interior minister Mahmudul Hasan and former industries secretary Mosharaf Hossain and his wife, Zeenat. All remained in detention without charge at the end of the year.

New cases of torture of criminal and political suspects by the police were reported; seven suspects were said to have died as a result. Wazed Ali, a rickshaw-puller, died in custody in February at Kotwali police station, Jessore, reportedly after a severe beating. His death was followed by clashes between protesters and police during which at least four people died. The police said that Wazed Ali had committed suicide, but they apparently disposed of his body themselves.

In May Hasanul Karim, known as "Manik", a student leader, died a few hours after his arrest in Chittagong. A post-mortem attributed his death to shock and brain haemorrhage, and found that the injuries that caused his death had been inflicted with blunt weapons. The police said that he had been attacked by members of the public at the time of his arrest but in a photograph taken shortly afterwards there was no sign of the injuries later found on his body.

Manirul Murshed, an asylum-seeker who had been active in the student wing of the AL, was tortured after Swedish authorities returned him to Bangladesh in October. He was detained by airport police on his arrival. During the 13 hours of his detention he was beaten with a truncheon, including on the soles of his feet and his genitals, whipped with electric cable and kicked.

During anti-government demonstrations from October to December scores of demonstrators were reportedly shot dead by police and the paramilitary Bangladesh Rifles, sometimes in circumstances which suggested they were victims of extrajudicial executions. For example, on 10 October police reportedly shot three people dead near Gulistan, Dhaka. Witnesses said police officers dragged one person away who had been shot in the chest but was still alive. Officers then struck him on the head with a rifle butt, causing his death, and took his body away in a van.

At least 19 people were known to have been sentenced to death; 17 for murder and two for drug-smuggling. However, the true figure was believed to be considerably higher. It was not known if there were any executions. The government informed Amnesty International that there had been one execution in 1987 and two in 1988.

Amnesty International raised with the government four cases of death in custody which occurred in 1988 and 1989 and requested information on the inquiry the government said it had initiated into reprisal killings in the Chittagong Hill Tracts in June 1989 (see *Amnesty International Report 1990*). The government responded in each case, but did not provide evidence that full and impartial investigations had been held.

In November Amnesty International urged the government to hold full and impartial investigations into the deaths of anti-government demonstrators and to ensure that law enforcement officers were instructed to use lethal force only when strictly necessary. The organization urged the government to release all prisoners detained for the non-violent expression of their political views, and to charge any prisoner against whom there was evidence of involvement in a recognizably criminal offence. Amnesty International also urged the government to abolish the death penalty. After the change of government in December, the organization urged the interim authorities to ratify international human rights instruments and to introduce strict limits on powers of administrative detention.

BENIN

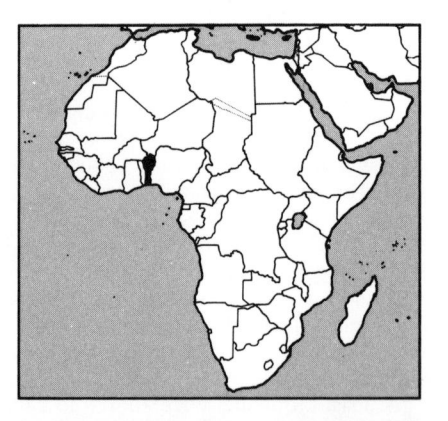

Political reforms at the beginning of the year were followed by important changes affecting human rights and strengthening the rule of law. All remaining political prisoners were released in an amnesty announced in March. In contrast to previous years, there were no reports of torture and the few people arrested for political reasons were referred to the courts instead of being held unlawfully or in administrative detention. A political activist was killed in September by a security officer.

After several months of strikes and demonstrations advocating political change, the government convened a national conference in February to discuss reforms. At the conference, representatives of some previously banned opposition groups and other political leaders called for an inquiry into torture allegations, the dismantling of all torture centres, and the release of all remaining political prisoners. A High Council, chaired by the Roman Catholic Assistant Archbishop of Cotonou, Monsignor Isidore de Souza, was set up to oversee the implementation of the conference's recommendations. President Mathieu Kérékou retained his post as head of state, but an interim government was appointed, headed by Nicéphore Soglo, to hold power until elections scheduled for 1991. A new constitution was prepared and approved by a national referendum on 2 December. It included important human rights safeguards prohibiting arbitrary detention and making torture a criminal offence.

The national conference also approved the formal establishment of a 42-member National Human Rights Commission which included government appointees and elected representatives of the country's non-governmental organizations. The conference recommended the creation of a national committee to investigate past torture allegations, but apparently no investigation was initiated.

The last remaining political prisoners were released under an amnesty announced in March. Three prisoners arrested in 1977 and held either without charge or after a grossly unfair trial, as well as two groups of prisoners accused of plotting to overthrow the government in 1988, were among those released. However, no official inquiry into prisoners' allegations of torture or other human rights abuses had opened by the end of the year.

Some government critics and opponents were arrested, but most cases were quickly referred to the procuracy and the courts to determine whether offences had been committed. This contrasted with the official practice throughout the 1970s and 1980s of detaining political opponents without trial, outside the jurisdiction of the courts. Most of those arrested were members of the *Convention du Peuple*, People's Convention, an umbrella organization representing several political groups including the *Parti communiste du Dahomey*, Communist Party of Dahomey, many of whose members had been detained without trial in past years (see *Amnesty International Report 1990*).

One person who appeared to be a prisoner of conscience was Laurent Metognon, a trade unionist. He was arrested in January and held for two weeks for allegedly inciting disobedience against the government and for threatening behaviour in connection with strikes at the Ministry of Finance where he worked. The procuracy ordered his release.

Three other people, including Augustin Voyémé, a medical doctor, were arrested in August at So-Ava for attending an unauthorized meeting. They were taken before the procurator and charged with using violence against the authorities and organizing prohibited demonstrations. They were acquitted at a trial two weeks later.

Other *Convention du Peuple* supporters were arrested when they tried to arrange the replacement of unpopular mayors outside the normal administrative framework. One person was arrested in Savé in February and charged with trying to substitute an illegal authority for legal authority. He was released to await trial, but no proceedings had started by the end of the year. In another case, Jean-Marie Yacoubou, a former prisoner of conscience held from 1985 to 1989, was detained for three weeks from 10 February without charge.

Sègla Kpomassi, a teacher and member of the *Convention du Peuple*, was reportedly shot dead by a security officer on 16 September in Azové, Mono province, where there had been demonstrations and protests against the authorities. No attempt appeared to have been made to arrest him. The Minister of the Interior said Sègla Kpomassi had been shot when officers returned fire from the crowd, but the only other casualty reported was another protester. An inquiry into the circumstances of Sègla Kpomassi's shooting had not concluded at the end of the year.

Amnesty International welcomed the improvements in human rights in 1990 and submitted proposals to the commission drafting the constitution, urging the abolition of the death penalty and the introduction of a procedure to allow all detainees to question the legality of their detention before the courts. In May an Amnesty International delegation visited Benin and discussed measures to protect human rights with government officials, including the establishing of responsibility for past human rights violations. Amnesty International also investigated the cases of those arrested for political reasons in 1990 and was informed by the government that an inquiry into the circumstances of Sègla Kpomassi's death was under way.

BERMUDA

One death sentence was imposed and later commuted. A referendum on capital punishment was held. There were no executions; the last hangings were carried out in 1977. No one was under sentence of death at the end of the year.

Leroy Dunlop was sentenced to death in January after being convicted of premeditated murder. He defended himself at his trial and chose not to exercise his right of appeal. He was scheduled to be executed on 21 February. However, on 16 February the Governor, Sir Desmond Langley, commuted the sentence to life imprisonment following consideration of the case by the Committee on the Prerogative of Mercy.

The referendum on capital punishment approved by an Act of Parliament in June 1989 (see *Amnesty International Report 1990*) took place in August. Voters were asked whether they favoured retaining the death penalty for premeditated murder. Only about one third of registered voters participated in the ballot: some 79 per cent of them favoured retention. The result was not binding on Parliament and a parliamentary debate and vote were pending at the end of the year.

Amnesty International urged the Governor to exercise clemency in the case of Leroy Dunlop and later welcomed the commutation of his death sentence. The organization publicly called for the abolition of the death penalty in Bermuda before the referendum.

BHUTAN

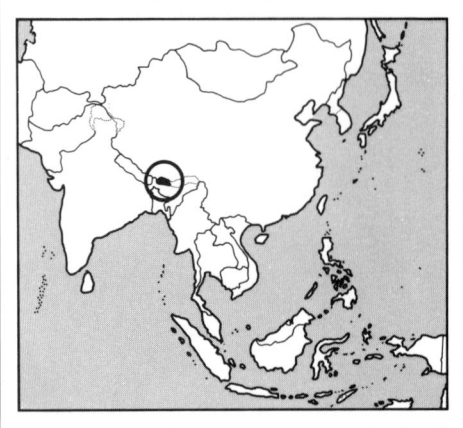

Six prisoners of conscience were detained without trial throughout the year for alleged "anti-national" activities.

Protests by groups of Nepali-speaking southern Bhutanese against the government policy, introduced in 1989, of national cultural integration intensified, and from February or March included the use of intimidation and violence. This policy involved the compulsory wearing of distinctive Bhutanese dress, the promotion of Dzongkha — the language of the majority northern Bhutanese — as the national language, and the promotion of *driglam namzha*, the northern Bhutanese "code of conduct".

The government of King Druk Gyalpo Jigme Singye Wangchuck informed Amnesty International in June that 42 people had been arrested between October and December 1989 in connection with "anti-national" activity in southern Bhutan (see *Amnesty International Report 1990*). Three further prisoners were extradited from Nepal in November and imprisoned in Bhutan. All but six of the prisoners were released on the King's orders.

The six, whom the authorities regarded as ringleaders, were believed by Amnesty International to be prisoners of conscience. They were held without trial throughout 1990 at unknown places of detention. The government said that all of them had committed treason by writing, publishing and distributing literature critical of the government's policy of cultural integration.

Under Bhutanese law, treason is punishable by death. However, King Druk Gyalpo Jigme Singye Wangchuck said that the prisoners would not be executed.

Further detentions in southern Bhutan were reported during the year as political unrest continued. During a tour of southern districts in September the King reportedly released all but 47 of more than 400 prisoners held in the south at that time. Amnesty International did not know the identities of the remaining 47 prisoners or whether they were charged or tried.

Amnesty International appealed throughout the year for the release of the six prisoners of conscience detained since 1989. In June the government told Amnesty International that the six had been involved in violent criminal activity in southern Bhutan and could not be considered prisoners of conscience. However, the government produced no evidence to show that they had been involved in violent crime, and the crimes for which they were apparently being blamed had clearly been committed by other people months after the six had been imprisoned.

At a meeting with Amnesty International in September, the Foreign Minister explained the context of unrest among "anti-nationals" in southern Bhutan, and provided details on the rise of violent criminal acts by these groups during 1990. He said the six had not been tried and that the King hoped to release them after a solution to the problems of southern Bhutan had been negotiated. In December Amnesty International requested further information from the government about the 47 prisoners reportedly detained in southern Bhutan.

BOLIVIA

A man was allegedly tortured and killed by the police. Police officers shot dead a university student in suspicious circumstances warranting an independent investigation. No official investigation was initiated into allegations that intelligence officials had tortured three detainees in 1989.

During the year a wave of public demonstrations against the economic policies of the government of President Jaime Paz Zamora took place across the country. Miners, trade unionists and students protested against the privatization of the state oil company and key mining districts of the state mining company, and against cuts in the education budget. Scores of demonstrators were arrested and detained for short periods of time.

There was a marked increase in the violent activities of armed opposition groups. In October one Bolivian policeman was killed and another injured during an attack on the United States of America (USA) marines' residence in the capital, La Paz. An armed group identifying itself as *Comisión Néstor Paz Zamora – Ejército de Liberación Nacional* (CNPZ-ELN), Néstor Paz Zamora Commission – National Liberation Army, claimed responsibility for the attack. In communiques to Bolivian radio stations, the group demanded the annulment of agreements with the USA to fight drug-trafficking and expressed regret at the death of the policeman. Following the attack dozens of people, most of them students, were detained for short periods and released without charge.

Alejandro Escobar Gutierrez, a Peruvian citizen, was killed in Bolivia. According to morgue officials, his corpse was delivered to the morgue in La Paz between 6 and 7 December by police agents without any explanation. Autopsy reports indicated that his death was caused by gunshot wounds and noted that his body showed clear signs of torture. The authorities alleged that Alejandro Escobar Gutierrez was a member of the CNPZ-ELN, which had held the Bolivian businessman Jorge Lonsdale in captivity after his abduction in June. A joint military-police operation was undertaken on 5 December to rescue Jorge Lonsdale, during which a number of people were killed or arrested. Four bodies were reportedly recovered: three were identified as CPNZ-ELN members and one was said to be that of Jorge Lonsdale.

On 20 July Juan Domingo Peralta, a university student, was killed by agents of the *Grupo Especializado Antiterrorista* (GEA), Anti-Terrorist Special Force, a police unit under the authority of the Ministry of the Interior. According to a statement by the Interior Ministry, Juan Domingo Peralta had been identified as a member of the armed group, *Fuerzas Armadas de Liberación Zarate Willka* (FAL-ZW), the Zarate Willka Armed Liberation Forces. The statement said that he was killed during an armed confrontation with GEA agents while resisting arrest. According to reports, however, no warrant for his arrest had been issued and there was no indication that he was being sought by the authorities. He was not in hiding and regularly attended his classes at the university. Juan Domingo Peralta was the brother of Jhonny Peralta, who was wanted by the police for alleged FAL-ZW activities. By the end of the year no investigation into the killing was known to have been carried out.

Three of the five detainees originally charged with the killing of two Mormon missionaries alleged in 1989 that they had been tortured by intelligence agents (see *Amnesty International Report 1990*). According to reports, no investigation was conducted into these allegations. The trial of the five – Nelson and Felix Encinas Laguna, Constantino Yujra Loza, Gabriel Rojas and Simón Mamani – was repeatedly delayed and was continuing at the end of the year.

The *Juicio de Responsabilidades* (responsibilities trial) of former president General Luis Garcia Meza and 54 co-defendants, which started in 1984, continued during the year. The charges against them included killing and torturing government opponents between 1980 and 1982 (see *Amnesty International Reports 1981* to *1983*). In October hearings opened against 22 defendants charged with the 1980 killings of trade union leader Gualberto Vega, national deputy Carlos Flores Bedregal, and political leader Marcelo Quiroga Santa Cruz, and with the related attack on the *Central Obrera Boliviana* (COB), Bolivian Workers Confederation. Eight witnesses for the prosecution identified some of the defendants as participants in human rights violations. Lawyers acting for the prosecution and representing relatives of the victims received death threats during the year, which they attributed to people linked with former government-sponsored paramilitary groups active during the military government.

Amnesty International wrote to the government urging a thorough and impartial investigation into the circumstances surrounding the death of Alejandro Escobar Gutierrez. The organization also made inquiries about the deaths connected with the 5 December joint military-police operation and sought information about those who had been detained. No reply had been received by the end of the year.

The organization called for a thorough and impartial investigation into the circumstances of Juan Domingo Peralta's killing by the security forces. Amnesty International reiterated its concern that the authorities had failed to investigate allegations that three of the defendants originally accused of killing two Mormon missionaries were tortured. The organization urged the government to ensure that the defendants receive a fair trial conforming to international standards.

BRAZIL

Death squads killed hundreds of people, often in circumstances that suggested extrajudicial executions. Rural trade union leaders were threatened with death or killed, reportedly by off-duty police officers and gunmen. Members of indigenous communities continued to be subject to armed attacks, in which at least four Indian villagers were killed. Eleven people reportedly "disappeared" during the year. The remains of more than 1,000 people were discovered in a secret burial ground in São Paulo; at least eight were thought to be "disappeared" political prisoners killed during the 1960s and 1970s. Torture and ill-treatment of detainees continued. Official inquiries about abuses in prisons made little or no progress, and conditions remained harsh. Peasants involved in land disputes were detained without warrant, charge or trial, held incommunicado and subjected to ill-treatment. Local, state and federal authorities made little progress in bringing to justice those responsible for extrajudicial executions, torture and other human rights violations.

Fernando Collor de Mello, Brazil's first civilian president to be directly elected in 30 years, took office on 15 March.

Death squads, often composed of off-duty or on-duty police officers, killed hundreds of people, including young adults and children, and allegedly undertook contract killings for businesses and professional criminals. Authorities in Rio de Janeiro reported that nearly 500 minors were killed in the state in 1990, most of them by death squads. The members of death squads were often difficult to identify, as they reportedly made a practice of killing people who witnessed their activities.

On 30 April in Diadema, a poor suburb of São Paulo, armed men in plain clothes shot and killed Marcello Rosa de Oliveira, aged 17, and his brother Marcos Rosa de Oliveira, aged 18, when the youths did not present labour cards. About an hour later, four or five armed men in plain clothes approached six youths at a nearby street corner. Reports said the six, ranging in age from 15 to 21, were forced to lie face down on the ground. The gunmen then shot five of them dead and seriously wounded the sixth. These killings were typical of those reportedly committed by death squads.

Two military policemen were convicted in September of the 1989 murder of five young people in Nova Friburgo, Rio de Janeiro state, and sentenced to 71 years' and 42 years' imprisonment respectively. The policemen were said to be members of a death squad.

Four other military policemen were convicted in October of the 1988 abduction, torture and murder of Disney Erwin Rodrigues, aged 18, and Simone Amaral Cerqueira, aged 17, also in Nova Friburgo (see *Amnesty International Report 1989*). Three of the defendants were sentenced to more than 30 years' imprisonment each; the fourth, convicted as an accessory, received a sentence of six months. Among hundreds of such cases, these were the only convictions of alleged death squad members that came to Amnesty International's attention during the year.

Wolmer do Nascimento, a director of the National Movement of Street Children, received written and oral death threats in November after he denounced death squad killings of minors in suburban Rio de Janeiro. He subsequently received federal police protection on orders of the Justice Minister.

The northern state of Pará was a focal point for land conflicts in which rural workers, church workers, trade unionists and others were threatened or killed. Official investigations into these killings or those of previous years failed to result in trials by the end of the year.

In April men claiming to be federal police officers abducted three brothers, all linked to a rural trade union, from their home in Rio Maria, Pará. Paulo Canuto de Oliveira and José Canuto de Oliveira were shot dead, but Orlando Canuto Pereira escaped. An official investigation later identified the killers as military police officers. Their trial had not yet started by the end of the year.

At least five other trade unionists were murdered in Pará during the year. Some 250 peasants, rural trade unionists and lawyers connected with land disputes were reportedly killed in Pará between 1985 and 1990, but none of those responsible for the killings was known to have been brought to justice.

Trade unionists in Acre state, including successors of the murdered union leader Chico Mendes, received death threats and some went into hiding or left the area. In most cases the authorities did little to provide protection or investigate the threats. Ilzamar Mendes (Chico Mendes' widow), José Alves Mendes Neto (Chico Mendes' brother), Gomercindo Clóvis Rodrigues, Raimundo de Barros, Júlio Barbosa de Aquino, Francisco de Assis Monteiro de Oliveira and Osmarino Amâncio Rodrigues were reportedly on a death list of 25 people drawn up by local landowners.

The trial of Chico Mendes' accused murderers took place in December, almost two years after he was killed (see *Amnesty International Reports 1989* and *1990*). Darli Alves was sentenced to 19 years' imprisonment for ordering the murder, and Darci Alves received the same sentence for carrying it out. This was the first time that anyone was convicted in Brazil of ordering the killing of a rural activist.

Indigenous Indian communities suffered violent incursions by hired gunmen, miners and landowners that resulted in deaths and injuries. For example, two Makuxi Indians, Mário Davis and Damião Mendes, were killed in June by hired gunmen, allegedly employed by a local landowner. In September miners reportedly attacked a Yanomami-Yekuana village in Roraima, killing the community's leader Lourenço Yekuana and his son, and seriously wounding one other. Despite the widespread and persistent nature of such attacks, the authorities failed to bring to justice those responsible for the killings and failed to implement promised measures to protect members of indigenous communities. Outside observers continued to find access to indigenous areas restricted by the National Indian Foundation, a government agency, making documentation of human rights violations difficult.

On 26 July police officers allegedly abducted 11 people, including five minors, from a farm in Magé, Rio de Janeiro state. It was believed that the police went to the farm to steal valuables from the group, one of whom was alleged to be a drug-trafficker. Although the authorities announced an investigation, the whereabouts of the 11 remained unknown at the end of the year.

In September an unmarked burial ground near Perus cemetery in São Paulo was found to contain the remains of more than 1,000 people, possibly including eight "disappeared" political prisoners from the 1960s and 1970s. Brazilian human rights organizations believed that victims of death squads active against criminal suspects in that period might also have been interred there. In October forensic scientists began work, expected to take at least a year, to identify the remains.

At least 122 "disappearances" which took place between 1964 and 1985 have been documented by Brazilian human rights organizations, but the remains of only a few of the "disappeared" have been recovered. In November the body of José Maria Ferreira de Araújo, who "disappeared" in 1970, was found in a São

Paulo cemetery, buried under a false name. Local human rights groups were searching for the remains of more "disappeared" people in other cemeteries in or near São Paulo.

Torture and ill-treatment of detainees continued to be widespread. The Brazilian Bar Association's branch in Mato Grosso do Sul reported the torture of 10 prisoners in 1990. In April, for example, maximum security prisoner Eribaldo de Araújo Menezes testified that guards beat and tortured him with electric shocks, left him alone in a wet cell overnight and warned him his life would be in danger if he reported his torture.

Four air force enlisted men, Rober Soares da Silva, Uziel Bernardo da Costa, Walter Félix de Oliveira and Cleuton Eurípedes Inácio, were allegedly tortured on 8 August at the Anápolis, Goiás, air force base. Six air force officers, assisted by four military policemen, reportedly administered electric shocks to the soldiers, who were hooded to prevent them from seeing their interrogators. The officers were investigating the theft of two revolvers from the base. After extensive press coverage, an official investigation resulted in charges against the base commander, two air force officers and four military police officers. Their trial had not started by the end of the year.

A presidential spokesman commenting on the case said: "In this government, torture never again", paraphrasing the title of a report on torture under the former military government published by human rights organizations.

Additional cases of torture of soldiers were later reported in Piauí and São Paulo states.

Official inquiries into the February 1989 beatings of more than 1,000 prisoners at a São Paulo detention centre made little progress during the year (see *Amnesty International Report 1990*). Military and civil police officers were charged with the February 1989 suffocation to death of 18 prisoners at a São Paulo police station, but no trial had begun by the end of the year.

After a peaceful demonstration in June, landless peasants from Cruz Alta, Rio Grande do Sul, were allegedly attacked by military police officers. One of the protesters, Ivo Martins de Lima, was shot in the back of the head, reportedly at close range while lying on the ground. He was later said to be recovering.

The increasing tension between the Landless Rural Workers Movement and the military police in Rio Grande do Sul led to a confrontation in Porto Alegre on 8 August. This resulted in the killing of a policeman by peasants and a 12-hour police blockade of the City Hall, where demonstrators had sought refuge.

In many cases peasants seeking land rights were detained without a warrant, held incommunicado and ill-treated. On 21 July military and civil police officers, reportedly armed and dressed in plain clothes, entered the Jandaia estate near Curionópolis, Pará state, and threatened women and children with summary execution if they did not reveal the whereabouts of the men of the community.

Eleven of the men were detained without warrants, including Valdo José da Silva, who was reportedly shot in the back and legs as he tried to flee from police. The other arrested men were taken 100 kilometres to Marabá police station, and were reportedly denied food and water for two days. Four of the men said they were beaten to coerce them into making self-incriminating statements. A *habeas corpus* petition was filed on their behalf, but the police obtained an order for up to 10 days' "temporary detention". However, the men were kept in Marabá jail for over two months. They were granted a *habeas corpus* order in October and released.

Sandra de Oliveira Souza and Maria Divina da Silva Santos were detained without any judicial order on the Jandaia estate on 22 July and secretly taken to Marabá police station, allegedly to force them to reveal the whereabouts of their husbands. Lawyers who saw the women on 25 July reported that they were covered with bruises. The two women were released within a few days.

A March 1989 attack by military police battalions on landless peasants at Salto do Jacuí (see *Amnesty International Report 1990*) led to an official investigation, but no disciplinary action resulted during 1990.

In an oral statement to the United Nations Commission on Human Rights in February, Amnesty International described its concerns about torture and other ill-treatment in Brazilian prisons and police stations.

In São Paulo in June Amnesty International launched its publication, *Beyond the*

Law: Torture and Extrajudicial Execution in Urban Brazil, which called on the Brazilian Government to stop widespread violations of human rights by civil and military police. Also in June Amnesty International representatives visited Brazil and met government officials, representatives of non-governmental organizations and the press.

In a nationally televised speech on 22 June, President Collor said, "We cannot and will not again be a country cited as violent in reports by Amnesty International.... We will not allow the 'new Brazil' to accept any form of disrespect for human rights."

In August President Collor and other officials met Amnesty International representatives to discuss the organization's report. The President said that his government did not consider Amnesty International's work an interference in Brazil's internal affairs and promised that his ministers would study the organization's recommendations. Amnesty International subsequently sent the Brazilian Government 12 recommendations for safeguards against torture and other human rights violations.

In September Amnesty International issued a statement on the torture and killing of Brazilian children by police officers and death squads. On the same day President Collor called for a federal investigation of all the cases featured in the statement. Federal authorities had previously denied responsibility for investigating human rights violations, claiming that this rested solely with state and local authorities.

By the end of the year, however, the reported number of children killed by police and death squads had not dropped, the killings of rural trade unionists continued to be reported, allegations of torture and ill-treatment of detainees were still being made, and when state and local investigations and judicial proceedings were initiated, they were subject to long delays.

BRUNEI DARUSSALAM

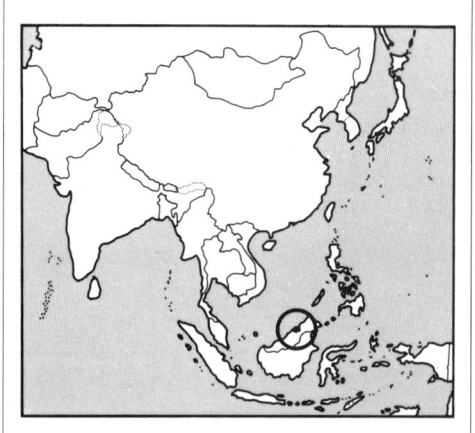

Seven prisoners of conscience, four of whom had been held since 1962, were released. Criminal offenders continued to be sentenced to mandatory whippings which constitute a cruel, inhuman or degrading form of punishment.

After spending 27 years in prison without charge or trial, Sarponin bin Sarpo, Suhaili bin Badas, Tinggal bin Muhammad and Baha bin Mohammed were released in January, along with Sheikh Nikman bin Sheikh Mahmud who had been held without trial for 14 years. The first four were detained soon after an abortive armed rebellion staged in December 1962 by the *Partai Rakyat Brunei* (PRB), Brunei People's Party, against the then Sultan. The fifth, Sheikh Nikman, who was not a member of the PRB, was apparently held because he was the brother of the PRB president-in-exile.

Abdul Latif Hamid and Abdul Latif Chuchu, who had been the leaders of the Brunei National Democratic Party, were conditionally released in March. They had been detained without charge or trial since January 1988 apparently for advocating parliamentary democracy under a constitutional monarchy. Their conditions of release included staying indoors between 10pm and 6am, not leaving their district without police permission, and not engaging in any political activity for one year. Abdul Latif Hamid died of asthma in May. His death did not appear to be related to his detention.

Whipping continued to be a mandatory

punishment for 42 criminal offences including assault, extortion, rape, robbery and vandalism. In one case in July, a 21-year-old man was sentenced to three lashes and three years' imprisonment for having unlawful sex with a minor, a girl aged 13.

In January Amnesty International wrote to the government welcoming the release of five prisoners of conscience and urging the release of the two others. In April Amnesty International welcomed their release but urged the government to lift the restrictions imposed on them.

BULGARIA

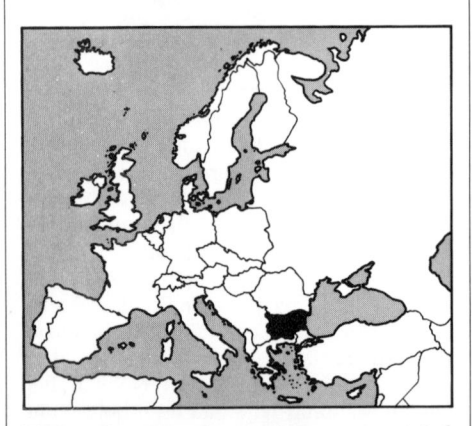

Two prisoners of conscience were tried and sentenced for espionage but later released. A number of ethnic Turks remained imprisoned until late December in connection with their resistance to the enforced assimilation of the ethnic Turkish minority from 1984 to 1989. A moratorium on executions was introduced.

In January an amnesty affecting 31 people was announced for those imprisoned after 1 January 1984 under specified articles of the criminal code for opposing the assimilation campaign against the ethnic Turkish minority (see *Amnesty International Reports 1986* to *1990*). The assimilation campaign was officially recognized as having been illegal, although no prosecutions for the attendant large-scale human rights abuses, including loss of life, were undertaken (see *Amnesty International Report 1990*). In March parliament passed legislation which allowed ethnic Turks and other Bulgarian Muslims, whose names had been forcibly changed in past assimilation campaigns, to use their original names. Also in March, legislation was introduced which reorganized the judicial system and guaranteed the right to defence in all phases of the legal process.

Elections held in June to a new parliament, the Grand National Assembly (GNA), an assembly empowered to rewrite the Constitution, were won by the Bulgarian Socialist Party (BSP) – the former Communist Party – with 211 of the 400 seats. The main opposition, the Union of Democratic Forces (UDF), won 144 seats. In July President Petar Mladenov resigned after it was revealed that he had suggested calling in tanks to disperse anti-government protesters in December 1989. In August the GNA elected UDF leader Zhelyu Zhelev President. In September President Zhelev pardoned 314 prisoners, including 17 ethnic Turks sentenced for espionage during the assimilation campaign. In November, following major demonstrations and strikes, the BSP government led by Prime Minister Andrey Lukanov resigned. In December a coalition caretaker government was appointed until new elections could be held.

In late December another amnesty was announced for all those sentenced for "treason and espionage". All remaining detainees convicted of political offences were subsequently released.

After the January amnesty over 60 ethnic Turks remained imprisoned for opposing the assimilation campaign, many of them having been convicted of espionage under Article 104 of the criminal code. Some of these prisoners had reportedly been charged with espionage after they attempted to give foreign observers information about human rights abuses which had occurred during the assimilation campaign.

In February an ethnic Turkish medical doctor, Enver Ahmedov Hatibov (whose "Bulgarian" name was Belchin Perunov Perunov), was sentenced to 10 years' imprisonment under Article 104. He was accused of identifying undercover agents of the Ministry of Internal Affairs to two Turkish citizens, including Yusuf Mutlu, an ethnic Turk who emigrated from Bulgaria to Turkey in 1978. The ministry had been responsible for human rights abuses against the ethnic Turkish minority during the assimilation campaign. Yusuf Mutlu was arrested while on a trip to Bulgaria. He was tried with Enver Hatibov and sentenced to 12 years' imprisonment. However, both were released early; Enver Hatibov was freed in May and Yusuf Mutlu in September. Early releases of ethnic Turks imprisoned for opposing the assimilation campaign occurred throughout the year.

In July the GNA introduced a moratorium on executions. In August President Zhelev commuted the sentences of the 11 people on death row to 30 years' imprisonment. They had all been convicted of murder. No executions were carried out in 1990.

In February an Amnesty International delegation visited the country and discussed its concerns with officials in the Foreign Ministry. The organization called for the release of Enver Hatibov and Yusuf Mutlu, and throughout the year sought further information on ethnic Turks imprisoned during the assimilation campaign. The Bulgarian Government made information available on a number of cases. Amnesty International called for a civilian, non-punitive alternative service to be introduced for conscientious objectors to military service. It welcomed the moratorium on the death penalty and called on the GNA to abolish it completely.

BURKINA FASO

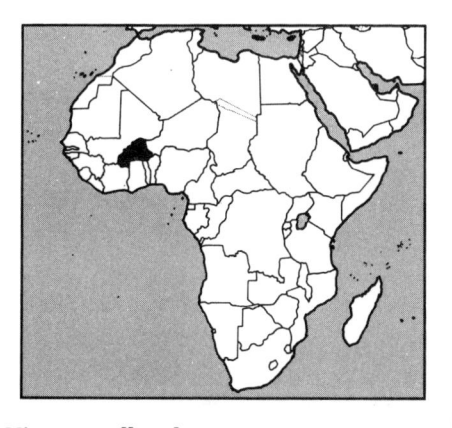

Nineteen alleged government opponents, including possible prisoners of conscience, were held throughout 1990 following their arrest in December 1989. Eight others arrested at the same time were released and four were officially said to have escaped: one of these, however, was reported to have died in detention under torture. More than 40 other people were arrested for political reasons. Most were released uncharged but at least 12 were still held without charge or trial at the end of the year, including eight students who had been forcibly conscripted into the armed forces. There were reports of torture and ill-treatment of political detainees, two of whom were said to have died as a result.

A new draft constitution to replace the constitution suspended in 1980 was prepared by a government-appointed commission and submitted to President Blaise Compaoré for approval in October. It was scheduled to come into force after a referendum in 1991. It allows for political parties but excludes any based on particular religious denominations or regions of the country, and those considered "pro-imperialist". Presidential and legislative elections were scheduled for 1991.

Nineteen people arrested in December 1989 in connection with an alleged conspiracy against the government were detained throughout the year without being brought to trial. In all, 31 people had been arrested, most of them associates of former president Thomas Sankara, who was killed in the coup in October 1987 which brought President Compaoré to power. They included Raymond Train Poda, a former minister of justice, Guillaume Sessouma, a university lecturer, and Moumouni Traoré, an economist, all members of the *Union de lutte communiste-reconstruite* (ULC-R), Union of Communist Struggle-Reconstructed, which had supported the Sankara government. The 31 also included former soldiers, some of whom had previously been detained without trial for almost two years following the 1987 coup.

Four of the 31, including Guillaume Sessouma, were said by the government in January to have escaped from detention. However, there were persistent reports suggesting that Guillaume Sessouma had died under torture: later in the year, Amnesty International received information which confirmed this, although the government continued to maintain that he had escaped. Eight of the prisoners had been released by September, four of them provisionally, but the others remained in custody. Their cases had been referred to the courts and pre-trial judicial proceedings began in March, but no trial date had been set by the end of 1990. They were permitted access to lawyers but were denied family visits until

August. Neither Raymond Train Poda nor Moumouni Traoré had been formally charged by the end of the year: it appeared that they, and possibly others, might be prisoners of conscience.

Further political arrests occurred in March and May. Lambert Ouedraogo and Aboubacar Traoré were detained without charge for five days in March at security police headquarters in the capital, Ouagadougou. They were questioned about the distribution of documents produced by the *Parti communiste révolutionnaire voltaïque* (PCRV), Revolutionary Communist Party of Upper Volta (Burkina Faso was called Upper Volta before 1984).

Over 40 students were arrested by police in May after demonstrations at the University of Ouagadougou calling for improved conditions and permission to hold meetings of the *Association nationale des étudiants burkinabè* (ANEB), National Association of Burkinabè Students. Among those arrested was ANEB's President, Seni Konanda. At least 12 students were still held illegally without charge or trial at the end of the year. Eight of them were forcibly conscripted into the armed forces and confined to barracks in Pô, Dedougou and Koudougou. In July the government denied that any students were being detained and said that the eight were undertaking obligatory military service. At least four others, however, were held incommunicado in detention centres in Ouagadougou: one, Boukary Dabo, a medical student, was reported in October to have died in detention, possibly as a result of ill-treatment. No inquest had been held by the end of the year.

Several of the detainees arrested in December 1989 were reported to have been tortured or ill-treated. Tibo Ouedraogo, an army officer, was said to have been kept handcuffed throughout the year. Following reports of their torture, the government sought to allay fears about the prisoners' safety: in January, representatives of a local human rights organization were invited to see them and in November they were presented to the local press.

During their detention in March, Lambert Ouedraogo and Aboubacar Traoré were reportedly blindfolded, beaten on the back, stomach and genitals, and denied food and water while under interrogation. Aboubacar Traoré was also allegedly taken into a courtyard and told that he was to be shot. Some of the students arrested in May were also said to have been tortured, although no details were available.

The cases of seven people sentenced to death for criminal offences in 1989 (see *Amnesty International Report 1990*) were referred to the Court of Appeal in Ouagadougou for a retrial. The outcome had not been reported by the end of the year.

Amnesty International sought information from the government about those arrested in December 1989. The authorities said they would be tried according to the law, but did not respond to the organization's repeated inquiries about the charges against them. Amnesty International also pressed for the unconditional release of the students arrested in May, including those forcibly conscripted into the armed forces.

Amnesty International called on the authorities to treat all prisoners humanely and to protect them from torture, in particular by ending the use of prolonged incommunicado detention. In October it called for an investigation into the death in detention of Boukary Dabo and the death under torture of Guillaume Sessouma, but without response.

BURUNDI

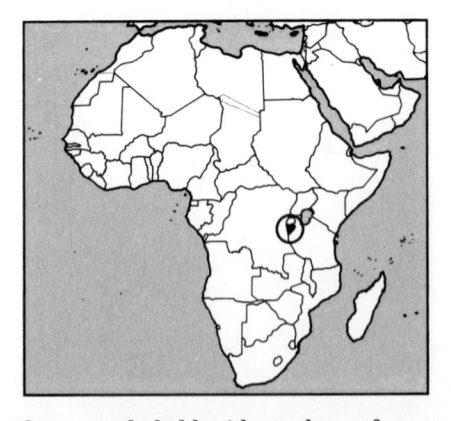

Three people held without charge for one week appeared to be prisoners of conscience. More than 60 political prisoners, some of whom had been detained without trial since 1988, were released. Several prisoners reportedly continued to be held in deliberately harsh conditions. An amnesty announced in August resulted in the commutation of all death sentences.

In April a government commission completed preparation of a draft charter of national unity, which was presented to the nation by President Pierre Buyoya in May. It proclaims every citizen's right to personal security, fundamental human rights and equality with others. It was unanimously adopted at the end of December by an extraordinary congress of Burundi's only legal political party, the *Union pour le progrès national* (UPRONA), Union for National Progress. The congress elected an 80-person UPRONA Central Committee, composed of members of the Hutu and Tutsi ethnic groups, replacing the military committee which had ruled Burundi since President Buyoya came to power in September 1987. The charter was expected to be submitted to a referendum in early 1991. President Buyoya stated that a new constitution would be drawn up in early 1991 and that the electorate would eventually be allowed to choose between the existing one-party state and a multi-party political system.

On 9 May Burundi acceded to the International Covenant on Civil and Political Rights and to the International Covenant on Economic, Social and Cultural Rights.

Three people arrested and detained for one week in February appeared to be prisoners of conscience. Albert Nsezeye, a lay preacher from Gisuru in Ruyigi province, was arrested with two others apparently because he had typed a letter to the Minister of the Interior on behalf of villagers in Gisuru. They were complaining about alleged embezzlement by a local government official. When they were released, the three were required to pay a fine on the grounds that they had distributed tracts, although they had been neither charged nor tried.

A number of political prisoners were released. In January the last of some 20 Jehovah's Witnesses who had been arrested in mid-1989 (see *Amnesty International Report 1990*), were freed. In April Manara Elonga Nsamba, a Zairian national held since June 1989 for allegedly possessing "anti-government" tracts, was released. All had been held without charge or trial.

In August President Buyoya announced an amnesty on the eve of a visit to Burundi by Pope John Paul II. Among those freed were over 40 members of the Hutu ethnic group who had been arrested in August and September 1988 in connection with serious intercommunal disturbances. They were said by the authorities to have been involved in intercommunal killings, but none of them was ever charged or brought to trial. Some appeared to be imprisoned on account of their prominence in the Hutu community, rather than because there was evidence of any involvement in violent offences. The amnesty also led to the release of at least 15 soldiers and civilians arrested in March 1989, who had been accused of conspiring against the government (see *Amnesty International Report 1990*).

At least four people were reported to have been severely beaten at the time of their arrest, during a violent assault in August on Mabanda military camp by an armed group which had apparently infiltrated the country from Tanzania. At least seven people died in the attack. The four were still held without charge or trial in Rumonge prison at the end of 1990.

Two untried political detainees died in custody in mid-1990: one had been arrested in connection with the intercommunal disturbances in August 1988 and the other in connection with the alleged conspiracy against the government in March 1989. The authorities attributed their deaths to natural causes, but other sources suggested that ill-treatment at the time of their arrests and harsh conditions of imprisonment may have contributed to their deaths. Neither was the subject of an inquest.

Three former government ministers imprisoned for corruption after the coup which brought President Buyoya to power continued to be held in deliberately harsh conditions (see *Amnesty International Report 1990*). They were kept in isolation cells and denied regular contact with their families.

At the time of the August amnesty President Buyoya commuted all death sentences to life imprisonment; the number of sentences commuted was not announced. Amnesty International did not learn of any new death sentences imposed during the year and no executions were reported.

Amnesty International welcomed the releases of uncharged political prisoners and the commutation in August of all death sentences. In response to inquiries from Amnesty International, the government said that the deaths of the two political detainees were due to natural causes.

CAMBODIA

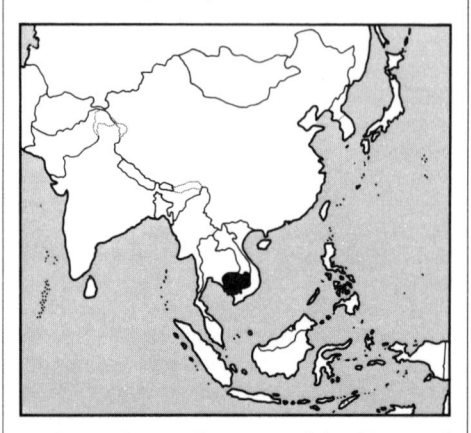

At least six people arrested in May and still held at the end of the year were believed to be prisoners of conscience. More than 200 political prisoners arrested in previous years were believed to be held, either without charge or trial or after unfair trials, and the situation of more than 700 others was not known. New information was received about the alleged torture of political detainees in 1989. Guerrilla forces fighting the Phnom Penh government reportedly detained and summarily killed members of their own armed forces as well as captured civilians.

The Government of the State of Cambodia, headed by Chairperson of the Council of Ministers Hun Sen, maintained its opposition to the establishment of political parties other than the ruling Kampuchean People's Revolutionary Party (KPRP) despite provisions in favour of the "right to set up associations" in the 1989 Constitution.

The government continued to face armed opposition from the guerrilla forces of the National Government of Cambodia (NGC), formerly known as the Coalition Government of Democratic Kampuchea. It comprised the *Partie* of Democratic Kampuchea (the "Khmer Rouge") and two other groups. A framework for the settlement of the Cambodian conflict put forward by the five permanent members of the United Nations Security Council contained provisions on safeguards for human rights, but these appeared to be inadequate.

In Phnom Penh, six government officials and possibly other people were reportedly detained in May in connection with attempts to form a political party. They included Ung Phan, the Minister of Transport and Telecommunications, Thun Saray, the acting Director of the Institute of Sociology, and Khay Mathury, an architect and former army lieutenant-colonel. They had reportedly written and attempted to publish the charter of a new political party. No charges were known to have been brought against them by the end of the year.

According to official media reports, 775 political suspects were detained by the police and military forces between January and August, mainly in the western provinces. They were alleged to have been involved in the activities of the armed coalition opposing the government. Some apparently remained in detention without charge or trial at the end of the year but no details of these cases were known to have been made public. There was no new information on the fate of political suspects whose detention was reported in the official news media in 1989 (see *Amnesty International Report 1990*). However, Amnesty International learned of the names of 213 political prisoners arrested between 1979 and 1988 and believed still held without trial or after unfair trials.

Three former political prisoners who had been held in 1989 for suspected involvement in armed opposition to the Phnom Penh government in Sisophon, capital of the northwestern province of Banteay Meanchey, alleged that they were tortured in detention by local security authorities. Two of them, both rice farmers from Thmar Puok district, were reportedly detained by soldiers in early 1989 and handed over to the police in Sisophon. They said they were held without charge or trial for more than one year during which they were tortured three times about their alleged links with locally active guerrilla forces. They said they were shackled by the hands and feet and severely beaten, and in one case denied "reasonable amounts" of food and water for over four months, in an attempt to make them confess to planting land mines and acting as guides for the guerrillas. The third former political prisoner said he had been shackled by both feet and both hands during three months' detention at the Corrections Offices of Military Region 4 in western Cambodia after he was arrested in late 1989.

Opposition guerrilla forces operated near the Thai border and staged attacks on lines of communication deeper inside Cambodia. In one train attack in July, guerrilla forces said to belong to the "Khmer Rouge" reportedly captured and subsequently murdered about 26 civilian passengers on a train travelling from Batdambang to Phnom Penh.

Thirty members of the "Khmer Rouge" armed forces were reportedly detained and summarily executed on 27 July in an area known as Zone 1003 in northern Cambodia, after "Khmer Rouge" military police accused them of leading a movement demanding greater personal and economic freedoms in accordance with earlier "Khmer Rouge" statements. Six of those killed, including Buntheuan, the chairman of a company of Division 616 special forces, were reportedly shot dead in their beds at dawn on 27 July. The other 24 were reportedly taken to a nearby forest and executed. The 30 victims had apparently been named in "confessions" extracted by military police interrogators from some of the 70 people detained in underground cells in Choam Sla, in Zone 1003, and allegedly severely ill-treated.

In September Amnesty International wrote to leaders of the NGC guerrilla forces to express grave concern about the reported killings of train passengers by "Khmer Rouge" forces. It reiterated its call for those responsible for the killing of prisoners to be brought to justice. In December the organization wrote to NGC leaders to express concern about the reported summary execution of 30 members of the "Khmer Rouge" armed forces and to urge an independent and impartial investigation, the results of which should be made public.

In March the Phnom Penh government wrote to Amnesty International indicating its agreement in principle to the organization's long-standing request to visit the country. It promised to set a date for the visit, but had not done so by the end of the year.

In September Amnesty International expressed its concern to the Phnom Penh government about the May arrest and detention of government officials. It called on the authorities to make public their whereabouts and either to charge them with recognizably criminal offences or release them.

In October and November Amnesty International answered a request by the Phnom Penh Ministry of Foreign Affairs to submit a list of prisoners of concern to the organization. The organization provided the names of the 213 political prisoners known to it and asked the Cambodian Government to name and indicate the whereabouts of hundreds of political prisoners reportedly detained in recent years. It further called for investigations into allegations that detainees held in Sisophon had been tortured.

In November Amnesty International wrote an open letter to governments involved in the peace process and to the Cambodian parties themselves, highlighting the organization's concerns about political prisoners, torture, executions and the need to bring to justice those responsible for human rights violations. Amnesty International urged that human rights provisions in the peace settlement should be strengthened and that they should provide for political prisoners to be either released or given a new and fair trial. Amnesty International added that information about political prisoners should be made public and urged that appropriate international and non-governmental organizations be granted access to such prisoners.

CAMEROON

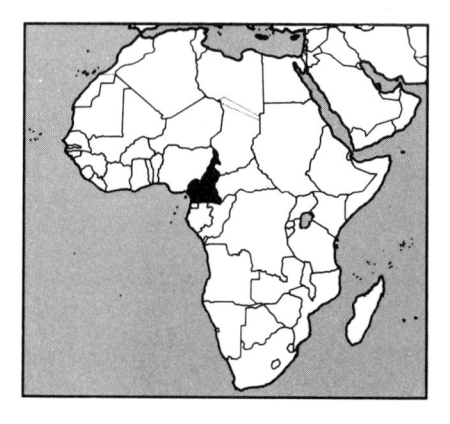

At least 21 prisoners of conscience had been released by the end of the year. Others remained imprisoned. Over 140 other political prisoners, including prisoners of conscience, were also released, although most were placed under restriction orders. At least 80 others remained in prison despite an official undertaking to release them. At least three prisoners of conscience were reportedly tortured or

ill-treated. Several government opponents were killed in suspicious circumstances. Eight death sentences were passed but no executions were known to have been carried out.

Several laws were amended or replaced in December which maintained the government's powers under previous laws to imprison its critics. Broad powers of administrative detention were maintained without any safeguards against arbitrary imprisonment. A state of emergency could still be imposed by decree without control by the legislature or the judiciary. Special military courts to try political cases were replaced by a special State Security Court, whose judges were still to be appointed by the government and which allowed no right of appeal. Three new political offences were created, all punishable by long prison sentences, concerning the spreading of false information and incitement to revolt and rebellion.

At least 21 people were prisoners of conscience during 1990. Yondo Black, former president of the Cameroon Bar Association, and Anicet Ekané, a company director, were arrested in February. In April they were sentenced to three and four-year prison terms respectively for attending meetings to discuss multi-party democracy and the formation of a new political party. They were tried by a special military court with nine other civilians, including one *in absentia*. The other defendants received suspended prison sentences or were acquitted. Details of the charges – subversion and showing contempt for the Head of State – were withheld throughout the trial, and no convincing evidence was brought to justify the convictions. At least three of the defendants were reportedly tortured or ill-treated; Anicet Ekané said that he had been stripped, beaten and forced to stand without food and water for two days. Yondo Black and Anicet Ekané were freed in August following an announcement in July by President Paul Biya that all political prisoners were to be released.

Other prisoners of conscience were released. They included Samuel Zézé, released in July, who had been held without charge or trial almost continuously since December 1985 for allegedly distributing literature on behalf of the opposition *Union des populations du Cameroun* (UPC), Union of Cameroonian Peoples (see *Amnesty International Report 1990*).

Isidore Nkiamboh was released in June after more than five years' detention without charge or trial. He was apparently arrested in April 1985 after entering Cameroon with a letter to President Biya requesting registration for the Cameroon Democratic Party (CDP), an opposition group based abroad. Three other people arrested in September 1990 for allegedly bringing CDP documents into the country were released uncharged after about three weeks.

Djeukam Tchameni Dominique, a computer company director who had been arrested in November 1988, was convicted of importing subversive material and sentenced to three years' imprisonment by a special military court in March. He was released unconditionally in August.

In April President Biya announced that all prisoners still held in connection with a coup attempt in April 1984 would be released. This announcement was made shortly after Amnesty International had publicized reports that two political prisoners had died in custody in December 1989 as a result of torture or ill-treatment. At least 140 prisoners were reported to have been freed but the authorities did not identify those who were released. Most had been held in administrative detention after completing prison sentences. Others had been detained either without trial or after being acquitted in 1984 of involvement in the coup attempt.

Suzanne Lecaille and Issa Tchiroma, who had been acquitted in 1984, were released unconditionally. At least 18 of those released, and possibly many more, were forbidden to leave their home areas without official authorization. Many had become ill due to harsh prison conditions: Haman Toumba and Jean-Pierre Dia, who were administratively detained after completing five-year sentences, were both reportedly deaf and blind when they left prison and Haman Toumba was barely able to walk.

At least 80 prisoners held in connection with the coup attempt, including possible prisoners of conscience, were believed to be still held at the end of 1990. Of these, about 60 were still serving prison sentences of 10 years or more, imposed after unfair trials before special military courts in 1984. At least 20 others remained in administrative detention; they included Paul Daïssala Dakolé, a senior transport official detained without charge or trial since 1984, and Ahmadou Alfaki, a police officer rearrested following his acquittal in 1984.

Following the deaths of two prisoners at Yaoundé's Central Prison in December 1989 (see *Amnesty International Report 1990*), new information was received suggesting that as many as 26 political prisoners had died between 1984 and 1989. Most were reportedly untried detainees held in connection with the 1984 coup attempt who had died from malnutrition, disease and medical neglect. One, Moudio Hildina, a former government official, had apparently been paralysed for years before his death in June 1989 as a result of being denied medical treatment. He had remained in prison despite completing a two-year prison sentence imposed in 1984. Neither his death nor those of other political prisoners were the subject of inquests.

Several government opponents were killed in suspicious circumstances, accompanied by allegations of official complicity. In April Pierre Bouobda was shot dead by security police. He was one of 200 lawyers who had nominally joined Yondo Black's defence team and was questioned by police shortly before his death. Witnesses alleged that he was followed and killed by police officers who subsequently tried to make his death appear to be the result of an armed robbery. Following protests, it was announced that investigations involving several police officers had been opened, but none was known to have been charged by the end of 1990.

A cover-up was also alleged after six supporters of a new opposition political party, the Social Democratic Front (SDF), were shot dead by the security forces in May at an unauthorized rally in Bamenda. Government-employed journalists later said that they had been made to report falsely that the six had been killed in the crush of the crowd. Some sources also alleged that two women students were raped and killed by the police following subsequent clashes between student supporters of the SDF and the security forces in Yaoundé, although Amnesty International was unable to verify this. Hundreds of students were briefly detained and reportedly ill-treated.

Eight death sentences were imposed during the year for attempted murder and aggravated theft. No executions were known to have taken place.

Amnesty International appealed for the release of prisoners of conscience and for a review of the cases of those in administrative detention or imprisoned after unfair trials. In July it published a report, *Cameroon: Imprisoned for Advocating a Multi-party System – the Yondo Black Affair*, which described the trial of Yondo Black and others as a travesty of justice. Amnesty International also called for an official inquiry into all deaths of prisoners, for major improvements in prison conditions, and for the commutation of death sentences. Announcing the release of Yondo Black and others in July, President Biya said that Amnesty International was welcome to visit Cameroon. However, efforts by Amnesty International to follow up this invitation had received no response from the government by the end of 1990.

CANADA

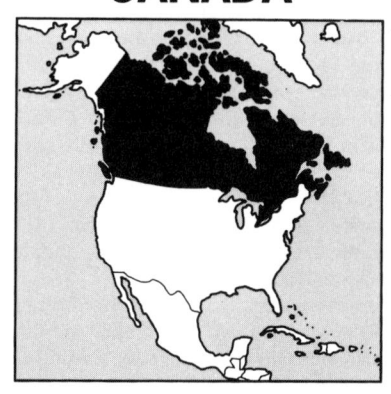

Several Mohawk Indians were allegedly ill-treated by the Quebec police after their arrest during an armed confrontation following from a land dispute. Extradition proceedings were started in the case of a prisoner charged with murder in the United States of America (USA) whose laws provide for the death penalty.

Conflict broke out in Quebec in early July between Mohawk Indians and the Canadian authorities over a land dispute. Armed Mohawk Warriors erected a blockade in the town of Oka, near Montreal, in protest at the town's proposals to extend a golf course on to ancestral land claimed by the Mohawk Nation. The conflict escalated on 11 July when armed provincial police tried to storm the barricades using tear-gas; a police officer was killed during the confrontation. In the following weeks, several hundred Mohawks held out behind barricades. Following negotiations with the federal and provincial governments, and after the federal government had promised to buy the disputed land for the Mohawks, most of the barricades were dismantled peacefully in the presence of international observers in late August and early September.

The conflict ended on 26 September when the last remaining group of 20 Mohawk Warriors and some 30 Mohawk women and children surrendered to the Canadian army. This followed federal government assurances that it would consider the Mohawks' grievances and speed up land claims. The army had been brought in on 1 September with the stated aim of maintaining the peace as tension mounted between the Mohawks and the provincial police and local population.

Several Mohawks arrested during the dispute alleged that they were ill-treated by the Quebec police in late August. Some claimed that they were initially denied access to lawyers. There were also allegations that Mohawks were ill-treated by police officers while detained at a military base in late September. About 100 Indians involved in the conflict were charged with offences which included possession of unlawful weapons and participation in a riot. Most were released on bail after their initial appearance in court.

An Amnesty International representative visited Montreal in November to collect information on the allegations of ill-treatment. Amnesty International was still investigating the allegations at the end of the year.

Lee Robert O'Bomsawin, an American Indian, faced possible extradition to the state of Florida, USA, on a charge of first-degree murder. If convicted, he could be sentenced to death. In September 1990, 313 people were on death row in Florida. The state carried out 25 executions between 1976 and December 1990.

Amnesty International wrote to the Canadian Minister of Justice in April requesting that Lee Robert O'Bomsawin not be returned to Florida unless the state offered assurances that he would not be sentenced to death. The minister replied that all submissions made on Lee Robert O'Bomsawin's behalf would be considered before any decision on extradition was made.

CENTRAL AFRICAN REPUBLIC

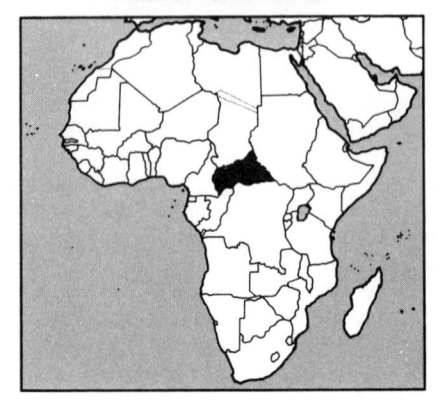

At least 37 pro-democracy activists were arrested; 25 were still being held but had not been tried at the end of the year. Most appeared to be prisoners of conscience. More than a dozen other suspected government opponents arrested in previous years, including prisoners of conscience, remained in detention without trial. One was reportedly beaten and ill-treated. Three prisoners remained under sentence of death. No death sentences were known to have been imposed or carried out in 1990.

The government faced increasing pressure for political reform and multi-party democracy but maintained that all shades of political opinion were being accommodated within the ruling *Rassemblement démocratique centrafricain* (RDC), Central African Democratic Alliance, the only political party allowed by the Constitution. In May more than 200 people signed an open letter to President André Kolingba, calling for a national conference to discuss the introduction of a multi-party system. A *Comité de coordination pour la convocation de la conférence nationale* (CCCCN), Coordination Committee for the Convening of a National Conference, was formed in mid-May by the leading advocates of multi-party democracy. In June the CCCCN published a memorandum calling for an end to one-party rule.

Twenty members of the CCCCN were arrested on 12 September, when a meeting called to plan a national conference was broken up by the security forces. Among those arrested were two former prisoners of conscience: Abel Goumba, a former vice-president and leader of the *Front patriotique oubanguien-Parti du travail* (FPO–PT), Oubangui Patriotic Front–Labour Party; and Aristide Sokambi, President of the CCCCN. At least 17 more arrests were made in the days after a peaceful CCCCN meeting on 13 October; the meeting was followed by violent demonstrations in which around 40 people were injured. At least four CCCCN members were among the 17 people arrested, including Thomas Koazo, a journalist and former prisoner of conscience released in September 1989 (see *Amnesty International Report 1990*), and General Timothée Malendoma, a former army officer. All of those arrested on 12 September and five of those arrested on 13 October remained held; the 25 detainees were charged with state security offences but none had been tried by the end of the year.

In July Maître Nicolas Tiangaye, a lawyer supporting the CCCCN campaign, was officially restricted from leaving the capital, Bangui, by the Minister of Public Security while disciplinary proceedings against him were being considered. The restrictions were imposed after he criticized the army in a way which the authorities apparently considered seditious. The Justice Minister said the restrictions were unlawful; as a result he was dismissed from office. The restrictions on Nicolas Tiangaye were lifted in October, when a panel of judges acquitted him of professional misconduct.

Untried political detainees arrested in previous years continued to be held. They included Jacques Ngoli, who was arrested in May 1987 apparently for helping to draft a tract which criticized the government, and Jeanne-Marie Ruth Rolland, a former prisoner of conscience (see *Amnesty International Reports 1989* and *1990*). Jeanne-Marie Ruth Rolland was arrested in December 1989 after refusing to move out of the way of a government motorcade. She was initially held at the Bangui headquarters of the paramilitary *Compagnie Nationale de Sécurité*, national security agency, where she was kept handcuffed and reportedly denied medical treatment. In mid-1990 she was moved to an undisclosed place of detention.

Twelve political opponents of the government, who were forcibly returned from Benin in 1989 (see *Amnesty International Report 1990*), remained in detention without charge or trial and were held incommunicado. One of the detainees, General François Bozize, was reportedly beaten severely and ill-treated in July; the authorities said he had tried to escape. General Bozize's brother, Honoré Cocksiss Ouilébona, and several others who were arrested in late 1989 as suspected political supporters of the General, also remained in detention throughout 1990 without being charged.

Three people convicted in 1982 remained under sentence of death (see *Amnesty International Report 1990*). Amnesty International did not learn of any new death sentences or executions during the year.

Amnesty International appealed for the release of pro-democracy activists and other prisoners of conscience, and sought information about other political detainees held without trial. Amnesty International called for an inquiry into allegations that General Bozize had been beaten and urged the authorities to take steps to protect all prisoners from beatings and other ill-treatment, and to allow prisoners regular access to their families, doctors and lawyers.

CHAD

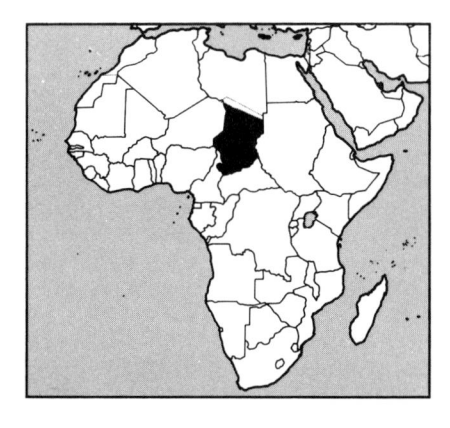

More than 300 political prisoners were extrajudicially executed shortly before the government of President Hissein Habré was overthrown on 1 December. Hundreds of others, including prisoners of conscience, survived and were released. They had all been held without charge or trial in secret detention centres where conditions were harsh and torture was frequent.

Many had effectively "disappeared". Released prisoners said that hundreds had died in prison, with several deaths from starvation occurring each day. Dozens of other extrajudicial executions by President Habré's troops were reported before the change of government.

Armed clashes in eastern Chad continued until the end of November between government troops and insurgents belonging to the *Mouvement patriotique du salut* (MPS), the Patriotic Front for Salvation, a coalition of armed opposition groups led by Idriss Deby, a former army commander. President Habré and other senior government officials fled Chad on 1 December after military victories by the MPS. Idriss Deby appointed himself President of Chad and installed a new government. However, the situation remained uncertain. There were attempts on the lives of two new government ministers, and one army officer, Gabaroum Demtita, was reportedly arrested and killed by members of the security service in late December.

Before the MPS take-over, President Habré's government continued to be responsible for gross human rights violations including arbitrary arrests, secret detention, torture and extrajudicial executions. As one of their last acts before President Habré fled the country, members of his Presidential Guard extrajudicially executed more than 300 political prisoners in the capital, N'djamena. The victims had been secretly detained at the President's headquarters. Some of their bodies were apparently thrown into the Chari river, but many others were found in the headquarters.

Gross and persistent abuses of human rights had taken place under President Habré's rule despite the adoption by referendum in December 1989 of a new constitution containing strong human rights guarantees. Released prisoners alleged that the former president had been directly involved in the day-to-day workings of the *Direction de la documentation et de la sécurité*, the Directorate of Documentation and Security, the security service which was responsible for holding political prisoners and had a record of severe human rights violations. No political detainees had been charged or brought to trial, or even allowed to challenge their detention in the courts or elsewhere since President Habré came to power in 1982.

Several hundred political prisoners were released on 1 December following the MPS take-over. They had been detained at various secret detention centres in N'Djamena. Many had been held at a converted swimming pool, where torture was frequently used. Other prisoners were found alive at a house used by the former interior minister and at other secret detention centres.

Fewer than 20 of the more than 200 people known to have been arrested in 1989 were among those released (see *Amnesty International Report 1990*). The others, who were members of the Zaghawa community, as well as several hundred members of the Hadjeraï community arrested in 1987, had apparently died or been killed in detention. Released prisoners said that hundreds of people had been secretly executed in 1987 and 1989, in many cases at President Habré's headquarters. The victims included 11 brothers of Hassan Fadoul, a senior MPS official who became Minister of Planning and Cooperation in the new government in December, and Ahmed Dadji, the director of a state company. Others were said to have died as a result of torture, malnutrition or illness, in the absence of medical care. Released prisoners said that there were usually several prisoners' deaths each day due to starvation.

Before losing power, President Habré's government had refused to account for those arrested or to disclose any information about them.

People arrested in 1990 before the MPS take-over were subjected to torture and to brutal beatings and whippings during interrogation. Some were tortured with electric shocks to sensitive parts of the body. Others had two sticks tied together with cords along the sides of their heads; the cords would then be twisted, causing severe pain and bleeding from the nose.

President Habré's forces were responsible for dozens of extrajudicial executions in March after recapturing the eastern towns of Bahai and Tine, after they had been briefly occupied by the MPS. Dozens of government soldiers who had been held prisoner during the MPS occupation were reportedly executed extrajudicially by Chadian army officers, apparently because their failure to hold the towns against the MPS was attributed by the government to a lack of will to fight. The victims were said to be mostly southerners from the Mayo Kebi prefecture.

Government soldiers reportedly crossed the border in March and took seven wounded insurgents from their hospital beds in Kutum, Western Sudan, and summarily executed them. In April, 24 civilians were reportedly arrested, tortured and extrajudicially executed by government forces who recaptured the town of Iriba after it had been occupied by the MPS. Those killed included Take Hissein and Noura Markou, two sisters-in-law of Idriss Deby.

At least nine people were arrested in August, after leaflets criticizing the government and calling for democracy in Chad were circulated in N'Djamena. They included Gatta Gali Ngothe, a lecturer and former adviser to President Habré, Joseph Madjimbang, a former ambassador, and Laoukein Bardé, an army officer. They were all held incommunicado and without charge or trial at secret detention centres until they were freed in December following the change of government.

Dozens of refugees who had voluntarily returned to Chad, some with the assistance of the United Nations (UN) High Commissioner for Refugees, were arrested shortly after their return and either secretly detained without charge or trial, or killed by government forces. They included Daïenhl Gabriel, a trader, Anhoul Jean, a former local government official, and Metel Ernest, a priest, all of whom were reportedly arrested and extrajudicially executed by government soldiers only a month after they returned in July after living for several years at a refugee camp in northern Cameroon.

Amnesty International repeatedly urged President Habré's government to release prisoners of conscience and called for urgent official clarification of the fate and whereabouts of people who had "disappeared" or were believed to be secretly detained. Amnesty International also pressed the government to stop torture and extrajudicial killings, and introduce full safeguards to prevent such abuses.

In February Amnesty International submitted information about its concerns in Chad for UN review under a procedure established by Economic and Social Council Resolutions 728F/1503, for confidential consideration of communications about human rights violations.

In March Amnesty International published a detailed account of its concerns, *Chad: Political Prisoners Held in Secret – Calling the Government to Account*.

Following the change of government in December, Amnesty International welcomed the release of political prisoners and urged the new authorities both to establish an inquiry into the cases of "disappeared" prisoners and to introduce strong safeguards for the future protection of human rights. In response, the new government said it had dissolved the political police and released all political prisoners, and that no one would be detained in the future because of their opinions.

CHILE

Shortly after the civilian government of President Patricio Aylwin took office in March, a commission was set up to investigate human rights violations committed during more than 16 years of military rule. On the basis of an amnesty law passed in 1978, the Supreme Court ruled in August that cases of human rights violations committed before 1978 could be closed before they had been properly investigated. Military courts used the amnesty law to close investigations even as further evidence of the involvement of members of the army and security forces came to light. Most cases not covered by the amnesty law remained unresolved, although limited progress was reported in some investigations. At least three journalists were briefly detained on the orders of the military courts for writing articles discussing the role of the armed forces in past human rights violations. Forty-nine prisoners convicted of politically motivated offences received a presidential pardon but around 230 political prisoners whose trials were marked by serious irregularities remained in prison at the end of the year. Allegations of torture and ill-treatment were reported, although significantly fewer than in previous years. Nine political prisoners remained under recommended death sentences.

One of the most important human rights initiatives taken by President Aylwin was the creation in April of the *Comisión Nacional de Verdad y Reconciliación*, National Commission for Truth and Reconciliation. The Commission was charged with gathering information to establish the truth behind cases of "disappearance", illegal execution and death resulting from torture carried out by agents of the state, as well as death resulting from politically motivated acts of violence by private individuals, between September 1973 and March 1990. The Commission was also mandated to recommend measures aimed at preventing the recurrence of human rights violations and to advise on reparations to victims. The scope of its responsibilities did not include investigating hundreds of complaints of torture presented to the courts in past years. The Commission had no formal legal powers but transmitted information on cases within its mandate to the courts for judicial investigation. The Commission's report was expected to be presented to President Aylwin in early 1991.

The government took other measures to address the legacy of past human rights violations. For example, it proposed reforms which aimed to guarantee the right to a fair trial and eliminate the death penalty.

The scope of the government's human rights initiatives was limited by factors inherited from the previous government. The 1980 Constitution, for example, ensured the continuing presence of the former president, General Augusto Pinochet, as Commander-in-Chief of the armed forces and enabled the Pinochet administration to appoint nine senators to the Congress, reopened in March for the first time since the 1973 military coup. This prevented the elected civilian government from achieving a Senate majority. The Supreme Court, composed of judges appointed during the military government, continued to curb investigations into past human rights violations.

A dissident faction of the extreme left-wing group, the *Frente Patriótico Manuel Rodríguez* (FPMR), Manuel Rodríguez Patriotic Front, remained active. It claimed responsibility for the attempted assassination in March of General Gustavo Leigh, a former commander of the air force, and for the death in May of a former member of the security forces. The *Movimiento Juvenil Lautaro*, Lautaro Youth Movement, an armed group with unclear origins, claimed responsibility for numerous bombings and the deaths of several *carabineros* (uniformed police officers).

In August Chile ratified the American Convention on Human Rights. The government also withdrew all but one of the important reservations of the former administration to the United Nations Convention against Torture and Other Cruel, Inhuman or Degrading Treatment or Punishment. It withdrew reservations to the Inter-American Convention to Prevent and Punish Torture and recognized the competence of the Human Rights Committee to examine inter-state complaints under Article 41 of the International Covenant on Civil and Political Rights.

In August the Supreme Court upheld the decision by lower tribunals to use the 1978 Amnesty Law to close a case that originated in 1978 with a criminal complaint against senior members of the *Dirección de Inteligencia Nacional* (DINA), Directorate of National Intelligence, concerning their responsibility for the "disappearance" of 70 people between 1974 and 1976 (see *Amnesty International Report 1990*). The intelligence agency, formally disbanded in 1978, was implicated in a significant number of "disappearances" in the 1970s. The court's ruling established a legal precedent which undermined hopes that the fate of the victims would be clarified and that those responsible for human rights violations before 1978 would be brought to justice.

Other cases were closed by the military courts on the basis of the 1978 Amnesty Law. They included that of Dr Claudio Tognola Ríos, who "disappeared" following his detention by a military patrol in 1973. His remains, discovered with those of other victims in a disused mine in Tocopilla, northern Chile, were positively identified in November. The remains of other "disappeared" prisoners were identified after being discovered in secret graves. The victims included Vicente Atencio Cortés, a former member of the House of Deputies, and Eduardo Canteros Prado, who both "disappeared" following their arrest by the DINA in 1976.

The military courts successfully contested the competence of a civilian court to conduct investigations arising from the discovery of a clandestine grave in Pisagua, northern Chile, leaving little prospect that investigations would continue. Political prisoners were held by the army at a camp set up in Pisagua after the 1973 military coup and some illegal executions were carried out there. At least 18 of the bodies were identified.

Most cases of human rights violations not covered by the 1978 Amnesty Law remained unresolved. However, some progress was reported in a few investigations by civilian court judges, such as an investigation reopened in July into the 1982 murder of trade union leader Tucapel Jiménez. He was killed in circumstances that suggested the involvement of members of the *Central Nacional de Informaciones* (CNI), the state security police. The CNI, which was disbanded in February, had been accused of participating in serious human rights violations, including extrajudicial executions and torture.

In September three journalists were arrested on the orders of military courts on charges of "offending the armed forces" because they had written articles discussing the role of the armed forces in past human rights abuses. Juan Pablo Cárdenas was released unconditionally in October when the Military Court of Appeal revoked the charges against him. The other two, Juan Andrés Lagos and Alfonso Stephens, were released on bail. About 30 journalists continued to face legal proceedings in the military courts at the end of the year, most of them on charges of "offending the armed forces" or "offending the *carabineros*".

Charges pending since 1986 against Dr Ramiro Olivares and Gustavo Villalobos of the *Vicaría de la Solidaridad*, Vicariate of Solidarity, a church human rights organization, were dropped by the Supreme Court in June (see *Amnesty International Report 1990*).

Forty-seven convicted political prisoners were granted a presidential pardon in March and two others were pardoned later in the year. The government announced proposals to modify legislation that had seriously undermined the right to a fair trial of prisoners charged with politically motivated offences. The majority faced legal proceedings in military courts on charges of membership of armed opposition groups or of armed offences. The proposed reforms included provisions to prevent statements extracted under torture from being used as evidence, to reduce penalties for politically motivated offences, to transfer cases to civilian courts, and to restrict the jurisdiction of military courts to military offences. Some of the proposals were blocked in the Senate, although provisions were eventually approved to allow President Aylwin to pardon a number of political prisoners still detained. At the end of 1990 the reforms were still under discussion and the situation of about 230 political prisoners, many still awaiting judgment after long delays in their trials, remained unresolved.

At least 17 people, some of them charged with politically motivated offences, alleged that they were tortured or ill-treated while in police custody. Eight or more of these cases reportedly occurred in the Third Police Station of the *carabineros* in the capital, Santiago. Alvaro Rodríguez Escobar, for example, was arrested in August and held for seven days before his transfer to prison. He was reportedly subjected to electric shocks and other methods of torture.

In January the Military Court of Appeal commuted the death sentences of Juan Díaz Olea and Cristián Vargas Barahona to life imprisonment. They had been sentenced to death by a military judge in 1989 following a trial marked by serious judicial irregularities (see *Amnesty International Report 1990*). A government bill calling for elimination of the death penalty was rejected by the Senate in December. Death sentences recommended by the prosecution in 1989 continued to stand against nine political prisoners.

In meetings with President Aylwin and senior government officials in October, Amnesty International welcomed the measures adopted by the administration but urged that every effort be made to thoroughly investigate past human rights violations and to bring those responsible to justice. Amnesty International also called for the release of the detained journalists and for a thorough review by civilian courts of the proceedings against remaining political prisoners under conditions that guaranteed a prompt, full and impartial hearing. In addition, Amnesty International expressed concern at the cases of torture reported during the year; the government informed the organization that investigations would be opened into any case brought to its attention. Amnesty International called for the abolition of the death penalty. In December, at the invitation of the National Commission for Truth and Reconciliation, Amnesty International submitted a series of recommendations for preventing the recurrence of human rights violations in Chile.

CHINA

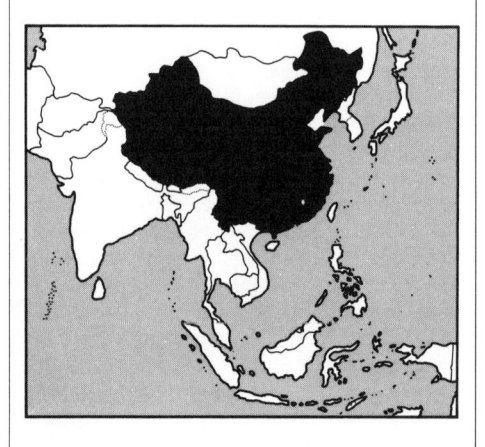

Hundreds of prisoners of conscience remained in prison throughout 1990, including many detained without charge or trial. There were many new arrests of political and religious activists, advocates of Tibetan independence and others. Some government opponents were sentenced to prison terms after unfair trials. Torture of detainees by police and harsh conditions of detention continued to be reported. A dramatic increase in the number of death sentences and executions was recorded, particularly after the launch in May of a new campaign against crime. Amnesty International recorded over 960 death sentences, including 750 which were carried out, but believed the true number was far higher.

Martial law, in force for over six months, was lifted in Beijing on 11 January. In Lhasa, capital of the Tibet Autonomous Region (TAR), where it had been in force for 14 months, it was lifted on 1 May. However, the police and security forces retained extensive powers of arbitrary arrest and detention without trial under regulations in force throughout the country. Public meetings and demonstrations remained severely restricted under legislation which came into force after the June 1989 crackdown on the pro-democracy movement. No public inquiries were known to have been carried out into the killings of unarmed civilians by government forces in Beijing and Lhasa in 1989.

According to the government, 881 untried political detainees arrested since June 1989 were released in the first half of 1990. They were freed in three groups, but the identities of only 11 were officially disclosed. Prisoners of conscience were among those released.

Hundreds of people arrested in connection with the 1989 protests remained in prison throughout 1990, but the fate of thousands of others remained unknown. The authorities stated that 881 people had been released and 355 were still in pre-trial detention in Beijing in mid-1990. However, they did not disclose how many had been detained in Beijing or nationwide, nor how many had been tried or assigned to labour camps without trial. Released detainees confirmed that thousands had been arrested in Beijing alone.

Students, workers and others who had not played a major role in the protests were reportedly sent to labour camps under a law on "re-education through labour" which permits detention without charge or trial for up to four years. An official at the Tuanhe "labour-re-education" camp, in Beijing's suburbs, told foreign journalists in May that 300 "counter-revolutionaries" had been sent to the camp after the June 1989 crackdown. According to unofficial sources, other groups were sent to labour camps further away from Beijing.

Hundreds of political detainees were also held without charge or trial in prisons and detention centres throughout the country. Officials stated in June that 355 people detained since June 1989 were still held "for investigation" in Beijing. Student leaders and intellectuals who had played a major role in the protests were held at Qincheng, a maximum security prison for prominent political prisoners several miles north of Beijing. Over 100 of them were still held there without charge in May, according to a released detainee.

Prolonged detention without charge or trial was facilitated by illegal practices which had become the norm, and by regulations which permit administrative detention without judicial approval or review, contrary to provisions in the Constitution and Chinese law. Regulations on "shelter and investigation" – which give police the authority to detain suspects without charge for renewable periods of three months – were used frequently to detain people suspected of involvement in the protests.

In November several dozen leaders of the 1989 protests were charged with "counter-revolutionary" offences after being held for over one year without charge. They included student leader Wang Dan, who was charged with "counter-revolutionary propaganda and agitation". Two intellectuals, Wang Juntao and Chen Ziming, faced trial on the same charge as well as that of "conspiring to overthrow the government", which carries penalties from 10 years' imprisonment to death. The trials had not taken place by the end of 1990.

In Tibet, the lifting of martial law in Lhasa in May was followed by a decree requiring prior police permission for any public assembly. New regulations prohibited the use of "religion or other activities" in "demonstrations or parades [which] ... endanger national unity or social stability". Buddhist monks and nuns were expelled from monasteries and convents near Lhasa, particularly from April to July. Some were reportedly restricted to their village of origin.

Tibetans suspected of opposition to the government continued to be arrested. Agyal Tsering, a monk, was reportedly held incommunicado for several weeks following his arrest in February in Qinghai province. He was later sentenced to 18 months' imprisonment for allegedly printing and distributing a leaflet advocating Tibetan independence. At least nine nuns and a monk arrested in Lhasa in August, apparently for chanting pro-independence slogans, were still held at the end of 1990.

Political and religious activists were also arrested elsewhere. Among those held were 11 poets who were arrested in March in Sichuan province and accused of belonging to an underground poets' society and of publishing "subversive poetry". They were reportedly planning to publish a collection of poems commemorating those killed in Beijing in June 1989. They were still detained at the end of 1990.

Other arrests were unconnected with the 1989 protests. Some reflected a tightening of the official policy on religion and a continuing crackdown on independent church groups.

In north China, over 30 Roman Catholic priests, bishops and church members were arrested in late 1989 and early 1990. They belonged to the "underground" church, which remains loyal to the Vatican and refuses to join the official church. Most had participated in the formation of a Chinese Bishops' Conference, which declared its allegiance to the Pope, and they were still held without charge at the end of 1990. Liu Guangdong, the 71-year-old bishop of Yixian in Hebei province and Chairman of the Conference, and Su Zhemin, a priest, were accused of taking part in "illegal activities". They were administratively "sentenced" in May to three years' "re-education through labour". Further arrests of dissident Catholics took place in several provinces during the year.

Members of independent Protestant groups were also detained and harassed by police. Some were released after short periods, but others were still held at the end of 1990. Those still held included Xu Guoxing, a preacher arrested in November 1989 in Shanghai who was sent to a labour camp without trial for three years' "re-education through labour". He was accused of having founded an independent "house-church" without official approval. He was considered a prisoner of conscience.

Other prisoners of conscience held throughout 1990 included people serving long prison sentences for their involvement in the democracy movement of the late 1970s, Tibetan advocates of independence and people arrested for their religious activities.

In Xinjiang, over 6,000 people were reportedly arrested and accused of "fomenting rebellion" after unrest in Baren Township. Although few details were available, at least 50 civilians were apparently killed by security forces in clashes when several hundred Muslim Kirghiz on a pilgrimage were barred access to a mosque by police. Official reports described the clashes as a "counter-revolutionary riot" engineered by Muslim "separatists" and said that only 16 civilians and six police officers had been killed. However, local television reportedly said that 50 civilians and eight police officers had died. In September the authorities in Xinjiang announced regulations severely restricting religious activities.

Some prisoners of conscience were convicted on "counter-revolutionary" charges and sentenced to prison terms. Chen Zhixiang, a Guangzhou teacher, received a 10-year sentence in January for allegedly displaying a slogan criticizing government leaders shortly after the 4 June 1989 massacre. Li Haitao, an academic held since June 1989, received a four-year sentence in August for "counter-revolutionary propaganda and agitation" and "disrupting traffic": he had circulated information about the 4 June massacre and organized public protests in Wuhan, Hubei Province. Tashi Tsering, from Shigatse, southern Tibet, was reportedly sentenced to seven years' imprisonment for having written "slogans and leaflets" in support of Tibetan independence. He had been arrested in November 1989.

Few such trials were publicly reported. Most trials publicized by the authorities were of people accused of committing ordinary criminal offences during the 1989 protests. However, hundreds of secret trials related to the protests reportedly took place. A report by the *Washington Post* in January that 800 people were sentenced in such trials was denied by the official New China News Agency. In February, however, the official *Beijing Daily* said that "more than 200 cases" stemming from the "counter-revolutionary rebellion" had been tried by the Beijing municipal courts in 1989, without specifying how many defendants were involved in each case. It added that Beijing courts had also handled 3,459 cases involving "crimes of seriously disrupting social order" – some of which may have been related to the 1989 protests.

New reports of torture and ill-treatment of prisoners emerged. Released detainees said that beatings and other abuses, as well as harsh conditions of detention, were commonplace in Beijing after the June 1989 crackdown. Cases of torture were also reported in other areas, particularly Tibet. Topgyal, a tailor arrested in April for possessing a video-cassette of the Dalai Lama, was reportedly severely beaten while held incommunicado in police custody in Lhasa. Lhakpa Tsering, a student arrested in late 1989 and accused of belonging to a "counter-revolutionary" organization, was allegedly beaten to death in December in Drapchi prison, Lhasa. A doctor and judicial officials reportedly examined his body at the request of his family, but no formal inquest was reported by the end of 1990.

In a report presented to the United Nations (UN) Committee Against Torture in April, the authorities acknowledged that torture still existed in China but gave no details of the procedures followed to investigate individual cases. According to official sources, more than 4,700 cases of "infringement of citizens' rights" were investigated and dealt with in 1988, and 2,900 cases of "perverting justice for bribes, extorting confessions by torture, illegal detention and neglect of duty" were investigated from January to March 1990. Of these, more than 490 "major" cases involved "deaths and injuries as well as serious economic losses".

There was a dramatic increase in the use of the death penalty. The authorities do not publish statistics on the death penalty, but it appeared that several thousand people may have been sentenced to death in 1990. Amnesty International recorded over 960 death sentences, including some with a two-year stay of execution. At least 750 executions were known to have been carried out. There were 270 in June and July alone, following the launch in May of a new campaign "to sternly crack down on crime". Courts were ordered to impose "severe and swift" sentences, using 1983 legislation which provides for summary procedures. The widespread practice of deciding sentences before trial added to the summary nature of the proceedings. Some death sentences were officially described as a means of ensuring "social order" and "stability" before the Asian Games held in Beijing in September. Some prisoners sentenced to death were reportedly paraded in public before execution, a practice which in Amnesty International's view constitutes degrading treatment and is prohibited under Chinese regulations.

Amnesty International continued throughout the year to press for the release of prisoners of conscience, for the fair trial or release of other political prisoners, and for commutation of all death sentences. However, despite numerous appeals and inquiries to the government, there was no direct reply.

In May Amnesty International sent the government a list of 700 detainees believed held since June 1989, and requested information about them and others being held. In September it sent the government a detailed account of its concerns relating to the death penalty and called for an immediate halt to executions and the introduction of fair trial safeguards. In November it called on the authorities to disclose what had happened to hundreds of political detainees who had vanished since their arrest the previous year. Following reports that leaders of the 1989 protests might soon face secret trials, the organization called on the government to ensure that the trials were conducted in accordance with international standards, and to allow international observers.

In January Amnesty International submitted to the UN Secretary-General a document describing its concern at the killings of unarmed civilians in Beijing in June 1989, the large-scale arbitrary arrests carried out subsequently and persistent reports of torture and ill-treatment. This document was included in a report debated in March by the UN Commission on Human Rights. In an oral statement to the Commission in March, Amnesty International reiterated its concern about extrajudicial executions carried out in June 1989.

Amnesty International again expressed its concerns in China in an oral statement to the UN Sub-Commission on Prevention of Discrimination and Protection of Minorities in August.

The organization also published several reports and documents about human rights violations in China. They included in March, *Tibet Autonomous Region; One Year Under Martial Law: An Update on the Human Rights Situation*, and in April, *China: The Massacre of June 1989 and its Aftermath*, as well as *Catholics Imprisoned in China: Recent Arrests and Long-term Prisoners* and *People's Republic of China: Torture and Ill-treatment*. In May it published *List of People Detained for Activities Related to the 1989 Pro-Democracy Movement*, and in September three documents entitled *The Continuing Repression*, including one on the death penalty and anti-crime campaigns.

COLOMBIA

Hundreds of people were executed extrajudicially or "disappeared" after being seized by members of the armed forces or paramilitary groups associated with them. Victims included political activists – including two presidential candidates – and human rights, trade union and church activists. Scores of peasants were arbitrarily detained, tortured and killed by government troops in counter-insurgency operations. In urban areas "death squad"-style killings of suspected delinquents increased. Political detainees held illegally in army installations were reportedly tortured. Most cases of human rights abuses remained unresolved despite investigative efforts by the Procurator General and some judges. Two army officers were convicted for their part in the killing of 12 judicial officials.

Peace negotiations initiated during 1989 with the guerrilla organization, the *Movimiento 19 de Abril* (M-19), 19 April Movement, culminated in the group's formal surrender of weapons in March after 16 years' armed opposition. Its members, who were granted an amnesty, formed a political party, *Alianza Democrática M-19*, M-19 Democratic Alliance. Three other guerrilla organizations also entered peace negotiations with the government.

The principal remaining guerrilla forces, *Fuerzas Armadas Revolucionarias de Colombia* (FARC), Revolutionary Armed Forces of Colombia, and the *Ejército de Liberación Nacional* (ELN), National Liberation Army, maintained their campaigns of armed opposition throughout the year. They carried out scores of kidnappings, bomb attacks on economic targets and ambushes of government forces in which civilians were also killed.

Some of the estimated 140 paramilitary organizations, many of which were created and supported by the Colombian army, offered to disband and return their weapons to the armed forces in exchange for a general amnesty for those accused of human rights violations. Two did disband. However, the government publicly stated that members of paramilitary organizations responsible for criminal abuses must stand trial.

A renewed escalation in political violence in the run-up to congressional and municipal elections in March and presidential elections in May left scores of people dead, including two left-wing presidential candidates. Bernardo Jaramillo Ossa, presidential candidate for the coalition party *Unión Patriotica* (UP), Patriotic Union, and M-19 Democratic Alliance leader Carlos Pizarro Leongómez, were shot dead in March and April respectively. The UP withdrew from the elections.

Liberal party candidate César Gaviria Trujillo was elected President and assumed office in August. The electorate also voted to form a constituent assembly to reform the Constitution, and this was elected in December.

Scores of UP activists were again among the victims of human rights violations. In February Diana Cardona Saldarriaga, UP Mayoress of Apartadó in the Urabá region of Antioquia department, was abducted from her home in Medellín and subsequently killed by men who claimed to be her officially assigned bodyguards from the *Departamento Administrativo de Seguridad* (DAS), Administrative Security Department, shortly before the genuine escorts arrived. The Procurator General publicly called on the Minister of Defence to explain how the gunmen had obtained confidential information about the whereabouts and plans of Diana Cardona. She was the sixth UP mayor to have been killed since the first direct municipal elections in March 1988. Both of her predecessors in Apartadó had resigned following death threats. Two days after Diana Cardona's killing six UP members were shot dead by unidentified gunmen in the town of Unguía, Chocó department, at a commemorative meeting.

Paramilitary groups – whose legal basis was withdrawn in 1989 – continued to operate with virtual impunity and were responsible for the majority of killings and "disappearances". Peasant community leaders in conflict zones were among the victims. Josué Vargas, Miguel Barajas and Saúl Castañeda, leaders of the *Asociación de Campesinos de Cararé*, Cararé Peasants' Association, and journalist Silvia Duzán were shot dead in February by two gunmen in the community of La India, municipality of Cimitarra, Santander department. Silvia Duzán was interviewing the peasant leaders about their association's attempt to obtain guarantees for the safety of civilians from the military, paramilitary and guerrilla forces operating in the area. Shortly before the killings, a paramilitary leader had reportedly accused the Cararé Peasants' Association of having links with guerrilla groups and had threatened its leaders.

The banana plantation area of Urabá continued to be severely affected by paramilitary abuses. In January a group of approximately 40 armed men, some in military uniform, entered the village of Pueblo Bello in Urabá. They rounded up 43 men and drove them away in two lorries in the direction of the nearby San Pedro army base. In a meeting with Amnesty International representatives in April, the military commander of Urabá denied that the lorries had passed by the army base. However, in April the Procurator General opened disciplinary proceedings against two army officers from the San Pedro base. Investigators had established that they had ordered the permanent road-block outside the army base to be inexplicably lifted shortly before the abduction.

In April, 24 bodies were found in clandestine mass graves on a ranch in Córdoba department. Judicial investigations had previously implicated the ranch owner – together with members of the armed forces – in a series of multiple killings in Antioquia department in 1988 and 1989. Seven of the 24 bodies were identified as inhabitants of Pueblo Bello. Five civilians arrested on the ranch and charged in connection with the "disappearance" and presumed killing of the 43 men were released by a Superior Court Judge in May after a petition of *habeas corpus* was filed on their behalf. Several warrants for the arrest of the ranch-owner were not carried out by the security forces.

María Restrepo Quinceno, the regional Procurator of Urabá who had participated in the investigation of the Pueblo Bello "disappearances", was shot and killed in July together with her bodyguard in Apartadó. Three civilians arrested in connection with the killings reportedly claimed to work for the army and told investigators that an army officer from the Voltígeros Battalion had provided the guns used in the attack on the Procurator.

An increasing number of reports were received of human rights violations committed by counter-insurgency troops deployed in remote rural areas where armed opposition groups were active. In April, two days after an armed confrontation between the FARC and members of the army's counter-insurgency *Brigada Móbil*, Mobile Brigade, in Puerto Valdivia, Antioquia department, six peasants from Puerto Valdivia were arrested by members of the Girardot Battalion. Five days later the peasants' bodies were found in a common grave on a nearby farm. They were bound and showed signs of torture. The Commander of the army's IV Brigade claimed the six were "guerrillas killed in combat". However, the Procurator General opened disciplinary proceedings against 11 members of the army, including two captains, for the unlawful killing of the peasants. The results of the proceedings had not been revealed by the end of the year.

Members of the National Police, which under the state of siege reimposed in 1984 comes under the authority of the armed forces, were also responsible for extrajudicial executions. Fifteen-year-old Fredy Pérez Solano, 17-year-old Jaime Béltran Pérez, Eliécer Suárez Suárez and Saúl Ortíz Nisperuza, members of the Zenú Indian community, were detained by members of the National Police in January near the community of Arroyo de Piedra, in the San Andrés de Sotavento Indian reserve in Córdoba department. Eye-witnesses testified that the four were beaten and forced into a police van. Their bodies were found the next day showing signs of torture as well as gunshot wounds. In June the Procurator General opened disciplinary proceedings against eight police agents allegedly responsible for the killings. However, the Public Ministry's efforts to investigate the killings and bring those responsible to justice did not lead to convictions by the courts. In October the eight police agents were acquitted by a public order judge in Montería, Córdoba department. The police agents were later reportedly dismissed.

The Procurator General also opened investigations into allegations that the Elite Police Corps, created in 1989 with the declared aim of combating paramilitary organizations, was responsible for a series of multiple killings of youths in poor neighbourhoods of Medellín during the government's continued offensive against drug-trafficking organizations. The attacks were carried out in apparent retaliation for the killing of over 150 police officers in Medellín in the first half of the year.

Reports of "disappearances" increased. In July the then Minister of the Interior, Dr Horacio Serpa Uribe, presented a draft bill to Congress designed to incorporate "disappearances" into the Colombian Penal Code explicitly as a crime punishable with five to 10 years' imprisonment. Dr Serpa stated that "...disappearances have occurred continually in recent years. The courts are full of denunciations and the Public Ministry is saturated with investigations, [which are] generally inconclusive." The bill had not been debated by the end of the year.

In June the Procurator General ordered disciplinary proceedings against an army major and three police officers accused of complicity in the "disappearance" of at least 16 people from the town of Trujillo and surrounding communities in Valle de Cauca department in March and April. The "disappearances" were apparently carried out in reprisal for an ELN ambush on a military patrol in which seven soldiers were killed. According to the Public Ministry's initial report, the army major, attached to the 3rd Infantry Battalion, ordered the illegal detention and participated in the torture and "disappearance" of the 16 people. A local priest who had been assisting relatives of the "disappeared" in Trujillo, Father Tiberio Fernández Mafla, himself "disappeared" shortly afterwards. His mutilated body was found a week later.

There were an increasing number of attacks on human rights workers. In July Dr Alirio de Jesús Pedraza Becerra, a lawyer, was seized in Bogotá's Suba district by eight armed men who identified themselves to two police agents nearby as members of the security forces. Military and police authorities denied his detention and reportedly obstructed the Public Ministry investigation by refusing to identify the police officers who witnessed the abduction. Following Dr Pedraza's "disappearance", other human rights workers received anonymous threats warning them to stop their activities or face the same fate.

Dr Pedraza had been working on behalf of a number of trade unionists detained and tortured by the army's III Brigade in Cali, Valle de Cauca department, in March. The trade unionists testified that they were subjected to beatings, electric shocks, "*submarino*" (near-drowning) and mock executions. A human rights worker who was detained when she went to the Brigade to inquire about them alleged that she was raped by soldiers and threatened with death. After several days' incommunicado detention the detainees were brought before a judge and eventually acquitted of violating the anti-terrorist statute, Law 180. In May the Public Ministry opened disciplinary proceedings against four officers of the III Brigade, including the Brigade's second-in-command, for illegal detention and torture. The results were not known by the end of the year.

In the vast majority of cases, members of the armed forces accused of human rights violations continued to be shielded from prosecution by their superiors, and criminal proceedings in both civilian and military courts generally resulted in acquittals. However, in June two army officers and six civilian members of a paramilitary organization were convicted of the killing of 12 members of a judicial commission of inquiry in January 1989 in La Rochela, Santander department (see *Amnesty International Report 1990*). The army lieutenant and sergeant were sentenced to eight and 12 years' imprisonment respectively for "aiding and abetting terrorist activities" after the court found them guilty of providing the weapons used to kill the judicial officials. However, the lieutenant escaped from custody in the Boyacá Battalion in Pasto shortly before the trial ended.

In November the Procurator General and his deputies resigned. They had recommended that two senior military commanders be dismissed from the armed forces in connection with the siege of the Palace of Justice in November 1985 (see *Amnesty International Report 1986*). This recommendation was severely criticized by high-ranking army officers and members of Congress. The Procurator General said that General Jesús Arias Cabrales, then commander of the XIII Brigade, had failed to take the necessary measures to protect hostages, and Colonel Edilberto Sánchez Rubiano, then head of the army's B-2 Intelligence Unit, had been involved in the "disappearance" of Irma Franco, who was taken alive from the building by the army but was not seen again.

Throughout the year Amnesty International urged the government to take measures to halt human rights violations. The organization repeated calls for paramilitary forces responsible for widespread abuses to be disbanded and for effective investigations into human rights violations leading to the prosecution of those responsible.

In January Amnesty International submitted information about its concerns in Colombia for United Nations (UN) review under a procedure, established by Economic and Social Council Resolutions 728F/1503, for confidential consideration of communications about human rights violations.

In an oral statement to the UN Commission on Human Rights delivered in February, Amnesty International included references to its concerns in Colombia.

COMOROS

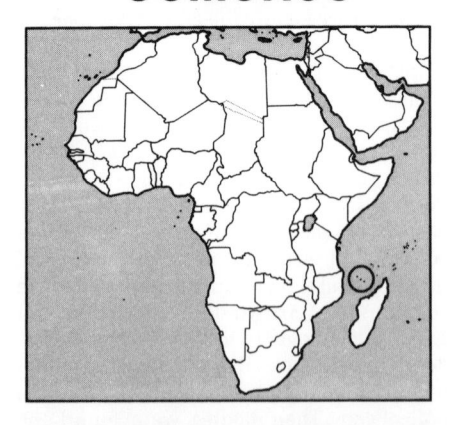

At least 20 people were detained in connection with an alleged conspiracy against the government but they had not been brought to trial by the end of 1990. One of them died in custody, apparently as a result of torture, and another was also reported to have been tortured.

Saïd Mohamed Djohar, who had been Acting President since December 1989, was elected President in March for a six-year term. After the result was announced, there were clashes in early April between security forces and opposition demonstrators.

At least 20 people were arrested in August following an announcement by the authorities that an attempt to destabilize the government, involving European mercenaries, had been foiled. In October the government said that Max Veillard, described as a French mercenary who promoted the alleged plot, had been killed in an exchange of fire with the security forces. Those arrested were supporters of Mohamed Taki, leader of the *Union nationale pour la démocratie aux Comores*, National Union for Democracy in the Comoros, who was a candidate in the March presidential elections. Mohamed Taki himself was not arrested. One of the detainees, Saïd Mlindé, died in custody on 15 September apparently as a result of torture, although the authorities did not clarify the circumstances of his death. Ali Soihili, a journalist detained in connection with the same alleged coup plot, was also said to have been tortured. He reportedly told another journalist who saw him when he was taken before the *juge d'instruction* (examining magistrate), that he had been tortured for more than five hours, handcuffed to a wall for two days shortly after his arrest, and denied food.

Those arrested in August were charged with involvement in an attempt to destabilize the government but they had not been brought to trial by the end of the year.

Amnesty International expressed concern about reports of torture and the death in custody of Saïd Mlindé, and urged the government to initiate a full and impartial investigation. The organization also sought information about the legal status of those arrested in August.

CONGO

All known political prisoners were released in August following a presidential amnesty. At least 50 such prisoners were freed, including prisoners of conscience. At least four prisoners remained under sentence of death but no new death sentences or executions were reported.

President Denis Sassou-Nguesso announced political reforms in July, including the end of the one-party state and the unchallenged position occupied by the *Parti congolais du travail* (PCT), Congolese Labour Party, since 1969. The PCT Central Committee decided in July to allow other parties to compete for power in 1991 after the introduction of a new constitution providing for multi-party democracy. It recommended that a law should be enacted to strengthen basic rights to freedom of expression, press, association and assembly: these rights had been guaranteed under the 1985 Constitution but not respected in practice. The Chief of Staff of the National People's Army announced in November that from January 1991 the army, which had dominated successive Congolese governments since 1969, would be required to be apolitical and that soldiers would return PCT membership cards and medals awarded by the PCT. The reforms were announced following mounting pressure on the government to increase political freedom and the standard of living: protests included workers' strikes, and petitions and demonstrations by political and social groups.

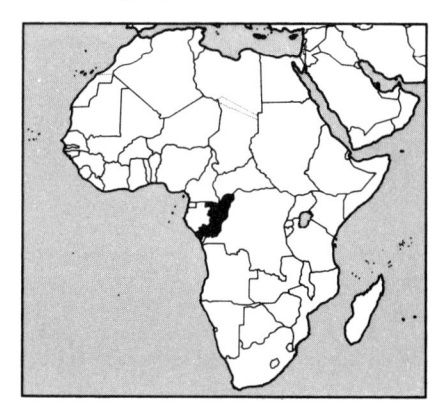

At least five people – civilians and members of the armed forces – were arrested in July and accused of involvement in a plot to overthrow the government. Among them were Célestin Nkoua, a former radio journalist and manager of a printing company; a former leading trade unionist and member of the PCT Central Committee; and Lieutenant-Colonel Michel Ngangouo. A government minister said that documents seized at Célestin Nkoua's home showed that the men had been planning a coup since 1987, that they had planned to establish a new form of government in January 1990 and had conspired in May 1990 to incite the army to rise against the government. Despite these assertions, however, it appeared that those detained had been arrested solely because of their opposition to the one-party state and their support for a national conference to debate political reforms. They were held as prisoners of conscience without charge at the central police station in the capital, Brazzaville, until August when they were released.

President Sassou-Nguesso announced on 14 August that all political prisoners were being released. At least 50 prisoners were freed: 26 of them were members of the Kouyou ethnic group arrested in 1987 and 1988 in connection with an alleged conspiracy to overthrow the government (see *Amnesty International Report 1990*). The 26, who included prisoners of conscience such as Father Joseph Ndinga, a Roman Catholic priest, had all been detained without charge or trial in military and civilian prisons in Brazzaville.

Claude-Ernest Ndalla, who had been sentenced to death in 1986 after an unfair trial before the Revolutionary Court of Justice, and others convicted with him, were also released under the amnesty. His death sentence had been commuted in 1988 (see *Amnesty International Report 1989*).

Four people convicted of murder in 1989 remained under sentence of death. Amnesty International did not learn of any new death sentences imposed by the courts or of any executions carried out during the year.

In May Amnesty International published a report, *The People's Republic of Congo: Unlawful Political Detentions and Amnesty International's Concern about Unfair Trial*, detailing violations of the basic rights of those detained since 1987 and 1988, and the organization's fears that their trials might be unfair. It urged the courts to investigate all allegations of torture and not to accept evidence extracted under torture. Before August, Amnesty International called for the release of prisoners of conscience and for prompt and fair trials for all political prisoners. It welcomed the release in August of all political prisoners and called for the commutation of all death sentences.

CÔTE D'IVOIRE

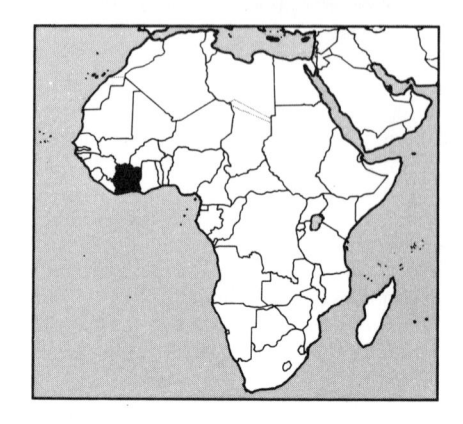

At least 250 people, including opposition political party supporters, were detained and held for short periods. None of them was charged or brought to trial. A government opponent convicted on criminal charges in 1989, who may have been prosecuted for political reasons, remained in prison.

The year began with protests against the one-party state. They were led by the *Front populaire ivoirien* (FPI), the Ivorian Popular Front, which had been refused legal recognition by the government. Following reforms announced in April to allow opposition parties, the FPI was the main challenger to the ruling *Parti démocratique de la Côte d'Ivoire* (PDCI), Democratic Party of Côte d'Ivoire, in a series of elections from October to December for the presidency and the National Assembly. President Félix Houphouët-Boigny was re-elected at the end of October.

At least 50 people, including FPI supporters, were detained for their peaceful opposition activities. None was known to have been referred to the procuracy or brought to trial, suggesting that they may have been arrested on account of their political views rather than because they had committed any offence. Some of them were held for more than 48 hours – the period for which the security forces are legally allowed to detain suspects for questioning before referring them to a judicial authority. Many appeared to be prisoners of conscience. All were believed to have been released by the end of the year.

In February five people, including

Tubene Gabriel and Seibi Sie, were arrested and held for up to 12 days for distributing a new FPI newspaper, *l'Evénement*, (*Events*), in Gagnoa and Yamoussoukro. The apparent reason for the arrests was that government officials had not authorized the newspaper's sale. The case against them was dropped and they were released.

On 26 March a group of 127 teachers were arrested in the capital, Abidjan. They were arrested when they drove in convoy into the city centre to protest against the banning of a meeting which had been called to discuss a recently announced reduction in teachers' salaries. They were taken to Akouédo military barracks, outside the capital. On 28 March several of their wives and daughters staged a peaceful protest in Abidjan. They were dispersed by police officers using tear-gas and some were detained. All the teachers and their relatives were released uncharged on 30 March.

On 2 April Bah Bernard Doh and Kouato Charles Magli were among 30 trade unionists arrested for demonstrating in support of a free trade union in Abidjan. All but one of them were kept in custody for 11 days and then released without charge.

More than 40 FPI supporters were reportedly arrested in Abidjan and Daloa on 28 October, when they alleged that the presidential elections were being unfairly conducted. They were released uncharged after a few days.

Innocent Kobena Anaky, a leading member of the FPI who was convicted on charges of tax and customs fraud in February 1989, remained imprisoned (see *Amnesty International Report 1990*). It appeared that his prosecution might have been politically motivated and that he did not receive a fair trial.

Amnesty International expressed its concern to the government about the short-term detention of trade unionists, teachers, opposition political party activists and others apparently imprisoned for their non-violent political activities, and appealed for their release. The organization continued to seek information from the authorities about the imprisonment of Innocent Kobena Anaky, on the grounds that he may actually have been charged and convicted because of his non-violent political activities, but received no further response.

CUBA

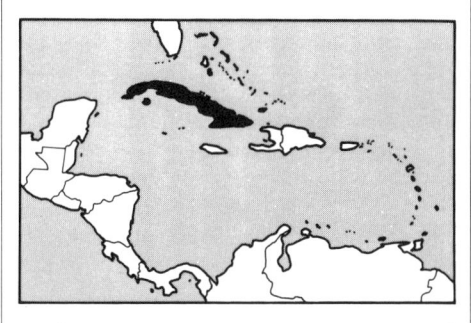

At least 70 government critics, most of them probable prisoners of conscience, were detained. Many of them were released after short periods; others were held for up to eight months without access to lawyers. At least eight prisoners of conscience were serving prison sentences at the end of the year; five others were released, most after completing their sentences. Trials of political prisoners continued to fall short of international standards for fair trial. No executions were known to have taken place but at least two death sentences were believed to be pending appeal before the People's Supreme Court.

The changing situation in Eastern Europe had serious political and economic repercussions on Cuba. The Cuban Government called on the public to openly discuss the weaknesses of the country's political system, but continued to take harsh action against small unofficial opposition and human rights groups calling for radical political change or an extension of civil rights.

In March large crowds attacked the homes of two former political prisoners, brothers Gustavo and Sebastián Arcos Bergnes, leaders of the *Comité Cubano Pro Derechos Humanos* (CCPDH), Cuban Committee for Human Rights, when meetings of human rights activists were taking place there. Security forces reportedly stood by and watched the crowds shout insults and throw stones, causing serious damage to the buildings.

In August the Attorney General said that fewer than 200 people were in detention for "counter-revolutionary" crimes. This figure, however, did not include those prisoners convicted of certain criminal offences for which prisoners of conscience are often held, such as illegal association, clandestine printing and trying to leave the country illegally.

Between January and March about 50 people were arrested apparently in connection with their political, human rights or religious activities. Most were believed to have been released within a few days, but some were held for several months.

In January two mathematics students at Havana University, Jorge Quintana and Carlos Ortega, were arrested and taken to the Havana headquarters of the *Departamento de Seguridad del Estado* (DSE), Department of State Security. Both were members of the *Unión de Jóvenes Comunistas* (UJC), Union of Young Communists, the youth wing of the Cuban Communist Party (the only legal political party in Cuba). They were accused of belonging to an opposition group and of criticizing President Fidel Castro. They were held until November, when the prosecutor changed the charge against them from "enemy propaganda" to the criminal offence of "disrespect". Jorge Quintana and Carlos Ortega were given non-custodial sentences of three years' and two years' "restricted liberty" respectively, which required them to report regularly to the police.

Six people were reportedly arrested in Sagua La Grande, Villa Clara Province, in January and charged with illegally producing religious literature for the banned Jehovah's Witnesses. It was not known whether they remained in detention.

Also in January Aurea Feria Cano and Jesús Contreras, said to be leaders of an unofficial political group, the *Unión Democrática Indio-Feria*, Indio-Feria Democratic Union, were detained in Havana and taken to the DSE headquarters. They were held until November when they were tried with four other people for "enemy propaganda" on the grounds that they were planning to distribute "counter-revolutionary" pamphlets. The outcome of the trial was not known.

In March eight members of the *Partido Pro Derechos Humanos en Cuba* (PPDHC), Party for Human Rights in Cuba, were arrested in Havana. Shortly afterwards a senior official announced that they were being accused of serving the interests of the United States of America by trying to change Cuba's socialist government and constitution, and of belonging to a "counter-revolutionary organization". In July two of the detainees – Tania Díaz Castro and Pablo Roberto Pupo Sánchez – appeared on Cuban television alleging that Cuban human rights groups, including the PPDHC, were being manipulated by foreign diplomats. This coincided with the attempt by several Cubans to obtain asylum in foreign embassies in the capital, Havana. Two months later, the two, together with the six other PPDHC members detained with them, were released. In November the eight were convicted of "illegal association" and given sentences ranging from three months' to one year's "restricted liberty".

PPDHC Secretary General Dr Alfredo Samuel Martínez Lara was also arrested in March, only a few days after he had been released from prison (see *Amnesty International Report 1990*). He had completed a nine-month sentence for "illegal association, demonstration and meeting" in December 1989, and was then given an additional sentence for "disrespect", allegedly for insulting President Castro. He was released on 27 February. After his rearrest in March, Dr Martínez Lara was apparently taken to the DSE headquarters where he was still being held at the end of the year. Reports were received that he was being subjected to psychological pressures. In November he was allowed one brief visit from a lawyer who reportedly found that no formal charges had been brought against him. However, some sources said that the authorities were investigating the possibility that he was connected with 11 young people who were arrested in January and tried in July on charges including terrorism and rebellion. The 11 were accused of belonging to the *Asociación Juvenil Pro Derechos Humanos* (AJPDH), Youth Association for Human Rights, said by the authorities to be the armed wing of the PPDHC. They received sentences ranging from three years' "restricted liberty" to 15 years' imprisonment. Little information was available concerning the circumstances of their arrest and trial.

In June the trial took place of Esteban González González and six other prisoners of conscience who had been arrested in September 1989. They were charged with rebellion and "other acts against state security" on the basis of their membership of the unofficial *Movimiento Integracionista Democrática* (MID), Movement for Democratic Integration, of which Esteban González González was the founder and leader. They were convicted on charges including possessing and disseminating "counter-revolutionary propaganda" and planning to carry out a campaign of civil disobedience with a view to changing the political and social system and restoring capitalism. Esteban González González was sentenced to seven years' imprisonment; the others to between three years' "restricted liberty" and six years' imprisonment. The MID calls for political reform and full respect for human rights in Cuba but specifically rules out the use of violence. The seven had been held for several months in the DSE headquarters without access to lawyers before being transferred to prison.

Information was received concerning six other prisoners who may be prisoners of conscience. Juan Mayo Méndez, held in Boniato Prison; Agustín Figueredo, Ernesto Bonilla Fonseca and Alexis Maestre Savorit, held in Las Mangas Prison, Bayamo; and CCPDH member Alexis Morejón Rodríguez, held in Camaguey Province, were all accused of "enemy propaganda", mainly for writing or shouting anti-government slogans. Pedro Alvarez Martínez, a PPDHC delegate for Pinar del Río, was arrested in December 1989 and given a five-year sentence for offences including "clandestine printing".

CCPDH member José Irene Padrón Dueñas was detained in Havana on 4 September and taken to the DSE headquarters, possibly because he had denounced the arrest of his brother-in-law Alexis Morejón Rodríguez (see above). At the end of the year it was not known whether he was still in detention.

Reports continued to be received that several hundred people were imprisoned for trying to leave the country illegally, some of whom may have been prisoners of conscience. A letter smuggled out of Combinado del Este Prison in July 1990 said that 335 people were being held in the prison for that offence. However, little detailed information on individual cases was available.

Prisoner of conscience Hiram Abí Cobas Núñez was released from prison in November on grounds of illness and allowed to serve the remainder of his sentence at home. In March 1990 he and co-defendant Elizardo Sánchez Santa Cruz had appealed unsuccessfully against the sentences imposed on them in November 1989 (see *Amnesty International Report 1990*).

Prisoner of conscience Elizardo Sánchez Santa Cruz remained in prison at the end of the year.

Four other known prisoners of conscience were released, most after completing their sentences: Manuel González González in January; Edita Esther Cruz Rodríguez in February; Javier Roberto Bahamonde Masot in July; and David Moya Alfonso in October (see *Amnesty International Report 1990.*)

Alfredo Mustelier Nuevo, one of three remaining *"plantados históricos"* (political prisoners held since the 1960s and 1970s who refused to take part in prison rehabilitation programs or to obey certain prison regulations), was released in March.

No executions were known to have taken place during 1990. At least two death sentences, including that of Jorge Luis González Norona who was convicted of triple murder, were believed to be pending appeal before the People's Supreme Court. There was concern at reports that the authorities were considering extending the already wide range of offences punishable by death to include serious drug-related crimes.

Amnesty International continued to appeal for the release of prisoners of conscience and sought information from the authorities about the legal status of political prisoners. In March the organization expressed concern about the attacks on the homes of CCPDH members. No written response was received to these communications. However, Amnesty International delegates to the Eighth United Nations (UN) Congress on the Prevention of Crime and the Treatment of Offenders, which took place in Havana from 27 August until 7 September, were able to raise the organization's concerns with senior Cuban officials, including the Attorney General and the President of the People's Supreme Court.

In August Amnesty International referred to the cases of Elizardo Sánchez Santa Cruz, Hiram Abí Cobas Núñez and Hubert Jérez Mariño in an oral statement about prisoners of conscience made to the UN Sub-Commission on Prevention of Discrimination and Protection of Minorities.

CYPRUS

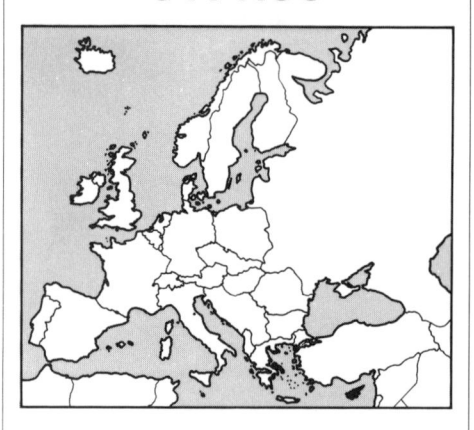

Some 30 prisoners of conscience were held, all of them Jehovah's Witnesses who had refused on conscientious grounds to perform military service or reservist exercises.

Draft legislation announced in 1988, which would recognize for the first time the right to conscientious objection, had not been debated in parliament by the end of the year. The draft legislation proposes three years' unarmed military service or four years in the Civil Defence Force or a social service as alternatives to ordinary military service of 26 months. The draft legislation provides for conscientious objection only on religious grounds. It was not clear how conscientious objectors to reservist exercises would be treated or whether the social service would be of a purely civilian character. It was also unclear whether a conscientious objector would have the right to choose between the alternatives. Conscientious objectors to military service in 1990 were given prison sentences of up to six months; those refusing to perform reservist exercises were given sentences of up to four months' imprisonment. Conscientious objectors who continued to refuse either military service or reservist exercises following their release faced further prosecution and imprisonment.

A number of conscientious objectors imprisoned during the year had already served sentences of up to 12 months prior to September 1985, when all imprisoned conscientious objectors were released following a decision by the Supreme Court (see *Amnesty International Report 1986*). Georgios Anastasi Petrou, who had served a 12-month prison sentence between 1984 and 1985 for refusing to perform military service, was sentenced to two months' imprisonment in January and a further three months' imprisonment in September for refusing to participate in reservist exercises.

On 1 October, Independence Day, President George Vassiliou granted an amnesty to five imprisoned conscientious objectors. In December one other conscientious objector was granted early release.

Amnesty International appealed repeatedly for the release of all imprisoned conscientious objectors. It urged the government to introduce alternative civilian service of non-punitive length; to widen the grounds for objection in the draft legislation; and to provide for objection which develops after conscription into the armed forces. In July President Vassiliou informed Amnesty International that it was likely that the draft legislation would be enacted before the end of the year.

CZECH AND SLOVAK FEDERAL REPUBLIC

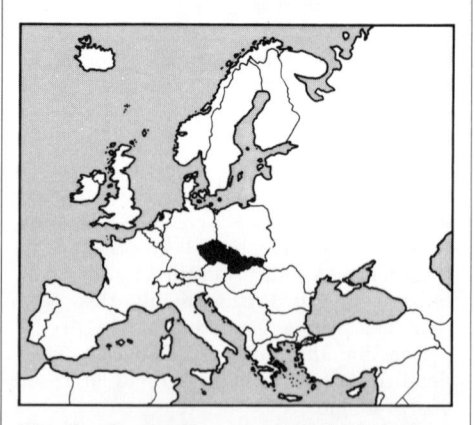

The death penalty was abolished in May. A Soviet soldier's asylum request was not properly considered. He was returned to Soviet military authorities who reportedly imprisoned him briefly as a prisoner of conscience.

The major political changes which began in late 1989 (see *Amnesty International Report 1990*) continued. Elections in

June gave the Civic Forum party a majority in the Federal Assembly, and former prisoner of conscience Vaclav Havel was re-elected President. Throughout the year major reviews of the legal and political systems, including the Constitution, continued.

In March a civilian alternative to military service lasting 27 months was introduced. Normal military service is 18 months. There were no reports of people imprisoned for refusing conscription.

In May the Federal Parliament voted to abolish the death penalty and this became effective on 1 July. The last execution reportedly took place in February 1989.

In April Aleksandr Vitalyevich Maslyayev, a 19-year-old soldier with the Soviet army stationed in the Czech and Slovak Federal Republic (CSFR), requested asylum at the Office of the President of the CSFR on the grounds that he did not wish to perform his military service in an occupying army because of his conscientiously held beliefs. He was reportedly informed that his request would be processed by the Federal Ministry of the Interior. Instead, he was handed over to Soviet diplomatic staff and subsequently returned to his unit where he was reportedly detained for 10 days before being transferred to the USSR.

Amnesty International welcomed the abolition of the death penalty. In May the organization wrote to the government concerning the introduction of alternative service. In August it raised its concerns regarding the return of Aleksandr Maslyayev.

DENMARK

Investigations continued into allegations that asylum-seekers had been ill-treated in 1988. It was alleged that a foreign visitor had been ill-treated while in police custody.

In February Denmark signed the Second Optional Protocol to the International Covenant on Civil and Political Rights Aiming at the Abolition of the Death Penalty. It had not yet ratified this instrument by the end of the year.

In January 1990 a court began to hear a civil suit brought by the Prison Officers' Union against two prison nurses for making allegedly defamatory statements. The nurses had alleged in an article published in *Amnesty Nyt* in September 1988 that asylum-seekers, who were being detained with ordinary prisoners, had been beaten by prison officers and subjected to racist insults in Copenhagen prisons. They reported that special cells existed in which detainees were strapped down and bright lights were left on continuously. Following the publication of the article, the Danish Parliament decided that asylum-seekers should be detained at a special centre and not with criminal prisoners.

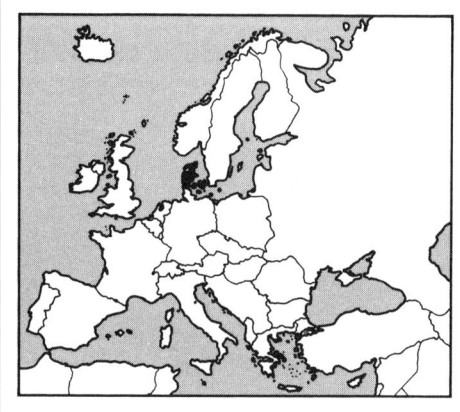

In April the court ruled against the Prison Officers' Union on four of its five complaints about the nurses' allegations of racist abuse, ill-treatment and forcible restraint of asylum-seekers. However, the nurses' unqualified statement about an alleged severe beating was found to be unjustified and they were fined.

In September Himid Hassan Juma, a Tanzanian national, was allegedly beaten by guards at the prison of Copenhagen Central Police Station. He had been visiting Denmark as a tourist when he was detained by police on suspicion of possessing a false passport. The government announced in November that a judicial investigation would be established to look into the case.

Amnesty International sent an observer to the civil proceedings brought by the Prison Officers' Union. In May Amnesty International wrote to the government inquiring whether it had initiated an independent investigation into the allegations of ill-treatment and whether it had taken steps to prevent the recurrence of such treatment.

The government replied in August that it was initiating an independent judicial inquiry into the allegations and had taken a number of other measures, including new and extended training of prison officers and a mechanism to interview detainees who were punished by solitary confinement. Amnesty International welcomed the initiatives and requested to be kept informed about their implementation.

In October Amnesty International urged the government to initiate a prompt and thorough investigation into the allegation that Himid Hassan Juma had been ill-treated, and to make the findings public.

DJIBOUTI

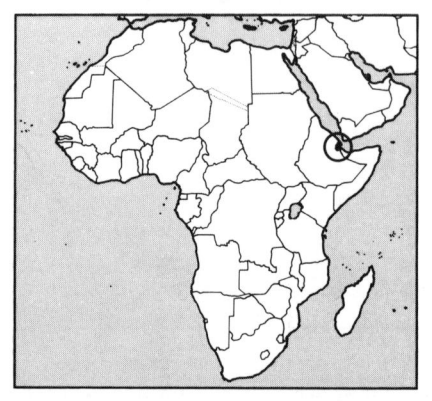

Scores of suspected government opponents were arrested but most were released after a few days or weeks. Some were alleged to have been tortured or ill-treated.

There were bomb attacks in June and September, the second of which killed a child and injured 17 people and was attributed to a little-known opposition group, the *Mouvement de la jeunesse djiboutienne*, Djibouti Youth Movement.

Dozens of people belonging to the Afar ethnic group were arrested after the June bomb attack, in many cases apparently because of their suspected opposition to the government rather than because of any evidence of their involvement in such violence. All were released within a few days, except for one man, Omar Daoud Banoita, who was reportedly accused of responsibility for the bombing. He had not been tried by the end of the year.

In August four Afars were arrested in the capital, Djibouti, in connection with a leaflet which criticized the government and called for a multi-party system. They included Kassim Ahmed Dini, son of a former prime minister; Mohamed Dileyta, a journalist; and Adam Mohamed Dileyta, a United Nations employee. All four were released uncharged after a few days. They were alleged to have been tortured or ill-treated. Another government critic arrested in August, Aka Der, was detained for two months and then released without being charged.

Scores of people, mainly from the Somali ethnic group's Gadabursi clan, were arrested following the September bomb attack and detained for several days. There appeared to be no evidence that they had been involved in causing the explosion and some of them were allegedly tortured.

In October four men accused of carrying out the September bomb attack were referred to the procuracy for a formal judicial investigation and were remanded in custody. A fifth, a taxi-driver, was reportedly kept in incommunicado detention without being brought before a magistrate, and there was concern for his safety. All five were still held at the end of the year.

Amnesty International sought information from the authorities about the arrests of suspected government opponents after the September bombing and expressed concern that some appeared to have been detained without being brought before a judge. It asked for details of the legal proceedings against the four people charged in connection with the September attack and inquired about the taxi-driver who was said not to have been seen since his arrest.

The Minister of the Interior confirmed that a number of people had been referred to the procuracy for judicial investigation in connection with the September bombing. In November he said that nine people were still held, but that they had regular access to their families, lawyers and doctors of their choice.

DOMINICA

A prisoner remained under sentence of death and there were fears of his impending execution. There were no executions during the year; the last execution was carried out in 1986.

Eric Joseph, a Rastafarian sentenced to death in 1983, was the only prisoner on death row at the end of the year (see *Amnesty International Report 1987*). His appeal to the Judicial Committee of the

Privy Council (JCPC) in London, which acts as the final court of appeal for Dominica, was heard in July 1988: the decision to dismiss his appeal was issued in October 1988. His case was subsequently reviewed by Dominica's Advisory Committee on the Prerogative of Mercy which advised the President that the sentence of death should be carried out. In June there were fears that preparations were under way for his execution but at the end of the year he was still on death row. According to reports, the death sentences of other prisoners were commuted to prison terms in 1989 on the advice of the Advisory Committee on the Prerogative of Mercy.

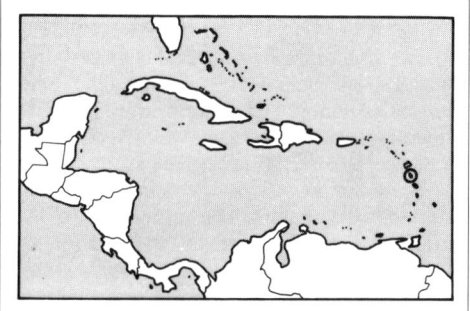

Amnesty International wrote to Prime Minister Eugenia Charles in January appealing for clemency to be granted to Eric Joseph and appealed on his behalf again in June. The organization also urged the Prime Minister to initiate moves towards the total abolition of the death penalty.

DOMINICAN REPUBLIC

One person was killed in circumstances suggesting he may have been extrajudicially executed. A detainee remained in prison despite the fact that a judge had reportedly ordered his release, and many detainees were not brought before a judge after arrest. A community activist received death threats from the police.

President Joaquín Balaguer of the *Partido Reformista Social Cristiano*, the Social Christian Reformist Party, was re-elected in May by a slim margin over Juan Bosch of the *Partido de la Liberación Dominicana*, the Dominican Liberation Party. He was inaugurated for his fifth term as President in August amid claims from opposition leaders of election fraud. On the eve of his inauguration, disturbances throughout the country culminated in a 48-hour general strike, with confrontations between police and protesters leaving over a dozen dead and hundreds wounded.

Further general strikes were held in September and November, in protest against the government's economic measures. The police and army used firearms and detained briefly hundreds of demonstrators in their attempt to control mass protests, some of them violent. At least three demonstrators reportedly died in these clashes.

On 28 September Jesús Diplán Martínez, a young community leader, was killed in the town of Salcedo in circumstances suggesting he may have been extrajudicially executed. According to eye-witness reports, he was shot in the street by members of the security forces after being arrested. A commission of inquiry to investigate the case was reportedly set up, but to Amnesty International's knowledge the results had not been made public and no one had been charged by the end of the year.

Luis Lizardo, who was arrested in May 1989 for alleged involvement in a bombing, remained in detention (see *Amnesty International Report 1990*). A judge had reportedly ordered his release after a *habeas corpus* petition was filed in May 1989, but the police apparently refused to comply with the order. There was no official response to requests for information about his exact legal situation.

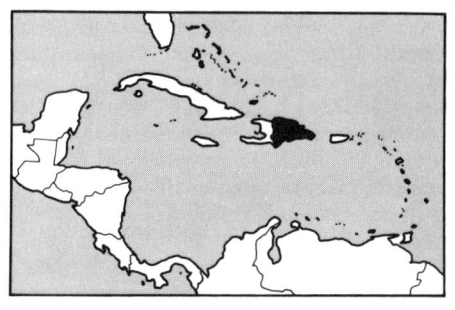

Many detainees were reportedly not brought before a competent judicial authority within 48 hours of their arrest, as specified by Article 8 of the Constitution. For example, Ramón Almánzar, a community activist affiliated to the *Colectivo de Organizaciones Populares*, the Collective of Popular Organizations, was detained on

1 October by the police in connection with their inquiries into the use of violence by protesters during countrywide demonstrations. He was reportedly held without charge for at least 12 days before being released.

Another political activist involved in mobilizing opposition to the government's economic policies, Fernando Peña Segura (see *Amnesty International Report 1990*), reportedly received numerous death threats from the police.

Following the death of Jesús Diplán Martínez, Amnesty International appealed for a thorough and impartial inquiry into the killing.

ECUADOR

Torture and ill-treatment of detainees by the police and security forces continued to be reported. One person was reportedly killed and several injured as a result of army and police operations to disperse members of indigenous communities involved in land disputes. The Supreme Court declared it outside its jurisdiction to initiate proceedings against security forces personnel allegedly responsible for an extrajudicial execution in 1985.

Against a background of heightened political tensions between Indian communities and the security forces over territorial rights, the government of President Borja Cevallos issued an official communiqué in August claiming that the *Confederación de Nacionalidades Indígenas del Ecuador* (CONAIE), the Confederation of Indigenous Nationalities of Ecuador, was seeking to set up "a state within a state". In September talks were held between indigenous leaders, human rights defenders, church leaders and government representatives in an attempt to resolve the demands of the Indian organizations.

In August a faction of the armed opposition group *Alfaro Vive, Carajo*, Alfaro Lives, Dammit, suspended negotiations with the government about reintegrating its members into civilian life and handing over weapons to the authorities.

In August Ecuador signed the Protocol to the American Convention on Human Rights to Abolish the Death Penalty; it had not ratified this treaty by the end of the year.

Members of the police forces reportedly continued to ill-treat and torture detainees suspected of committing common crimes. In January two prison directors responsible for holding untried criminal suspects transferred from police custody resigned and publicly denounced the torture and ill-treatment some detainees had allegedly suffered during police interrogation.

René Sangolqui was detained in May on suspicion of having committed a double murder. He was taken to the headquarters of the *Servicio de Investigaciones Criminales* (SIC), the Criminal Investigation Service, in the town of Loja. He later claimed that during his interrogation he was beaten, hung by his thumbs, and had a bag placed over his head into which gas was fed, causing him near-asphyxiation. The government stated in June that it had ordered an investigation into the allegations, but its findings had not been published by the end of the year.

Marco Antonio Espín, a soldier, stated that he had been held for over three weeks in February and March at the headquarters of the *Batallón de Transmisiones de Rumiñahui*, the Rumiñahui Communications Battalion, in Quito, the capital. He was accused of using illicit drugs. He reported that members of the army threw water over him and a fellow soldier, and applied electricity to their necks, backs and genitals. Marco Antonio Espín testified that he had been denied access to a doctor during his detention and warned not to inform human rights organizations about his torture. No investigations into his case were known to have been initiated by the end of the year.

In June Indian communities in the sierra region organized a series of protests over territorial rights. They took over highways and occupied the church of Santo

Domingo in Quito. In June Oswaldo Cuvi, an Ecuarunari Indian community activist, was reportedly shot and killed by the army during attempts to disperse protesters peacefully blocking the highway in Gatazo Grande, Chimborazo province. Several other Ecuarunari Indians were reportedly injured by army gunfire in the same incident. In early October César Morocho, an Ecuarunari Indian leader, failed to return home after leaving a meeting in Quito. He was not seen again. César Morocho had led a march denouncing the killing and injuring of Indians involved in the Gatazo Grande protest, and had reportedly received numerous telephone calls threatening him with death.

In separate operations between 9 and 13 November, large numbers of armed police entered three Indian communities in the provinces of Pichincha and Imbabura in the context of land disputes. Reports indicated that a number of unarmed community members protesting over land rights were severely beaten by the police and injured by gunshot pellets, including Cayetana Farinango. She died on 14 November. No official investigations into these incidents were known to have opened by the end of the year.

The Supreme Court declared it was not within its competence to initiate judicial proceedings against navy and police officers named in 1989 by a multi-party congressional committee as responsible for the killing of Consuelo Benavides in 1985 (see *Amnesty International Reports 1987* and *1990*). The government also failed to clarify the fate of people who "disappeared" between 1984 and 1988.

In May Amnesty International published a report entitled *Ecuador: Torture Continues*. It described the common practice of torture and ill-treatment of suspected criminals by the police and documented 21 cases. The organization pressed for thorough investigations into the allegations. In August the government responded to allegations raised both in the report and in a November 1989 letter from Amnesty International (see *Amnesty International Report 1990*). The government reaffirmed its commitment to investigate fully all the cases and to comply with its human rights obligations. It provided information on 26 cases of reported torture, including those of Héctor Vinicio Arteaga Carpio, Gonzalo Quintero Mina, Sélfido Ilves Camacho, and of Héctor Mejía and five colleagues (see *Amnesty International Report 1990*). The government denied that Héctor Vinicio Arteaga had ever been detained by the SIC in Azuay. It stated that the Attorney General's department had established the causes of Gonzalo Quintero's death and had submitted its report to the competent authorities. The government reported that judicial proceedings had been initiated against the alleged torturers of Sélfido Ilves, and that an investigation into the reported torture of Héctor Mejía and his fellow workers had also been initiated.

In September Amnesty International representatives held talks in Ecuador with government officials about alleged torture and ill-treatment by members of the police. The officials said the government was taking initiatives to implement a program of reforms and training, including human rights education, for its police forces.

Amnesty International wrote to the authorities calling for allegations of torture by the police to be investigated fully and the findings published. It also called for thorough investigations of the violent incidents during police operations directed against members of indigenous communities, and for an investigation into the fate of César Morocho. In December the organization urged the authorities to investigate fully cases of reported torture within the armed forces.

EGYPT

Several thousand members and sympathizers of Islamic groups, including prisoners of conscience, were detained without charge or trial under state of emergency legislation. A number of political prisoners were acquitted after courts found that their confessions had been extracted under torture and were inadmissible as evidence. Allegations of torture and ill-treatment, although fewer than in 1989, were once again reported. At least 38 death sentences were passed during the year, some of them *in absentia*. Five prisoners were executed.

In January a new Minister of the Interior, General Muhammad 'Abd al-Halim Musa, was appointed. Like his predecessor, he made extensive use of the special powers granted to him under the state of emergency, in force since 1981, to order administrative detention and to contest judicial decisions to release political detainees. Sporadic clashes in Upper Egyptian villages, mostly between the police and members of Islamic groups, resulted in dozens of deaths. On 12 October the Speaker of the People's Assembly, Dr Rifa'at al-Mahgoub, and five guards were shot dead in Cairo. Thousands of arrests followed, initially among nationals of other Arab countries and then among members of Islamic groups and their sympathizers. Elections for the People's Assembly held on 29 November were boycotted by most opposition parties, who alleged that the new election law was biased in favour of candidates standing for the ruling National Democratic Party (NDP) of President Hosni Mubarak. The NDP gained nearly 80 per cent of the seats in the assembly, but voting in some parts of the country was accompanied by violent clashes between rival groups, resulting in at least five deaths, and there were allegations of ballot rigging.

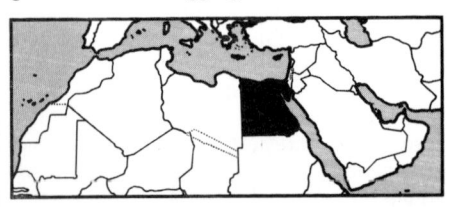

Political arrests under emergency legislation took place throughout the year. The authorities frequently justified detention orders on the grounds that the person concerned was a "threat to national security". At hearings held a month or more after the arrests in question, the courts frequently declared that this constituted insufficient grounds for detention and ordered detainees to be released. These decisions were regularly challenged by the Minister of the Interior, often leading to prolonged detention without charge or trial. Moreover, some of these detainees did not appear in court when their initial appeals for release were heard, and thus spent several months in detention without appearing before a judicial authority. These included Hassan Ibrahim Mar'iy, a former parliamentary candidate for the Socialist Labour Party, and 16 others held with him between April and July.

The overwhelming majority of those detained under the emergency laws on political grounds, including prisoners of conscience, were members or sympathizers of Islamic groups, many of them students. Most were eventually released uncharged after weeks or months in detention.

In June 'Ala' al-Din Hamid, a writer, was arrested. The authorities later said that his novel, *Masafa fi 'Aqli Rajul* (*Distance in a Man's Mind*), "offend[s] and degrade[s] religions in a way which has jeopardized national unity and... threatened social peace". He appeared to be a prisoner of conscience. He was released on bail on 22 August.

Five Muslim converts to Christianity detained since November 1989 were held without trial for several months. One of them, 'Abd al-Hamid Bishari 'Abd al-Muhsin, died in prison in February as a result of heart failure, according to official sources.

Other Muslim converts to Christianity detained during the year included Mustafa Muhammad Sa'id al-Sharqawi, Muhammad Hussein Muhammad Ibrahim Sallam and Hassan Muhammad Isma'il Muhammad, who remained in prison at the end of 1990 without charge or trial after three months in detention, during which they were reportedly subjected to torture and ill-treatment.

Some of those arrested in 1990 were tried before (Emergency) state security courts, while numerous other such trials continued from previous years. Under state of emergency legislation, verdicts of (Emergency) state security courts are not enforced until approved by the President of the Republic, who is also empowered to reduce the sentence imposed or reject the verdict and order a retrial. These powers seriously undermine the independent functioning of the judicial process.

Fourteen prisoners of conscience were released on 24 April by order of the Prime Minister, acting in his capacity as Deputy Military Governor. They had been serving prison sentences originally imposed in 1986 (but only enforced in 1989) in connection with the so-called Egyptian Communist Party case of 1981 (see *Amnesty International Report 1990*). All of the defendants in a similar case dating from 1979, in which the defendants had previously succeeded in having their sentences quashed by the Court of Cassation, were retried and acquitted in March. In November the retrial began of 176 people arrested in the wake of food riots which occurred in January 1977. The charges against them included membership of illegal political organizations, instigating the 1977 riots, and distributing leaflets. In April 1980 a state security court had acquitted 155 of them, and sentenced the others to either one or three years' imprisonment. The President did not accept this verdict.

Several other groups of political prisoners indicted in previous years were acquitted on the grounds that their confessions had not been freely given but resulted from torture or coercion. By the end of the year the President had not approved these judgments, and those acquitted, most of whom were members of Islamic groups, remained at risk of retrial.

Allegations of physical and psychological torture continued during 1990. The most common forms of torture reported were beatings, suspension, burning with cigarettes and electric shocks, often accompanied by threats, invariably inflicted by members of the State Security Intelligence Police. Khalid al-Sharif, a journalist working for the weekly *Al-Haqiqa* (*The Truth*) newspaper, was detained in August for the fourth time under state of emergency legislation. He alleged that security police suspended him by the wrists and tortured him with electric shocks applied to sensitive parts of the body, cigarette burns and beatings. It was not clear what action, if any, was taken by the authorities to investigate this allegation.

Reports of torture were received in the wake of the mass arrests which followed the assassination in October of the Speaker of the People's Assembly. At least 10 people accused of participating in the murder, including Mamdouh 'Ali Youssef, Safwat 'Abd al-Ghani, and the brothers Ahmad and Muhammad Mostafa Zaki, were reportedly severely beaten while in incommunicado detention. Mamdouh 'Ali Youssef suffered injuries to his spine and had to be carried to his interrogation sessions on a stretcher. The suspects were reportedly held for several weeks at the State Security Intelligence Police Directorate at Lazoghly, Cairo, and were denied access to their lawyers and medical treatment.

The health of Nabil al-Maghrebi, a political prisoner serving a sentence of life imprisonment in Tora Prison, continued to give cause for concern following reports that his condition was deteriorating as a result of ill-treatment and lack of adequate medical care.

No information came to light concerning the whereabouts of Mostafa Muhammad 'Abd al-Hamid 'Othman, a medical student who "disappeared" after his arrest in Zagazig in December 1989. Fellow students reported seeing him at the State Security Intelligence Police Directorate in Lazoghly in January, but official sources stated that he had been released in December, 10 days after his arrest.

Dr 'Ala' Mohy al-Din 'Ashour, a prominent member of *Al-Gama'at al-Islamiyya*, the Islamic groups, was shot dead in a Cairo street on 2 September, reportedly by people shooting from an unmarked car. There were allegations that he may have been extrajudicially executed.

At least 38 people were sentenced to death, including some *in absentia*, most of whom had been convicted of drug-trafficking or murder. No executions were recorded of people convicted of drug-trafficking (see *Amnesty International Report 1990*). At least five people who had been convicted of murder and other offences were executed. At least one death sentence was quashed by the Court of Cassation.

Amnesty International continued to press for the release of prisoners of conscience, including those held because of their religious beliefs. The government said that some of those detained had been arrested because their activities offended religion and threatened social peace.

In February Amnesty International submitted a memorandum to the Egyptian Government concerning the use of administrative detention and torture. The organization called for changes in detention procedures to safeguard detainees from torture and arbitrary imprisonment. In the memorandum and again later in the year Amnesty International urged the authorities to investigate torture allegations thoroughly and impartially in accordance with the provisions of the United Nations (UN) Convention against Torture and Other Cruel, Inhuman or Degrading Treatment or Punishment, to which Egypt acceded in 1986. However, there was virtually no progress with such investigations.

In May an Amnesty International delegation visited Cairo to discuss human rights with the government and to urge the implementation of the recommendations contained in its May 1989 report, *Egypt: Arbitrary Arrest and Torture under the State of Emergency*, and in its memorandum. In October 1990 Amnesty International published the updated text of its February memorandum and said that torture and arbitrary detention under emergency laws "could well continue as long as the security forces can detain and torture with apparent impunity".

In August Amnesty International delivered an oral statement to the UN Sub-Commission on Prevention of Discrimination and Protection of Minorities, outlining its concerns about emergency legislation permitting lengthy administrative detention.

EL SALVADOR

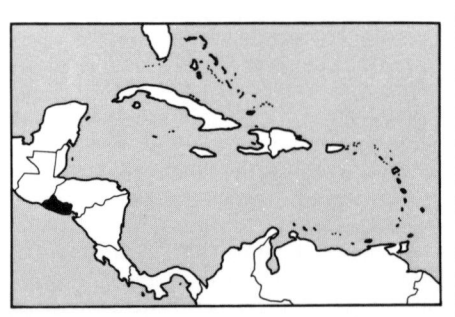

There was a sharp rise in the number of "death squad" murders in the first eight months of the year. Other people were killed in overt military operations in circumstances suggesting extrajudicial executions. Members of the armed opposition reportedly killed several captives. Torture was frequently used during police and military custody and at least two people died in detention as a result. Irregularities in legal proceedings against many of the approximately 200 political prisoners included the use of confessions extracted under torture as a basis for charges. New "disappearance" cases were reported and the authorities failed to clarify thousands of others reported in previous years. Virtually no measures were taken to bring those responsible for human rights violations to justice.

A state of siege remained in force until April by which time constitutional guarantees, suspended in November 1989 following a major offensive by the armed opposition *Frente Farabundo Martí para la Liberación Nacional* (FMLN), Farabundo Martí National Liberation Front, had been fully restored. By March most of the students, trade unionists, church representatives, and others who had been rounded up in November and December 1989 had been released. Many of them reported having been tortured during up to 15 days' incommunicado detention in police or military custody before their transfer to prison.

The lifting of emergency measures coincided with renewed talks between the government and the FMLN, this time under the auspices of the United Nations (UN) Secretary-General, to settle the armed conflict. Both parties signed an Agreement on Human Rights in July which committed them to take immediate steps to prevent killings, torture and "disappearances" and also provided for the establishment of a UN verification mission to monitor human rights once a cease-fire had been agreed. By the end of the year, peace talks had not been concluded and agreement was still pending, especially regarding army reforms and the punishment of those responsible for human rights violations. While the Agreement on Human Rights was regarded as a positive initiative, many of its provisions were already in force under existing legislation, which had been frequently violated in the past. The armed conflict intensified during the last two months of the year when the FMLN launched a series of attacks, the stated intention of which was to put pressure on the authorities to negotiate reforms.

The number of killings by "death squads" linked to the armed forces rose sharply between January and August, with a total of 51 cases reported – more than double the figure for the same period in 1989. Many of the bodies, often mutilated, were found dumped by the roadside: identity cards had been removed to prevent identification. Among the victims were cooperative members Angel Flores Aragón and Julia Ponce Flores, who were abducted in December 1989. A soldier told relatives that they had been handed over to the National Police but the police denied holding them. In mid-January their bodies were found by the side of a road.

In April Colonel Juan Manuel Zepeda, Vice-Minister for Defence, told Amnesty International delegates that he had detected a "typical" death squad unit, made up of three or four soldiers armed with handguns, but denied that such units operated under official orders.

Scores of unarmed civilians were killed by the military in circumstances suggesting extrajudicial executions. Many of these killings occurred in rural areas. Roberto Vásquez was shot dead on 20 April when soldiers raided the farming cooperative of which he was President. The government claimed he died in an armed confrontation but witnesses said there was no exchange of gunfire and alleged that he was killed deliberately.

Some detainees were apparently secretly executed after arrest by the military, among them 16-year-old José Acosta Castillo, whose body was found with bullet wounds on 5 May. He was not identified until 19 June when the body was exhumed at the request of *Tutela Legal*, the legal aid office of the Archdiocese of San Salvador. José Acosta had "disappeared" on 5 May after being taken into military custody with two members of his family who were later transferred to prison, accused of supporting the FMLN. Soldiers had reportedly said they were taking José Acosta to the mountains to indicate the location of FMLN camps.

Some reports were received of the execution of detainees by the FMLN. Most of the victims were alleged to be informers or to have other links with the military or security forces. Some of those killed were shot in front of witnesses. In October eight FMLN members were said to have taken a peasant and former soldier they had detained, Salvador Araña Martínez, to a farm and summoned those who lived there out of their homes. They reportedly made the detainee lie face down, accused him of killing a worker on another farm, and then shot him four times in the back. The army press agency known as COPREFA said he was tortured before he died but the autopsy report examined by *Tutela Legal* recorded only the four bullet wounds. A number of people were reportedly abducted by the FMLN and in some cases their bodies were subsequently found.

In December it was announced that the judge investigating the November 1989 killing of six Jesuit priests, their cook and her daughter had committed an army colonel and eight soldiers to trial for their role in ordering or carrying out the murders (see *Amnesty International Report 1990*). The colonel and seven of the soldiers had been arrested in January following investigations by the Special Investigative Unit and a specially appointed Commission of Honour. Military personnel repeatedly obstructed or delayed the proceedings by destroying evidence, giving false or contradictory testimony and failing to provide information or answer court summonses promptly. President Alfredo Cristiani, who had given public assurances on several occasions that the case would be clarified as soon as possible, publicly admitted for the first time in July that he had authorized a raid on the Central American University – where the killings occurred – two days before the murders. In October the United States (US) authorities presented the court with a statement, made 10 months earlier by a US colonel but retracted shortly afterwards, which suggested that high-ranking Salvadorian military officers knew of plans to kill the priests several days before the incident occurred. Chain of command responsibility for the killings had not been established by the end of the year.

The authorities failed to identify those responsible for most other apparent extrajudicial executions in 1990 and previous years. Those cases which were in the hands of investigative bodies, including the October 1989 bombing of the offices of the *Federación Nacional Sindical de Trabajadores* (FENASTRAS), National Trade Union Federation of Workers, in which 10 people died, made no significant progress. In May all but one of the 13 soldiers charged with killing 10 peasants in San Francisco in September 1988 were acquitted. The remaining defendant, an army major accused of ordering the massacre, was committed to trial but no trial date had been set by the end of the year (see *Amnesty International Report 1990*).

Irregularities in detention procedures, including illegal and often unacknowledged arrests, were repeatedly reported, even after new operational guidelines were issued to police and military units at the end of July. In August, an Office of Information on Detainees was opened within the judiciary to provide information about arrests. The security forces were required to present the office with a list of detainees every 24 hours. Initial reports suggested that they did not always do so, and that the office's information was often incomplete.

Military units, which frequently carried out arrests even when not empowered to do so, were not required to provide lists of those arrested.

Although the period of police-military custody was reduced from 15 days to 72 hours in March, the use of torture during incommunicado detention persisted, even after the inclusion of provisions banning such practices in the Agreement on Human Rights and the new directives on detention procedures. Beatings, sleep and food deprivation, suspension by the wrists, subjection to extreme hot or cold temperatures and near-suffocation in the *capucha*, a rubber hood sometimes filled with lime, were the most common methods of torture described. Torture was most likely to occur during the period before the arrest was acknowledged.

In September political prisoner Carlos López was removed from his prison cell in San Salvador in the middle of the night. He said that armed men, believed to be from the Treasury Police, forced him into a vehicle, in which he was repeatedly interrogated, beaten and threatened with death before being transferred to a prison in Gotera.

The same month 15-year-old Herson Rivera, detained by National Guard members, was reportedly kicked, punched, beaten and threatened with rape. Pressure was applied to his throat and a knife was placed at his neck to try to force him to confess to belonging to the FMLN.

At least two detainees reportedly died in custody as a result of torture. Julian Rosales López was arrested in February and taken to an unknown destination by soldiers of the Atlacatl Battalion. Several days later his family were informed that his body was in the National Police headquarters. An autopsy report showed severe injuries to his head and other parts of his body reportedly caused by torture. Mauricio Quinteros was abducted by armed men in plain clothes in San Salvador on 30 July. His family eventually located him in police custody but were not allowed to see him. On 10 August they were told that he had committed suicide by hanging. However, the autopsy carried out by the judicial authorities showed injuries which could not have resulted from hanging, and human rights workers concluded he had died under torture.

At the end of the year approximately 200 detainees accused of politically motivated offences remained in prison. Human rights lawyers alleged that many had been committed to pre-trial detention on the basis of confessions extracted under torture. Mauricio Gabriel Barrera Ardón alleged that when he was taken to court in May police officers threatened to kill him if he refused to ratify the statement they had drawn up on his behalf. When he tried to deny its contents before a court official, a policeman reportedly pulled his hair and discreetly hit him in the back. He alleged that while in police custody he had been beaten, denied food and sleep for five days, and had his head submerged several times in water.

Jorge Alberto Miranda Arévalo was acquitted in April of the 1987 murder of human rights worker Herbert Anaya Sanabria after the judge concluded that his confession had been extracted under duress (see *Amnesty International Reports 1988* to *1990*). However, he remained in prison pending an appeal by the prosecution and because he was facing other charges of "subversive association".

Among the "disappearance" cases reported to Amnesty International was that of Angel Sebastian Lico Matozo. He was reportedly abducted by uniformed soldiers of the *Destacamento Militar No. 7* (DM7), Military Detachment No. 7 in the town of Ahuachapán in March. DM7 officials denied he had been in detention, but a former detainee in the DM7 said he had heard Angel Lico being interrogated there. Amnesty International also received information about the "disappearance" of 17-year-old Erik Romero Canales following his arrest by First Brigade soldiers on 18 November 1989. His mother was allowed to take him food at the military checkpoint where he was held overnight. On the following day his mother saw him being taken away blindfold to an unknown destination. By the end of 1990 the case remained unclarified, in spite of eyewitness evidence of his arrest.

The authorities said they were investigating the "disappearance" of six members of the San Cayetano farming cooperative in Ahuachapán. All were abducted in December 1989 by individuals allegedly linked to the DM7 and at the end of 1990 their whereabouts remained unknown. The DM7 repeatedly denied allegations that they had been involved in the abductions. There was no progress in investigations into the "disappearances" of Sara Cristina Chan Chan Medina and Juan Francisco Massi Chávez, abducted in August 1989 (see *Amnesty International Report 1990*).

Throughout the year, Amnesty International called on the authorities to take steps to prevent arbitrary arrest, torture, "disappearances" and extrajudicial executions, to clarify the fate of the "disappeared", to investigate human rights violations and to bring those responsible to justice. An Amnesty International delegation visited El Salvador in April for talks with civilian and military officials, including from the DM4 and DM7, the Vice-Minister of Defence, and representatives of human rights and other non-governmental organizations. The delegation met victims of human rights violations or their relatives.

In October Amnesty International published a report, *El Salvador: Killings, Torture and "Disappearances"*, which was presented to the government. It detailed the organization's concerns, including the rise in the number of "death squad" killings, and contained 34 recommendations to the government for the protection of human rights. The organization called on the Salvadorian authorities to take effective measures to ensure that their stated commitments to human rights were fully implemented in practice. The Minister of Justice wrote to Amnesty International in November stating that he shared the organization's commitment to human rights. However, the letter did not address any of the issues or cases included in Amnesty International's report.

EQUATORIAL GUINEA

Seven people were reportedly arrested in December because of their political views or activities. Six prisoners of conscience continued to serve sentences imposed after an unfair trial in 1988: a seventh was released in February. Five political prisoners were released in August: they too had been sentenced after an unfair trial. There were new reports of torture of criminal suspects in both 1989 and 1990, and of at least 10 deaths as a result of torture. At least one death sentence was reported but was later said to have been commuted.

In late September the government of President Teodoro Obiang Nguema Mbasogo announced that a national human rights commission would be established. The announcement came one week after Amnesty International had published a report on torture of prisoners in Equatorial Guinea. The commission will reportedly be attached to the National Assembly. Its tasks are to include investigating reports of human rights violations and publicizing the government's actions in the field of human rights.

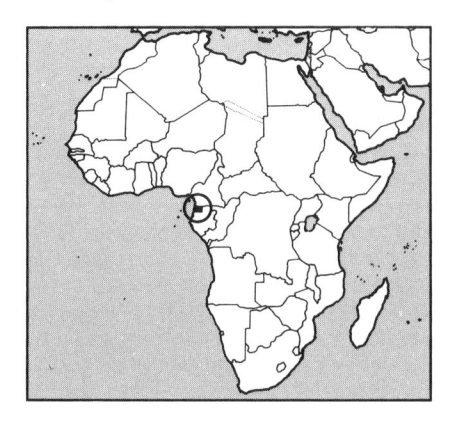

In late November the Vice-President of the Chamber of People's Representatives, Antonio Ebang Mbele, was reportedly placed under house arrest because of his support for political changes. A week earlier the Central Committee of the *Partido Democratico de Guinea Ecuatorial* (PDGE), Equatorial Guinea Democratic Party, the only party allowed by law, had said that the country "could adapt" to political pluralism. In early December there were reports that at least six people, including Marcelino Asumu Nsué, a former minister of agriculture, other civilians and soldiers, were arrested in Ebebiyin in the northeast of the mainland province of Rio Muni and later transferred to prisons in the capital, Malabo, or Bata in Rio Muni province. They were reportedly suspected of favouring political changes or of contacting government opponents in exile. Some of those detained were reportedly ill-treated.

At the beginning of the year seven prisoners of conscience were serving sentences imposed in September 1988. One of them, Primo José Esono Miká, was released in February at the President's orders. They had been convicted, on the basis of statements extracted under torture, of attempting to overthrow the government. However, the real reason for their imprisonment was their membership of, or suspected connection with an exile opposition party (see *Amnesty International Reports 1989* and *1990*).

Five political prisoners were released in August on the 11th anniversary of the government's accession to power. They had been convicted in 1986 of attempting to overthrow the government. One other, Sergeant Venancio Mikó, had his sentence reduced to just under nine years' imprisonment. He had been sentenced to death in 1983 for attempting to overthrow the government but the sentence was later commuted to 30 years' imprisonment (see *Amnesty International Reports 1984, 1987* and *1989*). All six had been tried unfairly by military courts. In September the government announced that it had released political detainees but did not provide further details.

New information became available during the year about the torture of criminal suspects in both 1989 and 1990. A total of 10 people reportedly died as a result.

At least 20 people from Ebebiyin were reported to have been tortured in early 1989, initially in Ebebiyin and again after they had been transferred to Bata. They were apparently suspected of using a form of sorcery, known locally as *kong*, to kill people and turn them into obedient spirits or "zombies". Nine of those held reportedly died as a result of torture: the others were acquitted of murder in mid-1989, although reports suggested that they may have been retried in May 1990 and sentenced to prison terms.

Two other criminal suspects were reportedly tortured in Bata in January 1990. José Eneme, Equatorial Guinea's consul in Douala in neighbouring Cameroon, and his friend Alberto Nsué were arrested in Equatorial Guinea and accused of using *kong* to cause the death of José Eneme's deputy, José Maseme, who had died in a road accident in Cameroon. Alberto Nsué was said to have died as a direct result of torture. José Eneme sustained injuries to his face, legs and feet. He was then apparently convicted of homicide in Ebebiyin in May and sentenced to death; the sentence was reportedly commuted to 30 years' imprisonment.

Juan Eyeme Nguema, a former director of the National Institute of Social Security, was also reported to have been tortured when he was detained from April until early June, apparently in connection with financial questions.

Amnesty International pressed for the release of the six prisoners of conscience still held at the end of 1990 after receiving information which confirmed that they and the three others sentenced with them had not used or advocated violence. In July it wrote to the government about the recent reports of torture and deaths in custody, and called for immediate action to prevent further abuses. Having received no response, Amnesty International publicized its concerns in September in a report, *Equatorial Guinea: Torture*. This described the use of torture to extract confessions and punish convicted prisoners. It also detailed the torture of dozens of political prisoners arrested in August 1988 and of criminal suspects in 1989 and 1990. Amnesty International urged the government to state publicly that torture would no longer be tolerated, to set up an independent and impartial inquiry into reports of torture, and to introduce effective safeguards against torture and ill-treatment of prisoners.

In October Amnesty International responded to a government invitation to visit Equatorial Guinea by confirming its wish to visit Equatorial Guinea and asking for previously requested information about its concerns to be made available in advance of any visit. It also asked the government to indicate the steps it would take to investigate and prevent torture.

ETHIOPIA

Hundreds of suspected government opponents continued to be detained, mostly without charge or trial, including some held since the late 1970s. They included prisoners of conscience. There were also new political arrests. In September some political prisoners in Eritrea were released. Twelve army generals arrested in 1989 for involvement in a coup attempt were executed and 23 army officers were sentenced to prison terms after trials which failed to satisfy international fair trial standards. Torture and ill-treatment

of political prisoners continued and there were new reports of extrajudicial executions by government troops. At least 60 people were under sentence of death at the end of 1990.

There was renewed fighting between government and opposition forces, particularly in Eritrea and central Ethiopia. Preliminary peace talks broke down in early 1990. In the north, the Eritrean People's Liberation Front (EPLF) captured the port of Massawa in February and controlled most of Eritrea, except for Asmara and the port of Assab. The Ethiopian People's Revolutionary Democratic Front (EPRDF), headed by the Tigray People's Liberation Front (TPLF), which had controlled Tigray since 1989, captured substantial territory in the central regions. The Oromo Liberation Front (OLF) was active in Asosa district in western Ethiopia. Unarmed civilians were killed in bombings by the Ethiopian air force and by soldiers in the areas of conflict.

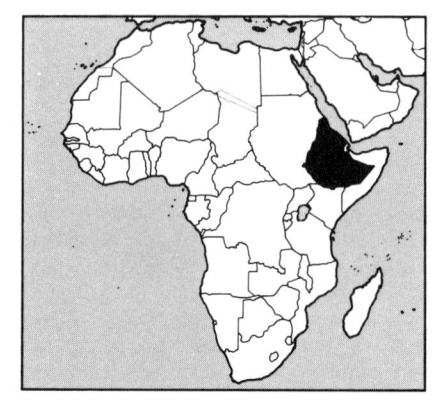

There were reports of human rights abuses by opposition groups. Opponents of the TPLF leadership were said to be still detained by the TPLF after several years and to be held in harsh conditions. There were reports of killings of government supporters by both the TPLF and the OLF – the latter denied killings reported in Asosa in February.

In March the central committee of the Workers' Party of Ethiopia (WPE), the only legal party, announced economic reforms. It also proposed to allow political opposition groups if they accepted the territorial unity of the country and the leadership of the WPE. However, no further announcement was made regarding the implementation of these proposals.

Details of political prisoners were, as in previous years, difficult to obtain. Hundreds of suspected political opponents, including prisoners of conscience, were held in secret and tortured by the security police. Most political prisoners were detained indefinitely without charge or trial, with no opportunity to challenge the legal basis or reasons for their detention, despite constitutional guarantees. Some allegedly "disappeared" after their arrest and may have been extrajudicially executed.

During 1990 there were reports of new political arrests, especially of people suspected of having links with opposition groups such as the EPLF, TPLF and OLF. People from Tigray region were particularly targeted for arrest in early 1990, in reprisal for the TPLF's advance south.

Three trade union leaders arrested in the capital, Addis Ababa, in January, apparently for political reasons, remained in detention without charge or trial at the end of the year. They included Alemayehu Tadesse of the official All-Ethiopia Trades Union. In May about 300 university students in Addis Ababa were arrested and held for a few days when they demonstrated against the execution of 12 army generals and called on the government to resign. Some demonstrators were wounded when security police fired on them but reports of killings were unconfirmed.

Two foreign journalists and two Ethiopians whom they had interviewed were arrested in May because the interview contained criticisms of the government. The two foreigners were expelled but the two Ethiopians were reportedly tortured and were detained until September, when they were released uncharged.

Reports continued to be received of people being forcibly conscripted into the armed forces, including boys as young as 12 years old. Some were punished with detention or beatings for attempting to evade or escape military service.

Over 100 known long-term political detainees arrested in previous years were still held at the end of 1990. Among them were prisoners of conscience such as Aregai Gebre-Igziabeher, a Tigrayan student held since 1978 for alleged links with the TPLF, and Mulugetta Mosissa, an Oromo civil servant detained since 1980 for alleged OLF links. Political prisoners still held included Tadelech Haile-Mikael, a journalist detained since 1979. Her husband, a leader of the opposition Ethiopian People's Revolutionary Party (EPRP), was killed in custody shortly after her arrest. Berhanu Mamo, mayor of Mekelle in Tigray region, also remained in detention. He was arrested in 1984 with numerous other Tigrayan officials, over 100 of whom were still held. They came under suspicion when detainees being tortured apparently claimed they were TPLF supporters. In addition, numerous Eritreans were in detention in Asmara and Addis Ababa on suspicion of involvement with the EPLF. Ajak Obuyi and 27 other farmers belonging to the Anuak ethnic group reportedly remained in detention in Metu prison in the southwest. Held since 1986, they were apparently suspected of belonging to an armed opposition group.

Some 130 military personnel arrested in connection with the coup attempt in May 1989 also remained in detention without charge. In addition, at least three civilians arrested after the coup attempt were still held without charge or trial. They included Genet Mebratu, a United Nations (UN) World Health Organization official and widow of one of the coup leaders, and Teferra Wonde, a former deputy prime minister. There was still no information about the "disappearance" in custody in June 1989 of Fanta Belay, a former minister of industry and air force commander.

Some 270 EPLF fighters captured in the late 1970s were still detained alongside political prisoners in Addis Ababa's Central Prison. In addition, 18 former members of a Somali armed opposition group opposed to the Somali government, the Democratic Front for the Salvation of Somalia (DFSS), remained in detention. They had been held in Ethiopia without charge or trial since 1985 and 1986.

Marking the 16th anniversary of the revolution which overthrew the previous government, the government announced the release in September of 620 Eritrean prisoners held in Asmara who were serving prison sentences of up to 20 years. They were said to include political prisoners, but no details were published.

A total of 47 military officers arrested after the coup attempt in May 1989 were tried during 1990. In May, 12 generals were sentenced to death by the military division of the Supreme Court and were immediately executed. Their trial on charges of treason and mutiny, which began in December 1989, was held mostly *in camera*, and the proceedings were kept secret. The presiding judge was reportedly removed shortly before the verdict was announced, allegedly because the government disagreed with his handling of the trial. The defendants had legal representation but were not allowed private access to their families and had no right of appeal. Some defendants reportedly told the court that they had been tortured. The death sentences and executions were announced together on 21 May but the executions probably took place at least two days earlier. Two other senior officers were sentenced to 10- and 15-year prison terms. A second secret trial of 21 middle-ranking officers began in January and ended in June. All were convicted and sentenced to between one and seven years' imprisonment. A third trial of higher-ranking officers started in January but appeared to have been adjourned indefinitely.

Torture of people arrested for political reasons continued to be reported. Those held by the security police were reportedly beaten on the soles of the feet, hung by the wrists or ankles, subjected to electric shocks, plunged into cold water or scalded with hot oil, or suffered injuries to their bones, hearing or eyesight from beatings.

Several long-term detainees were reportedly ill as a result of torture or denial of medical treatment. Among them were Abdulkadir Hassan Mohamed, known as "Isbarije", a 62-year-old former DFSS finance secretary who was suffering from pulmonary tuberculosis, and Nigist Ghiorghis, a woman arrested in 1978 as an alleged EPLF member, who had an untreated heart complaint.

Once again there were reports of extrajudicial executions by government soldiers, although confirmed details were difficult to obtain. A judge and seven other Tigrayans were reportedly extrajudicially executed in Arba Minch in southern Ethiopia in January, in reprisal for TPLF military successes in central Ethiopia. Thirty people were reported to have been rounded up in Asmara on 9 June, allegedly for breaking the curfew, and to have been extrajudicially executed.

At least 60 people were reported to be under sentence of death for criminal offences in Addis Ababa's Central Prison at the end of 1990. However, no details were available on court-imposed death sentences or executions during the year, apart from the executions of the 12 army generals in May.

Amnesty International continued to appeal to President Mengistu Haile-Mariam for the release of prisoners of conscience and for other political detainees to be brought to trial fairly and promptly, or released. The organization urged a full review of all cases of untried political detainees and appealed for those in poor health to be given proper medical treatment. The organization also sought information about the trials of those arrested after the May 1989 coup attempt, and asked to send an observer to assess the fairness of the trials, but no reply was received. Amnesty International also received no reply when it again urged the authorities to receive an Amnesty International delegation to discuss human rights in Ethiopia.

In an oral statement to the UN Sub-Commission on Prevention of Discrimination and Protection of Minorities in August, Amnesty International expressed concern about administrative detentions in Ethiopia.

FIJI

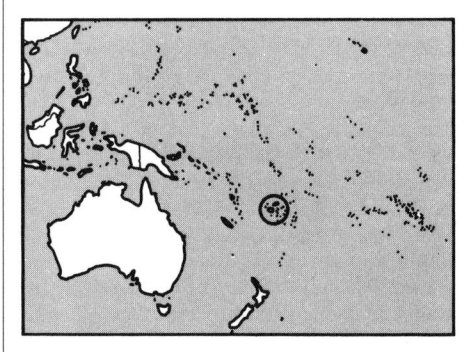

A leading critic of the government was abducted and tortured. After his release he and six others were charged with sedition and unlawful assembly. Three journalists also faced charges in connection with a newspaper report. All 10 were at liberty and had not been tried by the end of the year.

A new constitution was promulgated in July to replace the one suspended after the 1987 military coup. It guarantees power for indigenous Fijians, although they comprise just under half the population.

Dr Anirudh Singh, a lecturer at the University of the South Pacific (USP) and chairman of a local civil rights organization, the Group Against Racial Discrimination (GARD), was abducted by soldiers on 24 October, taken to woodland and tortured. He was held for 11 hours during which he was tied up, beaten severely and had his hair burned with cigarettes. He was apparently questioned about a peaceful protest on 18 October by around 200 ethnic Indians, during which a copy of Fiji's new constitution was burned. The government ordered an investigation into the protest, which it described as illegal, "despicable and treasonous".

Three journalists working for the *Daily Post* newspaper were arrested in October and charged under Section 15(a) of the 1976 Public Order Act. The arrests followed a report in the newspaper that a further protest was to take place at the university over the abduction and torture of Dr Singh, at which more copies of the Constitution would be burned. On the day that the report appeared, the government banned all meetings, processions and assemblies at the university campus in the interests of "public safety" and "public order". The GARD, however, reportedly denied that protests were planned.

Dr Singh and six others – four USP lecturers, a medical doctor and a former school teacher – were arrested and charged with sedition and unlawful assembly on 1 November. Their trial had not taken place by the end of 1990. If imprisoned, it appeared likely that they as well as the three journalists would be prisoners of conscience.

The trial of 21 people charged with arms-smuggling in 1988 (see *Amnesty International Reports 1989* and *1990*), resulted in 19 being conditionally discharged and one being acquitted. One of the accused had left the country before charges were brought.

Amnesty International expressed concern about the abduction and torture of Dr Singh to Prime Minister Ratu Sir Kamisese Mara and called for an urgent and impartial inquiry. The government replied that a police investigation had been initiated. It also said that there was no indication that the military or police had been involved in the incident. However, following the investigation five soldiers were charged with the abduction of Dr Singh with intent to cause grievous bodily harm. They pleaded guilty and on 21 November received suspended prison sentences.

FINLAND

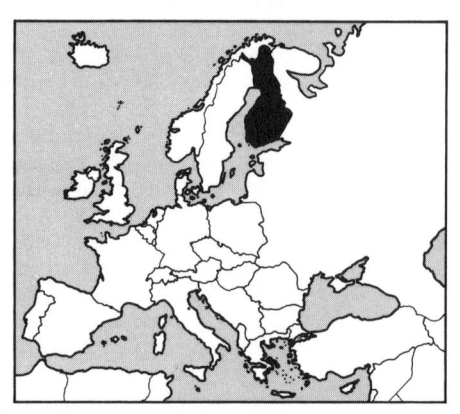

Three conscientious objectors to military service began serving prison sentences; two of them completed their sentences and were released. Four conscientious objectors imprisoned in 1989 were also released after completion of their sentences. All seven were considered prisoners of conscience.

In February Finland signed the United Nations Second Optional Protocol to the International Covenant on Civil and Political Rights Aiming at the Abolition of the Death Penalty. It had not yet ratified this instrument by the end of the year. In May Finland ratified both the European Convention on Human Rights and its Protocol No. 6 concerning the abolition of the death penalty.

Finnish law on unarmed and civilian service was last amended in 1987, increasing the length of alternative service from 12 to 16 months: twice as long as military service.

Three conscientious objectors began serving their sentences. Mauri Robert Ryömä, a hospital assistant, began serving a 12-month sentence in January. Timo Kinnunen, a student, began serving a seven-month sentence in March. Hannu Puttonen, an editor, began serving a 12-month sentence in October.

Three conscientious objectors were released in June after serving their sentences: Karri Dyrendahl-Nyblin, Tomi Saarinen and Juha Kanerva (see *Amnesty International Report 1990*). Veijo Heikkilä, another conscientious objector adopted as a prisoner of conscience, was released in August. Timo Kinnunen was released after completing his sentence in October.

Mauri Robert Ryömä and Timo Kinnunen, along with two other imprisoned conscientious objectors who were not considered prisoners of conscience, began a hunger-strike on 23 April. The action was aimed in part at drawing attention to the punitive length of alternative service. Timo Kinnunen ended his hunger-strike on 18 May as a result of his deteriorating health; the others continued. On 31 May President Mauno Koivisto reduced Mauri Robert Ryömä's sentence and he was released shortly afterwards. The two remaining hunger-strikers were granted a presidential pardon. Earlier in May Amnesty International had called on the government to release the two prisoners of conscience immediately and to guarantee them adequate medical care.

In a letter of 14 August to the Finnish President, Amnesty International expressed its concern that Timo Kinnunen had not received a pardon or reduction of sentence as had Mauri Robert Ryömä and the other two hunger-strikers.

Amnesty International considered that because of its punitive length, civilian service did not provide an acceptable alternative to military service and sought the release of conscientious objectors whom it considered prisoners of conscience.

FRANCE

Hundreds of conscientious objectors to the national service laws, the vast majority of them Jehovah's Witnesses, were considered prisoners of conscience. There were reports of ill-treatment in police custody.

Conscientious objectors who refused to conform to the national service laws continued to receive sentences of up to 15 months' imprisonment. The alternative civilian service available to recognized conscientious objectors remained twice the length of ordinary military service.

Thierry Daligault refused to perform military service because of his Christian and pacifist beliefs. He did not apply for civilian service because, among other objections, he considered its length to be punitive. He was arrested on 19 July and following a trial on 27 November was sentenced to 12 months' imprisonment for failing to obey call-up orders and refusing to put on military uniform.

At least three imprisoned conscientious objectors had been refused conscientious objector status because their applications had been made after their call-up orders were issued.

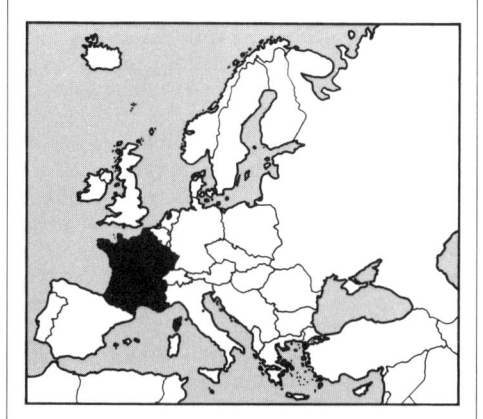

Ludovic Bouteraon stated that when he registered for national service in early 1990, he informed the authorities of his wish to perform an alternative civilian service compatible with his pacifist beliefs. He claimed that he received no indication that there were further procedures to be followed to obtain conscientious objector status. He therefore reported to an air force base on 1 August, as ordered, declared his conscientious objection and refused to perform military service. He was held under arrest at the base until 17 August, when he was tried under a summary procedure by a Strasbourg court. He was sentenced to 15 months' imprisonment and transferred to a civilian prison. On 8 September he submitted a formal application for conscientious objector status to the Ministry of Defence. This was rejected in October, on the grounds that it had been made outside the stipulated time limit. In November an appeal court reduced his sentence to 12 months' imprisonment, eight of which were suspended. He was released on conditional liberty in December and exempted from further military obligation.

Several judicial inquiries were under way into allegations of ill-treatment in police custody. These often concerned immigrants and French citizens of North African origin.

Abdelaziz Gabsi and Kamel Djellal alleged that they were ill-treated on the night of 11 December 1989 in Echirolles, near Grenoble, after a police officer asked to see Abdelaziz Gabsi's identity papers. They claimed that when Abdelaziz Gabsi offered a jacket containing the papers the police officer insulted him, struck him across the face with the butt of his shotgun and then hit him several more times on the head. The police officer then allegedly struck Kamel Djellal several times, handcuffed him and beat him to the ground. He was also bitten by a police dog in the charge of a second officer. Following the incidents Abdelaziz Gabsi's face was reportedly badly bruised and swollen, and Kamel Djellal required 20 stitches to wounds on his head and face.

The police stated that the accused officer had been attacked by Abdelaziz Gabsi and had acted only in self-defence. The Public Prosecutor's office in Grenoble opened a judicial inquiry into the allegations and ordered the General Inspectorate of the National Police to carry out an investigation. The inquiry was apparently continuing at the end of the year.

A judicial inquiry opened in September 1989, following Lucien Djossouvi's allegations of ill-treatment by the police in Paris (see *Amnesty International Report 1990*), had not concluded.

Amnesty International considered that because of its punitive length civilian service did not provide an acceptable alternative to military service. It also considered that individuals should be able to seek conscientious objector status at any time. It appealed throughout the year for the release of conscientious objectors whom it considered to be prisoners of conscience, including Thierry Daligault and Ludovic Bouteraon. The organization expressed concern to the authorities about allegations of ill-treatment in police custody and asked to be informed about the progress and outcome of inquiries opened into such allegations.

GABON

Seven prisoners of conscience were released. Eighteen people arrested in 1989 in connection with two alleged plots to overthrow the government were tried by

the State Security Court: they had only a limited right of appeal. Two detainees were reportedly ill-treated.

In May a new constitution was introduced to end the one-party state and allow political parties other than the ruling *Parti démocratique gabonais* (PDG), Gabonese Democratic Party, headed by President Omar Bongo. This followed a series of strikes, demonstrations and riots by students, workers and others calling for social and political reform and for the convening of a national conference to discuss the need for constitutional change. The conference, which was convened in March by the government and attended by about 170 political and other groups, came out in favour of a multi-party political system. It also adopted a Charter of Liberties reaffirming the rights guaranteed by the Universal Declaration of Human Rights and the African Charter on Human and Peoples' Rights.

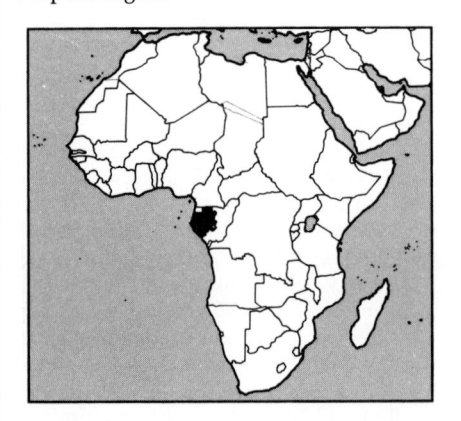

Further riots broke out in Libreville and Port-Gentil shortly after the introduction of the new constitution when the leader of a newly formed political party, the *Parti gabonais du progrès* (PGP), Gabonese Progress Party, died in suspicious circumstances. PGP supporters alleged that Joseph Rendjambe had been killed by government agents but the authorities denied the allegation. The government then declared a state of siege, which remained in force until August, and the army was called in to quell the disturbances.

National Assembly elections took place in September and October. The PDG won a majority of seats amid opposition allegations of ballot rigging.

Seven prisoners of conscience were released in January. They had been detained without charge or trial since December 1989 for allegedly distributing leaflets on behalf of an opposition party, the *Mouvement de redressement national* (MORENA), Movement for National Recovery (see *Amnesty International Report 1990*).

Five other prisoners who were among over 20 people arrested in late 1989 in connection with two separate alleged plots to kill President Bongo and overthrow the government (see *Amnesty International Report 1990*) were released in January. A pre-trial judicial inquiry concluded that they had no case to answer. Eighteen others, however, were brought to trial before the State Security Court for their alleged involvement in the two coup plots. Eight of them, including Lieutenant Colonel Georges Moubandjo, were sentenced in November to between five and eight years' imprisonment with hard labour. Six of the seven accused who faced charges at a second trial in December were present in court; Pierre Mamboundou, a leading government opponent recently expelled from France to Senegal, was tried *in absentia*. Four of the seven, including Pierre Mamboundou and Mathias Boussougou-Mapangou, a former commander of the presidential guard, were sentenced to between one and 10 years' imprisonment. Daniel Cohen, a French national, was given a six-year suspended sentence, and two, including Valentin Mihindou Mi Minzamba, a former minister and presidential adviser, were acquitted. All those sentenced were convicted of conspiring to overthrow the government. Defendants sentenced by the State Security Court are restricted on appeal to raising points of law. All those sentenced in November and December appealed for presidential clemency but this had not been granted by the end of 1990.

The government did not disclose the results of autopsies on two other prisoners arrested in connection with the alleged conspiracies to overthrow the government, who had died in detention in 1989 (see *Amnesty International Report 1990*). The authorities had told Amnesty International that the autopsy findings in both cases would be disclosed after the trials of the alleged coup plotters had been concluded.

Two PGP supporters arrested at the time of the May riots were reportedly ill-treated while detained incommunicado by the *Service de contre-ingérence*, Counter-intelligence Service. They were subsequently brought to trial in October with other PGP supporters but released.

Two people convicted in 1989 *in absentia* of attempted murder and one person convicted in 1989 of ritual murder remained under sentence of death. No new death sentences or executions were reported.

Amnesty International welcomed the release of prisoners of conscience, and called for the fair trial or release of other political detainees and the commutation of death sentences. It also urged the government to clarify the circumstances in which two political detainees had died in detention in 1989.

GAMBIA

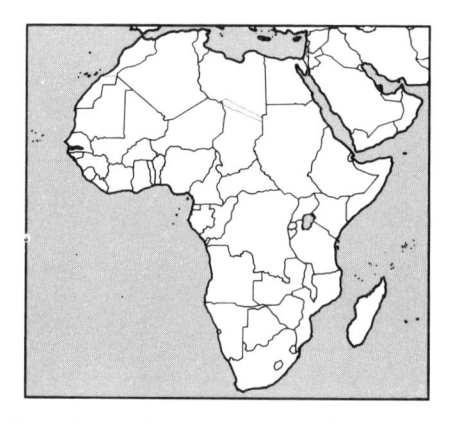

Ten Senegalese nationals who sought asylum in the Gambia were forcibly repatriated: one was subsequently reported to have died as a result of torture in police custody in Senegal. The 10 Senegalese, including Ibou Camara, a former political prisoner, fled to Gambia in June and July from Senegal's Casamance region following clashes there between Senegalese security forces and armed insurgents (see Senegal). Casamance villagers suspected of supporting the insurgents were reportedly tortured and extrajudicially executed by Senegalese soldiers. Many villagers fled to neighbouring Gambia to seek asylum.

The 10 men were arrested on 26 September in several villages by the Gambian security forces. They appeared in court in Kanifing on 8 October charged with entering the country without a residence permit and were remanded in Banjul's Mile 2 prison to face trial. On 12 October, before being brought to trial, they were handed over to immigration officers at Jiboro village by Gambian gendarmes. They were then taken to the border and forcibly returned to Senegal. At least one of them, Sékou Mary, known as Agnocoune, avoided arrest and returned to the Gambia where he was arrested on 23 October by police officers at Brikama. He was handed over directly to the Senegalese security forces without any court proceedings. He died in Diouloulou police station soon after, apparently as a result of beatings.

Amnesty International appealed to the Gambian Government to respect its international obligations by ensuring that asylum-seekers were not involuntarily returned to countries where they would be at risk of torture, imprisonment as prisoners of conscience, or execution. It also urged the authorities not to imprison asylum-seekers or refugees from Casamance for entering the country "illegally" or for having no residence rights in the Gambia. The government acknowleged that nine Senegalese had been forcibly returned to Senegal, saying that there was no reason to believe that any harm would come to them. It did not comment on the death in police custody of Sékou Mary.

GERMANY

On 3 October the German Democratic Republic (GDR) acceded to the Federal Republic of Germany (FRG). Most federal law came into force throughout the unified country. Before unification, laws which had been used in the GDR to imprison prisoners of conscience were reformed or repealed. In the FRG a defendant accused of defaming the state by publishing leaflets was acquitted. Political prisoners who may not have received a fair trial in the GDR continued to be detained. Prisoners detained under anti-terrorist legislation in the FRG continued to be held in virtual isolation.

In July a law revising the GDR Penal Code came into force which reformed or abolished provisions that had been used to detain people for exercising their rights to freedom of expression, association, assembly and movement.

Following the accession of the GDR

under Article 23 of the FRG Constitution, the unified country was named the Federal Republic of Germany. The Unification Treaty between the GDR and the FRG, signed in August, contained *inter alia* provisions on constitutional and legal reform. On 3 October the FRG Constitution and most federal law came into force in the five re-established *Länder* (states) – Brandenburg, Mecklenburg-Vorpommern, Sachsen, Sachsen-Anhalt and Thüringen – and international treaties and obligations undertaken by the FRG before unification became applicable. International treaty obligations of the GDR were to be reviewed as to their continued application, adjustment or expiry. Former GDR law remained valid as far as it was compatible with the Constitution. The Treaty provided that victims of politically motivated prosecutions and convictions of the "SED [the former ruling party] regime of injustice" would be rehabilitated, and would receive compensation. Judicial decisions by the former GDR courts remained in force, but those convicted by the criminal courts would be given the right to have their convictions and sentences reviewed.

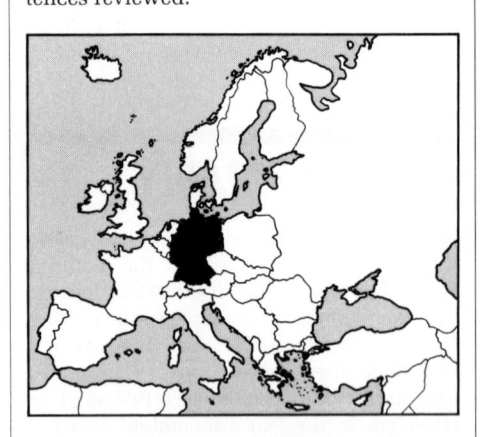

In February the FRG ratified the European Convention for the Prevention of Torture and Inhuman or Degrading Treatment or Punishment and in October ratified the United Nations (UN) Convention against Torture and Other Cruel, Inhuman or Degrading Treatment or Punishment. The FRG also signed in February the Second Optional Protocol to the International Covenant on Civil and Political Rights Aiming at the Abolition of the Death Penalty, which it had not ratified by the end of the year. The GDR ratified the Second Optional Protocol in August.

All-German elections took place on 2 December, in which the centre-right coalition led by Helmut Kohl won a decisive victory. Richard von Weizsäcker remained Head of State.

In April Christiane Schneider, who had been accused of maliciously defaming the state through the dissemination of written materials, was acquitted by the Cologne District Court. She had admitted publishing leaflets which included a declaration by a prisoner describing the government policy towards Red Army Faction prisoners as an "extermination program" and the isolation of prisoners as "isolation torture". An Amnesty International delegate attended the trial in order to assess whether, if imprisoned, Christiane Schneider would be a prisoner of conscience.

In September prisoners in 38 prisons in the GDR participated in rooftop occupations and hunger-strikes demanding, among other things, a review of their sentences. Later that month a law on remission of sentences came into force in the GDR reducing by one-third most prison sentences passed before July by GDR courts. In addition the law gave every prisoner sentenced before July the right to apply to have his or her sentence reviewed by an independent committee.

Prisoners detained under anti-terrorist legislation in the FRG continued to be held in virtual isolation. Prolonged isolation may have serious effects on the physical and mental health of prisoners and may constitute cruel, inhuman or degrading treatment (see *Amnesty International Report 1990*).

One woman was held in virtual isolation in Stuttgart (sometimes known as Stammheim) prison. Previously, the Baden-Württemberg Ministry of Justice had said that Stuttgart prison was not suitable for the long-term detention of women prisoners. Brigitte Mohnhaupt, imprisoned since 1982 under anti-terrorist legislation, was moved to Stuttgart prison in June. Reportedly, she spent 23 hours in isolation in her cell and had one hour's exercise a day, which she took alone every other day and on alternate days with three other women prisoners who were foreign. Communication with the three women was difficult, as reportedly only one of them spoke a little German. According to her lawyer, Brigitte Mohnhaupt's concentration had deteriorated owing to years of isolation. In November she was moved to Aichach prison in Bavaria, where she reportedly continued to be kept in virtual isolation.

The authorities said in August that Andrea Sievering (see *Amnesty International Report 1990*) was still held in Stuttgart prison as she was a witness in a trial taking place in Stuttgart.

The government informed Amnesty International in December that it had repeatedly looked into allegations that prisoners detained under anti-terrorist legislation were subjected to "inhuman isolation" by the authorities. The government said it did not believe that isolation occurred when there was regular contact with other people and the outside world through radio, television and correspondence. In its reply, Amnesty International expressed concern that the degree of social isolation in which prisoners detained under anti-terrorist legislation were held may have been harmful and therefore may have amounted to cruel, inhuman or degrading treatment. The organization referred to past examples, including the case of Brigitte Mohnhaupt, which indicated that in several cases the health of these prisoners had been impaired as a consequence of their prison conditions. It called on the government to consider increasing social contact for these prisoners and asked what steps it had taken to this effect. Amnesty International also asked to be informed in detail about the reviews carried out by the government of allegations that the prisoners were held in inhuman isolation.

During the year Amnesty International wrote to the GDR Procurator General and five regional public procurators requesting copies of court documents relating to the trials of 11 prisoners who had been convicted in the GDR. The organization expressed concern that they might not have been given a fair trial because trials in the GDR had in the past regularly been held *in camera* and court documents had often not been available. The public procurators replied that two prisoners had been released, and that some of the cases would be investigated to establish whether the sentences should be quashed. By the end of the year Amnesty International had not received the requested court documents.

In June Amnesty International wrote to the Chancellor of the FRG and to the Prime Minister of the GDR submitting a number of papers describing its concerns in both countries. The organization asked for the papers to be brought to the attention of the FRG and GDR representatives of joint commissions which had been set up to examine ways in which the social, economic and political systems of the two countries could be brought into harmony to facilitate unification. In July the FRG Federal Ministry of Justice replied that it had brought the information submitted by Amnesty International to the attention of the relevant representatives.

GHANA

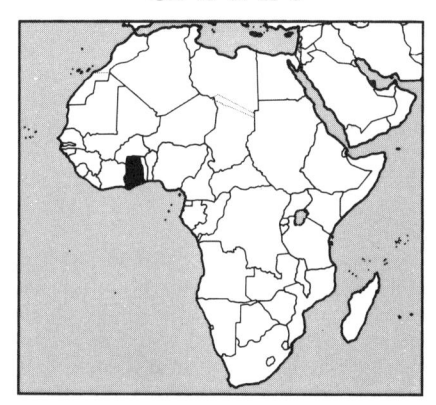

At least 11 prisoners of conscience were held in detention without trial. About 40 soldiers and civilians suspected of plotting against the government remained in detention without charge or trial at the end of 1990, including some who had spent more than five years in custody. Ten other detainees were released in June. Twenty people were sentenced to death and nine executed.

Under pressure to allow debate on whether political parties should be legalized, the government organized seminars about democracy but harassed critics calling for a return to constitutional rule. Members of the new Movement for Freedom and Justice were briefly arrested and charged with spreading false information (the charges were later withdrawn), and were refused permission to hold public meetings.

Major Courage E.K. Quarshigah, whom the authorities accused of plotting to overthrow the government, remained in detention without charge or trial together with four other members of the security forces arrested in September 1989. Five other military and security police officers were arrested in January in connection with the same case. One was subsequently released without charge and two were said to have escaped, but the two others remained in detention without charge or trial at the end of 1990. All the detainees were prisoners of conscience.

A board of inquiry set up to investigate the alleged conspiracy apparently found insufficient evidence to justify any prosecutions. A summary of its findings, published by the government, contained factual errors about certain detainees, apparently to attribute motives to them for joining a conspiracy. According to the summary, only two witnesses admitted to any conspiracy — Flight-Lieutenant William Kofi Domie, who died in security police custody in September 1989, and a soldier who was subsequently kept in incommunicado detention. No inquest was held into the circumstances of Flight-Lieutenant Domie's death (see *Amnesty International Report 1990*).

Kweku Baah, a lawyer and former government minister, was arrested in June and detained for five weeks before being released without charge. No reason was given for his detention but it seemed to be in connection with plans to commemorate the murder in June 1982 of three judges and a retired army officer. Members of the military government were allegedly involved in the murder and leading members of the Ghana Bar Association were detained in June 1989 when they planned commemorative lectures (see *Amnesty International Report 1990*).

Two possible prisoners of conscience continued to serve prison sentences after unfair trials in 1983 in which they were convicted of involvement in a coup attempt in November 1982. Andrews Kwame Asare Pianim, an economist and former chief executive of the Cocoa Marketing Board, was serving an 18-year prison sentence, and Jacob Jabuni Yidana, a former senior police officer, an eight-year sentence (see *Amnesty International Reports 1984 to 1987*).

At least 40 political detainees — possibly more — were still held in administrative detention at the end of 1990. The majority of the detainees had been held since the first half of the 1980s on suspicion of involvement in conspiracies against the government. Most were detained under the Preventive Custody Law, PNDC Law 4 of 1982, which allows the indefinite detention without charge or trial of anyone suspected of threatening the security of the state. Among them was Bombardier Mustapha Mohamed, a prosecution witness at the trial of those allegedly involved in the November 1982 coup attempt, who was not released after giving evidence. They included Corporal Daniel Dzane and Sergeant Nicholas Osei, held in connection with alleged coup attempts in 1983. Also held were at least 14 soldiers arrested in 1985, including Lance-Corporal Osho Kojo Ampah, some of whom were apparently suspected of planning to assassinate the head of state, Flight-Lieutenant J.J. Rawlings, in February 1985.

In June the release was announced of 10 political detainees who had been held for years without charge or trial. They included Kojo Adjei Brempong, detained since 1986, whose release was previously announced in an amnesty in February 1987. The others released were all believed to be former members of the security forces; five had been held since 1983 or 1984, the other four since 1985, 1986 and 1988.

Public Tribunals sentenced 20 prisoners to death for murder and armed robbery. Nine prisoners convicted of armed robbery in 1989 were executed in February, the first known executions since 1988.

Amnesty International appealed for the release of Major Quarshigah and those detained with him, and urged a review of the detention or convictions of prisoners held for alleged involvement in coup attempts or conspiracies against the government. Amnesty International continued to call for an end to the use of the death penalty and appealed for the commutation of death sentences. In July Amnesty International published a report, *Ghana: Detention without Trial — the Quarshigah "Conspiracy"*, in which it detailed its concerns about the cases of Major Quarshigah and his co-detainees. In response, the government invited Amnesty International to visit Ghana to discuss its concerns: such a visit was expected to take place in early 1991.

GREECE

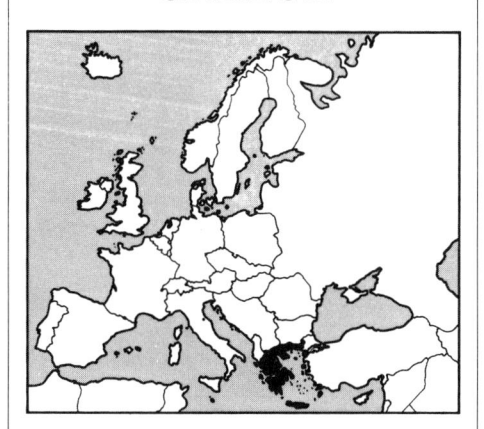

Some 400 conscientious objectors to military service, all of them Jehovah's Witnesses, were in prison: all were prisoners of conscience. Two ethnic Turks were also considered to be prisoners of conscience. There were allegations of torture and ill-treatment in police custody.

Draft legislation first announced in 1988 (see *Amnesty International Reports 1989* and *1990*), proposing alternative civilian service double the length of military service, had still not been debated in parliament by the end of 1990.

Most of the imprisoned conscientious objectors were serving four-year sentences, which could be reduced to about three years by working for part of the sentence.

Jehovah's Witness minister Daniel Kokkalis continued to be held in prison (see *Amnesty International Report 1990*). In March a further two ministers, Dimitris Tsirlis and Timothy Kouloubas, were detained. They were sentenced in April and May respectively to four years in prison. Their appeal hearings were postponed twice and had not been held by the end of the year. The imprisonment of Jehovah's Witness ministers was in direct contravention of Law 1763/1988 which exempts, among others, religious ministers of a "recognized religion" from their military obligations. The Jehovah's Witness faith has been legally "recognized" in Greece for many years.

In October the Council of State ruled that Daniel Kokkalis should have been discharged from military service as a minister of a recognized religion. However, he was still in prison at the end of the year.

Between 30 and 40 men, who were not Jehovah's Witnesses, had not been charged or imprisoned by the end of 1990 after publicly declaring their conscientious objection to military service on a variety of grounds.

In January two ethnic Turks, Sadik Ahmet and Ibrahim Serif, were sentenced to 18 months' imprisonment and three years' deprivation of civil rights under Article 192 of the Penal Code, which proscribes incitement to violence or mutual discord. The basis of the charge was their use of the word "Turk" to describe the ethnic Turkish minority in Western Thrace in a 1989 election manifesto. There was no indication that they had advocated violence. Ethnic Turks in Greece are officially considered to be Greek Muslims and are forbidden to organize associations whose names include the word "Turkish". In March Sadik Ahmet and Ibrahim Serif were released following appeal: the appeal court reduced their prison sentences to 15 months and 10 months respectively and allowed them to pay a fine instead of serving the rest of their sentences. In April Sadik Ahmet was elected as an independent deputy to the Greek Parliament.

A number of people alleged that they had been tortured and ill-treated by the police. Kostas Andreadis, taken into police custody in March, stated that he had been forced to confess to crimes after being tortured by *falanga* (beating on the soles of the feet), electric shocks and threats that he would be thrown out of a window at the Thessaloniki Police Headquarters. An official medical report certified injuries to both feet.

In September Emmanuel Kasapakis lodged a complaint against the police for beating him at his home in Athens after they had called in connection with loud music at a party there. An official medical report certified injuries to the head which had needed stitches and had caused concussion and amnesia, and injuries to the left hand.

An inquiry into Dimitris Voglis' complaint about police torture was not concluded (see *Amnesty International Report 1990*).

Amnesty International appealed repeatedly for the release of all imprisoned conscientious objectors and urged the government to introduce alternative civilian service of non-punitive length. The organization also raised a number of cases of alleged torture and ill-treatment with the authorities. The government responded in four cases, including that of Kostas Andreadis, stating that the allegations were unfounded. No response was received concerning other cases.

An Amnesty International delegate attended the appeal hearing of Sadik Ahmet and Ibrahim Serif in March.

GRENADA

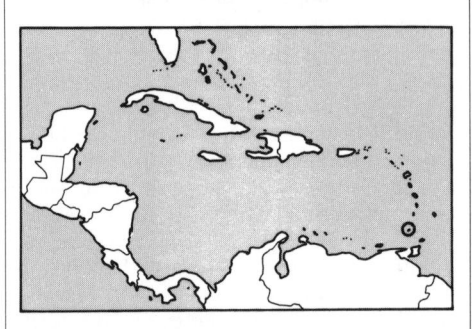

The appeal hearings ended in the cases of 14 former members of the People's Revolutionary Government (PRG) sentenced to death for murder and of three others convicted of manslaughter for the 1983 killings of Prime Minister Maurice Bishop and others. The appeal court's decision was pending at the end of the year. No executions had been carried out since 1978, although 21 prisoners were under sentence of death for murder. There were complaints about the prison conditions of one of the PRG prisoners sentenced to death.

The hearings before the Grenada Court of Appeal in the Maurice Bishop murder case concluded in September. They had started in May 1988. The 17 appellants had been convicted in December 1986 of the killings of PRG Prime Minister Maurice Bishop and 10 other people at the People's Revolutionary Army (PRA) headquarters at Fort Rupert on 19 October 1983. Fourteen of the defendants were sentenced to death for murder and three were convicted of manslaughter and sentenced to long prison terms.

The killings at Fort Rupert had taken place following a power-sharing dispute within the Central Committee of the PRG, during which Maurice Bishop was placed under house arrest. On 19 October he was freed from house arrest by several thousand supporters and taken to Fort Rupert. He and others were reportedly shot by a firing squad after the PRA regained control of Fort Rupert.

These events were followed by the invasion of Grenada by the United States of America and troops from six Caribbean states on 25 October 1983. Most of the defendants in the case had initially been detained by the occupying forces in late October or early November 1983 and were later transferred into Grenadian custody before being charged.

Ten of the 14 people sentenced to death were members of the PRG Central Committee who had not been present when the killings took place but were found guilty of ordering or instigating them. They included the deputy leader of the PRG, Bernard Coard; his wife, Phyllis Coard; and the Commander-in-Chief of the PRA, General Hudson Austin. The three defendants convicted of manslaughter were PRA soldiers found guilty of having carried out the killings under orders.

More than 30 grounds of appeal were presented. These challenged, among other things, the selection and impartiality of the trial jury; the admissibility of statements made by several of the accused, who alleged that they had been extracted as a result of ill-treatment; and the trial judge's directions on the reliability of witness testimony. A key prosecution witness was Fabian Gabriel, who had originally been charged with murder but was granted a conditional pardon in return for testifying for the state.

Constitutional motions raised in earlier proceedings also formed part of the appeal. These included a motion that unfavourable pre-trial publicity had deprived the defendants of a fair trial. Another motion challenged the legitimacy of the Grenada Supreme Court: on this basis the defendants had refused to recognize the jurisdiction of the trial court and had dismissed their defence counsel when the trial began in April 1986. They had also refused to participate in the trial proceedings except to make unsworn statements to the court (see *Amnesty International Report 1987*). The appeal court had not yet ruled on the case by the end of the year.

In July Phyllis Coard reportedly started a hunger-strike in protest against her conditions of confinement at Richmond Hill Prison. Unlike other prisoners condemned to death, Phyllis Coard had been held mainly in solitary confinement since 1983 and had been periodically denied visits from relatives. She was also reportedly denied occupational facilities available to other women inmates. Phyllis Coard also complained that in 1990 the Prison Commissioner had frequently entered her cell area unaccompanied by women staff, which was contrary to prison regulations, and had looked into her cell even when advised that she was using her slop pail.

An Amnesty International observer attended the final summations in the Maurice Bishop murder appeal in September. Amnesty International had previously raised concerns about aspects of the proceedings, including questions about the impartiality of the jury and allegations that some of the accused had been ill-treated during police interrogation. Amnesty International continued to assess the proceedings.

In September Amnesty International wrote to the recently appointed official Prison Visiting Committee about the prison conditions of Phyllis Coard. The organization said it was concerned that her long-term solitary confinement could damage her physical and mental health and that her conditions of detention had apparently remained unchanged, or had worsened, despite reports about her deteriorating health. Amnesty International asked the Committee to investigate the allegations about the unaccompanied visits of the commissioner to Phyllis Coard's cell area, stating that this appeared to be contrary to the United Nations Standards Minimum Rules for the Treatment of Prisoners. The organization also expressed concern about reports that Phyllis Coard had been placed on seven-day restricted diets (usually bread and water) five times in a four-month period for protesting about her treatment. Amnesty International said it was disturbed by the reasons for this punishment and by the frequency with which it had been imposed. The organization asked the Committee to review this practice.

The Committee replied in October, stating that it had visited the prison to ensure there was no breach of regulations. The Committee's letter made no reference to the specific concerns raised by Amnesty International.

GUATEMALA

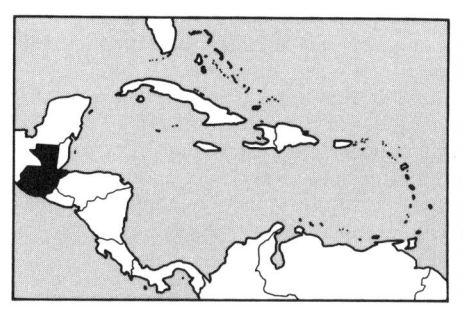

Reports were received of hundreds of "disappearances" and extrajudicial executions, continuing the pattern of gross abuses reported over more than two decades. Many victims appeared to have been tortured before being murdered. As in previous years, there was a pattern of harassment and assaults directed at suspected government opponents by the security forces acting both in uniform and in plain clothes.

Human rights workers and others who pressed for inquiries into past violations were particularly vulnerable to attack by military personnel and their civilian agents, who repeatedly characterized them as guerrilla supporters. Other victims included villagers who refused to serve in the ostensibly voluntary civil patrols, people in areas believed to be sympathetic to or controlled by the armed opposition, representatives to the National Dialogue consultative process set up under the 1987 Central American Peace Agreement, academics and students, trade unionists, street children, journalists and politicians.

Some victims were shot outright by security force personnel, acting either in uniform or in plain clothes in the guise of "death squads". Other victims were forcibly seized; their bodies were found later, sometimes far from the original place of abduction, often badly tortured or mutilated to obscure identification. Others remained "disappeared". Civil patrols, formed at the behest of the military and operating under military control, were also blamed for human rights violations.

Abuses intensified as November elections approached to replace the government of President Vinicio Cerezo Arévalo, which took office in 1986 and was Guatemala's first elected civilian government in almost 20 years. President Cerezo's election had brought new hope for an end to the long-term pattern of human rights violations in Guatemala and for a public accounting for crimes committed by the security forces. However, his administration did little to investigate abuses committed under military governments or to bring those responsible to justice. After a brief initial decrease, reports of abductions, torture, "disappearances", and political killings escalated throughout his term of office.

The perpetrators of human rights violations appeared to operate with impunity. Very few instances were known of official personnel being charged with abuses even when specific evidence, including eye-witness testimony, pointed to their guilt. In the one known case in recent years where official agents were found guilty on such a charge, the six police officers involved were released in July 1990 after an appeal court overturned their conviction for the 1987 abduction and murder of two agronomy students, despite strong forensic and other evidence linking them to the crime.

The abuses were reported in the context of a continuing insurgency, and the government and military periodically charged that the armed opposition had carried out torture and murder, although details of individual cases were rarely conclusive. In the highly publicized killing of some 23 peasants in El Aguacate, Chimaltenango, in 1988, evidence presented by the authorities to support such allegations remained controversial and contrasted with findings of local and international human rights groups which alleged military responsibility (see *Amnesty International Report 1990*).

In January Guatemala acceded to the United Nations (UN) Convention against Torture and Other Cruel, Inhuman or Degrading Treatment or Punishment.

Human rights activists were among those targeted for abuse. At least two members of an organization known as the CERJ, which protects the human rights of Guatemala's indigenous peoples, "disappeared", and some six others were apparent victims of extrajudicial executions. Several CERJ members were reportedly victimized because they had been pressing for inquiries into human rights violations previously carried out against their relatives or for exhumation from clandestine graves of family members killed during army counter-insurgency campaigns in the early 1980s.

María Mejía was killed in March in Sacapulas, El Quiché department, by men in plain clothes in an attack in which her husband, also a CERJ member, was severely wounded. According to his testimony, the assailants included two civilian army agents, who appeared to be acting under army orders. Reportedly, the same agents subsequently threatened several other local villagers with death because they opposed service in the nominally voluntary civil patrols, and a number of families fled the area. On 27 March, as the families attempted to return to their homes accompanied by CERJ supporters and government officials, they were threatened and assaulted by approximately 25 armed men, believed to be soldiers in plain clothes and civil patrollers acting under military orders. Some of the attackers were masked. The group fled, but Assistant Human Rights Procurator César Alvarez Guadamuz suffered an injury to his hand. In October the Assistant Procurator was again assaulted by a group including civil patrollers in similar circumstances.

Leaders and members of a group known as GAM, which attempts to clarify the fate of members' "disappeared" relatives, were also targeted. In March a 100-person delegation led by GAM was attacked by civil patrollers, reportedly acting under army orders, as it was travelling to El Quiché to support villagers threatened for refusing to join the civil patrols. The group's President, Nineth Montenegro de García, whose husband had "disappeared" in 1985, was among those injured. In July unknown men opened fire on her mother's home, using bullets of the type reportedly used by the security forces. In August her eight-year-old daughter reportedly received death threats by telephone.

Ana Graciela del Valle also experienced continuing intimidation after she filed a protest following an incident in July 1989. Four armed men in plain clothes had held a gun to her two-year-old son's head and said he would be killed if her brother-in-law didn't stop his work as director of the human rights centre known as CIEPRODH. Police repeatedly questioned her, asking particularly about CIEPRODH's investigation of the 1988 El Aguacate killings.

In May Luis Miguel Solís Pajarito, representative to the National Dialogue of the displaced peoples' association known as CONDEG, "disappeared." He had evaded a kidnapping attempt in April, and reported being followed by men in plain clothes during a May Day march. In September one-month-old Josefa María "disappeared" along with her mother, María Tiu Tojín. The two were taken into custody by the military along with members of a peasant community who had fled during the army counter-insurgency campaigns of the early 1980s and did not wish to return to areas under army control. The army customarily treated all members of such communities as guerrilla collaborators and they, as well as those who tried to publicize their often desperate economic and health conditions, were targets of abuses. Also in September Myrna Mack, an internationally known anthropologist who had been researching displaced communities, died after a particularly brutal "death squad"-style attack.

In June a group of armed men identified by witnesses as military entered Pacoc in El Quiché and ordered the two deputy mayors to arrest 15 people denounced by civil patrollers as "subversives". Most were members of a group known as CONAVIGUA, which campaigns for compensation for widows of those killed by the army, and for exhumation of their husbands' bodies from clandestine graves. The attempt to apprehend the CONAVIGUA members foundered when the two deputy mayors refused to cooperate. The mayors were then reportedly threatened with abduction.

Academics were also victims of human rights violations in 1990. Early in the year Dr Carmen Angélica Valenzuela, a professor at the University of San Carlos (USAC) and President of the Guatemalan Association of Women Doctors, became one of the few survivors of abduction and "disappearance" in Guatemala in recent years. In February she was released from military custody following a widespread international outcry and diplomatic intervention on her behalf, and went into exile abroad. She had been abducted in the presence of witnesses by men armed with sub-machine guns and was tortured in custody. Reportedly, police and military authorities had initially denied that she was in detention.

In April four people, three of them reportedly law students at the USAC, were abducted by armed men driving a van with polarized windows – a type of vehicle customarily used by the security forces. They had been fund-raising for a student satire. The bodies of three, bearing apparent signs of torture, were eventually recovered from a cemetery in eastern Guatemala where they had been buried as "unknown".

Continuing human rights violations against academics, and the failure of the authorities to establish responsibility for a series of abductions and murders of USAC staff and students in the third quarter of 1989, were cited by Harvard Law School as major factors in its decision to terminate in 1990 an administration of justice program that it had been implementing under the aegis of the United States Agency for International Development (USAID).

Two trade unionists, brothers Carlos Enrique and Tyron Francisco Sagastume, who worked at the Guatemala City Coca-Cola bottling plant, were found dead in February, the day after they had gone missing near their homes. Their bodies showed apparent signs of torture. Leaders and members of their trade union, which has played a leading role in Guatemalan trade unionism, had been targets of abuses over a long period.

Politicians were also subjected to abuses. Among the victims was Socialist International (SI) leader Salvadorian Héctor Oqueli Colindres, who was abducted and apparently extrajudicially executed in Guatemala in January as he was on his way to observe the Nicaraguan elections on behalf of SI. In the same incident, Guatemalan lawyer Gilda Flores Arévalo was also abducted and killed. Both the Guatemalan and Salvadorian governments initiated inquiries, but neither had announced significant findings by the end of the year. A report commissioned by SI described the Guatemalan Government's inquiry as "gravely flawed" and suggested it may have been "designed to fail". Similarly, no findings were known regarding the abduction and torture of a United States (US) nun, Diana Ortiz, in November 1989 (see *Amnesty International Report 1990*), despite reports in April 1990 that the government would establish a special investigatory commission. Government officials initially said that Diana Ortiz had arranged her own kidnapping, but they later retracted this and promised an inquiry after pressure from US religious organizations.

At least 14 street children were apparently extrajudicially executed by

Guatemala City police during the year. They included 13-year-old Nahamán Carmona López, who was attacked on 4 March and died 10 days later in hospital of multiple injuries, including a ruptured liver, six fractured ribs, two broken fingers and severe bruising to 70 per cent of his body. In June pressure from children's and international organizations led to the arrest of four police officers in connection with his death. A number of street children whose witness testimony was crucial in the case against the detained officers were repeatedly assaulted and intimidated, apparently by other police officers. The case was also marked by judicial irregularities and delays. Staff of organizations which have been instrumental in calling international attention to abuses against the street children were also increasingly the victims of threats and police brutality. In December a street worker with Covenant House, a group associated with such efforts, narrowly escaped abduction. He may have been targeted because he had given testimony crucial in bringing charges against a Treasury Police agent for an attack on street children.

Amnesty International repeatedly made public its concerns and called on government authorities to initiate inquiries into many incidents of human rights violations and to bring those responsible to justice. No instances were known where those allegedly responsible were convicted for the abuses reported, even in cases where eye-witness testimony explicity identified the alleged perpetrators.

In April the organization called attention to the organization's concerns about escalating violence against human rights monitors, an issue also raised at an April meeting in London with Guatemala's Interior Minister and the Director General of the Treasury Police. In July Amnesty International published a document outlining its concerns regarding abuses against street children. In October an Amnesty International delegation to Guatemala held a press conference to publicize these and other concerns and to release an open letter calling on candidates in the November presidential elections to make clear the steps they intended to take to improve the human rights situation in the country. The delegation also met government officials, local human rights groups and other independent groups, and victims of and witnesses to recent abuses.

In the lead-up to the November elections, the organization expressed special concern at the escalating attacks on politicians and journalists, noting that in October alone, two journalists were victims of "death squad"-style murders, and a third, Byron Barrera, survived an attack in which his wife died.

In a written statement to the UN Commission on Human Rights in February, Amnesty International expressed grave concern at the deteriorating human rights situation in the country and the failure of the authorities to adequately investigate the reported incidents.

GUINEA

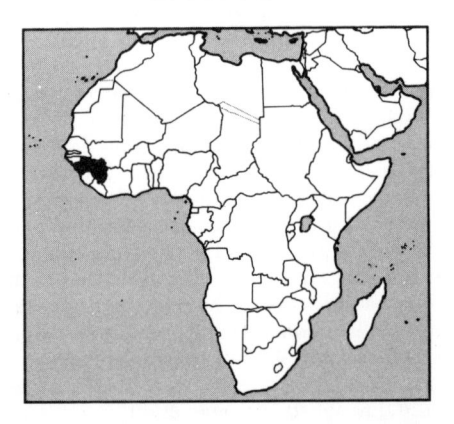

More than 50 people, including possible prisoners of conscience, were arrested for political reasons, but most were freed before the end of the year. Two were sentenced after an unfair trial. Some detainees were reportedly tortured and at least one was said to have died in security police custody as a result. There was no further information about the fate or whereabouts of 63 people who "disappeared" following their arrests in 1984 and 1985.

In February the government of President Lansana Conté announced an amnesty for all people convicted of political offences. In practice, this appeared to apply only to prisoners convicted at secret trials in 1986 and did not result in the release of any more of these prisoners, 63 of whom were still unaccounted for. The amnesty allowed some convicted *in absentia* in 1986 to return to Guinea.

A new constitution drafted by a constitutional commission appointed in 1989 was approved by a referendum in December. It includes safeguards against illegal detention and torture. However, in accordance with guidelines set by the government, it allows for only two political parties. The new constitution will not enter into force until 1995. In practice, all political parties remained prohibited during 1990.

Twenty-two supporters of the *Rassemblement du peuple guinéen* (RPG), Guinean People's Rally, an umbrella opposition organization, were arrested in August for allegedly distributing the party's newspaper, *Malanyi* (Unity). Most were released uncharged a few weeks later, but three were brought to trial in November before a criminal court in Conakry, whose procedures did not satisfy international fair trial standards. They were charged with distributing a newspaper without indicating the names of the authors or publishers. All three were convicted. However, two who received three-month sentences and who appeared to be prisoners of conscience were released immediately in view of the time they had already spent in custody. The third, who had returned to Guinea following the February amnesty, was also convicted of using a false identity card and received an 18-month prison term.

Two other alleged RPG members, Jean Sefa Camara and Joseph Soumah, known as Aïto, were tried by a criminal court in Conakry in February 1990. Both had been arrested in January 1988. Few details emerged about their trial but they were apparently accused of undergoing military training abroad as a prelude to organizing violent opposition to the government in Guinea. They were sentenced to two and five years' imprisonment respectively. The two prisoners did not benefit from the February amnesty.

Mohamed Ali Bangoura, another suspected RPG member who had been arrested in November 1989 when found in possession of the party newspaper, was released uncharged.

Further arrests occurred after student demonstrations in November and December, in which at least five people were killed, including Sékou Traoré, a Conakry University student. He was shot dead when security forces fired on a student march to the presidential palace. Dozens of other students were said to have been injured. At least four student leaders were then arrested: they were released uncharged after a few days. When a further march was organized, a foreign journalist and four members of a non-governmental human rights monitoring group, the *Organisation guinéenne des droits de l'homme*, Guinean Human Rights Organization, were arrested. They were initially accused of holding an unauthorized demonstration but were released uncharged after a few days. The government issued a public apology for the deaths of students and said an inquiry would be held, but its outcome was not known at the end of 1990.

In July, 34 residents of Liberia, including both Guinean and Liberian nationals, were arrested at Macenta. They had crossed the border into Guinea to escape the conflict in Liberia (see **Liberia**). Ten women were released uncharged after five days, but the 24 men were all held until October, when 17 of them were released uncharged. One other detainee was reportedly released in November. All the men were apparently detained on suspicion of being supporters of the Liberian rebel leader Charles Taylor, whose forces had killed a number of Guineans living in Liberia and to whom the Guinean authorities were opposed.

The 24 men were reportedly beaten in detention with their hands tied behind their backs. They were moved to the Alpha Yaya military camp in Conakry and later to security police custody. They were held in harsh conditions and reportedly kept naked: one of them was said to have died in custody in October as a result. At least four refugees appeared before a court in Conakry in December. They were charged with endangering state security, illegal possession of arms, looting and other offences. One of them was sentenced to five years in prison and three were acquitted; one other was sentenced *in absentia* to 20 years' imprisonment.

No new information was received about 63 people arrested in 1984 and 1985 and convicted in secret and unfair trials in 1986 (see *Amnesty International Report 1989*). The government did not respond to relatives' requests for information.

No further information was received about the official inquiry which the government had announced in November 1989 after a prisoner was reported to have been tortured to death and six demonstrators were said to have been shot dead by soldiers in Labé.

Amnesty International sought information about the arrested RPG supporters and urged that any held for their non-violent opinions or activities should be released. In April Amnesty International urged the commission drafting a new constitution to include full human rights safeguards. In particular, it stressed that the legality of all detentions should be open to challenge in the courts to prevent any recurrence of the arbitrary detentions, torture and "disappearances" which had occurred in the past in Guinea. No such provision was made, however, in the Constitution adopted in December.

GUINEA-BISSAU

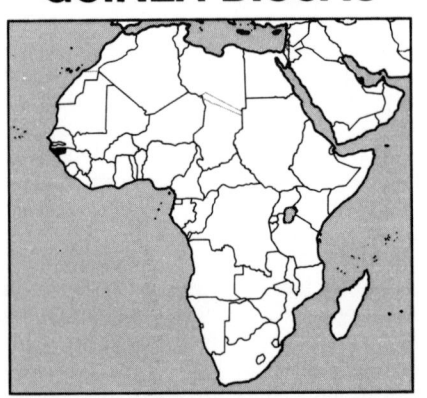

Twenty-two political prisoners sentenced after an unfair trial in 1986 were released from prison in an amnesty, but six of them were restricted. The whereabouts of others remained unclear. A senior government official was arrested for apparently political reasons.

At a congress in December the ruling party, *Partido Africano de Independência da Guiné e Cabo Verde* (PAIGC), African Party for the Independence of Guinea and Cape Verde, agreed on a program of constitutional and legal changes to introduce a multi-party political system in 1991. President João Bernardo Vieira had earlier announced that anyone was free to form a political party, but there were no legal guarantees to protect freedom of association or information.

In January the government announced an amnesty for all prisoners still serving sentences imposed in July 1986. They had been convicted, after an unfair trial, of plotting to overthrow the government. According to official sources, 16 prisoners were released and six others, whose death sentences had previously been commuted to 15-year prison terms, were ordered to remain on the islands where they had been held on prison farms. Although official reports indicated that all those serving sentences imposed in July 1986 had been released in 1990 or in previous years, it appeared that at least two were still held and that some of those reportedly freed in previous years remained restricted.

According to Amnesty International's understanding, 24 of those convicted in July 1986 were still in prison at the beginning of the year, including 18 who had been sentenced to prison terms of between 13 and 15 years and the six who were originally sentenced to death. As the names of the prisoners released in January were not reported it was impossible to say which two had apparently not been released. However, one of them may have been Buota Nam Batcha, a former National Assembly deputy, who was said to have died in custody after the trial. The government did not clarify this, nor did it respond to reports that another prisoner, Nfono Tchuda Nalagna, had died in custody in 1987 (see *Amnesty International Report 1989*). Once again there were claims that some of those convicted at the 1986 trial and who were officially reported to have been released in previous years were restricted to remote villages.

Guinea-Bissau's Vice-President and head of the armed forces, Iafai Camara, was reportedly placed under house arrest in November. He was said by official sources to have helped supply arms to separatist rebels in the Casamance area of neighbouring Senegal in breach of a bilateral agreement. Iafai Camara had not been charged or brought to trial by the end of the year and was apparently subsequently released.

Several other people were allegedly arrested or had restrictions placed on their movements for political reasons. Two men were reportedly detained, one for some days and the other for a few hours, after they returned from abroad: they were questioned about their suspected contacts with government opponents in exile. Former political prisoners who had been arrested in 1980 after a successful coup and released a few years later were also reportedly harassed by security police or instructed not to leave their home areas.

Amnesty International welcomed the January releases. It sought information from the government about the two prisoners who had apparently not been released and those who were reported to have died in custody. It also requested information from the government in response to reports that political prisoners released in previous years remained under restrictions. There was no reply.

GUYANA

Three people charged with treason were acquitted when confession statements allegedly signed as a result of ill-treatment in police custody were ruled inadmissible by the trial court. A trial was pending in the case of six others charged with treason, which carries a mandatory death sentence. Eight people were hanged for murder; in one case there was new evidence raising questions about the prisoner's guilt. At least 24 people convicted of murder were under sentence of death.

In October the treason trial opened in the cases of Karran Persaud Deokarran, Bhoj Pertab Singh and Neville Wordsworth, members of the opposition People's Progressive Party (PPP), who had been charged with plotting to overthrow the government in 1989 (see *Amnesty International Report 1990*). After hearing two weeks of testimony about the circumstances of their arrest and police detention, the court ruled that the defendants' confessions had not been made freely and voluntarily and were therefore inadmissible. The prosecution offered no further evidence in the case. The defendants, who had spent nearly 18 months in custody, were acquitted of all charges and released.

The accused had alleged that unidentified police officers arrested them at their homes in Mahaicony (East Demerara) in the early hours of 28 April 1989 and took them blindfolded to an unknown place of detention. They said they were held incommunicado for six days in dark, unsanitary cells and subjected to threats and violence by police officers during repeated interrogation. The accused alleged that, on the night of 3 May 1989, they were taken to a roadside and immediately rearrested by other police officers. They said they signed confessions at police headquarters on 4 May after further threats and beatings.

The police had acknowledged that the defendants were being detained only after *habeas corpus* proceedings were initiated by the prisoners' lawyers on 3 May 1989, but denied that the defendants had been in custody since 28 April. During the trial two lawyers testified about their unsuccessful attempts to locate the defendants after having been contacted by relatives who had witnessed them being taken from their homes. The lawyers did not see the defendants until 5 May 1989, despite repeated inquiries at police stations from 28 April onwards.

Six people, including an assistant police superintendent and an army officer, were charged with treason on 9 October. They were accused of having been involved in military training with unknown people between June and October as part of a conspiracy to overthrow the government. Warrants were issued for the arrest of three others detained for the same offence who had reportedly escaped from police custody. The trial was pending at the end of the year.

A bill passed by the National Assembly in 1989, which would extend the death penalty to certain drug-related offences, had not been signed into law by the end of the year (see *Amnesty International Report 1990*).

Eight prisoners were hanged for murder, bringing to 18 the number of executions since 1985, when hangings resumed after a 15-year moratorium. Several of those hanged in 1990 had been sentenced to death during the moratorium.

Sylvester Sturge was executed in February despite new evidence raising questions about his guilt. He and two co-defendants were convicted and sentenced to death in 1987 for the murder of two men on a coconut plantation. The evidence against Sylvester Sturge at his trial consisted largely of his confession, which he later retracted. He alleged that he had signed the statement after four police officers beat him in an unoccupied building on the way to the police station. Those alleged to have been involved in the ill-treatment included the chief investigating officer, who was related by marriage to one of the murder victims. The court ruled that the confession statement was admissible despite contradictions in police testimony as to who was present when the confession was taken and the submission by the defence of a bloodstained shirt which Sylvester Sturge said he was wearing when he was beaten.

When warrants were issued for the execution of Sylvester Sturge and a co-defendant, Elroy Aaron, in February, Elroy Aaron told prison officials that Sylvester Sturge was innocent and had not been present during the murder. This statement was brought to the attention of President Desmond Hoyte and the Attorney General. Although a judge advising the Mercy Committee was reportedly asked to review the case shortly before the execution, the prisoners themselves were not interviewed. Both executions went ahead as scheduled. The third defendant in the case had earlier had his murder conviction quashed on appeal.

Amnesty International appealed for clemency whenever it learned that an execution was scheduled. In Sylvester Sturge's case, the organization also urged President Hoyte to grant a stay of execution to allow time for the new evidence to be considered by the courts.

An Amnesty International observer attended part of the treason trial of Karran Persaud Deokarran, Bhoj Pertab Singh and Neville Wordsworth.

HAITI

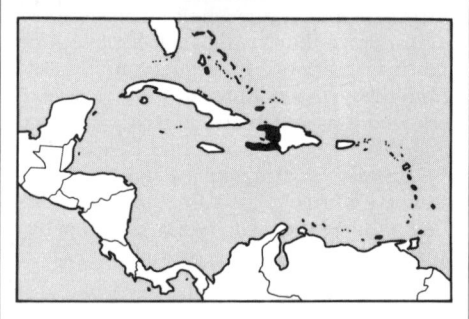

Hundreds of people, including prisoners of conscience, were arrested without warrant and detained without charge or trial for short periods of time. Many detainees, including children, were ill-treated or tortured, and at least four died, apparently as a result of torture. Prison conditions continued to be harsh. The security forces were reportedly responsible for indiscriminate shootings and extrajudicial executions of civilians.

In January President Prosper Avril declared a state of siege and imposed restrictions on news broadcasts, following the assassination of army Colonel André Neptune. During the state of siege, which lasted until the end of January, there were widespread arrests and raids on several independent radio stations.

In March President Avril resigned following widespread popular protest against his government, and a transitional government took over, headed by Ertha Pascal-Trouillot and a Council of State (*Conseil d'Etat*). Presidential elections held on 16 December were won by Father Jean-Bertrand Aristide, the candidate for the *Front national pour le changement et la démocratie*, National Front for Change and Democracy. He was expected to succeed President Pascal-Trouillot in February 1991.

Violent crime, indiscriminate shootings and killings by heavily armed men, sometimes in military uniforms, continued to be widespread. There appeared to be no political motivation for their actions. Haitians referred to the situation as *"l'insécurité"*, the insecurity. There was evidence that many of these acts were committed by members of the security forces.

In January over 20 politicians, journalists and human rights activists were arrested following the assassination of

Colonel Neptune and accused of terrorist activities. Most of them were ill-treated by the security forces at the time of arrest or while in custody. Some were released shortly after arrest and others were deported without judicial proceedings. The remaining detainees were released in February, when the government declared an amnesty for those accused of crimes against the security of the state.

Political leaders Evans Paul, Jean-Auguste Meyzieux, Marino Etienne and Patrick Beauchard were among those who benefited from the February amnesty. They had been arrested in late 1989 and charged with plotting to assassinate President Avril and overthrow the government (see *Amnesty International Report 1990*).

Arbitrary arrests by the security forces throughout the country continued to be reported. Victims included members of grassroots organizations and human rights groups, journalists and peasants. The Port-au-Prince police were reportedly responsible for the arbitrary arrest and ill-treatment of street children. There was also an increasing number of reports that local police and military authorities arrested civilians and held them for up to several days, sometimes with the acquiescence of local judicial authorities, with the aim of extracting money.

In March two directors of Radio Cap-Haïtien were arrested without warrant following the broadcast of a statement asking for President Avril's resignation. They were released uncharged several days later. In May radio reporter Tony Vergniaud was arrested and beaten by soldiers in Port-de-Paix while investigating reports of a local judge's involvement in corruption. Arrested under the orders of the judge he was investigating, he was released the same day. In June Logique Paris and Narcisse Orellien, members of the peasant organization *Tèt Kolle*, Heads Together, were arrested by the local police chief in Mahotière, Northwest Department, and severely beaten after they protested against the arrest of two others. They were released three days later.

Ill-treatment and torture of detainees by the security forces was widespread. Methods of torture included severe beatings with fists and sticks on the soles of the feet, the genitals, the eyes and the head. At least four prisoners died in police or prison custody, apparently as a result of severe beatings. In August Méhus Laroche was reportedly arrested without a warrant in Plaisance, Northern Department, and severely beaten at the police headquarters in Cap-Haïtien. He died nine days later at Cap-Haïtien penitentiary. Also in August farmer Michel Fontaine was arrested without a warrant in La Gonâve district and was reportedly severely beaten by a deputy rural police chief. His body, later returned to his family, showed signs of severe injuries to the head, eyes and legs. The deputy police chief was subsequently arrested, but to Amnesty International's knowledge, he had not been charged or tried by the end of the year.

Prison conditions in the National Penitentiary, Saint Marc, Gonaïves, Cap-Haïtien and other detention centres throughout the country continued to be extremely harsh, and many inmates were reportedly ill because of malnutrition, poor hygiene and lack of medical treatment.

As in previous years, the security forces ill-treated civilians during demonstrations and protests, as well as during disputes over land rights. In some of these incidents the security forces were said to have deliberately wounded or killed demonstrators and peasants. In April at least four people were wounded when local military personnel reportedly opened fire to disperse a peaceful demonstration by the *Mouvement des Paysans de Borgne*, Borgne Peasant Movement. Also in April demonstrators in Cabaret threw stones after soldiers had fired warning shots in the air. The soldiers directed their fire on the crowd, and killed two civilians.

The security forces were allegedly involved in "death squad"-style killings. In June four gunmen, two of whom wore military uniforms, shot and killed Council of State member Serge Villard and trade unionist Jean-Marie Montès, and wounded politician Emmanuel Magni. In September a United States Federal Bureau of Investigation team arrived in Haiti to assist in the investigation. By the end of the year no findings had been made public. In July Mariano Delaunay, a teacher and member of the Saint Jean Bosco Roman Catholic Community, was killed by a gunman identified by witnesses as an army sergeant.

The government was not effective in bringing those responsible for human rights violations to justice, despite announcing inquiries into several cases and arresting and dismissing some officials implicated in abuses. In April judicial proceedings were initiated against one of those allegedly responsible for the killings at the Saint Jean Bosco church in September 1988 (see *Amnesty International Report 1989*), but by the end of the year no progress was evident. In July Roger Lafontant, a prominent member of the government of deposed President Jean-Claude Duvalier, and publicly accused of responsibility for gross human rights violations, returned to Haiti. The government issued warrants for his arrest which were not, however, based on alleged involvement in human rights abuses. The security forces did not enforce the warrants and Roger Lafontant remained at large at the end of the year.

Amnesty International wrote to President Avril and later to President Pascal-Trouillot raising cases of concern to the organization, requesting details of any inquiries and measures taken against officials implicated in human rights violations and expressing concern at the absence of investigations into past human rights abuses. No response was received.

HONDURAS

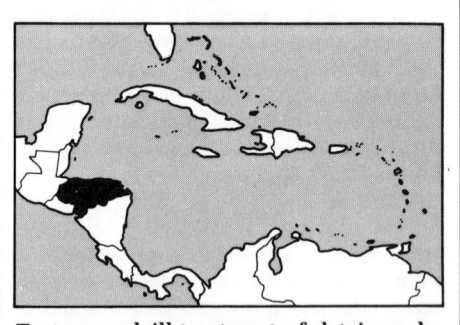

Torture and ill-treatment of detainees by the army and police were frequently reported. Charges against some political detainees were reportedly based largely on statements extracted under torture. Two trade unionists and a student leader were killed in circumstances suggesting that they had been extrajudicially executed by groups allegedly linked to the armed forces. Several criminal suspects may have been extrajudicially executed by police. The fate of approximately 150 people who had "disappeared" following arrest under previous governments remained unclarified.

In January Rafael Leonardo Callejas took office as president following his election in November 1989. Although the President emphasized the importance of safeguarding human rights in his inaugural speech, human rights violations persisted.

Some actions attributed to armed opposition groups were reported, including attacks on United States military personnel based in Honduras.

In May Honduras signed the Second Optional Protocol to the International Covenant on Civil and Political Rights Aiming at the Abolition of the Death Penalty; it had not ratified this treaty by the end of the year.

Detainees were often arrested without warrant and held beyond the 24-hour constitutional limit before being taken before a judge. Political and criminal suspects were reportedly tortured or otherwise ill-treated while held incommunicado in the detention centres of the *Dirección Nacional de Investigaciones* (DNI), the investigative branch of the national police force, or in military barracks. Methods of torture included food and water deprivation; suspension from the ceiling by a rope passed through the detainees' handcuffs, which were fastened behind their backs; electric shocks to hands and feet; near-suffocation in the *capucha*, a rubber hood sometimes impregnated with lime (*cal*); beatings; and death threats against detainees' families.

Manuel Castillo Reyes was among five people arrested in April and accused of smuggling weapons to the armed opposition in El Salvador. He was reportedly held incommunicado for almost five weeks before being transferred to prison. During his first 15 days in custody he was reportedly beaten repeatedly, subjected to the *capucha*, and suspended by his feet. He said that military personnel lit fires around him in the middle of the night and threatened to burn him alive. He was released after several months in prison, but two others held with him, who also alleged they were tortured, remained in prison at the end of the year. In an exceptional move, a judge hearing the *habeas corpus* petition presented on Manuel Castillo's behalf began an investigation into his claims of illegal arrest.

Lawyer Julio Francisco Lagos Holman, arrested in Tegucigalpa in May by members of the DNI, was taken to different centres belonging to the *Fuerza de Seguridad*

Pública (FUSEP), the Public Security Forces, who accused him of arms possession. He claimed he was beaten, kicked and given electric shocks by FUSEP agents. He was released without charge on 8 June.

The circumstances of the detention and interrogation of other political detainees led to fears that their right to a fair trial may have been undermined, particularly as it was alleged that charges had been based mainly on confessions extracted under torture. Five prisoners arrested in 1989 and accused of arms-trafficking were reportedly charged on the basis of statements extracted under torture. Some said they had been held without legal representation for several months.

Physical attacks and other intimidatory acts were reportedly directed against trade unionists, government opponents, human rights activists and students. Honduran human rights groups attributed these abuses to clandestine groups allegedly linked to the armed forces. Former student leader Roberto Zelaya left Honduras in April after being seriously injured in an attack the previous month. Three unidentified men had reportedly abducted him, beat him over the head and stabbed him in the stomach.

Several priests working with peasants, particularly near the border with El Salvador, were also among the victims. Father Felipe Quintanilla, for example, reported that shots were fired at his home from a passing car in May. Other priests received anonymous death threats.

Two trade unionists and a student leader were killed in circumstances suggesting that they may have been extrajudicially executed. The cases were similar to other extrajudicial executions reported in previous years which were allegedly carried out by groups linked to the armed forces.

On 20 March Dennis Hernán Rodríguez García, a member of the *Organización Campesina de Honduras* (OCH), Honduran Peasants' Organization, was abducted from his home in Talanga, Morazán province, by a man who reportedly identified himself as a member of the DNI. The man told Dennis Rodríguez' wife that he was being taken to the headquarters of the *Batallón Fuerzas Especiales*, Special Forces Battalion. Dennis Rodríguez' body was found the next day on a road near Talanga, showing bullet wounds and signs of torture. The DNI and the Special Forces Battalion denied having arrested him.

On 31 May Francisco Javier Bonilla Medina, a leader of the *Sindicato de Trabajadores del Instituto Hondureño de Seguridad Social* (SITRAIHSS), Union of Workers of the Honduran Social Security Institute, was shot dead in Tegucigalpa by an armed man in civilian clothing. The gunman also tried to kill Consuelo Valladares, a union colleague who was with Francisco Bonilla at the time. She and her husband subsequently received death threats. The incidents occurred in the context of strikes and other union activities in protest against government measures. President Callejas appointed an army commission to investigate Francisco Bonilla's killing. It concluded that student leader Martin Pineda had ordered the murder. Martin Pineda presented himself to a court, which found no evidence to incriminate him, and he was released without charge after six days in custody. The commission also accused three men of carrying out the murder, but they denied the allegations, saying they were forced to confess to the crime after being tortured.

The body of Ramón Antonio Briceño, student leader of the *Frente de Reforma Universitaria* (FRU), University Reform Front, was found in June with 11 bullet wounds and signs of beatings. Shortly before he was killed, the *Alianza de Acción Anticomunista* (AAA), Anticommunist Action Alliance, painted the message "Briceño, you are dead" on the walls of the National University.

Investigations into these and other political murders which took place in previous years, such as the 1988 killings of Miguel Angel Pavón Salazar and Moisés Landaverde (see *Amnesty International Reports 1989* and *1990*), made little progress. By the end of 1990, no one had been brought to justice for any of the killings.

Some criminal suspects were reportedly killed in circumstances suggesting that they were victims of extrajudicial executions by police officers. In May Walter David Cruz Torres and Kemer Javier Andino López were arrested by four DNI agents in Tegucigalpa and accused of stealing. They were reportedly interrogated, beaten and shot on a road near Olancho. Walter Cruz died instantly but Kemer Andino escaped.

Three Salvadorian tradesmen reportedly "disappeared" following their arrest without warrant by Honduran soldiers in November, after they had crossed the border into Honduras to buy food and clothes. The army denied holding them. It was later reported that they had been deported to El Salvador in early December.

In a report presented to the Honduran Government in December 1989, the United Nations Special Rapporteur on Torture made a series of recommendations for the prevention of torture in Honduras, including the creation of an office of public prosecutor within the Attorney General's Office, and the transfer of control of the police from military to civilian authority. To Amnesty International's knowledge, none of the recommendations had been implemented by the end of 1990, although some initial steps were taken towards the eventual creation of a judicial police.

In June Amnesty International wrote to President Callejas welcoming his declared commitment to human rights and urging him to take steps to ensure that human rights abuses, including killings, were fully investigated and those responsible brought to justice. The organization continued its appeals for clarification of the fate of approximately 150 detainees who had "disappeared" under previous governments.

In December the Minister of the Interior and Justice announced that the Honduran Government would investigate these "disappearance" cases. Amnesty International welcomed the announcement and requested further details of the proposed investigations. It also asked for clarification of the whereabouts of the three Salvadorian tradesmen who "disappeared" in November. No reply was received.

Also in December the Honduran Government finally paid the compensation to the families of "disappearance" victims Angel Manfredo Velásquez and Saúl Godínez which had been ordered by the Inter-American Court of Human Rights in 1988 and 1989 (see *Amnesty International Reports 1989* and *1990*).

HONG KONG

Five pro-democracy activists were briefly detained and charged under a little-used law with illegally using megaphones and soliciting funds. The refugee-determination ("screening") process for Vietnamese asylum-seekers remained deficient despite some improvements. At least 10 people were sentenced to death but there were no executions.

The Basic Law of the Hong Kong Special Administrative Region (SAR), due to come into force in July 1997 when the People's Republic of China assumes sovereignty over Hong Kong, was adopted in April by the National People's Congress in Beijing. It failed to fully recognize and protect specific human rights and to indicate how the International Covenant on Civil and Political Rights, as applied in Hong Kong, would remain in force (see *Amnesty International Reports 1989* and *1990*).

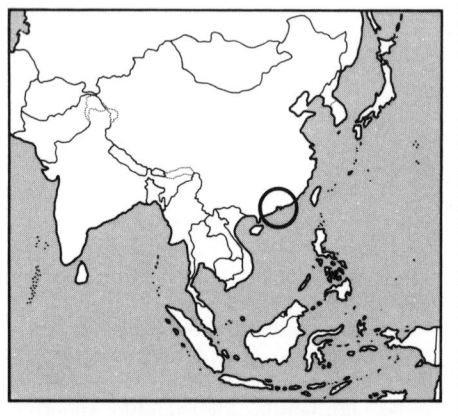

A draft of the Hong Kong Bill of Rights Ordinance, due to be adopted in 1991, did not recognize the international monitoring procedures used in Hong Kong and lacked certain safeguards against the imprisonment of prisoners of conscience. It provided for protection of the right to life but did not contain an assurance that Hong Kong's policy of not carrying out executions would be maintained.

Shortcomings in the screening process for Vietnamese asylum-seekers remained, raising the prospect that some of those denied refugee status ("screened out") might include people who could be at risk of imprisonment as prisoners of conscience or other serious human rights violations if returned to Viet Nam. However, some improvements were made to the screening process and the proportion of Vietnamese asylum-seekers who were granted refugee status increased during the year.

A judicial inquest was held into the death of an asylum-seeker. He had died from a ruptured spleen after an incident in which asylum-seekers were allegedly assaulted by police in the Shek Kong Detention Centre in July 1989 (see *Amnesty International Report 1990*). During the inquest two police officers reportedly admitted kicking the man. In March the inquest returned an open verdict. The outcome of an investigation into the incident by the Complaints Against the Police Office had not been disclosed by the end of the year.

In December, 23 "screened-out" Vietnamese asylum-seekers who neither volunteered nor objected to return to Viet Nam were flown back under a program established by the Hong Kong Government and the Office of the United Nations High Commissioner for Refugees.

Five prominent pro-democracy activists were briefly arrested in February, following a week-long sit-in to protest against alleged flaws in the Hong Kong Basic Law. They were convicted under the Summary Offences Ordinance of having illegally used megaphones to address the public and of collecting money without permission. At their trial in May lawyers suggested that the charges against the five were politically motivated. They refused to pay fines imposed by the court but these were paid anonymously in August. An appeal against the convictions was still pending at the end of the year. In July and September Amnesty International wrote to the Hong Kong Government to express concern at aspects of the case, including the uncommonly rigid application of a public order regulation. The Hong Kong authorities replied stating that the prosecutions had not been politically motivated.

At least 10 death sentences – mandatory for murder – were pronounced during the year. The Hong Kong Government continued the practice of commuting all death sentences.

Following the visit of an Amnesty International delegation to Hong Kong in November 1989 (see *Amnesty International Report 1990*), the organization published in January a *Memorandum to the Governments of Hong Kong and the United Kingdom Regarding the Protection of Vietnamese Asylum-Seekers in Hong Kong*. This documented flaws in the screening process, made recommendations for its improvement and expressed opposition to any forcible repatriations until these flaws had been satisfactorily addressed. The memorandum also called for prompt and impartial investigations into allegations that detained asylum-seekers had been assaulted and ill-treated by police and other officers. In a report in July on these developments, Amnesty International made public its concern that no asylum-seekers should be forcibly sent back to Viet Nam while significant flaws in the procedure remained.

In June Amnesty International outlined its concerns on the draft Bill of Rights in a memorandum addressed to the Governor, Sir David Wilson. The organization recommended that anyone involved in criminal proceedings whose rights might have been violated should be allowed to invoke the Bill of Rights, which should not include reservations that infringe on the internationally recognized rights of prisoners and asylum-seekers. The organization also recommended that the Bill of Rights provide for the abolition of the death penalty.

INDIA

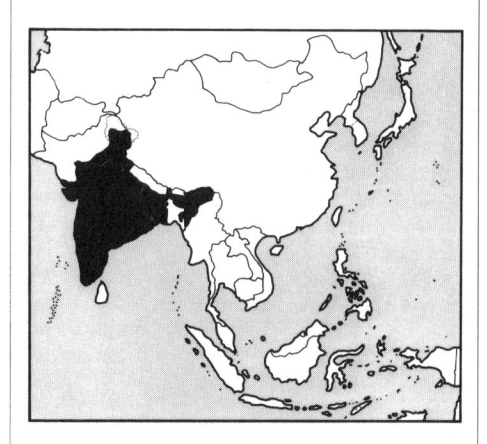

Several thousand political prisoners, including prisoners of conscience, were held without charge or trial under special or preventive detention laws. Increasingly, politically motivated arrests were not officially acknowledged. Torture and ill-treatment were widespread and in some states systematic, resulting in scores of deaths in police custody. Dozens of people "disappeared" or appeared to have been extrajudicially executed in "encounters" staged by the police. Over 100 peaceful demonstrators were believed to have

been victims of extrajudicial executions. A small number of death sentences were carried out.

Prime Minister Vishwanath Pratap Singh's National Front (NF) coalition government lost its majority in Parliament and resigned on 7 November. There had been widespread controversy over its plan to reserve more jobs in the public service for members of the underprivileged castes and its opposition to attempts by Hindus to take over a Muslim shrine in Ayodhya. A new minority government led by Prime Minister Chandra Shekhar, who had formed a breakaway faction of the Janata Dal party, called the Janata Dal (Socialist), took office three days later, after obtaining the support of the Congress party.

Earlier in the year the NF government, which had stated its commitment to accountability and respect for human rights, faced increasing violence by armed separatist groups, notably in Jammu and Kashmir, Punjab and Assam. According to Jammu and Kashmir's Director General of Police, 1,044 people were killed in the state by armed separatists between January and September, including 107 members of the security forces and 377 civilians – mostly alleged informers or victims of abductions. In Punjab at least 3,800 politically motivated killings were reportedly committed by government forces and armed separatists during the year – an unprecedented level of such deaths. In October alone Sikh separatists were officially said to have killed 265 people, including 68 members of the security forces. President's rule (direct rule from New Delhi) was extended for the eighth time in October for a further six months. In Jammu and Kashmir, the state assembly was suspended in January and direct rule was imposed. In July the government applied to Jammu and Kashmir the Armed Forces Special Powers Act – already in force in northeast India – which empowered the security forces to shoot to kill with immunity from prosecution.

Well over 10,000 political prisoners were held under preventive detention laws – the National Security Act (NSA) and the Jammu and Kashmir Public Safety Act – or under special "anti-terrorist" laws, notably the Terrorist and Disruptive Activities (Prevention) Act (TADA) and the Arms Act. Some political prisoners were held on criminal charges.

The NSA permits detention without charge or trial for up to one year. Nagaimugan was ordered to be detained for one year under its provisions in Tamil Nadu in April for making statements "likely to disrupt the country's unity". On 10 September a court ordered his release on technical grounds. Lal Advani, leader of the Bharatiya Janata Party, and many party members were also briefly detained under NSA provisions in October, when communal violence was feared in Ayodhya. The TADA allows up to one year's detention for investigation of suspected "terrorist" or broadly defined "disruptive" activities. Its provisions make bail difficult to obtain. The act was used mainly in Punjab, Assam, Manipur, Andhra Pradesh, and Jammu and Kashmir, where some 1,700 people were reportedly being detained under its provisions in mid-1990. Despite its name, those detained under the TADA have included peaceful critics of the government in states where there was no armed opposition to the government. In Gujarat, for example, the act was used to detain trade union leaders and landless labourers demanding fair wages and land. One of 600 people held there under the TADA in January was Zohrabibi, a 60-year-old woman who was said by the Indian press to have been detained by the Baroda police because she complained about the killing of her husband during communal rioting in 1982.

It was difficult to estimate the precise number of political prisoners held in India at any one time owing to the large numbers involved, their geographical spread and the rate of turnover. Official statistics were rarely given and often proved to be contradictory. For example, before releasing 600 untried political detainees, the government in New Delhi said in January that 12,000 people were being held in Punjab alone: the state government, however, put the number at 6,000.

Hundreds more arrests were reported during 1990. No official figures were given in 1990 about the number of those being held for political reasons at any one time in Jammu and Kashmir, although unofficial sources in July estimated that between 10,000 and 15,000 people had been detained without trial in the state since January. Semi-official sources put the number held in September at 2,800, of whom 2,000 were said to be suspected armed secessionists and the others political leaders. One of the latter, Abdul Ghani Lone, was arrested in April for advocating a separate state. He was initially held without trial at Jodhpur Central Jail in Rajasthan, where it was difficult for relatives to visit him. The Director General of the Jammu and Kashmir police said that 602 people were arrested under the Jammu and Kashmir Public Safety Act between January and September. About 1,000 others, mostly male youths aged between 14 and 18, were arrested in the state on the border with Pakistan.

Most of those arrested for political reasons were detained without charge or trial. They included some prisoners of conscience and in some cases their detention was not acknowledged. Yusuf Yameel, a Srinagar-based journalist reporting on developments in Jammu and Kashmir, was abducted by army officers on 2 June, detained for two days and interrogated. His detention was initially denied by the state government, but an inquiry was subsequently ordered. Its outcome was not known.

Trials of political prisoners were rare and subject to delay. "Naxalite" (Maoist revolutionary) political prisoners in West Bengal were denied the right to prompt and fair trial: four of them had awaited trial for over nine years.

Torture remained widespread. In Jammu and Kashmir there were well-documented reports of women being raped by members of the security forces, especially during house-to-house searches. Released prisoners said they had been beaten, tortured with electric shocks, burned with cigarettes and suspended upside-down. In Punjab, torture was also systematically used: methods included rolling wooden bars across the thighs and inserting chilli powder into sensitive parts of the body. Relatives of alleged armed secessionists were among those arrested and tortured. Elsewhere, victims of torture included villagers detained in connection with demands for greater autonomy or separatism in Assam, Nagaland and Manipur, criminal suspects and people belonging to lower castes or tribal populations. In Bihar, people were tortured to deter them from asserting their demands to land rights and better pay.

Scores of people, including many members of the lower castes, died in police and military custody allegedly as a result of torture. In Manipur, S. Joel was reportedly beaten and given electric shocks by members of the 20th Assam Rifles, who were seeking information about insurgent activities. His body was handed over to the police in late May: he was said to have been shot while trying to escape. Relatives who had seen him on the previous day, however, said that he was then unable to walk because of injuries he had sustained under torture. In some cases, medical evidence corroborated torture allegations. In July Raju Mohite, a member of the Scheduled Castes, died in a Bombay hospital one day after his release from 10 days' detention at Oshiwara police station. The police denied torture but a post-mortem revealed extensive injuries to his body, attributed to beatings with a "hard and blunt object".

Increasingly, political suspects were held in unacknowledged detention, sometimes for months. Some "disappeared" after arrest, especially in Punjab, where arrests were made and subsequently denied by plainclothes police or paramilitary forces. *Habeas corpus* applications resulted in the courts ordering some of those held to be produced, but such orders were often ignored by the security forces. In one case, the Punjab and Haryana High Court instituted contempt of court proceedings against Central Reserve Police Force officers who failed to produce three men – Devinder Singh Pujari, Rajinder Singh Pappu and Jurbaj Singh Jago – in court on 22 March, although a High Court official had located them in secret detention two weeks earlier. At the end of the year, the whereabouts of the three men remained unknown.

Extrajudicial executions of suspected government opponents were reported, notably in Jammu and Kashmir, Punjab and Andhra Pradesh. In Jammu and Kashmir unarmed demonstrators demanding independence were shot dead by the police without warning, including in May, when at least 47 people in a funeral procession were killed after anti-Indian slogans were shouted. The police said the victims had been caught in "cross-fire", but witnesses said that the police officers fired into the crowd without warning. Fifteen other unarmed civilians were shot dead on 1 October by the paramilitary Border Security Force in retaliation for the murder of one of their men by Kashmiri separatists.

In Punjab extrajudicial killings in

"encounters" staged by the police continued to be reported. These allegations were hard to corroborate because there were rarely survivors of or witnesses to such killings. However, the Attorney General acknowledged that a policy of killing government opponents existed: he told the Supreme Court in April that an order issued by the Director General of Police, Punjab, promising financial awards for the "liquidation" of 53 men described as "terrorists", had lapsed. In June the Governor of Punjab appealed to the police to stop fake encounters. Yet allegations of staged "encounter" killings continued to be made: Harpal Singh and Baljit Singh, both members of the All India Sikh Students Federation, were shot dead in June in what police maintained was an armed encounter near Kotla Ajner village. However, villagers said the two had been tortured for several hours and then killed by police officers. Official investigations into such reports were rare but this case was investigated by a magistrate who found that the "death of the two was not in the ordinary course of an encounter". The state's Home Secretary reportedly urged criminal prosecutions of those allegedly responsible, but the Director General of Police apparently opposed this because he thought it would demoralize the police.

During a campaign to build a Hindu temple at the site of an existing mosque at Ayodhya, Uttar Pradesh, the security forces allegedly killed several unarmed Hindus inside houses in early November. In November and December members of the Provincial Armed Constabulary were said to have deliberately killed several Muslims, including women and children, not connected with communal violence which had erupted in various towns in Uttar Pradesh.

Police officers allegedly responsible for human rights violations were sometimes suspended but rarely prosecuted. Moreover, when official investigations were conducted into alleged large-scale human rights violations, their outcomes were often withheld. The NF government had stated its commitment to repealing that part of the 1952 Commission of Inquiry Act enabling governments to withhold the findings of inquiries on grounds of state security. Despite this, it refused to disclose the findings of an official inquiry into alleged extrajudicial killings of Muslims in Meerut in May 1987, saying the inquiry had "been treated as 'secret' by the government of Uttar Pradesh".

Dozens of people were sentenced to death and some executions were believed to have been carried out. However, the exact figures were not known. At least one mercy petition was rejected by the President.

Amnesty International sought information about possible prisoners of conscience and victims of "disappearances", and pressed the government to investigate and prevent extrajudicial killings, notably in Punjab, Jammu and Kashmir, and Uttar Pradesh. It urged full and impartial investigations into all deaths in custody, and appealed to the government not to execute prisoners sentenced to death. In October Amnesty International published two reports: *Operation Bluebird*, a case study of torture and extrajudicial executions in Manipur; and *India: Summary of Amnesty International's Current Concerns*.

In June the NF government partially lifted a 10-year-old ban on all Amnesty International visits to India, and said that the organization would be allowed to conduct "private visits" or talks with the government in New Delhi. The government subsequently failed to schedule such meetings although Amnesty International proposed dates in July, August, September and October. An Amnesty International delegation attending the World Congress on Human Rights in December met the Cabinet Secretary and Foreign Secretary, who said that there had been no change in the previous government's policy that Amnesty International could visit New Delhi for discussions with the government. However, the government had not decided whether to allow the organization to visit Punjab and Jammu and Kashmir.

In an oral statement to the UN Sub-Commission on Prevention of Discrimination and Protection of Minorities, Amnesty International included reference to its concerns in India about the torture of detainees.

INDONESIA/ EAST TIMOR

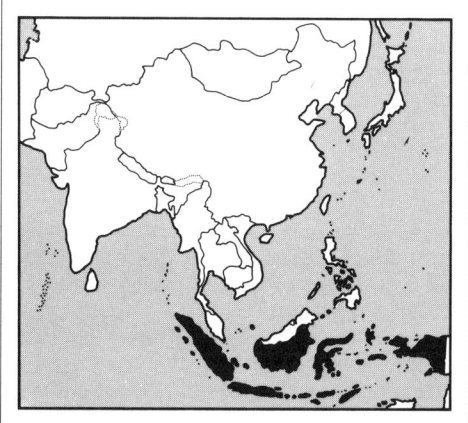

At least 20 alleged opponents of the government were imprisoned as prisoners of conscience during 1990. Together with more than 100 other prisoners of conscience convicted in previous years, they were sentenced after trials whose fairness was in serious doubt. Some had been imprisoned for more than 20 years. Hundreds of other political opponents of the government were detained in Aceh, Irian Jaya and East Timor; most were released uncharged but some were still held at the end of the year. There were new reports of torture and ill-treatment of political detainees, peaceful protesters and criminal suspects, some of whom died as a result. Hundreds of bodies were found in Aceh and North Sumatra; scores of the victims were alleged to have been extrajudicially executed by government forces. Three people were sentenced to death and four political prisoners were executed after more than 20 years in prison; eight other political prisoners remained in imminent danger of execution.

The government of President Suharto faced armed resistance from advocates of independence in the territories of East Timor, Irian Jaya and Aceh, and open political opposition from pro-democracy activists throughout the country. In East Timor, scores of people were briefly detained when hundreds of protesters, many of them students, took part in a series of peaceful demonstrations. In Aceh, where more than 5,000 government troops were deployed to combat armed rebels, hundreds of people were killed and hundreds arrested. Elsewhere, university students, Islamic activists and national opposition figures criticized what they said was the government's authoritarian rule.

In August President Suharto and other government officials called publicly for greater political openness and respect for human rights. In practice, however, serious human rights violations continued. Hundreds of thousands of former Indonesian Communist Party (PKI) members and prisoners continued to be required to report regularly to local military authorities. A new system was introduced – known as "Special Research" (*Penelitian Khusus* or *Litsus*) – for vetting former PKI prisoners and other possible communist sympathizers. This broadened the criteria by which people could be considered "influenced" by communist thinking and then subjected to restrictions on their employment and civil rights.

At least seven university students sentenced to prison terms during the year were believed to be prisoners of conscience. One, Bonar Tigor Naipospos, a student at Gajah Mada University in Yogyakarta, was jailed for eight and a half years after an apparently unfair trial. He was convicted of subversion for possessing and distributing literature said to contain communist ideas, and of disseminating Marxist teachings in university discussion groups and through his own writings. Six students were sentenced to three-year prison terms in February for "expressing feelings of hostility, hatred or contempt" towards the government after a peaceful demonstration at the Bandung Institute of Technology in August 1989 (see *Amnesty International Report 1990*).

At least 50 of some 140 political prisoners in Irian Jaya were believed to be prisoners of conscience. About 20 were sentenced during 1990 for advocating the independence of the province of Irian Jaya. They included Jacob Rumbiak and three others who had sought refuge in the Papua New Guinea Consulate in Jayapura in December 1989. They apparently received assurances that they would be fairly treated but were later arrested, tried for subversion and sentenced to between 12 and 15 years in prison. Dr Thomas Wainggai and 36 others convicted of subversion in 1989 remained in prison (see *Amnesty International Report 1990*). Dr Wainggai and his wife were transferred to Jakarta, making visits by relatives extremely difficult.

At least 20 Islamic activists, some of whom appeared to be prisoners of conscience, were convicted in a series of subversion trials which began in 1989 in Aceh, Bandung, Bima, Bogor, Jakarta, Lampung and Madura. Most were accused of undermining the state ideology *Pancasila* and attempting to establish an Islamic state. Their trials may not have been fair. At least 40 of an estimated 300 imprisoned Islamic activists sentenced for subversion in previous years were prisoners of conscience. They were convicted of involvement with *usroh* groups, which advocated closer ties among Muslims and a stricter adherence to Muslim teachings. Haji Abdul Ghani Masykur's sentence was reduced from 11 to eight years on appeal (see *Amnesty International Report 1990*).

About 50 prisoners arrested in the late 1960s for alleged involvement in the 1965 coup attempt or for PKI membership remained in prison throughout 1990. Many were believed to be prisoners of conscience, such as Pudjo Prasetio, an alleged PKI member in Bali who was arrested in 1967 but only brought to trial in 1979. He was serving a life sentence imposed for subversion and was reportedly in poor health.

One prisoner of conscience, Lieutenant General Dharsono, was released in September (see *Amnesty International Reports 1985* and *1986*). Amnesty International learned of the release of two political prisoners who had been in prison for more than 20 years; they had been convicted of involvement in the 1965 coup attempt after trials whose fairness was in doubt. In January it was learned that Abdul Syukur, arrested in 1969 and sentenced to 20 years' imprisonment in 1976, had been released in August 1989. Murdjani, arrested in 1968 and sentenced to 19 years' imprisonment in 1977, was released in May.

There continued to be serious doubts about the fairness of political trials, particularly those held under the broadly worded Anti-Subversion Law. Defendants were frequently held for months before being charged or tried and some were apparently convicted on the basis of uncorroborated confessions extracted under duress. Bonar Tigor Naipospos, for example, was held for almost one year before being formally charged and tried. Before his trial, senior military officials with responsibility for political trials had publicly implied his guilt. He was reported to have been convicted on the basis of witnesses' statements obtained by coercion. A witness who alleged that he had been forced to make a statement by interrogators was prevented from testifying about this by the court.

Torture and ill-treatment of political detainees and criminal suspects were widespread and reportedly caused several deaths. In East Timor, scores of people were beaten by security forces during peaceful pro-independence demonstrations or were detained without charge and tortured or ill-treated in custody. Donaciano da Costa Gomes was one of several young people detained for over two weeks after peaceful demonstrations in Dili in January. He said that he and other detainees had been tortured with electric shocks, immersed for long periods in fetid water, kicked, punched, slashed with knives and hung from the ceiling.

Members of the police and police auxiliary forces beat or tortured criminal suspects to extract confessions, sometimes causing serious injury or death. Cecep Suherman, a boy of 13, died after being clubbed on the head and kicked in the chest by two police auxiliaries at a Jakarta recreation park in June. The police authorities originally said that he might have died as a result of a fall but according to four eye-witnesses, the dead boy and at least two of his friends had been beaten for entering the park without paying. The two police auxiliaries allegedly responsible were brought to trial and sentenced to three years' imprisonment.

Dozens of other police and military personnel were also tried for torturing or ill-treating criminal suspects. Some were convicted but generally received short prison sentences. In March, 12 Semarang city police officers were convicted by a military court of torturing three young criminal suspects, one of whom died of his injuries within hours. Witnesses testified that 10 of the police officers had taken turns to kick and beat their victims on the head and body with lengths of wood, an iron pipe and a police helmet for over eight hours. They were jailed for between 15 days and one year.

Extrajudicial executions by government forces and paramilitary groups backed by local military commanders were reported in East Timor, Irian Jaya and Aceh. In some cases, victims were tortured and ill-treated before being killed. In March Candido Amaral, a father of five, was detained by members of the Indonesian security forces in East Timor. He was said to have been kicked and punched during questioning about armed opposition activities and then had his genitals burned with cigarettes. The following day he was taken away and shot by firing-squad without any form of trial. The military authorities said that those responsible would be disciplined but it was not clear whether anyone had been brought to justice by the end of the year.

In Aceh, where government forces faced armed opposition from rebel forces who themselves committed acts of violence including murder, scores of people were reportedly victims of extrajudicial executions. From September onwards, villagers in parts of Aceh and North Sumatra discovered hundreds of corpses in shallow graves, ditches and rivers. Some were still blindfold with their hands and feet bound, and many bore signs of torture and had bullet wounds to the head. Government and military officials admitted killing more than 40 suspected rebels during the year, but said that the corpses were those of the victims of rebel attacks. However, human rights activists and local political and religious leaders said that some were the victims of extrajudicial killings by government troops and government-backed paramilitary forces.

Four elderly political prisoners – Satar Suryanto, Yohanes Surono, Simon Petrus Soleiman and Noor Rohayan – were executed by firing-squad in February, more than 20 years after being imprisoned for alleged involvement in the 1965 coup attempt. It was confirmed that two others – Mochtar Effendi bin Sirait and Tohong Harahap – who were accused of similar offences had been executed in October 1989. These executions brought the total number of death sentences carried out since 1985 to 28. Of these, 22 were "PKI" prisoners, four were Islamic activists and two had been convicted of murder.

Three people were sentenced to death for murder, bringing the number on death row to at least 29. Of these, eight were believed to be in imminent danger of execution: seven had been convicted of involvement in the 1965 coup attempt or of PKI membership; and one was an Islamic activist convicted of subversion in 1982. The death penalty was retained in a revised version of the Criminal Code proposed in October but not adopted by the end of the year.

Amnesty International appealed throughout the year for the release of prisoners of conscience and for a review of other cases involving unfair trials. The organization expressed concern about the detention, torture and ill-treatment of political detainees and peaceful protesters in Indonesia and East Timor. It expressed dismay at the execution of four political prisoners in February and urged the government to commute all outstanding death sentences.

In an oral statement to the United Nations (UN) Sub-Commission on Prevention of Discrimination and Protection of Minorities in August, Amnesty International included reference to its concerns in Indonesia. In a submission to the UN Special Committee on Decolonization in the same month, it drew attention to continued reports of extrajudicial executions and "disappearances" in East Timor and the emergence of a pattern of short-term detention, ill-treatment and torture of alleged political opponents of Indonesian rule in the territory.

In meetings with representatives of the Indonesian Government, Amnesty International reiterated its proposal, submitted in 1989, to visit Indonesia and East Timor. The government said that the proposal was still under consideration but there was no progress on this by the end of the year.

IRAN

Hundreds of people imprisoned for political reasons, including prisoners of conscience, remained in prison and hundreds more were detained during the year. Some were held indefinitely without charge or trial, others were sentenced to prison terms after unfair trials held *in camera* and in the absence of defence lawyers. Many arrests occurred after political demonstrations, or as a result of ethnic unrest. Torture and beatings of prisoners were widely reported, and some elderly and infirm prisoners of conscience were allegedly denied necessary medication. Over 750 people were executed after

being convicted of criminal offences, according to Iranian press reports, including at least 400 sentenced for alleged drug-trafficking. Many executions took place after summary trials. A number of government opponents resident abroad were believed to have been victims of extrajudicial executions carried out by Iranian Government agents.

The Special Representative of the United Nations (UN) Commission on Human Rights on the situation of human rights in the Islamic Republic of Iran was granted access to the country for the first time in January, and returned for a second visit in October. President Ali Akbar Hashemi Rafsanjani's government promised to provide detailed responses to specific allegations of abuse as requested by the Special Representative but had done so only partially by the end of the year. Information about the detention and treatment of political prisoners, particularly from more remote parts of the country, continued to be difficult to obtain because human rights groups were not allowed access to the country.

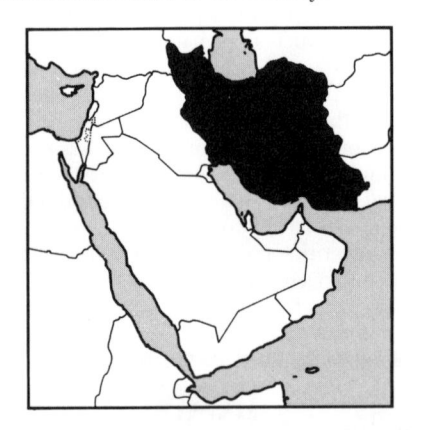

Approximately 100 women allegedly connected with two left-wing political parties, the Tudeh Party and the People's Fedaiyan Organization of Iran (Majority), were still held at Evin Prison, Tehran, at the beginning of 1990. They were arrested in 1983 just prior to the dissolution of the two political parties. Some were detained without charge or trial; others had been held for some years and then sentenced at secret summary trials. About half of those sentenced had completed their prison terms, but the authorities refused to release them until they agreed to sign prepared statements denouncing their former political activities, or, in some cases, those of their executed husbands. They had been tortured and, without exception, denied access to legal counsel.

About 50 of the women were granted unconditional temporary release from prison in August for an initial 10-day period, which some of them were able to extend. Most were forced to return to prison by the end of October.

Mariam Firouz, the former head of the Democratic Organization of Iranian Women and a prisoner of conscience aged over 70, was not among the women offered temporary release. However, she was visited by the UN Special Representative in October.

In June a number of signatories to an open letter to President Rafsanjani were arrested. The letter, signed by 90 people, criticized the lack of rights and freedoms in Iran as well as other aspects of government policy. The identities of more than 20 of those held became known but others may also have been arrested. Some of the detainees were members of the Association for the Defence of the Freedom and Sovereignty of the Iranian Nation (ADFSIN), led by the first prime minister of the Islamic Republic, Mehdi Bazargan, who was not himself arrested. However, several former ministers in Mehdi Bazargan's short-lived 1979 government were among those detained, including 75-year-old Ali Ardalan, who suffers from chronic heart disease, and Nour Ali Tabandeh, who is over 70. At least 16 were still held without trial at the end of the year.

Some of those detained were beaten at the time of arrest, and there were persistent reports that they had been ill-treated in detention to make them confess in televised interviews to government allegations of espionage and counter-revolutionary activities. Some of the prisoners were reportedly denied necessary medication thereby further endangering their health.

In common with other political prisoners in Iran, these detainees were not permitted access to a lawyer, and they had no right to challenge the legality of their detention before a judicial authority. ADFSIN's stated aims and objectives made clear that its activities were aimed at upholding the rule of law and respect for the Constitution of the Islamic Republic. These detentions, and the banning of ADFSIN, restricted yet further the already narrow scope for legal political opposition to the government.

More than 50 supporters of the opposition group, the People's Mojahedine Organization of Iran (PMOI), were held in incommunicado detention. Their whereabouts were unknown and there had been no news of some of them since 1988.

Hundreds of other people were reportedly arrested following political demonstrations in various parts of the country. In February disturbances after the postponement of two football matches in Tehran turned into protests about government policy and clashes between demonstrators and police, resulting in the detention of scores of people. In April the official press reported the arrest of 65 people for taking part in a political demonstration in Mellat Park in north Tehran. Throughout the year there were reports of unrest in Kurdistan and Baluchistan resulting in the arrest of hundreds of people, some of whom may have been involved in armed attacks on members of the security forces, or smuggling. There were no reports of alleged participants in political demonstrations being brought to trial, and it is not known how many of those arrested remained in prison at the end of the year.

In March, 10 men were sentenced to death for spying for the United States of America (USA) in closed trials before Islamic Revolutionary Courts. They were arrested at the end of 1988, with no reason being given for their detention, and held incommunicado in Evin Prison until August 1989, when family visits were permitted. Confessions by the prisoners were reported in the press in November 1989. Three of the condemned prisoners were met by the UN Special Representative in October, but the fate of the other seven was not known.

Torture of prisoners in pre-trial detention continued, and arbitrary brutality towards convicted prisoners was common. One of the women prisoners of conscience released temporarily in August said that prisoners were beaten by the guards on the slightest pretext.

At least 12 people had the fingers of one hand amputated as judicially imposed punishments for repeated theft, and floggings were imposed for a wide variety of offences.

Former prisoners who had escaped from Iran to seek political asylum in Europe described the torture they had suffered during 1988 and 1989. One man, accused of having monarchist sympathies, described how, in 1989, he had been taken for execution in Qasr Prison, Tehran, with 10 other prisoners. He was blindfolded and forced to stand against a wall, and then heard gunshots. As he was being led away, he lifted his blindfold and saw that eight of the prisoners had been killed.

A man arrested in 1988 in Zahedan and suspected of activities for *Peykar*, a banned left-wing political organization, described how he had been taken to a detention centre, strapped to a bed face down, and beaten with whips and cables. He said that on one occasion an interrogator had held a pistol to his neck while another guard fired a pistol into the air.

A number of political opponents of the government were killed outside Iran in circumstances suggesting that they were the victims of extrajudicial executions carried out by Iranian Government agents. In April Dr Kazem Rajavi, a representative of the PMOI, was shot dead while driving near his home in Geneva. A Swiss judicial investigation revealed evidence that agents of the Iranian Government were directly involved in this killing. In August an Iranian Kurdish activist was found shot dead on the Konya to Ankara road in Turkey. It was alleged that Iranian Government agents may have carried out this killing, as well as a letter bomb attack in Sweden in September in which the wife of an Iranian Kurdish exile was killed. In October Sirous Elahi, a prominent member of the Flag of Freedom Organization, was found shot dead in his Paris apartment building, and Iranian Government involvement in the killing was alleged. Several other attempts on the lives of Iranian exiles were reported.

There were 757 executions of people convicted of criminal offences. Many of these executions took place in public, often after summary trials which failed to comply with international standards. More than 400 of the executions were for drug-trafficking; over 100 of these took place in a two-week period in September when an intensification of the long-running anti-narcotics campaign, including further proposals to speed up the punishment of offenders, was announced.

It was not possible to estimate the number of political executions which routinely took place in secret. It was alleged that among those executed for criminal offences were a number of political opponents falsely accused of involvement in criminal activity. For example, Dr Sepah Mansour, executed in January in Karaj, was said to have been falsely accused of drug-trafficking, and to have been killed because of his opposition to the government.

In December a Christian pastor, the Reverend Hossein Soodmand, was executed in Mashhad apparently on charges of apostasy, punishable by death under the Islamic Penal Code of Iran. He had converted to Christianity from Islam more than 20 years ago.

In May the Islamic Consultative Assembly passed a new law extending the death penalty to offences such as profiteering and food-hoarding, described as "economic terrorism". This new law, which was seen as a political attack on influential *bazaari* merchants, was blocked because of an objection from the Council of Guardians, which is empowered to veto parliamentary decisions which it finds incompatible with Islamic principles.

Four men accused of rape of minors were beheaded, and at least six people were stoned to death. One man was put to death by being thrown from a precipice. Kazem Shirafkan, aged 17, was executed in Mashhad for the murder of a 10-year-old boy.

Amnesty International campaigned throughout the year for an end to executions in Iran, expressing particular concern about the very large number of executions and the lack of procedural safeguards for defendants facing charges punishable by death.

In February Amnesty International submitted a written statement to the UN Commission on Human Rights which drew particular attention to its concerns about the death penalty and torture.

In August Amnesty International made reference to the execution of minors in Iran in an oral statement to the UN Sub-Commission on Prevention of Discrimination and Protection of Minorities.

In April Amnesty International wrote to President Rafsanjani asking to be informed of the reasons for the arrest of 65 people in Mellat Park in Tehran, and seeking further information on their situation. The letter also sought information about other reported arrests, but no reply was received.

Amnesty International also pressed for the release of all prisoners of conscience and for fair trials for all political prisoners. In May it publicized the plight of the women prisoners from left-wing opposition groups imprisoned since 1983, eight of whom it named as prisoners of conscience. Amnesty International made renewed appeals in August following the imprisonment of more than 20 prisoners of conscience for criticizing the lack of rights and freedoms in Iran, and expressed particular concern about their torture and ill-treatment. The organization wrote to Ayatollah Yazdi, the Head of the Judiciary, about its wish to send a delegation to observe the trial of these prisoners, but there was no response and no indication from the authorities as to when the trial might take place.

In June Amnesty International wrote to President Rafsanjani expressing its deep concern at the preliminary conclusions reached by a Swiss judge investigating the killing of Dr Kazem Rajavi which indicated "the direct involvement...of one or more official Iranian services". Amnesty International expressed its unreserved opposition to extrajudicial executions and sought urgent clarification of the role of the Iranian authorities in Dr Kazem Rajavi's killing. No reply was received.

In December Amnesty International published a major report, *Iran: Violations of Human Rights 1987-1990*, which contained detailed information about torture, executions and political imprisonment, and criticized the Iranian authorities' failure to halt persistent gross violations of human rights.

IRAQ AND OCCUPIED KUWAIT

Thousands of political prisoners, including prisoners of conscience, were detained without charge or trial or imprisoned after unfair trials. Some of them had been detained in Iraq in 1990 or previous years but thousands of others, including Iraqi exiles, foreign nationals and Kuwaitis, were imprisoned after Iraq's invasion of Kuwait on 2 August. Torture of prisoners was routine and widespread. Hundreds of people, including Iraqi refugees who returned to Iraq under official amnesties and Kuwaitis detained after the invasion, reportedly "disappeared" in custody.

There were hundreds of extrajudicial executions: the victims included Kurdish opponents of the Iraqi Government and Kuwaiti opponents of Iraq's occupation, including children. Two people were executed after unfair trials. It was not clear whether other executions were preceded by any judicial proceedings.

On 2 August Iraqi troops invaded Kuwait, and on 8 August it was annexed as Iraq's 19th province. On 3 August the United Nations (UN) Security Council passed a resolution imposing economic sanctions on Iraq and demanding the immediate withdrawal of Iraqi troops from Kuwait. At the end of the year, Iraqi troops remained in Kuwait, despite nine other Security Council resolutions calling for withdrawal and for the restoration of the sovereignty of Kuwait.

In March a general amnesty was declared for all Iraqi Kurdish government opponents living abroad. Initially valid for two months, the amnesty was extended until 11 July. Between April and June, some 2,900 Iraqi Kurds, Assyrians and Turcomans reportedly returned from Turkey to Iraq under the amnesty. However, there was no independent international monitoring of the return process, and many refugees were reportedly coerced into returning (see **Turkey**). Scores of returning Iraqi Kurds were arrested and later "disappeared", and others, including four Turcomans, were reportedly executed. In December another general amnesty was declared for all Iraqi government opponents living abroad and army deserters.

Thousands of political prisoners, including possible prisoners of conscience, remained in detention without charge or trial, or were serving prison sentences imposed after unfair trials; hundreds of others were detained for political reasons during the year. They included suspected members of prohibited political parties, such as the Kurdistan Democratic Party (KDP); the Patriotic Union of Kurdistan (PUK); the Iraqi Communist Party (ICP); and *al-Da'wa al-Islamiyya,* the Islamic Call. Relatives of suspected government opponents, including children, continued to be imprisoned while the authorities sought the suspects.

Two people were executed after unfair trials, from which there was no right of appeal. Farzad Bazoft, a British-based Iranian journalist arrested in September 1989 (see *Amnesty International Report 1990*) and convicted with two others of espionage by the Revolutionary Court, was sentenced to death and executed in March. One of his co-defendants, British nurse Daphne Parish, was sentenced to 15 years' imprisonment but pardoned by President Saddam Hussein in July and released. The third defendant, an unnamed Iraqi national, received a 10-year prison sentence. On 13 July an Iraqi with Swedish citizenship, Jalil Mahdi Saleh al-Nu'aimi, was executed by hanging. He had been convicted of espionage by the Revolutionary Court and sentenced to death on 30 April.

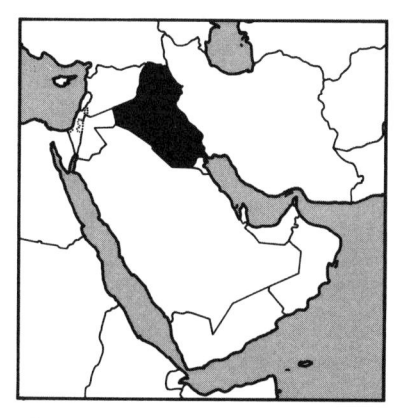

There were new reports of "disappearances" of government opponents. One, a KDP member sentenced to death *in absentia* in 1988, "disappeared" after he was extradited from Turkey to Iraq in May, despite having been recognized as a refugee by the United Nations High Commissioner for Refugees (UNHCR). Reports suggested that he was executed following a trial in June.

The fate and whereabouts of thousands of other prisoners who "disappeared" in previous years also remained unknown. Among them were 353 Kurds who "disappeared" in custody in August 1988, and 33 Assyrian Christians and a number of Kurds who "disappeared" following their return from camps in Turkey and Iran in 1988 and 1989 under official amnesties (see *Amnesty International Report 1990*).

Hundreds of people were reportedly executed, although in most cases it was difficult to determine whether they had received any form of trial. Among them were 23 Iraqi Kurds who were executed in the Shahrazar region of northern Iraq between December 1989 and February 1990. They were reportedly arrested following anti-government demonstrations and held at a military camp in the city of Khurmal prior to their execution.

In February Amnesty International received reports that large numbers of people, including unarmed civilians and army deserters, were killed or wounded following armed incursions by government forces in southern Iraq between 10 and 21 January. Troops were said to have attacked more than 30 towns and villages in the predominantly Shi'a provinces in the south.

Following the invasion of Kuwait on 2 August, thousands of people were reportedly arrested there by Iraqi forces, and either detained in Kuwait or taken to prisons in Iraq. They included Iraqi exiles suspected of having links with *al-Da'wa al-Islamiyya*: membership of this organization carries the death penalty in Iraq. Hundreds of Kuwaitis, including children, were also arrested, as were former members of parliament, civil servants and students. Many of them were prisoners of conscience, held for their peaceful opposition to the Iraqi occupation. Some were soon released, but hundreds, possibly thousands, were believed still held at the end of the year.

Hundreds of foreign nationals were also detained. Some were held at military and industrial installations in Iraq and Kuwait as so-called "human shields", but all were believed to have been released by the end of 1990.

According to the testimonies of former detainees, torture was routine and widespread. The methods used reportedly included prolonged beating all over the body, breaking of limbs, extinguishing cigarettes on the body and in the eyes, gouging out of the eyes, electric shocks, sexual assault and mock executions. The majority of victims were Kuwaiti males, among them minors as young as 13. Rape victims were said to include women and young men. A 17-year-old Kuwaiti student arrested in September and held for one month in Kuwait City and Basra alleged that he was severely kicked and beaten, subjected to *falaqa* (beating on the soles of the feet) for prolonged periods, had electric shocks applied to his chest until he lost consciousness, had his skin pierced with pins, was threatened with the insertion of a bottle into his anus and was subjected to mock execution. Most victims said their torturers sought information about those opposing the Iraqi occupation. Some detainees reportedly died under torture and had their bodies dumped in the street or outside their homes.

Scores of Kuwaitis reportedly "disappeared" following arrest; it was feared that many were extrajudicially executed. Relatives who inquired about them were in some cases themselves arrested and tortured.

In August Iraq's Revolutionary Command Council (RCC) introduced the death penalty for looting, hoarding food for commercial purposes and harbouring Western nationals. A man said to be an Iraqi soldier was executed by firing-squad. His body was publicly displayed in Kuwait City on 16 August: he was said to have been convicted of looting. Ten others, including Kuwaiti, Syrian, Egyptian and Iraqi nationals, were executed for the same offence later in August and seven more were publicly hanged in November. It was not known whether any of them had received a trial.

Iraqi troops were said to have deliberately killed hundreds of unarmed civilians. According to eye-witnesses, Kuwaiti men and young boys were shot in the head at close range, often in front of their families. Many had already been detained and tortured. Some were killed after being found in possession of opposition literature, the Kuwaiti flag or photographs of the Amir of Kuwait. Others were reportedly killed for refusing to display photographs of President Saddam Hussein. According to medical personnel working in hospitals in Kuwait, scores of bodies of young men were brought in off the streets; many of them had been shot in the head or heart at close range. Some of the bodies were mutilated and bore marks of torture. A Kuwaiti woman and two youths aged 13 and 16 were reportedly shot dead after Iraqi troops fired without warning on a peaceful demonstration in the Jabiriyya district of Kuwait City of 8 August. On 9 September, five employees of al-'Addan Hospital were summarily executed for allegedly neglecting an injured Iraqi officer who was brought in for treatment but died subsequently. Patients were also said to have died after Iraqi troops forcibly removed them from life-support machines at hospitals in Kuwait City.

Some 120 Iraqi soldiers and officers were reportedly executed in early August for allegedly refusing to take part in the invasion of Kuwait. Amnesty International received the names of some of those reportedly killed, including Major General Kamal 'Abd al-Sattar and air force Brigadier Saleh Muhammad Jaber. Reports were also received of the execution of Iraqi army deserters following the invasion of Kuwait.

Amnesty International continued throughout the year to call for the release of prisoners of conscience, for the fair trial or release of other political prisoners detained without trial or after unfair trials, and for urgent government action to halt torture and ill-treatment and to account for the "disappeared". Amnesty International also campaigned against the death penalty, and called for the commutation of all death sentences, including that imposed on Farzad Bazoft after a grossly unfair trial, and for an end to extrajudicial executions. Amnesty International expressed particular concern to the government in January about reported mass killings of unarmed civilians and army deserters by government forces in southern Iraq. In May the organization called for full human rights protection for more than 2,500 returning Kurdish refugees in view of past reports of "disappearances" and the lack of independent international monitoring of the return program. In June Amnesty International published a report, *Iraqi Kurds: At Risk of Forcible Repatriation from Turkey and Human Rights Violations in Iraq*, which drew attention to these concerns. In response to the report, the Iraqi Government stated that "refugees – on their return to Iraq – will be free to reside in their original areas or wherever they may wish..."

Following the invasion of Kuwait, Amnesty International expressed grave concern about the arrests there of Iraqi exiles, many of whom were taken to Iraq, and the imprisonment of all those detained for political reasons. Amnesty International called publicly on the Iraqi Government to end the gross human rights violations – torture, "disappearances" and executions – committed by its forces in Kuwait. In December Amnesty International documented these violations in a major report, *Iraq/Occupied Kuwait: Human Rights Violations Since 2 August*, and repeated its call for an immediate end to human rights violations. The government denied violating human rights and rejected Amnesty International's findings.

In an oral statement delivered to the UN Commission on Human Rights in February, Amnesty International drew attention to its concerns in Iraq. After the Commission had rejected a resolution calling for a Special Rapporteur to be appointed to study Iraq's human rights record, Amnesty International issued a statement saying that it was deeply disturbed at the decision of the UN's central human rights body to take no action on the systematic and wide-ranging abuses in Iraq.

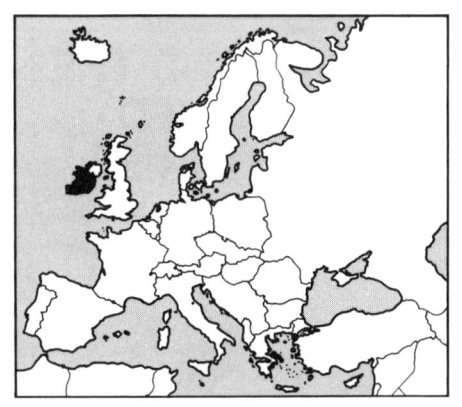

IRELAND
(REPUBLIC OF)

The death penalty was abolished in July: no execution had taken place since 1954. A former prisoner was prevented from raising his allegations of ill-treatment in custody in a civil action against the state.

Parliament passed a law abolishing the death penalty in June; the law was signed by the President on 13 July and became effective immediately.

The High Court ruled in March that Osgur Breatnach could not raise his allegations of police assault in civil proceedings because of the criminal court's ruling in 1978 that he had not been ill-treated. Osgur Breatnach, Nicky Kelly and Brian McNally had been convicted in 1978 of involvement in the 1976 Sallins mail train robbery solely on the basis of confessions allegedly obtained by ill-treatment during incommunicado detention. The Court of Criminal Appeal in 1980 ruled that the confessions of Osgur Breatnach and Brian McNally had been involuntary and quashed their sentences. Nicky Kelly was released on "humanitarian grounds" in 1984.

All three have attempted to bring civil actions for damages against the state (see *Amnesty International Report 1990*). Nicky Kelly was prevented from proceeding with his civil action in 1986; no decision has yet been reached on whether to allow Brian McNally's action.

Amnesty International was concerned that Osgur Breatnach and Nicky Kelly appeared to have been prevented from having their claims of police ill-treatment fully and impartially investigated. The organization urged the government to establish an independent inquiry into all the allegations of ill-treatment in custody made in connection with the 1976 Sallins mail train robbery, and to make the findings public.

ISRAEL AND THE OCCUPIED TERRITORIES

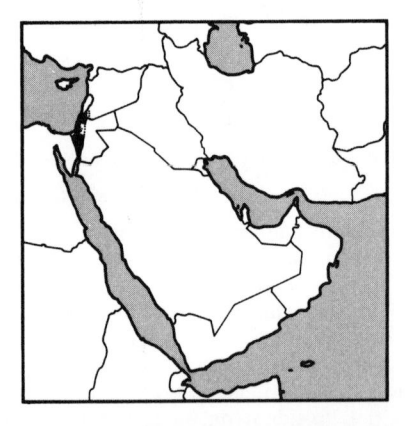

Some 25,000 Palestinians, including prisoners of conscience, were arrested in connection with the *intifada* (uprising) in the Occupied Territories. Over 4,000 were administratively detained without charge or trial, and thousands of others were tried by military courts. By the end of the year about 13,000 were still detained or imprisoned. Dozens of Israelis, including Druze and Jewish objectors to military service, were imprisoned as prisoners of conscience. Thousands of Palestinians were punitively beaten or otherwise tortured or ill-treated. About 120 Palestinians, including children, were shot dead by Israeli forces, often in circumstances suggesting unjustifiable killings. Israeli soldiers misused tear-gas, endangering lives. Investigations into abuses and related prosecutions appeared to be inadequate. One person remained under sentence of death.

Palestinians in the West Bank and Gaza Strip continued to protest at the Israeli occupation. They organized regular strikes and demonstrations. Young people, often masked, frequently attacked Israeli soldiers and sometimes Israeli civilians, mainly with stones or petrol bombs. Some Israelis were stabbed to death. A dozen Israeli civilians and members of the security forces were killed in such attacks. Some 150 Palestinians were killed apparently by other Palestinians, the vast majority on suspicion of collaborating with the Israeli authorities.

The Israeli authorities responded to disturbances with widespread arrests and restrictions of movement. They also used excessive or indiscriminate force. They closed educational institutions, imposed prolonged curfews and closed off areas to outside observers as military zones. They also demolished or sealed houses as a form of punishment.

Over 4,000 Palestinians were held in administrative detention for renewable periods of up to one year. A two-step process of judicial review of detention orders was available, but appeals by detainees took place weeks, sometimes months, after arrest. In almost every case, detainees and their lawyers were not provided with crucial information about the reasons for their detention. With few exceptions, appeals resulted in confirmation of the original detention order or slight reductions in detention periods. Almost all administrative detainees were held in the Ketziot detention camp in the Negev desert in Israel. Despite improvements in accommodation facilities, conditions in the camp remained harsh, particularly as detainees did not receive visits from relatives.

Among the administrative detainees were prisoners of conscience. They included three human rights fieldworkers: Sha'wan Jabarin and Iyad Haddad were released in September and December after 11 months and two and a half months in detention respectively; Wafiq Abu Siddu was served with a six-month detention order in November, reduced on appeal to four and a half months. Other political detainees included Radwan Abu 'Ayyash and Ziad Abu Zayyad, two journalists served with six-month orders in November, and Dr Ahmad al-Yazji, a surgeon served with a one-year order in November.

Israeli prisoners of conscience included Michel Warschawsky, head of the Alternative Information Centre, who was imprisoned between July and November for agreeing to typeset a booklet without adequately checking its legality according to Israeli law. The booklet was issued by the Popular Front for the Liberation of Palestine and advised on how to withstand interrogation.

Two Israeli prisoners of conscience imprisoned in 1989 were released when their sentences expired. Abie Nathan, an Israeli peace campaigner, was released in February but was charged again for having met officials of the Palestine Liberation Organization (PLO) during the year. Yacov Ben Efrat, a political activist, was released in October (see *Amnesty International Report 1990*). Trial proceedings initiated in previous years against 12 Israelis accused of unauthorized contacts with the PLO continued, but had not been completed by the end of the year.

Other prisoners of conscience released during the year included Hamzi Smeidi, a Palestinian journalist sentenced in January to 15 months of actual imprisonment. He was found guilty of drafting non-violent parts of a leaflet issued by the clandestine Unified National Leadership of the *intifada*. He was released in June.

Dozens of Israeli Druze were imprisoned for several months for refusing to perform military service on grounds of conscience. 'Urwa Salim served a total of over nine months in prison between 1988 and 1990. Fu'ad Humayd was imprisoned for 45 days in May and June for refusing to do reserve duty in a prison containing Palestinian political prisoners. Some 46 Israeli Jews served periods of imprisonment of up to 35 days for refusing to perform certain types of military service, such as duties in the Occupied Territories. Nir Keinan, a career officer, was imprisoned for 35 days after refusing to serve in the Gaza Strip. He was released in November and was dismissed from the army. Amnesty International considers such objectors to be prisoners of conscience.

Thousands of Palestinians faced trial by military courts, most charged with violent offences such as throwing stones or petrol bombs. After being arrested, they could be held for 18 days before being presented to a judge. Many were denied access to lawyers and family for much longer periods. Confessions allegedly extracted during incommunicado detention were often the primary evidence against them. Those contesting charges faced delays which could postpone trials for months and sometimes years. Bail was rarely granted and many pleaded guilty in order to avoid periods of pre-trial detention which would exceed likely sentences. The much heavier sentences imposed on those convicted after trial also reportedly deterred many from contesting charges.

The systematic use of ill-treatment during interrogation was widespread and there were reports of punitive beatings immediately after arrest and of torture. Methods included beatings with truncheons and rifle butts; hooding with dirty sacks; sleep deprivation by prolonged shackling in contorted positions; confinement in small, darkened cells often referred to as "closets"; and squeezing of testicles. Riad Shehabi, a shop-owner in Jerusalem arrested on suspicion of throwing stones, was severely beaten in July while in police custody. 'Abd al-Ra'uf Ghabin, a journalist, was held incommunicado for over three weeks in September. During this time he was allegedly deprived of sleep and beaten on his head, genitals and other parts of his body. In May Ghaleb Zallum died apparently as a result of beatings by soldiers after he refused to clear a road of stones in Hebron (al-Khalil).

Mordechai Vanunu, an Israeli former nuclear technician, continued to serve his 18-year prison sentence in solitary confinement with severely restricted access to visitors (see *Amnesty International Reports 1988* to *1990*).

About 120 Palestinians, including children and young people, were shot dead by Israeli forces using live ammunition and special types of plastic and other bullets. Firearms continued to be used as a common means of riot control under official guidelines which appeared inconsistent with the internationally recognized principles of necessity and proportionality in the use of force. Many resulting killings seemed unjustifiable. In October at least 17 Palestinians were shot dead by police at the Haram al-Sharif (Temple Mount) in

Jerusalem during a riot. An official commission of investigation found that the shootings were justified by a life-threatening situation, although it also established that at some point firing was indiscriminate and that two nurses were injured when an ambulance attending the wounded was shot at. Reports from local human rights groups and other sources suggested that many of the victims died as a result of the indiscriminate and unjustifiable use of firearms. A judicial inquest into these killings was also initiated and was continuing at the end of the year.

There were reports of Israeli soldiers possibly deliberately misusing tear-gas, which can be lethal in confined spaces. Scores of babies needed urgent treatment after tear-gas canisters were thrown into a Gaza maternity clinic in June and into the infant ward of Makassed Hospital in October. A soldier received a 10-day prison sentence in connection with the incident in Gaza. A few elderly or very young Palestinians reportedly died after exposure to tear-gas in confined spaces.

Several soldiers and police officers were convicted or disciplined for offences related to the *intifada* during the year. Investigations were mostly conducted internally by the police or armed forces and took a long time to conclude. In October one soldier was sentenced to two months of actual imprisonment and three received suspended sentences of up to five months for having beaten two Palestinians in their custody in February 1988. One of the victims, Iyad 'Aql, died after the assault. One soldier was reportedly sentenced to three months of actual imprisonment and two others to prison sentences of 14 and 28 days in connection with the torture of Sha'wan Jabarin (see *Amnesty International Report 1990*). In June a soldier was sentenced to four months of "unpleasant" work at a military base for having shot dead in June 1988 'Abd al-Ra'uf Hamed, who was apparently fleeing arrest. Another soldier was reportedly sentenced to one month's imprisonment for the killing in August 1989 of Yaser Abu Ghawsh (see *Amnesty International Report 1990*). The official investigation established that the treatment of the victim after he had been shot, when a doctor was reportedly prevented from giving aid, was "inappropriate under the circumstances".

John Demjanjuk, convicted in 1988 of offences including crimes against humanity, remained under sentence of death. His appeal proceedings before the Supreme Court began in May and continued during the year.

Amnesty International called for the release of prisoners of conscience and for administrative detainees to be released unless they were given an adequate opportunity to challenge their detention. It also appealed on behalf of victims of torture or ill-treatment. In January Amnesty International published a report, *Israel and the Occupied Territories: Killings by Israeli Forces*. The report said that existing guidelines for the use of firearms, as well as the pattern of killings and subsequent investigations, suggested that the Israeli authorities were effectively condoning if not encouraging extrajudicial executions as a means of controlling unrest. After the killings in Jerusalem in October, it called for an independent judicial inquiry to investigate the incident and to review official guidelines on opening fire and methods of riot control.

In January Amnesty International submitted a written statement to the United Nations (UN) Commission on Human Rights about human rights violations in the Occupied Territories. In August it drew attention to its concerns about administrative detention to the UN Sub-Commission on Prevention of Discrimination and Protection of Minorities.

Amnesty International delegates visited the country in July and October. They met several civilian and military officials and observed administrative detention hearings and military court trials.

The Israeli authorities told Amnesty International that every administrative detention order was based on reliable information, although reasons of security precluded disclosure of sources. They stressed violent aspects of the *intifada*, arguing that Israel's response had been proportionate in that context. They said that some soldiers had understood orders issued in early 1988 on the use of nightsticks as authorizing "excessive force, including the use of force as a punitive or deterrent measure", but that this had been redressed and offenders punished. The authorities also said that the decision to impose solitary confinement on Mordechai Vanunu was found to be reasonable by the Israeli judiciary.

Amnesty International received replies on six cases of fatal shootings by Israeli forces which were among those submitted to the authorities in 1989. The official version of events was sometimes inconsistent with the allegations which Amnesty International had received. Nevertheless, in five of the six cases official investigations had established that the guidelines for opening fire had been violated. In one case a soldier was charged with causing death by negligence; in two cases soldiers were charged with illegal use of arms; and in two others soldiers were reprimanded or censured.

ITALY

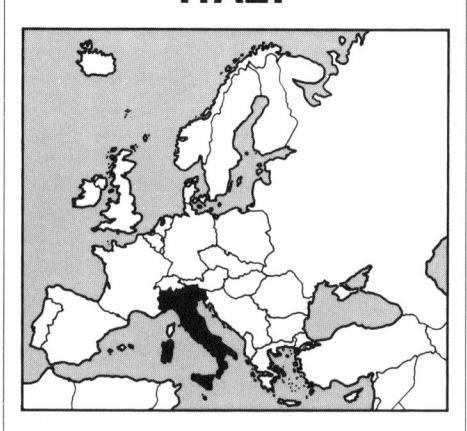

Reports of ill-treatment in prisons and police custody continued. Excessive delays were reported in the investigation and judgment of a number of such allegations made in previous years. Several trials involving law-enforcement agents and prison guards accused of torture and ill-treatment resulted in suspended prison sentences or amnesties.

A draft law on conscientious objection to military service, replacing existing legislation and pending final parliamentary approval since April 1989, had still not been introduced (see *Amnesty International Report 1990*).

International standards requiring trial within a reasonable time had been breached in a number of cases during the 1980s and, despite the introduction of a new code of penal procedure in October 1989 (see *Amnesty International Report 1990*), the criminal justice system continued to be criticized for being slow and inefficient. There were reported difficulties in implementing the new code and the government was criticized for making inadequate provision for essential structural and administrative reforms.

No progress was reported in the preparation of legislation to abolish the death penalty from the Wartime Military Penal Code and thus for all offences under Italian law, as requested by the Chamber of Deputies in August 1989.

In February Italy signed the Second Optional Protocol to the International Covenant on Civil and Political Rights Aiming at the Abolition of the Death Penalty. It had not yet been ratified by the end of the year.

Reports of the ill-treatment of prisoners continued. On 30 January around 20 prisoners in Novara Maximum Security Prison attempted to remain in the exercise yard for an extra 30 minutes, in protest at disciplinary action taken against a fellow prisoner. It was alleged that when they refused to disperse, water hoses were turned on them and about 80 guards attacked them with truncheons and iron bars. Some of the prisoners were reportedly beaten after they had been knocked to the ground. It was claimed that a number of prisoners were beaten again during transfer to the prison infirmary and that at least two prisoners, Nicola De Maria and Bruno Ghirardi, were also beaten the next morning. Nicola De Maria's lawyer visited the prison on 2 February and, after interviewing some of the prisoners and receiving reports about the physical condition of others, he submitted a written complaint to the Novara Public Prosecutor's office. He estimated that between 10 and 15 prisoners had suffered fractured bones during the disturbances, and that a similar number had required treatment for head wounds. Judicial and administrative inquiries were opened into the incidents but no results had been published by the end of the year.

Several criminal prosecutions opened in previous years in connection with the alleged torture and ill-treatment of prisoners were concluded, some after long delays.

In May, nearly five years after Salvatore Marino's death in a Palermo police station in August 1985, the verdicts were announced in the trial of 15 law-enforcement agents charged with participating in involuntary homicide (see *Amnesty International Reports 1986* to *1990*). A forensic report established that Salvatore Marino had been forced to swallow large quantities of salt water and had sustained numerous injuries all over his body. The court found 10 defendants guilty of the lesser offence of manslaughter, and sentenced them to two years' suspended imprisonment and a two-year suspended prohibition on holding state employment. The charge against two other defendants was reduced to "causing involuntary physical injury", qualifying them for an immediate amnesty. The remaining three defendants were acquitted. The public prosecutor appealed against the verdicts.

A number of judicial inquiries opened in previous years into allegations of ill-treatment in police custody remained unresolved (see *Amnesty International Reports 1987* to *1990*). No progress was reported in an inquiry into the alleged ill-treatment of at least 47 detainees in Milan in 1988 nor in an investigation into around 30 such cases opened in Naples in 1986. However, according to unconfirmed reports, criminal proceedings brought against a *carabinieri* officer who shot and injured 15-year-old Antonio Leone in a Naples police station in July 1988 ended in an amnesty (see *Amnesty International Report 1989*).

The judicial investigation into the case of three police officers accused of ill-treating Francesco Badano in a Padua police station in May 1988 ended in April 1990 (see *Amnesty International Report 1989*). The police had stated that Francesco Badano's various injuries were attributable to a violent struggle at the time of arrest, but forensic reports concluded that injuries to the soles of his feet could not have been incurred in this way. Francesco Badano was transferred to Padua hospital the evening of his arrest to receive urgent treatment for his injuries. An autopsy concluded that the circumstances of his death in the maximum security wing the following morning were consistent with suicide. The investigating magistrate considered it "reasonably proven" that Francesco Badano had been physically ill-treated while in police custody but stated that it had not been possible to collect sufficient evidence to prove that the accused officers were those responsible; they could not, therefore, be committed for trial. The magistrate also commented on the lack of cooperation shown by other police officers interviewed about the case. However, no administrative inquiry appeared to have been opened into Francesco Badano's treatment in police custody.

Administrative inquiries into allegations of ill-treatment, if opened, rarely resulted in disciplinary proceedings against those responsible, even when the ill-treatment had been judicially proven.

There were claims that immigrants, particularly those of North African origin, were frequently subjected to ill-treatment by law-enforcement agents but that they rarely made formal complaints because they feared police harassment, further ill-treatment or counter-charges of calumny. As a result it was difficult to assess the number of such cases.

Amnesty International continued to seek information from the government and other sources on the steps taken to investigate allegations of ill-treatment. It expressed concern about the lack of progress in a number of judicial and administrative inquiries opened into such allegations in previous years. Amnesty International pressed the authorities to make further efforts to identify those responsible for Francesco Badano's treatment in police custody. The organization also investigated cases where charges of calumny were brought against detainees, apparently without full investigation of their original complaints.

JAMAICA

Nineteen people were known to have been sentenced to death for murder, at least one of whom was under 18 at the time of the crime. Over 250 prisoners were under sentence of death at the end of the year. No executions were carried out; the last executions took place in February 1988. The Human Rights Committee adopted the view that there had been violations of the International Covenant on Civil and Political Rights (ICCPR) in the case of a prisoner under sentence of death. Three prisoners died during a prison riot, allegedly as a result of ill-treatment by prison officials.

Jamaica's Minister of Justice told Parliament in June that consideration was being given to commuting the death sentences of certain categories of prisoners, but no decision had been taken by the end of 1990. In November an opposition senator tabled a motion calling on the government to ratify the Second Optional Protocol to the ICCPR Aiming at the Abolition of the Death Penalty.

Adrian Campbell, sentenced to death for murder in February, was under 18 at the time the crime was committed; international standards and Jamaica's Constitution forbid sentencing minors to death. His co-defendants, Barrington Clarke and Conrad Henricks, were reportedly 18 at the time of sentencing and therefore may also have been under 18 in June 1989 when the murder took place. All three remained on death row at the end of the year.

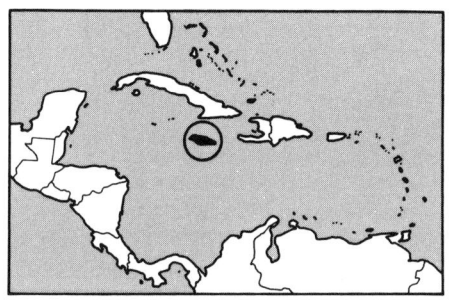

In July the Human Rights Committee, which supervises implementation of the ICCPR, held that Jamaica had violated its treaty obligations under the Covenant in the case of death row prisoner Carlton Reid. It expressed the view that he was "entitled to a remedy entailing his release". The Committee found a violation of Article 14(3)(b) because the court failed to grant defence counsel sufficient time to prepare his examination of witnesses, and a violation of Article 14(3)(d) because Carlton Reid had been denied effective representation at the appeal proceedings. The Committee also concluded that Article 6 of the Covenant (the right to life) had been violated since a death sentence had been imposed after judicial proceedings which fell short of international standards. Carlton Reid was still on death row at the end of the year.

Earl Pratt and Ivan Morgan remained on death row despite the fact that in April 1989 the Human Rights Committee had expressed the view that their sentences should be commuted (see *Amnesty International Reports 1989* and *1990*).

Three death row inmates died during attempts by police and soldiers to end disturbances at St Catherine's Adult Correctional Centre on 28 May. The increasing number of prisoners on death row had created serious overcrowding. Tension had further increased among death row inmates following a statement by the Minister of National Security in early May, expressing his personal support for the resumption of executions. The riot reportedly broke out after prison warders stopped work to protest against low wages and poor working conditions. As a result, they did not open cells or provide morning meals for inmates. Prisoners in the death row and general population areas broke their cell locks and some of them set fire to unused materials in a store room. Warders reportedly later ordered prisoners to leave their cells, made them strip, and beat them with batons and guns. Tear-gas was also used to subdue the prisoners. The riot lasted for about one hour.

The results of the autopsy performed on the three dead prisoners were not made public, but reports allegedly emanating from hospital workers said that Calvin Green and Paul Grey died as a result of haemorrhaging caused by blows to the head and other parts of the body. Warders reportedly tear-gassed Denny Wilson in his cell, sprayed him with high pressure water, and then took him out of his cell and beat him to death. Injured prisoners were allegedly not given prompt medical attention; Anthony Bernard had his jaw broken as a result of being beaten by warders and allegedly did not receive prompt medical care. Prisoners were denied visits for about one week after the disturbance. An investigation was reported to have been started by the Corrections Department and the Police Department but there had been no public report of their findings by the end of the year.

Five warders charged with murder for the killing of a prisoner beaten to death at the Gun Court Rehabilitation Centre in July 1988 (see *Amnesty International Reports 1989* and *1990*) went on trial in July; three were convicted of manslaughter and sentenced to nine years in prison; two were released.

Amnesty International expressed concern about the sentencing to death of Adrian Campbell in contravention of international standards and Jamaican law, and sought clarification about the ages, at the time of the crime, of his two co-defendants. Amnesty International called for the immediate commutation of the death sentences.

Amnesty International wrote to the authorities in June about the death of the three prisoners in the May prison riot, urging a full and impartial inquiry. It also expressed concern about the death of two prisoners at the General Penitentiary in July 1989 and one at St Catherine's Adult Correctional Centre in September 1989; they reportedly died from injuries inflicted by warders or members of the security forces brought in to quell disturbances at the prisons (see *Amnesty International Report 1990*). Amnesty International reiterated its view that the uncertainty of the situation of death row prisoners had led to growing tension and had had an adverse effect on both warders and prisoners; it urged the authorities to take steps towards commuting all death sentences. No replies had been received by the end of the year.

JAPAN

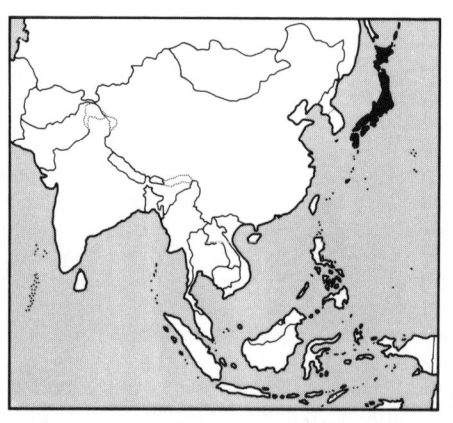

The Supreme Court upheld five death sentences but there were no executions. Two prisoners had their death sentences commuted on appeal and one other prisoner, who had been under sentence of death for 15 years, was acquitted after a retrial. There was concern about the lack of safeguards to prevent the ill-treatment of detainees.

Some 90 prisoners convicted of murder were believed to be under sentence of death. The Supreme Court had confirmed 36 of these sentences, five of them in 1990. No executions took place.

In February the Fukuoka High Court commuted the death sentence on Hika Masanao and in March the Tokyo High Court commuted the death sentence on Shinohara Shinichi. The courts stressed that the death penalty should be imposed only when unavoidable. Shimogami Norio, who had been sentenced to death for murder in 1975, was retried before the Nagoya High Court. In July the court acquitted him after finding that there was no material evidence to support his conviction for murder.

In April Amnesty International sent a memorandum to the government outlining its concerns about the use of the death penalty and about detention procedures in the light of claims by some detainees that they had been ill-treated during interrogation. Amnesty International urged the authorities to examine all allegations of ill-treatment – including cases publicized by the Japan Federation of Bar Associations – and to identify and eventually amend regulations and practices which could facilitate ill-treatment. Amnesty International urged the government to consider strengthening certain safeguards against ill-treatment, including prisoners' right of access to lawyers and the complaints procedure. It also urged it to review the policy of allowing prisoners to be detained in police holding cells instead of the normal detention centres administered by the Ministry of Justice. The Secretary General of Amnesty International discussed the memorandum with Justice Ministry officials during a visit to Japan in May and June. In September the ministry sent its written comments to Amnesty International pointing out, among other matters, that some restrictions on lawyers' meetings with their clients had recently been lifted. In its memorandum Amnesty International also urged the commutation of all death sentences and the abolition of the death penalty.

In April Amnesty International wrote to the Minister of Justice and to the Tokyo High Court about the case of Zhang Zhenhai, a Chinese national who had hijacked an aircraft to Japan in what he said was an attempt to avoid arrest in China for his political activities. His extradition was requested by the Chinese authorities but Amnesty International was concerned that if returned to China to face charges in connection with the hijacking, he could face additional charges in connection with his involvement in the pro-democracy protests in May and June 1989, for which some people had been summarily executed and others allegedly tortured or ill-treated. It urged the Japanese authorities to respect the internationally agreed principle of non-*refoulement* of individuals at risk of human rights violations. Zhang Zhenhai was extradited to China at the end of April after the Chinese authorities had given guarantees to their Japanese counterparts that he would not be charged with a capital offence or for his political activities. He was sentenced in July 1990 to eight years' imprisonment for hijacking.

JORDAN

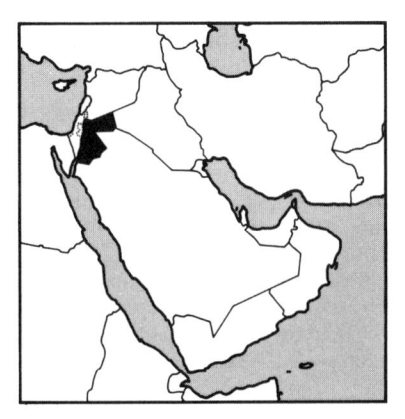

Dozens of real or suspected opponents of the government, including possible prisoners of conscience, were held in administrative detention without charge, trial or judicial review. At least 26 were sentenced to prison terms by the Martial Law Court, whose procedures did not satisfy international standards of fair trial. Thirty-six political prisoners sentenced by this court in previous years were released, but some 30 others remained in prison. There were reports of torture or ill-treatment of detainees. At least four people were executed.

The government undertook a major review of existing state of emergency and other legislation relevant to human rights. A new draft Defence Law which, if adopted, would replace the 1935 Defence Law, was presented to Parliament in June. The draft proposed that administrative detention orders be reviewable every 30 days by the High Court of Justice but retained provisions for the indefinite administrative detention of security suspects and lacked other legal safeguards. The draft was still under discussion at the end of the year.

In January and July new Martial Law Directives greatly reduced the jurisdiction of the Martial Law Court with a view to its abolition. However, the court continued to have jurisdiction over offences relating to membership of illegal associations, for which almost all political prisoners have been charged and sentenced. Martial law, declared in 1967 and officially "frozen" since December 1989, was still in force at the end of 1990.

In January the government also proposed the repeal of the 1953 Law of Resistance to Communism, which has been used to imprison prisoners of conscience. The proposal was still being discussed by Parliament at the end of 1990.

Dozens of real or suspected opponents of the government were arrested during the year and detained incommunicado under state of emergency legislation by the General Intelligence Department (GID) and other security agencies. Many were released within a short time of their arrest and included possible prisoners of conscience. Among them were known or suspected members of the Islamic *Hizb al-Tahrir fi al-Urdun*, Liberation Party in Jordan (LPJ), such as Sheikh Taher 'Abd al-Hamid al-Taher, a religious leader aged over 70. He was held incommunicado by the GID for almost three weeks in November apparently after he had spoken against the political system during a Friday sermon. Also detained was 'Abd al-Hamid al-Khalayfah, who was arrested in June apparently after he had publicly criticized the security forces' handling of riots in May. The riots were in protest at killings of Palestinians in the Israeli Occupied Territories. In August Samir Abu Hilalah was detained for six days by the Preventive Security, a wing of the security forces, apparently for his peaceful political activities; he had organized a debate on political issues in Ma'an.

At least 26 people, including possible prisoners of conscience, were sentenced to prison terms by the Martial Law Court. Bakr 'Abd al-Latif al-Khatib, who was arrested in March 1988, was sentenced early in 1990 to four years' imprisonment on charges of membership of an illegal association, the Popular Front for the Liberation of Palestine (PFLP), but he was pardoned and released in June. Twenty-five others were reportedly sentenced to six-month prison terms after being tried by the Martial Law Court in connection with the May riots. As in previous years, the Martial Law Court was not bound by the normal rules of judicial procedure and defendants were denied any right of appeal to a higher tribunal, contrary to international fair trial standards.

Thirty-six alleged members of illegal organizations who had been sentenced to prison terms by the Martial Law Court in previous years were released, 27 of them after an amnesty was declared in February. They included Kamal Khalil and Hasan Shahin, both alleged members of the PFLP arrested in 1988, and four alleged members of the LPJ, including Muhammad Khattab, who had been arrested in 1989. They were serving sentences of up to four years' imprisonment and may have been prisoners of conscience. Seven other prisoners serving sentences of up to life imprisonment for violent political offences were pardoned and released in November. Also freed were Munir 'Akrush, who was released in January shortly after starting a four-year sentence imposed under the Law of Resistance to Communism, and Brik al-Hadid, who was freed in September under a royal pardon. He had been arrested in 1978 and sentenced to death for his alleged involvement in a plot to assassinate King Hussein bin Talal.

Some 30 people sentenced after unfair trials by the Martial Law Court in previous years were still in prison at the end of the year. Most were serving life sentences imposed for violent political offences.

There were new reports of torture or ill-treatment of detainees. The alleged victims included people arrested during the May riots, including 10 Palestinians who were said to have been beaten while in police custody and at Qafqafa Prison. In another case, Jihad Abu Falah was allegedly subjected to *falaqa* (beatings on the soles of the feet) and cigarette burns while in police custody between May and June. Four men arrested apparently after a personal confrontation with security officers were allegedly burned with cigarettes and beaten in May while held for a few days by the Military Intelligence Department. In most cases torture is said to have occurred while detainees were held incommunicado and after lawyers' requests for visits had been refused.

There were concerns that two prisoners who died in custody might have been subjected to cruel, inhuman or degrading treatment. Mu'taz Hamdan, who was serving a life sentence imposed by the Martial Law Court, was reported to have been shackled by his hands and feet to a hospital bed while terminally ill with leukaemia. He died in May. Sufyan al-Shamasnah was also reported to have been shackled to his hospital bed while critically ill prior to his death in August. He reportedly did not receive prompt medical attention after suffering a burst appendix while in police custody. Those detaining him apparently thought he was faking an illness.

At least four people were executed after being convicted of murder. Two others were also convicted of murder and sentenced to death, but they were not known to have been executed by the end of the year. Those under sentence of death included two prisoners convicted by the Martial Law Court for a bomb attack in 1982.

Amnesty International welcomed the human rights initiatives taken by the Jordanian Government during the year, specifically the review of emergency legislation and the releases of prisoners, and urged that further initiatives be taken. It called for a full judicial review of the cases of political prisoners convicted by the Martial Law Court and for the adoption of internationally recognized safeguards relating to administrative detention, fair trial and torture and ill-treatment. It also urged the ratification of international human rights standards and appealed for the commutation of all death sentences.

In March an Amnesty International delegation discussed extensively the organization's concerns and the Jordanian Government's proposals for reform with Prime Minister Mudar Badran and other cabinet and government officials in Amman. The delegation also met members of parliament and local professional associations, and visited the GID interrogation centre and the Swaqa Rehabilitation Centre, Jordan's largest prison. GID and prison officials denied that torture had taken place in the cases raised by Amnesty International. Jordanian authorities also stated that they would not detain political activists, even if they were members of illegal organizations, unless they had been involved in violence or constituted "a clear danger to the security of the citizens and the state".

In June Amnesty International published a report, *Jordan: Human Rights*

Protection After the State of Emergency. This detailed the organization's outstanding concerns, the outcome of its discussions with the government in Amman, and recommendations for further safeguards to protect human rights.

KENYA

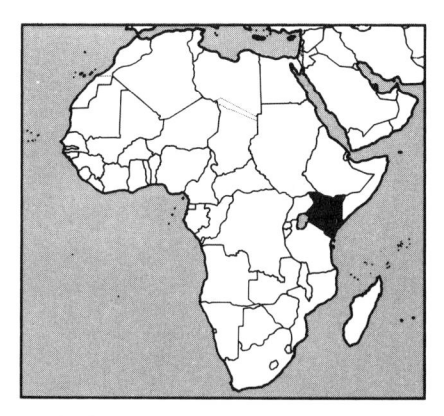

Hundreds of people were arrested in connection with a campaign for multi-party democracy. Most were released within a short time but three out of six prisoners of conscience detained without charge or trial were still held at the end of the year, and at least six others were sentenced to prison terms. Some 30 people were awaiting trial at the end of the year on charges of treason, sedition or possessing prohibited publications. Some political prisoners were reportedly tortured or ill-treated. At least 40 people were sentenced to death but it was not known if there were any executions. Hundreds of refugees and asylum-seekers were arrested and several were forcibly returned to Uganda.

There were frequent arrests, interrogations and other harassment, including death threats, of government critics, particularly church leaders, lawyers and others advocating a multi-party political system. The government's response to a strengthening campaign for multi-party democracy in July was to detain the leaders or charge them with sedition, and arrest demonstrators. The government insisted on retaining one-party rule but proposed some reforms to the ruling party – the Kenya African National Union (KANU) – the electoral system, and the security of tenure of judges and the Attorney General.

In February Foreign Minister Robert Ouko was abducted, tortured and murdered by unknown people, who then burned his body. British police were brought in to help investigate amid suggestions that there might have been government involvement in his death. Their findings were not made public. A judicial commission of inquiry into the case was established in October and was still taking evidence at the end of the year.

A government minister resigned after the death of Anglican Bishop Alexander Muge in a car crash in August. The minister had made a public death threat against the bishop, who was an outspoken government critic.

In June over 50 people were arrested for selling or producing cassette tapes of popular songs criticizing the government. However, sedition charges against record producer Joe Mwangi Mathai and over 50 street vendors who were kept in custody for some weeks were later withdrawn.

The main leaders of the multi-party movement, Kenneth Matiba and Charles Rubia, both former government ministers, were arrested in July and detained under administrative detention orders. Four others were also detained in July under the same Public Security Regulations – Raila Odinga, son of former vice-president Oginga Odinga, and three human rights lawyers, including John Khaminwa, who was arrested when he sought access to Kenneth Matiba, and Gitobu Imanyara, editor of the *Nairobi Law Monthly*. The lawyers were released after three weeks but the three others remained in indefinite detention without charge or trial at the end of the year.

Four former prisoners of conscience – George Anyona, a former member of parliament, Edward Oyugi, a university professor, Augustus Kathangu, a local politician, and Ngotho Kariuki, an accountant and former academic – were arrested in July and charged with holding a "seditious meeting". If convicted of this offence, they could receive 10-year prison sentences. Judges rejected their bail applications and ignored their complaints of torture and ill-treatment. They had not been tried by the end of the year.

Over 1,500 people were arrested and over 30 were shot dead by police at a banned demonstration in July and in subsequent disturbances. Most of those arrested were eventually released but several were charged with public order offences, such as making a two-finger V-sign meaning "two parties" and shouting political slogans. At least two demonstrators received six-month prison terms.

At the end of the year over 20 people, some of whom had been released on bail, were awaiting trial on charges of possessing seditious or prohibited publications which were mostly non-violent. Some were held in connection with leaflets produced by the clandestine opposition organization *Mwakenya* (*Muuangano wa Wazalendo wa Kukomboa Kenya*, Union of Patriots for the Liberation of Kenya), which called for the violent overthrow of the government. Gitobu Imanyara, editor of the *Nairobi Law Monthly*, which had published articles on human rights, the death penalty and multi-party democracy, was charged with publishing a seditious publication. A subsequent ban on the journal was temporarily suspended by a court order.

At the beginning of the year 26 people, including at least four prisoners of conscience, were serving prison sentences of up to seven years which had been imposed after unfair political trials between 1986 and 1989. Ten of the 26 prisoners received one-third remissions of sentence and were released during the year. At least five others had their sentences reduced on appeal.

Six people were sentenced to prison terms following political trials in 1990. In March the Reverend Lawford Imunde, a Presbyterian minister, was jailed for six years for possessing a "seditious publication" – his private and unpublished diary, which contained some criticism of the government. He applied to the High Court to declare the conviction unconstitutional on the grounds of violations of his fundamental rights, saying that he had only pleaded guilty because he had been tortured during incommunicado detention and given false promises of a non-custodial sentence. The court dismissed the case.

Koigi wa Wamwere, a former member of parliament and exiled leader of the Kenya Patriotic Front, an opposition organization which he founded while living in exile, was arrested on 9 October in Nairobi. The police said he was captured at the home of Rumba Kinuthia, a lawyer and pro-democracy activist, and that arms and ammunition were found there and at the home of Mirugi Kariuki, another lawyer. Police alleged that Koigi wa Wamwere had entered Kenya clandestinely to plan a violent campaign to destabilize the government. Rumba Kinuthia and Mirugi Kariuki had been arrested the day before Koigi wa Wamwere, but at that time police had not reported finding any weapons. At the end of 1990, the three were awaiting trial on treason charges together with five other people, including relatives of Koigi wa Wamwere and Rumba Kinuthia. Charges of misprision (concealment) of treason against two women related to Rumba Kinuthia were withdrawn and they were released after two months in custody.

Some political detainees were reportedly tortured or ill-treated in security police custody. At remand hearings George Anyona alleged that he and his three co-accused had been put in cells flooded with water and that their treatment in Kamiti prison was "inhuman and cruel". Allegations of torture and ill-treatment were also made by Koigi wa Wamwere and the others charged with him.

At least 40 people were sentenced to death after being convicted of robbery with violence or murder. The government did not disclose the number of prisoners on death row but it was believed to exceed 200. It was not known if any prisoners were executed or had their death sentences commuted during 1990.

In October and November hundreds of refugees and asylum-seekers were arrested after President Daniel arap Moi announced that refugees and illegal aliens were to be expelled. Despite interventions by the Office of the United Nations High Commissioner for Refugees, at least five recognized refugees were forcibly returned to Uganda.

Amnesty International appealed for the release of prisoners of conscience, both those held without charge and those facing sedition or other charges. It also intervened on behalf of detainees in security police custody in an effort to protect them from torture or ill-treatment, illegal detention or unfair trial. Amnesty International called for independent investigations into all torture allegations and criticized the courts for failing to act on prisoners' complaints of torture and harsh treatment. The organization also appealed for the commutation of all death sentences. In October Amnesty International requested information from the Attorney General about the disputed

KOREA
(DEMOCRATIC PEOPLE'S REPUBLIC OF)

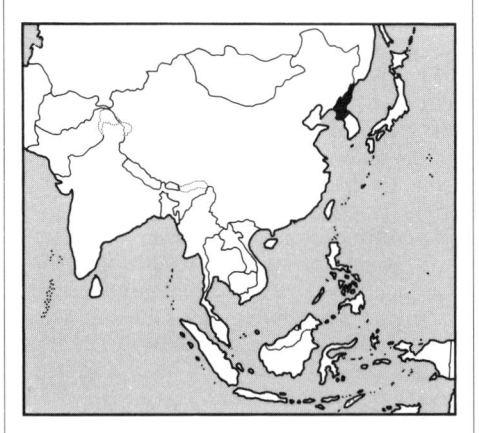

Two Japanese nationals who may have been prisoners of conscience were released after seven years in detention. It was impossible to confirm reports that there were thousands of political prisoners owing to the difficulty of obtaining information about human rights. All news media were controlled by the state and those available to foreigners did not report any political arrests, trials or executions.

Two Japanese seafarers, Beniko Isamu and Kuriura Yoshio, were released in October as a result of an agreement between the Korean Workers' Party and Japan's Liberal Democratic Party and the Japan Socialist Party. Both men had been held since 1983, accused of spying and helping a North Korean soldier defect to Japan aboard their ship. Both denied the accusations. On their return to Japan, Beniko Isamu told reporters that they had neither been formally charged nor tried, although the authorities had previously announced that they had been tried and sentenced to 15 years of "reformation through labour" in December 1987 (see *Amnesty International Report 1989*).

The situation of others reportedly detained in previous years, including about 40 university staff and students said to have been arrested in 1988 (see *Amnesty International Report 1989*), remained unclear. Likewise, it was not possible to confirm other reports that tens of thousands of people might be held for political reasons at corrective camps throughout the country (see *Amnesty International Report 1990*).

There was concern that a number of students who were recalled from their studies in Eastern Europe at the end of 1989 might have been detained on suspicion of criticizing their government while abroad, but this could not be confirmed. On several occasions, however, the ruling Korean Workers' Party called on its members to intensify ideological indoctrination in the advantages of socialism over capitalism, apparently as a reaction to political changes in Eastern Europe, and some sources suggested that returning students were made to attend ideological "re-education" sessions.

Amnesty International welcomed the release of Isamu Beniko and Kuriura Yoshio and sought information from the government about others reportedly detained, but without response. Amnesty International also wrote to the government about its wish to visit the Democratic People's Republic of Korea to discuss human rights with government officials but received no reply.

KOREA
(REPUBLIC OF)

Around 150 people were believed to be prisoners of conscience or possible prisoners of conscience. Thirty prisoners, including several prisoners of conscience held for over 15 years, were released in amnesties. Several prisoners convicted of national security offences complained that they were ill-treated during interrogation. Fourteen people convicted of criminal offences were executed, double the number of executions in 1989.

The National Security Law continued to prohibit contacts with North Korea and activities beneficial to anti-state organizations and North Korea. However, the South–North Exchange and Cooperation Law came into force in August. Under this law, the South Korean Government can authorize its citizens to visit North Korea, to invite North Koreans to the south and to trade and engage in joint ventures with them. Unauthorized contacts with North Koreans continued to result in arrests.

The Constitutional Court made two rulings related to basic freedoms. In January it upheld the constitutionality of Article 13 (2) of the Labour Dispute Mediation Act under which third parties – people not directly connected with the workplace – have been imprisoned for intervening in labour disputes. In April the court ruled that paragraphs (1) and (5) of Article 7 of the National Security Law – which prohibit activities and publications praising anti-state organizations – were constitutional but open to political abuse. Arrests under these provisions continued.

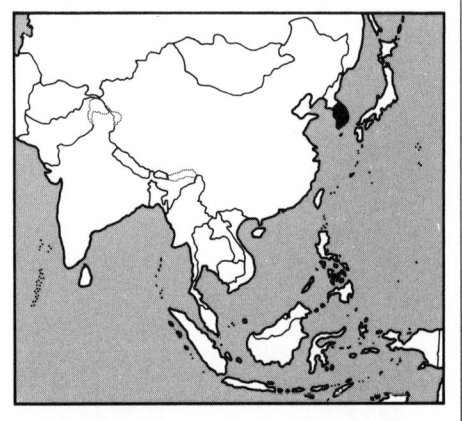

In April the government acceded to the International Covenant on Civil and Political Rights (ICCPR) and its first Optional Protocol. It made reservations on four provisions of the ICCPR, including the right of government employees to organize trade unions. In October the government acceded to the International Covenant on Economic, Social and Cultural Rights.

Over 1,500 people were imprisoned for politically motivated activities. More than half of them were students and workers charged with taking part in illegal demonstrations or committing violent acts. According to a government report to the National Assembly, the number of arrests under the National Security Law increased and 759 people were officially reported to have been charged under this law in the 12 months prior to September 1990. About 250 of them were charged with sympathizing with, or espionage for, North Korea; most of the others were charged with establishing "anti-state" organizations and producing and distributing materials benefiting North Korea.

At least 25 writers and publishers and a number of students were among those tried under the National Security Law for disseminating written or other material said to benefit North Korea. Most received suspended sentences of up to two years' imprisonment. Oh Pong-ok was arrested in February after writing a poem, *Red Mountain, Black Blood*, which the authorities said praised the role played by North Korean leader Kim Il-sung during the Japanese occupation. Oh Pong-ok was released in May with a two-year suspended sentence. Another prisoner of conscience, Kim Song-kyu, was released in April. The President of the student council of Dongguk University, he had been arrested in December 1989 for organizing a student performance of a North Korean revolutionary play.

Over 140 prisoners convicted of espionage continued to serve sentences ranging from five years to life imprisonment. Some had been held since the 1950s but most of those arrested since 1971 had been convicted of visiting North Korea or contacting North Korean agents abroad, notably in Japan. Under the National Security Law, information useful to North Korea, even if it is freely available, is considered a state secret. Many prisoners serving sentences for espionage were believed to have received unfair trials and to have been forced to confess under torture in pre-trial detention. They included prisoners of conscience such as Park Ki-rae, detained since 1974, who served eight years under sentence of death before his sentence was commuted to life imprisonment. Like others, he was denied an early release because he refused to write a statement of conversion to "anti-communism".

Unauthorized contact with North Korea continued to be punished by imprisonment. Dissident artist Hong Song-dam was sentenced to seven years' imprisonment in January on charges including sending photographic slides of his painting, *A History of the National Liberation Movement*, to North Korea where they were reproduced for exhibition. He was a prisoner of conscience. In September the Supreme Court upheld sentences of 18 months' imprisonment imposed on four members of *Minjatong*, the Central Council for National Peaceful Reunification. They were arrested in June 1989 because *Minjatong* espoused certain views on reunification which were similar to those of the North Korean authorities. They too were prisoners of conscience. In November three members of the dissident organization *Chonminnyon*, the National Coalition for a Democratic Movement, were arrested for participating in an unauthorized meeting in Berlin with North Koreans.

Accusations under the National Security Law of organizing or participating in anti-state organizations were brought against members of alleged underground revolutionary socialist or communist groups, composed mostly of students, former students and workers. Around 200 people were believed to have been arrested on such charges in the second half of the year in connection with groups called *Hyukromeng*, the Alliance for the Struggle of the Revolutionary Working Class, *Sanomaeng*, the Socialist Workers League, *Chamintong*, Independent National Unification Group, and *Chonminhangnyon*, the Democratic Students League. The authorities accused them of planning to overthrow the government by force and replace it with a socialist government.

Thirty prisoners who had been convicted on national security charges were released in presidential amnesties in February and May, and it was confirmed that 27 others had been freed in December 1989. Those released included Suh Song, a prisoner of conscience held since 1971, and three other prisoners of conscience – Chin Tu-hyon, Choi Chol-kyo and Paek Ok-kwang – held since 1974 and 1975. Another prisoner of conscience, the Reverend Moon Ik-hwan, was released in October on health grounds after serving one year of his seven-year sentence for an unauthorized visit to North Korea.

Several prisoners complained of beatings and sleep deprivation during interrogation, principally prisoners who were arrested late in the year on suspicion of belonging to "anti-state" organizations. Criminal suspects also alleged that they were beaten, particularly some who were arrested after the government declared a "war on crime" in October. In December the Ministry of Justice told the National Assembly that 53 lawsuits alleging torture and assault had been filed against 115 police officers during the 12 months prior to October 1990. Most such lawsuits were believed to have been unsuccessful.

A former marine officer was sentenced to two years' imprisonment for torturing a marine in military custody in 1983. Compensation was awarded to the relatives of two people who died, in 1986 and 1989, as a result of police ill-treatment.

Some 100 prisoners alleged that they were beaten and tied in painful positions for several hours at a time as a punishment for taking part in a prison protest in August in Seoul Detention Centre. The authorities denied the reports, but the prisoners and their families reportedly filed a complaint with the courts.

Fourteen people who had been convicted of rape, robbery or murder were executed, and two prisoners had their death sentences commuted. Kim Hyun-hui, a North Korean sentenced to death in April 1989 for planting a bomb which blew up a Korean Airlines aircraft, was released under a special amnesty granted by President Roh Tae-woo in April. Suh Sun-taek, sentenced to death in July for spying for North Korea, had his sentence commuted by the Seoul Appeal Court in November.

Amnesty International welcomed the releases of prisoners of conscience and appealed for those still held to be freed. The organization called for the cases of prisoners convicted of espionage to be reviewed to establish whether they had received fair trials. Amnesty International urged the authorities to amend the National Security Law, to enforce safeguards against torture and ill-treatment of prisoners and to abolish the death penalty. In January it published two reports: *South Korea: Return to Repressive Force and Torture?* and *South Korea: Long-term Political Prisoners*. The government responded to these reports and other Amnesty International documents and appeals by reiterating its commitment to human rights and referring to recent prisoner releases and legal reforms in 1989. The government said that they were not holding any prisoners of conscience, arguing that those arrested had "threatened the rule of law and national survival" and were "radical anti-state forces intent on overthrowing our free democratic system". The government also denied that prisoners had been tortured or refused access to their lawyers or relatives.

In October an Amnesty International delegation visited South Korea and discussed human rights concerns with Ministry of Justice officials.

KUWAIT

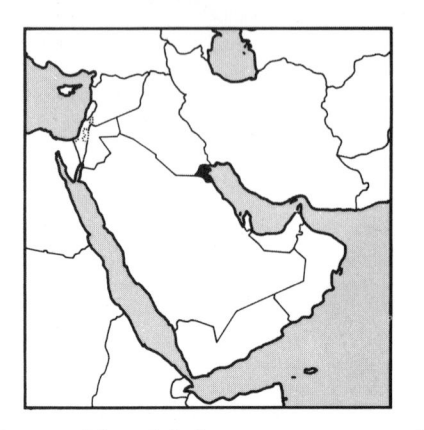

Human rights violations were perpetrated on a massive scale by Iraqi forces following their invasion of Kuwait on 2 August. Hundreds, possibly thousands, of Kuwaitis and other nationals were arbitrarily arrested and detained or restricted. Torture was widespread, resulting in a number of deaths, and hundreds of people reportedly "disappeared" in detention. The death penalty was introduced for new offences and scores of summary executions and extrajudicial killings were carried out by Iraqi forces (see Iraq/Occupied Kuwait).

Earlier in the year, the Kuwait Government carried out political arrests. At least 26 suspected opponents of the government were detained without charge or trial for up to three weeks. Some may have been prisoners of conscience. Four political prisoners who were brought to trial before the State Security Court were acquitted. They and some of the untried detainees said they had been tortured. Twenty-nine other political prisoners sentenced after unfair trials in recent years were believed to have escaped after the Iraqi invasion.

Thirteen suspected opponents of the government of the Amir of Kuwait, all Shi'a Muslims, were arrested in February and detained without charge or trial at Amn al-Dawla Prison in Kuwait City, where some were reportedly tortured or ill-treated. Some of those held, who included Hassan Habib al-Salman, a municipal councillor, Saleh Jawhar Hayat, imam of the Imam al-Hussain Mosque in Kuwait, and Faisal al-Saffar, a university student, had previously been detained in 1989. All 13 were released on bail in March, although none was formally charged or brought to trial. 'Abd al-Rida Karoun, an untried political detainee held since November 1989, was also released in March.

Thirteen other people, prominent advocates of parliamentary democracy, were arrested in May following months of protests and demonstrations supporting the restoration of parliamentary democracy. They included former members of parliament Ahmad al-Khatib, Ahmad al-Nafisi and Jassem al-Qatami. Eleven of them were charged with holding illegal meetings, and the other two with distributing leaflets without a licence. They were all released on bail after four days, and the Amir pardoned them in June.

Four Shi'a Muslims who had been arrested in September and November 1989 in connection with bomb attacks in Mecca, Saudi Arabia, were tried by the State Security Court in May and June (see *Amnesty International Report 1990*). The four, Sayyid Muhammad Baqir al-Musawi, Faisal al-Mahmid, Walid al-Mazidi and 'Abd al-Hamid al-Saffar, faced 10 charges, including membership of a prohibited organization aiming to overthrow the government, inciting sedition and illegal possession of weapons. Their trial was held *in camera*. All four defendants, who alleged in court that they had been tortured in pre-trial detention, were acquitted and released in June.

Twenty-nine Shi'a Muslim political prisoners, including possible prisoners of conscience, were still serving prison sentences ranging from three to 15 years at the beginning of 1990. All had been convicted by the State Security Court after trials which failed to satisfy international fair trial standards. Seven had been convicted between 1985 and 1987 on charges including the distribution of leaflets inciting violence. The other 22 were tried in 1989 on charges including membership of banned organizations and publicly defaming the Amir of Kuwait. All remained in Kuwait Central Prison until 3 August, when they were believed to be among an estimated 60 political prisoners who escaped from the prison following the Iraqi invasion.

Political detainees who had been held at Amn al-Dawla Prison alleged that they had been tortured. Some of those released in March said they had been kicked and beaten, subjected to *falaqa* (beating on the soles of the feet), deprived of sleep and threatened with sexual assault. The four defendants acquitted by the State Security Court in June also alleged that they had been tortured to force them to make confessions. One of them, Sayyid Muhammad Baqir al-Musawi, said he had been given electric shocks after water was poured over his body, and was forced to keep his arms raised for long periods during the five months in which he was held incommunicado.

Amnesty International expressed concern to the authorities about the arrests of suspected opponents of the government and the alleged torture of political detainees. In March the government replied that "the offenders were given the opportunity to defend themselves without pressure or torture". In May an Amnesty International delegation visited Kuwait and discussed the organization's concerns with government officials and members of the judiciary. The delegation also attended two *in camera* sessions of the trial of four defendants before the State Security Court.

LAOS

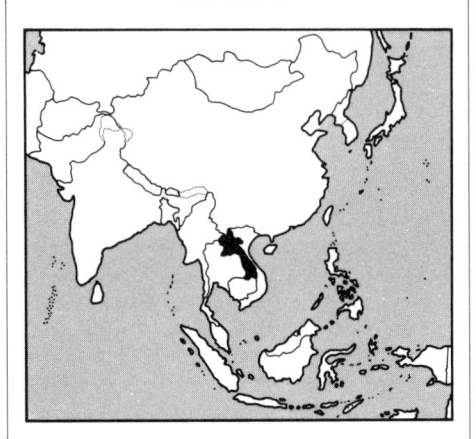

Three people arrested in October and later charged with treason appeared to be prisoners of conscience. At least 33 other suspected opponents of the government held since 1975, including five prisoners of conscience, remained under restriction without charge or trial. No information became available on the fate of over 200 people detained since 1975. The official media indicated that judgments in political trials held in Savannakhet province were based on "guidance" from non-judicial authorities.

The ruling Lao People's Revolutionary Party (LPRP) reiterated its opposition to a multi-party system in Laos amid signs that some officials and intellectuals were critical of its policies. In April the LPRP Political Bureau approved a draft constitution describing Laos as "a popular democratic state under the leadership of the LPRP". The draft, published in June, failed to incorporate specific guarantees relating to freedom of conscience and expression, and against torture. It also failed to safeguard the right to life. The new constitution was scheduled to be adopted by the legislative Supreme People's Assembly during 1991.

On 8 October the authorities detained at least three people suspected of involvement in an unofficial "Social Democrat Club". They were Thongsouk Saisangkhi, who reportedly called for "a multi-party system" when he resigned as Deputy Minister of Science and Technology on 26 August; Latsami Khamphoui, another former deputy minister who had reportedly circulated letters criticizing government policy; and Feng Sakchittaphong, a former senior official in the Ministry of Justice. In early November the authorities announced that the three detainees would be charged with treason under Article 51 of the Criminal Law, which carries a possible death penalty, but they were not known to have been brought to trial by the end of the year. They appeared to be prisoners of conscience detained solely for their non-violent advocacy of multi-party democracy.

At least 33 people held without charge or trial since 1975, including five prisoners of conscience, remained under restriction in a camp near the village of Sop Pan in the northeastern province of Houa Phanh (see *Amnesty International Report 1990*).

Poor housing conditions in Sop Pan deteriorated in March after a rainstorm destroyed some of the camp's dwellings. The inmates, mostly elderly men, had little access to medicine and medical treatment. Sop Pan's chief medical officer, Tiao Sisoumang Sisaleumsak, himself a 72-year-old prisoner of conscience, resigned his post in July owing to poor health. A member of parliament and minister in the pre-1975 government, he had been held without charge or trial since November 1975.

There was no further information on the

fate of the 12 Lao whose arrests on political grounds were officially reported in 1989, or about 185 people previously reported to be held in Attapeu province for "re-education".

In June the president of the Savannakhet provincial People's Court told the official newspaper *Pasason* that of 446 cases tried by the court in 1989, "79 were political". He added that the court had jurisdiction over all cases except "difficult or political cases" which were referred for "guidance" to the Party Committee and the local government. No other reports relating to political trials were received.

The Criminal Law adopted in November 1989 was implemented. It maintained the death penalty for a wide range of criminal and political offences. No death sentences were reported during the year.

In October Amnesty International wrote to Prime Minister Kaysone Phomvihan and to members of the Constitution Drafting Committee to urge that the draft constitution be amended to include comprehensive safeguards for human rights in line with international standards. Amnesty International recommended that the right to life should be recognized and the death penalty abolished, that torture should be specifically prohibited, and that the freedoms of thought and association should be fully protected. Amnesty International also repeated its request to visit Laos to discuss its concerns there.

In November the organization expressed concern about the arrest of Thongsouk Saisangkhi, Latsami Khamphoui and Feng Sakchittaphong, and urged that they be immediately and unconditionally released if detained for their non-violent political activities and beliefs.

LEBANON

Hundreds of people were arbitrarily arrested by government forces and armed militias. Some may have been prisoners of conscience, but few details were available. A few were released in prisoner exchanges, but the fate of most of them was not known. Among those arrested were scores of people who reportedly "disappeared" or were tortured. Others were extrajudicially executed.

A continuing lack of central governmental control, together with violent conflicts between governmental and non-governmental forces, made it particularly difficult to obtain accurate information about human rights violations. However, all sides were believed to have carried out abuses.

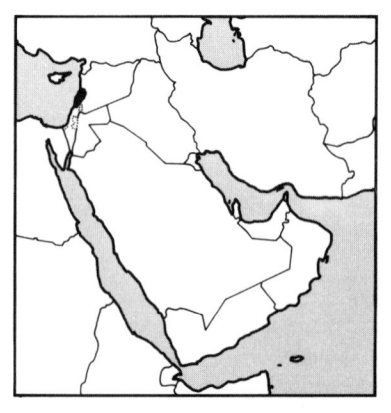

General Michel 'Aoun, appointed as interim prime minister in September 1988 by the then outgoing president Amin Gemayel, continued to challenge the legitimacy of President Elias Hrawi's government. In October, however, General 'Aoun's predominantly Christian militia were driven from their East Beirut base by Syrian forces and Lebanese Army units. The "Green Line" dividing East and West Beirut was then dismantled, and various armed militia forces reportedly withdrew from the city.

Syrian military forces maintained control of northern Lebanon, the Beka' Valley, southern and West Beirut, and the coastal region towards Sidon. In October they extended their control to East Beirut and surrounding areas previously held by General 'Aoun's forces. Israeli military forces maintained control of the so-called "security zone" along the Lebanese/Israeli border.

Parts of the country remained under the control of four armed militias – the Lebanese Forces (LF), a Christian militia; the mainly Shi'a Muslim Amal Movement; the predominantly Druze Progressive Socialist Party (PSP), and the South Lebanon Army (SLA), a Christian militia which controlled a strip of territory in the south bordering on Israel. These groups all exercised effective control over particular areas and their populations, and thus had the means and responsibility to respect human rights. Other non-governmental groups also committed human rights abuses but lacked such extensive or effective territorial control. They included Hizbullah (Party of God), Islamic Jihad and various Palestinian factions.

Government forces and armed militias arrested both combatants and civilians. Among those arrested by Syrian military forces and Syrian-sponsored militias were an estimated 200 Christian supporters of General 'Aoun. Most were military personnel arrested in October in East Beirut and its suburbs: 24 were later released but others reportedly remained in prisons in Syria and at 'Anjar detention centre in the Beka' Valley (see **Syria**).

Hundreds of people, including civilians, were reportedly taken prisoner during armed clashes between the LF militia and General 'Aoun's forces between January and July. The LF was said to have captured some 600 people, mainly combatants, from General 'Aoun's forces, of whom 89 were released in July and October. The fate of the others remained unknown. In May and June, 189 LF detainees held by General 'Aoun's forces were released. A further 300 LF detainees held in East Beirut were reportedly released in October after General 'Aoun's forces were ousted by Syrian forces and Lebanese Army units. At the same time, Syrian forces reportedly freed 23 Syrians and seven Lebanese nationals who had been held in Roumieh Prison in East Beirut.

The SLA continued to detain without charge or trial an estimated 300 prisoners, including youths, women and old men, in Khiam detention centre in southern Lebanon. The majority of them were Shi'a Muslims from villages inside the Israeli "security zone". Some had been held for up to five years. Among those detained was Salma Salam, an interpreter for the United Nations' Norwegian battalion in southern Lebanon, who was arrested in July 1989. The reason for her detention was not disclosed.

The SLA released 73 detainees held in Khiam, including 40 who were freed on 1 October. Some had been held without charge or trial for two years.

The fate and whereabouts of an estimated 625 detainees reportedly arrested by Amal in previous years remained unknown (see *Amnesty International Report 1990*). Many of those held were said to be members or supporters of Hizbullah. In August Amal announced that it had arrested a self-confessed participant in the kidnapping of a US citizen, Colonel William Higgins, in 1988, and that he would stand trial. However, it was not known whether the trial had taken place.

Former detainees at Khiam alleged that they had been tortured in SLA custody, including with beatings and electric shocks. Muhammad Hussain Balhus, released in November 1989 after five years' detention without trial, reportedly suffered neurological and urological disorders as a result of his torture. Murtada Amin, a doctor released in June 1988 after 28 months' detention, said he was beaten and hung upside-down during interrogation.

Both the LF and the SLA were reported to have executed prisoners. The LF was said to have executed 16 of its militiamen in February, allegedly for refusing to fight against General 'Aoun's forces. In the same month 13 Sunni Muslim detainees held by the LF were also reportedly executed. In March the SLA reportedly executed one of its members who had been accused of plotting to assassinate an SLA officer.

Syrian government forces and Syrian-sponsored groups reportedly carried out scores of extrajudicial executions following the ousting of General 'Aoun's forces from East Beirut in mid-October. The victims included both military personnel and civilians (see **Syria**). Many others were also deliberately killed, apparently for political reasons, outside the immediate context of armed conflict, but there was insufficient information to attribute responsibility for these and other apparent extrajudicial executions.

Amnesty International sought information about those detained by the contending forces in Lebanon. In October it urged President Hrawi's Government to establish an impartial inquiry into alleged extrajudicial killings of General 'Aoun's supporters by Syrian troops. The organization also urged the government to ensure the physical safety of all those held by Lebanese and Syrian government forces, and to ensure that detainees were either given a fair and prompt trial, or released. The Lebanese authorities responded in November: they strongly denied the alleged extrajudicial executions, in particular that children had been extrajudicially executed, but expressed regret at the "possible loss of life" during "military action".

LESOTHO

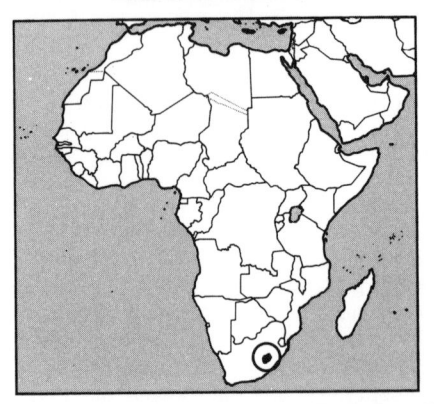

At least 11 people were briefly detained without charge or trial for political reasons: some appeared to be prisoners of conscience. There were new allegations of torture and the authorities admitted that a criminal suspect had been tortured by police in 1989. One prisoner was executed.

Three members of the ruling Military Council and one member of the Council of Ministers were dismissed and detained in February. Three of them were released uncharged within a few weeks but Colonel Sekhobe Letsie was charged with the murder of two government ministers and their wives in 1986 (see Amnesty International Report 1989).

In March King Moshoeshoe II was forced into exile by the Military Council. The Chairman of the Military Council, Major General Metsing Lekhanya, assumed the king's executive and legislative powers and on 6 November King Moshoeshoe was formally deposed in favour of his eldest son who became King Letsie III, with purely ceremonial powers.

In June a constituent assembly was inaugurated to prepare for a return to civilian government in 1992, but all party political activity remained banned under a 1986 decree. Teachers, students and workers involved in a wave of strikes and demonstrations during the second half of the year were subjected to tear-gas, and whipped and shot at by the police. At least two youths were shot dead by the police during these incidents. In December the police raided the office of a human rights organization in the capital, Maseru, seized documents and interrogated staff.

Five leaders of a nationwide teachers' strike were arrested in August. They appeared to be prisoners of conscience but were released uncharged after three days' detention.

In January the Court of Appeal ruled that Johnny wa ka Maseko, a newspaper editor, had been unlawfully detained for four weeks prior to his deportation in December 1988 (see Amnesty International Report 1989).

Michael Sefali, a former government minister detained without charge or trial for eight days in March, brought a damages claim before the High Court alleging that he had been stripped naked and made to stand on crushed stones during police interrogation. The outcome of the case was not known. However, in another case the authorities conceded in May that a criminal suspect had been tortured at Maseru Police Headquarters in July 1989 and agreed to pay him damages. Lakia P. Pholo had been assaulted and made to jog barefoot on crushed stones while handcuffed and with a blanket and tyre placed over his head. He was also subjected to deliberately humiliating assaults. There was no indication that those responsible for his torture had been identified and brought to justice.

An inquest into the 1986 killings of government ministers Desmond Sixishe and Vincent Makhele and their wives resumed briefly in January but was postponed indefinitely when murder charges were brought against Colonel Sekhobe Letsie and a former army sergeant. Their trial concluded in December but no judgment had been given by the end of 1990. During the trial a statement made by one of the defendants in pre-trial custody was ruled inadmissible after he alleged that it had been obtained by torture.

One prisoner convicted of murder was executed in September. At least one other convicted prisoner remained under sentence of death.

Amnesty International welcomed the authorities' decision to prosecute those allegedly responsible for the 1986 killings, which appeared to have been extrajudicial executions, and the releases of teachers and others detained without charge or trial.

LIBERIA

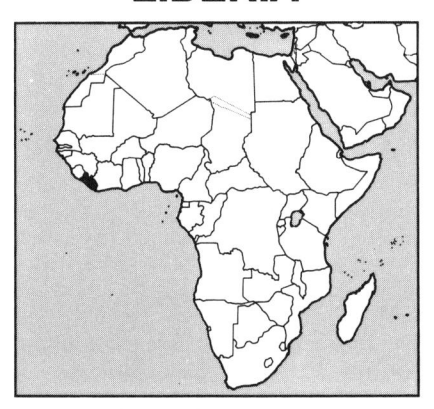

Human rights violations on a massive scale were perpetrated throughout the year by the Armed Forces of Liberia and by rebel forces. Thousands of people were extrajudicially executed or executed after grossly unfair trials. Ten prisoners of conscience were released. Three possible prisoners of conscience were sentenced to life imprisonment after an unfair trial.

The government of President Samuel Doe was overthrown in a rebellion in which thousands of civilians were killed by both sides. An estimated 700,000 people fled the country and the infrastructure of the state collapsed. Following an invasion of Nimba County in northeast Liberia by a force of about 100 exiled government opponents in December 1989, government forces destroyed villages and killed civilians not involved in the uprising. People belonging to the local Gio and Mano ethnic groups, previously the target of army killings in 1985, swelled the ranks of the rebel National Patriotic Front of Liberia (NPFL), led by Charles Taylor, a former government official. Human rights violations escalated dramatically as the NPFL and a breakaway group of rebels, the Independent National Patriotic Front of Liberia (INPFL), led by Prince Yeduo Johnson, pushed towards the capital, Monrovia. The flight of refugees and displaced people became a flood as the government's position grew increasingly insecure and as the rebels took control of parts of Monrovia in July.

In late August member governments of the Economic Community of West African States (ECOWAS) sent a joint military force to Monrovia to try to enforce a cease-fire. This force became engaged in fighting the NPFL, which surrounded Monrovia and opposed intervention from abroad. President Doe was captured and brutally killed by the forces of Prince Johnson in September. At a meeting of ECOWAS heads of state in November, the NPFL agreed to a cease-fire. However, the NPFL refused to recognize an interim civilian government led by Dr Amos Sawyer, which had been installed in Monrovia by the ECOWAS force, saying that it had already established its own government in Gbarnga, Bong County.

Thousands of people were killed, tortured or brutally ill-treated both by President Doe's forces and by those opposed to them, and these abuses continued after the President's death. Most victims were civilians targeted because of their ethnic group.

The predominantly Gio and Mano rebel forces summarily killed government officials and others considered to be supporters of President Doe's government, particularly members of his Krahn ethnic group and the Muslim Mandingo community in areas they took over or while the victims were fleeing Monrovia. Further large-scale killings occurred when they entered Monrovia in July. One rebel leader was said by eye-witnesses to have personally shot four people dead in cold blood, including a Red Cross worker and a woman whom he shot in the face in front of her child. In Grand Gedeh County, President Doe's home area, Charles Taylor's NPFL forces were responsible for indiscriminate killings of people belonging to the Krahn ethnic group. In August former government minister Senator Fred J. Blay and Congressman William T. Jabbah were reportedly executed by the INPFL; they did not appear to have had any form of trial.

In response to the invasion, government troops exacted brutal reprisals against members of the Gio and Mano ethnic groups in Nimba County, leading to a mass exodus into neighbouring countries. Gios, Manos and Americo-Liberian critics of the government were also arrested in Monrovia and extrajudicially executed, particularly as the rebels approached the capital. On 30 May at least 30 Gio and Mano men, women and children were abducted by government soldiers from a United Nations compound where hundreds were seeking protection. They were then apparently executed extrajudicially; the bodies of some of them were found the next day. In July about 600 defenceless people – including many women and children from the Gio and Mano communities – were extrajudicially executed by government troops who broke into a church refuge for displaced people in Monrovia.

It was impossible to estimate how many people were taken prisoner by government and rebel forces. In January the government said a number of rebels had been captured and would be brought to trial, but they appeared to include Gio and Mano civilians arrested in Monrovia. None was brought to trial and their fate was unknown. In June several hundred Gio and Mano soldiers were reported to have been arrested. Some appeared to have been extrajudicially executed – their bodies were found in the streets – although the government later said that 150 had been released.

An unknown number of prisoners were executed after unfair trials before special courts set up by the rebels. At least 100 people – government officials and members of the Krahn and Mandingo ethnic groups – were reportedly executed after being convicted of "crimes against the people" or of supporting the government. They had been tried by three courts set up by the NPFL in June, one of which was reportedly presided over by a school teacher.

In August both the NPFL and INPFL seized a number of foreigners in an attempt to influence the actions of other governments. About 50 foreigners, including Americans, were detained by the INPFL, which sought direct United States intervention in the conflict. The NPFL took prisoner at least 30 Nigerians, as well as nationals of Guinea and Ghana, in an attempt to deter their governments from contributing to the ECOWAS force. There were reports of widespread arrests among the Ghanaian community living in areas under the NPFL's control. All foreigners known to be held by the INPFL were believed to have been released by the end of the year but the NPFL was still holding an unknown number. Two Nigerian journalists detained by the NPFL, Tayo Awotunsin and Krees Imodibie, were reportedly executed extrajudicially in October. Both were said to have been deprived of food and water for several days and forced to bury abandoned corpses.

Before the collapse of the government, Gabriel William Kpoleh and nine other prisoners of conscience were released in a presidential amnesty in March. They had been convicted of treason in 1988 (see *Amnesty International Reports 1989* and *1990*). In January the Supreme Court found that the trial court had made a "patent and blatant blunder" and ordered a retrial. In April charges against them were formally withdrawn.

Three people sentenced to life imprisonment in May for complicity to murder appeared to be prisoners of conscience. Angeline Watta Allison and two others were convicted of involvement in a ritual murder allegedly ordered by her husband, former defence minister Major-General Gray Dioh Allison, as part of a plot to overthrow the government. Major-General Allison had himself been sentenced to death in 1989 after an unfair trial before a special military court (see *Amnesty International Report 1990*). Angeline Watta Allison's two co-accused told the court that they had been threatened with death and ill-treated to make them confess and implicate the Allisons.

Two others charged in the case died in detention in 1989, apparently as a result of torture and medical neglect, and three prosecution witnesses were still held in detention although charges against them had been withdrawn. All the defendants lodged appeals with the Supreme Court, but it was not known whether they and Major-General Allison, who was awaiting a presidential decision on his clemency appeal against the death penalty, survived the subsequent killings.

No death sentences were known to have been passed by the ordinary courts, but one government soldier was executed by firing-squad in June after being convicted by a court-martial of murdering a civilian.

Amnesty International publicly appealed for an end to torture, extrajudicial executions and other abuses by both government and rebel troops. It also urged governments worldwide, particularly those with influence over the Liberian Government or the rebels, to use every effort to protect prisoners, civilians and others from human rights violations.

LIBYA

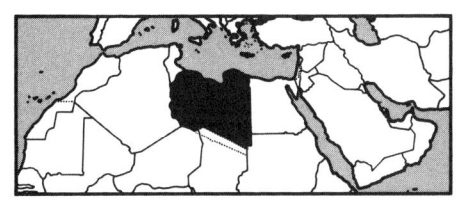

Five prisoners of conscience remained in prison. At least 445 other suspected opponents of the government, including possible prisoners of conscience, continued to be detained without trial. At least 18 political prisoners were serving sentences imposed after unfair trials, and one prisoner remained in detention after being acquitted. No death sentences or executions were announced.

Five prisoners of conscience serving life sentences continued to be held in Abu Salim Prison, Tripoli. All had been arrested in April 1973 and convicted of membership of the Islamic Liberation Party (ILP), an illegal political party. The five included 'Ali Muhammad al-'Akrami and 'Ali Muhammad al-Qajiji.

At least 445 people arrested for political reasons, including possible prisoners of conscience, were still held without trial at the end of 1990. Of these, 394 were arrested in Benghazi, Tripoli and other towns between January 1989 and April 1990 in connection with demonstrations and violent clashes between supporters of Islamic opposition groups and government forces in early 1989 (see *Amnesty International Report 1990*). Most of those held were said to have been arrested as suspected members or supporters of various banned Islamic opposition groups, rather than for any involvement in violence. They included alleged members or supporters of the *Wahabiyya* Islamic doctrine; *Al-Tabligh*, Preaching; *Al-Jihad*, Holy War; *Al-Da'wah al-Islamiyah*, Islamic Call; the Muslim Brotherhood; and the Islamic Liberation Party.

All but one of the 394 detainees were reportedly held incommunicado and their whereabouts were unknown to Amnesty International. The exception, 'Adil Rajab Husayn al-Karghalli, a businessman reportedly arrested in March 1989 after returning from Saudi Arabia, was held at Abu Salim Prison. Others detained included 'Abdul-Naser al-Bashir Abu-Lseyen, a doctor, and Abu Bakr al-Sadiq Mahmud, an engineer, who were arrested in January 1989 in Tripoli and Benghazi respectively; Muhammad al-Furtiya, a lecturer apparently regarded as a religious leader by some followers of the *Wahabiyya* Islamic doctrine, who was arrested in February 1989 in Misrata and detained along with two of his sons, both in their twenties; and 'Umar Hafidh al-Buri, a computer engineer who was reportedly arrested in March 1990 in Benghazi.

The 51 other political detainees were arrested between 1974 and 1986 and did not benefit from the March 1988 amnesty in which 400 political prisoners, including prisoners of conscience, were released (see *Amnesty International Report 1989*). In 1988 the authorities had agreed to review their cases as well as those of all other political prisoners still held. However, no such review was known to have taken place by the end of 1990. The 51 still held included 'Ali 'Abdullah al-Sanussi al-Darat, a journalist and writer who was reportedly arrested in 1974 or 1975 for political reasons, and Ahmad 'Abdul-Qadir al-Thulthi, detained since 1986, who had reportedly been denied family visits since the beginning of 1989. Most of the others were said to have been allowed monthly family visits.

One political prisoner held since 1984, 'Abdullah Menina, remained in detention despite having been tried in 1985 and acquitted on charges related to illegal political activities (see *Amnesty International Report 1990*).

At least 18 other political prisoners – 14 civilians and four soldiers – were serving prison terms imposed after unfair trials. Two of the civilians, arrested in 1984, were convicted in separate trials in 1984 and 1987 before courts composed of members of the Revolutionary Committees (local groups set up to support official policies) on charges including having links with opposition groups abroad. The other 12 civilians were Islamic activists reportedly arrested in 1983 and subsequently convicted of membership of an illegal organization by a Revolutionary Committees' court. The whereabouts of the 12 were still unknown. The four soldiers were convicted of attempts to overthrow the government and sentenced to death in three separate military trials between 1970 and 1985. In all these trials, the defendants were reportedly denied legal counsel and any right of appeal. Their death sentences were commuted by Libyan leader Colonel Mu'ammar Gaddafi in June 1988.

No death sentences or executions were recorded in 1990. However, in March, following a fire which allegedly broke out at al-Rabita factory, the Libyan Secretary of the People's Bureau in Rome was reported in the international media as having stated that several people had been detained and that those responsible for the incident would "be executed". The Secretary did not identify those held, and the government did not provide Amnesty International with any clarification of his statement.

Amnesty International continued to appeal for the immediate and unconditional release of all prisoners of conscience and for clarification of the cases of other political prisoners and detainees. The organization repeatedly sought assurances that all those who were held incommunicado and whose whereabouts were unknown were being treated humanely and given access to their relatives, lawyers and medical attention. Amnesty International also sought information on the reported execution of eight people in Ghut al-Ruman region near Tripoli in April 1989 and the killing of a medical student in Tripoli in January 1989, when security forces reportedly fired at demonstrators. No response to any of these inquiries was received.

The Secretariat of the General People's Congress responded to Amnesty International's attempt to clarify reports of mass arrests carried out in October 1989 (see *Amnesty International Report 1990*) by stating that Amnesty International should not rely on the Western press because it was biased against Libya. The response also questioned Amnesty International's reasons for expressing concern about political prisoners who used violence. Amnesty International replied that it did not rely on any single source for its information and that it was standard practice for the organization to seek a government's views on its concerns prior to making public statements. It also reaffirmed its view that the whereabouts of all political detainees should be made known and that they should have access to legal counsel and their families, and should receive a prompt and fair trial.

MADAGASCAR

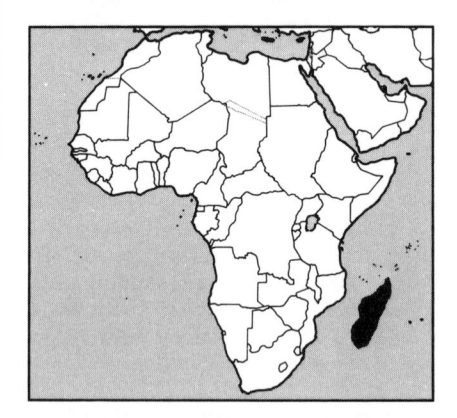

Two political prisoners sentenced in 1983 after what may have been an unfair trial were released in June. At least 14 other people were sentenced in connection with a coup attempt in December. Some of them were reportedly ill-treated.

Richard Andriamaholison, a former government minister and head of the Gendarmerie, and Marson Rakotonirina, a former army officer, were pardoned by President Didier Ratsiraka in June on the 30th anniversary of Madagascar's independence, and released. Both had been sentenced to life imprisonment in 1983 for planning to assassinate President Ratsiraka after a trial which may have been unfair. Lawyers who attended the proceedings said that prosecution witnesses had been interrogated before the trial by members of the security service, who forced them to make statements under duress.

Dozens of people were arrested following an attempted coup in May, when armed government opponents occupied the national radio station and announced that the government had been overthrown. They urged people to demonstrate in support of the coup attempt but a crowd which gathered outside the radio station was dispersed by troops who later stormed the building. Six people were officially said to have been killed and 45 injured in this operation. In addition, 13 of the armed government opponents were captured. On 29 May Alex Oheix, a French national and husband of one of the 13, was arrested. The 13, together with Alex Oheix, were brought to trial in December on charges of endangering the security of the state, illegal possession of weapons, and other offences. Alex Oheix and his wife, Elisabeth Rasoazanay, were acquitted but the other 12 were convicted and sentenced to prison terms ranging from six to 18 months. The detained men were apparently denied visits from relatives before they were brought to trial. Several were said to have been beaten after their arrest.

Several people arrested for apparently supporting the 13 May coup attempt were also imprisoned: two people received six-month prison terms in August while others received suspended sentences.

Amnesty International was concerned by the alleged ill-treatment of people arrested following the coup attempt in May. The organization continued to investigate the cases of those who were apparently detained for supporting the attempted coup.

MALAWI

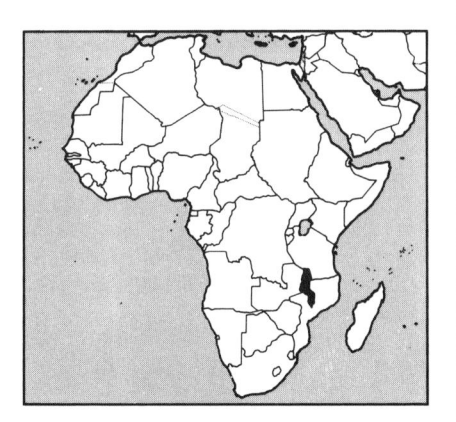

At least 28 prisoners of conscience remained in prison throughout the year; most were held without charge or trial. They included people from the Northern Region arrested in the first half of 1989 and others held for even longer. At least 15 other political prisoners were also held without charge or trial and it was believed there were many dozens more whose identities were not known. The torture and ill-treatment of persistent criminal offenders continued in at least two prisons.

In February Malawi acceded to the Organization of African Unity's African Charter on Human and Peoples' Rights. However, no action was taken during the year to guarantee basic human rights as outlined in the Charter.

New political arrests were reported in 1990, but widespread fears that providing information about human rights issues would result in arrest made it impossible to obtain further details. All 28 prisoners of conscience known to be in detention at the start of the year were held throughout 1990. The majority were held without charge or trial under administrative detention orders imposed under the 1965 Public Security Regulations, which permit indefinite detention without charge or trial. The regulations require Life-President Dr Hastings Kamuzu Banda to review detention orders every six months, but even this limited safeguard was not known to have been implemented. Most political prisoners were therefore denied any opportunity to challenge the legal basis or reasons for their detention.

New information was received about one prisoner of conscience. Ishmael Mazunda, a medical instructor at a mission hospital, was arrested in November 1989. As secretary of a disciplinary committee at the hospital, he had expelled a number of students in July 1989. Subsequently, government officials were apparently told that he had made disrespectful references to Life-President Banda while teaching, as a result of which he was detained.

Also detained without charge or trial as prisoners of conscience were 16 people from the Northern Region who were arrested between February and May 1989 following public criticism of northerners by Life-President Banda (see *Amnesty International Report 1990*). They included George Mtafu, Malawi's only neurosurgeon, Thoza Khonje, a senior employee of the Sugar Company of Malawi, other employees of state-owned companies, civil servants, a teacher and a student. All were held in Mikuyu Prison near Zomba. Some were believed to be allowed monthly visits by their families, but it remained unclear whether all prisoners had this right.

Some prisoners of conscience were still held several years after they had been arrested. L.E. Chaloledwa was detained in 1977 apparently because of his family ties to a government opponent, and Kalusa Chimombo, a teacher, was detained in 1978 for allegedly showing disrespect to the Life-President. Jack Mapanje, an internationally respected poet whose work had increasingly dealt with political themes, had been held since September 1987. Orton and Vera Chirwa, the only prisoners of conscience known to have been charged and tried, also remained in prison. Their trial in 1983 before a traditional court was grossly unfair (see *Amnesty International Reports 1983* to *1990*).

Other political prisoners detained without charge or trial had also been held for long periods. Machipisa Munthali was originally arrested in 1965 for allegedly smuggling arms into Malawi. He is believed to have been sentenced to 11 years' imprisonment, but once his sentence expired he remained in Mikuyu Prison under a detention order. Gomile Kuntumanji, a former government minister and rival to the Life-President, died in Chichiri Prison in April. He had been detained without charge or trial since 1969.

Harsh prison conditions and apparently deliberate neglect had a serious effect on the health of a number of prisoners. George Mtafu was reported to have become ill in mid-1990 and two other prisoners of conscience, Blaise Machira and Margaret Marango Banda, were reportedly denied appropriate medical treatment (see *Amnesty International Report 1990*).

Some criminal prisoners were reportedly subjected to a form of gross ill-treatment known as the "hard-core" regime. Under this, persistent offenders nearing the end of their sentences were reportedly taken to either Nsanje or Dzaleka Prison, chained naked to the floor of a cell, and denied adequate food for 30 days. Some criminal prisoners were also reported to have been beaten by prison staff with batons.

Amnesty International continued to press for the release of all prisoners of conscience and for the fair, prompt trial or release of other political detainees. The government did not respond at all to Amnesty International's extensive and concerted appeals, other than in January when it told the organization that Malawi government agents had played no role in the killing of Mkwapatira Mhango and nine others in October 1989 (see *Amnesty International Report 1990*). In an oral statement to the United Nations Sub-Commission on Prevention of Discrimination and Protection of Minorities in August, Amnesty International included reference to the plight of prisoners of conscience detained without charge or trial in Malawi.

MALAYSIA

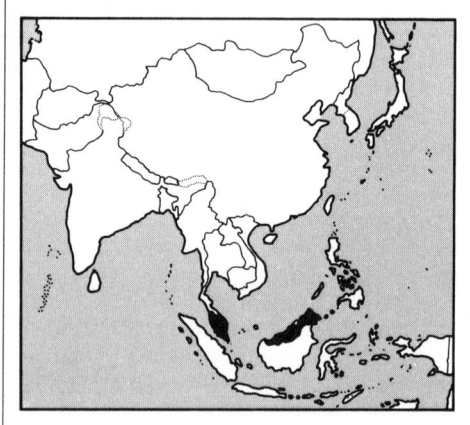

Four alleged advocates of the secession of Sabah state from Malaysia were detained without charge or trial. There were new allegations of police ill-treatment of criminal suspects. Three people were reported to have died in police custody, one of whom was said to have been ill-treated. At least 54 death sentences were imposed and 12 people executed, of whom 11 had been convicted for drugs offences.

The National Front coalition led by Prime Minister Mahathir Mohamad was re-elected in October with a two-thirds majority in parliament. Soon after the election, the Prime Minister indicated that his government would retain the Internal Security Act (ISA) which permits detention without charge or trial.

Four people from Sabah state were arrested in May and June 1990 and detained under the ISA, accused of advocating secession from Malaysia. All four – Abdul Rahman Ahmad, Benedict Topin, Wencelous Damit Undikai and Albinus Yudah – were arrested at a time of tension between the federal authorities and the state government of Sabah, which is dominated by the *Parti Bersatu Sabah* (PBS), United Sabah Party. The four, who were known to be close to the PBS, were publicly accused by the police of involvement in a conspiracy to take Sabah out of Malaysia. They had not been charged or brought to trial by the end of the year. It appeared that they might be prisoners of conscience.

There were new reports of ill-treatment of criminal suspects during police interrogation. In at least one case the Kuala Lumpur High Court ruled that a statement made by a defendant in a kidnapping case after he had been assaulted by the police was inadmissible evidence at his trial.

Ang Soon Kheat, a criminal suspect, died in custody in Pandamaran police station, Selangor state, in August. His wife said that he had complained of police brutality and that she had found bruises on several parts of her husband's body and injuries on his neck and face. The police, however, said that he had died as a result of slipping from a cell door on to which he had climbed while suffering from drug withdrawal symptoms.

In April a directive was issued to police officers instructing them not to use force against suspects detained for investigation. Four police officers were subsequently charged at a magistrate's court in Kajang, Selangor state, with causing injury to a burglary suspect.

At least 54 people were sentenced to death after being convicted of criminal offences – 49 for drugs offences, four for murder and one for a firearms offence. The Supreme Court confirmed the death sentences on 14 people. Their last recourse was to make a final appeal to the Pardons Board of the state where the offence was committed. At least 12 executions were carried out: 11 people were hanged for drugs offences and one for a firearms offence.

Amnesty International called for the four political detainees from Sabah to be brought to trial in accordance with internationally accepted legal standards, or released. It also urged the commutation of all death sentences.

MALDIVES

At least 10 journalists and a member of parliament were detained, apparently without charge or trial: they appeared to be prisoners of conscience. The death penalty was extended to additional crimes under new legislation.

In December the *majlis* (parliament) passed the Prevention of Terrorism Act which extended the death penalty to offences associated with terrorism. Full details of this legislation were not known by the end of the year.

At least 10 journalists and editors working for a news magazine, *Sangu,* and two newspapers, *Hukuru* and *Manthiri*, were arrested between June and the end of the year, apparently for having criticized the government during a period of greater freedom of expression following parliamentary elections in November 1989. It was not known how many remained in detention at the end of 1990. *Sangu* was ordered to close, and all copies of the first issue of *Manthiri* were reportedly confiscated. In September an independent member of parliament, Mohammad Latheef, was also arrested. He had reportedly criticized corruption in government and called for a vote of no confidence. He remained in detention with no known charge against him at the end of the year.

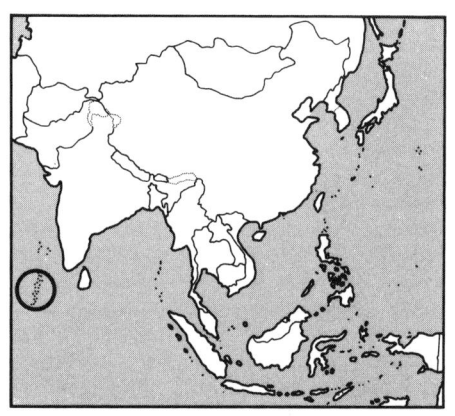

Amnesty International expressed concern to the government about the arrests and urged that those held should be released if they had been detained for the peaceful expression of their opinions. Amnesty International also told the government in December of its concern about the extension of the death penalty and urged President Maumoon Abdul Gayoom to continue to commute death sentences, as had been the practice in the Maldives since 1951.

MALI

At least one prisoner of conscience and several possible prisoners of conscience were detained without charge or trial. Two possible prisoners of conscience were tried for insulting the Head of State and one was sentenced to two years' imprisonment. Government forces were responsible for extrajudicial executions following an

uprising by members of the Tuareg ethnic group during which civilians as well as government troops were killed. One detainee reportedly died as a result of torture or ill-treatment. Four death sentences were passed *in absentia*. No judicial executions were known to have been carried out.

Bassirou Diarra, an opposition leader based in France, was detained without charge for one week when he visited Mali in July. His detention appeared to have no legal basis and he was considered a prisoner of conscience.

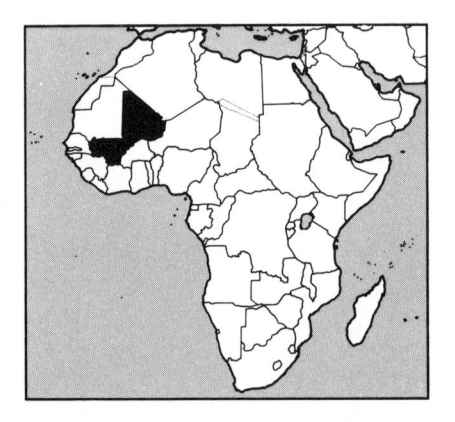

Two people tried in February on charges of insulting the Head of State may have been prisoners of conscience. Mamadou Alpha Idrissa Niang was sentenced to two years' imprisonment for allegedly insulting the Head of State, General Moussa Traoré, although he had made no written complaint as required by law for a prosecution. The outcome of his appeal was unknown. Mamadou Camara, who had been held since October 1988, was acquitted and released.

There was an uprising by members of the Tuareg ethnic group in June, apparently sparked by the government's perceived lack of concern for the Tuareg community. Tuareg insurgents launched attacks in the northeast, killing government officials, members of the security forces and civilians. After an attack on Ménaka, in which about 14 people were killed, they abducted at least two people, one of whom was known to have been released.

In response, the government declared a state of emergency in the sixth and seventh administrative regions around Timbuktu and Gao, and sent troops to the area. Under the emergency, the security forces were empowered to detain without charge for up to two months any person considered a threat to public safety. Severe reprisals were taken against the Tuareg community: army units attacked encampments, beat, raped or killed the inhabitants, and destroyed property. More than 50 Tuareg were reported to have been extrajudicially executed by government forces in August. In Gao, about a dozen Tuareg men and one woman were said to have been publicly shot by firing-squad near the airport on 4 August, after which their bodies were mutilated by onlookers and crushed by an armoured vehicle. A further 24 Tuareg were reportedly executed extrajudicially by soldiers in Gao on 14 August, as well as 18 others in Ménaka, Kidal, Tin Essako and the Tamesna area. One of the alleged victims, Akhmed Ag Makhakha, leader of the Ichadanharen clan, was in his eighties.

Tuareg encampments in the remote desert area near the Algerian border were also reportedly attacked by government forces but few details were available. At In Teguift Well, three men and a paralysed woman were said to have been killed on 8 August and other Tuareg, including children, were driven away and later died of thirst. At Alkit, near Kidal, government soldiers who attacked an encampment of members of the Idnan clan on 9 August reportedly stripped both men and women, and then flogged and shot the men, killing about 10.

The government said in August that 30 people had been killed in the uprising. Other sources suggested that the real figure was much higher, with possibly more than 300 people killed by Tuareg insurgents, and almost as many by government forces, including elderly people and children. The government denied that anyone had been executed. Further sporadic clashes between Tuareg and government forces were reported after September but on a smaller scale than before.

Several leading members of the Tuareg community and others were arrested at the height of the crisis and detained or placed under house arrest. Some were released within a short period but others were held for several weeks. They were possible prisoners of conscience. Among those detained were Sikaye Ag Ekawel, director of a government-sponsored food aid project, and Ouéfane Ag Soulaymane, a merchant. In September some 70 Tuareg were reported to be held at Djikoroni military camp near the capital, Bamako. None of those arrested was known to have been charged or tried and it was not clear whether they and others had been released by the end of the year.

Political detainees were reportedly held in harsh conditions and, in some cases, ill-treated. In August Habib Ben Wahab reportedly died in custody at Gao police station after torture or ill-treatment. He was apparently suspected of passing military information to the rebels. No inquest or other inquiry into his death was reported. In one incident, the head of the Idnan clan and another man were reportedly stripped in public and beaten by soldiers in Kidal in early August.

Four people were sentenced to death *in absentia* in December. They were convicted of embezzlement by the Special State Security Court. This special court allows no right of appeal, although procedural questions may be contested in the Supreme Court. No executions were reported.

Amnesty International appealed for the release of prisoners of conscience and for other political detainees to be brought to trial promptly and fairly on recognizably criminal charges or released. It also called on the government to halt extrajudicial executions by the security forces, to safeguard detainees from ill-treatment and to establish an independent investigation into the killings.

MAURITANIA

Thousands of people, all of them black Mauritanians, were detained and held without charge or trial for up to several months. Others, including some who had been arrested in 1989, were still held without charge or trial at the end of 1990. Some of those held were prisoners of conscience and many were reportedly tortured. At least 15 black Mauritanians died as a result of torture. Dozens of others "disappeared" following arrest. At least 100 people were extrajudicially executed by government forces and pro-government militia.

Expulsions of black Mauritanians from the country continued throughout the year. Over 50,000 Mauritanians had been expelled in mid-1989, following intercommunal violence between Mauritanians and Senegalese (see *Amnesty International Report 1990*). Several thousand people were expelled to Senegal and Mali during 1990 and thousands of others fled the country to escape persecution. Following the 1989 expulsions, the government settled Haratines (descendants of black slaves of the Moors) on land in the south belonging to those who had been expelled, and reportedly armed them. Mauritanians expelled to Senegal and Mali carried out armed raids across the border to recover property and cattle confiscated at the time of their expulsion, and attacked government forces and people who had been settled on their land. Acts of violence against government targets, such as military posts, were also committed by armed opposition groups.

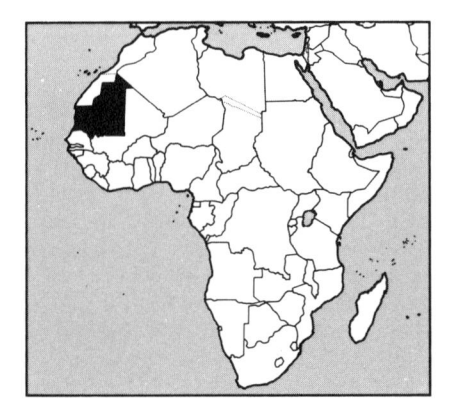

Large-scale human rights violations continued, targeted mainly at black Mauritanians of the Halpulaar ethnic group (known as Fulanis) in the south of the country, along the Senegal river valley. While conducting searches and enforcing curfews, the National Guard and Haratine militia supporting them arrested, tortured and killed Halpulaar villagers apparently with impunity. However, information was difficult to obtain and relatively few incidents could be documented in detail.

In November and December some 3,000 or more black Mauritanians were arrested in the capital, Nouakchott, and in Nouadhibou. The authorities later alleged that there had been a conspiracy to overthrow the government. Most of those arrested were members of the armed forces and civil servants. They included Abdoulaye Malikel Sy and Ly Moussa, two former prisoners of conscience. At the end of 1990 the majority were held without charge or trial in various military barracks.

Arrests occurred throughout the year in the south. At least 350 villagers were said to be held in a military barracks at Azlat in Aleg region in mid-1990. Although a number were released in July, it was unclear what had happened to others. No legal procedures were observed in such cases, and those detained were held incommunicado without any information being revealed about them. Some relatives who made inquiries about detainees were themselves arrested. The secrecy surrounding detentions meant that many people who were openly arrested were subsequently classified as "disappeared" when no news could be obtained about them.

Some of those arrested in mid-1989 were still held without charge or trial at the end of 1990. Most were detained simply because of their race or ethnic origin. Those held included alleged government opponents, all of them black, who were arrested in Nouakchott and elsewhere. Among those released was Ladji Traoré, a former prisoner of conscience from the Soninké ethnic group, who was detained unlawfully from October 1989 to October 1990. The authorities gave no reasons for his detention, but it was believed to be connected to his opposition to the expulsions of black Mauritanians from the country.

Dozens of people, foreigners as well as black Mauritanians, were arrested and held without charge for several weeks before being expelled from the country. In one case, a Mauritanian woman was held in Nouakchott's Central Police Station from March until May, and then summarily expelled to Senegal with 50 other people.

Some villagers were detained on suspicion of harbouring returned refugees, after people who had sought refuge in Senegal or Mali came back over the border to recover confiscated property or cattle. Others were held because they opposed the expulsions or protested against the confiscation of their goods. Yoro Lam, a herdsman from Zereyga near Foum Gleita, in M'Bout area, was held in Nouakchott prison from June 1989 to September 1990 because he and his brother had resisted the expropriation of their cattle by police (see *Amnesty International Report 1990*).

Many detainees were reportedly tortured by security forces. Following the November arrests as many as 15 prisoners were said to have died after torture including Ly Moussa, a former prisoner of conscience. Methods of torture used included burning with hot irons and cigarettes, and the "Jaguar", during which the victim is suspended upside-down from a bar and beaten on the soles of the feet. Gorel Bâ, a farmer from Gourel-Mamoudou village, was among about 10 people arrested in April in M'Bomé who were chained up, beaten and subjected to the "Jaguar" by soldiers. Many Halpulaar women were also reportedly raped while held by the security forces. One woman was said to have been repeatedly raped in February by soldiers at the military post of the Ould Mogheïna area, near Rosso, before being thrown into the Senegal river.

Dozens of villagers reportedly "disappeared" following arrest by government forces: many of them were believed to have been extrajudicially executed. Most were detained in the Aleg or Sélibaby regions. Sixteen people, including Kanni Sall and 15-year-old Oumar Thiam, were arrested in March at Dioudé-Diéry near Boghé, Aleg region, by the National Guard. They were taken to an unknown destination and their fate was unknown at the end of 1990. In the Sélibaby region, whole families "disappeared". Adama N'Diaye, his wife and nine children were arrested in February at Gourel-Amadou Mamadou, near Ould Yengé, and taken into the bush. They were not seen again.

Reports of extrajudicial executions by the army, the National Guard and Haratine militia rose dramatically in the first half of the year. There were killings reported in most towns and villages along the Mauritanian bank of the Senegal river. Virtually all the victims appeared to be unarmed Halpulaar villagers. The killings had begun in May 1989 with the operation to expel black Mauritanians (see *Amnesty International Report 1990*). The victims were often singled out following routine patrols of villages. On 10 April, for example, a patrol of soldiers and armed Haratines entered Moudji village near Sélibaby. After searching houses, they arrested seven men including Silly Youmé Bâ and Mamadou Demba Sall. The seven were taken a few kilometres out of the village and extrajudicially executed: three were shot and four had their heads crushed with stones. All were found with their hands tied behind their backs, indicating that they were being held as prisoners when they were killed.

Several people were also killed when members of the National Guard reportedly fired at villagers deliberately and for no apparent reason. For example, Thierno Saïbatou Bâ, a religious leader, was killed on 12 April in Ngoral-Guidal near Boghé. Eye-witnesses said that soldiers shot him just after he had finished bathing in the river in preparation for afternoon prayers. In another case, at least four people suspected of returning illicitly to Mauritania after being expelled were said to have been beheaded by members of the National Guard in July and August in the Maghama area.

Fourteen political prisoners were released in September, their sentences having been reduced by one year as a result of a measure ordered by President Maaouya ould Sid'Ahmed Taya in December 1989 which affected all sentenced prisoners. Thirteen of the 14 were serving five-year prison terms imposed after unfair trials in 1986 and 1987. They had been convicted in connection with the distribution of an opposition group manifesto, the *Manifeste du négro-mauritanien opprimé*, Oppressed Black Mauritanian's Manifesto. The 14th had been sentenced to three years' imprisonment in September 1988 when eight members of the pro-Iraqi Ba'th Socialist Party were convicted of state security offences. However, at the end of 1990, 32 members of the armed forces and one civilian remained in prison in Aïoun El Atrouss. They had been convicted in October 1987 of plotting to overthrow the government, after trials which failed to satisfy international fair trial standards.

Amnesty International repeatedly expressed concern to the Mauritanian Government about persistent reports of grave human rights violations. In a statement to Amnesty International in June, the Minister of Justice intimated that the security forces' actions constituted a legitimate response to the acts of violence committed by armed opposition groups.

In October Amnesty International published *Mauritania: Human Rights Violations in the Senegal River Valley*. The report expressed concern that the rule of law had been virtually abandoned in the river valley area and called on the authorities both to disarm the irregular Haratine militia and to instruct members of the security forces and militia to respect human rights. The government did not respond to these appeals. However, it dismissed the organization's concerns and accused Amnesty International of favouring Senegal in the conflict between the two countries and of ignoring the persecution of Mauritanians in Senegal. After the November arrests Amnesty International appealed to the authorities to end the use of torture and to release those held solely because of their ethnic origin. The government acknowledged that numerous arrests had occurred but denied that anyone had been tortured. In an oral statement to the United Nations Commission on Human Rights, Amnesty International included reference to its concerns in Mauritania.

MAURITIUS

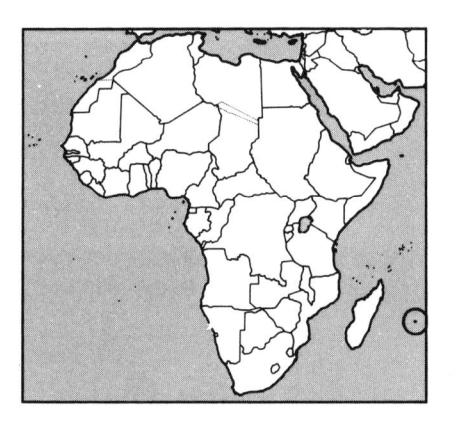

Four people faced charges that could result in their becoming prisoners of conscience. No new death sentences were reported, but six prisoners remained under sentence of death. There were no executions.

In June the government established a committee to review laws with provisions that provide for imprisonment in violation of human rights. The laws included the 1970 Public Order Act, which permits detention without charge or trial, the 1973 Industrial Relations Act, which limits the right to strike, and the 1984 Newspaper and Periodicals (Amendment) Act, which makes it illegal to publish false news. The committee had not reported by the end of the year.

Harish Boodhoo, leader of the *Parti socialiste mauricien* (PSM), Mauritian

Socialist Party, and Vedi Ballah, editor of the PSM newspaper, *Le Socialiste* (*The Socialist*), were awaiting trial on charges of giving out false information. If convicted they could become prisoners of conscience. They were charged in January 1989 after publicly calling for an inquiry into the alleged involvement of government ministers in the sale of Mauritian passports (see *Amnesty International Report 1990*); they were expected to stand trial in 1991. In November the Supreme Court rejected an application by the two men, who were at liberty throughout 1990, to have the charges against them declared unconstitutional.

In May 1990 Sydney Selvon, Vice-President of the Mauritius Union of Journalists and Chief Editor of the daily newspaper, *Le Mauricien* (*The Mauritian*), and Harish Chundunsing, a journalist employed by *Le Mauricien*, were also charged with publishing false news. This followed publication by the newspaper of an article which wrongly reported that the government had dropped charges against a sea captain accused of illegal fishing in Mauritian waters. They remained at liberty and were expected to stand trial in 1991.

Charges brought in August 1989 against seven trade unionists and a journalist accused of participating in an illegal demonstration were dropped in July (see *Amnesty International Report 1990*).

In March the Supreme Court turned down the appeal of Radha Krishna Kunnath, an Indian national sentenced to death in August 1989 for drug-trafficking (see *Amnesty International Report 1990*). The court granted him permission to appeal to the Judicial Committee of the Privy Council (JCPC) in the United Kingdom, the highest Court of Appeal for Mauritius. Five other prisoners under sentence of death, four for drug-trafficking and one for murder, continued to wait for their appeals to be heard by the JCPC. There were no executions.

Amnesty International continued to appeal to the Mauritian Government to commute all death sentences. It also urged the government to abolish the death penalty.

MEXICO

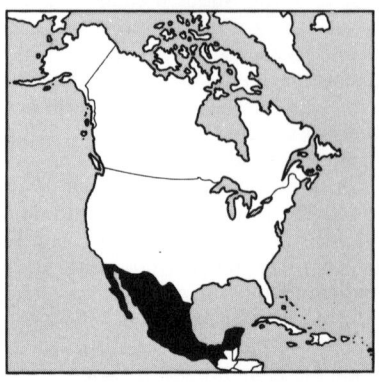

The widespread use of torture and ill-treatment by law enforcement agents, in some cases leading to the death of detainees, continued to be reported. Hundreds of people were arbitrarily detained and ill-treated by security forces in the context of forced evictions of peasants and of widespread protests against alleged electoral fraud. Dozens were detained for political reasons; in a number of such cases, charges were based on forced confessions. At least six people "disappeared" and little progress was reported in clarifying the whereabouts of several hundred who "disappeared" in previous years. Evidence suggested that at least three people were extrajudicially executed. Several others, including a renowned human rights lawyer, were believed to have been killed because of their peaceful human rights or political activities.

Following an increasing number of reports of human rights violations, President Carlos Salinas de Gortari announced in June the creation of the National Human Rights Commission, which incorporated its predecessor, the Directorate of Human Rights. The main functions of the Commission are to investigate human rights abuses and to issue recommendations to the authorities. By the end of the year it had received hundreds of complaints and had issued 33 recommendations regarding well-documented cases of human rights abuses. Most of these recommendations had not been implemented by the end of the year.

Allegations of electoral fraud by the governing *Partido Revolucionario Institucional* (PRI), Institutional Revolutionary

Party, during state and local elections in December 1989 triggered widespread protests, principally involving members of the centre-left *Partido de la Revolución Democrática* (PRD), Democratic Revolutionary Party. Following accusations of electoral fraud in previous years, the Inter-American Commission on Human Rights issued a series of recommendations in May 1990, calling on the government to "assure the free and full exercise of political rights and judicial protection" for those participating in electoral processes.

Torture was frequently used by law-enforcement agents throughout the country, particularly by the state and federal judicial police. It was often used to extract confessions from detainees, and such statements continued to be admissible as evidence in courts. Torture methods reported included beatings, electric shocks, near-asphyxiation in water or by covering the head of the victim with a plastic bag, forcing carbonated water with chilli pepper into the nose, and psychological torture. Adequate medical treatment was rarely made available to victims and official forensic doctors frequently failed to fully document cases of torture. Despite a public outcry and numerous formal complaints to the authorities about torture and other human rights violations, very few of those responsible were brought to justice.

Scores of torture cases were reported in the context of federal judicial police operations aimed at preventing the cultivation and trafficking of drugs.

In March Rubén Oropeza Hurtado was detained in the town of Tijuana by the federal judicial police. He was reportedly forced to confess under torture to drugs offences and was denied adequate medical treatment. In July he was admitted to a local clinic in a critical condition, apparently resulting from beatings suffered in detention, and underwent a major abdominal operation. He died in October. Those allegedly responsible were not brought to justice, despite recommendations on this case by the National Human Rights Commission.

In October Pedro Yescas Martínez died in detention, five days after his arrest in the town of Durango, reportedly as a consequence of torture inflicted by the federal judicial police. According to witnesses, he was forced to confess to drugs offences and was later denied medical treatment, despite his injuries. Protests in the press and complaints by relatives prompted an investigation, but those responsible had not been brought to justice by the end of the year.

Children and youths were among those reported to have been tortured and ill-treated by the security forces. Seventy-six well-documented complaints against the Tijuana juvenile justice system were filed in April by the *Centro Bi-Nacional de Derechos Humanos*, Bi-National Human Rights Centre, in Tijuana. No investigations into these allegations were known to have been initiated by the end of the year.

Between January and April at least 15 people were killed by the security forces during the protests against alleged vote-rigging. Scores of people were arrested, dozens reportedly suffered torture or ill-treatment and four "disappeared" after their arrest. Most of the victims belonged to opposition parties, principally the PRD. Government officials reportedly ill-treated protesters, particularly during forced evictions of activists occupying local municipal buildings as a form of protest.

The most serious abuses were reported in the states of Guerrero and Michoacán, two strongholds of the PRD. In March at least 250 police agents surrounded the municipality of Omatepec, Guerrero, to evict approximately 50 PRD protesters. According to witnesses the police shot at the protesters, wounding many and killing at least one, Román de la Cruz Zacapela. Many were detained for short periods during which some were reportedly tortured. Vicente de Jesús, Miguel Silverio, Daniel Alvarez and Andrés de la Cruz Zacapela were reported to have "disappeared" after their arrest. Despite formal complaints by victims and their families, proceedings were not initiated against those responsible.

Hundreds of people were arbitrarily detained and ill-treated during forced evictions of peasants by security forces, usually aided by local landowners and *pistoleros* (gunmen), in rural areas. In April police agents and *pistoleros* forcibly evicted more than 100 peasant families from the communities of Paso Achiote, Unión y Progreso and Emiliano Zapata in the State of Chiapas from communal land which they claimed had been promised to them by the authorities. Men, women and children were arrested and dozens suffered ill-treatment and injuries; 14 of them were held until September.

Sócimo Hernández, a peasant activist from Embocadero, continued to be imprisoned on a murder charge. He was reported to have confessed after being tortured with beatings, near-asphyxiation and threats. He had been arrested in November 1989 and accused of the murder of Pedro Hernández Hernández (see *Amnesty International Report 1990*).

In May Salomón Mendoza Barajas, PRD mayor of Aguililla and well known for his denunciations of human rights violations by anti-narcotics squads operating in the region, was arrested. He had complained to the police about the alleged harassment, arbitrary arrest and ill-treatment of local residents. While in custody he was said to have been subjected to near-asphyxiation and beatings to force him to confess to murder and drugs possession. He was also reportedly denied adequate medical treatment and as a result is permanently disabled. In November the National Human Rights Commission recommended that he should be released, together with other Aguililla residents who had been detained and reportedly ill-treated. It also recommended that charges against them should be dropped and that those responsible for the abuses in Aguililla should be brought to justice. In December Salomón Mendoza Barajas and one other detainee were released, after the Attorney General's Office dropped the charges against them. However, at the end of the year several other detainees from Aguililla remained in prison, despite a recommendation by the National Human Rights Commission that they should be released.

The authorities promised to investigate cases of "disappearance" – more than 500 people were known to have "disappeared" in Mexico, mostly during the 1970s and early 1980s. However, little progress was reported. The whereabouts of José Ramón García (see *Amnesty International Report 1990*) remained unknown and no progress was reported in bringing to justice those responsible for his "disappearance". At least six new cases of "disappearance" were reported in 1990.

In June Francisco Quijano García, who was investigating the alleged murder of his three sons by federal judicial police, "disappeared" in Mexico City. He had allegedly received several anonymous death threats before his "disappearance". No progress was made by the end of the year in establishing his whereabouts.

Among the killings reported were those of Francisco Quijano García's sons Hector, Jaime and Erik in the State of Mexico in January. The police stated that they died during an armed confrontation. However, according to witnesses and forensic evidence, they were unarmed at the time of the killings and were extrajudicially executed by an anti-narcotics squad. The same squad had reportedly also tortured Hector García in the cells of the Attorney General's Office before taking him to the site of the killings. At the end of the year, no developments in the investigation into these killings had been reported.

In February three Venezuelan teachers and a Mexican lawyer were reportedly abducted in the town of Culiacán by members of the federal judicial police. In response to inquiries from the Venezuelan Ministry of Foreign Affairs, the Mexican authorities at first confirmed, but later denied, that the three Venezuelans were being held by the Federal Attorney General on arms-smuggling charges. Their bullet-riddled bodies, all showing signs of torture, were found in March. No progress was reported in the investigations announced into these killings.

Norma Corona Sapién, a human rights lawyer, was murdered in May in the town of Culiacán. She had been investigating the alleged participation of federal judicial police agents in the reported torture and killing of the three Venezuelans and the Mexican. The federal government established a commission of inquiry and five people allegedly responsible for her killing were detained and charged, including two former federal judicial police agents. Local human rights organizations expressed concern that the full truth about Norma Corona's killing had not been established and continued to call for further investigations.

Amnesty International repeatedly called for full investigations into human rights violations including extrajudicial executions, torture and "disappearances" and urged the authorities to bring all those responsible to justice. In September it published *Mexico: Human Rights Violations Against the Triquis in Oaxaca*, which examined past human rights violations reportedly suffered by members of the Triqui indigenous communities in western

Oaxaca, including killings, torture and the "disappearance" of two children.

In November the Executive Secretary of the National Human Rights Commission met Amnesty International to discuss the Commission's work. Amnesty International welcomed the creation of the Commission but expressed concern about the apparently limited effectiveness, thus far, of its recommendations.

MOROCCO AND WESTERN SAHARA

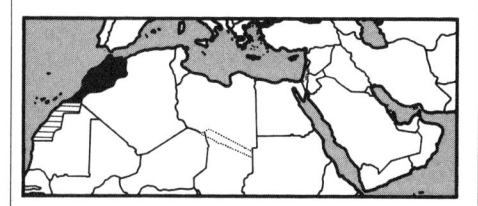

More than 50 suspected government opponents were prisoners of conscience; some had been held continuously for more than 16 years. Others were arrested and imprisoned in 1990. Hundreds of other political prisoners, some of whom were possible prisoners of conscience, were serving sentences imposed after trials which fell short of international fair trial standards. There were new reports of torture and ill-treatment of prisoners, and of deaths in custody, possibly following such abuse. No steps were taken by the authorities to clarify hundreds of cases of "disappearances" reported since 1975. More than 140 people were believed to be under sentence of death but no executions were known to have been carried out.

National elections due in 1990 were postponed in anticipation of a negotiated settlement to the long-running dispute over the Western Sahara. A plan for a cease-fire to be followed by an amnesty for political prisoners and a referendum in the Western Sahara, worked out under United Nations auspices in June, was agreed by both the Moroccan Government and the *Frente Popular para la liberación de Seguia el-Hamra y Rio de Oro*, Popular Front for the Liberation of Seguia el-Hamra and Rio de Oro, known as the Polisario Front.

Riots took place in Fes, Tanger and other towns during a one-day general strike on 14 December called by two major trade unions in support of a number of social and economic demands including a higher minimum wage. The government said five people were killed but other sources suggested that at least 50 people had died, mostly as a result of attempts by the police and army to restore order.

More than 40 prisoners of conscience and many others who may have been prisoners of conscience were held throughout the year. The former included Abraham Serfaty and seven other alleged members of clandestine Marxist groups sentenced after an unfair trial in 1977 (see *Amnesty International Report 1978*), and Ali Idrissi Kaitouni, a painter and poet sentenced to 15 years' imprisonment in 1982 for his writings. All nine were held at Kenitra Central Prison.

Fatima Oufkir also remained in custody. Her husband, former interior minister General Mohammed Oufkir, died in suspicious circumstances after his alleged involvement in a coup attempt in 1972; Fatima Oufkir, her six children and one of her cousins continued to be held under house arrest and virtually incommunicado near Marrakech. They had been held continuously since 1972, when the youngest child was only three years old, although no charges had ever been brought against them.

Some 25 members of the armed forces were also prisoners of conscience. All remained in prison without facing further charges after completing their sentences: they had been among over 100 military personnel sentenced in 1972 for allegedly attempting to kill King Hassan II. In 1973, 61 of the prisoners were moved to a remote prison at Tazmamert and since then had been subjected to such harsh and grossly inadequate conditions that at least 29 of the group had reportedly died in custody.

Suspected government opponents jailed during the year were also prisoners of conscience. They included six alleged members of an illegal Islamic group, *al-'Adl wa'l-Ihsan*, Justice and Charity, who were tried by the Court of First Instance at Salé. They were each sentenced in March to two years' imprisonment for membership of an unauthorized organization, illegal fundraising and other offences. Their sentences were confirmed on appeal in August. Between December 1989 and March 1990, 32 other people were tried on similar charges; six were acquitted after trial and the others were acquitted or given reduced sentences on appeal.

The trial of the six prisoners at Salé was marked by gross irregularities. Defendants' dates of arrest were falsified to conceal the length of time they had been held incommunicado in pre-trial (*garde à vue*) detention, and the court refused to allow the defence to call witnesses to testify to this: defence lawyers walked out of the court in protest.

Abdessalam Yassine, the leader of *al-'Adl wa'l-Ihsan*, was also a prisoner of conscience. He was placed under house arrest in January and still confined at the end of the year.

Other prisoners of conscience included Ahmed Benjelloun, director of the weekly newspaper *al-Tariq* (*The Way*), who was sentenced to four months' imprisonment in May after being convicted under Article 44 of the Press Code. An article he had published in April 1989 was held to have defamed certain institutions.

Two others, Mohammed El-Brini and Abdelkader Himer, journalists with the newspaper *al-Ittihad al-Ishtiraki* (*Socialist Union*), were also charged under the Press Code in connection with an article published in August which criticized corruption and delays in the courts. Their trial had not concluded by the end of the year and both men were at liberty.

Many other people brought to trial during the year, including a number arrested in the wake of widespread demonstrations on 14 December, may have been prisoners of conscience. More than 40 students were brought to trial before the December unrest on charges such as disturbing public order, and received sentences of up to five years' imprisonment. Some alleged in court that they had been tortured while held in *garde à vue* detention, often beyond the maximum period permitted by law. Nine Fes University students who were tried in the *Chambre criminelle*, criminal chamber, in Fes in July 1990, alleged that they had been tortured while held in *garde à vue* detention for up to 49 days following their arrests in 1989. They then remained in custody for nearly one year before being brought to trial.

Over 1,000 people were arrested following the riots on 14 December. More than 200 of them had been sentenced to prison terms of up to 10 years by the end of the year.

More than 300 political prisoners sentenced after unfair trials in previous years continued to be held throughout 1990. They included 14 prisoners serving sentences of up to 20 years' imprisonment imposed in September 1981 following riots in Casablanca and at least 110 others, including alleged members of illegal Marxist and Islamic groups, who were sentenced after demonstrations and riots in January 1984. Other alleged Marxists, convicted of belonging to *Ila'l-Amam*, Forward, and of conspiring against the government, had been sentenced in 1986, and more than 30 out of 85 students sentenced for public order and other offences in 1989 were also still held. Their trials failed to satisfy international fair trial standards.

There were new reports of torture and ill-treatment of prisoners, particularly untried detainees held in *garde à vue* detention. Seven of the Fes University students who were tried in July alleged that they had been tortured at Derb Moulay Cherif detention centre in Casablanca while held incommunicado in 1989. They said that they were beaten, including on the soles of the feet, kicked, suspended in contorted positions, partially suffocated and given electric shocks. No investigation of these allegations was known to have been initiated by the court or the detaining authorities.

Abdelkader Migou, a trader, was also allegedly tortured at Oujda police station where he was taken following his arrest in August as a criminal suspect. He was said to have lost consciousness after being kicked and to have sustained three broken ribs as a result of the alleged assault. He received hospital treatment and a medical report found injuries consistent with his allegations. His lawyer sought an official inquiry, but no investigation was known to have been initiated.

Reports of five deaths in custody suggested that the victims may have been tortured. Saida Habiba died in Azilal police station two days after her arrest in January. Mohammed Hirchi, a 17-year-old criminal suspect, died in hospital in Oujda in July, 12 days after his arrest. In both cases reports suggested that these prisoners had been tortured or ill-treated in *garde à vue* detention before their deaths. In January the Moroccan Government said an inquiry would be held into Saida Habiba's death, but Amnesty International received no information to indicate whether any such inquiry was established. Following Mohammed Hirchi's death his lawyer pressed for a judicial investigation into the cause and circumstances of his death but it was not known whether any such inquiry was held. The Moroccan Government informed Amnesty International delegates in February that the cases of Larbi Charrat and Abdeljalil Yakouti, who died in custody in 1989, had been put before the *juge d'instruction* (examining magistrate).

Reports of cruel, inhuman or degrading treatment in prison continued. In Kenitra Civil Prison women were reportedly slapped, kicked, and beaten with sticks and on the soles of the feet (*falaqa*); in February one criminal prisoner, Malika Rabali, was allegedly tortured and put in a straitjacket for 24 hours. Political prisoners in Meknes, Safi and Ghbila prisons claimed to have been assaulted by prison officers. Severe overcrowding continued in many detention centres and prisons, and there were reports of over 100 prisoners being confined in cells measuring 24 square metres. Three political prisoners who had been on hunger-strike since June 1989 (see *Amnesty International Report 1990*), and one other who had been on hunger-strike since June 1985, ended their protests in February after they were transferred to Kenitra Central Prison. However, Hassan Aharrat and Noureddine Jouhari, who had been on hunger-strike since June 1985, were said to be still held incommunicado and secured to beds in Averroes Hospital in Casablanca at the end of the year. Both continued to be forcibly fed through gastric tubes (see *Amnesty International Report 1990*).

The government had still failed to account for the fate of hundreds of people of Western Saharan origin reported to have "disappeared" since 1975 in the custody of Moroccan security forces. There were persistent rumours that many were still alive and confined in secret prison camps or detention centres, one of which was said to be at Qal'at M'gouna, east of Ouarzazzate. However, this could not be confirmed.

No executions were recorded during the year. However, 147 prisoners reportedly remained under sentence of death in Kenitra Central Prison. They included 15 political prisoners who were convicted of plotting against the monarchy. Six of them were possible prisoners of conscience.

Amnesty International continued throughout the year to call for the release of prisoners of conscience, for other political prisoners to be brought to trial promptly and fairly or released, and for government action to prevent torture. Amnesty International also continued to press for an investigation into cases of "disappearance" and expressed concern over reports of life-threatening conditions and deaths among prisoners at Tazmamert.

In February an Amnesty International delegation visited Morocco and had discussions with King Hassan II, government ministers and officials. Before the visit, the organization had submitted details of its concerns relating to *garde à vue* detention, which were subsequently published in a report, *Morocco: Human Rights Violations in Garde à Vue Detention*. The delegation also met a specially constituted Committee for Dialogue with Amnesty International, which presented a lengthy response. However, the response failed to address adequately Amnesty International's concerns. Two Amnesty International delegates who travelled to Morocco to carry out research in advance of a proposed second visit in March were asked to leave the country. Subsequently, the Moroccan authorities informed Amnesty International that it would not be permitted to send representatives to the country before the next meeting with the Committee for Dialogue, and no such meeting with the Committee was arranged before the end of the year.

In May King Hassan II appointed a *Conseil consultatif des droits de l'homme* (CCDH), Human Rights Advisory Council. This set up two working groups, one to examine the use of *garde à vue* detention and the remand system, *détention préventive*, and the other to review the prison system. The full findings of the two groups had not been officially announced by the end of the year.

In November Amnesty International published a report, *Morocco: "Disappearances" of People of Western Saharan Origin*, and reiterated its call for an inquiry into "disappearance" cases. The government did not respond to the report or the renewed appeal.

MOZAMBIQUE

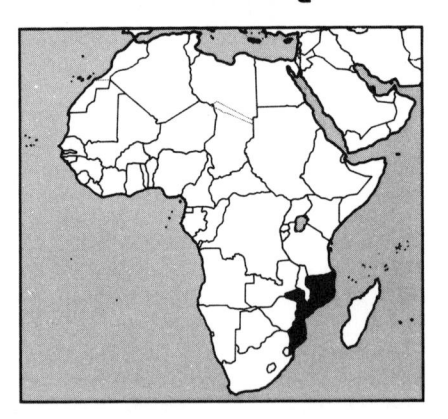

A new constitution abolished the death penalty and extended human rights guarantees. Over 500 untried political detainees were released, but more than 200 were still held at the end of 1990. Dozens of prisoners were convicted of political offences and jailed: it was not clear whether their trials satisfied international standards for fair trial. An escaped prisoner was reportedly recaptured and tortured to death. The authorities punished some members of the security forces for abusing human rights.

The new constitution came into force in November, following country-wide discussions of a draft published in January. The Constitution provided for a multi-party political system in place of a one-party state. It abolished the death penalty, which had not been imposed since 1986. New safeguards for prisoners included the prohibition of torture, arbitrary arrest and indefinite detention without charge, as well as the inclusion of the right to challenge the legality of imprisonment through *habeas corpus* procedures. The Constitution thus invalidated a 1975 law which prevented prisoners suspected of crimes against the security of the state from using *habeas corpus* procedures and which permitted their indefinite detention without charge or trial. However, proposed new legislation to limit the period during which a suspect may be detained by the security forces before referral to the judicial authorities had not been introduced by the end of 1990.

The conflict continued between government forces, aided by Zimbabwean troops, and the armed opposition group *Resistência Nacional Moçambicana* (RENAMO), Mozambique National Resistance, which was said to have received financial or military assistance from sources in South Africa. Talks between the government and RENAMO aimed at ending the war were inconclusive, although a limited cease-fire was agreed in December. Hundreds of civilians were killed in the fighting. Millions of displaced people continued to be dependent on emergency relief supplies and hunger was widespread.

There were further reports of abuses by RENAMO including the abduction and killing of civilians. RENAMO released eight foreign nationals captured in 1989 and 1990 and two others escaped. There were also reports that government soldiers killed civilians suspected of assisting RENAMO. However, it was not possible to obtain independent corroboration of reports of abuses committed in areas affected by the fighting.

On 7 March Mozambique acceded to the Organization of African Unity's African Charter on Human and Peoples' Rights.

Several hundred people were reportedly captured or arrested on suspicion of committing crimes on behalf of RENAMO. According to government sources, by the end of October 60 prisoners, including people accused of politically motivated crimes and soldiers accused of military offences, had been tried and convicted. A further 519 people had been released untried, 180 others were awaiting trial and the cases of about 40 people were under investigation.

At the beginning of 1990 there were about 140 untried political prisoners in the custody of the national security service, some of whom had been held for over two years. Some were tried and convicted of politically motivated violent crimes during the year but few details of the trials were reported. Others were released on the grounds that they had already spent at least half as long in detention without trial as any prison term to which they might be sentenced if tried and convicted. Over 20 political prisoners captured in previous years were still awaiting trial at the end of 1990.

Insufficient information was available to assess whether the trials of political prisoners were fair. Franz Sam Tembe, one of the prisoners whose cases were referred to the ordinary courts after the abolition of the Revolutionary Military Tribunal (see *Amnesty International Report 1990*), had been arrested in Maputo in 1987. He was sentenced to eight years' imprisonment in April 1990 after he had apparently admitted to recruiting for RENAMO. Later, however, he said that his officially appointed defence counsel had spent only 10 minutes with him before the trial.

It was reported in the local press in July that António Sitoi, a RENAMO member who had escaped from a prison in Gaza province, had been killed by members of the militia. After his recapture he had apparently been taken to a cemetery and forced to dig his own grave, in which he was then buried alive.

The authorities investigated several cases of alleged human rights violations by members of the security forces. Tomé Griche, a radio journalist, was arrested in July by soldiers after he published an article about the reorganization of the army in Sofala province. The authorities ordered his release and the procuracy began an inquiry into the circumstances of his arrest, which could lead to the prosecution of the soldiers involved.

A soldier convicted in July of killing one prisoner and mortally wounding another in November 1989 received a 16-year prison sentence. The victims had been arrested in Dondo, Sofala province, and questioned about the movements of a RENAMO group. Amnesty International learned in 1990 that three soldiers accused of arresting and torturing a radio journalist in May 1989 were tried in mid-1989 and each sentenced to 18 months' imprisonment. The results of an inquiry into allegations that prisoners convicted of fraud in September 1989 had been tortured while they were interrogated by the criminal investigation police had not been published by the end of 1990 (see *Amnesty International Report 1990*).

There was no news of dozens of people who "disappeared" in "re-education" camps after being arrested in the mid-1970s (see previous *Amnesty International Reports*).

After the draft constitution was published Amnesty International called for the inclusion of strong human rights guarantees. It welcomed the abolition of the death penalty and the additional human rights guarantees in the Constitution which was adopted in November. Amnesty International continued to ask for information about "disappeared" prisoners.

MYANMAR (BURMA)

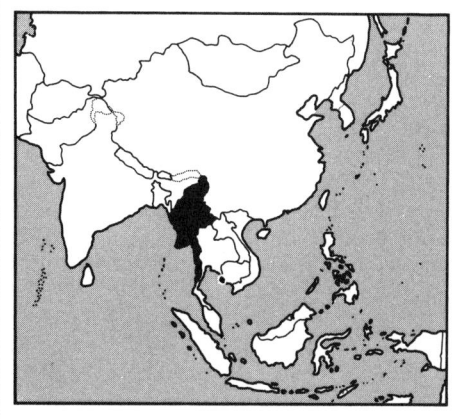

More than 350 prisoners of conscience and possible prisoners of conscience were known to be among thousands of people believed held for political reasons. Many were detained without charge or trial but others were sentenced after unfair trials by military tribunals. Torture and ill-treatment of prisoners were reportedly common. There were continuing allegations of extrajudicial executions by government troops in ethnic minority areas affected by armed insurgency. At least 100 people remained under sentence of death, but it was not known if any executions took place.

The ruling State Law and Order Restoration Council (SLORC), headed by General Saw Maung, continued to enforce Martial Law Order 2/88, which prohibits gatherings of more than five people, and Notification 8/88, which prohibits public criticism of the military. Scores of people were arrested for contravening these provisions and Order Number 3/90, issued in February, which severely restricts freedom of expression during election campaigning activities.

Parliamentary elections were held on 27 May. The opposition National League for Democracy (NLD) won an overwhelming majority, despite the detention or imprisonment of its leaders. However, by the end of the year the SLORC had not announced a firm timetable for convening the National Assembly or for handing over power to the elected civilian government.

More than 350 prisoners of conscience and possible prisoners of conscience had been identified by the end of 1990, but the actual number of people held for political reasons was thought to be in the thousands. Hundreds of people were arrested for their peaceful election campaigning activities or for protesting against the SLORC's refusal to hand over power and its continuing repression of government critics. In February at least 25 parliamentary candidates were reportedly arrested in the Yangon (Rangoon) area: it was not known whether any of them were released. Thirty other political activists were arrested in April and May during the election campaign. U Hla Wai, a candidate for the Democratic Party for a New Society (DPNS), was reportedly arrested at his home by 40 armed security officials on the day before the election. He was apparently still in detention at the end of the year. U Nu, a former prime minister, and the NLD's leaders, Aung San Suu Kyi and Tin U, remained in custody throughout 1990 and were officially barred from participating in the elections. Many other people arrested in 1989 apparently remained in prison throughout 1990.

Zar Gana, a former prisoner of conscience, was rearrested in May apparently for satirizing on stage the military authorities. He was said to have been sentenced to at least five years' imprisonment and held at Insein Prison, near Yangon. Another prisoner of conscience, Nay Min, a lawyer sentenced to 14 years' imprisonment in 1989, was reported to be suffering from an acute heart ailment. Torture with electric shocks may have exacerbated his condition.

Further political arrests occurred after the May election. Kyi Maung, the acting Chairman of the NLD, and the NLD's acting Party Secretary, Chit Khaing, were arrested in September. They were reportedly accused of passing sensitive information to unauthorized recipients, and in November were both convicted of violating the 1923 Official Secrets Act. Kyi Maung was sentenced to 10 years' imprisonment and Chit Khaing to seven years. Other political activists were arrested in September for writing, possessing or publishing anti-government material. Those held included NLD Information Officer Kyi Hla, and two DPNS leaders – Kyi Win and Ye Naing. Kyi Win and Ye Naing were each sentenced to seven years' imprisonment. All were considered to be prisoners of conscience.

It was unclear in many cases whether individual political prisoners were being detained without charge or trial under the 1975 State Protection Law or had been tried and sentenced. However, some were known to have been tried by military tribunals which were established in July 1989 in order to try alleged martial law offenders. Such tribunals used summary trial procedures which contravened international fair trial standards; they could waive "unnecessary" witnesses, and defendants had no right to judicial appeal. Those convicted were liable to one of three sentences: at least three years' hard labour, life imprisonment, or the death penalty.

Among the prisoners of conscience who were sentenced was U Thein Han, a lawyer and NLD candidate from Pabedan Township, who was arrested in February and sentenced to three years' imprisonment with hard labour. Another was 82-year-old U Oo Tha Tun, a well-known Arakan historian and election candidate for the Arakan League for Democracy. He was reportedly sentenced to three years' imprisonment with hard labour under Section 5/J of the 1950 Emergency Provisions Law, which prohibits promoting disloyalty to the state. In addition, two NLD leaders, Ohn Kyaing and Thein Dan, were sentenced to three years' imprisonment in October by a military tribunal at Insein Prison. They had reported the alleged killings of two Buddhist monks and two students by security forces during a demonstration on 8 August in Mandalay.

The demonstration, led by monks, commemorated mass anti-government protests in 1988 during which hundreds of demonstrators were shot dead by security forces. At the 1990 demonstration, at least 17 monks were beaten or arrested, and eight others were shot by security forces. The four alleged killings, which the SLORC denied, could not be confirmed.

Following the 1990 demonstration, Buddhist monks in Mandalay and other cities refused to provide religious services for military personnel and their families, and demanded that General Saw Maung apologize for the injuries inflicted on monks at the demonstration. They also called for the release of all detained monks, for an accurate account of the 1990 demonstration to be published, and for troops to be kept out of monasteries. In October, after a directive that monks must end their boycott had failed, the SLORC issued Order Numbers 6/90 and 7/90. The first order required all unofficial monks' organizations to disband and the second empowered military tribunals to try monks. Between 22 and 25 October troops systematically searched monasteries and arrested as many as 40 monks, only one of whom – U Laba "U Wayama" – was known to have been officially identified. Troops arrested at least 300 other monks in the following days. The SLORC then introduced decree Number 20/90, which provided for the imprisonment of monks belonging to unofficial monastic organizations or who criticized official monastic organizations.

Official suppression of the monks' protest was accompanied by searches of NLD and other political party offices and the arrests of more than 50 NLD leaders in late October. Those held included Khin Maung Swe, Kyaw Min, Chan Aye and Soe Thein, all NLD Central Executive Committee members, and at least 16 elected members of the National Assembly. All appeared to be prisoners of conscience. More than 40 NLD activists were also detained, as was the entire DPNS leadership, comprising at least eight people. Most were believed still held at the end of the year.

Nita Yin Yin May, another prisoner of conscience, was sentenced in November to three years' imprisonment under the Official Secrets Act. A Myanmar national employed by the British Embassy in Yangon, Nita Yin Yin May may have been imprisoned because she was suspected by the SLORC of involvement in discussions about non-violent opposition to military rule with foreign diplomats.

Reports of torture and ill-treatment of prisoners were received throughout the year from prisons in urban centres and in ethnic minority areas affected by armed insurgency. In the latter, civilians continued to be forcibly conscripted as porters by government forces and were apparently used as human minesweepers by troops as well as to carry supplies. Conscripted porters were said to have been beaten and kicked, and some reportedly died as a result.

Several prisoners were reportedly beaten in September, when 89 inmates at Insein Prison staged a hunger-strike to demand a transfer of power to the elected opposition. Nine prisoners apparently required hospital treatment and there were suggestions that six may have died. The SLORC later said that "internationally recognized batons" were used to control the hunger-strikers, and that only three prisoners were "slightly injured".

At least one person was reported to have died as a result of torture. Maung Ko, a senior member of the NLD, died in a military detention centre near Yangon on 9 November. His family reportedly said that they believed torture was the cause of his death because his body was covered in bruises and one of his legs was broken. However, General Saw Maung denied the allegation and said that Maung Ko had committed suicide by hanging himself with a blanket.

Extrajudicial executions continued to be reported from ethnic minority states: government troops were alleged to have deliberately killed civilians suspected of being political opponents as well as porters conscripted by the army. At least 100 people reportedly remained under sentence of death, including Moe Kyaw Thu who was 17 years old when convicted. It was not known if there were any new death sentences imposed during the year or if any executions were carried out.

Amnesty International pressed for the release of all prisoners of conscience, for the fair trial or release of other political prisoners, for investigations into all reports of torture, and for the commutation of all death sentences. In May Amnesty International published *Myanmar: Prisoners of Conscience and Torture*, and in November a full report on its concerns, *Myanmar: In the National Interest*. In these publications, the organization called for urgent steps to be taken to end widespread and systematic human rights violations by Myanmar's military government. Amnesty International informed the SLORC that it wished to visit Myanmar to discuss human rights but received no response.

In January Amnesty International submitted information about its concerns in Myanmar for United Nations (UN) review under a procedure, established by Economic and Social Council Resolutions 728F/1503, for confidential consideration of human rights violations. In February

Amnesty International submitted information about human rights abuses in Myanmar to the UN Commission on Human Rights in both a written and an oral statement to the Commission. These included reference to its concern about the government's failure to investigate torture allegations. In August Amnesty International delivered an oral statement to the UN Sub-Commission Working Group on Detention which drew attention to the continued imposition of a death sentence on Moe Kyaw Thu, who was 17 at the time of the offence. The SLORC responded to Amnesty International's reporting of human rights violations in Myanmar by categorically denying that torture is used or that political prisoners are held.

NAMIBIA

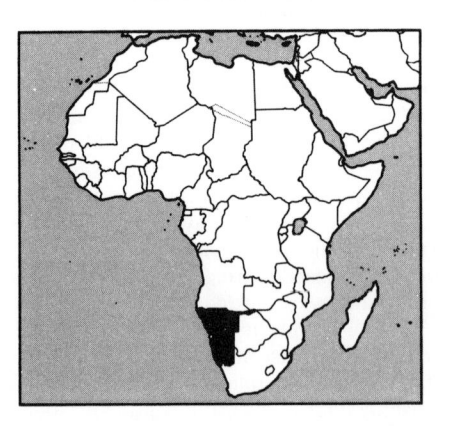

Namibia became an independent republic on 21 March after more than 60 years' administration by South Africa. The Constitution abolished the death penalty and guaranteed human rights. However, there were some reports of prisoners being tortured or ill-treated by police. Moreover, hundreds of people who had died or "disappeared" before independence in the custody of the South African authorities in Namibia or in detention camps run by the South West Africa People's Organisation (SWAPO) in Angola remained unaccounted for.

After multi-party elections in March, SWAPO's leader, Samuel Shaafishuna Nujoma, became President. The human rights guarantees of the new constitution broadly accord with relevant provisions of the principal international human rights standards. The United Nations (UN) Transition Assistance Group which helped to administer the independence process left Namibia in May. A new police force and army were recruited from former SWAPO guerrillas and the former South African-controlled security forces: some, including senior officers, had allegedly been responsible for killing or torturing prisoners in the past. In February a 1989 amnesty law exempting returning exiles from prosecution for abuses committed in the past was extended to South African security force personnel with respect to crimes committed in the course of their duties before independence.

Nine white men suspected of stealing a large quantity of weapons from arsenals as part of a right-wing plot to overthrow the government were arrested between August and October. They were charged with high treason and related offences. Their trial was set for early 1991. In a separate case, 15 people arrested in September were suspected of politically motivated offences as they were found in possession of ammunition. They included two relatives of Hans Diergaardt, a leader of the ethnically based local administration at Rehoboth before independence, who had barricaded himself in his state-owned residence until his eviction in September. He had apparently hoped to declare Rehoboth independent from Namibia. Hans Diergaardt's son was convicted in November and ordered to pay a fine; the others were acquitted of the same charges.

Nine convicted political prisoners were released under amnesty decrees connected with the independence process. Five who were imprisoned in Walvis Bay (a South African enclave in Namibia) for public violence offences during a protest in Walvis Bay in June 1988 against the siting of military bases near schools in northern Namibia were freed by the South African authorities in February. Four SWAPO members who did not qualify for release during Namibia's transition to independence were released soon after independence (see *Amnesty International Report 1990*). The case of another SWAPO member was referred to a commission which reviewed the cases of all prisoners and reduced the sentences of many.

There were dozens of allegations of torture or ill-treatment. Some criminal suspects alleged they had been tortured in police stations. For example, Malakia Endjambi, a diamond mine employee, alleged he had been severely beaten at Oranjemund in June. The Oranjemund police commander was subsequently charged with assault but he had not been tried by the end of 1990. Most complaints of torture or ill-treatment concerned "special constables", former soldiers who had received minimal training before being posted as border police. In a widely reported case in August, "special constables" allegedly tortured two South African tourists and forced them to confess that they had been spying for South Africa. One was reportedly beaten with a pole while suspended horizontally from a tree. The "special constables" were withdrawn in September and a Cabinet Committee was set up to recommend measures to prevent abuses by the police. The committee had not reported publicly by the end of 1990.

There was little progress in accounting for hundreds of people who had "disappeared" before independence, both in the custody of the South African authorities and in SWAPO detention camps in Angola. SWAPO failed to comply with a Supreme Court instruction of May 1989 to account for five of them by December 1989 (see *Amnesty International Report 1990*). It did, however, draw up a list of over 600 missing people. A heated controversy arose in October over the appointment as Army Commander of a SWAPO official allegedly responsible for detaining and torturing SWAPO members in Angola.

An all-party parliamentary committee set up in June to consider how to account for those who had died or "disappeared" in custody before independence apparently held no substantive discussions. However, Prime Minister Hage Geingob consulted various interest groups and reported to the National Assembly in November. As a result, the National Assembly requested the International Committee of the Red Cross to investigate the cases of those still unaccounted for in both Angola and Namibia.

Little further information became available about deaths in 1989 which appeared to be extrajudicial executions (see *Amnesty International Report 1990*). Amnesty International learned in 1990 that inquests into the deaths of about 300 SWAPO combatants killed by South African security forces in April 1989 had not found evidence of unlawful killings. An inquest in February found that the policeman who shot Petrus Joseph in August 1989 had acted in self-defence but the court noted that the police had not kept proper records of the incident.

At the beginning of the year 10 prisoners were under sentence of death for murder. In early March two had their sentences commuted on appeal to 15-year prison terms. The eight remaining death sentences were necessarily commuted when the death penalty was abolished, but by the end of 1990 the authorities had not yet decided on substitute prison terms.

Soon after independence, and again later in the year, Amnesty International wrote to the government to call for an independent and impartial inquiry to establish the fate or whereabouts of people who had died or "disappeared" or had been tortured in custody before independence. It also urged the authorities to ensure, at the very least, that those directly responsible for human rights abuses should not again be given any authority over prisoners. In addition, Amnesty International urged that police and military personnel should receive thorough training in human rights.

In August Amnesty International published a report, *Namibia: the Human Rights Situation at Independence*, which summarized human rights developments since September 1989.

NEPAL

Thousands of government opponents were detained during the first part of the year. Most were prisoners of conscience held without trial in harsh conditions. Torture and ill-treatment were widespread until mid-April. Scores of people, killed when security forces opened fire on unarmed demonstrators, may have been extrajudicially executed. The death penalty was abolished for ordinary offences.

In February the centrist Nepali Congress party and the communist United Left Front launched a largely peaceful campaign for multi-party democracy, in defiance of a 30-year ban on political party activity under the country's non-party *panchayat* (assembly) system. The campaign of strikes and demonstrations rapidly gained nationwide support. The authorities attempted unsuccessfully to suppress the protests by force:

NEPAL

there were thousands of arrests and numerous reports of torture and police attacks on demonstrators. In mid-April, after scores of unarmed demonstrators were shot dead by police in the capital, Kathmandu, King Birendra dismissed the government, lifted the ban on political parties and announced the release of political detainees. A multi-party interim government was then appointed to oversee constitutional reform and preparations for multi-party elections.

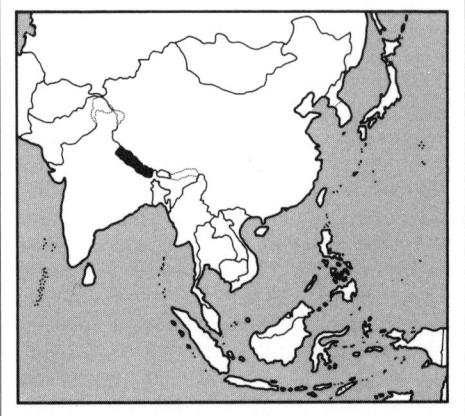

Most political detainees, including some who had been imprisoned for several years, were released by the end of April and all charges against them were dropped.

A new constitution was introduced in November, which provides increased human rights protection. It prohibits torture, which was not previously a specific offence, and forbids provision for the death penalty under future legislation. The application of the death penalty under existing legislation was restricted.

Over 8,000 democracy campaigners and sympathizers were arrested throughout Nepal between January and mid-April, including hundreds of students and agricultural workers, at least 50 lawyers, over 40 journalists, and several teachers, doctors, nurses and paramedics. Members of Amnesty International were among those held, as were leaders of banned political parties. Those detained were kept in police custody or jails for up to four months. Most were held under the Public Security Act which permits detention without charge or trial for up to 18 months, but others, including three members of the national *panchayat*, were charged under the Treason (Crime and Punishment) Act for criticizing the non-party system, or were charged with criminal offences. The police failed to keep records of all detainees, and ignored the legal requirements to bring detainees before a court within 24 hours of arrest. Scores of people were held incommunicado in unacknowledged detention for up to several weeks.

Most of those charged were released before being brought to trial, but some were given summary trials. In Hetauda, Man Nath Timilsina was brought to trial in early April after spending 44 days in police custody, during which he was allegedly tortured. He was unaware of the charges against him until he was met at the court by a state-appointed lawyer who reportedly told him that he was being charged under the State Offences Act and that any witnesses he named would be tortured. He was sentenced but then released in mid-April after the case was withdrawn.

Thirty Christians, arrested in previous years and sentenced to up to six years' imprisonment for religious conversion or proselytization – both of which remained illegal – were released in June, after King Birendra granted an amnesty to all such detainees.

Scores of detained pro-democracy activists were tortured during interrogation by police, in some cases apparently on the orders of senior police officers who personally threatened detainees and their relatives with death. Methods of torture reportedly included electric shocks, insertion of pins under the finger-nails, being made to stand in cesspits, sleep deprivation and, most commonly, severe beating with *lathis* (bamboo canes) – including on the soles of the feet – while bound and in some cases hung upside-down. Scores of people suffered broken bones as a result of such beatings. Torture victims included several Nepali Red Cross workers, who were detained after giving medical assistance to people injured when police fired on demonstrators, and several injured demonstrators arrested from their hospital beds.

Widespread torture and ill-treatment ceased after mid-April, but isolated reports of torture in police custody continued to be received throughout the year.

Conditions in police stations and jails were harsh. During the period of mass arrests, detainees were held in severely overcrowded conditions: hundreds were kept in *ad hoc* detention centres such as grain warehouses which were damp and lacked sanitation. In February over 150 people arrested in Chitwan were held by police for 48 hours without food or access to toilet facilities in a windowless, unventilated room measuring about 60 square metres. Many detainees, including torture victims, were denied proper medical treatment by police and needed hospital treatment after release.

Between 18 February and 9 April security forces fired on unarmed, largely peaceful demonstrators in several areas of Nepal, injuring scores and killing at least 50 people – some reports put the number of dead in the hundreds. Many victims suffered head and chest wounds, indicating that legal requirements to aim below the knee had not been met. Some of the dead may have been victims of extrajudicial executions.

In July the death penalty was abolished for murder and subversive activities. The reintroduction of the death penalty for these or any other offences was prohibited under the new constitution. Legislation providing the death penalty for espionage and for attacking the royal family was not repealed, but under the new constitution existing law must be reviewed within one year to ensure its compliance with constitutional provisions, including prohibition of the death penalty.

During the period of mass arrests, Amnesty International urged the *panchayat* government to release prisoners of conscience, charge or release other political detainees, and investigate allegations of torture and extrajudicial killings. The government replied that reports of arrests and deaths were exaggerated and denied that torture had occurred.

An Amnesty International delegation visited Nepal in April to investigate reports of mass arrests, torture and extrajudicial executions. It met members of the interim government, including several former political detainees, who stated their commitment to human rights protection. The interim government established investigations into the "loss of life" during the pro-democracy campaign, and into six "disappearances" which took place in the mid-1980s (see *Amnesty International Report 1988*). It also stated its intention to ratify international human rights treaties, although it had not done so by the end of the year.

Following the visit, Amnesty International submitted and published a memorandum to the government, containing recommendations for the prevention of further human rights violations in Nepal.

NICARAGUA

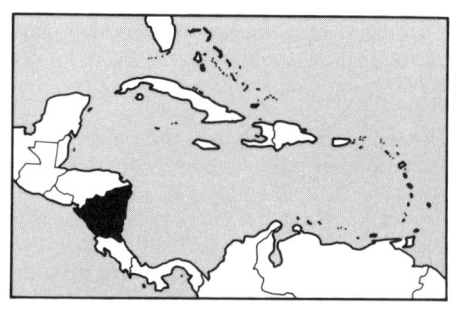

All remaining *contra* prisoners and detained former members of the National Guard were released before the new government took office in April. Two amnesty laws were passed effectively blocking investigations into past human rights violations. At least two clandestine graves were discovered; a local human rights group claimed they contained the remains of detainees who had "disappeared" in 1982 and 1983.

In April Violeta Chamorro, representing the 14-party *Unión Nacional Opositora* (UNO), National Opposition Union, took office as President after defeating President Daniel Ortega in February elections.

Following the election, leaders of the Nicaraguan Resistance, an armed opposition group commonly known as the *contra*, agreed to an internationally supervised demobilization program which officially ended at the beginning of July, although weapons continued to be collected after that date. *Contra* members and their families, many of them returning from Honduras, were to be resettled mainly in rural areas which were designated "development poles". A special rural police force made up of former *contra* members was established in the resettlement zones.

Political violence increased towards the end of the year, sparked off by complaints from former *contra* members about delays in providing land. Protest actions took the form of land seizures, hostage-taking, attacks on police stations, the occupation of churches, government and other public buildings, and road blockades. At least 25 people, including police officers, were reportedly killed between October and December. Some died in clashes between police and protesters; a few were killed during counter-actions by cooperativists whose land had been occupied by former *contra* members.

In February Nicaragua signed the Second Optional Protocol to the International Covenant on Civil and Political Rights Aiming at the Abolition of the Death Penalty. In August the government signed the Protocol to the American Convention on Human Rights to Abolish the Death Penalty. It had not ratified either of these instruments by the end of the year.

On 15 November the police arrested former *contra* adviser Arístides Sánchez, whom the government accused of plotting to destabilize the country. There were claims that he was subjected to psychological pressure by police officers and forced to sign a letter naming people alleged to be involved in the destabilization plot. The authorities denied the allegations and told a National Assembly commission looking into the incident that he had been alone in his cell when he wrote the letter. Arístides Sánchez was allowed to leave the country "on humanitarian grounds" shortly after his arrest.

Four leaders of the Sandinista-led *Frente Nacional de los Trabajadores*, National Workers Front, were held by police for two hours on 4 July during a national strike protesting against the government's economic policies. There were violent clashes when armed government supporters tried to prevent the strike. A 17-year-old youth was reportedly killed when two armed men on a motor cycle shot at a group of strikers. Three other men were killed in another strike incident in unclear circumstances.

By 25 April, when Daniel Ortega left office, the authorities had released all remaining *contra* detainees, 39 former National Guardsmen who had been imprisoned for alleged offences under the Somoza government, and some members of the Popular Sandinista Army accused of human rights violations. Some were released under the Law of General Amnesty and National Reconciliation (Law 81), which was passed in March. This granted an unconditional amnesty to all those who had committed crimes against state security, and civil and military personnel who may have committed crimes during the investigation of such offences between 1979 and 12 March 1990.

In May a second amnesty law revoked Law 81 but granted an amnesty to anyone responsible for "political crimes or common crimes related to them" committed at any time prior to the passing of the law, including those not yet sentenced or detained. The two amnesty laws effectively blocked investigations into past human rights violations, including those which had been opened into a number of cases of "disappearances" and killings of civilians carried out by government troops in previous years (see *Amnesty International Report 1990*).

Several unmarked graves were found in areas near the Honduran border which had been affected by *contra* and counter-insurgency activity in the past. The *Asociación Nicaragüense pro Derechos Humanos* (ANPDH), Nicaraguan Association for Human Rights, announced the discovery in June of an unmarked grave in Mokorón, Wiwilí, containing the partial remains of at least 10 people as well as items of clothing and nylon rope of the type used to tie wrists together. The organization claimed that the remains included those of seven peasants who had "disappeared" after their arrest in October 1983. Six of them had reportedly been arrested by soldiers in a house in San José de Bocay, not far from Wiwilí, when they tried to evade military service. The owner of the house had also been detained. A forensic report on the remains requested by the ANPDH suggested that the cause of death could have been *degollamiento*, slitting of the throat, because there was no evidence of bullet wounds, although not all the remains had been found. The examining doctor based his conclusions regarding the identity of the bodies on statements by relatives, who said they recognized some of the clothing and gold-filled teeth also found in the grave. However, another human rights group, the *Centro Nicaragüense de Derechos Humanos*, Nicaraguan Centre for Human Rights, concluded that these forensic investigations were insufficient to establish the time and cause of death, or to confirm the identity of the bodies. An investigation was reportedly initiated by the military authorities but the results were not known by the end of the year.

In August reports emerged of the discovery of another unmarked grave in Murra containing 16 skulls, some of them with bullet holes, and other human remains and clothing. Identity cards from an agricultural workers' union were also said to have been found. The cards belonged to six members of a group of 14 evangelists who were reportedly arrested in April 1982 by government troops. They were reportedly detained when they left a Sunday religious gathering after receiving a message summoning them to a meeting. The arrests were never acknowledged. The grave was said to have been discovered a few days after the men's alleged arrest but its existence was not made public until after the change of government because of fear of reprisals. Relatives of the six people whose identity cards were found, and of four others, said they recognized pieces of clothing or other items found in the grave as belonging to the missing detainees.

Amnesty International was investigating the cases of the unmarked graves. The organization was concerned that full and effective investigations should be carried out by the authorities, with the collaboration of forensic anthropologists, to determine the identity and fate of those who died, and to bring to justice those responsible.

On 11 April Amnesty International wrote to President Ortega expressing concern that Law 81 would block investigations into extrajudicial executions and "disappearances". The outgoing President of the official National Commission for the Promotion and Protection of Human Rights replied shortly afterwards stating that the Commission was opposed in principle to amnesty laws but that Law 81 should be seen in the context of reconciliation in that it favoured not only army personnel but also members of the *contra* involved in serious crimes. The Commission denied that the law was an invitation to impunity, pointing out that the Sandinista Government had made efforts to punish members of the army responsible for human rights violations.

In a letter to President Chamorro in July, Amnesty International reiterated its concern about the blocking of investigations into human rights violations following the passing of a second amnesty law in May. It also requested information about steps being taken by the authorities to clarify the fate of those who "disappeared" in previous years after their abduction by either the military or the *contra*. No response was received.

NIGER

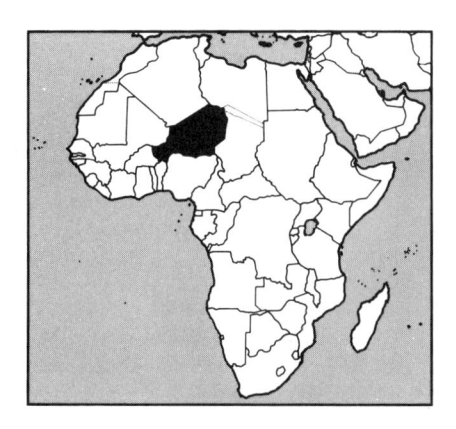

Hundreds of people belonging to the Tuareg ethnic group were arrested, tortured or extrajudicially executed. Some of those held appeared to be prisoners of conscience. Others reportedly died in detention as a result of torture or ill-treatment. At least three students were shot dead when the security forces opened fire on a demonstration.

There were calls for the introduction of a multi-party political system and in November the government announced the end of the one-party state set up in 1989. Multi-party elections were scheduled for 1992.

Tension between the government and the Tuareg community erupted into violence in May when an armed group of Tuareg attacked a prison and police station at Tchin-Tabaraden, killing three officials and three civilians. Government troops who were sent to the area attacked Tuareg encampments and were reported to have committed hundreds of extrajudicial executions. The victims included children. Two Tuareg prisoners were reportedly shot dead by soldiers in the centre of Tchin-Tabaraden on 7 May. At least two other Tuareg were said to have died in Tchin-Tabaraden on the same day, and other Tuareg were summarily killed at Gharo and In Gal. At Tilia, at least 25 people were said to have been extrajudicially executed including Hamazoutou Ag Naïssoun.

Hundreds of Tuareg were arrested, with about 500 reportedly detained in the Tahoua area alone. The arrests had begun in mid-March, when at least 28 people, including Attawa Egour and Karimoun Matachi, were arrested in Iférouane and Agadez area. They were reported to have been stripped naked, beaten and subjected to electric shock torture while in custody.

Among those arrested in May were prominent members of the Tuareg community such as Abdoulahi Mohamed, a former government minister, and Khamed Ibrahim El Moumine, a village leader. Some appeared to be prisoners of conscience, detained because of their position in the community rather than for any involvement in the violence. At least eight of the detainees, including Abdoullatif Mohamed, were transferred to Niamey after reportedly being tortured in Tahoua. Others were moved to Bilma and Nguigmi, where 93 were apparently being held in May, as well as to Tillabéry and Kollo. Seven of the eight detainees moved to Niamey were reportedly released by the end of August: the eighth was moved to Kollo prison. However, the authorities later said that 70 others were to be charged with state security offences and would remain in custody to await trial. None had been brought to trial by the end of the year.

Many of those arrested in May were reported to have been tortured in Tahoua military barracks. People were said to have heard screams from the barracks and at least four prisoners reportedly died in custody. They included Abdoulmoumine Ag Mohamed, a teacher, and Mouhamadou Ag Abdourabahi, known as "Daragat". One former prisoner alleged in a radio interview that he and his relatives had been tortured in Tahoua barracks and that his brother and other relatives had died.

Earlier in the year, at least three school students were shot dead in Niamey in February when security forces opened fire on a student demonstration against government plans to reduce student grants and restrict civil service recruitment. Two university lecturers were detained but released uncharged after five days. One, Sanoussi Jackou, was a former prisoner of conscience. President Ali Saïbou publicly apologized for the students' deaths, and an inquiry was announced. Several senior government officials resigned or were dismissed and a number of junior police officers were reportedly arrested. A magistrate was appointed to investigate, but his findings were not made public by the end of 1990 and no one was brought to trial.

Amnesty International expressed concern to the government about the allegations of torture and extrajudicial executions of Tuareg, and called for an urgent inquiry. It also called for the release of all those held solely on account of their ethnic origin or non-violent opinions. In response, the government denied the use of torture and extrajudicial executions, saying that all 63 people who had been killed had died in clashes between armed Tuareg and the security forces. The government said no prisoners or unarmed civilians had been killed by soldiers, and refused to investigate specific cases in which torture or extrajudicial executions were alleged. The government also invited Amnesty International to visit Niger: such a visit was arranged for November but then delayed at short notice at the government's request. It was expected to take place early in 1991.

Following the February shootings, Amnesty International called for an official investigation and urged the authorities to ensure that standing orders issued to security forces concerning the use of live ammunition conformed fully to international standards.

NIGERIA

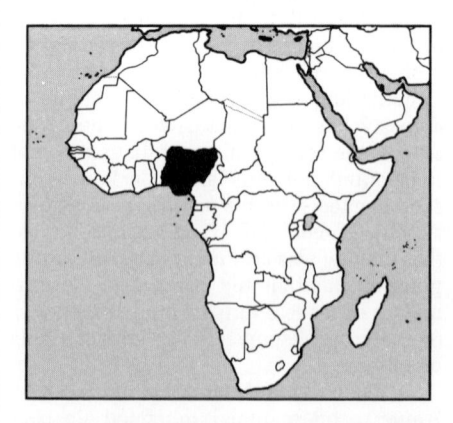

Over 120 people were executed, including 69 soldiers sentenced to death after secret, unfair trials for alleged involvement in a coup attempt in April. At least 106 prisoners were sentenced to death during

the year: 72 after being convicted of involvement in the attempted coup, and the rest after being convicted of murder or armed robbery. Over 60 civilians, detained without charge or trial following the coup attempt, were prisoners of conscience: most were released but at least nine were still held at the end of the year. Harsh prison and detention conditions continued to be reported.

Hundreds of soldiers and civilians were detained following an attempt on 22 April to overthrow the government, the Armed Forces Ruling Council (AFRC). At least nine soldiers and an unknown number of civilians were reportedly killed in the coup attempt, which was led by Major Gideon Orkar. In a radio broadcast before his capture, he claimed to represent the interests of people from central and southern Nigeria against domination by northerners.

Following the coup attempt, the government said that 863 soldiers and civilians had been tried by a special military court between May and July and that 764 of them had been acquitted and released. A further 38 people were tried and convicted in September. Of the 72 people sentenced to death, 42 were executed on 27 July, including Major Orkar and nine other officers; 27 more were executed on 13 September. The executions were carried out the day after the court's verdicts were submitted to the AFRC for approval. On both occasions, the sentences were not announced until after the executions had been carried out. The AFRC was believed to have commuted three death sentences. The military court sentenced 18 defendants, including three civilians, to prison terms; the AFRC subsequently reduced some of the sentences and ordered the release of two people sentenced to life imprisonment.

The trials were unfair. The defendants were detained incommunicado prior to the trial and there were allegations that some were tortured or ill-treated. Defendants were not permitted defence counsel of their choice, but were represented by military officers. It was not clear whether they had sufficient time to prepare their defence. The Special Military Tribunal, a court set up in 1986 following a previous coup attempt, tried the cases *in camera*, and details of the proceedings were not available. The court could not be considered independent: it was composed of senior military officers and presided over by members of the government, in most cases by Major-General Ike Nwachukwu. A member of the AFRC, he had been Minister of External Affairs until December 1989, and was reappointed to this position in September 1990. Defendants had no right of appeal. Their only recourse was to apply for clemency to the Joint Chiefs of Staff, whose recommendations would be considered by the AFRC.

Journalists, academics and religious leaders were among at least 50 civilians who were detained without charge following the attempted coup. Many were detained after publishing articles or speaking publicly about the coup attempt, in one case apparently after calling for the rebels not to be executed. Most were released uncharged within six weeks. However, three university lecturers – Omotoye Olorode, Idowu Awopetu and Obaro Ikime – were held uncharged for three months and subsequently dismissed from their posts, although their interrogation in detention apparently focused on their political views rather than any involvement in the coup attempt.

At least nine relatives of people sought by the authorities in connection with the coup attempt were reportedly still detained without charge or trial at the end of the year. They included two sisters of a business executive who was wanted by the authorities for allegedly financing the coup attempt. They appeared to be detained solely because of their family ties and were believed to be held under the 1984 State Security Decree. This decree had been amended in January to empower the Chief of General Staff to order the indefinite detention without charge or trial of anyone suspected of threatening national security, and to provide for review of all detentions within six weeks by a committee headed by the Minister of Justice.

There was an increase in the number of people reported to have been sentenced to death or executed for criminal offences. During 1990 at least 34 people were sentenced to death for murder or armed robbery and at least 52 criminal prisoners were executed. Most executions were carried out in public by firing-squad. All of the executed criminal prisoners appeared to have been convicted by Robbery and Firearms Tribunals, special courts from which there is no right of appeal and whose procedures do not ensure fair trial.

Death sentences continued to be passed on defendants under the age of 18 at the time of the offence. Five men aged between 17 and 21 when they were arrested in 1983 were reportedly sentenced to death in December for murder and armed robbery.

In July the Military Governor of Lagos State refused to commute the death sentences on 12 young men convicted of armed robbery in 1988, although one was revealed after the trial to have been 14 years old at the time of the offence and Lagos State's own Justice Department had said that an appeal court would have overturned the convictions (see *Amnesty International Report 1989*). One of the prisoners, Mohammed Ibrahim, died in December from pulmonary tuberculosis, apparently as a result of harsh prison conditions and medical neglect.

There continued to be a high incidence of prison deaths due to malnutrition and lack of medical care, particularly among prisoners awaiting trial. In March the judge in a Robbery and Firearms Tribunal in Oyo State expressed concern that seven of the 29 defendants in one case, most of whom were in their twenties, had died in Agodi Prison, Ibadan, before they could be brought to trial.

In November President Ibrahim Babangida ordered the release of 11 senior electricity employees serving sentences imposed for conspiring to interfere unlawfully with power-generating equipment and inducing others to do so during a strike in 1988 (see *Amnesty International Reports 1989* and *1990*).

Amnesty International expressed concern to the government about the use of the death penalty and appealed for the commutation of all death sentences. The organization was particularly disturbed by the speed with which prisoners sentenced in connection with the coup attempt were executed after having been tried unfairly and denied any right of judicial appeal. Amnesty International also pressed for the release of prisoners of conscience and for all other political detainees to be brought to trial promptly and fairly on recognizably criminal charges or released, and urged that all deaths of prisoners be officially investigated.

In an oral statement to the United Nations Sub-Commission working group on detention, Amnesty International included reference to its concerns about the imposition of the death penalty on juveniles in Nigeria.

NORWAY

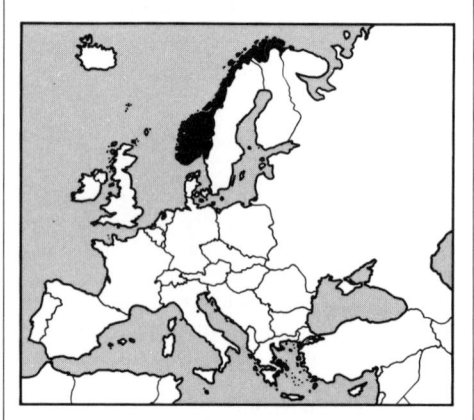

One prisoner of conscience, a conscientious objector to military service, served a three-month prison sentence. Two people were convicted of making false statements against the police, related to their allegations of ill-treatment.

On 13 February the government signed the Second Optional Protocol to the International Covenant on Civil and Political Rights Aiming at the Abolition of the Death Penalty; it had not yet been ratified by the end of the year.

Tore Guneriussen was imprisoned in February for 90 days because of his refusal, based on his political beliefs, to perform military service. Norwegian legislation at the time only accepted absolute pacifist convictions as acceptable grounds for exemption from military service. In June parliament adopted a new law, to come into effect in January 1991, extending the right of conscientious objection to those refusing to perform military service on the grounds of their opposition to nuclear weapons.

Two people, who had alleged that they were ill-treated by police officers in Bergen in previous years, were convicted of making false statements and given suspended sentences. Some 140 people had reportedly made allegations of police misconduct to a police inquiry in Bergen in 1987. In one case the inquiry proposed that a police officer be fined. The other cases were dismissed for various reasons. The Bergen

District Attorney subsequently initiated investigations into 50 of the 140 people who had made allegations to the inquiry. Fifteen of them, including the two convicted in 1990, were charged with making false statements against the police. One died before the court hearing took place and two cases were dropped by the prosecution. Nine people were convicted in 1989; eight of them were imprisoned for between two and seven months, and one was fined. One person was acquitted.

In 1989 and 1990 an Amnesty International delegate observed the trials of two people charged with making false statements. In December Amnesty International wrote to the government expressing concern that the criminal investigation and prosecution of people who made complaints about ill-treatment could act as a deterrent to others with similar complaints. The organization recognized that some complaints might be exaggerated or untrue and that police officers were entitled to protection of their reputations. However, it urged the government to take any necessary steps to ensure that those with genuine complaints about police ill-treatment should not be deterred from making them.

Amnesty International also called for the release of imprisoned conscientious objector Tore Guneriussen.

PAKISTAN

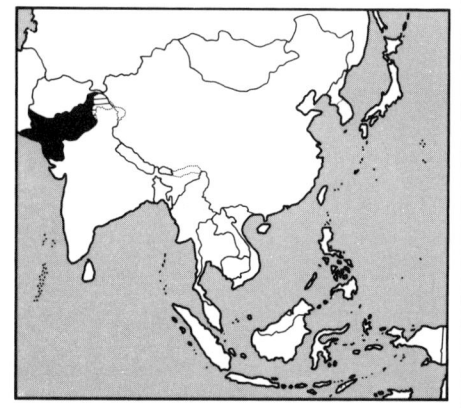

Scores of people arrested for non-violent political or religious activities were prisoners of conscience. Most were released after short periods. Torture was widespread, and reportedly caused the deaths of at least 24 prisoners. The President **promulgated ordinances affecting the application of the death penalty and extending its scope. No executions were reported.**

President Ghulam Ishaq Khan dismissed the government of Prime Minister Benazir Bhutto in August and dissolved the national and provincial assemblies. A state of emergency was declared but no emergency legislation was promulgated. An interim government was appointed until elections in October, which were won by the *Islami Jamhoori Ittehad* (IJI), Islamic Democratic Alliance. Mian Nawaz Sharif became Prime Minister in November and the state of emergency was then lifted.

Criminal and ethnic violence continued in Sind province, where hundreds of people were killed. In February rivalry between the ruling Pakistan People's Party (PPP) and the opposition *Mohajir Qaumi Mahaz* (MQM), Mohajir National Movement, led to conflict in Karachi in which supporters of each group kidnapped, imprisoned, tortured or killed members of the other. An exchange of prisoners was negotiated by the army. The alliance between the two parties had ended in November 1989.

Shortly after the dismissal of the PPP government in August investigations led to charges of corruption against former prime minister Benazir Bhutto and several of her former ministers. Their trials – which took place before a court which was empowered to disqualify them from public office but not to imprison them – were not completed by the end of the year. Benazir Bhutto's husband, Asif Ali Zardari, was arrested in October and charged with several offences, including involvement in a kidnapping case.

Several aides and associates of former prime minister Benazir Bhutto and her husband were detained without charge or trial in Karachi under the Maintenance of Public Order Ordinance (MPO), apparently in connection with the investigations into corruption. They included Ahmed Fahim Moghul, a former private secretary to Benazir Bhutto, who was released after spending over 40 days in custody.

The Sind High Court ruled that some of these detentions were unlawful: criminal charges were then brought against those held, who remained in custody until granted bail. Other PPP members were detained under the MPO in the interior of Sind during the pre-election period. Most were released within a few weeks, either unconditionally or on bail after criminal charges were brought against them.

Both under the PPP government in June and under the IJI government in December, the Sind provincial authorities allegedly arrested hundreds of political opponents during a campaign against crime. In some cases, members of the PPP arrested after the change of government were repeatedly charged with offences which could not be substantiated, and then placed under 30-day detention orders under the MPO. For example, a former member of the National Assembly, Afaq Shahid, was arrested in November and charged with three criminal offences in turn; each new case was brought against him after he had been cleared of the last, with the effect that he remained in police custody continuously and was still held at the end of the year. A PPP member of the Sind provincial assembly, Manzoor Hussain Wasan, was held in unacknowledged detention for over one week in December. During this period the Chief Minister of Sind denied his arrest. After his detention was challenged in the Sind High Court, criminal charges were brought against him.

The MPO empowers the authorities to detain prisoners without trial for up to three months if they are considered to be "acting in any manner prejudicial to public safety or the maintenance of public order". Under Article 10 of the Constitution, a review board can extend such detentions up to a limit of eight or 12 months, depending on the grounds for detention.

Members of the Ahmadiyya community continued to be arrested for the peaceful expression of their faith, and at least 13 were sentenced to terms of imprisonment. In Abbotabad, North West Frontier Province, a group of 12 Ahmadis, five of whom were arrested, faced criminal charges and a possible prison sentence for holding a prayer meeting in a private house in January. They were released on bail in late April. Their trial had not started by the end of the year. In Multan, Punjab province, two Ahmadi brothers, Muhammad Hanif and Muhammad Ahsan, were each sentenced to six years' imprisonment and a fine for offences connected with preaching their faith.

G.M. Syed, the 87-year-old leader of the Sind National Alliance, was released by the interim government in September when charges against him of sedition and desecrating the national flag were withdrawn. He had been held since October 1989 (see *Amnesty International Report 1990*). Others facing charges in the same cases were released on bail, some before and others after the change of government.

Information was received in 1990 of the release from Karachi Central Jail in July 1989 of a political prisoner who had been held in unacknowledged detention without charge or trial for over four years. Rahmatullah had been arrested by police and army personnel in December 1984, and was released following the filing of a constitutional petition on his behalf in the Sind High Court.

The torture of criminal and political suspects continued to be reported throughout the year. In over two dozen reported cases, torture allegedly caused the death of the prisoner. The true number of deaths in custody resulting from torture was believed to be higher. In December five people were reported to have died in the custody of the Criminal Investigation Agency in Karachi in the previous few weeks, allegedly as a result of torture. Most reports concerned torture in police custody, including the rape of women prisoners, but there were also allegations of torture by the paramilitary Rangers in Karachi and by prison staff in both Punjab and Sind provinces. In Karachi, Sind province, Abdul Rehman Thebo, a student of engineering accused of illegal possession of arms, required hospital treatment after he was reportedly tortured by Rangers in January. His injuries, including multiple bruises and abrasions, substantiated his allegation that he had been stripped, lashed and beaten on the soles of his feet and elsewhere, and had received electric shocks to his genitals. Two women, one of whom was deaf and dumb, were reportedly raped in August by prison officers at Sheikhupura District Jail, Punjab province. After a local human rights organization filed a writ petition, the prison officers were charged and transferred from Sheikhupura District Jail.

Inquiries into several cases of alleged torture were announced. Some police officers were apparently charged in connection with the torture of prisoners, but none was known to have been brought to trial.

Sentences of lashing continued to be imposed for crimes including rape and the possession of illegal drugs. In July police in Lahore, Punjab province, reportedly took 18 men to a mosque and lashed them publicly, without sentence having been passed by any court. The 18 had been arrested for watching pornographic films. They were moved to jail the following day.

Dozens of men, women and children were reportedly extrajudicially executed in May at Pucca Qila in Hyderabad, Sind province, when police opened fire on a procession of apparently unarmed protesters who were defying curfew regulations. The demonstrators were demanding the withdrawal of police from the area, which is inhabited by ethnic Mohajirs, and were protesting that they had been deprived of water for over 28 hours. The government announced in May that a judicial inquiry would be held into the recent violence in Sind province, which would include investigation of the Hyderabad killings. However, its work was reportedly hampered by lack of cooperation from the parties involved. It recommenced in November after the change of government, and was not completed by the end of the year.

The President promulgated three ordinances which affected the application of the death penalty, and a fourth which reintroduced Special Courts for Speedy Trials with the power to sentence convicted prisoners to death. Ordinances promulgated in August and September removed the powers of the President and provincial governors under the Pakistan Penal Code to commute death sentences for murder without the consent of the victim's heirs. They also enabled relatives of the victim to accept compensation from the murderer. The third ordinance, issued in December, made kidnapping for ransom an offence punishable by death.

Special Courts for Speedy Trials, which can condemn prisoners to death after trials lasting only a few days, were reintroduced through an ordinance promulgated in August. These courts, formerly in operation from 1987 to 1989, have jurisdiction over crimes which provincial governments deem "gruesome, brutal and sensational... or shocking to public morality", or which had "led to public outrage". Their procedures do not wholly conform to international fair trial standards. Prisoners convicted and sentenced by these courts retain the right of appeal.

Ordinances remain in force for 120 days; they must then be approved by the National Assembly or promulgated again.

At least 52 people were sentenced to death for murder. At least nine death sentences were passed by Special Courts for the Suppression of Terrorist Activities, the procedures of which do not wholly conform to international fair trial standards. No executions were reported.

Amnesty International pressed for the release of prisoners of conscience, including Ahmadis charged in connection with the practice of their faith, and sought information about government opponents detained without trial, both before and after the change of government. It called for the abolition of whipping and, following the reported extrajudicial executions in Hyderabad in May, asked for details of the composition and terms of reference of the inquiry announced by the government. It also urged the authorities to ensure that police were instructed to observe international standards relating to the use of lethal force as a means of preventing possible extrajudicial executions. No replies were received to specific requests for information.

Following the change of government, Amnesty International expressed concern that members of the outgoing administration might be tried and imprisoned for political reasons under the Holders of Representative Offices (Punishment for Misconduct) Order of 1977, noting that it lays down procedures which fall short of international fair trial standards. In the event, this legislation was not used in the corruption cases against former ministers.

Amnesty International submitted a memorandum on its concerns to the federal and provincial governments in April, and published the memorandum in May. Among its recommendations to the government the organization urged the review and limitation of powers for administrative detention and the implementation of effective safeguards against torture. It again submitted its concerns and recommendations for improved human rights protection following the formation of Prime Minister Nawaz Sharif's government.

PANAMA

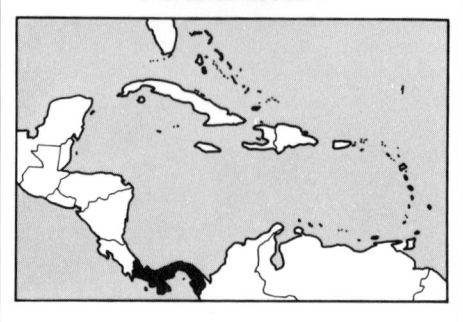

Several thousand prisoners detained by United States (US) troops after the US military invaded Panama in December 1989 were in custody at the beginning of 1990. They were reportedly held without legal counsel or access to families in conditions which many described as severely overcrowded and lacking sufficient food and medical care. Many were released within weeks or months. However, some were transferred to Panamanian prisons on criminal charges, including corruption, money-laundering and drug-trafficking. Prison facilities, particularly medical care, were reportedly insufficient and there were complaints of delays in legal proceedings and inadequate access to legal counsel.

In November Panama signed the protocol to the American Convention on Human Rights to abolish the death penalty.

Many of those in detention at the beginning of the year were members of the Panamanian Defence Forces (PDF), loyal to former *de facto* ruler Defence Forces' Chief Brigadier General Manuel Noriega. Other detainees were members of the civilian adjuncts to the PDF organized by General Noriega, known as the Dignity Battalions, some of which had offered armed resistance to the US invasion. US troops also detained residents of poor neighbourhoods where support for the Dignity Battalions was believed to be strong.

After initially seeking asylum in the Papal Nunciature, General Noriega was taken into custody by US troops in January 1990; he and several associates were detained in the United States of America on criminal charges related to drug-trafficking and money-laundering.

In the months following the invasion, further large-scale, frequently short-term, arrests were reportedly carried out by US troops and the restructured Panamanian security forces. Those arrested included leaders of political parties and trade unions which had supported General Noriega, those believed to have been Dignity Battalion activists and journalists allegedly arrested solely for having written articles critical of US policy in Panama or the administration of President Guillermo Endara Galimany. President Endara had been inaugurated during the invasion on the grounds that he had been the front-runner in the May 1989 elections before General Noriega declared them invalid.

Reports were also received that US troops may have used excessive force and not taken adequate care to avoid injuring civilians during military operations, leading to unwarranted deaths of non-combatant civilians, particularly in neighbourhoods believed to be Dignity Battalion strongholds. Allegedly, many victims were buried in mass unmarked graves in order to conceal the number of civilian casualties; some of the victims may have been extrajudicially executed.

Prisoners transferred to the custody of the Panamanian authorities during 1990 included journalist Escolástico Calvo, who managed the government-controlled media under General Noriega. His detention at a US military base in December 1989 was initially denied, but his family eventually visited him there. He complained of solitary confinement, not receiving medicines for diabetes, and being kicked by his guards. In February he was transferred to a Panamanian prison on what the authorities said were criminal charges, and in March to hospital for an operation. He was taken from hospital shortly afterwards by police officers, but following international protest he was returned for further care. His family repeatedly complained about his medical care; the government insisted it was adequate. In November he was released without explanation.

In April Panama's National Assembly voted to appoint a special prosecutor to probe the 1985 murder of Dr Hugo Spadafora, a former vice-minister of health whose decapitated body was found in 1987 just over the border with Costa Rica. High-level Panamanian officials had repeatedly charged that General Noriega ordered the PDF to kill Dr Spadafora (see *Amnesty International Reports 1985, 1988* and *1990*).

In December the Panamanian authorities announced charges against General Noriega and 11 other people, including senior military officials of his administration, for Dr Spadafora's murder.

In June a US soldier was convicted of murdering a Panamanian woman during the invasion and sentenced to seven years' imprisonment by a US military court. Along with two other soldiers, he had been accused of staging an exchange of fire for purely personal reasons, in which the woman was killed. The soldiers had apparently intended to use the staged fight as an explanation for the loss of a pistol.

In October Panamanian newspapers announced the arrest of a former PDF member, the 10th person to be detained in connection with the murders of a US citizen and a Panamanian. The victims had been seized and extrajudicially executed in the course of the invasion, reportedly in a combined PDF-Dignity Battalion operation.

Amnesty International wrote to Panamanian authorities including President Endara, with copies to US officials, urging the new government to investigate human rights violations reported under the previous administration and subsequently. Amnesty International asked how many prisoners remained in detention in the aftermath of the invasion, the specific legal basis for their detention and the procedures implemented to ensure that all of them were treated in conformity with international standards, particularly regarding protection from physical or mental ill-treatment. The organization urged that care should be taken to ensure that criminal charges were not being used to mask political persecution of General Noriega's supporters. In that context, any penalties imposed should be appropriate to the alleged offences, otherwise the punishments could be seen to be politically motivated. The organization also requested details of any investigations initiated into "disappearances" and extrajudicial executions reported under the previous administration, and regarding those held prior to General Noriega's overthrow.

In April President Endara responded to a number of the issues raised by Amnesty International, stating his administration's commitment to human rights. The President outlined judicial proceedings initiated with respect to certain cases reported prior to the invasion, including the extrajudicial executions of Father Nicolas Van Kleef during the 1989 elections, and of PDF members after a coup attempt in October 1989 (see *Amnesty International Report 1990*). In July the government expressed its willingness to discuss Amnesty International's concerns regarding conditions in Panamanian prisons; other officials maintained that the new government was doing its best to improve "inherited" facilities.

PAPUA NEW GUINEA

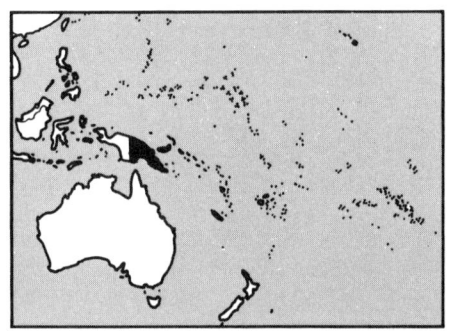

Dozens of people suspected of supporting an armed opposition group on the island of Bougainville in North Solomons Province and several criminal suspects in other parts of the country were tortured or ill-treated by government security forces. At least nine people were killed in apparent extrajudicial executions on Bougainville, some after torture or ill-treatment by government forces. The government announced plans to draft legislation to restore the death penalty for wilful murder.

Armed conflict between government forces and the Bougainville Revolutionary Army (BRA), which began in 1989, continued until mid-March when all government troops were withdrawn from Bougainville and the state of emergency there was ended. This followed the signing of a cease-fire agreement on 2 March. The BRA sought Bougainville's independence and financial compensation for land occupied by a copper mining company and for resulting environmental damage.

There were widespread reports that BRA forces committed acts of violence, including the torture and killing of civilians, both before and after the withdrawal of government troops. BRA forces were said to be responsible for a raid on the Kuveria jail complex in January which left four prison officers and two civilians dead. On 17 May an interim government formed on Bougainville with BRA backing unilaterally declared the island's independence. Following talks with representatives of this government in early August, the national government agreed to restore essential services to Bougainville as soon as possible and without resort to force. However, there were renewed clashes between BRA and government forces beginning in September and both the resumption of services and negotiations over Bougainville's political status were postponed.

Reported human rights violations by members of the security forces on Bougainville were not systematically investigated. The Supreme Court initiated procedures to streamline the hearing of human rights cases before the courts but by the end of the year no cases from Bougainville had been heard.

Papua New Guinea Defence Force (PNGDF) soldiers and members of police riot squads ill-treated or tortured dozens of Bougainvilleans and reportedly threatened some with death. Most of the victims were suspected members or sympathizers of the BRA and included journalists, medical professionals, government workers and local villagers.

In February four PNGDF soldiers beat and stabbed Wilfred Seamus, a Bougainvillean, after abducting him and taking him to an army barracks in Port Moresby. The soldiers reportedly tied his hands, blindfolded him and told him to sit on the ground. They kicked him repeatedly in the head and joints and stabbed him in the arms until an off-duty soldier intervened. Government authorities confirmed that the beating had taken place and said that a full investigation would be set up. To Amnesty International's knowledge, however, those responsible had not been brought to justice by the end of the year.

Some criminal suspects were also reportedly ill-treated in police custody. In one case, three young men detained in connection with a series of robberies in February were said to have been paraded around town on a truck with slogans such as "Pigs for Sale", "Dogs" and "Criminals" hung from their bodies. Witnesses said that the detainees, whose hands were tied, were hit over the head with gun butts by police officers before a crowd of onlookers. No disciplinary action or prosecutions were known to have been initiated against the police officers allegedly responsible.

At least nine people were killed in apparent extrajudicial executions on Bougainville, some of them after torture or ill-treatment. PNGDF soldiers reportedly beat and then shot dead Kevin Kokiai Lalai in custody on 25 January. The military authorities said that he had been shot while trying to escape but a post-mortem report found multiple bullet wounds and evidence that he had been shot from the front, not while running away. It was reported that Kevin Kokiai Lalai had previously been ill-treated in December 1989 by police and soldiers, and again on 17 January, when soldiers and prison warders assaulted several people whom they suspected of involvement in the attack on Kuveria jail.

The government announced plans in June to draft legislation to restore the death penalty for wilful murder but the proposed legislation had not been introduced by the end of the year.

Amnesty International several times expressed concern to the government about reported human rights violations on Bougainville and continued previous efforts to engage the government in constructive dialogue about the protection and promotion of human rights. In April an Amnesty International delegation visited the country for 10 days. Despite repeated efforts both before and during the visit the delegation was unable to meet any government ministers or military authorities. The organization expressed concern about the government's plan to draft legislation restoring the death penalty. The government acknowledged some of Amnesty International's communications but provided no substantive response to the concerns raised.

In an oral statement to the United Nations Commission on Human Rights in February, Amnesty International included reference to its concerns about torture in police and military custody in Papua New Guinea. In November Amnesty International published a report, *Papua New Guinea: Human Rights Violations on Bougainville, 1989-1990*. It documented 19 apparent extrajudicial executions and dozens of cases of torture and ill-treatment by government forces; it also examined the

PARAGUAY

Members of peasant communities involved in land disputes were detained in increasing numbers. Many were held without charge or trial for several weeks and some were ill-treated or tortured. Criminal suspects, including minors, were tortured or ill-treated by police officers while in custody. Little progress was made in judicial investigations into past human rights violations. Two convicted criminals were sentenced to death, although the last execution took place in 1928.

In March Paraguay ratified the United Nations Convention against Torture and Other Cruel, Inhuman or Degrading Treatment or Punishment and the Inter-American Convention to Prevent and Punish Torture.

In November President Andrés Rodríguez vetoed a bill passed by Congress which had proposed establishing a bicameral human rights commission mandated to investigate past and future human rights violations.

The unprecedented wave of land occupations which followed the change of government in 1989 continued throughout 1990. Hundreds of landless peasant families invaded large landholdings, often the property of absentee landowners, throughout the country. Dozens of peasant communities attempting to establish land claims were violently expelled by army and police personnel, sometimes operating in conjunction with armed civilians reportedly paid by landowners. In many cases forcible expulsion was accompanied by mass arrests, sometimes without judicial order, and torture or ill-treatment of detainees. The majority of detainees were released without charge or trial after weeks or months in custody.

In January some 120 families were forcibly expelled from land they had been occupying since 1986 in Curepi-cue, Naranjito, San Pedro department. A group of about 15 armed civilians, believed to have been hired by the landowner, burned the peasants' huts and destroyed their belongings, before forcing several of the peasants on to lorries and driving them to a police post in General Resquin. During the journey at least two of the peasants were said to have been beaten. The peasants were handed over to the local police chief who reportedly held them for over 12 hours before releasing them without charge.

The department of Alto Paraná bordering Brazil was one of the areas most affected by violence in the context of land conflicts. Peasants detained during expulsions and held in regional prisons repeatedly complained about conditions of detention and ill-treatment by prison staff. In June 132 detainees held in the prison at the regional governmental headquarters in the provincial capital, Ciudad del Este, sent an open letter to judicial and congressional authorities denouncing police torture of prisoners. They accused the police of using methods such as beatings, near-asphyxiation, high-pressure water hoses directed into the mouths of prisoners and electric shocks. An investigation of the prisoners' complaints was publicly announced by judicial officials, but it was not known whether it had been initiated by the end of the year.

In some instances peasants were arbitrarily detained and ill-treated by police forces with the apparent intention of pre-empting possible land occupations. In October a group of 130 peasant families were reportedly arrested without judicial order in Itá Cajón, Naranjito, Itapúa department. The peasants had been camped for over one year outside a property they had formally requested be expropriated in their favour. Several of the peasants, men and women, alleged that the police had beaten them with rifle butts during the operation to expel them from their camp.

In November the director of the Emboscada juvenile detention centre testified before the human rights commission of the Chamber of Deputies (the lower house of Congress). According to the prison director, a 16-year-old youth had been tortured in Lambaré police station, on the outskirts of Asunción. He stated that the boy had been beaten and kicked by police as a result of which he had suffered a hernia and sustained injuries to his arms and legs. In December several inmates of Emboscada prison testified before a criminal court judge investigating allegations of the ill-treatment of minors by police and anti-narcotics personnel. A 17-year-old youth told the judge that he had been arrested in July and held for two days in the *Departamento de Investigaciones de la Policía* (DIPC), Police Investigations Department, and that he had been beaten with truncheons and subjected to electric shocks.

Judicial investigations into human rights violations which had occurred under the previous government continued, although little progress was made (see *Amnesty International Report 1990*). Some senior police officers in the former administration of General Alfredo Stroessner remained in custody while trial proceedings against them continued. They faced a variety of charges, including the arbitrary arrest, torture and murder of scores of political opposition figures in the 1960s and 1970s.

Victims of human rights violations under the previous administration continued to come forward to present complaints to the courts. In October a formal criminal complaint was lodged by former prisoner of conscience Captain Modesto Napoleón Ortigoza against former president General Stroessner, former minister of the interior Edgar L. Ynsfrán, and several former high-ranking police officials. He accused them of abuses including arbitrary detention, torture and defamation. Captain Ortigoza had been released in December 1987 after completing a 25-year sentence for his alleged part in a conspiracy to overthrow President Stroessner in 1962 (see *Amnesty International Reports 1988* and *1989*).

No information was made available concerning the inquiry into the killings of two construction workers by army personnel during a strike at the Itaipú hydroelectric dam project in December 1989 (see *Amnesty International Report 1990*). The army officer who commanded the operation to break up the strikers' demonstration was suspended from duty immediately following the incident, pending results of the investigation. However, in May he was promoted by Congress.

At least two people were sentenced to death in separate cases in September; one for parricide and the other for homicide during an armed robbery. However, since 1928 death sentences imposed by trial judges have been commuted on appeal, generally to 30 years' imprisonment.

Amnesty International urged the authorities to introduce measures to prevent the use of torture and ill-treatment. The organization expressed its concern about reported attacks on peasant communities and ill-treatment of peasants and called for full and impartial investigations. It also reiterated the principle that all past human rights violations should be independently investigated, notwithstanding a change of government.

PERU

Over 300 men, women and children "disappeared" after arrest by security forces, mainly in the emergency zones under political-military command. Scores more were extrajudicially executed. The victims, most of whom were peasants, included human rights defenders, community leaders, politicians and trade unionists. Torture and ill-treatment by the security forces were widespread. Five prisoners of conscience were held, four of them on false charges of "terrorism". Three prisoners of conscience were released.

A campaign by armed opposition groups of sabotage, forced strikes and killings during the months leading up to the congressional and two-stage presidential elections in April and June, coupled with a severe economic crisis, formed the background to a deteriorating human rights situation. In July President Alberto Fujimori, leader of the Cambio 90 political party, took office. In his inaugural speech he stated that "the unconditional respect and promotion of human rights will be a firm line of action during my government" and promised to set up a national commission to guarantee respect for human rights. By the end of the year the government had not taken the initial step of establishing any terms of reference for such a commission.

The armed opposition group *Partido Comunista del Peru "Sendero Luminoso"*, Communist Party of Peru "Shining Path", remained active throughout most of the country. Shining Path called for boycotts of the congressional and presidential elections and murdered political candidates, government officials, leaders of popular organizations and other civilians, sometimes in execution-style killings following torture and mock trials. According to reports, in April and August respectively the former director of the Peruvian Institute of Social Security and the former labour minister were murdered. In October, seven civilians as well as 13 members of the army were reportedly murdered in Tingo María in a dynamite and machine-gun attack. A congressional commission formed to monitor political violence in Peru reported that 258 police and military personnel were killed in 1990 as a result of actions by armed opposition groups.

Approximately two-thirds of Peru, containing over half the population, remained under state of emergency measures. In August President Fujimori extended emergency legislation to a further 10 provinces for a period of one month, thereby placing most of the country's population under state of emergency measures. By December, 69 of Peru's 183 provinces were administered by the *Comando Conjunto de las Fuerzas Armadas*, the Armed Forces Joint Command. President Fujimori appointed a serving army general to the Ministry of the Interior, which is responsible for all police security services. The Peruvian authorities failed to investigate and punish violations committed by their security forces.

Law 24,150, introduced in 1985, remained the main legal instrument through which the political-military commands exercised their rule in the emergency zones. In practice its provisions facilitated the armed forces detaining people without notifying civil authorities or accounting for the fate of prisoners. The armed forces in the emergency zones maintained almost total independence from the civilian government. Torture, "disappearances" and extrajudicial executions were frequently reported without independent investigations being initiated; military courts, with few exceptions, were not known to have brought to justice security agents for human rights violations.

In the emergency zones *habeas corpus* was not suspended but the courts did not generally implement this right and the armed forces routinely denied legal representatives access to military establishments known to be holding prisoners incommunicado. As in previous years, the Public Ministry, headed by the Attorney General, failed to fulfil its constitutional responsibility to protect human rights: public prosecutors rarely took steps to remedy human rights abuses.

During the year 304 new cases of "disappearance" following arrest by the security forces were reported. Of these, 89 were reported to have been subsequently released or transferred to police custody. Twenty-four were reportedly found dead. The others remained unaccounted for. Most of the victims were members of isolated peasant communities in the emergency zones, although the number of reported "disappearances" increased in urban areas. The armed forces repeatedly denied holding prisoners, a policy which Amnesty International believes contributed to the high number of "disappearances".

Among the hundreds of victims of "disappearance" were Dora Gómez and her children, Nilton and Juan Carlos Gámez Gómez, aged 15 and 13 respectively. They were reportedly detained in April together with six other people when soldiers stopped a group of 30 peasants from Alto Río Chari in Junín's Satipo province. Their detention was denied and all nine remained "disappeared". In October

Ernesto Rafael Castillo Páez was detained in the Villa El Salvador neighbourhood of Lima, the capital. Witnesses said that he was handcuffed and forced into the boot of a police car before being driven away. A judge who ordered his release after a *habeas corpus* petition was filed reported that the register of detentions at the police station where Ernesto Castillo was allegedly taken had been tampered with. The authorities refused to acknowledge his detention and he remained "disappeared".

"Disappearances" were sometimes reported in conjunction with the multiple extrajudicial execution of men, women and children. Over a six-day period in April, 13 people were said to have been killed and eight others "disappeared", including an eight-year-old girl, after their detention by an army patrol in an operation that extended through several peasant communities in Chumbivilcas province, Cuzco department, and in neighbouring Apurímac. Eleven of those killed were dumped on a hillside, their bodies covered with *icchu*, a highland grass. Following repeated requests from leaders of the peasant communities, judges allowed the 11 bodies to be examined. The bodies bore multiple bullet wounds and marks consistent with torture.

In other cases the "disappeared" were subsequently discovered to be victims of extrajudicial executions. In mid-October a mass grave was discovered in the district of San Pedro de Cachi, in Ayacucho's Huamanga department, which reportedly contained the remains of at least 16 people. Initial reports indicated that nine of the bodies exhumed from this grave by a commission of investigation were those of peasants reported as "disappeared" on 22 September. They included three young women, Victoria Espinoza, Julia Mendoza and Irene Melgar, and two girls, Delia Melgar, aged 15, and Dina Tello, aged 13.

Extrajudicial executions were sometimes reported in the context of counter-insurgency operations conducted jointly by the armed forces and Civil Defence Committees – peasant-based patrols administered and controlled by the military zone commander. One report claimed that 12 men, three women and a 15-year-old boy were extrajudicially executed on 22 August near Uchuraccay, in Ayacucho's Huanta province, by a combined patrol of civil defence groups and some 50 soldiers from the Machente and Ccano military base. The victims had apparently refused to participate in a military operation against Shining Path.

Human rights activists were apparently targeted for "disappearance" or extrajudicial execution. Angel Escobar Jurado, secretary of the Human Rights Commission of Huancavelica, was last seen on 27 February being conducted through the streets by five men dressed in civilian clothing, one of whom was subsequently seen in the company of uniformed army personnel. On 10 June Guadalupe Ccallocunto, mother of four children and active in an organization assisting the families of the "disappeared", was taken away in the early hours of the morning from her home in Ayacucho city. The organization's offices were subsequently closed as a result of threats received by the staff. Human rights organizations in Lima and Ayacucho believe that she was detained by the army following repeated harassment by the security forces. The whereabouts of Angel Escobar Jurado and Guadalupe Ccallocunto remained unknown: the authorities denied detaining either of them. Both "disappearances" took place during a nationwide wave of attacks on human rights organizations and activists. The offices of both the Andean Commission of Jurists and the Peruvian Section of Amnesty International were damaged as a result of bombings in February and March. At least four human rights activists were repeatedly threatened over the telephone, sometimes with death.

Torture and ill-treatment as means of interrogating and intimidating political detainees were frequently reported. The rape of peasant women, either while in detention or during counter-insurgency operations, was common practice. In August Fidel Intusca, a mine worker, was detained by soldiers and taken to the military base at Puquio, Ayacucho department, where he was accused of collaborating with the armed opposition. In testimony later given to a human rights organization he described being submerged in water, burned on the neck and back, beaten and threatened with death. In late September a mother and her 17-year-old daughter were reportedly detained in a military base and raped repeatedly by soldiers. Both women were subsequently released but were threatened to prevent them from reporting the rape. Details of this case are known but cannot be revealed for fear of further reprisals. Effective investigations into cases of rape and other forms of torture following detention were not known to have taken place nor were the perpetrators brought to justice.

No official investigations were initiated into mass killings committed in previous years. For instance, troops killed 11 residents of Calabaza in the department of Junín in May 1989; the following month armed forces raided the communities of Santa Ana and Pampamarca in Ayacucho's Lucanas province, killing 17 people (see *Amnesty International Report 1990*). Neither incident was known to have been investigated.

In June the Court of Appeal of the Supreme Council of Military Justice heard the appeal of the two Republican Guard officers convicted in 1989 of offences connected with the 1986 massacre of 124 prisoners in Lurigancho prison (see *Amnesty International Reports 1987, 1988* and *1990*). The Court upheld the 15-year sentence imposed on one officer and increased the second officer's seven-year sentence to 10 years. The Court also heard appeals against 75 police and army personnel who had been acquitted in 1989 of similar offences. Eight Republican Guards were sentenced to prison terms ranging from one month to six months; the remaining 67 military and police officers were acquitted. In October a congressional commission concluded that former president Alan García bore constitutional responsibility for the 1986 massacre of about 250 inmates at Lurigancho and El Frontón prisons and Callao Women's Prison, but in November the Peruvian Congress defeated a move to bring criminal charges against him.

Almost all political prisoners, including those prisoners of conscience acknowledged to be in detention, were held on charges of "terrorism". One of five known prisoners of conscience, Noé Pastor Romo, was found not guilty of "terrorism" but remained in prison on charges of armed robbery. Three prisoners of conscience were released.

Amnesty International appealed to the authorities on numerous cases of "disappearance", extrajudicial execution and torture, urging them to conduct thorough and impartial investigations of the abuses and to bring the perpetrators to justice. The vast majority of appeals received no response from the government. Through the country's embassies, the authorities replied to inquiries on the killing of Dr Coqui Samuel Huamaní in August 1989 and the "disappearance" of Guadalupe Ccallocunto in June, but the information supplied did not clarify the fate of either victim. The organization also appealed for the release of five prisoners of conscience and continued to investigate the cases of 15 people arrested in previous years who may have been prisoners of conscience.

In May Amnesty International representatives held talks with presidential candidates Mario Vargas Llosa and Alberto Fujimori about the organization's concerns and specific proposals for improving human rights. Similar talks were held in June with Vice-President-elect Carlos García. In July Amnesty International wrote to President-elect Fujimori outlining its concerns and calling upon him to implement specific measures for investigating past human rights violations and preventing future abuses. The organization also recommended that the Attorney General's department be strengthened, that effective protection be given to human rights defenders and witnesses, and that the full rights of detainees provided for in domestic and international law be restored in practice. In November Amnesty International wrote to President Fujimori requesting that Ernesto Castillo's whereabouts be disclosed.

In January Amnesty International submitted information about its concerns in Peru for United Nations (UN) review under a procedure established by Economic and Social Resolutions 728F/1503, for confidential consideration of communications about human rights violations. In an oral statement to the UN Commission on Human Rights delivered in February, the organization included reference to its concerns in Peru.

PHILIPPINES

Scores of people were believed to have been extrajudicially executed and at least 50 others reportedly "disappeared" in police or military custody. Sixteen prisoners of conscience were known to have been released but at least 13 others remained in custody; there were many possible prisoners of conscience among the 700 or so other

political prisoners held. Some political detainees were reportedly tortured or ill-treated. The Senate postponed a vote on legislation seeking the restoration of the death penalty.

The government continued to face armed opposition from the New People's Army (NPA), the armed wing of the banned Communist Party of the Philippines (CPP), and from the Moro National Liberation Front (MNLF) and other rebel groups seeking independence for predominantly Muslim areas of Mindanao. Despite a constitutional ban on private armies, government and military authorities continued to encourage a wide range of armed groups commonly known as "vigilantes", which cooperated closely with the formal security forces in counter-insurgency operations. Government and military authorities labelled many lawful non-governmental organizations as "fronts" for the NPA and CPP in an apparent effort to weaken civilian organizations critical of government policy.

Tens of thousands of people were forced to leave their homes and there was widespread destruction and loss of life in parts of Mindanao, Northern Luzon, Negros, Samar and Mindoro as a result of the bombing by government forces of villages suspected of harbouring NPA or MNLF forces. A national state of emergency imposed by President Corazon Aquino in December 1989, following an attempted military coup, was lifted in June. In July a Supreme Court decision authorized law enforcement officials to arrest without warrant anyone they suspected of the crimes of rebellion or subversion.

Government forces clashed with demonstrators protesting against the continued presence of United States military facilities in the Philippines, and with trade unionists during a nationwide strike in October. Scores of people were arrested but most were released without charge.

The NPA was responsible for many killings, at least 80 of which were reportedly committed by NPA "sparrow units" – urban-based assassination squads. Victims included soldiers, police and civilians; among them was Mayor Xavier Hizon of Mexico, Pampanga province, who was killed in May. There was new evidence to suggest that three people earlier reported to have "disappeared" in 1988 had been detained by the NPA as suspected military spies.

The government took some steps to promote and protect human rights. It invited both the United Nations (UN) Working Group on Enforced or Involuntary Disappearances and the Special Rapporteur on Torture to visit the country and they did so in August and October respectively. The Presidential Committee on Human Rights, chaired by the Minister of Justice, began to meet regularly. The government-appointed Commission on Human Rights (CHR) openly opposed the restoration of the death penalty.

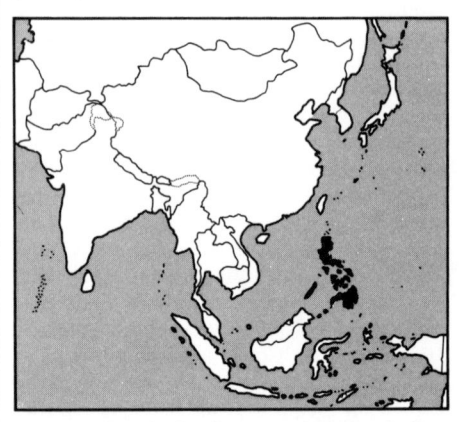

However, lack of cooperation by police and military authorities, judicial delays, witnesses' fear of reprisals and weaknesses in the CHR's mandate and procedures all combined to impede effective investigation of human rights violations and the prosecution of suspects. So too did Presidential Decree 1850, promulgated by former president Ferdinand Marcos, which protects members of the security services against prosecution in civilian courts. The failure of the authorities to exert effective control over tens of thousands of members of official and quasi-official paramilitary forces was also a major impediment to human rights protection.

Scores of suspected government opponents were killed in apparent extrajudicial executions by government or government-backed forces. The victims included human rights campaigners, peasant activists, journalists, church workers, trade unionists, suspected rebels and dozens of people living or working in areas of suspected NPA or MNLF activity.

Ruben Medina was killed in February shortly after members of the Philippines Constabulary (PC) and paramilitary auxiliaries of the official Citizens' Armed Forces

Geographical Unit (CAFGU) took him from a bus at Orani, Bataan province. Hours later, relatives found his body in a funeral parlour: an autopsy revealed that he had been shot 28 times, had his genitals severed and his skull destroyed by a bullet. The authorities gave no explanation of his death and no action was known to have been taken against those responsible.

A suspected Muslim rebel, Kamlon Mamindiala, and 18 members of his family, including a pregnant woman and six children aged between one and 13, were reportedly killed in August by soldiers of the army's 38th Infantry Battalion in Tacurong, Sultan Kudarat province. Kamlon Mamindiala was reportedly shot when he resisted arrest: soldiers then apparently ordered his relatives out of their houses and shot them. The military authorities initially said the family had been killed in an armed encounter between government forces and Muslim rebels, but investigations by the PC Provincial Commander and the CHR found that they had been massacred by "alleged members" of the 38th Infantry Battalion. The Defense Secretary reportedly ordered the temporary suspension of those allegedly responsible but they were not known to have been brought to justice by the end of 1990.

Cornelio "Oscar" Tagulao was shot dead in March, apparently because the trade union led by his brother was regarded by the military as a CPP and NPA "front". The three men in plain clothes who killed him in Mariveles, Bataan province, were said by eye-witnesses to have shouted, "For every NPA killing there will be 10 people killed in retaliation". The three were believed to be linked to the 24th Infantry Battalion. The local military commander later reportedly described the killing as a "good thing", warning that members of the family affiliated to the trade union in question would remain on the military's "Order of Battle".

Human rights lawyers and activists, church workers and members of legal organizations which the authorities accused of being NPA-CPP fronts received death threats believed to come from military or government-backed paramilitary sources. In Negros Occidental, Sister Aquila Sy, a well-known community and human rights worker, and others, including an 84-year-old parish priest, were threatened with death in August and September. Groups linked to local government and military officials circulated leaflets accusing them of supporting the NPA and calling for their deaths or expulsion. Sister Aquila Sy, known for helping "internal evacuees" displaced from their homes by military operations, had recently tried to locate three such people who had "disappeared" in military custody.

More than 50 people "disappeared" during the year after being detained by members of government or government-backed security forces. At least 15, whose detention had originally been denied by security forces, reappeared after a period in police or military custody. Five were believed to have died or to have been killed in custody. Most of the victims belonged to legal non-governmental organizations accused by the authorities of being NPA-CPP fronts; others were suspected NPA members.

Nestor Loberio and Diomedes Abawag, who worked with a farmers' organization in Catbalogan, Samar province, "disappeared" after they were abducted in January by armed men believed to be members of a military intelligence "death squad". Diomedes Abawag was thought to have been tortured and beheaded by his captors; his head, bearing signs of torture, was found by fishermen on 1 February. Nestor Loberio's whereabouts remained unknown at the end of the year.

Two women, Soledad Mabilangan and Alita Bona, who was then pregnant, "disappeared" after being taken by CAFGU and army personnel from a market-place in Wright, Samar province, in March. The military authorities denied that they were in custody for six weeks until two visiting Amnesty International representatives and two CHR officials found them in detention at the 802nd Infantry Battalion headquarters in Bagacay, Samar. However, they were not released; the military authorities said they would be held until their husbands, alleged NPA members, surrendered.

More than 1,500 suspected government opponents were arrested in 1990 but most were held briefly and released after questioning. Some of the 700 or so political prisoners still held at the end of the year were believed to have been prisoners of conscience, although most were accused of supporting the insurgency and charged with criminal acts such as murder and illegal possession of firearms in furtherance of rebellion.

Sixteen prisoners of conscience were released, including 12 who were among a group of 25 farmers from Leyte whose trial on rebellion charges ended in 1989 (see *Amnesty International Reports 1989* and *1990*). Judgment was delayed for more than 18 months before the court acquitted the 12. It had still not ruled on the remaining defendants, all prisoners of conscience, by the end of 1990, and they remained in prison.

Four members of the Alliance of Farmers of Central Luzon (AMGL) in Nueva Ecija, believed to be prisoners of conscience, were released on bail. They were among a group of 13 AMGL members arrested in 1988 and charged with subversion; the other nine had been released on bail in 1989 (see *Amnesty International Report 1990*).

There were continued reports that members of government and government-backed forces tortured and ill-treated political detainees and suspected rebels to extract confessions or for revenge. Ruben Abaigar alleged that he was beaten repeatedly and threatened with death by soldiers of the 52nd Infantry Battalion and CAFGU personnel who detained him in February as a suspected NPA member. He said the soldiers blindfolded him, tied his hands and beat him repeatedly, then threatened to stab him to make him admit to NPA membership. He was released without charge on 23 March.

Benedicto Mabilangan, a suspected NPA supporter, and his 15-year-old son Orlando were arrested without warrant by soldiers during a town festival in Catbalogan, Samar, and detained for 20 days. The boy, who was given one electric shock himself, witnessed his father being beaten and tortured with electric shocks and by having his face covered with cellophane into which holes were made so that water could be forced into his nostrils. A human rights lawyer who later helped to bring charges against the perpetrators received death threats believed to come from military sources.

The government named 43 police and military personnel said to have been sentenced between March 1986 and mid-1990 for "human rights violations", including two reportedly sentenced in 1990. It was unclear whether all had in fact been convicted of human rights-related offences or for common crimes. Other than the two listed by the authorities, no other member of the police or military was known to have been convicted of human rights offences in 1990, although a number were brought to trial. A military officer accused of killing labour leader Rolando Olalia in 1986 (see *Amnesty International Report 1987*) was acquitted after a three-year trial; others accused in the same case went into hiding or were given immunity to testify for the state.

Some alleged violations were officially investigated but generally the findings were not made public. An investigation was ordered into the killing of Jose Dy and Gilberto Lopez. The two had been shot dead in June by masked members of the PC while attending the funeral of an alleged NPA member in Manila. The outcome of the investigation was not known. Similarly, police in Northern Samar filed kidnap and murder charges against nine CAFGU members accused of killing three suspected NPA members in captivity in February. However, the nine were not known to have been arrested or to have stood trial by the end of the year.

The Senate Committee on Constitutional Amendments and Revision of Codes adopted a resolution in February postponing for one year any new legislative measures on the death penalty, which was provisionally abolished under the 1987 Constitution. There were continued calls for the restoration of the death penalty for certain "heinous crimes".

Amnesty International urged the government to ensure the independent investigation of alleged extrajudicial executions and "disappearances", and called for those allegedly responsible to be brought to justice before the civil courts. It called for the release of prisoners of conscience, for the prompt, fair trial or release of other political detainees and for the review of the cases of prisoners sentenced after apparently unfair trials. It urged the government to repeal Presidential Decree 1850 and to review the use of civilian paramilitary forces in its counter-insurgency campaign.

In April an Amnesty International delegation visited the Philippines to conduct research and to meet local human rights activists and organizations. The delegation also had discussions with the Commission on Human Rights. In September the organization testified before the UN Working Group on Enforced or Involuntary Disappearances.

POLAND

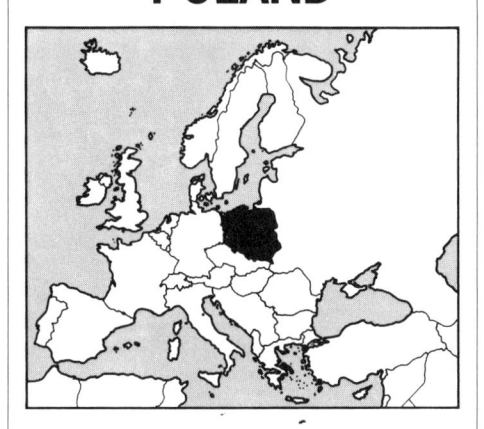

Several people were reportedly ill-treated in custody, leading in one case to death. A woman was killed in an arson attack for which members of the security forces were alleged to be responsible. The death penalty remained in force although there were no executions.

Under the government of the formerly banned trade union *Solidarnosc*, Solidarity, a comprehensive reform of the legal system continued. The National Judiciary Council was set up in February to promote the independence of the judiciary and freedom of the courts, and a new Supreme Court was inaugurated in July. A new system of appeal courts was also established and the misdemeanour courts, which had often been used for political cases, were transferred from the disbanded People's Councils to the Justice Ministry. In March the Prosecutor General's office was dissolved and the prosecution system put under the control of the Justice Ministry. The Penal Code and Petty Offences Code continued to be under review throughout the year. Investigations continued into past human rights abuses which occurred under former communist governments, including the murder of opposition activists. In December Solidarity Chairperson and former prisoner of conscience Lech Walesa was elected president.

In March the Ministry of the Interior stated that a detainee in Slupsk had died, apparently as a result of beatings in custody by a police officer. Reportedly, a special commission of inquiry was set up and proceedings were begun against the police officer.

In April an arson attack on the home of Jerzy Jachowicz caused the death of his wife, Maria Jachowicz. He had allegedly received a number of death threats following publication in the newspaper *Gazeta Wyborcza* of a series of reports he had written on the workings of the Polish security forces. A high-level commission of inquiry was set up to investigate the attack.

Amnesty International expressed its concern about reports of ill-treatment in detention and requested to be informed of the findings of special commissions set up to investigate the death in Slupsk in March, and the arson attack in April. The organization also urged the authorities to abolish the death penalty.

PORTUGAL

There were reports of ill-treatment in police custody and prisons.

In March Portugal ratified the European Convention for the Prevention of Torture and Inhuman or Degrading Treatment or Punishment. In October it ratified the Second Optional Protocol to the International Covenant on Civil and Political Rights Aiming at the Abolition of the Death Penalty.

The reports of ill-treatment concerned detained criminal suspects and convicted prisoners. It was claimed that many detainees and prisoners with substantive evidence of ill-treatment, such as medical reports, did not make official complaints because of intimidation and threats of counter-charges by police and prison officers.

According to press reports, in the early hours of 1 October José Luis Barros, Paolo Jorge Gomes Almeida and a friend were returning to their homes in Oporto when the friend was attacked without warning by an unidentified man who punched him in the face. The man then hit José Luis Barros and when the friend came to his aid, threatened them with a gun. They went immediately to a station of the Public Security Police to complain. José Luis Barros alleged that he and his companions were then attacked and hit by members of the Public Security Police at the entrance to the station. The man whom José Luis Barros recognized as having punched him in the street reappeared dressed in police uniform. When Paolo Jorge Gomes Almeida protested about the man having pulled a gun on them, a policeman reportedly seized him by the neck and threw him through a plate-glass door. He was taken to hospital and received 59 stitches to his right arm.

José Luis Barros was held in the station until morning. Paolo Jorge Gomes Almeida alleged that, while he was in hospital, the officer who had thrown him through the door told him to remember that he had tripped and fallen in the street and that it would be useless to complain to a court. Officers stationed in the police post within the hospital allegedly refused to register his complaint of assault. A judicial inquiry was opened in October.

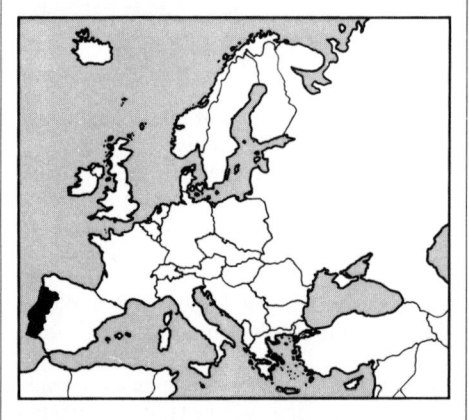

Daniel Rodríguez Perez continued to allege that he had been beaten by officers of the Public Security Police and the Judicial Police during three interrogations in 1988 (see *Amnesty International Report 1990*). In January the Prosecutor in Chaves indicted him for assaulting a member of the Judicial Police during his second interrogation on 6 May 1988. In February the authorities stated that he had fallen and cut his head before his first interrogation and that other injuries were self-inflicted. However, new information received during the year revealed that the Chaves prison doctor had examined him after each interrogation and, on 12 May 1988, had registered a formal complaint regarding his physical condition with the Chaves court. The doctor recorded a stitched scalp-wound, bruising of different degrees of severity to his face, chest, throat, shoulders and arms, and blood in his ears.

During the judicial investigation which was opened in 1988 into the alleged ill-treatment of Daniel Rodríguez Perez, the Judicial Police had informed the Prosecutor that the complaint should be archived because there was insufficient evidence to indicate any breach of discipline by police officers. The Prosecutor ordered the complaint to be archived in July 1989. Daniel Rodríguez Perez' trial on charges of assault, set for September 1990, was postponed at the last moment and had not taken place by the end of the year.

A number of allegations of ill-treatment concerned inmates of Linhó prison. On 5 March, following reported violent clashes between prisoners and prison guards, 19 prisoners were assembled in the exercise yard for transfer. Relatives of the prisoners alleged that officers of the Intervention Squad of the General Directorate of Prison Services then beat the prisoners with truncheons, insulting them and referring to complaints that Linhó prisoners had made to their families and the press about their ill-treatment. On 10 March the Director General of Prison Services stated that an administrative inquiry had been opened into the reported incident.

The results of an administrative inquiry carried out at Linhó prison following the death of Mário Manuel da Luz in June 1989 were made public in February. The autopsy had apparently concluded that he had died of bronchial pneumonia caused by injuries. Fellow prisoners at Linhó prison had alleged that during his detention in a punishment cell he was subjected to systematic ill-treatment by prison guards (see *Amnesty International Report 1990*). The Director General of Prison Services stated that acts committed in the prison's punishment cells and maximum security wing constituted "serious breaches of discipline and, probably, criminal offences". The prison governor had already been suspended by February 1990, in connection with allegations of ill-treatment involving four prisoners in the security wing. In August the Director General reported that disciplinary proceedings had been opened against the prison governor, the prison doctor and other prison officers.

Amnesty International sought information on the steps taken to investigate allegations of ill-treatment and asked to be informed of the progress and outcome of judicial and administrative inquiries into such allegations. In September an Amnesty International delegate visited Chaves to attend the trial of Daniel Rodríguez Perez and, in view of the prison doctor's medical report, asked the *Provedor de Justiça* (Ombudsman) for a review of the decision to archive the complaint of ill-treatment.

ROMANIA

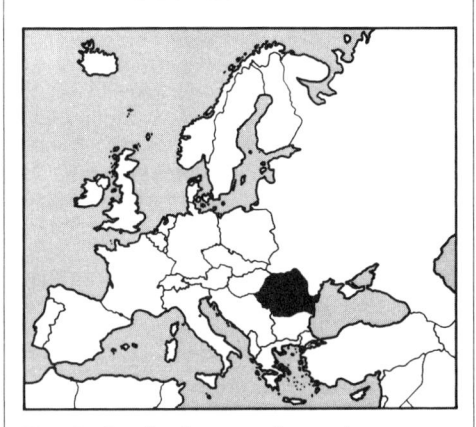

Hundreds of prisoners of conscience were detained for short periods and allegedly ill-treated following disturbances in June. Legal safeguards were lacking in some political trials. There were reports of torture and ill-treatment of detainees. Local officials allegedly colluded in violent attacks on people, in some cases apparently on the basis of the victims' ethnic origin.

Elections in May resulted in large majorities for President Ion Iliescu and the ruling National Salvation Front (NSF). Major reform of the legal system was initiated, and the Constitution, Penal Code and Code of Penal Procedure were under review. Throughout the year trials took place of people accused of having committed human rights abuses during the violent overthrow of the former government in December 1989 (see *Amnesty International Report 1990*).

In February the United Nations (UN) Commission on Human Rights extended for a further year, with the Romanian Government's agreement, the mandate of the Special Rapporteur appointed in 1989 to examine the human rights situation in Romania. In March Romania signed the Second Optional Protocol to the International Covenant on Civil and Political Rights Aiming at the Abolition of the Death Penalty, but had not ratified it by the end of the year. In December it acceded to the UN Convention against Torture and Other Cruel, Inhuman or Degrading Treatment or Punishment.

Hundreds of prisoners of conscience were detained following disturbances in June in Bucharest. On 13 June security forces evicted anti-government demonstrators from University Square where they had been encamped for seven weeks. Many were arrested and allegedly beaten by police. Later that day, a large crowd of anti-government protesters regained control of University Square. Sections of the crowd engaged in violence, including the burning of cars and attacking government buildings. The government, apparently unable to rely on the regular security forces, appealed to the population to "defend the democracy" and called thousands of workers, many of them miners, into Bucharest.

Over 1,000 people were reportedly detained; hundreds of them were prisoners of conscience unconnected with the violence. Costica Cojacaru, a retired telecommunications worker, alleged that he was attacked without provocation and "arrested" by miners on 14 June. He was taken to the Magurele military camp on the outskirts of Bucharest where he was detained in a garage with between 700 and 800 others until 16 June, when he was released. He alleged that he and the other detainees were repeatedly ill-treated by security officials and that miners were allowed to enter the base and threaten them.

Many of those detained were released after a few days, although some remained in detention for longer periods. Marian Munteanu, a student leader, was admitted into hospital on 14 June after miners broke into the University Architecture Faculty where he was sleeping, and savagely beat him. He was arrested in hospital on 18 June on charges of having incited the crowd to violence on 13 June, although eye-witnesses reported that he had categorically rejected the use of violence and called on the crowd to be peaceful. Other students who were arrested alleged that they had been forced to sign statements incriminating Marian Munteanu. He and many others arrested during these events were denied access to their families and lawyers, in some cases for over one month. Marian Munteanu was released on 3 August.

There were many reports of torture and ill-treatment in connection with the June disturbances in Bucharest. Iulia Horac alleged that after her arrest on 13 June, she and others arrested with her were beaten and kicked while being forced through a cordon of police officers armed with batons and shields. Miners and other workers called in by the authorities openly attacked those they considered to be government opponents with clubs, pickaxes and other weapons while the security forces stood by. The miners also "arrested" and severely beat hundreds of people, many of whom were also allegedly ill-treated after arrest by army and police officials. Many of the victims had no connection with the violence which had taken place earlier.

There were numerous eye-witness accounts of official encouragement, direction and control of the miners. Members of Bucharest's Rom (Gypsy) community appeared to be singled out in a way which suggested official coordination. Groups of miners, sometimes accompanied by police officers, reportedly targeted Rom homes, savagely beating the inhabitants, and attacked suspected Rom in the streets. A commission of inquiry into the June events was established but had not published its findings by the end of the year.

A number of people tried for public order offences were sentenced to up to six months' imprisonment under Decree 153/1970, which ostensibly deals with those "who lead a parasitic life". Those convicted included between 14 and 18 Rom sentenced in connection with inter-communal rioting in Tirgu Mures in March. These trials lacked essential legal safeguards and did not meet international standards for fair trials. Decree 153/1970 does not allow for an appeal to a higher tribunal and provides for an accelerated procedure which does not allow sufficient time to prepare a defence. The defence counsel for the Rom convicted in Tirgu Mures was reportedly permitted to see the dossier only minutes before the trial began.

There were many reports of ill-treatment of detainees, which in some cases amounted to torture. Some anti-government protesters arrested on 18 February were reportedly beaten by police officers until they signed confessions. They included Atila Rosianu, aged 16, who was reportedly beaten and forced by police to denounce one of his co-defendants. Some of the detainees – many of whom were minors including some under the age of 16 – were reportedly held incommunicado for as long as six weeks.

In Tirgu Mures on 19 March a large crowd of Romanians, many transported in from neighbouring villages and armed with axes, pitchforks and scythes, attacked the headquarters of the Democratic Alliance of Hungarians in Romania (RMDSZ). There were reports of collusion with local officials who allegedly welcomed the attackers and directed them to the RMDSZ headquarters. Ethnic Hungarians were brutally attacked and seriously injured in full view of police and military personnel who, eye-witnesses reported, did not intervene to protect them. Intercommunal tension had been rising in Tirgu Mures for some time, and the following day severe intercommunal rioting broke out. A commission of inquiry into the events was established but its findings had not been published by the end of the year.

Children detained in state-run psychiatric institutions were subjected to extreme neglect, amounting to cruel, inhuman or degrading treatment. The neglect had occurred over a long period of time under the former government, and resulted in scores of deaths, apparently from a combination of hunger and exposure to cold. Reports indicated that serious neglect continued in many of these state-run institutions after the change in government. Following widespread international attention, conditions reportedly improved.

An Amnesty International delegation visited the country in January and discussed its concerns with senior officials. The organization called for the immediate release of Marian Munteanu and other prisoners of conscience arrested in the June events. During the year it raised its concerns about alleged ill-treatment of detainees; the alleged complicity of local officials in violent attacks on people and the failure of the security forces to attempt to prevent such attacks; and the lack of legal safeguards in some trials. The authorities made a number of replies, most of which failed to address adequately the concerns raised. Amnesty International also called on the government to take immediate steps to prevent further ill-treatment of children in psychiatric institutions. In September a second Amnesty International delegation visited the country and met senior officials, including President Iliescu and Prime Minister Petre Roman.

RWANDA

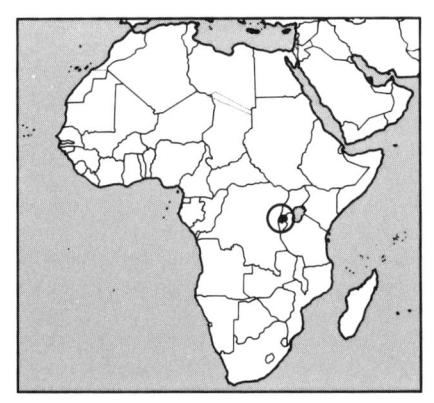

About 7,000 suspected government opponents were detained after armed Uganda-based exiles invaded northeast Rwanda in October. Over 4,000 were believed to have been released by the end of 1990 but the government announced that more than 1,500 others, who included possible prisoners of conscience, would be tried. Many of those arrested were reportedly tortured and ill-treated, and at least five of them died as a result of poor prison conditions. Six other people were prisoners of conscience after being convicted of political offences at unfair trials. The Head of State commuted 480 death sentences to life imprisonment and no executions were reported.

An armed force of Rwandese exiles, mostly members of the Tutsi ethnic group who had left Rwanda in the late 1950s and early 1960s, invaded northeast Rwanda from Uganda on 1 October in an attempt to overthrow the government of President Juvénal Habyarimana. Four days later, there was fighting in and around the capital, Kigali, when supporters of the rebels tried to open a second front. The rebels were said to have killed captured combatants and to have conscripted children into their ranks. The government declared a state of siege on 8 October, which was still in force at the end of the year, and took military action against the insurgents. The rebel-occupied territory was recovered and several rebel leaders were killed, but various parts of the north were still affected by the conflict at the end of the year. Hundreds of civilians were reportedly killed by rebel forces or government troops. A government minister said that more than 300 people killed by government troops were rebels in civilian clothes.

In November President Habyarimana announced that political reforms would be introduced to end the one-party state in 1991. He also approved a proposal for a regional conference to discuss the future of refugees and exiles from Rwanda, but this had not taken place by the end of the year.

About 7,000 people, the majority of whom appeared to be Tutsi, were detained in connection with the rebellion in the last quarter of the year. The detainees included members of the armed forces and civilians – some of them critics of the government – as well as relatives of the rebels and more than 200 Ugandan nationals. Among them were Alphonse Munyaneza, a Hutu and the son of a former government minister, and Thomas Kabeja, a Tutsi university lecturer: both men were among more than 4,000 people who were released uncharged before the end of 1990.

Following the first arrests in October the government set up commissions, composed of members of the security forces and the procuracy, to determine who should be released and who should be referred for possible prosecution. The grounds for their decisions were not made public, however, and some reports suggested that those still held at the end of 1990 included leading members of the Tutsi community and Ugandan nationals detained solely on account of their ethnic origin or nationality. The commissions ordered many releases, but numerous detainees had not appeared before them by the time their proceedings were suspended at the end of November. Eugène Rutagarama, a Tutsi biologist who appeared to be a prisoner of conscience held on the grounds that he had been in contact with government opponents while travelling abroad, was among more than 2,000 people still held at the end of the year.

In December the government announced that 1,566 people arrested in connection with the rebel incursion would be brought to trial. The first 12 defendants appeared before the State Security Court in late December, but their trial was adjourned to 1991.

Earlier in the year several other people were tried before the State Security Court. In March Innocent Ndayambaje, a university student who had been detained incommunicado for more than three years (see *Amnesty International Report 1990*), received a five-year prison term for forming a political party in violation of Rwanda's one-party constitution. He was a prisoner of conscience. In April Callixte Sinaruhamagaye and Claude Bahintasi, both held since 1987, Dr Aloys Sebiziga, who was arrested in 1989, and two others were acquitted on charges of assisting a former government minister living in exile (see *Amnesty International Report 1990*) and released.

Four Jehovah's Witnesses were sentenced to 10-year prison terms in April for disturbing the peace and organizing unauthorized meetings. All four were prisoners of conscience.

Two journalists, Vincent Rwabukwisi and Hassan Ngeze, were arrested in July. The State Security Court twice declined to pass judgment on the grounds of insufficient evidence but kept the journalists in custody. The Court reconvened in October, after the rebel incursion, and sentenced Vincent Rwabukwisi to 15 years' imprisonment for endangering state security by meeting Rwandese exiles in Kenya. There was no evidence to suggest that he had any prior knowledge of the armed incursion and he appeared to be a prisoner of conscience. Hassan Ngeze received a one-year suspended sentence for subversion as a result of a newspaper article he had published which claimed that the Tutsi dominated the Rwandese economy.

The State Security Court offered defendants little chance of a fair trial. All but one of the five judges were closely linked to the government and the security forces and could not be considered independent. Many defendants appeared in court without legal counsel and were unable to contest their cases on points of law. The court offered restricted and inadequate opportunities of appeal, and none of those convicted in 1990 was known to have lodged an appeal.

Many of those arrested in October were held for several days in Nyamirambo stadium, near Kigali, without food, drink or medical care, before being moved to various prisons. At least five people reportedly died in custody, possibly as a result of poor conditions and lack of medical care: only one such death was confirmed by the government.

Many detainees were also reportedly beaten by members of the security forces, especially at the time of their arrest. One person was said to have died under torture in December soon after his arrest by members of the security forces in the town of Rwamagana.

A family of three was possibly extrajudicially executed. Michel Karambizi, his wife and child were shot dead in Kigali by government soldiers in early October. Some sources suggested that they may have been targeted because Michel Karambizi's brother, a political exile, was a well-known government opponent, but the authorities said the family was killed in an armed clash with the security forces. No inquiry into the killings was known to have been carried out.

In September 480 prisoners had their death sentences commuted to life imprisonment by President Habyarimana. The courts were believed to have imposed further death sentences, but it was not known how many. No executions were reported.

Amnesty International appealed for the release of Innocent Ndayambaje and other prisoners of conscience.

Following the October incursion, Amnesty International sought information about those arrested, their legal status and their treatment and conditions of detention. It pressed the authorities to release all prisoners of conscience and to ensure the fair trial or release of other political detainees. The organization appealed to the government to take all possible steps to protect those in custody from torture, ill-treatment or other human rights abuses, to instruct members of the security forces to respect human rights, and to investigate alleged human rights abuses. In late December an Amnesty International representative visited Kigali to observe the trial of alleged rebel sympathizers and to collect information about political prisoners. Amnesty International welcomed those releases that did occur and the commutation of death sentences.

ST VINCENT AND THE GRENADINES

The death penalty for juveniles convicted of murder was introduced in late 1989. Four people were under sentence of death but no executions were carried out; the last execution took place in 1988.

An amendment to the Criminal Code, which came into force in November 1989, extended the use of the death penalty to people who were over the age of 16 at the time of the offence; previously the minimum age was 18.

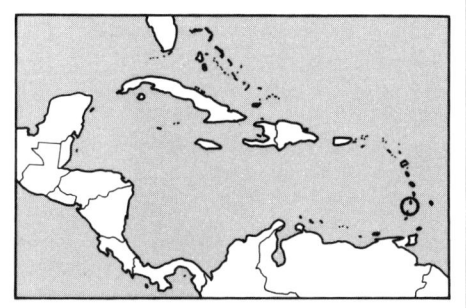

Amnesty International wrote to Prime Minister James Mitchell in April expressing concern at the new provision, pointing out that it contravened international standards which strictly prohibit death sentences being passed on people under the age of 18 at the time of the crime. Amnesty International urged the government to repeal the provision and to seriously consider abolishing the death penalty. Amnesty International also requested the commutation of all outstanding death sentences.

In an oral statement delivered in August to the United Nations Sub-Commission on Prevention of Discrimination and Protection of Minorities, Amnesty International included reference to its concern about the introduction of the death penalty for juveniles.

SÃO TOMÉ AND PRÍNCIPE

The death penalty was abolished under a new constitution which also increased protection for fundamental rights and freedoms. All political prisoners were released.

The new constitution came into force in September after it was approved by a referendum in August. It abolished the death penalty in law. No one had been sentenced to death since the penalty was introduced in 1979 for the offence of "mercenarism", or being a mercenary. Substantially increased protection for prisoners includes a prohibition on torture and the right to challenge the legality of a detention through *habeas corpus* procedures. The Constitution also guarantees freedom of expression and association, and introduced the right to form or join political parties. Three new political parties were formed to contest legislative and presidential elections in 1991.

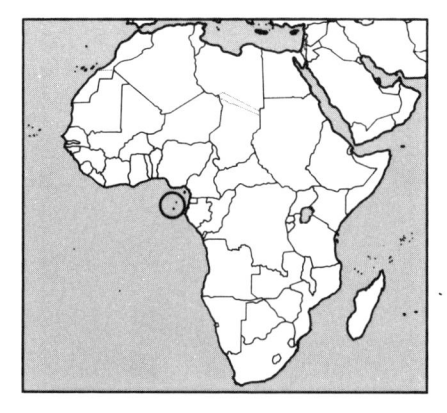

All 39 political prisoners were released. They had been convicted in September 1989 of armed rebellion and endangering the security of the state but had no right to appeal to a higher court against their convictions or sentences (see *Amnesty International Report 1990*). Three were released in March after completing their two-year sentences, which ran from the date of their arrest in 1988; the others were released in April on the orders of President Manuel Pinto da Costa.

Amnesty International welcomed the abolition of the death penalty and the increased human rights safeguards in the new constitution.

SAUDI ARABIA

More than 80 critics and opponents of the government were arrested and held as prisoners of conscience, 23 of whom remained in detention without charge or trial at the end of the year. Two possible prisoners of conscience arrested in 1990 were also still held. Five other prisoners of conscience arrested in 1989 and 12 political prisoners arrested in 1988 were detained apparently without charge or trial throughout 1990. At least 95 political detainees, including 26 prisoners of conscience, were freed under a royal pardon in April. Other prisoners of conscience

may have been among thousands of Yemeni nationals arrested between August and November. Four people were sentenced to prison terms after unfair trials. There were new reports of torture and ill-treatment, including of detained Yemeni nationals, and judicial amputations and floggings continued to be carried out. At least 13 people were executed.

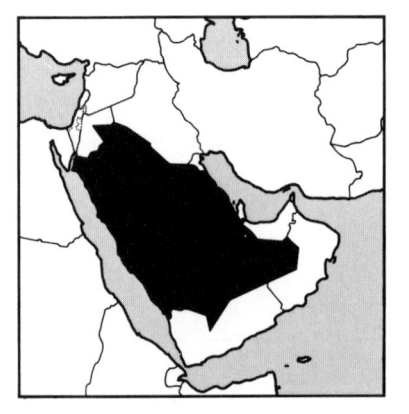

Following the Iraqi invasion of Kuwait on 2 August, military forces of the United States of America, the United Kingdom and eight other countries were stationed in the country. The Saudi authorities regarded Yemen as an unfriendly country and in September the hundreds of thousands of Yemeni migrant workers in the country were made subject to new visa and work permit requirements and in many cases were deported.

In November a consultative system of government was proposed when King Fahd bin 'Abdul-'Aziz announced that a Central Consultative Council, as well as Provincial Consultative Councils, would be set up as soon as the necessary legislation governing their functioning had been decreed. In the same month the Ministry of the Interior issued a decree introducing a legal ban on female drivers; this ban had previously existed in practice but not in law.

In April 7,681 detainees and sentenced prisoners were released following a royal pardon. Most were common law prisoners; however, 95 were suspected political opponents, most of whom had been detained without charge or trial. They included 26 prisoners of conscience suspected of being members of *Munadhamat al-Thawra al-Islamiyya fil Jazira al-'Arabiyya*, the Organization of Islamic Revolution in the Arabian Peninsula (OIRAP). Also among the 95 were nine possible prisoners of conscience, including five suspected supporters of *Hizbul 'Amal al-Ishtiraki al-'Arabi – al-Jazira al-'Arabiyya*, the Arab Socialist Action Party – the Arabian Peninsula, and four alleged supporters of *Hizbullah fil Hijaz*, the Party of God in Hijaz (see *Amnesty International Report 1990*).

At least 83 non-violent critics or opponents of the government were arrested between February and November. Of these, 23 were still held as prisoners of conscience at the end of the year. Six suspected supporters of OIRAP were arrested in February and April and held by *al-Mabahith al-'Amma*, General Intelligence, in al-Dammam. Among them was 'Abdullah Jabir Shahin from Safwa who was arrested in Kuwait in the last week of January and handed over to the Saudi authorities on 4 February. Four of the six were released in April under the royal pardon; the other two were released in June. Between August and October, 27 other suspected OIRAP supporters were arrested, 12 of them at Riyadh airport or other places when returning from abroad. Of these, 22 remained in detention apparently without charge or trial at the end of the year.

Another prisoner of conscience who remained in detention at the end of the year was Salih al- 'Azzaz, a well-known writer and journalist. He was arrested in Riyadh on 6 November on suspicion of helping to organize a protest that day by women against a ban on female drivers. During the protest, 49 women were arrested and held in custody for several hours. They were released only after their male relatives signed an undertaking that the women would not violate the ban. They included Fawzia al-Bakr, a professor at the University of Riyadh. She had previously been detained for several months in 1982 (see *Amnesty International Report 1983*).

Five students at King Saud University in Riyadh, arrested in July 1989, remained in detention without trial (see *Amnesty International Report 1990*).

Thousands of Yemeni nationals were arrested following the introduction of new visa and work permit requirements on 19 September. Among them were possible prisoners of conscience, apparently arrested for no reason other than their nationality or non-violent political views. Many were held for short periods in makeshift detention centres pending their deportation, while thousands of others were reportedly still held at the end of the year. It was not known whether any had been charged with a recognizably criminal offence.

Others arrested during the year included at least four possible prisoners of conscience, two of whom were still in detention apparently without charge or trial at the end of 1990.

Twelve alleged *Hizbullah fil Hijaz* supporters arrested in 1988 (see *Amnesty International Reports 1989* and *1990*) remained in detention, but it was not known whether they had been tried.

Four other *Hizbullah fil Hijaz* supporters were sentenced to between seven and 15 years' imprisonment in late 1989 or early 1990 after unfair trials. Their trials lasted only a few minutes and were held *in camera*. The defendants were denied lawyers, were not informed of the charges against them, and received no notice that they were to be tried until they were brought, in the early hours of the morning, before the Higher Shari'a Court in al-Dammam. In court they were asked to certify confessions extracted from them during interrogation. They had no right of appeal. Four Kuwaiti nationals sentenced in 1989 to between 15 and 20 years' imprisonment following similar procedures continued to be held (see *Amnesty International Report 1990*).

Torture and ill-treatment of political detainees and Yemeni nationals were reportedly widespread. Hundreds of Yemeni nationals were said to have been ill-treated or tortured in detention pending their deportation. For example, Amin Ahmad al-Shawafi, a mechanic from Ibb, who spent 16 days in Jeddah Central Prison before his deportation on 25 September, said he was questioned about his political views and continuously beaten over the head and body with a "sharp instrument".

Sayyid Tahir al-Shimimy, a religious scholar and alleged OIRAP supporter who was released in April, said he had been repeatedly tortured following his arrest in June 1989. He said he had been beaten, deprived of sleep and had his face pushed down a lavatory. He spent 130 days in solitary confinement in *al-Mabahith al-'Amma* prison in al-Dammam and required hospital treatment for spinal injuries following his release.

New information was received about the torture and ill-treatment in detention of 29 Kuwaiti nationals arrested in July 1989 (see *Amnesty International Report 1990*), 16 of whom were executed in 1989 and four of whom were still held at the end of 1990. Others who were released alleged that all the detainees were beaten with canes and whips, deprived of sleep and injected with unknown substances which induced a trance-like state. 'Adnan 'Abdul-Samad, a former member of parliament, was reportedly deprived of sleep for several days, beaten all over his body with an *'iqal* (a thick rope forming part of traditional Arab headwear) and had the *'iqal* tightened around his neck to the point of near-asphyxiation. He was later released uncharged.

At least five people, four Filipinos and one Egyptian convicted of repeated theft, had their right hands amputated in February or March. The imposition of the judicial punishment of flogging remained widespread, although the number of sentences carried out was not known. One victim, Jack Huissen, an American teacher, was reportedly sentenced in June to receive 160 lashes – 70 for alcohol consumption, and 90 for reasons not disclosed to him. Prior to his release and deportation on 15 August, he received 90 lashes. Four Kuwaiti nationals sentenced in September 1989 to floggings of between 1,000 and 1,500 lashes, continued to receive their punishments during the year (see *Amnesty International Report 1990*).

Between January and July, at least 13 Saudi and foreign nationals were publicly executed after being convicted of criminal offences including murder, drug-trafficking and rape. Among those executed was Rashash Sa'id Mubarak al-'Utaibi, who was beheaded in June following his conviction for murder and highway robbery. His decapitated body was crucified and displayed in Riyadh.

In January Amnesty International published a report, *Saudi Arabia: Detention Without Trial of Suspected Political Opponents*, which expressed concern about the continuing pattern of detention without trial of suspected political opponents and torture and ill-treatment of detainees. It urged the government to review current detention cases and to release all those detained on account of their non-violent political opinions or activities. The government denied it was holding political prisoners or that torture was used to extract confessions. However, it expressed willingness to discuss matters of concern to Amnesty International, and accepted in principle that Amnesty International should visit Saudi Arabia for this purpose.

While welcoming the releases of prisoners of conscience and others, Amnesty International continued to press for the release of other non-violent government opponents and to express concern about the detention of other political detainees without trial or after unfair trials. The organization also expressed concern about the torture and ill-treatment of prisoners, and about the use of the death penalty.

Following reports of torture and ill-treatment of detained Yemeni nationals, Amnesty International urged King Fahd to set up an immediate public inquiry and called for the release of anyone detained solely on account of their nationality. The government denied widespread torture or ill-treatment but undertook to examine information submitted by Amnesty International. The names and other details of over 400 Yemeni deportees, including victims of alleged ill-treatment, were then submitted to the government but no inquiry was known to have been established by the end of the year.

SENEGAL

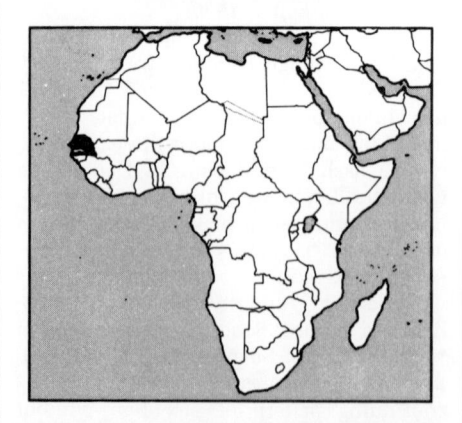

Hundreds of people suspected of supporting a separatist movement were arrested for political reasons; among them were possible prisoners of conscience. Some were released, but at least 300 were still held awaiting trial at the end of the year. **One prisoner of conscience convicted in 1989 began serving a six-month prison sentence and several government opponents were imprisoned after trials which did not conform to international fair trial standards. Torture and ill-treatment of detainees, sometimes leading to the victim's death, were widely reported after May. Government soldiers were alleged to have carried out several extrajudicial executions.**

The government continued to face armed opposition in the Casamance region. Most human rights violations occurred in May and the following months after a series of attacks on civilian targets by armed groups believed to be associated with the *Mouvement des forces démocratiques de la Casamance* (MFDC), Movement of Casamance's Democratic Forces, the main separatist organization.

Hundreds of people were arrested during the year in connection with the Casamance independence movement: most of them were suspected of being members of the MFDC but some may have been prisoners of conscience. Some were held for up to a few weeks in police custody in Casamance and then released uncharged. However, the majority, at least 300, were charged with endangering the security of the state and forming an unlawful association. They had not been brought to trial by the end of 1990. Those charged were transferred to Dakar and Rufisque prisons for their cases to be investigated by an examining magistrate. They included Father Diamacoune Augustin Senghor, a Roman Catholic priest and prominent supporter of Casamance independence previously imprisoned from 1982 to 1987, and Ankiling Diabone, a former African judo champion.

One prisoner of conscience began a six-month prison sentence in July. Cheikh Koureyssi Bâ, managing editor of the newspaper of the main opposition party, the *Parti démocratique sénégalais* (PDS), Senegalese Democratic Party, lost his appeal. He was convicted in 1989 on charges arising from his newspaper's claim that the PDS candidate won more votes than President Abdou Diouf in the 1988 presidential elections (see *Amnesty International Report 1990*). In another case heard in 1990, the PDS leader in the National Assembly, Ousmane Ngom, was sentenced to a three-month prison term for insulting the Head of State in a newspaper article. He appealed against the verdict and remained free.

At least one political trial took place which failed to meet international standards of fair trial. In mid-August five people from Casamance region, including Mamadou Sané "N'Krumah", a former political prisoner (see *Amnesty International Report 1990*), were convicted by the State Security Court in Dakar. They were found guilty of plotting against the internal and external security of the state, endangering public security and forming an unlawful association. They were accused of having asked officials in neighbouring Guinea-Bissau for military assistance for those seeking the independence of Casamance. They were sentenced to prison terms of between six and 10 years. All had been arrested in Guinea-Bissau, repatriated without any judicial proceedings, and arrested on arrival in Senegal in February 1988. The court did not investigate claims made by one of the defendants that he had been tortured in Senegalese police custody. Defendants convicted by the State Security Court have no right of appeal, although this is required by international law.

Torture and ill-treatment of detainees suspected of supporting the MFDC and of their relatives were increasingly reported after May in the context of counter-insurgency operations in Casamance. In one incident in June, government soldiers who entered Kabiline village, Bignona department, looking for suspected separatists, reportedly beat several of their relatives. One victim, Binta Niassy, apparently suffered a miscarriage after she was beaten, whipped and trampled on by soldiers. The soldiers also killed Famara Mary, a villager who escaped but was soon recaptured. Witnesses said that soldiers put a gun to his head and shot him dead.

Several people were reported to have died in custody as a result of torture or beatings. One, Assoua Diabone, a peasant farmer from Oussouye, died in Oussouye police station in June a few days after his arrest as a suspected separatist. Further deaths occurred in October: Younouss Djiba and a man known as Ampa Dakar, both suspected members of the MFDC, died after they were reportedly beaten by soldiers based at Kaguitte military barracks. Sékou Mary "Agnocoune" was apparently beaten to death by police based in Diouloulou, shortly after being forcibly returned to Senegal from the Gambia (see **Gambia**).

No formal inquiry by the procuracy was known to have been conducted into any of these deaths. Nor was any new information received about the findings of an inquiry into the alleged death under torture of Jean-Pascal Badji, a suspected MFDC member, in April 1989 (see *Amnesty International Report 1990*).

Several people were extrajudicially executed during the year. In May Jean-Marie Sagna from Kouring village, Ziguinchor department, was shot dead by soldiers based at Kaguitte military barracks. He was stopped by an army patrol and summarily killed, apparently because he was mistaken for a military leader of the separatists. The soldiers allegedly burned his body. The government said that there would be an inquiry into his death, but it was not known if this had been carried out.

In September dozens of soldiers entered Kanaw village, near the Gambian border, apparently with a list of people suspected of supporting the MFDC. Five men, including Kaoussou Tamba and Souleymane Goudiaby, were taken away by soldiers and were later found dead in a rice field.

In May Amnesty International published a report, *Senegal: Torture – the Casamance case*, which described the torture and ill-treatment of hundreds of alleged government opponents between 1982 and 1989. The government said that the allegations were "groundless" and were "an incredible story written by a Senegalese secessionist".

Amnesty International repeatedly urged the government to ensure prompt and impartial investigations into all allegations of torture and extrajudicial executions, and into all deaths in custody, and to bring to justice those found responsible. It also urged the authorities to take action to prevent further human rights violations.

SIERRA LEONE

Several people were detained without charge or trial, including possible prisoners of conscience. There was continuing concern about harsh prison conditions and the high death-rate of criminal

prisoners. At least 14 people were sentenced to death. It was not known if there were any executions.

Saidu Cham, a teachers' leader in Lunsar, Northern Province, and several teachers in Bo, Southern Province, were reportedly arrested in May in connection with a teachers' strike over pay and related demonstrations in which four people were said to have been killed. The teachers were apparently still held without charge or trial in July but no further information about their cases had been received by the end of the year.

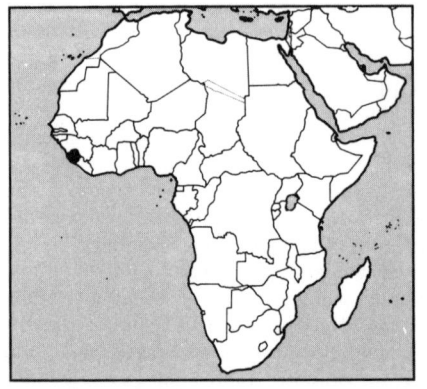

Three student leaders were briefly detained without charge or trial in November, apparently for organizing protests against the expulsion from university of six students accused of responsibility for criminal damage caused during demonstrations in June. The three included Mohamed Pateh Bah, who had been elected President of the National Union of Sierra Leone Students in August after the lifting of a 1986 ban on student unions.

Two journalists jailed on criminal charges in 1989 for what some alleged were political reasons were released. Both had worked for the *Chronicle* newspaper which had criticized government policies. The two men went on hunger-strike to protest against their imprisonment and the conditions at Pademba Road Prison in the capital, Freetown, complaining particularly that they were denied family visits and medical treatment. The authorities undertook to investigate their complaints but the two journalists, Karwigoko Roy Stevens and Lansana Fofana, were released in June and September respectively, the former after a successful application to the Court of Appeal.

As many as 100 prisoners out of a total prison population of about 1,000 were reported to have died from malnutrition and medical neglect at Pademba Road Prison during the first half of the year. The prisoners were held in overcrowded conditions and reportedly received inadequate food and practically no medical care. Many prisoners apparently contracted tuberculosis or skin diseases. Food supplies were halted for several days in October when suppliers said they had not been paid by the authorities.

The government made no public statement about the report of a commission of inquiry into the administration of prisons, which had submitted its findings in December 1989. The commission was set up following reports of grossly inadequate prison conditions leading to the starvation of prisoners in the mid-1980s (see *Amnesty International Reports 1984* to *1990*). It apparently recommended total refurbishment of the country's prisons and improvements in the nutrition and care of prisoners. It was unclear whether the government made any moves to implement any of these recommendations.

Three prisoners remained under sentence of death and at least 14 new death sentences were imposed for criminal offences. There were no known executions.

Amnesty International sought information from the government about the arrests of teachers and students, and urged the commutation of all death sentences.

SINGAPORE

Two prisoners of conscience were conditionally released from detention without charge or trial while a third who was released in 1989 remained confined at night to an offshore island. Criminal offenders continued to be sentenced to caning, which constitutes a cruel, inhuman or degrading form of punishment. The national media reported that 10 people were sentenced to death and three people were executed.

Vincent Cheng and Teo Soh Lung, both of them prisoners of conscience (see *Amnesty International Report 1990*), were released in June from detention under the Internal Security Act (ISA). However, restrictions were imposed on their freedom of movement, expression and association but they were not confined to live in any designated locality. In January the High Court had rejected Vincent Cheng's *habeas corpus* application challenging the legality of his detention. The Court of Appeal had rejected a similar application by Teo Soh Lung shortly before she was released.

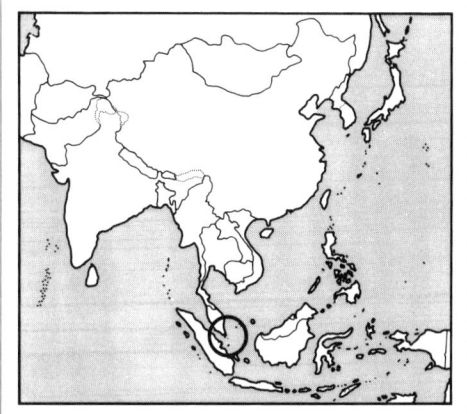

Chia Thye Poh, a former member of parliament who was released into internal exile in May 1989 after being detained without trial under the ISA since October 1966, continued to be regarded as a prisoner of conscience. He was exiled to the small island of Sentosa, off the main island of Singapore, on being released from prison. In September 1990 his restriction order was changed to permit him to visit and remain on the main island between 6am and 9pm daily and to seek a job with the approval of the Director of the Internal Security Department. At night he continued to be exiled to Sentosa.

Caning remained a mandatory punishment for around 30 crimes including attempted murder, armed robbery, rape, illegal immigration and drug-trafficking. Under amendments to the immigration law effected in March and August 1989, about 12 illegal workers from Thailand were reported to have been caned between November 1989 and March 1990. In January Mustaffa Ahmad was sentenced to 20 years' imprisonment and 15 strokes of the cane after being convicted of drug-trafficking. His three accomplices were sentenced to 12 years in jail and 10 strokes of the cane.

Ten people were reported to have received death sentences, of which eight were for drugs offences, one for murder and one for armed robbery. Three people were reported to have been executed, all for drugs offences.

Amnesty International continued to appeal for the unconditional release of and lifting of restrictions on Chia Thye Poh, Vincent Cheng and Teo Soh Lung. It also called for the commutation of all death sentences and for an end to executions.

SOMALIA

More than 50 critics and opponents of the government were arrested and imprisoned as prisoners of conscience but all were released before the end of the year. Fifteen prisoners of conscience arrested in 1989 and several untried political detainees were also freed. At least five detainees, including two held without charge or trial since 1976 and 1979, remained in prison. There were new reports of torture and ill-treatment, in two cases allegedly resulting in death. Hundreds of people were victims of extrajudicial executions by government forces in areas affected by armed conflict and in Mogadishu and other towns. Dozens of people were under sentence of death but the number of executions was not known.

In October a provisional constitution was introduced, which was to be submitted to a referendum within a year. It provided for the eventual legalization of political parties other than the ruling Somali Revolutionary Socialist Party (SRSP). Laws incompatible with the new constitution were abrogated, including the National Security Law, which had provided the legal basis since 1970 for the prolonged detentions and trials of government opponents. The National Security Court was abolished. A new "anti-sabotage" law was, however, being prepared to replace the National Security Law.

Armed conflict continued in the northwest where the Somali National Movement (SNM) had been fighting government forces since 1981, and in the central and southwestern parts of the country where the United Somali Congress (USC) and the Somali Patriotic Movement (SPM) were active. Opposition forces allegedly killed civilian supporters of the government, including some they had taken prisoner.

At the end of December USC guerrillas

seized parts of Mogadishu amidst heavy fighting. Hundreds of combatants and civilians were killed, foreigners were evacuated and President Mohamed Siad Barre's government was in danger of toppling.

In January the government acceded to the International Covenant on Civil and Political Rights, together with its first Optional Protocol, the International Covenant on Economic, Social and Economic Rights, and the Convention against Torture and Other Cruel, Inhuman or Degrading Punishment or Treatment.

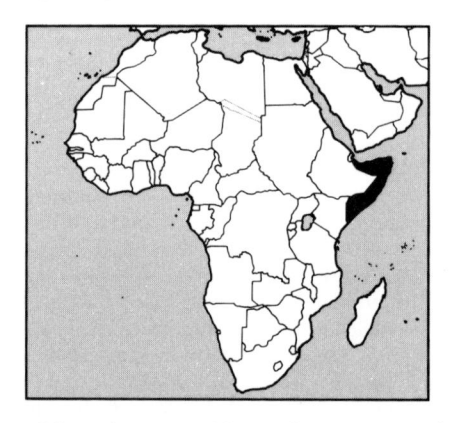

More than 50 critics and opponents of the government were arrested, but all were released by November. Several playwrights and actors from the Somali National Theatre were arrested in April after President Siad Barre walked out of a play which appeared to criticize his government. They were released after a few days. In July, 45 members of a newly-formed opposition group in Mogadishu, the Council for National Reconciliation and Salvation, were arrested for distributing an open "manifesto". This document criticized the government for human rights violations and urged it to hand over power to an interim government pending multi-party elections. Many of those arrested had previously held official posts, such as former police general Mohamed Abshir Musse, who had been a prisoner of conscience for 12 years, and Haji Musse Bogor, aged 82, a former government minister. The 45 detainees were held in Lanta Bur prison near Baidowa in harsh conditions. They were charged with treason, an offence for which the death penalty is mandatory. However, when they appeared before the National Security Court on 15 July, they were acquitted and released. Some of them were briefly redetained in early December.

Fifteen prisoners of conscience and several other political prisoners arrested in 1988 or 1989 were released. Sheikh Abdulaziz Ali Sufi, an Islamic preacher and university lecturer, Mohamed Ali Dahir, a businessman and religious writer, and four other prisoners of conscience held since July 1989, were brought to trial on capital charges before the National Security Court in January. The trial was adjourned and they were pardoned by President Siad Barre and released in March.

Several army officers who were arrested in late 1988 and mid-1989 for alleged links with the opposition SPM (which drew much of its support from disaffected army officers of the Ogaden clan), were released in October 1990 without having been charged or tried. One of the officers, Colonel Doctor Abdi Aideed Hirreh, had reportedly been denied medical treatment for injuries sustained in a car crash at the time of his arrest.

The trial of nine prisoners of conscience – including Abdirashid Abdi Kheyre, a businessman, and Farah Mohamoud Elmi, a veterinary science lecturer – arrested in Mogadishu in July 1989 and charged with treason, was postponed several times. The nine prisoners were reportedly in poor health as a result of torture and harsh prison conditions. In mid-October they went on hunger-strike, complaining that they should have been released under the terms of the new constitution. On 23 October demonstrations in Mogadishu called for the release of all political prisoners. The nine prisoners of conscience were released on 2 November, when an amnesty for political prisoners was announced. A total of 1,123 prisoners were released. Their names were not published but they apparently included many convicted criminal prisoners.

Despite the November amnesty, three long-term political prisoners were still held at the end of 1990: Hussein Mohamed Nur, an Ethiopian aircraft technician detained without charge or trial since 1976; Ahmed Dhore Farah, a district judge detained without charge or trial since 1979; and Mohamed Mohamoud Guleid, an army officer imprisoned after an unfair trial for espionage in 1981. Two former government ministers arrested in July 1989 – Major General Aden Abdullahi Nur and General Mohamed Abdullah Ba'adaleh – also remained in detention without trial.

There were new reports of torture which, in two cases, allegedly resulted in death. In February Mohamoud Mohamed Mohamoud, an 18-year-old student from Mogadishu, was arrested and tortured to force him to provide information about his brother, a government opponent who had fled the country. After two days in National Security Service custody he was taken to hospital seriously ill and died shortly afterwards. In June a visiting Italian medical scientist, Giuseppe Salvo, died in military custody in Mogadishu shortly after being arrested. A private autopsy found that he had been beaten to death. No official investigations into these deaths were known to have been initiated by the government. In July at least 20 Somali asylum-seekers were reportedly tortured or ill-treated after they were forcibly returned to Somalia and taken into custody. The asylum-seekers had been refused entry by Italian and Egyptian authorities. They were released several weeks later.

Hundreds of people were extrajudicially executed by government forces. In one incident, 17 people arrested by soldiers in the northern port of Berbera on 16 August were extrajudicially executed in the town that night. They appeared to have been arrested and killed in an arbitrary reprisal for SNM activities in the area. The victims included two employees of an international relief organization.

Indiscriminate killings of civilians by government soldiers were reported in all areas affected by armed conflict. In Belet Weyn in late May, over 100 men, women and children – unarmed villagers and nomads – were reported to have been indiscriminately killed in reprisal for a USC attack. Near Galkayu on 12 June, over 70 civilians were killed in an army reprisal raid. In Bulu Burti on 12 November, several prominent local people were extrajudicially executed and dozens of others arbitrarily killed in reprisal for a USC ambush of government troops nearby.

There were also many arbitrary killings of suspected government opponents by the army in Mogadishu and other towns. In July over 60 football spectators were shot dead in Mogadishu's main stadium by members of the presidential guard, who apparently thought that President Siad Barre might be attacked after people in the crowd shouted criticism of his opening speech. In Baidowa, dozens of people were reportedly shot dead by soldiers on 14 October for demonstrating against the President during an official visit. At least five others were killed and dozens wounded by soldiers during anti-government demonstrations in Mogadishu on 23 October. No inquiries were ordered by the government into these killings and no action was known to have been taken against those responsible.

Dozens of prisoners were under sentence of death, including some condemned during the year. It was not known how many executions, if any, took place. Some death sentences were commuted in the November amnesty. Two measures taken by the government suggested a possible reduction in the use of the death penalty in future years: the abolition in October of the National Security Court, which had sentenced hundreds of people to death since 1970, and the repeal of the National Security Law, which prescribed mandatory death sentences for 20 political offences. The death penalty, however, remained in force for some of these offences under existing laws.

In January Amnesty International publicly detailed its concerns on Somalia in a 29-page report: *Somalia: Report on an Amnesty International Visit and Current Human Rights Violations*. The organization urged the government to release prisoners of conscience and discontinue prolonged detention without trial and to stop torture and extrajudicial executions by the security forces, and recommended specific legal and institutional reforms to safeguard human rights. The report had been sent to the government for comment in late 1989; no response was received but several of the recommendations were implemented during 1990. Amnesty International welcomed the ratification in January of key international human rights instruments, urging that these standards be put into practice. It similarly welcomed the constitutional and legal changes in October, particularly the abolition of the National Security Court and the National Security Law. An Amnesty International visit to Somalia planned for June 1990 was postponed at the government's request and had not taken place by the end of the year.

Amnesty International appealed for the release of all prisoners of conscience. The organization urged that political prisoners should not be detained unlawfully or tortured, or given unfair trials before the National Security Court. It appealed for the commutation of all death sentences.

In July Amnesty International published new details (including the testimony of the sole survivor) of a massacre of 46 political prisoners by soldiers in July 1989 at Jezira beach near Mogadishu (see *Amnesty International Report 1990*). The report criticized the government for not releasing the findings of an official inquiry into the killings and for not taking action against those responsible. On this and other occasions Amnesty International called on the government to establish independent investigations into extrajudicial executions and bring to justice those responsible.

In January Amnesty International submitted further information about its concerns in Somalia for United Nations review under a procedure established by the Economic and Social Council Resolutions 728F/1503, for confidential consideration of communications about human rights violations.

SOUTH AFRICA

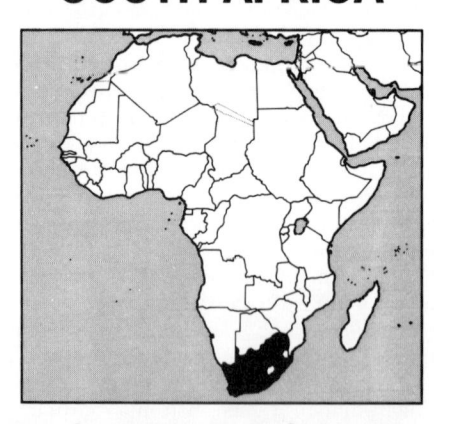

More than 1,500 critics and opponents of the government were detained without charge or trial for up to six months. Some were allegedly tortured. Those held included prisoners of conscience. At least 18 people died in police custody in suspicious circumstances, and there was evidence of security force complicity in extrajudicial executions of government opponents. A moratorium on executions was announced pending a review of the death penalty but there was one execution in the nominally independent Bophuthatswana "homeland".

In February State President F.W. de Klerk lifted bans imposed 30 years earlier on the African National Congress (ANC), the Pan Africanist Congress of Azania (PAC) and the South African Communist Party (SACP), and ordered the release of ANC deputy president Nelson Mandela, who had been serving a life sentence since 1964. Restrictions on other political and human rights groups opposed to *apartheid* were also removed and more than 700 government critics and opponents had their restriction orders lifted. Most had been restricted to local magisterial districts and held under overnight house arrest. The national state of emergency was lifted in three provinces in June and in the fourth in October. However, from August various magisterial districts were declared "unrest areas" in which security forces were given emergency powers of arbitrary arrest and detention. Preliminary negotiations began between the ANC and the government which were continuing at the end of 1990. As part of the process, exiled ANC leaders and others were given temporary immunity against prosecution to enable them to return to the country to participate in negotiations and in August the ANC agreed to suspend armed actions by its military wing. In November the government issued guidelines relating to pardon and indemnity for past political offences, making them applicable both to opposition activists and government personnel.

The year was marked by an unprecedented spiral of political violence resulting in thousands of deaths, many caused by fighting between ANC supporters and members of the Zulu-based Inkatha organization headed by Mangosuthu Buthelezi, Chief Minister of the Kwazulu "homeland". From July the violence spread from Natal to the area around Johannesburg and elsewhere. Some killings, for example, of black train commuters near Johannesburg in September and of residents of Pholo Park squatter camp in the East Rand in September, created suspicions that a "third force" of political extremists, including security force members, was orchestrating the violence to sabotage the process of negotiations between the government and the ANC.

About 450 government opponents were detained without charge or trial under national state of emergency regulations in force since June 1986. Those still in detention were released when the emergency was lifted in the Transvaal, Cape and Orange Free State in June and in Natal in October. Some had been arrested after the government lifted bans on opposition organizations in February. One, Magwedzha Phanuel Mphaphuli, a leading official of the United Democratic Front (UDF), was held without charge or trial for 41 days following his arrest in March.

About 200 other opposition activists were arrested in "unrest areas" declared by the Minister of Law and Order between August and the end of the year. In such areas the security forces were empowered to detain suspects without charge for an initial 30 days, which could then be extended indefinitely with the minister's authorization. Eight members of the Azanian People's Organization (AZAPO) were held for several months under this provision after their arrest in Soweto in September.

More than 600 people were detained in Bophuthatswana, where a state of emergency declared on 7 March was still in force at the end of 1990. Those held included ANC activists, some 55 of whom were arrested in November after Bophuthatswana President Lucas Mangope accused the ANC of conspiring to overthrow his administration by force. Dr Thabo Rangaka, a hospital superintendant, was one of those held but he and the others were all released uncharged within two weeks.

At least 217 opposition activists were detained throughout South Africa under Section 29 of the Internal Security Act, which permits indefinite incommunicado detention without charge or trial in solitary confinement for security police interrogation. The number of such arrests increased after the national state of emergency was lifted. Those held included prominent members of the ANC, SACP and other political organizations, as well as human rights lawyers and members of white extremist organizations. Some were held for six months, including J.B. Sibanyoni, a human rights lawyer arrested in June and released uncharged on 14 December.

Some Section 29 detainees were reported to have been tortured or ill-treated. David Madurai, a UDF activist held from January to May, said police officers had beaten him, threatened him with electric shocks and partially suffocated him while he was held in Durban.

Welverdiend police station near Carletonville was particularly identified with allegations of torture of political detainees. In October a local doctor was reported to have said that at least 30 youths he had treated had sustained burn marks as a result of being tortured with electric shocks by police. An official inquiry was apparently initiated into police methods at Welverdiend but its outcome was not known at the end of the year.

Torture of detainees was also frequently alleged against the police in Bophuthatswana: in one case in November a police constable disclosed in court that he had been taught at police college to assault prisoners "if a person does not want to tell the truth".

At least 18 people detained for political or criminal investigation reasons died in police custody in suspicious circumstances. In several cases the police said the detainee had committed suicide or had been shot while trying to escape. Some deaths, however, appeared to be the result of torture. Eugene Thokozane Mbulwana, a 15-year-old, was allegedly severely assaulted at Welverdiend police station before he died three days after his arrest in July. A youth detained with him was later shot dead by police in suspicious circumstances shortly after a statement he had made about Eugene Thokozane Mbulwana's death was publicized in the press.

Only one death in custody, that of Section 29 detainee Clayton Sizwe Sithole in January, was made the subject of an independent judicial inquiry. The judge concluded that, as the police had alleged, the detainee had committed suicide, but commented that the provisions of Section 29 are "drastic and make serious inroads into the normal rights and privileges of every citizen".

More than 5,000 people were brought to trial accused of politically motivated offences, but the situation of ANC members and others accused of violent offences was uncertain due to the government's agreement to grant indemnity to some opponents. Some trials were delayed while the accused applied for indemnity. Sathyandranath "Mac" Maharaj and eight other ANC and SACP members accused in connection with an alleged SACP plot to overthrow the government were among those who applied for indemnity. Arrested in July, they were released on bail in

November while the government considered their indemnity applications.

There was a notable development in March when the Cape Town Supreme Court ruled that the state should prove that contested pre-trial confessions made by four people accused in a major treason trial had been made freely and voluntarily. Eight of the 14 defendants were then released. Previously, the courts had accepted contested pre-trial confessions unless the defence could prove that they had not been given freely.

Two prisoners of conscience imprisoned for their conscientious objection to military service were released as a result of legal changes which halved the period of compulsory military service and an Appeal Court decision in March. The court ruled that the length of sentences imposed on conscientious objectors was discretionary and not mandatory under the 1957 Defence Act. David Bruce and Charles Bester were released when their six-year sentences were reduced to 20 months. Dr Ivan Toms' 18-month sentence was reduced by half. He had already been freed on bail.

Allegations of security force involvement in extrajudicial executions and other unlawful activities were considered by several judicial commissions of inquiry. In February the government appointed Judge Louis Harms to inquire into allegations made in 1989 by a former security policeman awaiting execution, Butana Almond Nofomela (see *Amnesty International Report 1990*). The Commission took evidence from former members of a security police counter-insurgency unit and from members of a covert military unit, the Civil Cooperation Bureau (CCB). Some of the witnesses alleged that they had been involved in officially sanctioned killings and attempted killings of government opponents. The inquiry's findings were published in November: it concluded that the CCB had taken unlawful action against ANC members and others held to be "enemies of the Republic", but said the evidence of the former security police personnel was too unreliable to permit findings in specific cases. However, it urged the Attorney General to investigate further the possible involvement of a CCB operative in the 1986 murders of Dr Fabian Ribeiro and his wife (see *Amnesty International Report 1987*).

Another judicial inquiry investigated the fatal shootings of 12 people and the wounding of 281 others by police at Sebokeng in March. In a report published in September, it concluded that the police had acted unlawfully by shooting without warning into a crowd of peaceful demonstrators, and recommended that the Attorney General should consider charging 34 police officers. The Attorney General had not made known his decision by the end of the year.

In November, while hearing an action for damages brought against two newspapers by the police, the Johannesburg Supreme Court was told by a former Military Intelligence agent that he had attempted to kill ANC members abroad with poisons provided by the police.

Despite these official inquiries and the announcement in July that the CCB was to be disbanded, further killings of political activists occurred, giving rise to speculation that the CCB or other clandestine security force units were still operating. In one case, Jeff Wabena, a trade union activist and ANC official, was shot dead by an unidentified gunman at a meeting in Mdantsane township on 12 October.

There was a dramatic reduction in the use of the death penalty. One execution was carried out in Bophuthatswana where 19 other prisoners were under sentence of death at the end of 1990, but there were no executions in the rest of South Africa.

In February the government declared a moratorium on executions pending a review of legislation relating to the use of the death penalty. More than 330 prisoners remained on death row in Pretoria at the end of the year. There was also a moratorium on executions in the nominally independent Transkei "homeland", where 89 prisoners remained on death row while a commission of inquiry reviewed the use of the death penalty. In the Ciskei "homeland" a draft bill of rights issued by a new military administration in September proposed prohibition of the death penalty and commutation of all death sentences to life imprisonment.

In July the Criminal Law Amendment Act came into force. This retained the death penalty as a discretionary but no longer mandatory sentence in murder cases, and provided for automatic appeal and clemency procedures for all prisoners sentenced to death. The amended law retained the death penalty for seven offences, ranging from attempted robbery with aggravating circumstances to treason in wartime, but provided for an *in camera* review by a nine-member panel of judges and academic lawyers of certain categories of cases of people sentenced under the old law. Prisoners and their legal representatives were entitled to make written submissions but not to attend the review hearings. By the end of the year the Department of Justice had indicated that at least 120 cases were to be reviewed.

Amnesty International appealed for the release of prisoners of conscience, for the prompt, fair trial or release of other political detainees and for impartial investigation of all reports of torture and deaths in police custody. The organization pressed for the abolition of the death penalty and welcomed the moratorium on executions, calling for all sentences to be commuted. In a report published in April, Amnesty International also criticized the imposition of judicial whippings by the courts and the involvement of medical personnel in the administration of the punishment.

Amnesty International representatives undertook two visits to South Africa for research purposes and an Amnesty International observer attended part of the proceedings of the Harms inquiry. The organization submitted a memorandum proposing additional human rights safeguards to a Law Commission appointed by the government to draw up a draft Bill of Rights. Amnesty International also submitted information on its concerns in South Africa to the United Nations (UN) Special Committee Against Apartheid and other UN bodies.

SPAIN

Six conscripts were imprisoned as deserters after declaring their conscientious objection to further military service. There were allegations that prison officers and members of the security forces had ill-treated detainees and prisoners. After long delays, significant verdicts were reached in trials of police and Civil Guard officers accused of ill-treatment. Inquiries were opened into disputed killings of members of an armed Basque group by security forces.

It was estimated that 32 people, including members of the security forces and civilians, were killed during the year in attacks by armed groups such as *Euskadi Ta Askatasuna* (ETA), Basque Homeland and Liberty, and *Grupos de Resistencia Antifascista Primero de Octubre* (GRAPO), First of October Anti-Fascist Resistance Groups. The special legal procedures applicable to detainees suspected of belonging to armed groups remained in force. Under these, extended incommunicado detention of up to five days may be imposed by judicial order and the detainee's lawyer may be appointed by the court.

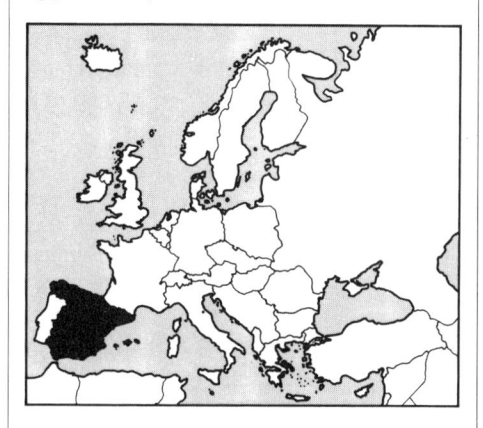

In April the Ombudsman, in a statement to parliament, expressed concern about the persistence of cases of alleged ill-treatment of detainees by members of the security forces. His report emphasized the deliberate obstacles to investigation created by officers accused of ill-treatment and the failure of the responsible authorities to clarify the facts.

In November parliament voted to ratify the Second Optional Protocol to the International Covenant on Civil and Political Rights Aiming at the Abolition of the Death Penalty. A reservation was entered retaining the death penalty under the Military Penal Code.

Six conscripts were imprisoned after they left their barracks and declared their conscientious objection to further military service. Under the law, the right to conscientious objection and alternative civilian service may only be exercised "until the moment of incorporation into the armed forces". Carmelo Sanz Ramiro, a baker who had completed several months' military service when he left his barracks, said he felt that continuing his service would be incompatible with his pacifist beliefs. He was arrested and imprisoned for desertion in February after he presented himself voluntarily to military authorities. He had applied for recognition as a conscientious objector about one week earlier. In March he was placed in isolation for several weeks for refusing to wear a military prison uniform. It was alleged that his civilian clothing was removed, leaving him in his underwear, and that his correspondence and reading material were withheld. His lawyer and girlfriend were denied visits. He was released in May but ordered to report back to barracks to continue his military service. According to news reports he was rearrested in October for refusing to comply with this order but released and exempted from all further military service for medical reasons.

In January the National Police stopped José Antonio Montoya and a friend in a car in Valencia and ordered them to get out and produce their papers. Reportedly, when they went to fetch them, the police assaulted them. José Antonio Montoya alleged that he was beaten on his head, neck and arm with truncheons before being handcuffed and taken to hospital for treatment. Medical evidence, including photographs, showed stitches to his head and severe contusions on his arm and back. José Antonio Montoya made an official complaint but the police failed to attend preliminary investigations in May and July. There was no further news regarding the progress of the investigation by the end of the year.

In May a judicial investigation was opened into allegations that 17 men had been beaten earlier that month by guards during a transfer of prisoners after a disturbance in the Modelo prison in Barcelona. A lawyer who interviewed the prisoners stated that some of them were badly bruised. The administrator and the deputy director of the prison were reportedly suspended following the incidents.

In November a court in Bilbao condemned nine Civil Guard officers to sentences including imprisonment, fines and disqualification from duty on charges relating to the torture of Tomas Linaza in 1981 (see *Amnesty International Report 1982*). Two officers were found guilty of torture and the other seven were found guilty of deliberately failing to perform their duty to prevent torture. In addition, the most senior officer was found guilty of refusing to cooperate with the law and tampering with evidence. Three other officers were acquitted. The judgment severely criticized the obstructive behaviour of the defendants and made specific reference to the "innumerable difficulties" the court had faced in obtaining basic information. The defence and prosecution entered appeals.

In June an exchange of gunfire occurred in the Foz de Lumbier in Navarre between members of an armed ETA group and the security forces. One Civil Guard sergeant was killed and another wounded. Two members of the ETA group were later found dead and a third was seriously wounded. The Minister of the Interior stated the next day that the ETA members had apparently committed suicide to avoid being taken alive and that the third member of the group had tried to kill himself, but failed. Doubt was thrown on this explanation by reports that one of the dead had been shot twice in the side of her head and the other had substantial quantities of water in his body. Judicial inquiries were opened into the circumstances of the deaths. In July there were reports that the Civil Guards had attempted to impede these inquiries, which had not been concluded by the end of the year.

On 18 September an ETA member, Mikel Castilló, was shot and killed in Pamplona while attempting to escape from a police officer. He was reportedly unarmed and his family brought a private petition alleging homicide. His companion, Bautista Barandalla, was arrested and alleged that he had been beaten and nearly asphyxiated while in custody. A third man escaped. Judicial inquiries into the allegations were opened but had not been completed by the end of the year.

Amnesty International considered that individuals should be able to claim conscientious objector status at any time and appealed for the release of conscientious objectors it considered to be prisoners of conscience, including Carmelo Sanz Ramiro.

Amnesty International expressed concern to the authorities about allegations of ill-treatment. In July it wrote to the Minister of Justice urging the fullest possible judicial investigation of the shootings in the Foz de Lumbier and subsequently expressed concern about the reported abuse of the judicial process by Civil Guard officers. No reply had been received by the end of the year. In October Amnesty

International wrote to the Attorney General expressing concern about the shooting of Mikel Castilló while reportedly unarmed and the allegations of ill-treatment made by Bautista Barandalla. The Attorney General replied in November with information about the two judicial inquiries then in progress.

SRI LANKA

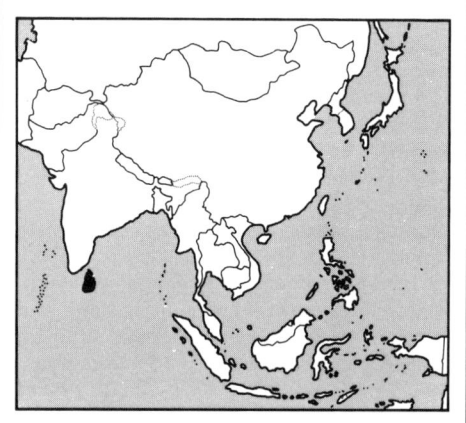

Thousands of people "disappeared" or were extrajudicially executed in the northeast; many were tortured and then killed in custody. An unknown number of others were detained in the area. In the south, "disappearances" and extrajudicial executions continued to be committed by government forces and "death squads" linked to them, but on a lesser scale than in 1989. About 9,000 political prisoners remained in detention without trial for alleged connections with an armed Sinhalese opposition group. The government took no steps to clarify the fate of thousands of people who had "disappeared" in the south since 1987, nor of over 680 people who had "disappeared" in the northeast in previous years.

Indian troops, who had been responsible for the security of the northeast since July 1987, completed their withdrawal by late March. Following heavy fighting with rival Tamil groups, the Liberation Tigers of Tamil Eelam (LTTE) – the "Tamil Tigers" – took control of Northeastern Province and continued negotiations with the Sri Lanka Government about the future administration of the province. Members of the Eelam People's Revolutionary Liberation Front (EPRLF) and allied groups, who had controlled the provincial council under Indian patronage, fled the area.

In June the LTTE captured numerous police stations in the east and took prisoner hundreds of police officers who surrendered. Most Sinhalese and Muslim officers among them were reportedly beaten and killed in captivity. Many Tamil officers were released but some reportedly remained in captivity at the end of the year. Fighting ensued between government forces and the LTTE, which evacuated major towns in the east as government forces moved in. Most of the Jaffna peninsula, where about 200 government soldiers and police remained besieged in Jaffna fort until September, remained in LTTE control at the end of the year.

Reprisal killings of Tamil civilians by Muslim groups in the east, some of whom were apparently armed by the government, were reported in August after hundreds of Muslim civilians were killed, apparently by the LTTE. In October the LTTE issued an ultimatum to Muslims in Mannar, Mullaittivu, Kilinochchi and Jaffna districts to leave the area or be killed: tens of thousands fled.

In the south, the government said in January that it had destroyed the armed opposition *Janatha Vimukthi Peramuna* (JVP), People's Liberation Front. According to government figures, the JVP had murdered 6,517 people between late 1987 and March 1990. There were markedly fewer reports of killings by the JVP in 1990 than in 1989. However, 15 members of a village "vigilance committee", which had reported on suspected subversives to the security forces, were murdered in Matara District in July. The government attributed the killings to the JVP.

In the northeast the LTTE was allegedly responsible for hundreds of killings, including the murder of many hundred Sinhalese and Muslim civilians. For example, the LTTE reportedly killed 27 Sinhalese civilians whom they dragged from a bus near Trincomalee in August and about 140 Muslim worshippers in mosques at Kattankudy in August. The LTTE also reportedly tortured and killed prisoners, killed or imprisoned numerous members or sympathizers of rival Tamil groups, and imprisoned Tamil civilians for ransom.

Outside the northeast, the LTTE was widely suspected of responsibility for the assassination in Colombo of an EPRLF member of parliament in May and for the murders in Madras, India, of 14 EPRLF central committee members in June.

In February President Ranasinghe Premadasa repealed Emergency Regulation 55FF which had permitted police to dispose of bodies without post-mortem or inquest. However, the remaining Emergency Regulations still enabled security forces to dispose of bodies secretly and extrajudicial executions continued. Several other regulations were repealed or amended, but the state of emergency remained in force at the end of the year.

Government forces in the northeast were reported to have extrajudicially executed thousands of defenceless civilians in areas they had regained, using counter-terror tactics similar to those employed in the south in 1989 (see *Amnesty International Report 1990*). Victims were reportedly shot, bayoneted, stabbed or hacked to death; some were said by witnesses to have been burned alive. In eastern areas, besides helping the army round up suspects, Muslim Home Guards also reportedly committed extrajudicial executions.

Victims' bodies were regularly left in the open. The identities of many remained unknown; others, presumably killed in custody, were identified as people who had been detained by security forces days earlier. Some had been burned beyond recognition or mutilated. In Amparai District, where the Special Task Force, a police commando unit, was especially active, bodies – some without heads – began to be washed up on the beaches from September.

In Amparai District alone at least 3,000 Tamil people were reportedly killed or "disappeared" between June and October, many of whom were believed to have been victims of extrajudicial execution. In Batticaloa and Vavuniya districts, as well as in other areas, widespread extrajudicial executions were also reported after government troops moved in.

Both the security forces and the government refused to acknowledge that many defenceless people had been deliberately killed. Government statements referred only to atrocities committed by the LTTE and the deaths in combat of "Tamil Tigers" and security forces personnel.

Thousands of men and women reportedly "disappeared" in the northeast after widespread arbitrary detentions by government forces, and were feared to have been killed in custody. Victims included babies and their mothers, children, and elderly men and women. In Batticaloa town alone over 1,200 people reportedly "disappeared" between June and October.

Government security forces often refused to acknowledge individual detentions and the authorities, despite widespread detentions, did not disclose how many political prisoners were held in the northeast nor whether any had been charged. Any person suspected of even minimal contact with the LTTE was at risk of detention, "disappearance" or extrajudicial execution. Members of Tamil and Muslim armed groups which opposed the LTTE helped the security forces to identify LTTE suspects, and in some areas armed cadres of certain Tamil groups were deployed alongside government security forces.

In the predominantly Sinhalese south, hundreds of extrajudicial executions and "disappearances" were reported, although this represented a marked reduction from 1989 (see *Amnesty International Report 1990*). In June scores of corpses were found near former army camps, apparently the bodies of prisoners killed at the camps before troops were redeployed to the northeast. Bodies of suspected victims of extrajudicial execution continued to be found in the following months.

Richard de Zoysa, a journalist who had reported on human rights issues, was among those killed in February. He was abducted by gunmen from his home in the capital, Colombo. The following day his naked body was found in the sea with bullet wounds to his neck and head. Although his mother identified one of the alleged killers as a senior police officer, a magisterial inquiry into his death was discontinued in August and no action was taken against the police officer allegedly involved. Richard de Zoysa's mother and her lawyer both received death threats in May when they pressed for a full inquiry into his murder. Other human rights defenders were also at risk: at least five members of parliament who had raised human rights cases received death threats. In September Kumaraguru Kugamoorthy, a radio producer and human rights activist, "disappeared" after being abducted in Colombo by an armed group believed to be connected with the security forces.

"Disappearances" continued to be reported from the south following detentions by uniformed police officers and abductions by plainclothes squads believed to be attached to the security forces. The victims included former JVP suspects who had previously been detained but then released, and young Tamil men apparently suspected of links with the LTTE. In Colombo and elsewhere hundreds of young Tamil men were detained by both uniformed and plainclothes personnel following the outbreak of hostilities in the northeast in June. Many were released after questioning but at least seven reportedly "disappeared". The Eelam People's Democratic Party, an anti-LTTE Tamil group, reportedly detained and interrogated suspects in Colombo with the assent of the government, before handing them over to the police.

The government took no steps to investigate the thousands of "disappearances" reported in recent years. Evidence mounted during 1990 of the massive scale of "disappearances" and extrajudicial executions which took place in 1988 and 1989 and were believed to number tens of thousands. In September the police confiscated details of 533 "disappearances" from an opposition member of parliament who was about to take them to a meeting of the United Nations (UN) Working Group on Enforced or Involuntary Disappearances in Geneva. The papers were returned to him in October after he filed a petition in the courts alleging infringement of his fundamental rights.

In January the government announced that detainees held without charge or trial in the south under Emergency Regulations would be screened for involvement with the JVP. Criminal charges would be brought where there was evidence of serious involvement; those marginally involved would be released on probation; those believed to have been involved but against whom there was no evidence would remain in detention for "rehabilitation", although the legal basis for such rehabilitation was unclear. At the end of 1990 about 9,000 prisoners remained in detention without trial.

Detentions of JVP suspects continued in the south. Suspects' relatives were at times detained in place of the wanted person. In one reported case a six-year-old child was detained in October by Kuliyapitiya police who had sought the father as a JVP suspect. The child was later released and the father arrested. The father spent one month in detention before his arrest was acknowledged.

Emergency Regulations provide for indefinite detention without charge or trial, and the Prevention of Terrorism Act (PTA) provides for up to 18 months' detention without charge or trial. Detainees are frequently held incommunicado, providing a ready context for torture and ill-treatment.

Charges were brought against security forces personnel for extrajudicial executions in only a few cases. Among those charged were eight police officers, who were accused of murdering 12 prisoners at Nittambuwa, Gampaha District, in February. A prisoner who survived with injuries witnessed the executions in a jungle clearing. The following morning he led people to the site, where the naked and charred bodies of the victims were found. The case was widely publicized, and an inquiry was held. No security forces personnel was known to have been charged in connection with "disappearances".

The trial of three police officers accused of murdering Wijedasa Liyanarachchi in September 1988 (see *Amnesty International Report 1989*) continued without conclusion.

Five people charged under the PTA and Emergency Regulations with a grenade attack on the parliament building in August 1987 (see *Amnesty International Report 1988*) and other offences were acquitted. The court found that their confessions had not been made voluntarily. On their release in December, two of the defendants were immediately detained under a fresh detention order and the state filed an appeal against the judgment.

The Supreme Court awarded damages to several victims of illegal detention and torture, including in April to a lawyer who had been illegally detained in 1987 for 10 months, and in July to a 16-year-old girl who had been illegally detained and tortured in 1988 (see *Amnesty International Report 1989*). There were reports of the intimidation of people who had filed fundamental rights petitions.

Throughout the year Amnesty International urged the government to implement effective safeguards against extrajudicial executions, "disappearances" and torture in all areas of the country. It urged that independent commissions of inquiry be established into reported extrajudicial executions and "disappearances", that those found responsible be brought to justice and that victims or their relatives be compensated.

In May Amnesty International called for an immediate halt to illegal killings and incommunicado detention by forces of the LTTE.

In oral statements to the UN Commission on Human Rights and the UN Sub-Commission on Prevention of Discrimination and Protection of Minorities, Amnesty International included reference to its concerns in Sri Lanka about extrajudicial executions and incommunicado detention under Emergency Regulations and the PTA.

In September Amnesty International published a major report, *Sri Lanka: Extrajudicial Executions, "Disappearances" and Torture, 1987 to 1990*, which covered the period to June 1990, and a further report including new violations committed by both government forces and the LTTE which had occurred in the northeast after June. Amnesty International publicly urged the government to take action to halt the long-standing pattern of gross human rights violations and to introduce effective safeguards for human rights.

In December Amnesty International expressed concern that a "Special Task Force" created by the government in November to "monitor and deal effectively with all violations of human rights" was not an independent body, and that its objectives placed too great an emphasis on countering international expressions of concern about Sri Lanka's human rights record rather than on the full investigation and remedy of past and continuing violations.

In January two government ministers claimed publicly that Amnesty International was a "terrorist organization" which had funded JVP propaganda, but were unable to produce evidence to support this false allegation when challenged to do so.

In December a letter to Amnesty International from a presidential adviser was published in a Colombo newspaper which argued that "when security forces have to deal with terrorist groups...excesses are bound to occur".

Amnesty International told the government several times of its wish to send a delegation to Sri Lanka to discuss its concerns, but received no response.

SUDAN

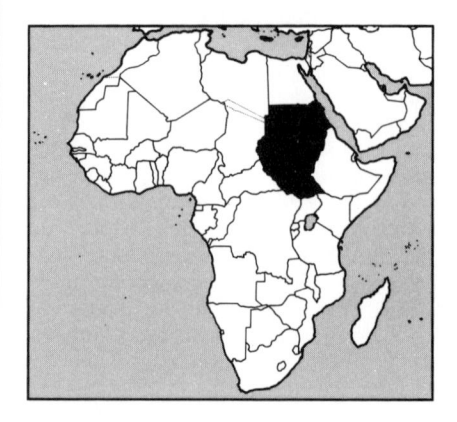

Hundreds of real and suspected government opponents were prisoners of conscience. Some were detained in 1989 and held without charge or trial throughout 1990. Over 150 others were arrested during the year. At least 90 prisoners of conscience were released. Some government opponents were sentenced to prison terms and 30 army officers were executed after grossly unfair trials. Government troops reportedly committed dozens of extrajudicial executions. At least three people convicted of criminal offences were executed. However, a prisoner of conscience sentenced to death in 1989 was pardoned and released.

The nationwide state of emergency declared by the National Salvation Revolution Command Council (NSRCC) following the June 1989 military coup (see *Amnesty International Report 1990*) remained in force throughout the year. Fighting continued in the south between government forces and the armed opposition Sudan People's Liberation Army (SPLA), which controlled large areas in the south. The SPLA continued to hold several senior members of its own organization who were suspected of opposing the SPLA leadership. At least 1,500 members of the Sudanese army were reported to be detained by the SPLA. In March the SPLA agreed to join a coalition of opposition groups, the National Democratic Forum (NDF), and endorsed the NDF's charter which calls for popular opposition to the military government and a return to democratic rule in Sudan.

On 31 December the Head of State, Lieutenant-General Omar Hassan al-Bashir, announced that *Shari'a* (Islamic law) would be immediately implemented in northern Sudan. However, it was not clear whether this meant that the "September Laws", enacted in 1983 and partially suspended in 1985, would be reintroduced. Based on an interpretation of Islamic jurisprudence, these laws had provided for the judicial amputation of limbs, flogging as a penalty for numerous offences, and stoning and crucifixion as methods of execution.

The state of emergency continued to give the government extensive powers of administrative detention. Detainees were held without charge or trial on an indefinite basis. No reasons for their imprisonment were given. The detentions could not be challenged by the courts and were not reviewed by any form of independent tribunal. However, some detainees were freed, apparently after their cases were reviewed by NSRCC officials.

At least 250 suspected opponents of the NSRCC were prisoners of conscience at the start of the year. Of these, 90 were released by the end of March: government officials thereafter said that there were no political prisoners being held although further releases took place in August and October. However, more than 150 other non-violent critics or opponents of the government were arrested during the year and at least 300 prisoners of conscience were being held at the end of 1990.

Those released included most of the 80 political leaders and former government officials arrested after the June 1989 coup (see *Amnesty International Report 1990*). Several members of the Umma Party, however, were rearrested in October. Former prime minister Sadiq al-Mahdi was released from prison in January but placed under house arrest: during April he was confined to one room and denied all visits and medical treatment. Thereafter, he continued to be denied visits but was permitted to see his doctor.

One of the prisoners of conscience who remained in detention without charge or trial throughout 1990 was Dr Ushari Ahmed Mahmoud, a university lecturer and prominent human rights activist who was arrested in 1989. In March he was moved to Shalla prison in Darfur where conditions were harsh, after he apparently refused to withdraw an allegation that an armed pro-government militia had been responsible for a massacre of civilians in al-Daien in 1987. At least 12 lawyers, including Mustafa Abdelgadir, and dozens of trade union activists were also held without charge or trial throughout the year.

New arrests of trade union activists occurred in May after a rail strike. Most were released within a short time, but at least five railway workers' leaders were believed to be in detention at the end of the year. More than 65 other men and women were also arrested in May, mostly in Khartoum, and remained in detention without charge or trial at the end of 1990. Among them were two prominent members of the Umma Party, members of the Socialist Arab Ba'th Party and academics known to support the NDF.

Many arrests were reported in areas affected by the conflict with the SPLA, notably in the south. In February about 200 suspected SPLA supporters were arrested and detained at an army barracks in Juba. Some were later released but an unknown number of others were apparently still held at the end of 1990. Dozens of other people of southern origin were arrested in Khartoum in February, March, September and December, including many who were still being held incommunicado and without charge or trial at Kober prison at the end of 1990.

A minority of those arrested were charged and brought to court, but they received unfair trials. In May, 24 army officers stood trial before military courts on charges of conspiring to overthrow the government: 23 were convicted and one was acquitted. Two of the convicted prisoners were sentenced to death but the Head of State immediately commuted their sentences to life imprisonment. Twenty others received prison sentences ranging from two years to life imprisonment, and one was set free. The trial was held *in camera* and the defendants were denied legal representation and the right to appeal to a higher court.

On 23 April the government announced that it had foiled a coup attempt and that army officers had been arrested. On the following day, 28 army officers were executed following a summary court-martial. Most had been arrested on 23 April, but two were already in custody before the alleged coup attempt. The trial lasted only two hours and the officers were denied legal representation and the right to appeal to a higher court. Fourteen other officers were tried by military courts in connection with the same alleged coup attempt: four were sent to prison for periods ranging from three to 15 years; four were dismissed from the armed services; and six were acquitted. Two other officers were executed in July after they were convicted of involvement in the April coup attempt.

Torture and ill-treatment of political detainees, particularly those held incommunicado by the security services in secret detention centres in Khartoum, continued to be reported. The purpose appeared to be to obtain information or confessions and to punish suspected opponents of the military government. Commonly reported methods of torture included beatings with rifle butts and truncheons, flooding of cells with cold water, mock executions and sleep deprivation. Victims were also burned with cigarettes, suspended from trees, and forced to crouch during interrogation with stones gripped between their legs while being whipped.

Dr Ali Fadul, a prisoner of conscience, died in April, apparently as a result of torture at a secret detention centre. He had been an active member of the Sudan Doctors' Union, which was banned after the 1989 coup. The authorities said that he had died of malaria but refused to show his body to his family and denied their request for an independent autopsy. Unofficial sources said that he had died of an internal haemorrhage and a skull fracture caused by torture.

Conditions in Shalla prison in Darfur Province were reportedly harsh and political prisoners were transferred there as a punishment. Inmates were said to be held in overcrowded cells, given insufficient water and, in many cases, to have become ill owing to inadequate sanitation. Urgent medical treatment was reportedly denied or unavailable although two seriously ill prisoners were moved to Omdurman military hospital in April. Prisoners at Shalla were denied family visits, as were some political prisoners held elsewhere in the country.

There was an increase in public floggings. Street vendors operating without a licence, most of them women, were summarily tried in market places by Public Order Courts. Convicted vendors were flogged on the spot.

Extrajudicial executions of civilians by government troops continued in southern Sudan. Between February and May, 13,000 government soldiers travelled from Malakal to Juba, reportedly burning and looting several villages and killing dozens of unarmed villagers. Among the dead were four elderly men who were burned inside their cattle shed by soldiers in Dior, near Ayod. In late May four men, including two Roman Catholic religious teachers, were arrested by government troops in Meridi in southern Sudan on suspicion of being SPLA supporters. They were tortured and set on fire by soldiers. One of them, Louis Laku, died in hospital on 16 September as a result of his injuries. Pro-government militias, known as the Popular Defence Forces, also extrajudicially executed unarmed civilians in Bahr al-Ghazal province and other areas in the south.

At least 33 people were executed, including the 28 army officers executed on 24 April and the two others executed in July. In addition, Gergis al-Ghous, who was sentenced to death in December 1989 for attempting to smuggle foreign currency out of the country (see *Amnesty International Report 1990*), was hanged in February. Two further executions were reported in August. The victims, who had been convicted of theft and murder, were hanged in al-Fasher before a large crowd: their bodies were then taken down and crucified. At least two other people were sentenced to death for drug-trafficking but had not been executed by the end of the year. An army colonel convicted of embezzlement was sentenced to death in early December.

People sentenced to death since the June 1989 coup were not allowed to appeal against conviction to a higher court and were not allowed proper legal representation at their trials. Dr Maamum Mohamed Hussein, a prisoner of conscience who had been sentenced to death in December 1989 (see *Amnesty International Report 1990*), was pardoned by the Head of State and released in May along with another prisoner of conscience who had been sentenced to life imprisonment. More than 100 people convicted of murder in previous years were believed to remain under sentence of death.

Amnesty International repeatedly urged the Sudanese Government to release all prisoners of conscience and allow all those detained since the 1989 coup to challenge their imprisonment in court. It protested about the use of torture and the increasing number of people sentenced to death. The organization also called for the commutation of the death sentence imposed on Dr Maamun Mohamed Hussein and of all other death sentences. It frequently urged the government to investigate reports of extrajudicial executions and to stop prisoners being killed by troops or militia. In August Amnesty International published a report, *Sudan: The Military Government's First Year in Power – A Permanent Human Rights Crisis*, which detailed the wide range of human rights violations recorded since the June 1989 coup. In October Amnesty International's Secretary General met the Head of State to explain the organization's concerns.

In oral statements to the United Nations (UN) Commission on Human Rights and the UN Sub-Commission on Prevention of Discrimination and Protection of Minorities in August, Amnesty International included reference to its concerns in Sudan. Amnesty International also submitted a communication under the African Charter on Human and Peoples' Rights concerning "a series of serious or massive violations" of human rights guaranteed by the Charter.

SURINAME

At least three people died in circumstances suggesting that they were extrajudicially executed. There were new reports that government soldiers killed people suspected of collaborating with the Jungle Commando, an armed opposition group. At least four members of an armed Amerindian group associated with the army were feared killed following an internal conflict. Most human rights violations committed before the civilian government took office in 1988 had still not been investigated.

The armed conflict which started in 1986 in opposition to the military government continued after the change to a democratically elected government in 1988. Negotiations to end the conflict had not succeeded by the end of 1990. In May the National Assembly passed a law withdrawing from the military police the power to arrest civilians and to conduct criminal investigations into offences involving civilians. The exercise of these powers over a number of years had led to human rights violations and a deterioration of the relationship between the police force and the army; police personnel investigating criminal offences allegedly committed by members of the army had received threats, including death threats. In late December Lieutenant-Colonel Desi Bouterse resigned as Army Commander following alleged disagreements with President Ramsewar Shankar. Two days later, on 24 December, the military took power in a bloodless coup which led to the resignation of the President. The National Assembly appointed Johan Kraag as President. The military promised to hold elections within 100 days. Lieutenant-Colonel Bouterse subsequently returned to the post of Army Commander.

Government soldiers killed three people in circumstances suggesting that they may have been extrajudicially executed. In March Stewart Deel and John Apai, bodyguards of Ronny Brunswick, the leader of the Jungle Commando, were killed while accompanying him to a meeting with the head of the army, held as part of the negotiations to end the armed conflict. The two men were reportedly shot by soldiers at Lieutenant-Colonel Bouterse's office in Paramaribo; the victims were reportedly unarmed. Ronny Brunswick and other members of the group were arrested and held for two days by the army, purportedly on suspicion of drug-trafficking, but were released on government orders.

In August police Inspector Herman Goodings was killed shortly after leaving the military headquarters at Fort Zeelandia where he and a colleague were investigating the arrest of two police officers by members of the army. His car was intercepted by a military vehicle and his colleague was allowed or forced to leave. Inspector Goodings' body, with gunshot wounds, was found the following day near the area where his car had been stopped. Inspector Goodings had investigated the involvement of an army officer in the killing of a group of people near Mungotapu in November 1986 (see *Amnesty International Report 1987*) and had expressed dissatisfaction when the officer was released on an order from Lieutenant-Colonel Bouterse. The government appointed a commission to investigate his killing but there was no indication that the investigation had been completed by the end of the year.

In July two men, believed to have been unarmed, were reported to have been killed in Nieuw Aurora because they were suspected of cooperating with the Jungle Commando. One of them was reportedly shot and then beaten to death with guns. There was no indication that the authorities investigated these deaths.

In February dissenting members of the *Tucayana Amazonas*, an armed Amerindian group generally associated with the army, sought asylum in Guyana but were returned to military custody in Suriname. While in custody four of them were taken away, allegedly by a group of unknown armed men. The authorities had not clarified their fate or whereabouts by the end of the year.

Most of the human rights violations committed before the civilian government took office were not investigated. The chances of such investigations ever taking place were considerably reduced when fires, reportedly started intentionally, destroyed several public buildings containing important evidence.

Amnesty International wrote to the President in September expressing concern about the killings of Stewart Deel, John Apai and Inspector Herman Goodings. The organization said it was concerned that Inspector Goodings could have been killed in retaliation for his investigation of members of the army. It requested information about the investigation into his death and about any investigation undertaken into the killing of Stewart Deel and John Apai. No reply had been received by the end of the year.

SWAZILAND

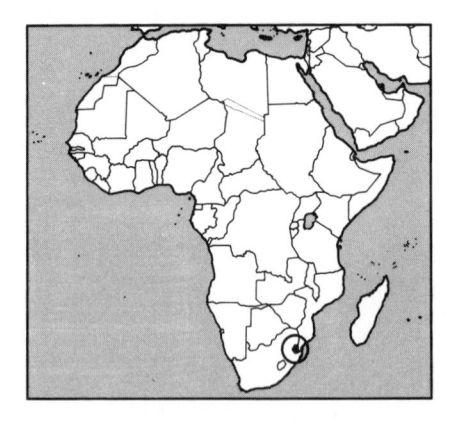

Eleven suspected government opponents were prisoners of conscience, of whom five were still held at the end of the year. All five were held without charge or trial after being acquitted of treason. A member of the royal family was rearrested and detained without charge or trial after being acquitted of treason. One detainee alleged ill-treatment in police custody and at least 80 students were injured, in three cases reportedly fatally, as a result of police beatings. Three people were sentenced to death and one person under sentence of death was reprieved. There were no executions.

Several dozen students, trade unionists and others were arrested in May and June as suspected supporters of the People's United Democratic Movement (PUDEMO), an illegal opposition party under a 1973 royal decree banning all political parties. Most were released within a few days, but 11 were charged with treason, sedition and other offences. They included Mpandlana Shongwe, President of the Swaziland National Union of Students, and Sabelo Dlamini, a law student who alleged that he was assaulted by the police after arrest.

Charges against one of the 11, Boy Magagula, were withdrawn in September. However, when he refused to testify for the prosecution, he was rearrested and charged again. He was released on bail and had not been tried by the end of the year. The 10 others stood trial in the High Court in October. They were accused of forming PUDEMO with the intention of forcibly overthrowing the government. Four were acquitted of all charges. The other six were acquitted of treason and sedition but convicted of contravening the 1973 decree by attending political meetings: four received six-month prison terms but were released in view of the time they had already been held; and two, Dominic Mngomezulu and Ray Russon, were each sentenced to serve one year in prison but were released on bail after lodging an appeal. During the trial, which was attended by an Amnesty International observer, the main prosecution witness and seven others said they had been threatened with prolonged detention to make them testify.

Five of the defendants, including Mpandlana Shongwe, were rearrested in November and held without charge or trial under renewable 60-day detention orders signed by Prime Minister Obed Dlamini. After three of them had been rearrested, Sabelo Dlamini and Ray Russon sought refuge in the American Embassy and then escaped to South Africa, only to be forcibly repatriated. No new charges were brought against the five, all of whom were believed to be prisoners of conscience.

A member of the royal family was also detained under a 60-day order after being acquitted of treason. Prince Mfanasibili Dlamini was due to be released in July after serving a prison sentence for defeating the ends of justice (see *Amnesty International Report 1987*), but was charged with planning to overthrow the government of King Mswati III. He was acquitted of this charge in August but immediately rearrested and was held under successive 60-day detention orders.

At least 80 students required hospital treatment in November as a result of beatings by police and soldiers inflicted when the authorities forcibly closed the university. Students had boycotted classes to protest against Sabelo Dlamini's expulsion from the university. Three students were reported to have died as a result of the beatings they received.

A prisoner sentenced to death in July 1987 for murder, whose case was the subject of Amnesty International appeals during 1989, had his sentence commuted in July. Three people were sentenced to death but there were no executions.

Amnesty International appealed for the release of prisoners of conscience and called for an independent inquiry into the beatings of students by police and soldiers in November, but received no response.

SWEDEN

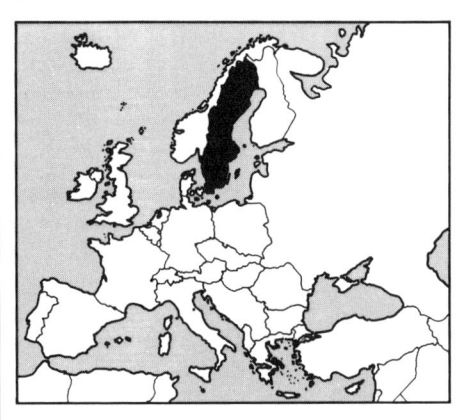

The government removed restrictions on the freedom of movement of six Kurdish refugees who had been under town arrest since 1984.

On 11 May the government ratified the Second Optional Protocol to the International Covenant on Civil and Political Rights Aiming at the Abolition of the Death Penalty.

Restrictions of town arrest had originally been imposed on nine Kurdish refugees whom the government considered to be terrorists. They could not be deported to Turkey because of fear of persecution (see *Amnesty International Reports 1989* and *1990*). Deportation orders and restrictions on two refugees were removed in August 1989 and restrictions on freedom of movement on six others in October 1990. However, the six refugees were still regarded as terrorists; they were required to report to the police weekly and their deportation orders remained in force. The ninth refugee, who was in prison for criminal offences, remained under restriction and deportation orders.

The government stated that the police believed that the Kurds' terrorist affiliations had become minor. In a hearing concerning two of the refugees in April, the Court of Appeal decided that the restrictions had "lasted so long that they must be considered as a deprivation of freedom" according to the Swedish Constitution. The judgment stated that the two refugees should be entitled to have their restrictions reviewed by a court. This decision was subsequently overturned by the Supreme Court.

In an exchange of correspondence with the government during the year, Amnesty International reiterated its concern that the government's decision to place indefinite restrictions on the refugees' freedom of movement was not open to judicial scrutiny. In October the organization welcomed the lifting of restrictions on the six refugees.

SWITZERLAND

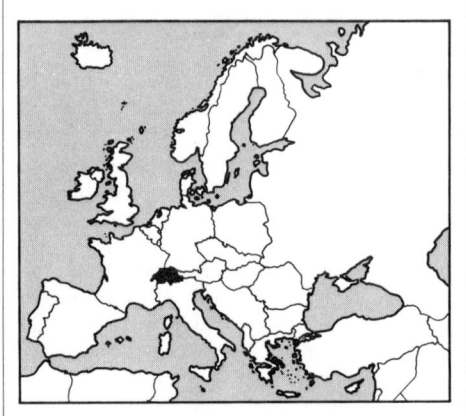

A total of 581 people were sentenced to prison terms for refusing to perform military service. Of these, 317 based their refusal on religious, ethical or political grounds, according to statistics published by the Federal Military Department. However, it was claimed that the number of people who had refused on conscientious grounds was far higher than reflected in the department's restricted categories. Many conscientious objectors served their sentences during 1990; all were considered prisoners of conscience. These included people sentenced in 1990 and earlier years, a large number of whom had expressed their willingness to perform an alternative civilian service.

Military service is a binding obligation under the Constitution and male citizens carry out a total of approximately 12 months' service between the ages of 20 and 50. Although there is limited access to unarmed military service, there is no provision for alternative civilian service, which could be introduced only by amending the Constitution through a public referendum.

In October the government issued an amendment to the Military Penal Code. Under its provisions, refusal to perform military service would remain a criminal offence. If a military tribunal concluded that a conscript was unable to reconcile military service with his conscience because of "fundamental ethical values", it would sentence him to a period of work in the public interest, ranging from one and a half times the length of military service to two years. This would not result in a criminal record. Conscripts considered to be refusing military service on unrecognized grounds would continue to receive prison sentences resulting in criminal records.

The amendment did not come into force during 1990 as it was liable to a referendum. A campaign organized by opponents of the amendment had until mid-January 1991 to collect the 50,000 signatures required to request the referendum.

During the year the Socialist and Christian Democrat parties sought wider support for initiatives, which they put forward in November 1989 and September 1990 respectively, aimed at introducing an alternative civilian service.

In October the National Council (one of the two chambers of parliament) requested the Federal Council to draft a revised Military Penal Code, eliminating the death penalty.

Although refusal of military service was punishable by up to three years' imprisonment, in practice sentences rarely exceeded 10 months during 1990. The law allowed a maximum of six months' imprisonment if a tribunal recognized a conscript's "severe conflict of conscience" on religious or ethical grounds; such sentences were served in the form of *arrêts répressifs* or *semi-détention*, allowing approved work outside the prison during the day.

Paul-Simon Dorsaz had spent over 12 years as an agricultural worker in religious communities when he refused military service. He began a sentence of three months' *arrêts répressifs* in November after a military tribunal recognized that his action was motivated by deep religious convictions and that he was facing a "severe conflict of conscience" and "moral distress". Caspar Schneider, a carpenter, served a seven-month prison sentence for refusing military service. He explained to the military authorities that his objection was based on his absolute belief in pacifism, influenced by the experiences of his mother's family in concentration camps and as refugees during the Second World War. A military tribunal acknowledged that ethical beliefs were a factor in his refusal but found that "egoistic" reasons were also present and concluded he was not suffering "a severe conflict of conscience". He was sentenced to 10 months' imprisonment, reduced on appeal.

Amnesty International continued to appeal for the release of prisoners of conscience. It wrote to members of parliament and the government expressing concern that the proposed amendment to the Military Penal Code would continue to punish people refusing military service on grounds of conscience and would not provide a genuine alternative service outside the military system. It also supported initiatives aimed at the introduction of such a service. In letters to Amnesty International, the federal authorities stated that they were "aware that the question of conscientious objection in Switzerland has to be solved" and acknowledged that the amendment to the Military Penal Code would not introduce "a real civilian service"; this required an amendment to the Federal Constitution, rejected by national referendums in 1977 and 1984.

SYRIA

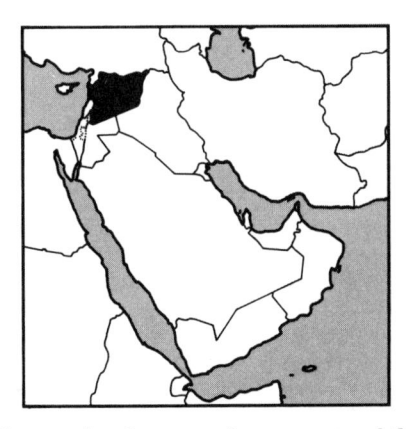

Thousands of suspected opponents of the government, including hundreds of prisoners of conscience, continued to be detained under state of emergency legislation in force since 1963. The majority were held without charge or trial, some for over 20 years. Others remained in prison after the expiry of their sentences. Some had been held incommunicado for long periods. Torture of political detainees continued to be reported, in at least four cases allegedly resulting in death. At least four people were executed. Scores of people, both soldiers and civilians, were reportedly extrajudicially executed by Syrian forces in Lebanon (see Lebanon).

Many of those detained, including at least 286 prisoners of conscience, were members of prohibited political parties, such as *Hizb al-'Amal al-Shuyu'i*, Party for Communist Action (PCA); *al-Hizb al-Shuyu'i al-Maktab al-Siyassi*, Communist Party – Political Bureau (CPPB); *Ittihad al-Nidal al-Shuyu'i*, Union for Communist Struggle (UCS); *al-Tanzim al-Sha'bi al-Nasiri*, Popular Nasserist Organization (PNO); *al-Ikhwan al-Muslimun*, Muslim Brotherhood, and the Arab Socialist Ba'th Party. Others were members of professional associations arrested in 1980 and 1981 after publicly demanding improvements in human rights in Syria. Some detainees had been arrested in place of relatives being sought by the authorities. Hundreds of Palestinians, including many suspected supporters of the Palestine Liberation Organization (PLO) and other Palestinian groups, were also still held.

Over 120 members of the CPPB and 154 PCA members, the majority of them prisoners of conscience arrested over the past decade, were among those who remained in detention without trial. They included Yusuf Ghaith, an engineering student, and Samir Haddad, a civil engineer, who were among 15 CPPB members or supporters arrested by *al-Amn al-Siyassi*, Political Security, in Yabrud in March and April, after anti-government slogans had reportedly been written on walls in the town. Twelve of the 15 were released during the year, one died in custody in April, and two were still detained without charge or trial in 'Adra Civil Prison at the end of 1990.

Over 160 members of the medical and engineering professions, including at least 10 prisoners of conscience, were believed to be still detained without charge or trial at the end of the year. They were arrested in 1980 and 1981 in connection with a one-day national strike in support of political reforms. One prisoner of conscience, Muhammad Nabil Salem, was held in 'Adra Civil Prison, but the whereabouts of most of those arrested with him remained unknown.

Other long-term political detainees included 18 Ba'th Party members, among them former government ministers. Some had been held without charge or trial for over 20 years. Muhammad 'Id 'Ashawi, a former minister of foreign affairs arrested in December 1970, was reported in September to be in poor health and to have been denied urgently needed treatment in prison and transfer to hospital.

Suspected supporters of the pro-Iraqi Arab Socialist Ba'th Party also continued to be detained without charge or trial. Among them was Ahmad 'Abd al-Ra'uf Roummo, a teacher who was reportedly held incommunicado and tortured for six months after his arrest in 1975. He was held in al-Mezze Military Prison in Damascus.

Four members of Syria's Jewish community also remained in detention without charge or trial in 'Adra Civil Prison. The authorities indicated in late 1989 that two of them, Eli and Selim Swed, were the subject of investigation and would be tried "as soon as possible". They had been arrested in 1987. However, no trial was reported to have taken place by the end of the year.

Scores of people arrested in previous years in place of relatives sought by the authorities also continued to be held without charge or trial. They included two women, Shafiqa al-'Ali and Fatima 'Abbas, who were arrested in March 1986 and remained in detention although their wanted relatives were themselves arrested in 1987.

Some political prisoners continued to be detained after serving sentences imposed by the courts, without further charges being brought against them. Khalil Brayez, a former Syrian army officer who was abducted from Beirut in 1970 by Syrian security agents and tried in Syria, had been due for release in October 1985. He was instead transferred to an unknown place in Damascus and was believed to be still held. 'Adel al-Zu'bi, a Syrian asylum-seeker who was returned involuntarily from the Netherlands in April, was reportedly arrested upon arrival at Damascus airport. He was apparently detained without charge or trial and was believed to be still held at the end of the year, although his whereabouts were unknown.

In October Syrian forces in Lebanon reportedly took prisoner scores of supporters of General Michel 'Aoun after a joint assault on his Beirut stronghold which they mounted with Lebanese government forces. The captives reportedly included 35 military officers loyal to General 'Aoun who were arrested at the Ministry of Defence in East Beirut and transferred to Syria. Most of these prisoners were reportedly held either in a prison at 'Anjar in the Beka' Valley in Lebanon or in prisons in Syria, including al-Mezze Military Prison.

Hundreds of other people arrested in Lebanon in previous years continued to be held. Some had been arrested by Syrian forces, others handed over to them by various Lebanese militias. They included Palestinians suspected of supporting PLO leader Yasser 'Arafat; members of *Harakat al-Tawhid al-Islami,* Islamic Unification Movement (IUM); members of various factions of the Christian Lebanese Forces; members of the Druze Progressive Socialist Party (PSP), members of the Arab Socialist Ba'th Party; and other critics of the Syrian Government. One, Mahmud Baidun, a Lebanese lawyer and former member of the Ba'th Party in Syria, was abducted from Tripoli in 1971. He was still detained without charge or trial in al-Mezze Military Prison.

There were reports of torture and ill-treatment of untried political detainees. At least four prisoners died in custody, allegedly as a result of torture. Munir Fransis, a civil engineer from Yabrud, died in custody in April, several days after being moved from detention to al-Muwassat Hospital in Damascus. His body was reported to have borne marks of torture when it was handed over to his family. Three Palestinians held in untried detention since 1985 were reported to have died in custody in Damascus during 1990. Among them was Ziad Musa Qatnani, whose body was returned to his family in July bearing marks of torture: one of his eyes had been gouged out, he had a broken skull, his nails had been extracted, and there were marks of torture by electricity. No official investigation into the causes of these deaths was known to have been carried out. Another political detainee, Samir Haddad, reportedly required intensive care in a Damascus hospital after his arrest in April when he suffered kidney failure following torture during interrogation. He was later moved to 'Adra Civil Prison, where he remained at the end of the year.

At least four people were executed: they were hanged publicly in Damascus in October after being convicted of smuggling.

At least 200 people were reported to have been extrajudicially executed by Syrian forces in October after the defeat of General Michel 'Aoun in East Beirut. The victims were said to include both military personnel and civilians, among them women and children. At least 30 of General 'Aoun's soldiers who had been captured were reportedly stripped, bound, lined up and shot in retaliation for an ambush in which Syrian soldiers had been killed. At least 14 men were reported to have been extrajudicially executed by Syrian forces in the village of Bsouss.

Amnesty International expressed concern to the government about new political arrests and the continued detention without charge or trial of hundreds of prisoners of conscience and other political prisoners, as well as reiterating its unconditional opposition to the death penalty. Amnesty International renewed its proposal to visit Syria to discuss its human rights concerns with the government but received no response. Similarly, there was no response to the organization's call in October for an impartial inquiry into reported extrajudicial executions by Syrian forces in Lebanon and for assurances about the physical security of Lebanese captives being held in Syria.

In an oral statement delivered to the United Nations Commission on Human Rights in February, Amnesty International expressed its concern about continued reports of torture and deaths in custody.

TAIWAN

One advocate of an independent Taiwan state was imprisoned as a prisoner of conscience. Six other prisoners of conscience were released. Five military officers were arrested after a prisoner died in military custody. Over 70 people convicted of criminal offences were reportedly executed. The death penalty was abolished for corruption.

President Lee Teng-hui was elected for a new term by the National Assembly and at his inauguration in May declared an amnesty under which nine political prisoners were released. He also promised to abolish the 1948 Temporary Provisions Effective During the Period of Communist Rebellion and to make "forward-looking and necessary revisions to portions of the Constitution". Subsequently the authorities started to review the laws and regulations affected by the Temporary Provisions, including the National Security Law and the offences of sedition and treason.

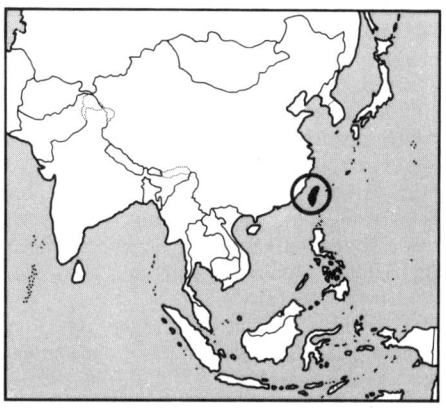

Huang Hua, a leading opposition activist, was arrested and tried in November on charges of sedition. He was accused of advocating an independent Taiwan state in speeches, by organizing demonstrations as part of his New Country Movement, and by supporting pro-independence candidates in the 1989 parliamentary elections. He was convicted in December and sentenced to 10 years' imprisonment. He was considered a prisoner of conscience.

Six other prisoners of conscience were released (see *Amnesty International Report 1990*). Hsu Tsao-teh was released on parole in April, after serving half his sentence. Three were released under the presidential amnesty: Shih Ming-teh, held since 1980, and Tsai Yu-chuan and Dr Huang Kuang-hsiung, held since 1987. Chuang Kuo-ming also benefited from the amnesty but remained in custody on criminal charges. Luo Yi-shih was released in December after completing a 10-month prison sentence (see *Amnesty International Report 1990*). In October the High Court had acquitted him of a charge of sedition arising from speeches he had made advocating independence for Taiwan. Chen Sheng-nan, sentenced to seven years and two months' imprisonment in 1989 (see *Amnesty International Report 1990*), was also released on bail. Amnesty International had no information on the result of his appeal.

Cheung Ki-lok was allowed to return to Hong Kong in November (see *Amnesty International Report 1990*). The High Court acquitted him in January and again in October of belonging to a seditious group, but the prosecution appealed against the verdicts.

In October five military officers were arrested for causing the death of an inmate in a military prison. They reportedly admitted beating him and applying an electric prod to various parts of his body.

The Statute for the Punishment of Corruption was amended in October and the death penalty abolished under that law. However, over 70 people convicted of criminal offences were reported to have been executed. The execution in July of three young kidnappers who had released their victim unharmed generated particular controversy in Taiwan.

Amnesty International urged the government to release prisoners of conscience and expressed concern about the executions. In response, the Ministry of Justice stated in August that the sentences on the three kidnappers had been lawfully passed and that both an official commission which had studied the death penalty in 1974 and public opinion supported the retention of this punishment.

In September the Judicial *Yuan* (council) made public its response to the report on Taiwan contained in *Amnesty International Report 1990*. It denied that prisoners convicted by the courts included prisoners of conscience and stressed that the courts had applied existing laws. It also said that three police officers whose arrests were referred to in the report had been given suspended sentences for torturing a suspect. It stated that the courts imposed death sentences with great care and for a limited number of offences.

TANZANIA

More than 120 government opponents were arrested in Zanzibar. At least 40 were prisoners of conscience, of whom three were believed to be still in prison at the end of the year. Fifteen of those arrested were detained without charge or trial. The others were charged and released on bail after short periods in custody, with some still awaiting trial at the end of the year. On the mainland a government opponent was detained without charge or trial following his return from exile. A Burundi national arrested for political reasons in 1989 died in prison; 14 others arrested with him remained in custody throughout the year. There were reports of executions and 12 people were sentenced to death.

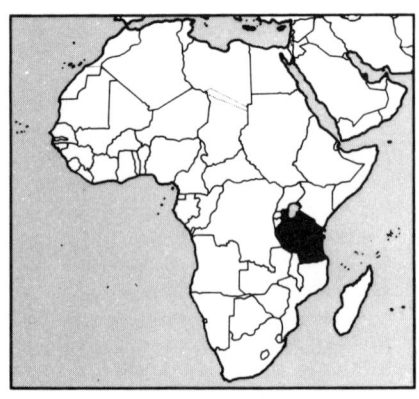

Opposition in Zanzibar and Pemba to continued union with mainland Tanzania increased in the run up to nationwide elections in October. Advocates of secession in the two islands called for a boycott of the electoral roll registration process. Hundreds who supported the call were dismissed or suspended from state employment and leaders of the campaign were detained. In all, more than 120 people were arrested in Zanzibar and Pemba, including former Zanzibar Government ministers. At least 40 were prisoners of conscience, although most were held only briefly. Shabaan Mloo, a former senior official of the *Chama Cha Mapinduzi* (CCM), Party of the Revolution, the only legal political party, was arrested in June with five other leading advocates of secession. They included the former Zanzibar chief justice, Ali Haji Pandu, and Mkubwa Makame. The latter was held for five days, apparently unlawfully, on successive 24-hour detention orders without being brought before a magistrate, and then released. The five others were held until December. They were detained under the 1964 Zanzibar Preventive Detention Decree, which permits indefinite detention without charge or trial, rather than the more recent 1985 Preventive Detention Act, which permits the legality of detention orders to be challenged in court. Shabaan Mloo had previously been detained for several days in January with 11 others.

Mkubwa Makame was rearrested in

August with two others, the day after they had met Amnesty International representatives visiting Zanzibar. At the same time, Juma Ngwali, a former government official, and two others were arrested on Pemba. All six were detained under the 1964 decree and held incommunicado until they were released in December. Two of the Pemba detainees were reported to have been denied appropriate medical care after becoming ill in detention. All those held under the 1964 decree were prisoners of conscience.

Three government critics sentenced to prison terms on Zanzibar in July were also prisoners of conscience. Rashid Ali Dadi received a one-year sentence and Omar Salum Hamad and Kombo Hassan Bakar were each jailed for six months after being convicted of holding an illegal meeting in 1989. They were convicted despite the prosecution's failure to prove that there was any unlawful purpose to the meeting.

Other government critics were also charged with holding illegal meetings or breaches of the peace. They were generally released for lack of evidence when their cases came to court, often after they had been held in custody and denied bail for up to two weeks. At least 50 government opponents were still facing such charges at the end of the year.

In April, 15 prisoners serving sentences imposed in 1989 for participating in an illegal demonstration and destroying property were pardoned and released. However, Seif Shariff Hamad, a former chief minister of Zanzibar and a leading advocate of secession, remained in custody throughout 1990 awaiting trial on charges of illegal possession of documents (see *Amnesty International Report 1990*).

At least one government opponent was detained in mainland Tanzania. Musa Membar, leader of the opposition Tanzania Youth Democratic Movement, was arrested in September when he entered Tanzania from Kenya, apparently to participate in the elections. He was detained without charge or trial under the 1985 Preventive Detention Act and was still held at the end of 1990. He was previously imprisoned in the United Kingdom for hijacking an aircraft flying from Tanzania to London in 1982.

On the mainland 15 possible prisoners of conscience from a Burundi opposition movement, the *Parti pour la libération du peuple Hutu* (PALIPEHUTU), Hutu People's Liberation Party, remained in detention pending deportation. They had been arrested in 1989 and accused of political activity detrimental to Tanzania's relations with Burundi (see *Amnesty International Report 1990*). In August their leader, Remi Gahutu, died as a result of illness possibly exacerbated by harsh prison conditions and poor medical facilities.

In January the authorities announced that since 1985 the Court of Appeal had dismissed 188 prisoners' appeals against the death sentence and that 25 executions had taken place. Further executions were believed to have been carried out in 1990. At least 12 people were sentenced to death after being convicted of murder.

Amnesty International appealed for the release of prisoners of conscience and investigated the cases of other political prisoners. In August Amnesty International representatives visited Zanzibar and met Attorney General Idi Pandu Hassan. He said that Shabaan Mloo and others detained without charge or trial under the 1964 decree were being held to prevent them from "disrupting" the October elections. In September Amnesty International published a report, *Tanzania: The Harassment of Government Opponents in Zanzibar*, which detailed recent arrests and reiterated the organization's call for the release of prisoners of conscience.

THAILAND

Three prisoners of conscience remained in prison throughout 1990. There were new political arrests in connection with antigovernment protest rallies. It was possible that some of those held might be prisoners of conscience. The police were accused of beating demonstrators and criminal suspects in custody. At least 13 death sentences were imposed or confirmed by the courts, but there were no reports of executions. Government soldiers were accused of extrajudicially executing 12 Cambodian asylum-seekers. About 2,000 asylum-seekers and others from Myanmar (Burma) were forcibly repatriated.

Three prisoners of conscience continued to serve sentences imposed in November 1988, when they were convicted of "lese majesty" (see *Amnesty International Report 1989*).

THAILAND

In March about 20 people were arrested for organizing a series of non-violent rallies in the capital, Bangkok, on behalf of the National Democratic Movement, which reportedly called on the government to "hand over administrative power to the people". They were charged with breaching the peace and refusing to disperse, but were released on bail. About a dozen of them were reportedly rearrested in October after a rally by a group called the People's Council. About 10 leading members of a group called the Revolutionary Council were also rearrested in October. They had previously been detained in May and June 1989, reportedly after distributing leaflets which falsely proclaimed the abolition of parliament and assumption of power by an interim government. They had been released on bail while awaiting trial on charges of inciting unrest. Before their rearrest, the authorities alleged they were behind the protest activities of the National Democratic Movement and the People's Council. All those rearrested in October remained on trial at the end of 1990.

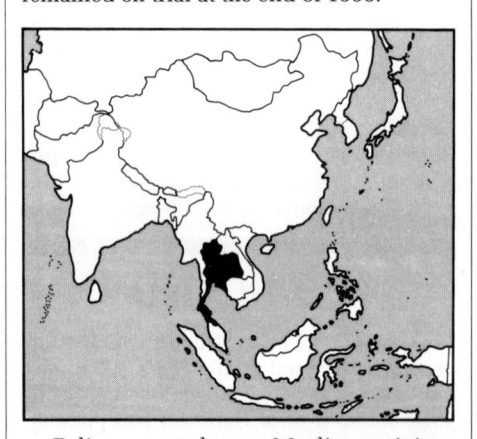

Police arrested two Muslim activists, Abdul Rahman Yuso and Hayi Mae Bueheng, in July and August respectively. They were among about 20 Muslim activists sought by police following a gathering in June of over 10,000 people at a mosque in the southern province of Pattani. During the gathering some demonstrators allegedly called for separation of Muslim-populated provinces from Thailand, threatened or attacked local authorities and insulted King Bhumibol Adulyadej. Abdul Rahman Yuso and Hayi Mae Bueheng apparently acknowledged that they had been present at the gathering, but denied involvement in any violent or other illegal act. Both prisoners were on trial at the end of 1990.

Amnesty International continued to investigate whether any of those detained in connection with the activities of the Revolutionary Council, the National Democratic Movement, the People's Council and Muslim protest rallies were prisoners of conscience.

Some of the 22 political prisoners sentenced after unfair trials in previous years for "communistic activities" and Muslim separatism remained in prison, but the precise number was not known. There was no further information about six alleged Muslim separatists and one alleged communist insurgent arrested in 1989 (see *Amnesty International Report 1990*).

Police officers reportedly beat people in custody. In April the police allegedly detained and severely beat several protesters during a rally by some 2,000 farmers and others in Mahasarakham province. The rally was in protest against pollution of land by rock-salt mining. Those injured included a farmer, who was beaten and kicked when he surrendered to the police, and a woman student. Also in April police officers in the southern province of Nakhorn Srithammaraat were said to have beaten a criminal suspect in an attempt to make him "confess". The suspect later collapsed from his injuries in court. In August police officers in Bangkok were accused of beating a 15-year-old criminal suspect during interrogation.

At least 13 people were either sentenced to death or had their death sentences upheld by the Appeals Court or the Supreme Court. All of them had been convicted of murder or drug-trafficking. No executions were reported.

Twelve Cambodian asylum-seekers were reportedly extrajudicially executed in June by Thai soldiers who detained them outside Site 2 refugee camp, apparently because they suspected them of involvement in an attack on a Thai village.

More than 2,000 asylum-seekers and others from Myanmar were reportedly repatriated against their will on separate occasions during the year, despite fears that they could be at risk of imprisonment as prisoners of conscience, or of torture or execution by the military authorities in Myanmar.

In June Amnesty International wrote to Prime Minister Chaatchai Chunhawan to express concern about the forcible repatriation of asylum-seekers to Myanmar and to seek information about the procedures by which they could apply for continued asylum in Thailand. Amnesty International also wrote to the government about the reported extrajudicial executions of Cambodian asylum-seekers and sought details about an army inquiry into the incident. The organization pressed for the release of prisoners of conscience and appealed to King Bhumibol Adulyadej to commute all death sentences finalized by the Supreme Court. No response was received.

TOGO

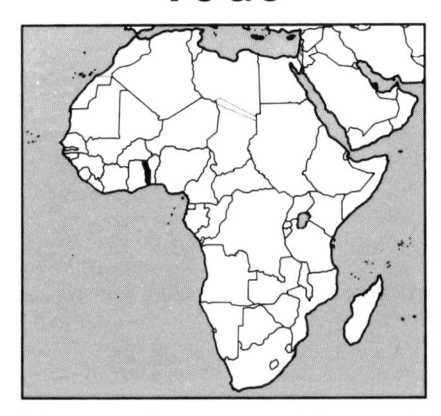

Thirteen pro-democracy activists arrested in August appeared to be prisoners of conscience: at least four of them were tortured. Eleven were released uncharged a week later. The other two were sentenced to five years' imprisonment in October but then released. Dozens of villagers in northern Togo were reportedly detained and tortured by government soldiers.

On 5 October there were violent demonstrations in Lomé, the capital, after the security forces violently dispersed crowds who had gathered peacefully to call for multi-party democracy and the release of two pro-democracy activists. Government vehicles and some police stations were destroyed, several people were reportedly killed and at least 170 demonstrators were arrested. They were all released uncharged in late October.

Following the demonstrations, the government announced that a commission would review the Constitution and that a new draft constitution would be submitted to a referendum by the end of 1991.

President Gnassingbé Eyadéma later announced that the one-party state would be replaced by a multi-party political system.

In late November the security forces used excessive force to disperse demonstrations of striking taxi drivers in the town of Sokodé and elsewhere. As a result several people were reportedly killed and dozens of others injured. Students in Lomé who demonstrated against government policies were also violently dispersed in November. Dozens of students were severely beaten by soldiers.

Thirteen pro-democracy activists were arrested in Lomé on 23 and 24 August. A week later 11 of them were released uncharged. The other two, Doglo Agbelengo and Logo Dossouvi, were brought to trial and on 5 October sentenced to five years' imprisonment for slander and inciting the army to revolt against the government on the grounds that they had distributed leaflets calling for multi-party democracy. They appeared to be prisoners of conscience. However, they were released a week after sentencing by order of President Eyadéma.

At least four of those arrested in August were tortured with electric shocks, whipped and beaten while being held incommunicado in the custody of the *Sûreté nationale*, the national security police. One of the detainees, Komlan Aboli, was subjected to severe beatings and electric shocks. The National Commission of Human Rights, established by the government in 1987, confirmed after an investigation that four detainees had been tortured and publicly urged the government to destroy the equipment used to inflict electric shocks. The head of the security police was subsequently dismissed but those allegedly responsible for torturing the detainees had not been brought to justice by the end of the year.

Earlier in the year, dozens of villagers were detained and tortured by soldiers. This occurred in February as soldiers attempted to forcibly resettle villagers living near a national park in the north of the country. The victims, including a number of elderly inhabitants from the villages of Koloware and Mparatao, were apparently accused of hunting in a wild game reserve. The National Commission of Human Rights carried out an investigation and submitted a report to President Eyadéma, which apparently confirmed that villagers had been unlawfully detained and tortured. As a result, President Eyadéma reportedly ordered the release of two villagers who remained in detention, that some of the victims should be compensated, and that the officer in charge of the soldiers responsible should be demoted.

Amnesty International called for the release of Doglo Agbelengo, Logo Dossouvi and others arrested in August. The organization also investigated reports that villagers in the north were tortured by soldiers, and urged the government to investigate all other reports of torture, to make the findings public and to take immediate steps to prevent the use of torture.

TRINIDAD AND TOBAGO

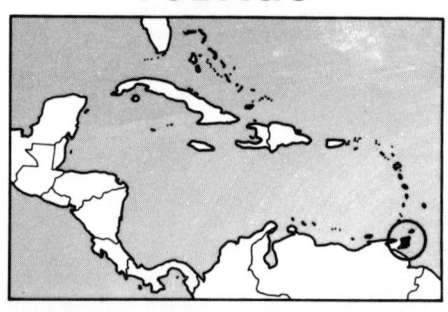

One hundred and fourteen people were charged with treason following an attempt to overthrow the government; if convicted as charged they would be sentenced to death. At the end of the year there were over 90 prisoners under sentence of death. There were no executions during the year; the last hanging was carried out in 1979. The Human Rights Committee adopted the view that there had been violations of the International Covenant on Civil and Political Rights (ICCPR) in the case of a prisoner under sentence of death. The Commission of Inquiry into the effectiveness and status of the death penalty submitted its report.

In an attempt to overthrow the government of Prime Minister Arthur Napoleon Raymond Robinson, an armed group occupied the parliament building and state television station from 27 July to 1 August. Members of the *Jamaat-al-Muslimeen*, Muslim Organization, a black Muslim group founded in the early 1980s and led by Yasin Abu Bakr, stormed the parliament building. They took 46 hostages including the Prime Minister and members of the cabinet, Senate and House of Representatives. The group's demands included the resignation of the Prime Minister and a general election within 90 days. As a result of confrontations during the five days, over 30 people were killed, including a member of the House of Representatives and police officers. Hundreds were injured, both inside the occupied buildings and in the streets. Among the injured was the Prime Minister who sustained gunshot wounds to his legs. A state of emergency was declared on 28 July and remained in force until 9 December. All members of the group engaged in the occupation surrendered unconditionally on 1 August.

As a result of the attempt to overthrow the government, 114 members of the *Jamaat-al-Muslimeen* were charged with treason, murder and other offences in August. The treason and murder charges carry a mandatory sentence of death on conviction. The trial was pending at the end of the year.

In July the Human Rights Committee, which supervises the implementation of the ICCPR, held that Trinidad and Tobago had violated its obligations under the Covenant in the case of death row prisoner Daniel Pinto, and that he was "entitled to a remedy entailing his release". The Committee found that Article 14(3)(d) had been violated, because the legal assistance provided at his appeal did not "adequately and effectively ensure justice". Daniel Pinto had complained about the quality of the court-appointed defence lawyer at his trial and objected to the same lawyer appearing for him at appeal. He made arrangements for a different lawyer to represent him at his appeal, but these arrangements were ignored by the Court of Appeal. The Committee also concluded that Article 6 of the Covenant (the right to life) had been violated since the death sentence had been imposed after judicial proceedings that fell short of procedural guarantees protected by Article 14 of the Covenant. Daniel Pinto was still on death row at the end of the year.

The Commission of Inquiry examining the death penalty, appointed in March 1989 (see *Amnesty International Reports 1989* and *1990*), held public sittings in March and April for members of the public to present their views. The Commission's report, submitted to President Noor Hassanali in September, concluded that the death penalty for murder and treason should be retained. The Commission recommended that prisoners sentenced to death over 10 years ago should have their sentences commuted to life imprisonment but that executions of those who had exhausted their appeals should be resumed. Amnesty International appeared before the Commission of Inquiry into the death penalty in March and called for total abolition and for the death sentences of all 96 prisoners then on death row to be commuted. It said that such moves would set an example of leadership in the upholding and advancement of human rights in the Caribbean and internationally. The organization pointed to the worldwide trend towards abolition and the various problems inherent in the death penalty.

TUNISIA

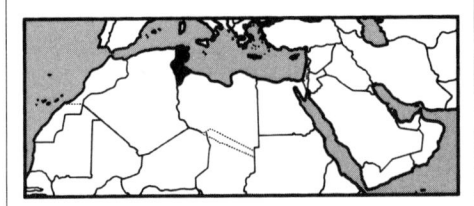

An Islamic activist was imprisoned as a prisoner of conscience. Hundreds of other religious or political activists, including possible prisoners of conscience, were arrested. Most, including at least 460 students who were forcibly conscripted into the army after demonstrations in February, were released during the year, but over 100 others were sentenced to prison terms. There were new reports of torture and ill-treatment of detainees. One execution was carried out, the first since 1987, and a second death sentence was passed.

Moncef Ben Salem, a university professor, was arrested in April after he criticized the government in a newspaper interview. A supporter of *Hizb al-Nahda*, Party of the Renaissance, an Islamic group not permitted to register as a legal political party, he was convicted in May of disseminating false information and defaming public order. He received a three-year prison sentence which he was serving at the end of the year. He said that after his arrest he was held at the Ministry of the Interior for more than 36 hours without food and was prevented from sleeping. He had previously been detained without charge or trial for 18 months until May 1989 (see *Amnesty International Report 1990*).

Bechir Essid was a possible prisoner of conscience. A lawyer and founder of the *Union démocratique unioniste* (UDU), Democratic Unionist Union, an unregistered political party, he was sentenced to four years' imprisonment in October by the Criminal Chamber of the Appeal Court in Tunis. He had been arrested 13 months earlier (see *Amnesty International Report 1990*). He was convicted of forming a gang and conspiring to attack persons and property, defaming the President, distributing false information and putting posters on public buildings without permission. He denied the charges, which were based on the uncorroborated testimony of a co-defendant.

Information was received in January that four possible prisoners of conscience, alleged members of the *Parti communiste des ouvriers tunisiens* (PCOT), Tunisian Workers' Communist Party (see *Amnesty International Report 1990*), had been acquitted in December 1989.

Over 1,000 students were arrested in February during demonstrations at five universities which resulted in violent clashes with the police. Most were released uncharged, but at least 460 students, including some who had already completed their military service or who had been certified medically unfit, were forcibly conscripted into the army. They were sent to isolated military camps where they were effectively held incommunicado. However, about 360 of them were released from military service in April and the remainder in June.

Hundreds of others were arrested in connection with frequent demonstrations by supporters of *Hizb al-Nahda* and other Islamic groups. Many were released uncharged but over 100, including possible prisoners of conscience, were tried and sentenced to up to two years and three months' imprisonment. Many such arrests occurred after Tayeb Hammasi, a Tunis school student, was shot dead by police in September during a demonstration in which Islamic activists reportedly distributed leaflets and threw stones at the police. The authorities said the death was accidental and that an inquiry would be held, but it sparked a wave of demonstrations and arrests of Islamic activists. At least 30 were arrested following a demonstration at Al-Fatah mosque in Tunis. Two – Salah al-Boughanmi and Lutfi Ghariani – were convicted in October of making speeches during an unauthorized demonstration and sentenced to one year in prison. Four others received six-month sentences for public order offences and 22 people received suspended sentences.

There were new allegations of torture and ill-treatment of both political detainees and criminal suspects. Hedi Ben Allala Bejaoui, a *Hizb al-Nahda* supporter, alleged that he was beaten, sexually abused with a stick and had faeces forced into his mouth at Ariana police station in Tunis after his arrest on 9 April. He also said that he was tortured with electric shocks at the Ministry of the Interior before being released uncharged after a few hours. A subsequent medical examination noted numerous injuries. The Interior Ministry said that there would be an investigation into his alleged torture, but it was not known whether this occurred.

In June Raouf Mthlouti, an 11-year-old boy accused of theft, alleged that he was beaten while in police custody in Ariana. A subsequent medical examination supported his allegations and his lawyer made a formal complaint to the procuracy, which apparently took no action.

Abdellatif Tlili, a *Hizb al-Nahda* supporter, was also reportedly tortured while being detained in November and December at the Ministry of the Interior in Tunis. Legally, suspects can only be held in pre-trial incommunicado detention for a maximum of 10 days, but he was held incommunicado for six weeks during which he was allegedly beaten severely, had a stick forced into his anus and was repeatedly suspended from a bar under his knees with his hands and feet bound together in front of him (the *rôti* position) for long periods. A medical examination after his release found injuries consistent with his torture allegations.

At least two people were sentenced to death. One of them was convicted of multiple murder in May and executed in November. This was the first execution to be carried out since President Zine El Abidine Ben Ali came to power in 1987. Former diplomat Lamari Dali was sentenced to death on 25 December after being convicted of treason at a trial conducted *in camera*. His sentence was confirmed on 28 December, but he had not been executed by the end of 1990.

Amnesty International wrote to the government in June to express concern at recent arrests and reports of torture and ill-treatment of suspects held in pre-trial incommunicado (*garde à vue*) detention. There had been no response by the end of the year.

In September Amnesty International published a report, *Tunisia: Summary of Amnesty International's Concerns*, which detailed recent evidence of torture and ill-treatment of detainees while held incommunicado and, sometimes, beyond the maximum time limit for *garde à vue* detention. Amnesty International also appealed for the commutation of the death sentence carried out in November and the one passed in December.

TURKEY

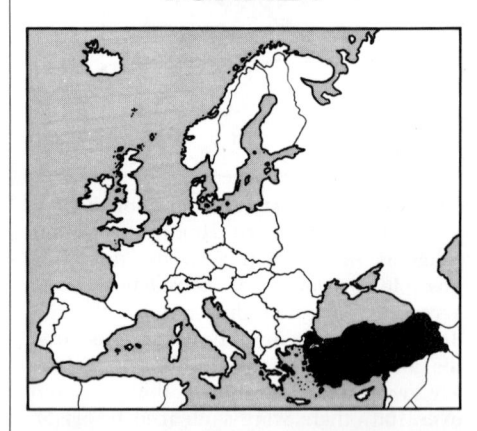

There were thousands of political prisoners, scores of whom were prisoners of conscience. Hundreds of political prisoners were sentenced to imprisonment and some to death after legal proceedings that did not meet international standards for fair trial. The use of torture continued to be widespread and systematic, in some cases resulting in death. There were reports of extrajudicial executions. Civilian and military courts passed at least eight death sentences. At the end of the year the total number of prisoners under sentence of death who had exhausted all legal remedies had reached 315. Seven Iraqi Kurds, some of whom were recognized as refugees by the Office of the United Nations High Commissioner for Refugees (UNHCR), were extradited to Iraq.

At the end of the year a state of emergency was still in force in 10 provinces in southeast Turkey where the security forces were engaged in counter-insurgency operations against Kurdish separatist guerrillas. Many human rights violations by the security forces were alleged to have taken place in the context of this conflict. The guerrillas were also reported to have attacked civilians, some of whom they abducted and killed. In August the armed organization *Devrimci Sol*, Revolutionary Left, claimed responsibility for the execution of three alleged police informers.

In May President Turgut Özal and the Council of Ministers introduced Decree 424 (replaced in December by Decree 430), which extended the already extraordinary powers of the Emergency Legislation Governor to allow for, among other things, the closure of printing presses, the banning of publications and the forcible resettlement from within the Emergency Powers region of individuals engaged in activities "harmful to the maintenance of general security and public order".

In August Turkey notified the Council of Europe that this decree might result in its derogation from Articles 5, 6, 8, 10, 11 and 13 of the European Convention on Human Rights, which contain guarantees of freedom of expression and assembly, and important safeguards against torture.

Turkish law allows detainees to be held in police custody for up to 15 days before being brought before a judge, or up to 30 days in the Emergency Powers region. Draft amendments to the Penal Code to shorten such detention periods, proposed in September 1989, had not been enacted by the end of the year. The right of access to a lawyer is provided by Article 136 of the Criminal Procedure Code, and this was reinforced by a circular issued by Prime Minister Yildirim Akbulut in April. However, lawyers in all parts of the country continued to be denied access to clients held in police detention.

Other proposed measures to protect detainees from ill-treatment also remained in draft form many months after they were originally announced. For example, in May the Judicial Committee began examining a draft law under which statements to the police would be admissible as evidence in court only if taken in the presence of a lawyer. However, no progress appeared to have been made by the end of the year.

Arrests and trials of prisoners of conscience continued throughout the year. Several people were taken into custody and charged under Penal Code Article 142 with "making separatist propaganda". İsmail Beşikçi was arrested in March in connection with books he had written about the Kurdish minority in Turkey. He had already served more than 10 years in prison for his writings about the Kurds. He was provisionally released in July, and his trial continued. Also in March Mehmet Fehim Işk, a journalist, was arrested for a speech he made which referred to the Kurds' "anti-colonial struggle". He was sentenced to four years and two months' imprisonment. In April the writer Musa Anter, aged 73, was arrested and imprisoned for a speech he had made about the Kurdish minority. In May he was acquitted and released. Doğu Perinçek, publisher of the magazine *İkibin'e Doğru (Towards 2000)* was arrested and charged in August, also for speeches allegedly containing Kurdish separatist propaganda. He was provisionally released in September, but his trial continued.

In October Vedat Aydın, Ahmet Zeki Okçuoğlu and Mustafa Özer were taken into custody and charged under Article 142 in connection with a speech made in Kurdish at the annual general meeting of the Turkish Human Rights Association (THRA). Mustafa Özer was released after one week; the two others were released by the court at the first hearing in December. The trial continued.

Haydar Kutlu and Nihat Sargın, leaders of the banned *Türkiye Birleşik Komünist Partisi* (TBKP), Turkish United Communist Party, who had been imprisoned in November 1987, were conditionally released in May, but their trial continued (see *Amnesty International Reports 1989* and *1990*).

Several prisoners of conscience who had been granted provisional release in the early 1980s were rearrested and imprisoned following confirmation of their sentences. Mehmet Ali Polat, Burhan Oktay, Orhan Ünal, Nezahat Moza Özden and Sabahattin İzcioğlu were reimprisoned during the year for membership of the *Türkiye Komünist Partisi* (TKP), Turkish Communist Party.

In November, 10 people attending a memorial service for the founder of the Islamic Nurcu sect, including the owner and eight staff members of the fundamentalist magazine *Yeni Asya* (*New Asia*), were detained for 14 days and investigated for "acting against the secular nature of the state" (Penal Code Article 163).

Hundreds of political prisoners were sentenced to imprisonment or death by military and state security courts after legal proceedings that did not meet internationally recognized minimum standards for a fair trial. These courts failed to investigate most allegations of torture made before them and in some cases permitted statements extracted under torture to be used as evidence.

The pattern of widespread and systematic torture continued, with many new allegations of torture and ill-treatment of political and criminal detainees and prisoners. Victims consistently reported similar methods of torture: being blindfolded and stripped naked, beatings on all parts of the body, hosing with cold water, squeezing of testicles and the application of electric shocks.

Among the hundreds of political prisoners who alleged they were tortured during 1990 was Mesut Bozkurt. He was detained at the İzmir office of the magazine *Yeni Çözum* (*New Solution*) when it was raided by police in February, and taken to İzmir Police Headquarters. He alleged that when he refused to sign prepared statements admitting membership of an illegal organization, he was hosed with cold water under high pressure, his testicles were squeezed, electric shocks were applied to his body and he was raped with a truncheon. Because he was blindfolded throughout the 16 days of his detention he was unable to identify the torturers.

People suspected of political offences were particularly at risk of torture in detention. However, as a result of the intensified military campaign to combat the guerrilla activities of the Kurdish Workers' Party (PKK), large numbers of villagers in southeast Turkey with no background of political activity were detained on suspicion of sheltering guerrillas and were reportedly tortured. One example was Mehmet Polat, imam of Bayramlı village, who was detained on 19 September. He alleged that he was kept blindfold, handcuffed, denied food and water, and forced to remain standing for long periods or to lie on the concrete floor of the lavatory. He was stripped naked, beaten on his genitals with a truncheon and forced to drink liquor as an affront to his religious beliefs. When the marks of torture had disappeared he was brought before the court, where he was formally arrested on charges of sheltering Kurdish guerrillas.

Some prisoners died in custody, reportedly as a result of torture and ill-treatment. On 4 June Serdar Çekiç Abbasoğlu was found dead in Ankara Closed Prison. Three days earlier he had been charged with burglary and brought to the prison from Ankara Police Headquarters. Fellow prisoners alleged that he had been bleeding from his mouth and nose and that his death was the result of torture while in police custody. On 18 November Yakup Aktaş of Derik in the province of Mardin was detained and taken to the Mardin Gendarmerie Regimental Headquarters. On 25 November his family was informed of his death, and received his body from Mardin State Hospital. Officials stated that an autopsy had found that he died of a heart attack. Yakup Aktaş was 24 years old. Those who washed his body before burial reported that there were bruises and cuts on his wrists, arms and back, and that the back of his head was crushed and bloodstained. They also said that there were wounds on his eyebrows and temples. His family demanded a second autopsy, the preliminary results of which emerged in late December and described widespread bruising and cuts on the head. Torture was established in several prosecutions during the year, but most of these cases nevertheless resulted in acquittal because the victims had been blindfolded and the torturers could not be positively identified. Seven court actions were known to have resulted in convictions.

Major Cafer Çağlayan, an army officer who was tried in Ankara Third Criminal Court for an incident in January 1989 when villagers of Yeşilyurt in the southeast were beaten, trampled, kicked and allegedly forced to eat human excrement, was convicted of ill-treatment. He was sentenced in June to two and a half months' imprisonment, which was converted to a fine of approximately $170, and a similar period of suspension from duties.

There were a number of reported extrajudicial executions, particularly in the southeast of the country where the security forces were most active. On 28 September soldiers and "special team" members arrived at Kayadeler (Uzkundos) village, near Bitlis, and cleared the mosque where the men of the village were at Friday prayers. Those present, with the exception of İbrahim Döner, whose family had a history of political activity, were told to go home. Shots were heard and two hours later İbrahim Döner's body, together with a pistol and a suicide note, were shown to his brother; Ibrahim Döner had been shot through the head. The brother stated that there were marks of blows on İbrahim Döner's neck and back.

At least eight people were sentenced to death by military and civilian courts during the year. Other death sentences were confirmed by appeal courts. By the end of the year, the number of people under sentence of death who had exhausted all judicial appeals had reached 315. Their sentences could be carried out if approved by the Turkish Grand National Assembly.

Thousands of Iraqi Kurds who fled to Turkey from Iraq in 1988 to escape chemical and conventional weapons attacks continued to be at risk of forcible return to Iraq. Iraq was seeking the extradition of 138 Kurdish political opponents of the Iraqi Government on ostensibly criminal charges: some of them were recognized as refugees by the UNHCR. Seven Iraqi Kurds, some of whom were also UNHCR-recognized refugees, were extradited to Iraq. Forty other Kurdish refugees were reported to have been forcibly repatriated to Iraq in January; their whereabouts were still unknown at the end of 1990. Over 2,500 Iraqi Kurdish refugees were repatriated between March and June under an amnesty announced by the Iraqi Government. Reports suggested that some had been coerced into returning to Iraq against their will by ill-treatment, intolerable camp conditions and intimidation by Iraqi officers who were allowed to visit the camps.

Amnesty International continued throughout the year to call for the release of prisoners of conscience, for fair and prompt trials for all political prisoners, and for an end to torture, extrajudicial executions and the death penalty.

Amnesty International repeatedly called on the Turkish Government to protect Kurdish refugees and other Iraqis from forcible return to Iraq. In February the Turkish Government claimed in a letter to Amnesty International that none of the Iraqis was forcibly sent back to Iraq against their will, and that no forced repatriation would take place. They denied having received a request from the Iraqi Government for the extradition of the 138 refugees.

During the year Amnesty International delegates observed hearings in several trials, including those of Haydar Kutlu, Nihat Sargın, Doğu Perinçek and the three THRA members.

The authorities responded to a number of specific torture allegations raised by Amnesty International. In some cases they stated that investigations or court proceedings were in progress, in others that official medical reports had stated that torture had not been inflicted.

In January the organization submitted information about its concerns for United Nations (UN) review under a procedure established by Economic and Social Council Resolutions 728F/1503, for confidential consideration of communications about human rights violations. In March Amnesty International submitted information about its concerns regarding torture in Turkey to the UN Committee against Torture, the monitoring body established under the UN Convention against Torture. In oral statements to the UN Commission on Human Rights in February and to its Sub-Commission on Prevention of Discrimination and Protection of Minorities in August, Amnesty International included reference to its concerns about the practice of torture during interrogation in police custody in Turkey.

UGANDA

At least 2,500 uncharged political detainees were released, but new arrests took place and more than 1,300 people remained in detention without charge or trial at the end of the year. Seventy-five prisoners were charged with treason, which carries a mandatory death sentence. Detainees were reported to have been tortured or ill-treated, and in some cases to have died as a result. Government forces allegedly committed over 100 extrajudicial executions in the course of counter-insurgency operations. At least 16 people were sentenced to death, six of whom, all soldiers, were executed.

The government of President Yoweri Museveni continued to face armed opposition in the northeast, north and southwest of the country. As in previous years, hundreds of people were detained by the government's National Resistance Army (NRA) and imprisoned outside the framework of the law, particularly in the northeast. However, a law passed in 1989 to allow suspected insurgents to be tried summarily was not invoked (see *Amnesty International Report 1990*). Rebels were responsible for the deliberate killing of captives.

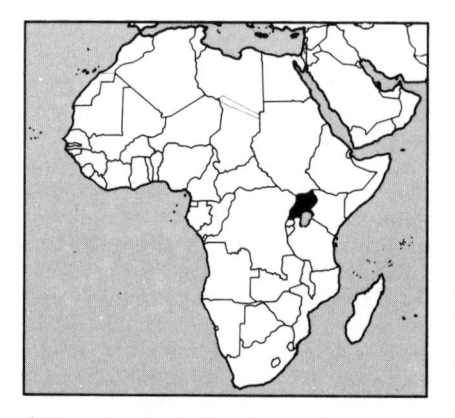

The Penal Code (Amendment) Bill enacted in June increased the number of offences punishable by death. The amendment, which made sexual relations with children under 13 or with prisoners capital offences, was presented as a measure to curb the spread of Acquired Immune Deficiency Syndrome (AIDS).

Hundreds of new arrests meant that at the end of 1990 there were over 1,300 people in detention without charge or trial, many in district prisons and military barracks. However, approximately 2,500 detainees were released uncharged during the year. The majority were civilians arrested by the NRA as suspected rebel supporters and held without any legal status in civil prisons where they were referred to as "lodgers". In January, 328 "lodgers" from Gulu District, some detained for over two years, were released, among them 11 children under the age of 13. A further 2,182 detainees from Kumi and Soroti Districts were released in April. Major Fred Mpiso, detained since being acquitted of treason in March 1988, was released in September following the filing of a writ of *habeas corpus* in February (see *Amnesty International Report 1990*).

Three journalists were arrested in February and charged with defamation after allegedly asking Zambia's President Kenneth Kaunda "impertinent" questions at a news conference in Entebbe. One, Hussein Abdi Hassan, was refused bail for five weeks but then acquitted in September. However, the government appealed against his acquittal and he and the two others still faced charges at the end of 1990. All were freed on bail.

Seventy-five prisoners, more than half of whom had already been held for a year or more, were charged with treason during 1990. Only four were brought to trial. It appeared that in some cases the long delays and the vague nature of the charges were being used to prolong the imprisonment of government opponents against whom evidence was lacking. Forty-three soldiers and civilians charged in January had been in military custody for 15 months: at least eight others arrested with them were still apparently detained without charge at the end of 1990.

There were reports of torture and ill-treatment of prisoners by NRA soldiers, Local Defence Unit militia personnel and prison staff. In March soldiers in Nebbi, northwest Uganda, were said to have beaten three suspected smugglers so severely that one of them died. Marks on the body indicated that his elbows, wrists and ankles had been tied together behind his back, a form of tying similar to the method known as *kandooya*, which was formally banned in the NRA in 1987 (see *Amnesty International Report 1988*). In Kampala, a detainee was alleged to have suffered brain damage after being beaten and given electric shocks by soldiers in Lubiri Barracks in September. Another detainee reportedly died in November after beatings by soldiers there. In August four prison warders in Mbarara were charged with murder after a prisoner died as a result of beatings.

Extrajudicial executions by NRA forces were reported from areas in which armed opponents of the government were active, including Gulu, Tororo and Kumi Districts. In March, 16 people were allegedly burned to death by soldiers at Got Ngur in Gulu District. Further extrajudicial executions reportedly occurred in Soroti District in August and September after the deployment there of an army brigade accused of human rights violations elsewhere. In Bugondo, 16 people were reportedly burned to death and in Soroti town, 20 were reportedly battered to death by soldiers. After this, 30 soldiers were arrested and the brigade was withdrawn.

The authorities announced investigations into some alleged abuses by government forces but the investigation process was protracted. Official investigations into alleged extrajudicial executions in 1988 and other years had still not been concluded by the end of 1990.

Two students were killed and three seriously injured in December when police opened fire without warning on a demonstration at Makerere University. On this occasion, the authorities suspended Uganda's two senior police officers, arrested 27 others and set up a commission of inquiry headed by a Supreme Court judge.

The General Court Martial, the highest military court, sentenced at least two NRA officers to death, one for treason and the other for robbery with violence. At least six soldiers were executed by firing-squad after appearing before other military tribunals on charges of murder or rape. Those convicted by such courts had no right of appeal.

The High Court also imposed a number of death sentences. In July, six people, including Captain Frank Kibuuka, were sentenced to death for treason (see *Amnesty International Report 1990*). Several hundred other prisoners convicted in previous years remained under sentence of death and at least two appeals against death sentences imposed in previous years were dismissed by the Supreme Court. However, no prisoners sentenced to death by the High Court were reported to have been executed.

Amnesty International representatives visited Uganda in February to seek information about individual prisoners and to discuss the organization's concerns with government officials. Amnesty International welcomed the releases of untried political detainees but urged the government to bring to trial promptly and fairly all political detainees, or release them. It also called for urgent and impartial investigation of reported extrajudicial executions and pressed for official action to prevent such killings. It expressed concern about the apparent failure of official inquiries into alleged extrajudicial executions by the NRA in 1988 to reach any findings or make any recommendations (see *Amnesty International Reports 1989* and *1990*). In response the government reaffirmed its opposition to extrajudicial executions and told Amnesty International in September that recent incidents in Gulu, Tororo and Kumi Districts were being investigated, and that a report into the 1988 killings in Gulu had been delayed by logistical problems but would be forthcoming. In December Amnesty International expressed concern at the killings of students at Makerere University and published a report, *Uganda: Death in the Countryside*, describing killings of prisoners and non-combatants by the army in 1990. It renewed its calls to the government to investigate reports of extrajudicial executions, to bring those responsible to justice, and to review army practices and procedures to prevent further killings.

UNION OF SOVIET SOCIALIST REPUBLICS

The USSR parliament continued to implement reforms aimed at bringing some laws closer to international standards on human rights. The number of known prisoners of conscience continued to drop, as some 14 benefited from early release and fewer arrests were reported. At the end of the year at least 30 known or suspected prisoners of conscience were believed to be imprisoned, or forcibly confined in psychiatric hospitals. Hundreds of people seeking to exercise their human rights were detained for short periods during the year. Some alleged that they were ill-treated. Proposals to restrict the death penalty, first published in 1988, had still not come before parliament. Fifty-five death sentences came to light and at least four people were executed. At least one person seeking political asylum was forcibly repatriated.

In March Mikhail Gorbachov was elected by parliament to the newly created post of executive President of the USSR. Elections in a number of union republics reflected a desire for increased autonomy; by the end of the year all 15 republics had passed declarations of sovereignty or independence. Some asserted the primacy of their laws over those of the USSR. The USSR Constitution was amended to remove the Communist Party's monopoly on power. Hundreds of people were killed in the southern republics as violence continued between ethnic and national groups, and troops were deployed to maintain order.

The USSR parliament continued to implement reforms intended to give Soviet citizens more of the human rights guaranteed by international standards. In January a law establishing a Committee for USSR Constitutional Supervision came into force. It appeared to provide, for the first time, a mechanism for systematically translating international standards into domestic law.

Religious believers were granted new rights under a Law on Freedom of Conscience and Religious Organizations which came into force in October. The law enabled religious groups to apply to become legal entities, which could then own property, establish religious and charitable institutions and engage in publishing, printing and manufacturing activity. The law also removed the requirement that congregations register (see *Amnesty International Report 1990*).

At least 14 prisoners of conscience benefited from early release. They included Bohdan Klymchak, imprisoned since 1978 for trying to leave the country without official permission and possessing "anti-Soviet" literature. He was released from his 20-year sentence of imprisonment and internal exile in October. Fewer arrests of prisoners of conscience were reported than in 1989. At least 30 people were believed still imprisoned, or forcibly confined in psychiatric hospitals, at the end of the year for peacefully exercising their human rights.

Most prisoners of conscience were conscientious objectors to military service, serving up to three years' imprisonment for "evading regular call-up to active military service". At least 16 new cases of imprisoned conscientious objectors came to light during the year: almost all concerned people sentenced before 1990. They included Vladimir Osipov from the Moldovan Republic, who was sentenced to three years' imprisonment in October 1988 for refusing his call-up papers. He had already served a three-year sentence on the same charge. Both refusals were based on his religious convictions. He was released early in November. In March the Soviet authorities gave a public assurance that they would not prosecute for "desertion" 30 Lithuanian soldiers who had left their units and had been arrested earlier that month, apparently because of their conscientious refusal to continue serving in the Soviet army. None of them appeared to have been charged with desertion by the end of the year. A number of republics adopted provisions for an alternative service for conscientious objectors. However, it was unclear how these regulations were to be applied, as the USSR authorities continued to assert the primacy of their laws, under which there is no legal provision for alternative service. In April the Estonian Republic abolished articles in its criminal code providing punishments for refusal to perform regular and refresher military service, and rehabilitated those convicted under these laws.

Hundreds of supporters of the Popular Front of Azerbaydzhan were reportedly arrested after troops moved into the republic's capital, Baku, following violent disorders in January. Many were apparently charged with "inciting racial hatred" and "organizing mass disorders". Most appeared to have been released, possibly pending trial, by the end of the year. As in other areas of ethnic conflict, a state of emergency and curfew made it difficult to obtain corroborative information on arrests and to investigate allegations that some people may have been detained for their peaceful opposition to official policies rather than for participation in violence.

Short-term detention and administrative measures (see *Amnesty International Report 1990*) were used against hundreds of people seeking to exercise their human rights. Valery Terekhov, for example, was placed under "administrative arrest" for the maximum 15-day term in February for carrying a placard in Leningrad calling for elections to be boycotted. Others were detained, sometimes repeatedly, for displaying nationalist symbols, distributing informal periodicals or, in one case, giving a religious sermon. Some detainees alleged that they were beaten. Leonid Zelenin is said to have received injuries, including a fractured lower jaw, when beaten in police custody in Moscow. He was detained from 9 to 11 April for distributing two informal publications and copies of the USA's Constitution.

Administrative procedures were also used to forcibly confine at least six people in psychiatric hospitals on what were believed to be political grounds. Nikolay Nosik and Pyotr Rikalo in the Ukraine and Kurbanberda Karabalakov in the Turkmenian Republic were held for distributing leaflets for opposition political groups. Artur Shtankov from Murmansk was allegedly confined after seeking to emigrate and renouncing his Soviet citizenship. He is said to have staged a hunger-strike in protest at his confinement and forcible medical treatment. At least five people believed confined in psychiatric hospitals on political grounds before 1990 were thought still held at the end of the year. They included Balazhon Boyev, a Muslim from the Tadzhik Republic, reportedly confined as a result of his religious activities. A draft law on psychiatry, said to include the principle that each compulsory confinement should be subjected to a judicial review, had not been debated in parliament by the end of the year. Existing appeal provisions introduced in 1988 had been widely criticized as inadequate (see *Amnesty International Report 1990*).

Although most known prisoners of conscience were serving their terms in less severe conditions than in previous years, those held in a corrective labour colony for political prisoners in the Urals – Perm 35 – alleged they were still subject to arbitrary punishment for continuing to express their beliefs. Prisoner of conscience Bohdan Klymchak, for example, was given a second term in the punishment cell in January after going on hunger-strike to protest against the confiscation of his mail following the visit of a USA congressman in August 1989. The congressman had apparently received prior assurances that there would be no reprisals against prisoners who spoke to him about their cases and conditions of imprisonment.

In January at least 30 Armenians were murdered in what is reported to have been a pogrom in the Azerbaydzhani capital of Baku. The official Soviet news agency TASS said that Azerbaydzhani police and soldiers took no steps to protect the victims. During the year the findings of the USSR parliamentary commission investigating the killings of civilians in the Georgian capital of Tbilisi in April 1989 became available (see *Amnesty International Report 1990*). The commission found that the army had used weapons and poisonous gas against demonstrators in violation of regulations. The commission's recommendations included legislation that would clearly define the procedures for introducing a state of emergency and martial law and for deploying riot troops and police to control public order disturbances. In 1990 parliament passed laws on procedures governing a state of emergency and on the use of Interior Ministry troops in maintaining public order.

In August a number of Somalis attempted to seek asylum in Finland. While travelling from Moscow to Helsinki, they were reportedly stopped by Soviet officials at the request of the Finnish authorities. They did not have entry visas for Finland and were returned to Moscow. However, towards the end of the year other such asylum-seekers were said to be arriving in Finland via the USSR. Also in August a Chinese military pilot seeking asylum was sent back to China.

The first known group seeking abolition of the death penalty was formed during the year, but parliament again deferred discussion of the draft Principles of Criminal Law, which would significantly restrict the scope of the death penalty (see *Amnesty International Report 1989*). Three death sentences were reported, all believed to have been imposed in 1989, on people who would have been exempt if the proposed changes to the criminal law had been adopted: two women and a man aged over 60. At least 52 other death sentences and four executions came to light, and a further seven people were thought to have been executed after their clemency petitions had been rejected. Between early 1987, when the authorities first announced they were reviewing the use of the death penalty, and the end of 1990, at least 159 death sentences and 49 executions were reported. Death penalty statistics remained secret, however, and the real number of death sentences and executions was probably much higher. Information given during an interview in October by the head of the USSR's parliamentary clemency body, to which all death sentences are referred, suggested that on average up to 360 death sentences are passed each year. He said the clemency commission recommends commutation in only three to five per cent of these cases.

Amnesty International urged the authorities to commute all death sentences and to impose a moratorium on the death penalty. It also appealed for the immediate release of all prisoners of conscience and for the restoration of their full civil rights, and sought information on others thought likely to be prisoners of conscience. The organization continued to urge the introduction of a non-punitive civilian alternative to military service, and a fair legal procedure for applying it.

Following the events in Baku in January, Amnesty International expressed concern that local authorities reportedly condoned the killings. It urged an immediate and impartial investigation into these allegations, and that the perpetrators of the killings be identified and brought to justice. By the end of the year Amnesty International had not been able to ascertain whether such measures had been taken.

In February Amnesty International wrote to the Chairman of the Committee on USSR Constitutional Supervision, welcoming its creation as it appeared to indicate increased respect for constitutional rights and the rule of law. It urged the committee to use its powers of legislative initiative to ensure that the laws and constitutions of the USSR are brought into line with internationally recognized standards. A report published by Amnesty International in July – USSR: *First Steps Towards Reform of the Criminal Justice System* – assessed recent legal changes in the light of international standards on human rights.

After participating states of the Conference on Security and Cooperation in Europe agreed at the June Conference on the Human Dimension to make death penalty statistics public, Amnesty International wrote to the USSR Minister of Justice and other officials asking what steps were being taken to make such figures available.

In September Amnesty International urged the Ministry of Foreign Affairs to ensure that no Somali asylum-seeker would be returned to Somalia without full and detailed consideration of each case and of the risks asylum-seekers faced if returned. It also asked that visa requirements not be enforced in such a way as to obstruct asylum-seekers from seeking protection. In October it expressed concern that the Chinese pilot returned to China might face human rights violations.

UNITED ARAB EMIRATES

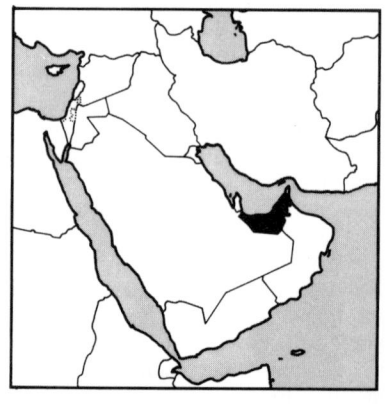

A possible prisoner of conscience held since 1987 was released. At least one person was sentenced to be lashed in public as a judicial punishment.

Mahmud Sulaiman 'Abdi, a 16-year-old Somali national who was arrested in 1987, apparently in connection with his father's political activities (see *Amnesty International Report 1990*), was released in mid-January after spending more than two years in prison. He was never charged or tried.

In September it was reported that a Pakistani national, 'Ala' al-Din Sulaiman, had been sentenced to 80 lashes after being convicted of drunkenness and other charges. It is not known whether the sentence was carried out. Two youths sentenced to 550 lashes each for drunkenness in 1989 (see *Amnesty International Report 1990*) were reported to have appealed against their sentences, which were not known to have been carried out by the end of the year.

Asylum-seekers from countries including Iran, Somalia and Uganda were allegedly threatened with involuntary return to their countries of origin where they might become prisoners of conscience or face torture or execution. However, no cases of such involuntary return were recorded.

Amnesty International wrote to the government to urge that sentences of judicial punishment constituting cruel, inhuman or degrading punishment, such as flogging, be commuted, and that such punishments be replaced with more humane penalties. The organization also appealed on behalf of asylum-seekers believed to be in danger of involuntary return to countries where they might become prisoners of conscience, or face torture or execution.

UNITED KINGDOM

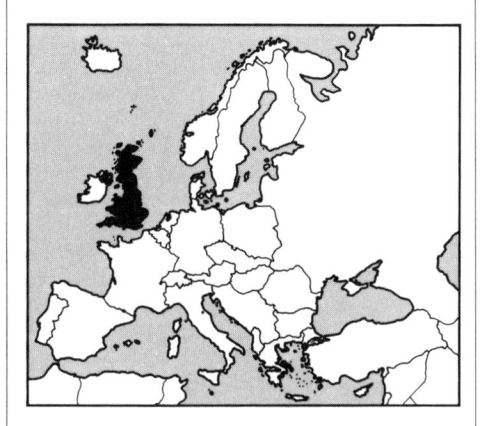

The cases of six prisoners sentenced in 1975 for bombings in Birmingham were referred to the Court of Appeal. A judicial inquiry into the wrongful convictions of the "Guildford Four" and related cases issued an interim report and three police officers involved in the "Guildford Four" cases were charged with conspiracy. The senior police officer who directed the investigation into a riot at Broadwater Farm in 1985 was found guilty by a disciplinary board of denying a 13-year-old suspect access to a lawyer, and new evidence cast doubt on the convictions of three people for the murder of a police officer during the riot. Six men of Kuwaiti and Bahraini origin were detained, possibly for their non-violent political activities. Suspects alleged ill-treatment while in police custody in Northern Ireland. The circumstances of several killings by security forces in Northern Ireland were disputed and coroners' inquests were delayed. A police inquiry into alleged collusion between security force personnel and Loyalist armed groups in Northern Ireland concluded that leaks of security information could not be eliminated.

There was an upsurge in violence in Northern Ireland by both Republican and Loyalist armed groups. Republican armed groups, notably the Irish Republican Army (IRA), are predominantly Catholic and seek a British withdrawal from Northern Ireland and a united Ireland. Loyalist armed groups, notably the Ulster Volunteer Force (UVF) and the Ulster Freedom Fighters (UFF), from the Protestant community, want Northern Ireland to remain a part of the United Kingdom. It was reported that in Northern Ireland during 1990, 44 people were killed by the IRA, two by the Irish People's Liberation Organization, 19 by Loyalists, and 10 by British soldiers.

The government continued to derogate from those articles of the European Convention on Human Rights (ECHR) and the International Covenant on Civil and Political Rights (ICCPR) which state that anyone arrested has the right to be brought before a judge promptly. The European Court of Human Rights had ruled that this right was violated by the Prevention of Terrorism Act (PTA) which allows suspects to be detained for up to seven days without judicial scrutiny.

The cases of the prisoners known as the "Birmingham Six", who have been imprisoned since 1974 for IRA bombings, were referred in August to the Court of Appeal. The government's decision was based on an interim report of a police investigation which suggested that police evidence at the trial concerning one prisoner's confession may have been fabricated.

Another police investigation examined allegations of grave misconduct by the West Midlands Serious Crimes Squad, which had been involved in interrogating the "Birmingham Six" and was disbanded in 1989 (see *Amnesty International Report 1990*). It had not been completed by the end of the year but an interim report disclosed that many vital documents had disappeared from police offices.

A judicial inquiry into the wrongful convictions of the "Guildford Four" and related cases was not completed. The "Guildford Four" had been convicted of murder in 1975 for bomb attacks; their convictions were quashed and they were released in 1989 as a result of evidence of police malpractice (see *Amnesty International Report 1990*). The judicial inquiry issued an interim report in July, dealing with the cases of seven members and friends of the Maguire family arrested in connection with the "Guildford Four" cases. The seven had been convicted in 1976 of possessing and handling explosives on the basis of forensic evidence, and served prison sentences of between five and 14 years. The report concluded that the convictions were unsound and criticized the judges, the prosecution and scientists for mishandling crucial forensic evidence. The Home Secretary immediately referred these cases to the Court of Appeal. The inquiry planned to look at wider issues relating to scientific evidence, as well as at the wrongful convictions of the "Guildford Four" once criminal proceedings against police officers had ended. Three Surrey police officers involved in the interrogation of the "Guildford Four" were charged in November with conspiracy to pervert the course of justice.

The police officer who led the inquiry into disturbances at the Broadwater Farm housing estate in London in 1985 faced a closed disciplinary hearing in June (see *Amnesty International Reports 1988, 1989* and *1990*). He was found guilty of denying 13-year-old Jason Hill access to a lawyer. Jason Hill, who was acquitted of murder, had been denied access to parents and lawyers during three days' detention and had made a confession while dressed only in underpants. In November disciplinary charges were brought against a police officer who had interrogated Jason Hill. New evidence, including psychological tests on two of the prisoners, cast further doubt on the convictions of three people for the murder of a policeman at Broadwater Farm. The case of Engin Raghip, one of the three, was referred to the Court of Appeal in December.

Six men of Kuwaiti and Bahraini origin, arrested in May under the PTA, alleged that they were detained because of their non-violent political activities. Four of them were released without charge; however, two were deported on national security grounds.

Suspects arrested under anti-terrorist legislation in Northern Ireland alleged that they had been ill-treated in police custody. Martin McSheffrey alleged that he had been ill-treated during interrogation at Castlereagh Police Centre in October 1989 and had confessed involuntarily as a result. He was acquitted in October 1990 after the judge heard medical evidence supporting the allegations and declared his confessions inadmissible. Brian Gillen obtained an out-of-court settlement of his claim for damages against the Royal Ulster Constabulary (RUC) for assault (see *Amnesty International Report 1989*). Ten people from Strabane alleged that they had been ill-treated during interrogation at Castlereagh in April and May. The allegations included slaps to the head, punches to the body, and fingers being bent back. The 10 were released without charge.

In January three men were killed in West Belfast by undercover soldiers during an attempted robbery. John McNeill was shot as he sat unarmed and unmasked in a getaway car. Six shots had been fired at his head and body and at least one had been fired from less than 24 inches away. Edward Hale and Peter Thompson had been shot 13 and 10 times respectively. They were reportedly carrying imitation firearms. Eye-witnesses said that no apparent attempt had been made to arrest the three; that they had not been challenged before being fired at; and that two of the three were shot again while lying on the ground. In December the Director of Public Prosecutions announced that no one would be prosecuted in connection with the killings.

In September Martin Peake, 17, and Karen Reilly, 18, were shot dead by soldiers while driving a stolen car in West Belfast. Officials alleged that they had driven through an army checkpoint and hit a soldier. However, eye-witnesses, including a 16-year-old passenger in the stolen car, claimed there was no checkpoint.

In December Fergal Caraher, a member of Sinn Fein (the political counterpart of the IRA), was shot dead and his brother Michael seriously wounded by British soldiers. Officials stated that the two unarmed men were shot after failing to stop their car at a border checkpoint in Armagh but this was disputed by eye-witnesses.

Police investigations continued into the killing in September 1989 of Brian Robinson, a member of the UVF. He was shot by undercover soldiers who had reportedly by chance seen him kill a Catholic man, and had then given chase. An eye-witness claimed that Brian Robinson was shot as he lay injured on the ground after soldiers had knocked him off his motor cycle.

Five House of Lords judges, sitting as the highest appeal court in the United

Kingdom, unanimously overturned a 1988 ruling of the Northern Ireland Court of Appeal that compelled security force personnel involved in disputed killings to give evidence at inquests (see *Amnesty International Report 1990*). The House of Lords decision held that such personnel do not have to attend or testify, to protect them from exposure to the "embarrassment, in circumstances where they may be the subject of criminal proceedings, of invoking the privilege against self-incrimination".

Long overdue inquests into over 20 killings by security force personnel were further postponed because of another legal challenge to the Coroner's Rules, objecting to written evidence being admitted from security force personnel not present to be cross-examined. The Northern Ireland Court of Appeal upheld the existing rule in December; an appeal against the ruling went to the House of Lords.

A police inquiry led by Deputy Chief Constable John Stevens into collusion between security force personnel and Loyalist armed groups in Northern Ireland released a summary report in May (see *Amnesty International Report 1990*). As a result of the inquiry, 59 people were charged or reported to the Director of Public Prosecutions. They were not charged with collusion but with lesser offences such as possession of security documents. The overwhelming majority of those arrested were civilians (32 were members of Loyalist organizations). They included Brian Nelson, who was charged with possessing documents containing information about IRA suspects likely to be of use to terrorists. Brian Nelson had reportedly been both a British military intelligence agent and the intelligence information officer of the Ulster Defence Association (UDA), which has links with the UFF. This gave rise to claims that the authorities had been aware for some years of collusion between the security forces and the UDA. Charges against five UDA men were dropped in October.

The Stevens inquiry report stated that "in the present climate" in Northern Ireland, leaks of official security information "may never be completely eliminated". However, it said that measures already taken had limited the opportunity for such leaks and that "the passing of information had been restricted to a small number of individuals". The inquiry was limited in its scope and failed to identify members of the security forces involved in passing on information to armed Loyalist groups.

In May Amnesty International expressed concern to the government about the decision to derogate indefinitely from ECHR and ICCPR articles guaranteeing detainees the right to be brought before a judge promptly after arrest. The government said that "a satisfactory procedure for the review of the detention of terrorist suspects involving the judiciary has not been identified". Amnesty International was not convinced that the search for a solution had genuinely been exhausted, and urged the government to meet international standards.

Amnesty International continued to press the government for a review of the "Birmingham Six" cases, in particular for a speedy resolution after the cases had been referred to the Court of Appeal. The organization sent an observer to the preliminary hearing in December, which set a date in February 1991 for the appeal hearing.

Amnesty International welcomed the referral of Engin Raghip's case to the Court of Appeal. However, it continued to urge the government to review the cases of all Broadwater Farm defendants convicted of serious offences on the basis of uncorroborated confessions obtained in the absence of a lawyer. It also urged the government to investigate a pattern of alleged police misconduct during interrogation of suspects. The government stated that it did not believe there was a need for a separate investigation into the overall pattern of police behaviour because the investigation supervised by the Police Complaints Authority had been wide-ranging.

Amnesty International asked the government about the detention of the Kuwaiti and Bahraini men and expressed concern that they might have been detained for their non-violent political activities. The organization was further concerned that one of them, Anwar al-Harby, was not allowed to appeal against the refusal of his asylum application and may have been expelled for his well-known human rights work on Kuwait.

Amnesty International expressed concern to the government about recent disputed killings in Northern Ireland, which raised some of the same questions posed in previous incidents, namely whether the people could have been arrested rather than killed; whether the use of lethal force was necessary in the circumstances; and whether they were planned operations (see *Amnesty International Reports 1989* and *1990*).

UNITED STATES OF AMERICA

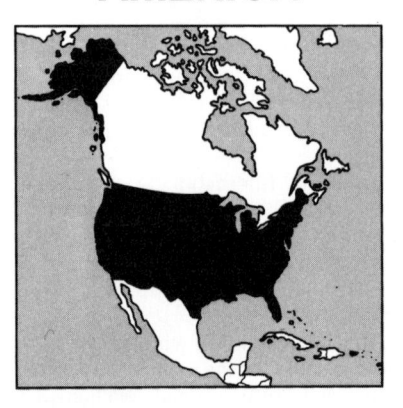

Twenty-three prisoners were executed in 1990. At the end of the year more than 2,300 people were under sentence of death in 34 states and under United States (US) military law. Proposals to extend the death penalty under federal law were dropped from a major crime bill. Amnesty International continued to investigate criminal cases in which it was alleged that the prosecutions were politically motivated. There were complaints of ill-treatment of prisoners.

A congressional committee removed all death penalty provisions from a federal crime bill which was then passed by Congress on 26 October. The US Senate and House of Representatives had earlier approved draft bills which would have reintroduced the death penalty for a number of federal crimes and extended it to crimes not previously punishable by death.

The House bill had contained an amendment giving defendants the right to seek reversal of their death sentences on the grounds of a demonstrated pattern of racial discrimination in death sentencing. This too was dropped from the legislation.

In October the United States of America (USA) ratified the United Nations (UN) Convention against Torture and Other Cruel, Inhuman or Degrading Treatment or Punishment.

Twenty-three prisoners were executed under state laws, bringing the number of executions since 1977 to 143. The states of Arkansas, Illinois and Oklahoma resumed executions after more than 20 years. Other executions were carried out in the states of Alabama, Florida, Louisiana, Missouri, Nevada, South Carolina, Texas and Virginia.

The states of Kentucky and Tennessee passed legislation prohibiting the death penalty for mentally retarded defendants. Only two other US states already had such legislation. Missouri raised the minimum age at which an offender could be sentenced to death from 14 to 16 years at the time of commission of the crime. This brought the state into line with a 1989 US Supreme Court ruling that offenders as young as 16 could be executed.

Evidence suggested that the death penalty continued to be applied in a racially discriminatory manner. In February the General Accounting Office (GAO), an independent agency of the federal government, published the findings of a survey it had conducted into the effects of race on capital sentencing practices. The GAO had examined numerous research studies on this issue carried out since the mid-1970s. Eighty-two per cent of these studies suggested that those convicted of murdering white victims were significantly more likely to be sentenced to death than those convicted of murdering black victims.

In September a pre-trial motion on racial discrimination was heard in Columbus, Georgia, in the case of William Brooks, a black defendant charged with the murder of a white woman. Lawyers from the Southern Prisoners' Defence Committee (SPDC) argued that the death penalty should not be available in this case as it had been applied in a racially discriminatory manner in the Chattahoochie Judicial Circuit, particularly in the city of Columbus where the case was being prosecuted. The SPDC presented data on homicide convictions in the circuit between 1973 and 1990 which showed that prosecutors had sought the death penalty in 34.3 per cent of white victim cases and only 5.8 per cent of cases involving black victims. This difference could not be accounted for by non-racial factors such as the presence of aggravating circumstances, additional felonies, multiple victims or the murder of strangers. Of the 27 cases which went to trial on a capital charge, 21 involved white, mainly single victims and six involved black victims, four of which were cases with multiple victims.

The SPDC also presented evidence to show that Chattahoochie prosecutors had consistently used their peremptory challenges (the right to reject potential jurors without explanation) to exclude blacks from trial juries in capital cases involving black defendants. Testimony given by the relatives of nine black murder victims suggested that their cases had been treated differently from those involving white families. On 19 September the court issued, without further elaboration, a four-word ruling: "The motion is denied." Amnesty International was represented at part of the hearing and concluded that the state had failed to offer a satisfactory explanation for the pattern of racial disparity in death sentencing.

Dalton Prejean, a black, mentally retarded juvenile offender, was executed in Louisiana in May. He was convicted in 1978 of the murder of a white police officer when he was 17 years old. He had been tried and sentenced by an all-white jury after the prosecutor had used his peremptory challenges to exclude all black prospective jurors from the jury panel. The Governor of Louisiana denied clemency despite a recommendation by the Louisiana Board of Pardons and Paroles that Dalton Prejean's death sentence should be commuted to life imprisonment without parole. Their recommendation was based on his history of childhood abuse and mental illness – factors which were not presented to the jury during the sentencing stage of his trial. International treaties and standards prohibit the execution of anyone under the age of 18 at the time of the crime.

In September Charles Coleman became the first prisoner to be executed in Oklahoma for 24 years. Eight years after his conviction his appeal lawyers discovered that he had a history of chronic schizophrenia and organic brain damage, first diagnosed in 1962 when he was aged 15. He had suffered head injuries in childhood and brain seizures since the age of nine – information which had not been presented at his trial. Amnesty International had written to the Oklahoma Board of Pardons and Paroles and to the Governor of Oklahoma arguing that Charles Coleman's brain damage, psychiatric history and deprived social background constituted compelling grounds for clemency. However, clemency was denied.

The first execution in Illinois since 1962 was carried out in September when Charles Walker was executed by lethal injection. Three physicians reportedly inserted an intravenous line through which non-medical staff later injected the lethal medication. This was believed to be the first time that doctors had participated so directly in an execution and was contrary to the guidelines of both the American Medical Association and the World Medical Association.

Earlier, the unique cruelty of the death penalty was graphically demonstrated when flames and smoke emitted from Jesse Tafero's headpiece during his electrocution in Florida in May. Three applications of high-voltage electricity were required before he was pronounced dead, owing to a malfunction caused by use of the wrong type of sponge in the headpiece. Executions in Florida were temporarily suspended until the state declared in July that the electric chair was working properly.

In September a Louisiana court issued a stay of execution for Frederick Kirkpatrick after his lawyers filed a petition arguing, among other things, that execution in the state's electric chair would be cruel and unusual punishment. Citing recent research by a United Kingdom physiologist, the petition argued that electrocution caused excruciating pain. The appeal was still pending at the end of the year.

Lawyers urged the Governor of Virginia to hold an inquiry into the use of the electric chair following Wilbert Evans' execution on 17 October. Blood had streamed from beneath the prisoner's mask and he had reportedly groaned as the electric current was applied.

In January a US district court denied a *habeas corpus* petition in the case of David Rice, a black political activist serving life imprisonment in Nebraska. He and Edward Poindexter had been convicted in 1971 of the murder of an Omaha police officer, although both denied involvement and alleged that they were "framed" because they were leading members of the National Committee to Combat Fascism, an offshoot of the Black Panther Party. At the hearing, lawyers for David Rice argued that evidence which might have damaged the credibility of the 16-year-old chief state witness had been improperly withheld by the prosecution at the time of trial. The witness, who was a major suspect in the murder, had been sentenced to youth custody in May 1971 after testifying for the prosecution and had proved untraceable since his release shortly afterwards. An appeal against the district court's denial of *habeas corpus* relief was heard in November and a decision was still pending at the end of the year.

Amnesty International wrote to the Attorney General of Nebraska in November, questioning the fairness of the original trial proceedings and noting that the continuing absence of the chief prosecution witness may have significantly hampered investigation of the defendant's post-conviction claims. Irregular conduct by the Federal Bureau of Investigation (FBI) during its "Cointelpro" (counter-intelligence) operations in the 1970s, Amnesty International said, had undermined the fairness of a number of trials of political activists, including members of the Black Panther Party.

In January the Governor of Louisiana rejected a recommendation by the Louisiana Pardons Board that Gary Tyler's life sentence be commuted to 60 years' imprisonment (see *Amnesty International Report 1990*).

Allegations of ill-treatment at Harrison County Youth Detention Center in Mississippi and at the Harrison County Jail, made public in September 1989, were reported to be under federal investigation. Inmates, including two boys aged 13 and 14, were allegedly beaten or otherwise abused by officials between 1986 and 1989. Amnesty International wrote to the Mississippi Field Division of the FBI in February to express concern and seek information about the investigation but had received no reply by the end of the year.

Reports suggested that US prison authorities may have been deliberately negligent in their treatment of Dr Alan Berkman, who developed Hodgkin's Disease while serving a federal prison sentence for politically motivated offences. The cancer had gone into remission in 1986 but recurred in 1990. The authorities reportedly failed to follow specific medical recommendations about regular monitoring of his condition and were said to have held him at the Washington, District of Columbia (DC) Jail, in conditions (including denial of fresh air and exercise) which had exacerbated his condition.

Amnesty International wrote to the Federal and Washington DC prison authorities in June expressing concern that the alleged medical neglect of Dr Berkman and his general conditions of confinement might be considered cruel, inhuman or degrading treatment. The Federal Bureau of Prisons replied, stating that Dr Alan Berkman – then in the custody of the Washington DC Corrections Department – was being treated by competent medical professionals and receiving chemotherapy.

Prisoners at Rikers Island Prison, New York, were reportedly ill-treated by guards on 14 August after a riot in the prison. It was alleged that guards took prisoners from their cells, lined them up against walls and beat them with batons. At least 142 prisoners and 20 prison guards were taken to hospital after the riot. Most had minor injuries but several inmates were still receiving hospital treatment days after the incident. An inquiry conducted by the New York State Commission of Corrections found that the guards had used excessive force.

Amnesty International wrote to the Mayor of New York City and to the New York State Commission of Corrections, welcoming the prompt decision to investigate the allegations and urging that those responsible for ill-treating prisoners after the riot should be brought to justice. In response, the authorities informed Amnesty International that several independent authorities (including the New York State Commission of Corrections) were continuing to investigate the allegations and that disciplinary action would be taken where appropriate.

In 1989 allegations came to light that police officers from the Area 2 police station in Chicago, Illinois, had systematically tortured or otherwise ill-treated more than 20 people suspected of killing police officers between 1972 and 1984. The suspects alleged that they had been beaten, kicked, subjected to electric shocks, had guns placed in their mouths or had plastic bags placed over their heads while in police custody during this period. At least 12 people filed complaints with the Chicago police department's Office of Professional Standards (OPS), which were dismissed as "not sustained", despite substantial medical evidence in at least one case. In February 1990 Amnesty International expressed its concern to the Illinois Attorney General about the apparent inadequacy of the OPS investigations and asked whether any action was being taken against police officers in light of the allegations. In response, the First Assistant Attorney General said that torture in police custody is prohibited in Illinois and that complaints to the OPS were investigated by independent civilian personnel. He suggested addressing further complaints to the Cook County State's Attorney or the US Attorney for the Northern District of Illinois (who are responsible for investigating alleged civil rights violations). Amnesty International wrote to both officials in December, asking them to investigate the allegations. Amnesty International also called on the Chicago city authorities to initiate a full inquiry.

There were allegations of human rights violations by US troops during the invasion of Panama (see **Panama**).

Amnesty International made numerous appeals on behalf of prisoners under sentence of death, urging clemency in all cases, and made interventions on behalf of David Rice, Dr Alan Berkman and others.

In an oral statement to the UN Sub-Commission Working Group on Detention, Amnesty International included reference to its concerns on the imposition of the death penalty on juvenile offenders in the USA.

URUGUAY

New evidence came to light linking senior officials in the military government of 1973 to 1985 to "disappearances" carried out in that period. Nevertheless the few remaining official investigations into "disappearances" failed to clarify the fate of the victims. Civil courts hearing compensation claims found the state responsible for the death in custody of a detainee in 1975 and for the illegal arrest and torture of several political prisoners under military rule. During 1990 several prisoners died in disputed circumstances in Libertad prison and there were further reports of ill-treatment of prisoners there.

Following the election victory of the *Blanco* National Party in November 1989, Luis Alberto Lacalle took office as President in March 1990.

In February and October respectively, Uruguay signed the Second Optional Protocol to the International Covenant on Civil and Political Rights Aiming at the Abolition of the Death Penalty and the protocol to the American Convention on Human Rights to abolish the death penalty. It had not ratified these treaties by the end of the year.

The few remaining official investigations into "disappearance" cases failed to clarify the fate of the victims. Investigations into "disappearances" had been entrusted to a military prosecutor under the 1986 Expiry Law (see *Amnesty International Reports 1987* to *1990*), which prevented the prosecution of military and police officials for human rights violations committed under military rule. In several cases the military prosecutor closed cases after concluding that the "disappeared" person had never been detained by the security forces. The prosecutor had made similar rulings in previous years, despite considerable evidence implicating members of the security forces.

Fresh evidence linking former senior government officials to "disappearances" continued to emerge. In April a Uruguayan newspaper revealed the existence of a classified memorandum, written by a Foreign Ministry official in 1976 to the then foreign minister, Juan Carlos Blanco, assessing the possible international repercussions of releasing Elena Quinteros, a teacher who "disappeared" following her 1976 abduction by police from the grounds of the Venezuelan Embassy. Further evidence implicating government officials in the Quinteros "disappearance" came to light in May when the results of a Foreign Ministry investigation carried out between 1987 and 1989 were made public. However, a parliamentary commission set up in June 1990 to investigate the involvement of Juan Carlos Blanco in this "disappearance" concluded that there was insufficient evidence to initiate proceedings against him. In 1983 the Human Rights Committee established under the International Covenant on Civil and Political Rights had concluded that the government had an obligation to investigate the case thoroughly, to clarify Elena Quinteros' fate and to bring to justice those responsible. In June 1990 the Foreign Minister announced that he would seek compliance with the Committee's 1983 conclusion. However, President Lacalle then stated publicly that neither legal channels nor public opinion supported a reinvestigation of the past. At the end of the year the case remained closed.

In February 1990 criminal proceedings brought by Sara Méndez against the adoptive parents of a 14-year-old boy, whom she believed to be her "disappeared" son, were closed following the government's decision that the case was covered by the Expiry Law (see Amnesty International Report 1990). Sara Méndez' son "disappeared" after being taken from his mother by police during her detention in 1976. However, her lawyers argued that the Expiry Law did not apply to alleged criminal offences committed by civilians, in this case the concealment of the identity of a minor. In May 1990 she took the case before a civil court, which in September ordered blood tests to ascertain the child's identity. However, the tests were delayed following a series of appeals by the adoptive parents, one of which was still pending at the end of the year.

Despite the barrier to criminal prosecution created by the Expiry Law, several relatives of people killed, "disappeared" or imprisoned under military rule obtained compensation from the state following civil court rulings in their favour. In April a judge ordered the Ministry of the Interior to pay compensation to the relatives of Alvaro Balbi, a Communist Party leader who died in police custody in July 1975. The judge concluded that Alvaro Balbi had died under torture, but stated that those responsible could not be brought to justice owing to the Expiry Law.

In November the Ministry of Defence accepted responsibility in a claim for damages presented to a civil court by the relatives of Vladimir Roslik, a doctor who died under torture at the Fray Bentos military headquarters in April 1984. In similar lawsuits, the Ministry of Defence agreed to negotiate a settlement with Sergio López Burgos and five other Uruguayans detained and tortured in Buenos Aires in a joint operation by Argentine and Uruguayan police in 1976 and later imprisoned in Uruguay. While acceptance of these claims was seen as a tacit admission of the Defence Ministry's responsibility for illegal detention and torture, the offer of an out-of-court settlement eliminated trial proceedings in which former members of the military would have been called to testify as witnesses. Other former political prisoners whose claims for damages were before civil courts expressed their dissatisfaction with any settlement that permitted the government to evade a thorough investigation and clarification of events as well as a public and unequivocal admission of state responsibility.

There was little progress in the investigations into two killings allegedly committed by police officers in 1989. Despite the presentation of new witnesses in the cases of Nestor Castillo Romero and Jorge Ricardo Inciarte Castells (see Amnesty International Report 1990), responsibility for their deaths had still not been established at the end of the year.

A police officer was tried for the illegal arrest of Guillermo Machado, who died in police custody in July 1989 (see Amnesty International Report 1990). To Amnesty International's knowledge, he was not convicted.

At least five criminal prisoners died in disputed circumstances in Libertad maximum security prison outside Montevideo. Among them was Jorge Barreiro Dorta, who was found hanging in his cell on 14 February. His cell-mate testified before a court that Jorge Barreiro Dorta had been subjected to ill-treatment by prison guards shortly before his death. His death provoked a hunger-strike by prisoners protesting against ill-treatment and harsh prison conditions. There were further reports of ill-treatment in Libertad prison during a cell search by prison guards on 2 July. According to relatives, scores of prisoners showed signs of having been beaten during the operation. A Supreme Court delegation, accompanied by judicial officials and forensic doctors, visited the prison in November and took statements from prisoners who said they had been ill-treated. In a number of cases judicial proceedings were initiated to investigate these allegations.

Detainees in some police stations in Montevideo also reported having been ill-treated. Three metalworkers detained in August later claimed in court that they had been hooded and beaten in order to make them confess to theft.

In December Amnesty International wrote to the Minister of the Interior expressing concern at reports of ill-treatment in Libertad prison and requesting information concerning the progress of official investigations initiated after the visit of the Supreme Court delegation. The organization asked what measures had been taken to clarify the death of five prisoners in Libertad and to guarantee the physical safety of those held there. Amnesty International continued to investigate allegations of ill-treatment of detainees in police custody.

VENEZUELA

Prisoners were allegedly tortured and ill-treated. At least one "disappearance" was reported. There were new reports of arbitrary killings by police officers, particularly in poor urban neighbourhoods. Investigations into human rights abuses in previous years continued to make little progress. The bodies of several people reportedly killed by the security forces in 1989 were exhumed from an unmarked mass grave.

Demonstrations took place throughout the year in response to the government's economic policies. In February one person, Italo Alberto Vargas, was fatally wounded and others were injured during clashes between police and trade union demonstrators in Caracas. Approximately 39,000 prisoners all over the country went on hunger-strike in March demanding better prison conditions and an end to overcrowding. Over 200 prisoners who were involved in organizing the hunger-strike were sent in April to the remote jungle camp of El Dorado, where conditions were reportedly harsh. At the end of July President Carlos Andrés Pérez announced an increase in public transport fares and petrol prices, which led to widespread protests, with some outbreaks of violence. Hundreds of people who had reportedly not engaged in violence suffered arbitrary arrest, and scores were injured by the security forces in the context of such demonstrations.

In July Venezuela signed the Second Optional Protocol to the International Covenant on Civil and Political Rights Aiming at the Abolition of the Death Penalty. In September Venezuela signed the protocol to the American Convention on Human Rights to abolish the death penalty.

Amílcar Rodríguez, a political prisoner, and at least nine other detainees allegedly suffered torture or ill-treatment during and after their transfer from different prisons to the remote jungle prison camp of El Dorado. The prisoners reported that following transfer to the prison camp, prison wardens beat them with *peinillas*, large blunted sabres, which were covered with excrement so that the resulting wounds would become infected. Amílcar Rodríguez was allegedly tortured, in the presence of two medical doctors, with electric shocks, blows with a baseball bat, and kicks. Ten prisoners, including Amílcar Rodríguez, were transferred to another prison in the state of Guárico in August, following a visit to El Dorado by three state attorneys and a forensic doctor who reportedly found the prisoners in poor physical condition.

At least one person "disappeared" after detention by members of the security forces. Fidel José Jiménez Fuentes was reportedly detained in March by the state police in Anzoátegui and taken to the local police station. His father went to the police station two days later and was told that his son was not being held there. The police subsequently said that Fidel Jiménez had been abandoned in a remote area because he had suffered a nervous breakdown. He was still missing at the end of the year. Seven police officers were arrested and accused of "abandoning a disabled person in a solitary place". A few days later, however, a judge ordered the seven to be released pending trial. The Attorney General's Office appealed against this decision.

There were renewed reports of arbitrary and unprovoked killings by police officers, particularly in the poor urban neighbourhoods of Caracas or in small provincial towns. José Gregorio Díaz, aged 15, and Jefferson Padilla, aged 16, were reportedly abducted in Caracas in broad daylight by officers from the *Policía Metropolitana*, metropolitan police, in January. Their bodies were found 13 days later. Both youths had been shot in the head. Four police officers were charged with the murders.

In June Pedro Muñoz Vásquez was intercepted in the streets of Caracas by three metropolitan police officers. According to witnesses, he was held by two of the officers while the third shot him at close range. A judge ordered the exhumation of Pedro Muñoz Vásquez's body in August and an autopsy confirmed the cause and manner of death reported by the witnesses. Arrest orders against the three officers were subsequently issued. No further information about the case was known at the end of the year.

Most investigations by military and civilian courts into alleged arbitrary killings by police and military personnel during previous years continued to make little progress. In June, however, the Supreme Court upheld the decision of a lower military court to bring charges against 19 members of a military and police patrol allegedly responsible for the deliberate killing of 14 fishermen in El Amparo in 1988 (see *Amnesty International Report 1989*). All 19 had been briefly detained in 1989, until the military court of appeal dropped the charges against them (see *Amnesty International Report 1990*). In August, following the Supreme Court's decision to reinstate charges, 15 of them were rearrested. In November it was announced that President Pérez – in his capacity as commander-in-chief of the armed forces – had ordered the investigations into this case to continue. The trial had not concluded by the end of the year.

Most complaints of alleged human rights abuses committed during the February to March 1989 protests remained before the military courts (see *Amnesty International Report 1990*). No new prosecutions or convictions were reported in connection with these cases. In November, however, a civilian judge investigating irregularities in the disposal of the bodies of many of those killed in Caracas during the 1989 protests ordered the exhumation of unmarked mass graves believed to contain the remains of victims.

Two police officers charged with killing two students – Yulimar Reyes and Juan Carlos Celis Pérez – during the February 1989 protests, were released in May pending trial after the charges against them were reduced from murder to manslaughter. Their trials were continuing at the end of the year.

In September criminal charges were brought against 16 members of the *Policía Técnica Judicial* (PTJ), criminal investigations police, accused of torturing six detainees in 1989 (see *Amnesty International Report 1990*). One of the detainees, Nelson Arvelo Ceballo, who was unconditionally released in 1989, sought refuge in the Attorney General's Office in March 1990 following a series of threats from members of the PTJ. Nelson Arvelo Ceballo died in August; the police said he was killed in a road accident. His family claimed that his body appeared to have a bullet wound in the head. The state attorney in charge of the case ordered the exhumation of the body to determine the cause of death, but this had not been done by the end of the year.

In March Amnesty International published a report, *Venezuela: Reports of Arbitrary Killings and Torture: February/March 1989*, which reiterated concerns expressed in a letter sent to President Pérez in January. The organization called for the publication of the official list of those who had died in the 1989 protests. It also called for the exhumation of all bodies buried in common graves, and requested information about any measures taken to prevent further arbitrary killings and ill-treatment. The government acknowledged Amnesty International's letter but no substantive reply was received. In March Amnesty International wrote to the President requesting information about the death of Italo Alberto Vargas following a trade union demonstration in February; no response was received. In November a forensic anthropologist visited the country on behalf of Amnesty International to monitor the exhumation of unmarked graves in Caracas reportedly containing the remains of several of those killed in February and March 1989.

VIET NAM

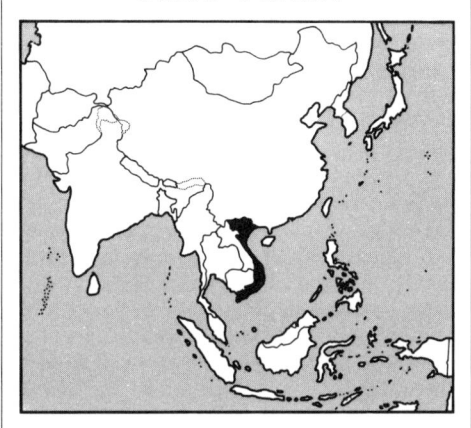

At least 60 known and possible prisoners of conscience remained in prison throughout 1990 and at least nine others were arrested during the year. The government confirmed that 128 prisoners detained in earlier years were still being held at a "re-education" camp. Six people were reportedly sentenced to death and there may also have been unreported death sentences. No executions were known to have been carried out.

The official policy of *dôi moi*, "renovation", under which reforms to protect human rights and to allow political debate were carried out between 1986 and 1989, suffered setbacks in 1990. In April the government confirmed that it was suppressing dissent and warned that force would be used to quash any attempt "to destabilize the socialist system". In June the official Vietnamese media announced the arrest of "many people accused of violating national security". Among those detained were known and suspected critics of the government.

At least 60 people who continued to be imprisoned throughout 1990 were believed to be prisoners of conscience or possible prisoners of conscience. At least four other prisoners of conscience and five possible prisoners of conscience were detained during the year, including two Roman Catholic priests, Chan Tin and Nguyen Ngoc Lan; Doan Than Liem, a lawyer; and Nguyen Dan Que, a doctor. The official Vietnamese media reported that the two priests had been arrested for offences including "carrying out activities aimed at opposing socialism". Chan Tin was also accused of giving anti-government sermons with the aim of "inciting Catholics to demand human and civil rights". Doan Than Liem was reportedly arrested on charges including involvement in the drafting of an unauthorized constitution. Dr Nguyen Dan Que, who had been imprisoned for political reasons from 1978 to 1988, was arrested in June after peacefully criticizing the government. In January he had become the first member of Amnesty International in Viet Nam. It remained unclear whether any of the nine detainees had been charged or tried.

Among the prisoners of conscience who continued to be held throughout the year were three Buddhist monks – Thich Tri Sieu, Thich Duc Nhuan and Thich Tue Sy – and a writer, Doan Quoc Sy. Dominic Tran Dinh Thu, a Roman Catholic priest who had been tried and sentenced with other defendants in 1987, was offered his release in January on the condition that he returned to live with his family. He refused, declaring that he would agree to be released only if his innocence was officially acknowledged, and on condition that he was allowed to return to his seminary and that all those tried with him were also released.

At least three prisoners of conscience were released. Ho Hieu Ha and Nguyen Huu Cong, two Protestant pastors convicted in 1987 of "preaching against the revolution", were freed in January (see *Amnesty International Reports 1988* and *1990*). Hoang Hai Thuy, a writer held since 1984, was released in February. Phan Van Lam Binh, a writer released from prison in 1989, reportedly continued to be subject to restrictions on his movement.

The government confirmed to Amnesty International in March that as of May 1989, 128 former soldiers and officials of the previous Republic of Viet Nam (RVN) government remained in a single "re-education" camp, referred to as K 1230D, at Ham Tan, Thuan Hai province. It provided no information to suggest that any of them had been freed since May 1989. Those detained included Tran Ngoc Diem, a former lieutenant-colonel in the RVN army who had been chief of security in Gia Dinh province. However, the situation of some former RVN military officers and civil servants who had been held in camps remained unclear. Among them were Truong Kim Cang, Nguyen Van Hao, Tran Ban Loc and Nguyen Khac Nghi.

The situation of a number of other prisoners, including possible prisoners of conscience, who were reported to have been detained without trial in previous years, remained unknown. They included Buddhist, Protestant and Roman Catholic clergy, former members of parliament, lawyers, teachers and students arrested for their political or religious beliefs and activities. Some of them were arrested after the collapse of the RVN Government in 1975. Among them were Nguyen Khac Chinh, a lawyer, and Truong Tuy Ba, a 72-year-old businesswoman.

In September the government declared an amnesty for around 700 prisoners on the occasion of the country's National Day, but the names of the released prisoners were not made public and it was not clear whether they included political prisoners.

Attempting to leave the country without official permission remained a crime under Articles 85, 88 and 89 of the Criminal Code. Anyone arrested for attempted "illegal departure" may be detained without trial or charged under the Criminal Code. There was no information about arrests of people attempting to leave the country illegally during the year. In March the Vietnamese media reported on the trial of 20 people, including five police officers, accused of organizing the illegal departure of some 1,000 people on payment of gold between September 1984 and March 1989. On 11 March the Ben Tre Provincial People's Court sentenced Phan Van Thanh, the leader of the group, to 20 years' imprisonment and his accomplices to jail terms ranging from three to 18 years. Lam Thi Tuyet and her five children, who had been detained without trial since February 1989 for attempting to leave the country by boat, were reportedly released in April 1990.

Political trials apparently continued with restricted rights to defence, contrary to the provisions of the Criminal Procedure Code introduced in 1989. Little information about such trials was available, although some details were received about a trial on 15 and 16 August in Ho Chi Minh City in which a Roman Catholic priest, Nguyen Van De, and 10 other Catholic priests and lay persons were convicted of spreading "counter-revolutionary propaganda through religious activities". Nguyen Van De was sentenced to 10 years' imprisonment and the other defendants to jail terms ranging from three to eight years.

Owing to restrictive legislation on the media adopted in December 1989 (see *Amnesty International Report 1990*), press reports of torture and ill-treatment were apparently discontinued. However, there were no firm indications that torture and ill-treatment had ceased to be used by police officers or as a form of discipline in "re-education" camps (see *Amnesty International Report 1990*).

Death sentences were rarely reported. In June the official army newspaper, *Quan Doi Nhan Dan*, reported that in the previous six months, during which an official crime suppression drive had been in progress, six people had been sentenced to death. No other details were published and there were no reports of executions.

In February Amnesty International published a report, *Viet Nam: "Renovation" (dôi moi), the Law and Human Rights in the 1980s*, which was partly based on the visit in May 1989 of an Amnesty International delegation to Viet Nam. While welcoming official moves to protect human rights, the report provided details of the organization's concerns in Viet Nam, including the continued detention without charge or trial of political prisoners, including prisoners of conscience; the imprisonment of prisoners of conscience on ill-defined charges of endangering national security; trials of political prisoners that fell far short of international standards; reports of torture and ill-treatment; and the use of the death penalty. The report was sent to the Vietnamese authorities with a request for their comments.

In March the Vietnamese Government replied that it had taken a series of measures "aimed at better guaranteeing the enjoyment of human rights and fundamental freedoms", and said that most of those sent for "re-education" had been released. The government also said that national security regulations did not hinder or restrict civil rights and that public trials and the right to legal defence were guaranteed by the Constitution and the Criminal

Code. It denied that there were any prisoners of conscience in Viet Nam, saying that some intellectuals had been imprisoned for violating the Criminal Code but not for their ideology or beliefs. The authorities said that people responsible for torturing or ill-treating prisoners would be brought to trial and that the death penalty was applied only in cases of serious crime as Viet Nam supports the long-term objective of abolishing the death penalty.

In a memorandum sent to the Vietnamese authorities in June, Amnesty International welcomed the government's comments but urged it to address urgently two aspects of Vietnamese law relating to human rights – legislation which appears to contravene international human rights standards, and discrepancies between the principles embodied in the legislation and their interpretation in practice. The organization appealed to the government to demonstrate that the human rights of its citizens were protected in practice, and to release those imprisoned for the peaceful expression of their beliefs or for their legitimate political or religious activities. The memorandum also referred to the detention in April and May of nine known or suspected government critics. In July Vietnamese officials said that two of the nine had not been detained. This statement could not be independently verified. The officials did not clarify the situation of the other seven detainees.

In August in an oral statement to the United Nations Sub-Commission on Prevention of Discrimination and Protection of Minorities, Amnesty International included a reference to prisoners of conscience being detained in Viet Nam on grounds of allegedly endangering national security.

YEMEN

In May the People's Democratic Republic of Yemen (PDRY) and the Yemen Arab Republic (YAR) united to form a single state – the Republic of Yemen. All known political detainees and prisoners arrested in 1990 and in previous years in the PDRY were released prior to unification. In the YAR, one prisoner of conscience was released in January; it was not possible to confirm the release or continued detention of one other prisoner of conscience and 25 suspected political opponents, including possible prisoners of conscience. Released detainees alleged torture and ill-treatment in both the former PDRY and YAR. The cases of 50 people who "disappeared" in the PDRY and YAR in previous years remained unresolved. Unconfirmed reports were received of three extrajudicial executions in the YAR. At least two death sentences were carried out in the YAR. Since unification no death sentences were known to have been ratified by the Presidential Council, which commuted eight death sentences in November.

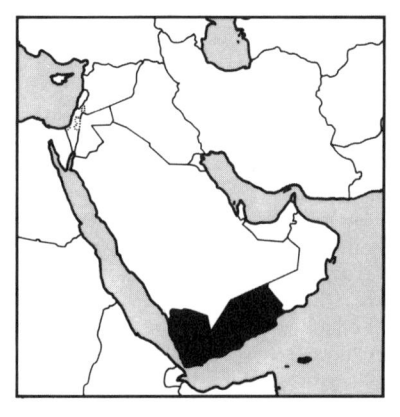

Following unification, a Presidential Council was set up to oversee the executive functions of the state during a 30-month transitional period, leading up to general elections. General 'Ali 'Abdullah Saleh, previously President of the YAR, became its Chairman, and 'Ali Salim al-Bidh, previously General Secretary of the Central Committee of the Yemeni Socialist Party of the PDRY, became its Vice-Chairman. The parliaments of the former PDRY and YAR merged and approved a new constitution.

Yemen's new constitution guarantees civil and political rights, and prohibits the use of "inhuman methods" of punishment and the promulgation of laws allowing such practices. In accordance with the Unity Agreement, the Republic of Yemen became a State Party to the International Covenant on Civil and Political Rights. In December the Presidential Council approved the government's decision to accede to the United Nations (UN) Convention against Torture and Other Cruel, Inhuman or Degrading Treatment or Punishment, and confirmed the decision taken in January by the Joint Council of Ministers to abolish the use of shackles in prisons.

YEMEN

Starting in May, the Parliament debated draft laws concerning freedom of the press and the judicial system. The Press Law was passed in December.

Between January and May, the authorities in the PDRY released 20 possible prisoners of conscience who had been held without trial. They included 11 suspected members of the previously banned *al-Ikhwan al-Muslimun*, Muslim Brothers, arrested in February 1988; seven suspected supporters of former president 'Ali Nasser Muhammad, who were arrested in March 1989; and Sa'id Aghbari and Muhammad Saleh al-Hammati, suspected government opponents arrested in 1987 and 1986 respectively (see *Amnesty International Reports 1989* and *1990*).

In January the government of the then PDRY released 33 other political prisoners in an amnesty. They had been convicted in connection with events in 1986 and 1989 of supporting former president 'Ali Nasser Muhammad who had been ousted in 1986 (see *Amnesty International Reports 1987* to *1990*).

In March between 100 and 150 people were arrested following demonstrations reportedly organized by Islamic groups in Aden and al-Mukalla in the then PDRY. The demonstrators, who included male and female students, reportedly called for the segregation of the sexes and the compulsory wearing of the *hijab* (veil) in schools. The majority of arrests took place in Aden on 20 March. Most of those detained were released the same day; five were released uncharged 10 days later. In al-Mukalla, 13 people were arrested on 24 March after a similar demonstration. Nine of them were released uncharged several days later. The four others were initially held at the State Security Detention Centre in al-Mukalla and later at the Central Prison of the Governorate of Hadhramawt. One of the detainees, Muhsin 'Ali Ba Surra, an agricultural engineer, was arrested by State Security officials while making inquiries about his brother who had been detained earlier in connection with the al-Mukalla demonstration. By the end of April all of them had been released.

In the then YAR, 'Abdo Fari' al-'Ubad, a prisoner of conscience who was only 16 years old when he was arrested in October 1989, was released uncharged in January. He had been detained because of his father's political activities. The situation of another prisoner of conscience, 'Ayesh 'Ali 'Ubad, who was only 12 years old when he was arrested in 1987 (see *Amnesty International Report 1990*), and of 25 other detainees, was unclear at the end of 1990. The 25, who included possible prisoners of conscience, were all suspected supporters of the prohibited National Democratic Front (NDF) who had been arrested between 1984 and 1988 (see *Amnesty International Report 1990*).

New allegations of torture and ill-treatment of prisoners in previous years in both former Yemeni states were received in 1990. Ahmad Nasser al-Fadhli, a Yemeni Socialist Party official who had been held in solitary confinement at al-Fateh detention centre in Aden for over six months following his arrest in January 1988, was reportedly beaten all over his body, deprived of sleep for three days and forced to stand for 48 hours. 'Ali Muhammad Nu'man, a trade unionist who had been held incommunicado and in solitary confinement in the YAR for six years up to 1989 (see *Amnesty International Report 1990*), said he had been tortured throughout his detention. He was held at *al-Amn al-Watani* (National Security) detention centres in Ta'iz and al-Hadda, where he was reportedly beaten all over his body with metal cables, confined for one year in a small cell, and kept permanently shackled.

In January the Joint Council of Ministers abolished the use of shackles in the YAR. This ruling was confirmed by the government of the Republic of Yemen in November. However, shackles were said to be still in use, including in prisons in Ta'iz and Sana'a, at the end of 1990.

The cases of 50 political detainees who "disappeared" after arrest between 1967 and 1986 in the PDRY and YAR remained unresolved. Among them were magistrates, engineers, army officers and senior state officials (see *Amnesty International Reports 1981*, *1982*, *1983*, *1987*, *1989* and *1990*). In some cases, the relatives of such detainees had themselves been arrested and had "disappeared" after making inquiries about the fate of their family members.

Three people were reportedly extrajudicially executed in the YAR in March because they were suspected of causing an explosion at the Grand Mosque in Sana'a.

At least two people convicted of murder in the YAR and whose sentences were ratified before unification, were executed during the year. At least 14 other death sentences were pending ratification by the Presidential Council at the end of 1990. In November eight members of the former NDF who had been sentenced to death by the YAR authorities in 1985 (see *Amnesty International Report 1990*) were given clemency.

The scheduled execution of Hassan Yussif al-Bishri, a former soldier in the YAR army who had been sentenced to death for murder in 1986, was postponed in November. His trial was allegedly marked by procedural irregularities, including the refusal of the court to allow at least one prosecution witness to retract the statements he had made against the defendant.

An Amnesty International delegation visited the Republic of Yemen in November at the invitation of the government, and met the Chairman and Vice-Chairman of the Presidential Council and other ministers and officials. The organization welcomed the releases of political prisoners in the former PDRY and submitted a memorandum to the unity government summarizing Amnesty International's outstanding concerns in Yemen. It sought clarification of the cases of 25 members of the former NDF arrested between 1984 and 1988, and of the fate of 50 suspected political opponents who "disappeared" in detention between 1967 and 1986. The organization requested details of the trial proceedings in the cases of seven people arrested in 1987 on charges of sabotage (see *Amnesty International Report 1990*). Amnesty International reiterated its request for an investigation into the deaths in custody in the past two years of seven political detainees. It called for the establishment of a judicial review into the legal proceedings in the cases of Hassan al-Bishri and eight members of the former NDF who had been under sentence of death, urged that no further death sentences be ratified and appealed for the commutation of all current death sentences. The organization also sought confirmation of the reported extrajudicial execution in March of three people in Sana'a. Amnesty International urged the government to accede to the UN Convention against Torture and Other Cruel, Inhuman or Degrading Treatment or Punishment.

In its response in December, the government denied holding any political prisoners. It stated that it had no information on 'Ayesh 'Ali 'Ubad, a prisoner of conscience. Of the 25 suspected NDF members whose cases were raised in Amnesty International's memorandum, the government said that six had been released, three were to be released by the end of the year, six had been tried and sentenced for criminal offences, and that it had no information on the remaining 10. The government asserted that allegations of torture were inaccurate, and that the deaths in custody referred to by Amnesty International had resulted from natural causes. Regarding "disappearances" and extrajudicial executions, the government attributed such violations in the former PDRY to "the regrettable events of January 1986". Of the 17 "disappearance" cases in the former YAR, the government said four had been released, one had died in custody of natural causes and that it had no information on the 12 other cases, including that of the former minister Colonel Sultan Amin al-Qirshi. The government also said that killings of suspected political opponents in the former YAR had resulted from acts of vengeance by individual citizens. It denied the extrajudicial execution of three people in March.

At the end of the year, Amnesty International was seeking further clarification on all of these concerns.

YUGOSLAVIA

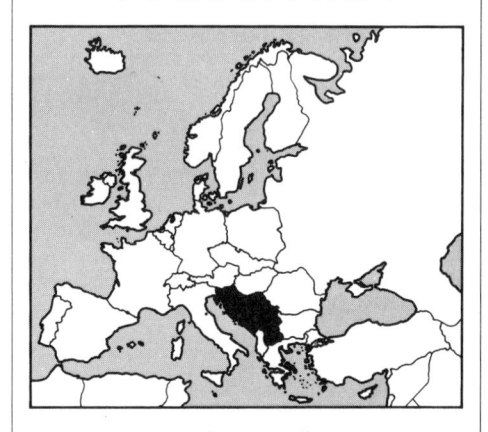

Over 1,000 ethnic Albanians were imprisoned in Kosovo province for up to 60 days for going on strike or for peacefully expressing nationalist sentiments. The number of prisoners of conscience serving long terms of imprisonment decreased significantly as a result of pardons, early releases and acquittals: by the end of the

year they numbered some 35. At least 30 ethnic Albanian demonstrators or onlookers were killed and several hundred others wounded during clashes between demonstrators and police. It was alleged that the police had used excessive and indiscriminate force. There were many allegations that police had beaten and otherwise ill-treated people under arrest. Conditions in some prisons were said to be harsh. At least four people were sentenced to death for murder, but no executions were reported.

Numerous opposition parties were legally established throughout the country and by the end of the year multi-party elections had taken place in all six republics. Nationalist parties won four of these elections, while communists retained power in Serbia (where they were renamed socialists) and in Montenegro. Slovenia and Croatia demanded that Yugoslavia cease to be a federation and become a confederation of states. Ethnic conflict intensified in Kosovo province; in July the Serbian parliament suspended the Kosovo parliament and government after ethnic Albanian members of the Kosovo parliament declared Kosovo independent of the republic of Serbia. Thousands of ethnic Albanians who refused to declare their approval for these measures lost their jobs, and the main local media in the Albanian language were banned. In September Serbia adopted a new constitution which deprived its two provinces, Kosovo and Vojvodina, of most of their autonomy.

Changes to the federal criminal code adopted in June significantly reduced the scope for prosecuting people for the non-violent exercise of their human rights. For example, Article 133, under which many prisoners of conscience had been imprisoned in the past for the non-violent exercise of their right to freedom of expression, was amended so as to prohibit only the advocacy of violent change to the constitutional order.

In March Yugoslavia signed the first Optional Protocol to the International Covenant on Civil and Political Rights; it had not yet ratified this by the end of the year.

Between 24 January and 3 February there were violent clashes between the police and ethnic Albanian demonstrators in many parts of Kosovo province after ethnic Albanians, who form some 85 per cent of the province's population, called for greater independence from Serbia, the resignation of local political leaders and the release of political prisoners. During the clashes at least 30 ethnic Albanians died and several hundred others, including police officers, were injured. An investigation carried out by police and judicial investigators claimed in a report in March that in almost all cases police officers had resorted to firearms only after being shot at by demonstrators. It stated that the police had used firearms improperly in only two incidents, and that the circumstances of four other deaths required further clarification. However, the report cited one incident in which police officers had used firearms although demonstrators had not fired at them. According to the report, on 31 January demonstrators in Košare village erected barricades and were throwing stones at police. After other "physical and chemical methods" had failed to restore order, police officers fired shots, allegedly into the air, killing 15-year-old Bekim Sejdiu.

Unofficial sources alleged that there were other incidents in which the police shot and killed people who had not fired on them. On 29 January Rexhep Aliu was killed by stray police bullets outside his garage on the outskirts of Uroševac as police chased a group of fleeing demonstrators. The report stated that the officers were returning fire; however, unofficial sources alleged that although there was violent rioting in the town at the time, there was no shooting by demonstrators in the vicinity. On 30 January Sadri Maksuti was severely wounded when police fired at demonstrators in Stanovac village. A local human rights committee in Kosovo alleged that police officers subsequently dragged Sadri Maksuti from a car which was taking him to hospital, and beat him to death. The driver of the car was also reportedly beaten.

Almost 600 demonstrators were sentenced and imprisoned for up to 60 days for their part in the protests; it was not possible to assess whether they included prisoners of conscience. In mid-March the press reported that police had filed 2,381 requests for proceedings against those who had contravened compulsory work orders, introduced under emergency measures, by striking in support of the demonstrations. Among them were 676 workers from Goleš mines, 85 of whom had been sentenced to between 30 and 60 days' imprisonment by 21 March. In June it was reported that proceedings were under way against 2,597 workers from Kosovo's Trepča mine alone.

By June, 391 ethnic Albanians in Kosovo had been arrested and proceedings had been initiated against 433 people for making a "V" (victory) sign to express their disagreement with official Serbian policy in the province – thus allegedly "disturbing public order" and "offending the socialist and patriotic sentiments of citizens". Scores of other ethnic Albanians were sentenced during the year to up to 60 days' imprisonment for alleged breaches of public order for peacefully expressing political dissent. In July Shefqet Haziri, Ramush Jashari and Islam Bjegova were sentenced in Priština to 30 days' imprisonment for hanging in their office a picture of Ibrahim Rugova, the leader of Kosovo's largest ethnic Albanian opposition party. In August Hajrullah Gorani and Ilir Tollaj, respectively President and Vice-President of the Union of Independent Trade Unions in Kosovo, were sentenced to 60 days' imprisonment for calling on ethnic Albanians to join in a general strike in Kosovo province on 3 September in protest against the dismissal of ethnic Albanians from their jobs. In October Qazim Kovaçi was sentenced to 45 days' imprisonment by a court in Montenegro for selling a book about the ethnic Albanian writer Adem Demaçi and an Albanian-language magazine.

In April the federal Presidency released 108 political prisoners and reduced the sentences of 115 others. Among the prisoners of conscience released was Adem Demaçi, whose 15-year prison sentence, his third for political offences, was due to expire in October. Officials stated in May that 190 political prisoners were still serving sentences, including 160 ethnic Albanians. Further releases followed: in May the federal Assembly granted an amnesty to all those prosecuted or convicted for "hostile propaganda" or "damaging the reputation of Yugoslavia" (under Articles 133 and 157). Press reports stated that there were only two prisoners serving sentences imposed under Article 133 at the time, but did not make clear how many were serving sentences imposed under Article 157. In June the Croatian Presidency released early on parole 37 political prisoners; the majority of them were ethnic Albanians.

According to official sources, only two political prisoners, who were not yet eligible for early release, remained in Croatian prisons. In November the federal Presidency granted pardons to or dropped charges pending against 564 people; 124 of them were released from prison and 69 had their sentences reduced.

In April Azem Vllasi, the former president of the Kosovo communist party, and 13 other ethnic Albanians were acquitted by the district court of Titova Mitrovica on grounds of lack of evidence. They had been charged with "counter-revolutionary undermining of the social order" for having allegedly organized or supported strikes at Stari Trg mine in February 1989 (see *Amnesty International Report 1990*). An appeal by the prosecution against the acquittal had not been concluded by the end of 1990.

On 7 September ethnic Albanian deputies of the suspended Kosovo assembly met clandestinely and adopted a constitution proclaiming Kosovo a republic within the Yugoslav federation. On 17 September four deputies – Raif Ramabaja, Nazif Matoshi, Ismail Sahiti and Fatos Pula – were arrested and charged under Article 116 of the federal criminal code with having aimed to unconstitutionally change Serbia's borders and proclaim Kosovo province a republic. The Serbian assembly revoked their parliamentary immunity from prosecution. However, on 25 October the Supreme Court of Kosovo ordered their release. On 21 September similar charges had been brought against Agim Mala, the former director of Priština television, and six former Kosovo government officials, including Prime Minister Jusuf Zejnullahu and Secretary of the Interior Jusuf Karakushi. Most of them were outside Kosovo at the time, but two – Seladin Skeja and Lekë Vuksani – were arrested. Zenun Çelaj, a journalist and human rights activist, was arrested on 27 September and charged under Article 116 for writing and publishing a report on the meeting of 7 September; he was released on 27 October. None of these men was accused of having used or advocated violence, but investigation proceedings continued against all of them.

In April the Serbian authorities took over policing in Kosovo province. Frequent reports continued to be received of police beating or otherwise ill-treating ethnic

Albanians in detention. For example, on 1 May, as large crowds were leaving a village near Dečani after a ceremony marking the end of a traditional blood feud, the police reportedly forced several dozen young people to get out of their cars after some people had made a "V" sign. The young people were beaten and taken to a local police station. Two of them, Lutfi Gashi and Sevdali Sherifi, were later taken with injuries to a local medical clinic where two police officers treated them after expelling the doctor on duty. On 18 May police allegedly stopped Bashkim Gërlica from Priština and asked for his papers. When they found in his possession a photograph of Anton Çetta, who had taken a leading part in a campaign to end blood feuds, they reportedly took him to a local police station, beat him and forced him to swallow his engagement ring. On 23 July Xhevdat Sadiku from Gnjilane was arrested and taken to a police station after police officers saw a photograph of Ibrahim Rugova in his shop window. He was reportedly beaten so badly in custody that he was admitted to hospital in Priština on 24 July. On his discharge four days later, he was issued with a medical certificate stating that he had suffered injuries to his head and body and that blood had been found in his urine. Many similar incidents were reported in subsequent months.

There were also reports of police violence in several incidents which took place outside Kosovo. On 13 June police officers reportedly beat a number of demonstrators who had gathered outside Belgrade television studios in a peaceful protest against editorial policy. Among those injured were Dragoljub Mićunović, a leader of a Serbian opposition party, and Ljubiša Mitić, whose collar bone was broken.

In September the Bar Association of Macedonia appealed for the release of nonviolent political prisoners. They stated that conditions at Idrizovo prison in Macedonia were poor and that punitive measures taken against prisoners on an almost daily basis had provoked a revolt by prisoners in October. Conditions in Stara Gradiška prison in Croatia and Zenica prison in Bosnia-Hercegovina were described by former prisoners as harsh. In February a court in Vranje sentenced four prison guards to three months' imprisonment each on charges of having beaten 18 ethnic Albanian detainees in March 1989 (see *Amnesty International Report 1990*). Twelve other prison guards were acquitted.

In March Xhafer Kurteshi and Rifet Hajrić, both convicted of murder and rape, were sentenced to death. Two people were sentenced to death for murder; Milan Tanić in April and Fikret Fehrić in December. No executions were reported. On 21 December a new constitution adopted in Croatia abolished the death penalty.

In May an Amnesty International delegation met federal and Serbian officials in Belgrade, discussed the organization's concerns in Yugoslavia and were informed about forthcoming legislative changes. In November the organization sent a memorandum to the authorities in which it welcomed certain legal reforms, but urged the release of all prisoners of conscience and expressed concern about allegations of police abuses in Kosovo province. It called on the government to initiate an independent investigation into the deaths of demonstrators in January and February and to ensure that security forces operated in accordance with internationally recognized norms.

ZAIRE

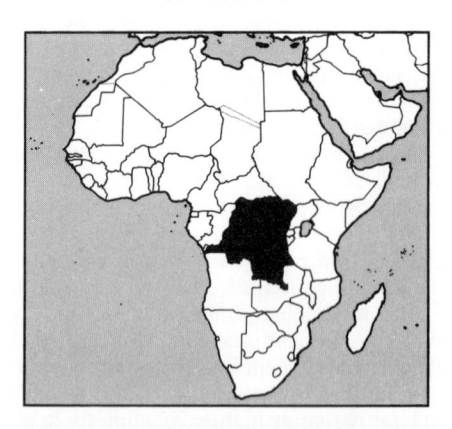

More than 100 government opponents were arrested and held without charge, including prisoners of conscience, but most were released by the end of the year. Many were beaten at the time of arrest, and two were said to have died as a result. Up to a dozen students were reportedly killed in an attack in which the security forces were implicated: at least 11 officials were arrested after a preliminary inquiry but the government did not respond to calls for a further inquiry. At least 24 people remained under sentence of death but no executions were reported.

In April President Mobutu Sese Seko announced that Zaire would cease to be a one-party state and that two new political parties and independent trade unions would be permitted. The ruling party – renamed in July the *Mouvement populaire pour le renouveau* (MPR), Popular Movement for Renewal – had been the only political party permitted by law since President Mobutu took power in 1965. A new constitution was adopted by the National Assembly in July, which eliminated references to the MPR's dominant role in government, and dozens of new political parties were formed before the end of the year.

In April President Mobutu said that the security forces were to become apolitical and in May the government's National Security Council announced that administrative and incommunicado detention and internal banishment would no longer be used. The National Security Council said that security service detention centres would be used only to detain suspects for short periods for questioning. In August the national security service was renamed the *Service national d'intelligence et de protection* (SNIP), National Intelligence and Protection Service. Despite these developments, however, the security services continued to carry out unlawful arrests and detentions.

Tshisekedi wa Mulumba, leader of *Union pour la démocratie et le progrès social* (UDPS), Union for Democracy and Social Progress, an unauthorized opposition party, was released. He had been under house arrest since March 1989 (see *Amnesty International Report 1990*). Most other prisoners of conscience were released either after the announcement of political reforms in April, or after the National Security Council announced in May that all uncharged political prisoners were to be freed. They included Albert Mola and Philippe Mamonekene, two members of Tshisekedi wa Mulumba's household arrested in July 1989. In May Kabongo Ntambwa (see *Amnesty International Report 1990*) had restrictions on his freedom of movement lifted. In July Tshitshinga Kanyinda and three other political prisoners sentenced after an unfair trial in 1987 (see *Amnesty International Report 1988*) were freed as a result of a presidential amnesty.

However, banishment orders imposed in 1987 on two high-ranking army officers, General Mukobo Mundende Popolo and Major Kayembe Mbandonkulu, apparently remained in force.

More than 100 suspected or known supporters of the UDPS and other political groups were detained during the year for short periods without referral to judicial authorities. Omene Samba was rearrested (see *Amnesty International Report 1990*) in January, together with dozens of other members or supporters of the UDPS, the day before a planned pro-democracy demonstration in the capital, Kinshasa. They were all released within several weeks.

At least 14 other UDPS members were detained in April after members of the security forces violently broke up a UDPS meeting at a house in Kinshasa. Two of those present – Denis Mwamba and Bwala Bwala – were said to have died as a result of injuries they sustained during the incident, in which dozens of others were wounded. Those arrested were released after a few days.

At least six journalists were also detained for short periods either because of their contact with Tshisekedi wa Mulumba or because they wrote articles critical of the government.

Government opponents still held at the end of the year included Digekisa Piluka, a Roman Catholic friar and student leader at Lubumbashi University. He was arrested in May apparently in connection with unrest at the university and possibly because he tried to publicize an incident at the university on 11 May in which a number of students were killed. About 30 other students arrested in connection with demonstrations in Lubumbashi and Kinshasa were also believed to be held with him at Makala prison in Kinshasa at the end of 1990. It was unclear whether a pre-trial judicial investigation of their cases had begun.

Other government critics arrested during the year included Ekongo Odimba and at least three other members of the *Mouvement national congolais–Lumumba* (MNC–L), Congolese National Movement–Lumumba wing, who were arrested while demonstrating peacefully in Kinshasa in July. They were held incommunicado for several weeks and then released uncharged. At least 15 members of the *Parti lumumbiste unifié* (PALU), Unified

Lumumbist Party, were arrested while demonstrating peacefully in Kinshasa in October. They were released in November. In both cases, those arrested were held by the security forces without having their cases referred to the procuracy.

Some political arrests were accompanied by violence on the part of the security forces. In July at least 12 UDPS members who were arrested at a meeting in Kinshasa's Kimbaseke district were beaten and two women among them were said to have been raped. All of them were released before the end of the month.

In May there were reports that up to a dozen students were killed during a night raid at Lubumbashi University campus by the security forces. Soldiers dressed in civilian clothes were said to have attacked the students; some sources suggested that between 50 and 150 students were killed and hundreds of others injured, but there was no independent evidence to support such estimates. The raid occurred after three students accused of being government informers were severely assaulted by other students. The government initially denied any responsibility for the killings. However, a parliamentary inquiry accused the governor of Shaba region and at least 10 other government and security officials in Lubumbashi of complicity in the attack and of failing to prevent it. The 11 officials were arrested but had not been tried by the end of the year. The inquiry did not establish how many students had been killed or injured, nor the identities of their attackers, and it recommended that a further, more thorough inquiry be carried out. The government maintained that only one student had died and did not order another inquiry.

Twenty-four people convicted of murder and robbery in September and October 1989, and an unknown number of other prisoners, remained under sentence of death. Amnesty International did not learn of any new death sentences or executions during the year.

Amnesty International appealed for the release of prisoners of conscience, including those under banishment orders, and for all death sentences to be commuted. The organization called for a full and impartial inquiry into the attack on students at Lubumbashi University to establish the number and identity of those killed and the nature and extent of official complicity, and urged that those responsible for the killings be brought to justice.

The Ministry for the Citizen's Rights and Freedoms told Amnesty International that government officials had been arrested and would be prosecuted in connection with the attack. However, the ministry, which has a responsibility to investigate alleged human rights abuses, rarely responded to other appeals or inquiries made by Amnesty International. In September Amnesty International published a report, *The Republic of Zaire: Outside the Law – Security Force Repression of Government Opponents, 1988-1990*, which described the organization's concerns about political imprisonment, security force violence and other abuses. The report included recommendations to the government regarding measures needed to protect human rights.

ZAMBIA

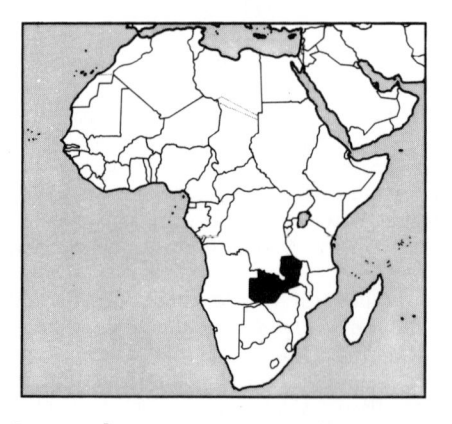

Suspected government opponents were detained without charge or trial for periods ranging from a few days to over one month and hundreds of people were reportedly beaten at the time of arrest during riots in June. However, all those arrested and all political prisoners were released in an amnesty in August. At least three people were sentenced to death but no executions were reported.

In June there were three days of violent demonstrations in Lusaka and other towns. According to official figures, 29 people were killed and over 150 injured. Many were shot dead by police or paramilitary forces while looting or breaking the curfew imposed by the authorities. Some were said to have been the victims of indiscriminate shooting by the security forces. Other people were reportedly beaten and arrested.

Shortly after the rioting, President Kenneth Kaunda survived an apparent coup attempt. Six soldiers and one civilian were arrested and held until August before being released in a government amnesty.

Following the riots, the Movement for Multi-Party Democracy (MMD) was formed to campaign for an end to the one-party state. The government initially resisted this demand. However, in September it announced that multi-party elections would be held in 1991 and amended the Constitution to allow political parties other than the ruling United National Independence Party.

The Penal Code was amended in June to allow the courts discretion when sentencing prisoners convicted of murder, which had previously carried a mandatory death sentence. However, there appeared to be no provision for a review of existing death sentences which had been imposed for murder. At least 200 prisoners who had received the mandatory death sentence for murder were believed to be awaiting execution.

More than 40 suspected government opponents were arrested in the wake of the riots. They included 32 University of Zambia students who were arrested in a dawn raid on the university campus the day after the riots had ended, some of whom were reportedly beaten at the time of their arrest. Six other students were arrested a few days later. All 38 were detained under the Preservation of Public Security Regulations, which permit indefinite detention without charge or trial, until August. They were then released in the amnesty granted by the government to alleged rioters, curfew-breakers and others. All 38 students were prisoners of conscience.

Others arrested for political reasons included Stephen Mukata, the Nkana Branch Chairman of the Union of Mineworkers, and Peter Chiko Bwalya, a former long-term political detainee. Stephen Mukata was released uncharged after a few days. Peter Chiko Bwalya was eventually charged in connection with an illegal demonstration, fined and released in August.

The August amnesty also resulted in the release of other political prisoners, including former army commander Lieutenant-General Christon Tembo and three other army officers charged with treason (see *Amnesty International Report 1989*). Their trial had begun in January but had not been completed. Former High Court commissioner Edward Shamwana and three others convicted of treason in 1983 were also released. Originally sentenced to death, their sentences were commuted to life imprisonment in 1986 after international appeals for clemency (see *Amnesty International Reports 1983* to *1987*).

As campaigning to promote multi-party elections intensified, Frederick Chiluba, the Vice-Chairman of the MMD, and eight local government officials were arrested in Choma in October. They were charged with holding an unauthorized meeting before being released on bail. Their case had not been heard by the end of the year.

At least three people were sentenced to death for murder but there were no reports of executions.

Amnesty International appealed for the release of prisoners of conscience and expressed concern about alleged beatings in custody.

ZIMBABWE

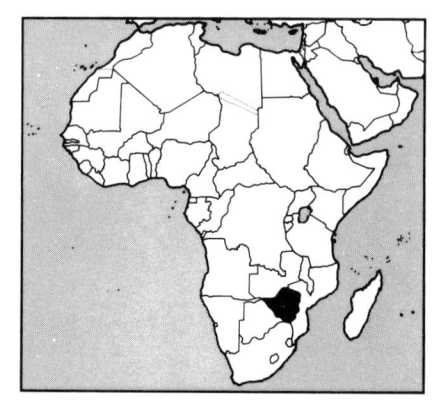

Several critics or opponents of the government were briefly detained without charge or trial; two were allegedly assaulted by intelligence officers. However, all long-term political detainees were released before the state of emergency was lifted in July and dozens of sentenced political prisoners were freed in an amnesty. They included over 50 prisoners who had been under sentence of death. At least three

other people were sentenced to death during 1990 but no executions were reported.

There was continuing insecurity along the eastern border owing to incursions and killings by guerrillas fighting the Mozambican Government. The national state of emergency which had been in force continuously since 1965 was lifted in July. As a result, the Emergency Powers (Maintenance of Law and Order) Regulations, which had provided for indefinite detention without charge or trial, were withdrawn; all untried political detainees, totalling at least eight, were released shortly after. In July the government also declared an amnesty for criminal prisoners, among them armed opponents of the government and prisoners serving sentences for human rights abuses committed in the early 1980s in Matabeleland. A committee set up to review cases had authorized the release of 1,400 people, most of them petty criminal offenders, by November.

In October the Supreme Court declared solitary confinement to be inhuman or degrading, and therefore unconstitutional. A similar ruling was expected to be made in November in relation to hanging, thereby effectively abolishing the death penalty, following an appeal to the Supreme Court by Douglas Chitiza, a soldier sentenced to death for murder. The appeal was not heard but Douglas Chitiza was released the day before it was due. However, the government introduced legislation in December to amend the Constitution so as to provide that neither hanging as a method of execution, nor corporal punishment for male juveniles (which the Supreme Court had declared unconstitutional in 1989) could be challenged on the grounds that they constitute inhuman or degrading punishment.

Several opposition activists were arrested following elections in March which saw the ruling Zimbabwe African National Union – Patriotic Front (ZANU-PF) headed by Robert Mugabe returned to office with an overwhelming majority. Before the election, Patrick Kombayi, a candidate for the opposition Zimbabwe Unity Movement (ZUM), was shot and seriously injured in suspicious circumstances. There were allegations that members of the government's Central Intelligence Organization (CIO) were involved, although this could not be confirmed. Those responsible for the shooting escaped arrest.

In April Paul Razika, Patrick Kombayi's election agent who had been with him at the time of the shooting, was arrested and held without charge or trial for 20 days. He was rearrested in May with three other ZUM activists: they were accused by the authorities of recruiting people for military training in South Africa. All four, however, were released uncharged within two weeks. They appeared to be prisoners of conscience.

Newman Ndlela, a defeated ZUM candidate, was also briefly detained in April. He was moved from place to place by police in Bulawayo, apparently to deny him access to his lawyer before he had made a statement and been brought to court. He was released on bail the day after he was charged with illegal possession of arms of war, a charge which arose from possession of a gun in the early 1980s. In July the case against him was dropped.

Five student leaders were arrested in October following demonstrations by students in Harare against legislative changes by the government which placed the university more directly under the control of its Vice-Chancellor and the Minister of Higher Education. This followed previous student unrest in 1989, which had resulted in arrests (see *Amnesty International Report 1990*). The five students were held without charge for a few days and then released.

Two detainees alleged that they were beaten in custody. Kembo Dube Bango and Soft Nhari, both ZUM activists, said they were ill-treated for 24 hours by CIO officers while held at Stops Camp, an interrogation centre within Mzilikazi police station in Bulawayo.

The amnesty declared by the government resulted in the release of more than 50 former government opponents under sentence of death. Most had been sentenced for murder and other violent crimes committed in Matabeleland in the early 1980s.

At least three people were convicted of murder and sentenced to death during 1990 and the Supreme Court confirmed one death sentence imposed for murder and rape. However, no executions were known to have been carried out.

Amnesty International appealed for the release of Paul Razika and other prisoners of conscience and urged an official investigation into the shooting of Patrick

Kombayi. Amnesty International also expressed concern to the government about its amendment of the Constitution to retain hanging and reintroduce whipping as a punishment for male juveniles. The organization urged that steps be taken to abolish the death penalty.

APPENDICES

APPENDIX I

AMNESTY INTERNATIONAL VISITS BETWEEN 1 JANUARY AND 31 DECEMBER 1990

DATE	COUNTRY	PURPOSE	DELEGATE(S)
January	Romania	Research	– Two staff members of International Secretariat
January	United Kingdom	Observe court hearing	– Staff member of International Secretariat
January/February	Morocco	Research	– Two staff members of International Secretariat
January/February	Namibia	Research	– Two staff members of International Secretariat
February	Uganda	Research/Discuss Amnesty International's concerns with government authorities	– Two staff members of International Secretariat
February	Denmark	Trial observation	– Per Stadig (Sweden)
February	Morocco	Discuss Amnesty International's concerns with government authorities	– Peter Duffy (International Executive Committee) – Alain Faure (France) – Staff member of International Secretariat
February/March	Trinidad, Barbados, Bahamas	Research/Discuss Amnesty International's concerns with government authorities	– Two staff members of International Secretariat
February/March	Bulgaria	Research/Discuss Amnesty International's concerns with government authorities	– Dick Oosting (Netherlands) – Staff member of International Secretariat
March	Jordan	Discuss Amnesty International's concerns with government authorities	– Secretary General of Amnesty International – Zaki Badawi (UK/Egypt) – Staff member of International Secretariat
March	Romania	Trial observation	– Nicolas Ulmer (Switzerland)
March	Yemen (People's Democratic Republic of)	Research	– Staff member of International Secretariat
March	Norway	Trial observation	– Lars Adam Rehof (Denmark)
March	Morocco	Research/Discuss Amnesty International's concerns with government authorities	– Two staff members of International Secretariat
March/April	Greece	Trial observation	– Staff member of International Secretariat
April	Taiwan (Republic of China)	Trial observation	– Carlye Chu (Hong Kong Resident)
April	Nepal	Research/Discuss Amnesty International's concerns with government authorities	– Stephanie Grant (UK) – Jorgen Thomsen (Denmark) – Staff member of International Secretariat
April	Brazil	Research/Discuss Amnesty International's concerns with government authorities	– Staff member of International Secretariat
April	Papua New Guinea	Research/Discuss Amnesty International's concerns with government authorities	– Dick Oosting (Netherlands) – Staff member of International Secretariat
April	Philippines	Research	– Two staff members of International Secretariat
April	Germany (Federal Republic of)	Trial observation	– Douwe Korff (Netherlands)

APPENDIX I

DATE	COUNTRY	PURPOSE	DELEGATE(S)
April	South Africa	Research	– Paul Gallagher (Ireland) – Staff member of International Secretariat
April	Turkey	Research/Trial observation	– Staff member of International Secretariat
April	South Africa	Observe proceedings of Judicial Commission of Inquiry	– Staff member of International Secretariat
April/May	Colombia	Research/Discuss Amnesty International's concerns with government authorities	– Marta Fotsch (Switzerland) – Two staff members of International Secretariat
April/May	El Salvador	Research/Discuss Amnesty International's concerns with government authorities	– Three staff members of International Secretariat
May	Egypt	Discuss Amnesty International's concerns with government authorities	– Secretary General of Amnesty International – Rashid Bel Alouna (Tunisia) – Two staff members of International Secretariat
May	Turkey	Research	– Staff member of International Secretariat
May	Yugoslavia	Discuss Amnesty International's concerns with government authorities	– Peter Baehr (International Executive Committee) – Stephen Owen (Canada) – Staff member of International Secretariat
May	USSR	Research	– Staff member of International Secretariat
May	Kuwait	Research/Discuss Amnesty International's concerns with government authorities	– Two staff members of International Secretariat
May	Benin	Research/Discuss Amnesty International's concerns with government authorities	– Two staff members of International Secretariat
May/June	Mexico	Research/Discuss Amnesty International's concerns with government authorities	– Two staff members of International Secretariat
June	Peru	Research/Discuss Amnesty International's concerns with government authorities	– Two staff members of International Secretariat
June	Brazil	Discuss Amnesty International's concerns with government authorities	– Bacre Waly Ndiaye (International Executive Committee) – Two staff members of International Secretariat
June	Tunisia	Research	– Staff member of International Secretariat
June	United Kingdom	Research	– Nanko Doornbos (Netherlands) – Staff member of International Secretariat
June	Greece	Research	– Staff member of International Secretariat
June/July	Romania	Research	– Staff member of International Secretariat
July	South Africa	Research	– Staff member of International Secretariat
July/August	Israel/Occupied Territories	Research/Observe Court Hearing	– Two staff members of International Secretariat
August	Honduras	Research/Discuss Amnesty International's concerns with government authorities	– Two staff members of International Secretariat

APPENDIX I

DATE	COUNTRY	PURPOSE	DELEGATE(S)
August	Brazil	Discuss Amnesty International's concerns with government authorities	– Bacre Waly Ndiaye (International Executive Committee) – John Alderson (UK) – Two staff members of International Secretariat
August	Brazil	Research/Discuss Amnesty International's concerns with government authorities	– Staff member of International Secretariat
August	Tanzania	Research	– Two staff members of International Secretariat
August	Turkey	Research	– Two staff members of International Secretariat
August/September	Egypt	Research	– Staff member of International Secretariat
September	Guyana	Research/Discuss Amnesty International's concerns with government authorities	– Bernard Simons (UK) – Staff member of International Secretariat
September	Ecuador	Research/Discuss Amnesty International's concerns with government authorities	– Two staff members of International Secretariat
September	Portugal	Research/Trial observation	– Two staff members of International Secretariat
September	USA	Observe court hearing	– Staff member of International Secretariat
September	Grenada	Trial observation	– Lawrence Kershen (UK)
September	Romania	Discuss Amnesty International's concerns with government authorities	– Peter Duffy (International Executive Committee) – Kodurayur Venkateswaran (India) – Staff member of International Secretariat
September/October	Swaziland	Trial observation	– Daniel Nsereko (Uganda)
September/October	Suriname	Research	– Yvonne Nederpel (Netherlands) – Staff member of International Secretariat
October	Guatemala	Discuss Amnesty International's concerns with government authorities	– Rodolfo Konder (Brazil) – Francisco Ottonelli (Uruguay) – Staff member of International Secretariat
October	South Korea	Research/Discuss Amnesty International's concerns with government authorities	– Paul Hoffman (USA) – Staff member of International Secretariat
October	Yemen (Republic of)	Research/Discuss Amnesty International's concerns with government authorities	– Two staff members of International Secretariat
October	Nepal	Research	– Evert Bloemen (Netherlands) – Staff member of International Secretariat
October	Guyana	Trial observation	– Gregory Denzil (Trinidad)
October	Italy	Research	– Staff member of International Secretariat
October	Tunisia	Trial observation	– Antonio Marchesi (Italy) – Staff member of International Secretariat
October/November	Israel/Occupied Territories	Trial observation	– Wesley Gryk (USA)
November	United Kingdom	Research/Observe court hearing	– Staff member of International Secretariat
November	Canada	Research	– Menno Kamminga (Netherlands)

DATE	COUNTRY	PURPOSE	DELEGATE(S)
November	Yemen (Republic of)	Discuss Amnesty International's concerns with government authorities	– Secretary General of Amnesty International – Two staff members of International Secretariat
November	Greece	Trial observation	– Alain Ottan (France)
November	Venezuela	Research	– Clyde Snow (USA)
November	Turkey	Trial observation	– Nicolas Madge (UK)
December	United Kingdom	Observe court hearing	– Staff member of International Secretariat
December	Rwanda	Trial observation	– David Weissbrodt (USA)
December/January	Thailand	Research	– Staff member of International Secretariat

APPENDIX II

STATUTE OF AMNESTY INTERNATIONAL
Articles 1 and 2

As amended by the 18th International Council meeting in Aguas de Lindóia, Brazil, 30 November to 6 December 1987

Object

1. CONSIDERING that every person has the right freely to hold and to express his or her convictions and the obligation to extend a like freedom to others, the object of AMNESTY INTERNATIONAL shall be to secure throughout the world the observance of the provisions of the Universal Declaration of Human Rights, by:

a. irrespective of political considerations working towards the release of and providing assistance to persons who in violation of the aforesaid provisions are imprisoned, detained or otherwise physically restricted by reason of their political, religious or other conscientiously held beliefs or by reason of their ethnic origin, sex, colour or language, provided that they have not used or advocated violence (hereinafter referred to as "prisoners of conscience");

b. opposing by all appropriate means the detention of any prisoners of conscience or any political prisoners without trial within a reasonable time or any trial procedures relating to such prisoners that do not conform to internationally recognized norms;

c. opposing by all appropriate means the imposition and infliction of death penalties and torture or other cruel, inhuman or degrading treatment or punishment of prisoners or other detained or restricted persons whether or not they have used or advocated violence.

Methods

2. In order to achieve the aforesaid object, AMNESTY INTERNATIONAL shall:

a. at all times maintain an overall balance between its activities in relation to countries adhering to the different world political ideologies and groupings;

b. promote as appears appropriate the adoption of constitutions, conventions, treaties and other measures which guarantee the rights contained in the provisions referred to in Article 1 hereof;

APPENDIX II

c. support and publicize the activities of and cooperate with international organizations and agencies which work for the implementation of the aforesaid provisions;

d. take all necessary steps to establish an effective organization of sections, affiliated groups and individual members;

e. secure the adoption by groups of members or supporters of individual prisoners of conscience or entrust to such groups other tasks in support of the object set out in Article 1;

f. provide financial and other relief to prisoners of conscience and their dependants and to persons who have lately been prisoners of conscience or who might reasonably be expected to be prisoners of conscience or to become prisoners of conscience if convicted or if they were to return to their own countries, to the dependants of such persons and to victims of torture in need of medical care as a direct result thereof;

g. work for the improvement of conditions for prisoners of conscience and political prisoners;

h. provide legal aid, where necessary and possible, to prisoners of conscience and to persons who might reasonably be expected to be prisoners of conscience or to become prisoners of conscience if convicted or if they were to return to their own countries, and, where desirable, send observers to attend the trials of such persons;

i. publicize the cases of prisoners of conscience or persons who have otherwise been subjected to disabilities in violation of the aforesaid provisions;

j. investigate and publicize the disappearance of persons where there is reason to believe that they may be victims of violations of the rights set out in Article 1 hereof;

k. oppose the sending of persons from one country to another where they can reasonably be expected to become prisoners of conscience or to face torture or the death penalty;

l. send investigators, where appropriate, to investigate allegations that the rights of individuals under the aforesaid provisions have been violated or threatened;

m. make representations to international organizations and to governments whenever it appears that an individual is a prisoner of conscience or has otherwise been subjected to disabilities in violation of the aforesaid provisions;

n. promote and support the granting of general amnesties of which the beneficiaries will include prisoners of conscience;

o. adopt any other appropriate methods for the securing of its object.

The full text of the Statute of Amnesty International is available free upon request from: Amnesty International, International Secretariat, 1 Easton Street, London WC1X 8DJ, United Kingdom.

AMNESTY INTERNATIONAL
NEWS RELEASES 1990

3 January
Amnesty International fears that killings of Palestinians by **Israeli forces** were condoned and even encouraged by the government

9 January
Amnesty International cites ill-treatment of detainees by **Austrian** police

11 January
Human rights abused in **Saudi Arabia** – most victims are Shi'a Muslims, says Amnesty International

15 January
Vietnamese asylum-seekers denied basic rights by **Hong Kong** and **United Kingdom**, says Amnesty International

17 January
Human rights abuses in **South Korea** reverse two years of positive trends, says Amnesty International

18 January
Sri Lanka: Amnesty International rejects "terrorist" label

25 January
Urgent reforms needed to protect **Somali** citizens against human rights abuses, says Amnesty International

2 February
Amnesty International welcomes announcement by **South Africa's** President de Klerk on suspension of executions

5 February
India: Amnesty International calls for an investigation into killings

15 February
Human rights violations in **Sri Lanka** reached unprecedented levels in 1989, says Amnesty International

20 February
Amnesty International calls on King Hassan II to end human rights abuses in **Morocco**

21 February
Human rights reforms introduced in **Viet Nam**, but violations continue, says Amnesty International

23 February
Amnesty International calls for release of prisoners of conscience and inquiry into reported torture in **South Korea**

1 March
Amnesty International cites torture reports in apparent crackdown on Shi'a Muslims in **Kuwait**

7 March
Secrecy over gross abuses in **Chad** – Amnesty International fears for fate of hundreds of political prisoners

12 March
Amnesty International appeals to **Iraqi** President to spare life of British-based journalist

15 March
Amnesty International condemns execution of journalist in **Iraq**

16 March
Moroccan Government orders Amnesty International delegates to leave

21 March
Amnesty International calls on **Peru's** presidential candidates to address human rights issues

22 March
Amnesty International asks **Taiwanese** authorities to release Cheung Ki-Lok unconditionally

28 March
Amnesty International urges inquiry into **Argentine** human rights abuses

9 April
Human rights activists attacked in **Guatemala** – Amnesty International reports growing violence

11 April
Amnesty International urges **Indian** authorities to protect human rights after killing of hostages

20 April
Amnesty International urges **Japan** not to return hijacker to China

APPENDIX III

2 May
Torture of political prisoners rife in **Myanmar**, reports Amnesty International

9 May
Turkey: government fails to act – torture and human rights abuses continue unabated, says Amnesty International

16 May
Amnesty International calls on **China** to account for pro-democracy prisoners and publicizes names of those known to be imprisoned

23 May
Human rights record improves in **Pakistan**, says Amnesty International, but further safeguards needed

24 May
Amnesty International calls for investigation into torture of political opponents in **Senegal**

30 May
Amnesty International calls for immediate trial or release of 26 political detainees held unlawfully for three years in **Congo**

6 June
Amnesty International calls for human rights safeguards after police torture and killings in **Nepal**

7 June
Amnesty International appeals for end to killings in **Liberia**

13 June
Amnesty International welcomes human rights moves in **Jordan** and calls for further safeguards

19 June
Amnesty International urges **Brazilian** Government to bring to justice police officers guilty of brutality and killings

21 June
Kurdish opponents "disappear" under amnesties in **Iraq** – Amnesty International fears for safety of refugees in **Turkey**

26 June
Amnesty International says human rights abuses persist in **El Salvador** despite government pledges

28 June
Amnesty International reports torture in secret centres after coup in **Sudan**

4 July
Amnesty International urges release of detained **Albanians**

11 July
Amnesty International details in annual report government targeting of **ethnic and national groups** for human rights violations

13 July
Hong Kong refugees screening process still flawed, says Amnesty International

23 July
Cameroon: Amnesty International appeals for release of prisoners after unfair trial

2 August
Amnesty International urges immediate release of government critics in **Iran**

3 August
Amnesty International reports **Iraqi** government opponents arrested after invasion of **Kuwait**

16 August
Prisoners of conscience are held in more than 70 countries, says Amnesty International

17 August
Televised "confessions" heighten concern about prisoners in **Iran**, says Amnesty International

20 August
Amnesty International appeals to **Iraqi** authorities on human rights violations

3 September
Amnesty International expresses grave concern about killings by Khmer Rouge in **Cambodia**

6 September
Children tortured and killed in **Brazil**, says Amnesty International

12 September
Government fails to curb torture in **Equatorial Guinea**, says Amnesty International

13 September
Executions in **China** increase dramatically in crime crackdown, says Amnesty International

19 September
Security forces continue to violate human

rights in **Sri Lanka**, says Amnesty International

25 September
Amnesty International calls for end to killings and torture of **children** worldwide

27 September
Violence and unlawful detentions continue in **Zaire** despite announcements of political reforms, says Amnesty International

2 October
Government killings of **black Mauritanians** escalate, says Amnesty International

3 October
Iraqi forces killing and torturing **Kuwaitis**, says Amnesty International

9 October
Amnesty International calls for immediate judicial inquiry into killings of **Palestinians** by **Israeli** forces

10 October
Amnesty International urges **Indian** Government to investigate human rights violations

15 October
Reported arrests of prisoners of conscience and extrajudicial executions in **Rwanda**, says Amnesty International

17 October
Government opponents detained and tortured by **Egyptian** forces, says Amnesty International

18 October
Amnesty International calls on presidential candidates for pledge on human rights in **Guatemala**

18 October
Government opponents forcibly repatriated and held without trial in **Central African Republic**, says Amnesty International

24 October
Amnesty International reports alarming rise in "death squad" killings in **El Salvador**

30 October
Amnesty International renews calls for inquiry into human rights abuses in **Namibia**

1 November
Amnesty International fears hundreds of **Yemenis** tortured by police in **Saudi Arabia**

7 November
Killings and arrests continue in military crackdown on opposition in **Myanmar**, says Amnesty International

14 November
Pro-democracy leaders may soon face unfair trials in **China**, warns Amnesty International

19 November
Cambodia: Amnesty International urges strong human rights provisions in settlement

21 November
Amnesty International calls for investigation into "disappearances" in **Morocco**

26 November
Amnesty International reports torture and killing of unarmed civilians in **Papua New Guinea**

29 November
Amnesty International reports government crackdown on opposition in **Kenya** – more than 20 face political trials

5 December
Amnesty International reports "relentless and ruthless" abuses of basic human rights in **Iran**, including hangings, torture and jailing of critics

13 December
Amnesty International says over 100 people killed in **Uganda** by soldiers in 1990, and calls for immediate investigations

14 December
Amnesty International expresses concern about hundreds of remaining political prisoners in **Albania**

19 December
Amnesty International urges end to torture and killings in **Iraqi-occupied Kuwait**

21 December
Amnesty International reports that more than 300 prisoners executed at ex-president's headquarters in **Chad**

APPENDIX IV

AMNESTY INTERNATIONAL AROUND THE WORLD

There are now more than 6,000 local Amnesty International groups in over 70 countries around the world. In 44 countries these groups are coordinated by sections, whose addresses are given below. In addition, there are individual members, supporters and recipients of Amnesty International information (such as the monthly *Amnesty International Newsletter*) in more than 150 countries and territories.

SECTION ADDRESSES

Australia:
Amnesty International,
Australian Section,
Private Bag 23, Broadway,
New South Wales 2007

Austria:
Amnesty International,
Austrian Section,
Wiedner Guertel 12/7, A-1040 Wien

Barbados:
Amnesty International,
Barbados Section,
PO Box 872, Bridgetown

Belgium:
Amnesty International,
Belgian Section (*Flemish branch*),
Kerkstraat 156, 2060 Antwerpen 6

Amnesty International,
Belgian Section (*francophone branch*),
9 rue Berckmans, 1060 Bruxelles

Bermuda:
Amnesty International,
Bermuda Section,
PO Box HM 2136, Hamilton HM JX

Brazil:
Anistia Internacional,
Seção Brasileira,
Rua Coropé 65,
05426 - São Paulo - SP

Canada:
Amnesty International,
Canadian Section (*English-speaking branch*),
130 Slater Street, Suite 900,
Ottawa, Ontario, K1P 6E2

Amnistie Internationale,
Section canadienne (*francophone branch*),
3516 ave du Parc,
Montreal, Quebec, H2X 2H7

Chile:
Amnistía Internacional,
Casilla 4062, Santiago

Côte d'Ivoire:
Amnesty International,
Section de Côte d'Ivoire,
04 BP 895, Abidjan 04

Denmark:
Amnesty International,
Danish Section,
Dyrkoeb 3, 1166 Copenhagen K

Ecuador:
Amnistía Internacional,
Casilla 240-C, Sucursal 15, Quito

Faroe Islands:
Amnesty International,
Faroe Islands Section,
PO Box 1075, FR-110 Torshavn

Finland:
Amnesty International,
Finnish Section,
Ruoholahdenkatu 24,
SF-00180 Helsinki

France:
Amnesty International,
French Section,
4 rue de la Pierre Levée,
75553 Paris (CEDEX 11)

Federal Republic of Germany:
Amnesty International,
Section of the FRG,
Heerstrasse 178, 5300 Bonn 1

Ghana:
Amnesty International,
Ghanaian Section,
PO Box 1173, Koforidua E.R.

Greece:
Amnesty International,
Greek Section,
30 Sina Street, 106 72 Athens

Guyana:
Amnesty International,
Guyana Section,
Palm Court Building, 35 Main Street,
Georgetown

Hong Kong:
Amnesty International,
Hong Kong Section,
Unit C, Third Floor,
Best-0-Best Building,
32-36 Ferry Street, Kowloon

Iceland:
Amnesty International,
Icelandic Section,
PO Box 618, 121 Reykjavík

India:
Amnesty International,
Indian Section,
c/o Dateline Delhi,
21 North End Complex,
Panchkuin Road,
New Delhi 110001

Ireland:
Amnesty International,
Irish Section,
Sean MacBride House, 8 Shaw Street,
Dublin 2

Israel:
Amnesty International,
Israel Section,
PO Box 14179, Tel Aviv 61141

Italy:
Amnesty International,
Italian Section,
viale Mazzini 146, 00195 Rome

Japan:
Amnesty International,
Japanese Section,
Daisan-Sanbu Building 2F/3F,
2-3-22 Nishi-Waseda, Shinjuku-ku,
Tokyo 169

Luxembourg:
Amnesty International,
Luxembourg Section,
Boîte Postale 1914,
1019 Luxembourg

Mexico:
Sección Mexicana de Amnistía
Internacional,
Ap. Postal No. 20-217, San Angel,
CP 01000 Mexico DF

Netherlands:
Amnesty International,
Dutch Section,
Keizersgracht 620, 1017 ER Amsterdam

New Zealand:
Amnesty International,
New Zealand Section,
PO Box 6647, Wellington 1

Nigeria:
Amnesty International,
Nigerian Section,
PMB 59 Agodi, Ibadan, Oyo State

Norway:
Amnesty International,
Norwegian Section,
Maridalsveien 87, 0461 Oslo 4

Peru:
Amnistía Internacional,
Sección Peruana,
Casilla 659, Lima 18

Portugal:
Amnistia Internacional,
Seção Portuguesa,
Apartado 1642, 1016 Lisboa Codex

Puerto Rico:
Amnistía Internacional,
Calle Robles No. 54 Altos,
Apartado I, Rio Piedras,
Puerto Rico 00925

Sierra Leone:
Amnesty International,
Sierra Leone, PMB 1021, Freetown

Spain:
Amnesty International,
Sección Española,
Paseo de Recoletos 18,
Piso 6, 28001 Madrid

Sweden:
Amnesty International,
Swedish Section,
Gyllenstiernsgatan 18,
S-115 26 Stockholm

Switzerland:
Amnesty International,
Swiss Section,
PO Box, CH-3001 Bern

Tanzania:
Amnesty International,
Tanzanian Section,

APPENDIX IV/APPENDIX V

National Secretariat,
PO Box 4331, Dar es Salaam

Tunisia:
Amnesty International,
Tunisian Section,
Secrétariat National,
48 Avenue Farhat Hached, 3ème Etage,
1001 Tunis

United Kingdom:
Amnesty International,
British Section,
99-119 Rosebery Avenue,
London EC1R 4RE

United States of America:
Amnesty International of the USA
(AIUSA), 322 8th Ave,
New York, NY 10001

Uruguay:
Amnistía Internacional,
Sección Uruguaya,
Yi 1333 Apto. 305,
Montevideo

Venezuela:
Amnistía Internacional,
Sección Venezolana,
Apartado Postal 5110,
Carmelitas 1010-A,
Caracas

COUNTRIES WITH LOCAL AMNESTY INTERNATIONAL GROUPS BUT NO SECTION*

Algeria	Egypt	Papua New Guinea
Argentina	Hungary	Philippines
Aruba	Jordan	Poland
Bangladesh	Korea (Republic of)	Senegal
Benin	Macau	Taiwan
Colombia	Mauritius/Rodrigues	Thailand
Costa Rica	Nepal	Yugoslavia
Curaçao	Pakistan	Zambia
Dominican Republic		

*Amnesty International groups in Sudan and Kuwait have ceased activities following the dissolution by government decree in Sudan in July 1989 and the Iraqi invasion of Kuwait in August 1990.

APPENDIX V

INTERNATIONAL EXECUTIVE COMMITTEE

Stephen R. Abrams/United States of America
Peter R. Baehr/Netherlands
Peter Duffy/United Kingdom
Anette Fischer/Denmark
Charles Henry/United States of America
Sofía Macher/Peru
Ravi Nair/India
Bacre Waly Ndiaye/Senegal
Malcolm Tigerschiold/International Secretariat

＃ SELECTED INTERNATIONAL HUMAN RIGHTS TREATIES

States which have ratified or acceded to a convention are party to the treaty and are bound to observe its provisions. States which have signed but not yet ratified have expressed their intention to become a party at some future date; meanwhile they are obliged to refrain from acts which would defeat the object and purpose of the treaty.

(AS OF 31 DECEMBER 1990)

	International Covenant on Civil and Political Rights (ICCPR)	Optional Protocol to ICCPR	Second Optional Protocol to ICCPR Aiming at the Abolition of the Death Penalty	International Covenant on Economic, Social and Cultural Rights (ICESCR)	Convention against Torture and Other Cruel, Inhuman or Degrading Treatment or Punishment
Afghanistan	x			x	x (28)
Albania					
Algeria	x	x		x	x (22)
Angola					
Antigua and Barbuda					
Argentina	x	x		x	x (22)
Australia	x		x	x	x
Austria	x	x		x	x (22)
Bahamas					
Bahrain					
Bangladesh					
Barbados	x	x		x	
Belgium	x		s	x	s
Belize					x
Benin					
Bhutan					
Bolivia	x	x		x	s
Botswana					
Brazil					x
Brunei					
Bulgaria	x			x	x (28)
Burkina Faso					
Burundi	x			x	
Byelorussian SSR	x			x	x (28)
Cambodia	s			s	
Cameroon	x	x		x	x
Canada	x	x		x	x (22)
Cape Verde					
Central African Republic	x	x		x	
Chad					
Chile	x			x	x
China					x (28)
Colombia	x	x		x	x

APPENDIX VI

	International Covenant on Civil and Political Rights (ICCPR)	Optional Protocol to ICCPR	Second Optional Protocol to ICCPR Aiming at the Abolition of the Death Penalty	International Covenant on Economic, Social and Cultural Rights (ICESCR)	Convention against Torture and Other Cruel, Inhuman or Degrading Treatment or Punishment
Comoros					
Congo	x	x		x	
Costa Rica	x	x	s	x	s
Côte d'Ivoire					
Cuba					s
Cyprus	x	s		x	s
Czech and Slovak Federal Republic	x			x	x (28)
Denmark	x	x	s	x	x (22)
Djibouti					
Dominica					
Dominican Republic	x	x		x	s
Ecuador	x	x		x	x (22)
Egypt	x			x	x
El Salvador	x	s		x	
Equatorial Guinea	x	x		x	
Ethiopia					
Fiji					
Finland	x	x	s	x	x (22)
France	x	x		x	x (22)
Gabon	x			x	s
Gambia	x	x		x	s
Germany, Federal Republic of	x		s	x	x
Ghana					
Greece				x	x (22)
Grenada					
Guatemala				x	x
Guinea	x	s		x	x
Guinea-Bissau					
Guyana	x			x	x
Haiti					
Holy See					
Honduras	s	s	s	x	
Hungary	x	x		x	x (22)(28)
Iceland	x	x		x	s
India	x			x	
Indonesia					s

APPENDIX VI

	International Covenant on Civil and Political Rights (ICCPR)	Optional Protocol to ICCPR	Second Optional Protocol to ICCPR Aiming at the Abolition of the Death Penalty	International Covenant on Economic, Social and Cultural Rights (ICESCR)	Convention against Torture and Other Cruel, Inhuman or Degrading Treatment or Punishment
Iran	x			x	
Iraq	x			x	
Ireland	x	x		x	
Israel	s			s	s
Italy	x	x	s	x	x (22)
Jamaica	x	x		x	
Japan	x			x	
Jordan	x			x	
Kenya	x			x	
Kiribati					
Korea (Democratic People's Republic of)	x			x	
Korea (Republic of)	x	x		x	
Kuwait					
Lao People's Democratic Republic					
Lebanon	x			x	
Lesotho					
Liberia	s			s	
Libyan Arab Jamahiriya	x	x		x	x
Liechtenstein					x (22)
Luxembourg	x	x	s	x	x (22)
Madagascar	x	x		x	
Malawi					
Malaysia					
Maldives					
Mali	x			x	
Malta	x	x		x	x (22)
Mauritania					
Mauritius	x	x		x	
Mexico	x			x	x
Monaco					
Mongolia	x			x	
Morocco	x			x	s (28)
Mozambique					
Myanmar (Burma)					
Namibia					
Nauru					
Nepal					

APPENDIX VI

	International Covenant on Civil and Political Rights (ICCPR)	Optional Protocol to ICCPR	Second Optional Protocol to ICCPR Aiming at the Abolition of the Death Penalty	International Covenant on Economic, Social and Cultural Rights (ICESCR)	Convention against Torture and Other Cruel, Inhuman or Degrading Treatment or Punishment
Netherlands	x	x	s	x	x (22)
New Zealand	x	x	x	x	x
Nicaragua	x	x	s	x	s
Niger	x	x		x	
Nigeria					s
Norway	x	x	s	x	x (22)
Oman					
Pakistan					
Panama	x	x		x	x
Papua New Guinea					
Paraguay					x
Peru	x	x		x	x
Philippines	x	x		x	x
Poland	x			x	x (28)
Portugal	x	x	x	x	x (22)
Qatar					
Romania	x		s	x	x
Rwanda	x			x	
St Christopher and Nevis					
St Lucia					
St Vincent and The Grenadines	x	x		x	
Samoa					
San Marino	x	x		x	
São Tomé and Príncipe					
Saudi Arabia					
Senegal	x	x		x	x
Seychelles					
Sierra Leone					s
Singapore					
Solomon Islands				x	
Somalia	x	x		x	x
South Africa					
Spain	x	x	s	x	x (22)
Sri Lanka	x			x	
Sudan	x			x	s
Suriname	x	x		x	
Swaziland					

APPENDIX VI

	International Covenant on Civil and Political Rights (ICCPR)	Optional Protocol to ICCPR	Second Optional Protocol to ICCPR Aiming at the Abolition of the Death Penalty	International Covenant on Economic, Social and Cultural Rights (ICESCR)	Convention against Torture and Other Cruel, Inhuman or Degrading Treatment or Punishment
Sweden	x	x	x	x	x (22)
Switzerland					x (22)
Syria	x			x	
Tanzania	x			x	
Thailand					
Togo	x	x		x	x (22)
Tonga					
Trinidad and Tobago	x	x		x	
Tunisia	x			x	x (22)
Turkey					x (22)
Tuvalu					
Uganda				x	x
Ukrainian SSR	x			x	x (28)
Union of Soviet Socialist Republics	x			x	x (28)
United Arab Emirates					
United Kingdom	x			x	x
United States of America	s			s	s
Uruguay	x	x	s	x	x (22)
Vanuatu					
Venezuela	x	x	s	x	s
Viet Nam	x			x	
Yemen	x			x	
Yugoslavia	x	s		x	s
Zaire	x	x		x	
Zambia	x	x		x	
Zimbabwe					

s – denotes that country has signed but not yet ratified
x – denotes that country is a party, either through ratification or accession
(22) denotes Declaration under Article 22 recognizing the competence of the Committee against Torture to consider individual complaints of violations of the convention
(28) denotes that country has made a reservation under Article 28 that it does not recognize the competence of the Committee against Torture to examine reliable information which appears to indicate that torture is being systematically practised, and to undertake a confidential inquiry if warranted

The countries listed in this chart are those included in the official United Nations publication entitled *Human Rights International Instruments: Signatures, Ratifications, Accessions etc.*

SELECTED REGIONAL HUMAN RIGHTS TREATIES
(AS OF 31 DECEMBER 1990)

ORGANIZATION OF AFRICAN UNITY (OAU)
AFRICAN CHARTER ON HUMAN AND PEOPLES' RIGHTS (1981)

Algeria	x	Gambia	x	Saharawi Arab	
Angola	x	Ghana	x	Democratic Republic	x
Benin	x	Guinea	x	São Tomé and Príncipe	x
Botswana	x	Guinea-Bissau	x	Senegal	x
Burkina Faso	x	Kenya		Seychelles	
Burundi	x	Lesotho	s	Sierra Leone	x
Cameroon	x	Liberia	x	Somalia	x
Cape Verde	x	Libya	x	Sudan	x
Central African Republic	x	Madagascar		Swaziland	
Chad	x	Malawi	x	Tanzania	x
Comoros	x	Mali	x	Togo	x
Congo	x	Mauritania	x	Tunisia	x
Côte d'Ivoire		Mauritius		Uganda	x
Djibouti		Mozambique	x	Zaire	x
Egypt	x	Namibia		Zambia	x
Equatorial Guinea	x	Niger	x	Zimbabwe	x
Ethiopia		Nigeria	x		
Gabon	x	Rwanda	x		

s – denotes that country has signed but not yet ratified
x – denotes that country is a party, either through ratification or accession
This chart lists countries which were members of the OAU at the end of 1990.

ORGANIZATION OF AMERICAN STATES (OAS)

	American Convention on Human Rights (1969)	Inter-American Convention to Prevent and Punish Torture (1985)		American Convention on Human Rights (1969)	Inter-American Convention to Prevent and Punish Torture (1985)
Antigua and Barbuda			Honduras	x (62)	s
Argentina	x (62)	x	Jamaica	x	
Bahamas			Mexico	x	x
Barbados	x		Nicaragua	x	s
Bolivia	x	s	Panama	x (62)	s
Brazil		x	Paraguay	x	x
Canada			Peru	x (62)	s
Chile	x (62)	x	St Christopher and Nevis		
Colombia	x (62)	s	St Lucia		
Costa Rica	x (62)	s	St Vincent and The Grenadines		
Cuba					
Dominica					
Dominican Republic	x	x	Suriname	x (62)	x
Ecuador	x (62)	s	Trinidad and Tobago		
El Salvador	x	s	United States of America		s
Grenada	x				
Guatemala	x (62)	x	Uruguay	x (62)	s
Haiti	x	s	Venezuela	x (62)	s

s – denotes that country has signed but not yet ratified
x – denotes that country is a party, either through ratification or accession
(62) denotes Declaration under Article 62 recognizing as binding the jurisdiction of the Inter-American Court of Human Rights (on all matters relating to the interpretation or application of the American Convention)
This chart lists countries which were members of the OAS at the end of 1990.

COUNCIL OF EUROPE

	European Convention for the Protection of Human Rights and Fundamental Freedoms (1950)	Article 25	Article 46	Protocol No. 6*	European Convention for the Prevention of Torture and Inhuman or Degrading Treatment or Punishment (1987)
Austria	x	x	x	x	x
Belgium	x	x	x	s	s
Cyprus	x	x	x		x
Denmark	x	x	x	x	x
Finland	x	x	x	x	x
France	x	x	x	x	x
Germany, Federal Republic of	x	x	x	x	x
Greece	x	x	x	s	s
Hungary	s			s	
Iceland	x	x	x	x	x
Ireland	x	x	x		x
Italy	x	x	x	x	x
Liechtenstein	x	x	x	x	s
Luxembourg	x	x	x	x	x
Malta	x	x	x		x
Netherlands	x	x	x	x	x
Norway	x	x	x	x	x
Portugal	x	x	x	x	x
San Marino	x	x	x	x	x
Spain	x	x	x	x	x
Sweden	x	x	x	x	x
Switzerland	x	x	x	x	x
Turkey	x	x	x		x
United Kingdom	x	x	x		x

s – denotes that country has signed but not yet ratified
x – denotes that country is a party, either through ratification or accession
Article 25: denotes Declaration under Article 25 of the European Convention, recognizing the competence of the European Commission of Human Rights to consider individual complaints of violations of the Convention
Article 46: denotes Declaration under Article 46 of the European Convention, recognizing as compulsory the jurisdiction of the European Court of Human Rights in all matters concerning interpretation and application of the European Convention

* Protocol 6 to the European Convention on Human Rights: concerning abolition of the death penalty (1983)

This chart lists countries which were members of the Council of Europe at the end of 1990.

APPENDIX VIII

OVERDUE REPORTS

A) BY STATES PARTIES TO THE INTERNATIONAL COVENANT ON CIVIL AND POLITICAL RIGHTS

Governments which have ratified or acceded to the International Covenant on Civil and Political Rights (ICCPR) are referred to as "States Parties" to that treaty. Article 40 of the ICCPR requires States Parties to submit reports to the United Nations (UN) "on the measures they have adopted which give effect to the rights recognized [in the ICCPR] and on the progress made in the enjoyment of those rights". The reports are supposed to "indicate the factors and difficulties, if any, affecting the implementation of the present Covenant".

The initial report is due within one year after the ICCPR enters into force for the particular state; subsequent reports are due every five years. They are reviewed by the Human Rights Committee, the body of 18 experts which monitors implementation of the ICCPR.

The Human Rights Committee has repeatedly expressed concern about the non-compliance of states with their reporting obligations.

The Committee noted that there may be various reasons for reports being overdue, including a shortage of resources, the assignment of insufficient priority, and in some cases the reluctance of states to expose themselves to scrutiny.

The UN General Assembly has urged States Parties to the ICCPR which have not yet done so "to submit their reports as speedily as possible".

As of 31 December 1990 the following states were at least one year late in submitting their initial, second or third periodic reports.

INITIAL REPORTS

State Party	Date due	Number of reminders sent
Gabon	20 April 1984	13
Niger	6 June 1987	7
Sudan	17 June 1987	7
Equatorial Guinea	24 December 1988	4

SECOND PERIODIC REPORTS

State Party	Date due	Number of reminders sent
Libyan Arab Jamahiriya	4 February 1983	15
Iran (Islamic Republic of)	21 March 1983	15
Bulgaria	28 April 1984	14
Cyprus	18 August 1984	14
Syrian Arab Republic	18 August 1984	14
Cook Islands (New Zealand)	27 March 1985	3
Gambia	21 June 1985	12
Suriname	2 August 1985	11
Venezuela	1 November 1985	11
Lebanon	21 March 1986	11
Kenya	11 April 1986	10
Mali	11 April 1986	10
United Republic of Tanzania	11 April 1986	10
Jamaica	1 August 1986	8
Netherlands Antilles	31 October 1986	3
Guyana	10 April 1987	8
Iceland	30 October 1987	7
Democratic People's Republic of Korea	13 December 1987	6
Peru	9 April 1988	5

APPENDIX VIII

Egypt	13 April 1988	5
El Salvador	31 December 1988	4
Central African Republic	9 April 1989	3
Gabon	20 April 1989	3
Afghanistan	23 April 1989	3
Belgium	20 July 1989	3
Guinea	30 September 1989	3
Luxembourg	17 November 1989	2

THIRD PERIODIC REPORTS

State Party	Date due	Number of reminders sent
Libyan Arab Jamahiriya	4 February 1988	6
Iran (Islamic Republic of)	21 March 1988	6
Lebanon	21 March 1988	6
Panama	6 June 1988	1
Madagascar	3 August 1988	5
Yugoslavia	3 August 1988	5
Bulgaria	28 April 1989	3
Romania	28 April 1989	3
Cyprus	18 August 1989	3
Syrian Arab Republic	18 August 1989	3

The Committee has extended the deadline for submission by the following countries whose reports were due on the dates indicated:

Second Periodic Reports

St Vincent and the Grenadines	8 February 1988
Bolivia	11 November 1988
Viet Nam	23 December 1988

Third Periodic Reports

Zaïre	30 January 1988
Dominican Republic	3 April 1989

B) BY STATES PARTIES TO THE CONVENTION AGAINST TORTURE AND OTHER CRUEL, INHUMAN OR DEGRADING TREATMENT OR PUNISHMENT

Governments which have ratified or acceded to the Convention against Torture and Other Cruel, Inhuman or Degrading Treatment or Punishment are referred to as "States Parties" to that treaty. Article 19 of the Convention against Torture requires States Parties to submit reports to the United Nations "on the measures they have taken to give effect to their undertakings [under the Convention against Torture]".

The initial report is due within one year after the Convention against Torture enters into force for the particular state; supplementary reports are due every four years and should cover "any new measures taken". The reports are reviewed by the Committee against Torture, the body of 10 experts which monitors implementation of the Convention against Torture.

As of 31 December 1990 the following states were at least one year late in submitting their initial reports.

INITIAL REPORTS

State Party	Date due	Number of reminders sent
Belize	25 June 1988	4
Bulgaria	25 June 1988	4
Uganda	25 June 1988	4

Uruguay	25 June 1988	4
Panama	22 September 1988	4
Luxembourg	28 October 1988	4
Togo	17 December 1988	4
Guyana	19 August 1989	2
Peru	7 October 1989	1

C) BY STATES PARTIES TO THE AFRICAN CHARTER ON HUMAN AND PEOPLES' RIGHTS

Governments which have ratified or acceded to the African Charter on Human and Peoples' Rights are referred to as "States Parties" to that treaty. Article 62 of the African Charter requires States Parties to submit reports every two years to the African Commission on Human and Peoples' Rights, established under the African Charter to monitor implementation of that treaty, "on the legislative or other measures taken with a view to giving effect to the rights and freedoms recognized and guaranteed by the [African Charter]".

The African Commission, composed of 11 experts, reviews these reports. As of 31 December 1990 the following States Parties were at least one year late in submitting their initial reports.

INITIAL REPORTS

State Party	Date due	Number of reminders sent
Benin	21 October 1988	1
Gabon	21 October 1988	1
Botswana	21 October 1988	1
Burkina Faso	21 October 1988	1
Central African Republic	21 October 1988	1
Comoros	21 October 1988	1
Congo	21 October 1988	1
Egypt	21 October 1988	1
Gambia	21 October 1988	1
Guinea	21 October 1988	1
Guinea-Bissau	21 October 1988	1
Liberia	21 October 1988	1
Mali	21 October 1988	1
Mauritania	21 October 1988	1
Niger	21 October 1988	1
Saharawi Arab Democratic Republic	21 October 1988	1
São Tomé and Príncipe	21 October 1988	1
Senegal	21 October 1988	1
Sierra Leone	21 October 1988	1
Somalia	21 October 1988	1
Sudan	21 October 1988	1
Uganda	21 October 1988	1
Tanzania	21 October 1988	1
Zambia	21 October 1988	1
Zimbabwe	21 October 1988	1
Equatorial Guinea	18 November 1988	1
Chad	11 February 1989	1
Algeria	20 June 1989	1
Zaire	28 October 1989	1
Cape Verde	6 November 1989	1

BASIC PRINCIPLES ON THE USE OF FORCE AND FIREARMS BY LAW ENFORCEMENT OFFICIALS

[*These Principles were adopted by the Eighth United Nations Congress on the Prevention of Crime and the Treatment of Offenders in Havana, Cuba, on 7 September 1990. The United Nations General Assembly subsequently welcomed these Principles in its Resolution 45/121 of 14 December 1990 and invited all governments to be guided by them in the formulation of appropriate legislation and practice and to make efforts to ensure their implementation. The text of the Principles is set out below.*]

General provisions

1. Governments and law enforcement agencies shall adopt and implement rules and regulations on the use of force and firearms against persons by law enforcement officials. In developing such rules and regulations, Governments and law enforcement agencies shall keep the ethical issues associated with the use of force and firearms constantly under review.

2. Governments and law enforcement agencies should develop a range of means as broad as possible and equip law enforcement officials with various types of weapons and ammunition that would allow for a differentiated use of force and firearms. These should include the development of non-lethal incapacitating weapons for use in appropriate situations, with a view to increasingly restraining the application of means capable of causing death or injury to persons. For the same purpose, it should also be possible for law enforcement officials to be equipped with self-defensive equipment such as shields, helmets, bullet-proof vests and bullet-proof means of transportation, in order to decrease the need to use weapons of any kind.

3. The development and deployment of non-lethal incapacitating weapons should be carefully evaluated in order to minimize the risk of endangering uninvolved persons, and the use of such weapons should be carefully controlled.

4. Law enforcement officials, in carrying out their duty, shall, as far as possible, apply non-violent means before resorting to the use of force and firearms. They may use force and firearms only if other means remain ineffective or without any promise of achieving the intended result.

5. Whenever the lawful use of force and firearms is unavoidable, law enforcement officials shall:
(a) Exercise restraint in such use and act in proportion to the seriousness of the offence and the legitimate objective to be achieved;
(b) Minimize damage and injury, and respect and preserve human life;
(c) Ensure that assistance and medical aid are rendered to any injured or affected persons at the earliest possible moment;
(d) Ensure that relatives or close friends of the injured or affected person are notified at the earliest possible moment.

6. Where injury or death is caused by the use of force and firearms by law enforcement officials, they shall report the incident promptly to their superiors, in accordance with principle 22.

7. Governments shall ensure that arbitrary or abusive use of force and firearms by law enforcement officials is punished as a criminal offence under their law.

8. Exceptional circumstances such as internal political instability or any other public emergency may not be invoked to justify any departure from these basic principles.

Special provisions

9. Law enforcement officials shall not use firearms against persons except in self-defence or defence of others against the imminent threat of death or serious injury, to prevent the perpetration of a particularly serious crime involving grave threat to life, to arrest a person presenting such a danger and resisting their authority, or to prevent his or her escape, and only when less extreme means are insufficient to achieve these objectives. In any event, intentional lethal use of firearms may only be made

when strictly unavoidable in order to protect life.

10. In the circumstances provided for under principle 9, law enforcement officials shall identify themselves as such and give a clear warning of their intent to use firearms, with sufficient time for the warning to be observed, unless to do so would unduly place the law enforcement officials at risk or would create a risk of death or serious harm to other persons, or would be clearly inappropriate or pointless in the circumstances of the incident.

11. Rules and regulations on the use of firearms by law enforcement officials should include guidelines that:
(a) Specify the circumstances under which law enforcement officials are authorized to carry firearms and prescribe the types of firearms and ammunition permitted;
(b) Ensure that firearms are used only in appropriate circumstances and in a manner likely to decrease the risk of unnecessary harm;
(c) Prohibit the use of those firearms and ammunition that cause unwarranted injury or present an unwarranted risk;
(d) Regulate the control, storage and issuing of firearms, including procedures for ensuring that law enforcement officials are accountable for the firearms and ammunition issued to them;
(e) Provide for warnings to be given, if appropriate, when firearms are to be discharged;
(f) Provide for a system of reporting whenever law enforcement officials use firearms in the performance of their duty.

Policing unlawful assemblies
12. As everyone is allowed to participate in lawful and peaceful assemblies, in accordance with the principles embodied in the Universal Declaration of Human Rights and the International Covenant on Civil and Political Rights, Governments and law enforcement agencies and officials shall recognize that force and firearms may be used only in accordance with principles 13 and 14.

13. In the dispersal of assemblies that are unlawful but non-violent, law enforcement officials shall avoid the use of force or, where that is not practicable, shall restrict such force to the minimum extent necessary.

14. In the dispersal of violent assemblies, law enforcement officials may use firearms only when less dangerous means are not practicable and only to the minimum extent necessary. Law enforcement officials shall not use firearms in such cases, except under the conditions stipulated in principle 9.

Policing persons in custody or detention
15. Law enforcement officials, in their relations with persons in custody or detention, shall not use force, except when strictly necessary for the maintenance of security and order within the institution, or when personal safety is threatened.

16. Law enforcement officials, in their relations with persons in custody or detention, shall not use firearms, except in self-defence or in the defence of others against the immediate threat of death or serious injury, or when strictly necessary to prevent the escape of a person in custody or detention presenting the danger referred to in principle 9.

17. The preceding principles are without prejudice to the rights, duties and responsibilities of prison officials, as set out in the Standard Minimum Rules for the Treatment of Prisoners, particularly rules 33, 34 and 54.

Qualifications, training and counselling
18. Governments and law enforcement agencies shall ensure that all law enforcement officials are selected by proper screening procedures, have appropriate moral, psychological and physical qualities for the effective exercise of their functions and receive continuous and thorough professional training. Their continued fitness to perform these functions should be subject to periodic review.

19. Governments and law enforcement agencies shall ensure that all law enforcement officials are provided with training and are tested in accordance with appropriate proficiency standards in the use of force. Those law enforcement officials who are required to carry firearms should be authorized to do so only upon completion of special training in their use.

20. In the training of law enforcement officials, Governments and law

enforcement agencies shall give special attention to issues of police ethics and human rights, especially in the investigative process, to alternatives to the use of force and firearms, including the peaceful settlement of conflicts, the understanding of crowd behaviour, and the methods of persuasion, negotiation and mediation, as well as to technical means, with a view to limiting the use of force and firearms. Law enforcement agencies should review their training programmes and operational procedures in the light of particular incidents.

21. Governments and law enforcement agencies shall make stress counselling available to law enforcement officials who are involved in situations where force and firearms are used.

Reporting and review procedures

22. Governments and law enforcement agencies shall establish effective reporting and review procedures for all incidents referred to in principles 6 and 11 (f). For incidents reported pursuant to these principles, Governments and law enforcement agencies shall ensure that an effective review process is available and that independent administrative or prosecutorial authorities are in a position to exercise jurisdiction in appropriate circumstances. In cases of death and serious injury or other grave consequences, a detailed report shall be sent promptly to the competent authorities responsible for administrative review and judicial control.

23. Persons affected by the use of force and firearms or their legal representatives shall have access to an independent process, including a judicial process. In the event of the death of such persons, this provision shall apply to their dependants accordingly.

24. Governments and law enforcement agencies shall ensure that superior officers are held responsible if they know, or should have known, that law enforcement officials under their command are resorting, or have resorted, to the unlawful use of force and firearms, and they did not take all measures in their power to prevent, suppress or report such use.

25. Governments and law enforcement agencies shall ensure that no criminal or disciplinary sanction is imposed on law enforcement officials who, in compliance with the Code of Conduct for Law Enforcement Officials and these basic principles, refuse to carry out an order to use force and firearms, or who report such use by other officials.

26. Obedience to superior orders shall be no defence if law enforcement officials knew that an order to use force and firearms resulting in the death or serious injury of a person was manifestly unlawful and had a reasonable opportunity to refuse to follow it. In any case, responsibility also rests on the superiors who gave the unlawful orders.

BASIC PRINCIPLES ON THE ROLE OF LAWYERS

[*These Principles were adopted by the Eighth United Nations Congress on the Prevention of Crime and the Treatment of Offenders in Havana, Cuba, on 7 September 1990. The United Nations General Assembly subsequently welcomed these Principles in its Resolution 45/121 of 14 December 1990 and invited all governments to be guided by them in the formulation of appropriate legislation and practice and to make efforts to ensure their implementation. The text of the Principles is set out below.*]

Access to lawyers and legal services
1. All persons are entitled to call upon the assistance of a lawyer of their choice to protect and establish their rights and to defend them in all stages of criminal proceedings.

2. Governments shall ensure that efficient procedures and responsive mechanisms for effective and equal access to lawyers are provided for all persons within their territory and subject to their jurisdiction, without distinction of any kind, such as discrimination based on race, colour, ethnic origin, sex, language, religion, political or other opinion, national or social origin, property, birth, economic or other status.

3. Governments shall ensure the provision of sufficient funding and other resources for legal services to the poor and, as necessary, to other disadvantaged persons. Professional associations of lawyers shall co-operate in the organization and provision of services, facilities and other resources.

4. Governments and professional associations of lawyers shall promote programmes to inform the public about their rights and duties under the law and the important role of lawyers in protecting their fundamental freedoms. Special attention should be given to assisting the poor and other disadvantaged persons so as to enable them to assert their rights and where necessary call upon the assistance of lawyers.

Special safeguards in criminal justice matters
5. Governments shall ensure that all persons are immediately informed by the competent authority of their right to be assisted by a lawyer of their own choice upon arrest or detention or when charged with a criminal offence.

6. Any such persons who do not have a lawyer shall, in all cases in which the interests of justice so require, be entitled to have a lawyer of experience and competence commensurate with the nature of the offence assigned to them in order to provide effective legal assistance, without payment by them if they lack sufficient means to pay for such services.

7. Governments shall further ensure that all persons arrested or detained, with or without criminal charge, shall have prompt access to a lawyer, and in any case not later than forty-eight hours from the time of arrest or detention.

8. All arrested, detained or imprisoned persons shall be provided with adequate opportunities, time and facilities to be visited by and to communicate and consult with a lawyer, without delay, interception or censorship and in full confidentiality. Such consultations may be within sight, but not within the hearing, of law enforcement officials.

Qualifications and training
9. Governments, professional associations of lawyers and educational institutions shall ensure that lawyers have appropriate education and training and be made aware of the ideals and ethical duties of the lawyer and of human rights and fundamental freedoms recognized by national and international law.

10. Governments, professional associations of lawyers and educational institutions shall ensure that there is no discrimination against a person with respect to entry into or continued practice within the legal profession on the grounds of race, colour,

sex, ethnic origin, religion, political or other opinion, national or social origin, property, birth, economic or other status, except that a requirement, that a lawyer must be a national of the country concerned, shall not be considered discriminatory.

11. In countries where there exist groups, communities or regions whose needs for legal services are not met, particularly where such groups have distinct cultures, traditions or languages or have been the victims of past discrimination, Governments, professional associations of lawyers and educational institutions should take special measures to provide opportunities for candidates from these groups to enter the legal profession and should ensure that they receive training appropriate to the needs of their groups.

Duties and responsibilities

12. Lawyers shall at all times maintain the honour and dignity of their profession as essential agents of the administration of justice.

13. The duties of lawyers towards their clients shall include:
(a) Advising clients as to their legal rights and obligations, and as to the working of the legal system in so far as it is relevant to the legal rights and obligations of the clients;
(b) Assisting clients in every appropriate way, and taking legal action to protect their interests;
(c) Assisting clients before courts, tribunals or administrative authorities, where appropriate.

14. Lawyers, in protecting the rights of their clients and in promoting the cause of justice, shall seek to uphold human rights and fundamental freedoms recognized by national and international law and shall at all times act freely and diligently in accordance with the law and recognized standards and ethics of the legal profession.

15. Lawyers shall always loyally respect the interests of their clients.

Guarantees for the functioning of lawyers

16. Governments shall ensure that lawyers
(a) are able to perform all of their professional functions without intimidation, hindrance, harassment or improper interference;
(b) are able to travel and to consult with their clients freely both within their own country and abroad; and
(c) shall not suffer, or be threatened with, prosecution or administrative, economic or other sanctions for any action taken in accordance with recognized professional duties, standards and ethics.

17. Where the security of lawyers is threatened as a result of discharging their functions, they shall be adequately safeguarded by the authorities.

18. Lawyers shall not be identified with their clients or their clients' causes as a result of discharging their functions.

19. No court or administrative authority before whom the right to counsel is recognized shall refuse to recognize the right of a lawyer to appear before it for his or her client unless that lawyer has been disqualified in accordance with national law and practice and in conformity with these principles.

20. Lawyers shall enjoy civil and penal immunity for relevant statements made in good faith in written or oral pleadings or in their professional appearances before a court, tribunal or other legal or administrative authority.

21. It is the duty of the competent authorities to ensure lawyers access to appropriate information, files and documents in their possession or control in sufficient time to enable lawyers to provide effective legal assistance to their clients. Such access should be provided at the earliest appropriate time.

22. Governments shall recognize and respect that all communications and consultations between lawyers and their clients within their professional relationship are confidential.

Freedom of expression and association

23. Lawyers like other citizens are entitled to freedom of expression, belief, association and assembly. In particular, they shall have the right to take part in public discussion of matters concerning

APPENDIX X

the law, the administration of justice and the promotion and protection of human rights and to join or form local, national or international organizations and attend their meetings, without suffering professional restrictions by reason of their lawful action or their membership in a lawful organization. In exercising these rights, lawyers shall always conduct themselves in accordance with the law and the recognized standards and ethics of the legal profession.

Professional associations of lawyers
24. Lawyers shall be entitled to form and join self-governing professional associations to represent their interests, promote their continuing education and training and protect their professional integrity. The executive body of the professional associations shall be elected by its members and shall exercise its functions without external interference.

25. Professional associations of lawyers shall co-operate with Governments to ensure that everyone has effective and equal access to legal services and that lawyers are able, without improper interference, to counsel and assist their clients in accordance with the law and recognized professional standards and ethics.

Disciplinary proceedings
26. Codes of professional conduct for lawyers shall be established by the legal profession through its appropriate organs, or by legislation, in accordance with national law and custom and recognized international standards and norms.

27. Charges or complaints made against lawyers in their professional capacity shall be processed expeditiously and fairly under appropriate procedures. Lawyers shall have the right to a fair hearing, including the right to be assisted by a lawyer of their choice.

28. Disciplinary proceedings against lawyers shall be brought before an impartial disciplinary committee established by the legal profession, before an independent statutory authority, or before a court, and shall be subject to an independent judicial review.

29. All disciplinary proceedings shall be determined in accordance with the code of professional conduct and other recognized standards and ethics of the legal profession and in the light of these principles.

PROTOCOL TO THE AMERICAN CONVENTION ON HUMAN RIGHTS TO ABOLISH THE DEATH PENALTY

Adopted by the General Assembly of the Organization of American States at its 20th Regular Session on 8 June 1990 in Asunción, Paraguay. At the end of the year the Protocol had been signed by five states: Ecuador, Nicaragua, Panama, Uruguay and Venezuela. It had not yet been ratified by any state.

The States Parties to this Protocol, Considering:
That Article 4 of the American Convention on Human Rights recognizes the right to life and restricts the application of the death penalty;
That everyone has the inalienable right to respect for his life, a right that cannot be suspended for any reason;
That the tendency among the American States is to be in favor of abolition of the death penalty;
That application of the death penalty has irrevocable consequences, forecloses the correction of judicial error, and precludes any possibility of changing or rehabilitating those convicted;
That the abolition of the death penalty helps to ensure more effective protection of the right to life;
That an international agreement must be arrived at that will entail a progressive development of the American Convention on Human Rights, and
That States Parties to the American Convention on Human Rights have expressed their intention to adopt an international agreement with a view to consolidating the practice of not applying the death penalty in the Americas,
Have agreed to sign the following Protocol to the American Convention on Human Rights to Abolish the Death Penalty

Article 1
The States Parties to this Protocol shall not apply the death penalty in their territory to any person subject to their jurisdiction.

Article 2
1. No reservations may be made to this Protocol. However, at the time of ratification or accession, the States Parties to this instrument may declare that they reserve the right to apply the death penalty in wartime in accordance with international law, for extremely serious crimes of a military nature.
2. The State Party making this reservation shall, upon ratification or accession, inform the Secretary General of the Organization of American States of the pertinent provisions of its national legislation applicable in wartime, as referred to in the preceding paragraph.
3. Said State Party shall notify the Secretary General of the Organization of American States of the beginning or end of any state of war in effect in its territory.

Article 3
This Protocol shall be open for signature and ratification or accession by any State Party to the American Convention on Human Rights.

Ratification of this Protocol or accession thereto shall be made through the deposit of an instrument of ratification or accession with the General Secretariat of the Organization of American States.

Article 4
This Protocol shall enter into force among the States that ratify or accede to it when they deposit their respective instruments of ratification or accession with the General Secretariat of the Organization of American States.

SELECTED STATISTICS

AMNESTY INTERNATIONAL MEMBERSHIP

At the beginning of 1991 there were more than 6,000 local Amnesty International groups in over 70 countries. There were more than 1,100,000 members, subscribers and regular donors in over 150 countries.

PRISONER CASES AND RELEASES

At the end of 1990 Amnesty International was working on more than 3,000 cases involving over 4,500 individuals adopted as prisoners of conscience or under investigation as possible prisoners of conscience. During the year action began on 1,683 new cases involving more than 2,000 individuals. A total of 1,609 cases involving the release of prisoners of conscience or those under investigation as possible prisoners of conscience was recorded.

URGENT ACTION APPEALS

During 1990 Amnesty International initiated 823 Urgent Action appeals on behalf of 3,626 people in 90 countries. Of these appeals, 139 were prompted by reports of torture and 21 were made on behalf of prisoners in a critical state of health and urgently in need of medical treatment. Some 83 appeals were issued in cases of arbitrary arrest, prolonged incommunicado detention, detention without charge or trial or unfair trial. Some 160 appeals related to extrajudicial killings or "disappearances" and 70 were made on behalf of prisoners sentenced to death. Twenty-six appeals related to death threats and 20 to ill-treatment. Others were issued in cases of deaths in detention, risk of *refoulement*, amputation, hunger-strike and political executions.

REGIONAL ACTION NETWORKS

Amnesty International's Regional Action Networks deal with human rights abuses in every country of the world. During 1990 participants in these 21 networks remained ready to take action when abuses occurred in Africa, the Americas, Asia and the Pacific, Europe and the Middle East and North Africa. In 1990 the Regional Action Networks worked on the cases of thousands of victims of human rights violations.

AMNESTY INTERNATIONAL FUNDING

The budget adopted by Amnesty International for 1990 was £10,100,000. This sum represents between 25 and 30 per cent of the estimated income likely to be raised during the year by the movement's national sections. Amnesty International's national sections and local volunteer groups are responsible for funding the movement. There is no central fund-raising program and no money is sought or accepted from governments. The donations that sustain Amnesty International's work come from its members and the public.